THE ORIGINS OF CONTEMPORARY

FRANCE

CLASSIC EUROPEAN HISTORIANS

A SERIES EDITED BY LEONARD KRIEGER

Hippolyte Adolphe Taine

THE ORIGINS OF CONTEMPORARY FRANCE

The Ancient Regime
The Revolution
The Modern Regime

Selected Chapters

Edited and with an Introduction
by Edward T. Gargan

THE UNIVERSITY OF CHICAGO PRESS

CHICAGO AND LONDON

944
T134a
1974

EDWARD T. GARGAN is professor of history at the
University of Wisconsin. Among his publications
are *De Tocqueville* and *Alexis de Tocqueville:
The Critical Years 1848-1851.*
[1974]

THE UNIVERSITY OF CHICAGO PRESS, CHICAGO 60637
THE UNIVERSITY OF CHICAGO PRESS, LTD., LONDON

International Standard Book Number: 0-226-78934-9 (clothbound)
Library of Congress Catalog Card Number: 73-87311

Contents

Series Editor's Preface

HIPPOLYTE TAINE's credentials for membership in the select group of Classic European Historians rest upon his preeminent representation of two movements seldom advocated by historians. Taine is the exemplar, first, of philosophical positivism in historiography, a rarity in that he actually wrote history while the custom of philosophical positivists is only to write about it—and even then not very kindly. Taine is also the exemplar of counterrevolutionary history, whereas the whole tradition of the profession has been overtly apolitical and covertly liberal; when there has been a challenge to the predominant Whig interpretation, it has usually produced bouts of frankly or euphemistically revolutionary history. Perhaps it has been this long addiction to antipositivist and progressive history that has made Taine a historian more caricatured than read, as Professor Gargan wryly indicates in his masterful introduction, and therefore more put upon than put right.

The fact is that in the writing of history no more than in literature proper can the quality of a composition be inferred from the theory or even from the untheoretical preconceptions putatively behind it, and this caution applies a fortiori to a historian who was also the aesthetician that Taine was. As do the other arts to their appreciators, history offers a crooked stick to its readers, and it is precisely the peregrination and the diffraction of an idea rather than its tedious recurrent identification and abstraction that constitute truth in the historical medium. We need not, consequently, enter into the debate about whether Taine really was a scholastic positivist by philosophy or even about whether his theory of history, with its psychological focus and its immediate relation to natural rather than to social science, can properly be called a historiographical version of philosophical positivism in any recognizable Comtean or Millian sense. Nor need we argue about the propriety of anyone so viscerally hostile to revolutionary upheaval concentrating his historical endeavor on the most violent and convulsive and enduring revolution in Western experience. We can casually agree, on the first count, that Taine's law, whereby cultural history is determined by the consequential interaction of race, milieu, and moment, is as close to positivism as we have gotten in a historian who professes to practice what he preaches; and on the second, that significant history can be written as much from repulsion as by attraction. What is important with Taine is neither point in itself, but rather the mutual penetration of the two approaches, which blunts the historiographical cutting-edge of either, and the refinement of both approaches through the imaginative reconstruction of the historical materials. From the reciprocal osmosis and the historical diffusion of Taine's theoretical stances come the surprises which make the reading of Taine such an unexpected experience and such a provocative case study in deciphering the historical language of ideas.

For the first of the surprises Professor Gargan prepares us very well, since the relationship between Taine's theoretical tenets becomes visible in his intellectual biography. There is in Taine's writing little of the rigorous legalistic or environmental determinism and little of the general conservative mentality that might have been expected from his reputation because his social conservatism manifested a passion that perforated his psychological determinism and because his defiant naturalism manifested an unconventional intelligence that made his reactionary politics the resultant of contexts themselves innovative in their conception. If we think of Taine as a radical in intellectual matters and as a romantic in his politics, certainly we exaggerate somewhat, but we also begin to see why his conservatism and his scientism should have been as qualified as they turned out to be in him.

Preface

The second of the surprises nothing short of reading Taine himself will deliver. This reading shows a vital interest in and understanding of the conditions in which real people lived, and it produces moving portraits of these people, both in the mass and in the depiction of individual intellectuals whom Taine presumably disliked. To read Taine's history is to incur a salutary reminder of the fruitful anomalies through which the nineteenth century developed the modern approach to history—the anomalies which caused "the father of scientific history," Leopold Ranke, to enshrine the sanctity of historical personality and which made romantic conservatives like the Grimms, Scott, and Chateaubriand pioneers in the concern with the popular social levels of the past.

Taine himself believed that every writer and every book could be epitomized in a summary formula. He is not the first historian, nor the last, who is unable to account for himself and to whom we are indebted for his failure.

LEONARD KRIEGER

Editor's Introduction

Two YEARS before his death Hippolyte Taine (1828–93) observed that the condition of a writer is like that of the artisan in the Gobelins tapestry factory.[1] There the worker busy behind the cloth can never know what the spectators in front understand of his art or even if his design is noticed at all. In his lifetime Taine did not lack universal praise as a literary critic, philosopher of science, psychologist, sociologist, and historian.[2] Today the flaws in his work are seen and more commented on than the splendor of his achievement. Taine would not have been surprised by the collapse of his reputation; he believed that each generation must of necessity judge and act according to its own time, history, and place. He would have expected historians sharing comparable values and historical experiences to reach conclusions that are fundamentally in agreement. In accordance with this law, for Taine an inescapable one, contemporary historians unanimously judge Taine's work as historian a failure.

1. Taine, *Sa vie et sa correspondance*, 4 vols. (Paris, 1907), 4:332 (Taine to Georges Lyon, 9 December 1891).

2. The last "life" of Taine is that of André Chevrillon, *Taine: Formation de sa pensée* (Paris, 1932); biographical material is also provided by Victor Giraud, *Essai sur Taine: Son oeuvre et son influence* (Paris, 1902) and Giraud's *Hippolyte Taine: Études et documents* (Paris, 1928); one of the few books in English is Sholom J. Kahn, *Science and Aesthetic Judgement: A Study in Taine's Critical Method* (New York, 1953); the most complete bibliography is in Carlo Mongardini, *Storia e sociologia nell'opera di H. Taine* (Milan, 1965).

Alfred Cobban perfectly summarized the historical profession's views on Taine when he suggested: "Of all those who have written histories of the Revolution, Taine possibly possessed the greatest genius and produced the worst history."[3] He considered that Taine's deplorable performance as a historian resulted from his hostility toward those who made the Revolution and his biased choice of facts to support his arguments. Characterizing this method as "vicious from its foundation," Cobban concluded: "Seldom has bad history been better written. Taine is the last and perhaps the most stimulating of the great primitives of revolutionary historiography. After him, history proper begins and unfortunately, for the most part, literature ends."[4] Georges Lefebvre, France's most honored historian of the Revolution, with equal severity regretted the tragic corruption of Taine's talent that allowed his antirevolutionary bias to dominate his history. Lefebvre added, however, that Taine understood social history more perceptively than any historian who preceded him and that he opened historians' eyes to social reality and collective psychology, the essential subjects of modern historical inquiry. Freed of his political prejudices and dread of the proletariat, Taine might have reached, Lefebvre proposed, an "incomparable grandeur."[5]

Yet the errors of geniuses are often more interesting and fertile than the attainments of more prudent scholars. Even today Taine's *Les Origines de la France contemporaine,* published in six volumes between 1875 and 1893, is frequently the point of departure for historians who consider their research important because they have decisively corrected Taine's mistakes and blunders. George Rudé's exciting book of 1959, *The Crowd in the French Revolution*, begins and ends by distinguishing its findings from those of Taine. In the last sentence of his study Rudé insists that his own major contribu-

3. Alfred Cobban, "Historians and the Causes of the French Revolution," in *Aspects of the French Revolution* (New York, 1968), pp. 43–44.

4. Ibid., p. 47.

5. Georges Lefebvre, *La Naissance de l'historiographie moderne* (Paris, 1971), p. 247.

tion has been his refutation of Taine's wrong treatment of the people during the revolutionary *journées*. [6] When Daniel Mornet published his fundamental *Les Origines intellectuelles de la révolution française* in 1933, he too believed that his own study was valuable because it exposed the distortions of Taine's historical presentation of the *philosophes*. [7] Mornet's and Rudé's criticism of Taine reaffirmed his academic excommunication first pronounced by Alphonse Aulard. Speaking ex cathedra and with an air of infallibility, Aulard devoted two years of public lectures from 1905 to 1907[8] at the Sorbonne to exposing, page by page, Taine's erudite sins. Virtue and sin alike on this occasion lost their attractiveness. Taine has remained on the historian's Index of Prohibited Books until the present. But despite his condemnation by all professional historians, Taine's volumes are discovered again and again in their hands and libraries. Creative scholars continue to regard Taine as the nineteenth-century historian whom they must put in the shade by the light of their studies.

The attraction and repulsion that Taine provokes cannot be attributed to his style, for this too, has been found wanting. Edmund Wilson, the American critic whose scope and energy resembled Taine's own force, noted that Taine's contemporary, Amiel, was correct when he objected to the mechanical character of Taine's writing. [9] A limited historian, an unacceptable moralist, a writer whose prose fatigues as often as it delights ought to have no claim on the attention of succeeding generations. But Taine continues to command our interest and to call forth our response to his voice. He himself offered an explanation of why this is so when he noted with satisfaction that modern psychology was beginning to know something of the "subterranean regions of the soul," to discover that the "breaking up and lasting doubling of the ego" makes it possible for two or more persons to exist distinctly and at

6. Georg Rudé, *The Crowd in the French Revolution* (Oxford, 1959), p. 239.

7. Daniel Mornet, *Les Origines intellectuelles de la révolution française* (1715–1787) (Paris, 1933), pp. 470–74.

8. Alphonse Aulard, *Taine historien de la révolution française* (Paris, 1907); for a reply to Aulard see Augustine Cochin, *La Crise de l'histoire révolutionnaire: Taine et Aulard* (Paris, 1909).

9. Edmund Wilson, *To the Finland Station* (New York, 1953), p. 45.

the same time within the same individual.[10] We cannot be done with Taine because the complexity of his own person and its changes in response to modernity anticipated our own alterations and ambivalences as we try to make sense of the modern condition of man. In his expectations as to what science might accomplish, what psychology might promise, what coherence history might offer, and what justification of life might be granted by literature, Taine encompassed our hopes in the use of intelligence. His experience of failure and despair haunts our own efforts, and when we find ourselves on his path, we are often desperate to detect a way out. This is possible, but we cannot escape the realization that he preceded us as historian, as literary critic, as psychologist, and we must acknowledge that his limits and shortcomings have often made possible our achievements.

The death of his father, a comfortable lawyer in the Ardennes, when Taine was not quite thirteen, affected his entire life. The consequences of this loss are testified to by an autobiographical novel which Taine began in 1861, but could not complete since he was then finding it almost impossible to read or work. An effort at self-analysis and therapy, the novel, *Étienne Mayran*, published posthumously, begins with a young boy's shocking discovery on the way home from his father's funeral that villagers who had previously addressed him as *Monsieur* Étienne now felt free to call him simply Étienne. For Étienne a life as a laborer or tradesman could only be escaped by a spectacular career as a student. Taine's inheritance of about twelve hundred francs a year was greater than · that of his hero, but he too had to succeed as a scholar if he was to know any independence. In Taine's case a family council determined that he enter Saint Honoré, a boarding school in Paris (as did Étienne in the novel), and from there attend the classes at the Bourbon college, to prepare for the examination that might admit him to the *École normale supérieure*. Within a year Taine's mother came to Paris to rescue him from Saint Honoré and the confinement he hated, though he continued on at the college. A key to her haste is perhaps furnished by the fictional student Étienne's horror

10. Taine, *The Modern Regime*, trans. John Durand, 2 vols. (New York, 1890–94), 2:103.

at the occasional indecencies of his fellow students and by his feelings that he was different. But Étienne, like Taine, was consoled by his "voluptuous response" to the Greek authors and by their lesson concerning the need of another soul to whom one could confide his thoughts and desires. Despite this need, however, "he would rather speak to the benches and walls than to his masters or to his companions."[11] Disgusted by the competitive, prize-seeking atmosphere of the school, Étienne was nevertheless graced by the realization that he loved learning and the interior life it nourishes. Through his study he achieves "the first view of totality," and perceives with joy "the great firm network by which all things and all ideas are tied together."[12]

Taine's attribution of a philisophical vision of such scope to an adolescent was not an extravagant claim, for he had acquired between his own fifteenth and eighteenth year precisely this grasp of the unity of being that encompasses consciousness and the world. Taine's own growth was such that a half century after he had entered the class in philosophy, his teacher, Charles Bénard, one of the professors of philosophy in the great tradition of the French lycée, insisted in a letter to Taine's biographer that he had had no decisive influence on his young student.[13] This was not because Taine was obdurate—indeed, he had welcomed a knowledge of Hegel from his instructor—but because when he began his philosophical studies, he was already a fervent disciple of Spinoza. All his life he would take for granted Spinoza's view of the chain of being that determines equally nature's action and human conduct. For Taine the student as well as for Taine the mature writer, it seemed obvious that all things and events are inextricably determined by the logic of nature. This determinism did not appall him as it did so many spiritualists, but rather delighted his intellect by the challenge of unraveling the web. The web, however, was not without its disturbing features.

At twenty, on the eve of his entrance to the École normale, Taine summarized his intellectual development in an essay that only a

11. Taine, *Étienne Mayran* (Paris, 1910), p. 215.
12. Ibid., p. 223.
13. Giraud, *Essai sur Taine*, pp. 282–83.

young man would have titled "Of Human Destiny." Here he established the freedom that followed once he had put aside his Catholic training—a tradition, he said, that attempted to make him a virtuous man through fear and a believer through obedience. He rejoiced in the fact that as master of himself he had "accustomed my body and soul to obey my will, and I had thus preserved myself from those bestial passions which blind and bewilder Man, take him from the study of destiny, and make him live like an animal, ignorant of the present, and careless of the future."[14] Taine's victory over the bestial passions, a success he would comment on in more than one letter, cannot be dismissed as a conventional adolescent struggle with sex. Throughout his life he would fear those moments when "the beast got out." And this dread of passion, so painfully experienced during his earliest efforts to possess a lucidity unclouded by the irrational, would echo and reecho through the pages of his history of the Great Revolution. This pursuit determined that he would live a life of celibacy until he was forty, and this same anxiety made him at times almost guilty of voyeurism as he watched others live. But his desperate need for a controlled existence gave urgency and intensity to his study of psychology as the key to the secrets binding nature, history, and the human condition. Taine worshipped Stendhal—he was to read *The Charterhouse of Parma* more than sixty times—for he recognized in him the psychologist of his century, the man who knew most about love and the poisons that destroy happiness. His own work in psychology would be confined to his great effort at collective psychology in his *Histoire de la littérature anglaise*, his analysis of the French Revolution, and the clinical pages of his masterpiece, *De l'intelligence* (1870). From his earliest days he sought to touch life as had Stendhal. Taine was, as his teacher in the lycée recognized, an artist manqué. His training as philosopher and scientist was merely the means he chose to attempt a flight he did not dare try as artist.

Students of Taine have analyzed and speculated at length about his indebtedness to Spinoza, Condorcet, and Hegel. But greater

14. Taine, *Life and Letters*, trans. R. L. Devonshire, 3 vols. (New York, 1902–8), 1:15.

attention must be paid to his teacher's intuition that Taine was in truth no philosopher; that he was not content with the philosophical modes of inquiry. The impact of the philosophers he did acknowledge as critical for his development can be briefly summarized in order to understand the experiences that truly shaped his vision after his formal education was over. Spinoza early and quickly convinced Taine that all things in this universe are determined; Hegel complemented Taine's indebtedness to Guizot's perception of universal history by his demonstration that the contradictions inherent in the historical process produce the moments of synthesis which dialectically convert the past and present into the future. Condorcet brought Taine the welcome information that our consciousness and egos are what our senses permit and convinced him that no further mysteries were at issue, but only the hard task of observation and experiment. Taine's debts to Condorcet would be repaid when in his *De l'intelligence* he described the ego as a series of events taking place in the "box" in the skull as it sorted out the messages of the senses. These ideas were all present to Taine in an undeveloped manner before he left the École normale in 1851. Other governing principles of his thought were also tentatively sketched out by the young *normalien.* His nephew and last biographer, André Chevrillon, astutely observed that as early as 1850 Taine's notes included his theme that the history of a people is to be captured by examining the dominating role of "la race; le moment; le milieu."[15] These concepts, so critical for Taine's thought, have also been traced to the influence of Montesquieu, Voltaire, and others. What he was to do with his hypotheses was determined, however, more by his life experiences than by any rigorous dependency on the books he mastered as a student. His ego, in accordance with Condorcet's prescription and his own later discoveries, was the target of a series of events that formed his person and works.

In the spring of 1848 Taine almost ignored the revolution as he prepared for his *baccalauréat* and the competition for the École normale. His only concession to these dramatic events was the

15. Chevrillon, *Taine,* pp. 399–400.

promise that after his schooling was over he would find out what the social, political, and physical sciences had to say about his society. When he became twenty-one in 1849, he further rationalized that he would not vote in the elections of that spring because he did not know anything about France. He shamefully admitted that he was without intelligent ideas on the manners, customs, and opinions of his own country. His education had offered only the self-evident proposition: "The true government is the one that is appropriate to the civilization of the people." He remained, however, uninstructed in any "empirical" methods for arriving at political truth.[16]

But Taine was not so detached from the real world as to be unaware that a civil war was taking place around him. He recognized that the conflict challenged the possessing classes and their indifference to the needs of men in want and hunger. From his privileged position as a student headed for the École normale, Taine concluded that stupidity and greed dominated the conduct of insurgents and incumbents alike. And he held to the rather unoriginal idea that property alone protects the individual against the state's abuse of its powers. He entertained the shallowest fantasies concerning socialism and communism, but he did accept universal suffrage as appropriate for the Second Republic.

Taine's neutrality and separation from the political passions of his contemporaries ended with the coup d'état of 2 December 1851. Before this event he had been living and teaching in Nevers as a substitute teacher of philosophy in the local lycée. He had been required to take this post in the fall of 1851 because he had surprisingly failed the examination for the *agrégé de philosophie* that summer. His lack of success has been attributed to his excessive self-assurance during the examination and to his aggressive rejec-

---

16. Taine, *Life and Letters*, 1:65 (Taine to L. A. Prévost-Paradol, 1 May 1849). Lucien-Anatole Prévost-Paradol was Taine's closest friend at the *École normale*. After leaving the École he became a famous political journalist, contributing to the *Journal des débats*, and founded the subsequently suppressed *Courrier du dimanche*. He went to Washington in 1870 as ambassador, but shortly after learning the news that the Franco-Prussian War had broken out, he committed suicide. On Prévost-Paradol see Pierre Guiral, *Prévost-Paradol (1829-1870)* (Paris, 1955).

tion of the conservative philosophical ideas of his examiners. While in the provinces he did not lose any of the *normalien's* obligatory disdain for lesser human beings, but he was gravely shocked by the response of his neighbors to power, violence, and dictatorship. Reporting to his friend Édouard de Suckau on the resistance efforts of peasants and townspeople in nearby Clamecy, Taine surrendered his philisophical composure: "The mob has taken Clamecy, a little town fifteen leagues from here; they burnt and pillaged the place and murdered some gendarmes. Some regiments have arrived from Paris with guns; it will be a butchery. What an ugly thing is politics! People in high places steal public liberty, shoot down four or five thousand men and perjure themselves; the lower classes, their adversaries, steal private property and cut throats; I dare wish success to neither side."[17]

Taine's fear of the mob, which would so dominate and unbalance his history of the French Revolution, did not in 1851 prevent him from equally detesting those who supported Louis Napoleon. He quickly perceived that liberals had a natural ability to become policemen in spirit and that they would give the prince president all the support necessary to prevail. And he predicted that Louis Napoleon would be very good at exploiting the self-interests, anxieties, and weaknesses of every group in society that could be frightened into assisting his dictatorship. "He will lean upon everything that is antagonistic to thought," Taine wrote, "the brutal discipline of the army, the selfishness and cowardice of landlords, the legends of the country, the clergy."[18]

When the authorities at Taine's school hastily prepared a document praising Louis Napoleon for having saved the nation, Taine refused to sign. His superior rather decently did not force the issue. On New Year's Day 1852, however, he was required as a *fonctionnaire* to call with his colleagues on the prefect and on the general who suppressed the insurrection. On this occasion the general boasted of how many he might have killed, or might still kill, and

---

17. Taine, *Life and Letters*, 1:137 (Taine to Edouard de Suckau, 9 December 1851).
18. Ibid., p. 138.

the prefect matched him with his promises to send hundreds into prison and exile. Somehow Taine managed to get back to his room, and that day he wrote to his mother: "It is better to be nothing as I am, or suspended, than to be a jailer or a licensed butcher." Philosophy offered no consolation, he could only cry out: "It is something not to be an executioner!"[19] A hundred years later Albert Camus, who shared some of Taine's reactions to the violence of his society, would ask also for a world where there were "neither executioners nor victims."

By 1852 Taine's view of man was less lovely than that he had received from Plato's dialogues. He now had to fit into his philosophy and science his realization that "stupidity, violence, ignorance, cowardice, were the principal ingredients that God mixed together, when making the human race."[20] For the rest of his life Taine would incorporate into his theories the ugly things people do to one another because of their self-interests and the passions of their class. From this time on he completely distrusted all rhetoric that blesses violence in the name of humanity. During the years 1848 to 1852 he first sensed something was wrong about such beautiful language when he pleaded with his fellow *normalien* Prévost-Paradol: "Those fine phrases after the manner of Rousseau, harmonious, rich, elegant, those long and happy inversions would seem out of place. In these times words are actions and we do not want flowers on the points of bayonets. Take your flowers away if you can."[21]

History in these few years pressed into Taine's consciousness the paradoxes he would never resolve and determined that he would be an outsider in a partisan world. "I detest," he wrote, "robbery and assassination, whether committed by the mob or the authorities."[22] Taine would never accept the idea that a choice must be made. He would finally attempt to make one in his history of the Revolution, but when that moment arrived he would not understand why his choice seemed disgraceful to so many.

19. Ibid., p. 155 (Taine to his mother, 1 January 1852).
20. Ibid., p. 137 (Taine to Suckau, 9 December 1851).
21. Ibid., p. 64 (Taine to Prévost-Paradol, 1 May 1849).
22. Ibid., p. 139 (Taine to Prévost-Paradol, 15 December 1851).

As a young man, however, Taine was not satisfied to admire his own virtue in contrast to the vices of his countrymen. Instead, when his doctoral thesis on sensation was rejected in 1852 for being insufficiently "spiritual," he set out to discover who were his fellow Frenchmen. Ostensibly he quickly wrote a thesis in literature on La Fontaine; in reality he began to uncover the historical conditions, climate, and behavior that made the French part of the human race, but distinguishable from their European cousins in Germany, England, Holland, and Italy.

Back in Paris, after resigning from the secondary school system in 1852, Taine attended courses on physiology, botany, and zoology. He sat entranced in classes on anatomy at the School of Medicine and took careful notes on the psychological disorders of the patients at the Salpêtrière clinic. The official philosophers found him wanting, but he knew that they were the ones who had no comprehension of science and modernity. Freed of the expectation of a respectable academic post, he divested himself of every orthodoxy. At each step in this process Taine used the organizing principles of the new sciences to analyze the morphological features of his society.

Taine now began to translate into very concrete statements the abstract concepts he had outlined in his notes of 1850 on the history of philosophy. As a philosopher he had concluded: "Philosophy is a form, a mode of existence of the human mind. It only really exists when it expresses in its own way the human mind of the time. If not, it does not exist; or else lacking personal force, it reproduces an old system. But then it still lacks the principle of life."[23] His limited experiences in the actual world and his study of the natural sciences confirmed Taine's earlier insight that the metaphysical and moral beliefs of any era must reflect the historical and social situation of that time. It was the lives that men lived that mattered to Taine, who regarded philosophy as a necessary outgrowth of their more mundane occupations. From this perspective Taine saw that La Fontaine, Stendhal, and Balzac had more to teach him than whole schools of metaphysics.

By 1860 when he published the third edition of his *La Fontaine*,

23. Ibid., pp. 310–11.

Taine believed that he understood some of the historical and psychological forces that had formed the French people, *les Gaulois*.
He praised La Fontaine because unlike so many "classical" authors
he had not been a captive of the artificial Latin civilization of the
court and nobles in the seventeenth century. La Fontaine was
worthy of respect as one of the few French writers from the
seventeenth to the nineteenth century who did not write solely for a
narrow, educated, wealthy, and powerful class. In language that
Marx, Sartre, or George Steiner would not find strange Taine declared: "Our letters, as our religion and our government, are super-
imposed on rather than rooted in the nation."[24] La Fontaine, by his
example, exposed the artificiality of the majority of France's writers, "the theoreticians of the sixteenth and of the nineteenth
century who write for a class and not for the nation."[25] He was
magnificent, according to Taine, because he had made a near perfect contact with the daily existence and spirit of *"le peuple,"* How
many great writers," Taine asked, "are understood by the people?"[26] Perhaps Rabelais and Molière, but certainly La Fontaine.

The great fabulist had the gift of being open to every experience
and saw as only a "stranger" can all that was happening around
him: "a peasant interested him as much as a prince, a donkey as
much as a man."[27] Without sentimentality, La Fontaine had depicted the almost magical authority that belonged to the office and
person of kings, but also their murderous appetites; he recorded the
brutal burdens of the peasants, but he gagged on their smells and
filth. Taine wanted to imitate and make his own La Fontaine's
unrivaled concreteness and to share his awareness of every possibility in this universe where the animal man philosophizes and
creates poems.

La Fontaine gave Taine his first realistic picture of the continuing habits and psychological character of the French people. In
his poetry they revealed themselves as rulers who insensitively

24. Taine, *La Fontaine et ses fables* (Paris, 1905), p. 61.
25. Ibid., p. 61.
26. Ibid., p. 59.
27. Ibid., p. 66.

crushed the innocent and as aristocrats who made the life of a parasite seem elegant and even honorable. The reader of La Fontaine understood that it is a fact of nature and not of morality that the rich bourgeoisie "have for the miserable a cold indifference, and suspicion and scorn for those who dispense charity."[28] La Fontaine enabled the student of France's history to see the peasant in his actual world rather than in a romanticized rustic tableau; to perceive what existence was for the exploiter of the smallest stubbled fields constantly overcome by debts and the demands of the relentless usurer. This was the reality of the peasants' life and "the pretended poetry and manners of the village."[29]

Taine delighted in the simple, plain, commonplace, and unlearned words of the poet fabulist. When writing his history he would try to borrow La Fontaine's language to describe the notables, bourgeoisie, artisans, and peasants. Yet in that context the honesty and simplicity of the poet would often elude the historian's reach, leaving an undesired impression of arrogance rather than of compassion and perfect clarity.

Often complaining that he labored by necessity and virtually as a slave, Taine wrote between 1855 and 1863 two of his minor and three of his major books. In 1856 he published his *Essai sur Tite-Live* and won the prize offered on this subject by the French Academy. The need to supplement his small inheritance and meager income as a tutor induced him to write his *Voyage aux eaux des Pyrénées* (1855), a guidebook that became a minor classic of this genre. At the same time he contributed a host of essays to such journals as the *Revue de l'instruction publique, Revue des deux mondes*, and the *Journal des débats*. Between 1855 and 1860 he managed an average of twenty long articles each year on literature, philosophy, and history, essays that became the basis of the books that would gain him status and recognition. In 1857 Taine published his *Les Philosophes français du xix*[e] *siècle*; and in 1858 the *Essais de critique et d'histoire* which included his almost book-length analysis of Balzac and his tribute to Michelet. Finally in

28. Ibid., p. 138.
29. Ibid., p. 149.

1863 he presented his astonishing tour de force, the *Histoire de la littérature anglaise.*

The diversity of Taine's interests, ideas, and theories during this decade almost defies any effort to give them unity. The diverse elements of his massive output cohere when they are seen in the context of his developing conception that the conduct and thought of any era are determined by its historical framework. This perspective made it possible for him, in *Les Philosophes français*, to destroy the prestige of the "official philosophers" who had dominated academic philosophy in France since the Revolution. *Doctrinaires* such as Royer-Collard (1763–1845), *spiritualistes* like Jouffroy (1796–1843), and the *éclectique* Victor Cousin (1792–1867) had succeeded, Taine proposed, because their vapid abstractions and self-serving ethical systems precisely fitted the superficial needs of their society and time. "If we had need," he wrote, "to believe that crocodiles are Gods, tomorrow in the *place Carrousel* they would build them a temple."[30] Victor Cousin as portrayed by Taine was a philosopher who even without a miter hastened to serve many kings and gods; he protected them by his moralizing and beautiful empty phrases that were unrelated to science and the actual world. After Taine's attack, French formal philosophy suffered a lack of confidence from which it has scarcely recovered. Neither Bergson nor Sartre are invulnerable to his pointed queries: Why are you moralizing? What are the positive facts behind your abstract words?

Taine was, of course, aware that his derisive criticism of the established philosophers could be attributed to his own rejection by the University. He readily confessed in his correspondence that when criticizing Victor Cousin, "mockery rose to my lips at every line."[31] His fundamental purpose was to expose all philosophical talk of virtue and beauty that disguised attempts at social control by "intellectual policemen." No revolutionary, incapable of violence, and unassailable because of his own disengagement from politics, Taine adamantly insisted: "Art and Science disappear as

---

30. Taine, *Les Philosophes français du XIX siècle* (Paris, 1857), p. 283.
31. Taine, *Life and Letters,* 2:99 (Taine to Suckau, 22 October 1855).

soon as they are turned into an instrument of education and government. That is why you find me so badly disposed toward Literature when it calls itself a teacher, and against Philosophy when it assumes the part of a guardian of public order."[32] A philosopher will be what his age and society permit, but he betrays his vocation if he believes that his utterances are universal and timeless when they are more likely to be limited and parochial.

Once Taine had purged himself of his hatred of the orthodox secular wisdom, he was able to celebrate the writers who had made honest contact with the human condition. "I adore," he wrote, "Balzac, who was a Christian, an Absolutist, and a Mystic, and also Beyle who was a Liberal, a Materialist, and an Atheist."[33] Taine's great essay on Balzac offered the praise he thought fitting and proper to the novelist who had succeeded in "abridging" the social history of the nineteenth century. This admiration for Balzac's genius was in part due to his realization that Balzac's novels confirmed Taine's historical conception of how any generation becomes one in the "totality" that unites the individual to his class, to his society, and to the world. Balzac's life and art perfectly illustrated the necessary relationship between a writer and the creative action open to him. His passion, indebtedness, aggression, and psychological penetration were precisely joined to the tendencies, dreams, and changes of his century.

Balzac was unsurpassed not because his novels reflected as in a mirror the realities of his time, but because as artist he co-created and gave consciousness to the forces that fashioned nineteenth-century France. The vulgar bourgeois, the faceless clerk, the omniscient village doctor, the confused virgin have a social identity because Balzac knew them and gave them life. When he describes money, "the great mainspring of modern life," Taine wrote, "he speaks to us of the interests that concern us, he satiates the covetousness that possesses us."[34] Language, gesture, the soil, the air, the

32. Ibid., p. 102.
33. Ibid., p. 132 (Taine to J. J. Weiss, 25 January 1858).
34. Taine, *Balzac: A Critical Study*, trans. Lorenzo O'Rourke (New York, 1906), pp. 90–91.

food you eat, the furniture you select, the virtues and vices you display are the only possible ones given your time and place. Balzac's fiction, according to Taine, demonstrated with the certainty of a laboratory experiment that "virtue is a product like wine or vinegar manufactured like other things, by a known series of determined operations having a measurable and certain effect."[35] The brilliant diagnoses in the *Human Comedy* included the elegant proof that a judge whose benevolence is much commented on is in reality a man "who loves the poor as the gambler does his game," and a lawyer who sacrifices his fortune for another is identified as having the compulsive "and involuntary fidelity of a dog."[36]

We would all like, Taine acknowledged, to revolt at this naturalism, but those committed to search for the causes behind human actions must accept the evidence that all natural and human events proceed from determined antecedents to appointed consequences. Historians seeking to explain the origins of human conduct were urged by Taine to partake of and participate in Balzac's art, to uncover with the artist's eye and the anatomist's scalpel the connections of the total structure.

Taine made three attempts to discuss how history was to be approached and written if it was to encompass as successfully as the good novel the whole experience of a society. His suggestions were offered in the preface to the first edition of his *Essais de critique et d'histoire* (1858), in the introduction to the *Histoire de la littérature anglaise* (1863), and in the longer preface to the 1866 edition of his *Essais*. On these three occasions Taine stated as clearly as possible his insight, corroborated by Balzac, that the psychology, society, institutions, beliefs, and thought of any historical generation must be symmetrically related. Thus: "In the same century, for example, philosophy, religion, art, the form of the family, and of government, public and private manners, all the parts in national life, imply one another, in such a fashion that one cannot be altered without the rest also changing."[37] History demands, Taine wrote,

35. Ibid., pp. 182–83.
36. Ibid., pp. 183–84.
37. Taine, *Essais de critique et d'histoire*, "Préface de la première édition," 12th ed. (Paris, 1913), p. iii.

the understanding that "mankind is not a collection of objects lying next to one another, but a machine of functionally interrelated parts; it is a system and not a formless pile."[38]

Critics objected that Taine's excessive stress on the homologous character of a historical epoch denied individuality, nuance, the chaos and incoherence of life. To this he replied that one had only to look at the totality of any period as one would look at a painting to recognize the necessary harmony of all of its parts. The "inner eye" must be used to perceive how the "imprint" of past experiences unites in any historical moment—as in the century of Louis XIV—religion and philosophy, the family and the state, industry, commerce, and agriculture.

It was true that on the surface all appeared to be in flux during Louis XIV's epoch; Jansenists seemed to dominate at one time, and at another it was the Jesuits; mystics prevailed at one hour, and still later Gallicans. But, Taine argued, the historian who observes the violent imagination of the previous century, the critical character of contemporary English philosophy, the skepticism of the age that followed will be able to isolate the essential traits of seventeenth-century France. The historian gifted by a holistic sense will see the links between the theological poverty of seventeenth-century France and the lucidity of its logic, the nobility of its moral doctrines, the "dryness" of its speculative talents, and its disdain for experience. He will recognize the relationships between the classical age's preference for mathematics and the concepts of King and God that were mutually dependent upon one another in a hierarchical society that was sustained by a way of reasoning and ordering things that united the philosophy of Malebranche, the sentences of Bossuet, the arrangement of the hedges at Versailles, the versification of Boileau, the laws of Colbert.[39]

The historian who successfully identifies the unifying features in a society's national character and establishes the structural factors that are the armature of its history does not deny individuality, but rather he locates the place of the unique within the collective

38. ibid., p. iii.
39. Ibid., "Préface de la deuxième édition," p. xvii.

psychological and historical experience of the whole society. Systematic analysis of this rigor does not deny freedom but makes it possible. When we understand the mutual interdependencies of all things, Taine believed, then we may be able "to modify to a certain degree the events of history."[40] When mankind approaches through history a kncwledge of the laws and necessary circumstances governing all forms of human association, then history may be profitable "to the intelligent insect" who penetrates the economy of the structure.

In the introduction to the *Histoire de la littérature anglaise* Taine presented his celebrated belief that three primordial forces determine the form and spirit of a people: *la race, le milieu, and le moment.* [41] The concepts of *milieu* and epoch have now an indisputable and indispensable place in the analytical language of critics and historians. Taine's views on the function of race have aroused bitter criticism. Sholom J. Kahn in his sensitive study of Taine's critical method has judiciously cited the great critic Leo Spitzer's harsh verdict: "Both in Tainism and Hitlerism civilization has been replaced by biology."[42] Kahn does not think this crime can be attributed to Taine, but proposes that Taine's use of race be understood as a consequence of the limited anthropological and biological theories of mid-nineteenth-century thought.

Taine did employ the concept of race to encompass the consistent characteristics and mental habits a people exhibit across their history. He undeniably thought heredity transmitted national traits and modes of historical behavior. But Taine also used the expression race in much the same way as historians who cannot be charged with Hitlerism. Winston Churchill, for example, in *A History of the English-Speaking Peoples*, wrote: "Thus by the end of the fifteenth century the main characteristics and institutions of the race had taken shape."[43] The conceit of race was of a similar

40. Ibid., p. xxiii.
41. Taine, *Histoire de la littérature anglaise*, 11th ed., 5 vols. (Paris, 1905, 1906), 1:xxii.
42. Leo Spitzer, "Race," in *Essays in Historical Semantics* (New York, 1948), p. 155, as quoted in Kahn, *Science and Aesthetic Judgement*, p. 87.
43. Winston S. Churchill, *A History of the English-Speaking Peoples*, 4 vols. (New York, 1956–58), vol. 1, *The Birth of Britain*, p. xix.

help to Taine when he was locating the significant periods of transformation in England's history.

The *Histoire de la littérature anglaise*, beginning with Tacitus and ending with Tennyson, elaborately develops the thesis, inherited from Balzac and Stendhal, that a literary work will always reveal more about a society than its histories or political documents. "I would give," Taine wrote, "fifty volumes of charters and a hundred volumes of state papers for the memoirs of Cellini, the epistles of St. Paul, the table-talk of Luther, or the comedies of Aristophanes."[44] This theme was not based on an underestimation of the realities of power and class. The preference for literature as the decisive historical witness was rooted in Taine's conviction that politics is in a sense the most rudimentary of social acts. Political systems and constitutions owe little to the genius or purposive action of statesmen, but virtually everything to their necessary responses to the social pressures of their times. "Social situations," Taine asserted, "create political situations; legal constitutions always accommodate themselves to real things; and acquired preponderance infallibly results in written right."[45]

Writing for the subjects of Louis Napoleon's Empire, Taine invited them to consider the English example as the most positive historical lesson for a society seeking a progressive and confident future. He considered the British too severe in their rejection of the French Revolution, but he thought that England had responded more intelligently than any other nation to the message of the Enlightenment and had made the most viable transition to the industrial nineteenth century. The French have a natural tendency to regard the English as dull performers in the theater of history, and Taine sometimes supported this stereotyping. Yet on viewing their entire historical repertoire, he could not restrain his sheer admiration for their virtuosity in a theater little inclined to be absurd:

44. Taine, *History of English Literature*, trans. H. Van Laun, 4 vols. (Philadelphia, 1896), 1:34.
45. Ibid., p. 78.

But they are patriots as well as innovators, conservatives as
well as revolutionary; if they touch religion and constitution,
manners and doctrines, it is to widen not to destroy them:
England is made; she knows it, and they know it. Such as this
country is, based on the whole national history and on all the
national instincts, it is more capable than any other people in
Europe of transforming itself without recasting, and of devoting itself to its future without renouncing its past.[46]

No French scholar has until this day attempted to tell again the full
history of England's literature and society. Voltaire, Guizot, and
Tocqueville had also, like Taine, looked to England to inform and
inspire their reflections on France's past and future. And Élie
Halévy's (1870–1937) *Histoire du peuple anglais au XIX siècle*
(1912–23; 1926–32) was a magisterial analysis of England's religious, economic, and political history. But with these important
exceptions, no other French thinkers have quite experienced
Taine's fascination for a society not his own or shared the quality of
his pleasure in England's literature and history.

England's attainments reinforced for Taine the depressing idea
that political and social failure was France's historical habit and
destiny. This discouraging feeling became an obsession at a time
when his own career was increasingly prospering. A literary celebrity, he could find no reason to celebrate the achievements of his
own nation. He enjoyed the friendship of Flaubert, Sainte-Beuve,
and Renan and attended the famous literary dinners at the restau-
rant Magny where those who mattered complimented one another
on their wit and fame. Money was still a problem, however, and in
1863 Taine accepted the post of admissions examiner for St. Cyr
Military College. In 1865 he succeeded Viollet-le-Duc (1814–79) as
professor of aesthetics and of the history of art at the École des
beaux-arts. The six weeks of lectures he gave each year paid less
than his examiner's position, but conferred a minimum dignity on a
man who no longer expected a major academic appointment, and
Taine stayed at the École until 1883. His courses published at the
end of the year in time constituted a series on the social history of
art. Incapable of not writing something every day, he also pub-

46. Ibid., p. 80.

lished in 1866 a thousand pages on his travels in Italy, pages flecked with comparative comments on Italy's and Europe's history since the Middle Ages.

Yet for all his activity Taine gave in these years the impression of a writer fleeing his proper subject—the analysis of his own society. Taine's *Carnets de voyage: Notes sur la province, 1863–1865*, which he kept while on tour for the army, did express some of his troubled impressions of his countrymen.[47] Writing in shabby inns that were little more than taverns, he asked himself again and again why he was unable to experience the happiness of other men. Every morning he began by admiring the sky, the landscape, old buildings, and the local types; by evening he would be recording his distaste for the citizens of Douai, Rennes, Toulouse, Marseille, Lyon, or Besançon. He had only contempt for the "democratic," egalitarian climate of the Second Empire as an atmosphere that gave life to a vulgar bourgeoisie competing against one another to make money, to push the careers of their sons, to excel by the vulgarity of their conspicuous consumption. France's bourgeoisie, even those of the upper middle classes, seemed shamefully inferior to the English higher classes, who brought their wealth and talent to the service of their neighbor and country.

Taine was never sentimental in his attitude toward the lower classes, but during these travels he did observe the harsh conditions of their lives. At Lyon he visited the heights of the Croix-Rousse, and while recalling the working class struggles there in 1831 and 1834, he confirmed the continuing exploitation, poverty, and ill-health of the silk workers. Their "washed out eyes" were indeed depressing as was the information that the middlemen in the trade degraded the daughters of the workers as the price for their help.[48] Such misery made clear why men become socialists, but Taine persisted in the conventional view that "unchangeable" economic laws do not permit wages to rise without endangering capital.

While collecting his notes on the provinces, Taine was submit-

47. Taine, *Carnets de voyage: Notes sur la province, 1863–1865* (Paris, 1896).
48. Taine, *Journeys through France* (London, 1897), p. 276.

ting similar material on Paris to the illustrated weekly *La Vie parisienne*. These comments were published in 1867 in his curious book *Notes sur Paris, vie et opinions de M. Frédéric-Thomas Graindorge*. It is almost impossible to believe that his caricatures of Parisian dance halls, prostitutes, kept women, and fashionable soirees were being written by the same author who was finishing *De l'intelligence*. Yet he wanted very much to have his Parisian sketches admired for their actuality and psychological penetration and was cruelly disappointed when Sainte-Beuve, in response to his impolite search for compliments, replied that the book was an embarrassment.

Taine believed that his sarcasm and irony were giving Parisians and Frenchmen a true glimpse of their damaged and banal souls. An unnerving effort in the *Notes sur Paris* to imitate a fable of La Fontaine captures all of this dreadful intent. Using the framework of an uncle instructing his nephew on the real world, Taine counseled his generation to accept life as being naturally harsh and unpleasant, requiring a stoical response to the experiences of brutality and failure that are the lot of most men. "My child," the uncle writes, "you enter life like a dining room, to take a seat at the table. You are mistaken; all the places are taken. It is not misfortune but happiness that is against the laws of nature. The normal condition of man, like that of a beast, is to be worn out by labor or to die of hunger."[49] The boy is reminded that in nature all animals prey on one another, leaving the last pieces of flesh to the insects and flies; and he is advised to acquire the resignation of field mice who are daily crippled and trampled on by elephants:

> Against these sorts of ills, the experience of all the rats and all the rat-holes has yet found no remedy; at the most after so many centuries, the little trotting race has found out some habits of the elephants, learned their paths, and to know their comings and goings from their cries. It is not quite so much crushed as it was fifty centuries ago; but it is still a victim, and will always so remain. Increase your skill as you may, poor rat; you will not add much to your happiness; rather try if you can to strengthen your patience and courage. Avoid all gro-

49. Taine, *Notes on Paris*, trans. John Austin Stevens (New York, 1897), p. 276.

tesque contortions and emotions; why make yourself the laughing-stock of your neighbors? Reserve the right to self-esteem, since you cannot escape the necessity of suffering. In time, the great feet of the elephants, and the calamities which they cause you, will seem to you quite in order. The best fruits of our science is cold resignation.[50]

The author of this gruesome tale did not need the Commune to confirm his view that ratlike victims cannot successfully revolt. But France's failures in the Franco-German War and the Commune did finally motivate Taine to write the history of his nation. His harsh philosophy would not be mitigated by that enormous work.

Poor health made Taine unfit for any kind of military service during the war, and he spent most of the period from July 1870 until after the disasters of Sedan and Metz away from the combat zones caring for the various needs of his family. France's defeat provoked a response in him that was neither very original nor unusually discerning. Like many others, he denounced the stupidity of the emperor, bewailed France's inferior preparations for the war (a war he had not desired), agreed that the Germans had revealed themselves to be perfidious brutes, and further concurred that the time had come for Frenchmen to "publicly confess their faults and to reform."[51] Taine welcomed the conservative composition of the National Assembly elected in February 1871, and anticipated that this beginning would permit France to adopt an Orleanist constitutional monarchy. The "reds" seemed thoroughly discredited in Paris, but he was afraid of the danger from "the discontent of the sixty or eighty thousand common people who have been fed for nothing during the siege."[52] In these months Taine felt a little ashamed of his previous frivolity in contributing to journals like *La Vie parisienne* and renewed his pledge that he would now seriously study and write France's history.

When the Commune was established in March 1871, Taine reacted to it in much the same way as did his famous literary

50. Ibid., p. 279.
51. Taine, *Sa vie et sa correspondance*, 3:35 (Taine to Albert Sorel, 16 December 1870).
52. Ibid., p. 51 (Taine to his mother, 12 February 1871).

friends. During the Second Empire, writers such as Flaubert, Alexander Dumas *fils*, Maxime du Camp, Théophile Gautier, and Renan had considered that their disdain for politics and their sophisticated gossip made them virtually members of the opposition![53] But they had done nothing to help the Republican minority, and Léon Gambetta's efforts to create Republican values and institutions earned their amused and superior contempt. The Commune gave such privileged, uninvolved men a chance to direct at the Communards the full arsenal of their rich vocabularies; words they would avoid using in polite conversation could now be hurled down on the people of the streets. Taine described the members of the Commune's municipal council as "narrow fanatics," "shoddy failures," "pickpockets," loudmouth "brawlers" from the political clubs.[54] He had often considered his country incompetent; he now had to admit that it was "grotesque, odious, base, absolutely incorrigible, and destined for criminal prison, or the insane asylum."[55]

During 1848 Alexis de Tocqueville had shown no great sympathy for the insurgents, but he had insisted that the problems of modern societies made obligatory careful discussion of the possibilities of socialism. Taine regarded the Communards as base fools and paraphrased their socialism in a dialogue suitable to their idiocy: "The patron, the bourgeoisie exploit us. They must be suppressed. There is no longer superiority, nor specialties. Me, a worker, I am capable, if I wish, of being the head of a business, magistrate, general. By good luck we have guns; we will use them and establish a Republic where workers like us will be ministers and presidents."[56]

On the eve of the "Bloody Week" of 21–28 May, when the Commune was crushed, Taine left Paris for England to give a series of lectures at Oxford. But before leaving France he had started

53. Paul Lidsky, *Les Écrivains contre la commune* (Paris, 1970), pp. 13–39.

54. Taine, *Sa vie et sa correspondance*, 3:78 (Taine to Madame H. Taine, 28 March 1871).

55. Ibid., p. 75 (Taine to Madame H. Taine, 26 March 1871).

56. Ibid., p. 92 (Taine to Madame H. Taine, 5 April 1871).

sketching out the work he now described as "my future book on contemporary France." When he returned home in the summer of 1871, he began the archival and library research on *Les Origines de la France contemporaine* that would possess him until his death twenty years later. He made a concrete attempt, however, to help insure that universal suffrage would not turn the Third Republic over to the socially defective and déclassés, and he cooperated in plans for a school of higher education whose elite students and well-born graduates would guarantee that the "enlightened and rich classes lead the ignorant and those who work and live from day to day."[57]

To further his first objective Taine wrote an important essay on universal suffrage advocating the indirect election of deputies in order to give predominant power to the notables of rural France. This procedure would save the nation, he believed, from the effects of a plebiscitarian system that had operated since 1848 like a strong blind horse turning to the left or right depending upon which way it was pulled. Admittedly workers of the large cities would object to surrendering all essential power to the provinces, but, he replied, "it is of no importance for they are only a minority, approximately one against nine, and have no right to impose their will on the nine others."[58] The Republic did not adopt Taine's proposal, yet the Senate was elected by indirect suffrage and assured the result he desired.

To advance his second goal Taine supported the founding of the *École libre des sciences politiques* as a means of insuring the rich and educated a monopoly of the administrative posts in the government. A major article in the *Journal des débats* brilliantly analyzed the empirical questions in political science, economic theory and practice, the comparative study of constitutions, diplomacy, and administrative policy that would be given a scientific base at the École.[59] The explosive ideas of the "enemy" would be defused by a critical examination of the "millenary" socialists from Babeuf to the

57. Ibid., p. 173 (Taine to John Durand, 29 November 1871).
58. Taine, *Du suffrage universel et de la manière de voter* (Paris, 1872), p. 62.
59. Taine, "Fondation de l'école libre des sciences politiques," in *Derniers essais de critique et d'histoire*, 16th ed. (Paris, 1923).

International, thus exposing the dreams of the ignorant implanted by the semi-ignorant. Ironically, seventy years later Marc Bloch in his moving account of the Third Republic's collapse attributed her social disunity in great part to the influence of the École. "The *École des Sciences Politiques*," he noted, "was always the spiritual home of the scions of rich and powerful families. Its graduates filled the embassies, the Treasury, the Council of State and the Public Audit Office."[60] Once the École was firmly established, Taine took up his history in earnest, predicting that his study would be faithful to the "anti-revolutionary" guidance of science.

Taine opened his inquiry into France's past and present by admitting in the first sentence of *L'Ancien régime* that at twenty-one, in 1849, he had not voted because he was too ignorant of his society's history, needs, and fundamental nature. No longer innocent or inexperienced, he now proposed to answer the question: "What is contemporary France?" An adequate reply would not only involve the research in archives incumbent on anyone who identified himself as a "documentary historian," but would also require that he draw upon all his past work, his understanding of man, art, psychology, and nature. The integrity of his own existence was at issue, and Taine accepted this risk.

Taine gave the last twenty years of his life to the research and writing of *Les Origines de la France contemporaine*. *L'Ancien régime*, published in 1875, required four years. *La Révolution*, in three volumes, took nine years to complete. *L'Anarchie*, on the opening of the Revolution, appeared in 1878; three years later, in 1881, *La Conquête jacobine*; and in 1884, *Le Gouvernement révolutionnaire*. His two volumes on *Le Régime moderne*, continuing the story from Napoleon's era until Taine's own time, came out in 1891 and in 1893, the year of Taine's death.[61]

No historian of France ever brought to conclusion a history with the scope of Taine's *Origines*. Before Taine, Tocqueville had sought

60. Marc Bloch, *Strange Defeat*, trans. Gerard Hopkins (New York, 1968), p. 159.

61. *L'Ancien régime* (Paris, 1875). *La Révolution*, vol. 1, *L'Anarchie* (Paris, 1878); vol. 2, *La Conquête jacobine* (Paris, 1881); vol. 3, *Le Gouvernement révolutionnaire* (Paris, 1884). *Le Régime moderne*, vol. 1 (Paris, 1891); vol. 2 (Paris, 1893).

to locate in the conflict between the Old Régime and the Revolution the clues to France's chronic fluctuations between free and unfree governments, between stability and disequilibrium. But Tocqueville did not finish his history and would, in any case, have been unwilling to go beyond the Empire. Taine designed his history to link in an unbroken fashion France's experience from the sixteenth century until the moment he put down his pen. The most recent effort to repeat his design was that announced in the spring of 1972 as the *Nouvelle histoire de la France contemporaine*; there will be eighteen volumes and seventeen authors, and so far six historians have been required to cover the years 1787 to 1815.[62] Historical specialization does not alone explain the difference between Taine's singular achievement and the practices of modern scholarship. Taine believed that without losing a thread he could trace out the continuity of France's history following the essential lines that converged on the revolutionary era and their pattern as they unraveled from that decisive moment. Modern historiography has at best been able to speak of a revolutionary legacy, a continuing spirit; Taine insisted that everything connected.[63]

Nineteenth-century France, according to Taine, inherited the contradictions between the scientific consciousness of modernity and the rhetorical democratic expectations of the previous revolutionary age. He proposed that a truly modern society would do well to give up the prescientific ideologies of the eighteenth century in preference for a precise knowledge of the workings of its productive systems; concrete information on the distribution of its literate and illiterate populations; an accurate reading on the range of talent spread through the social classes; a political balance between the heirs to great responsibility and those citizens of wealth and professional training aspiring to power; and a profound analysis of the

---

62. Michel Vovelle, *La Chute de la monarchie, 1787–1792* (Paris, 1972); Marc Bouloiseau, *La République jacobine 10 août 1792–9 Thermidor An II* (Paris, 1972); Denis Woronoff, *La République bourgeoise de Thermidor à Brumaire* (Paris, 1972); Louis Bergeron, *L'Épisode napoléonien: Aspects intérieurs 1799–1815* (Paris, 1972); J. Lovie and A. Palluel-Guillard, *L'Épisode napoléonien: Aspects extérieurs, 1799–1815* (Paris, 1972).

63. The best brief account of the historiography of the Revolution is Alice Gerard, *La Révolution française, mythes et interprétations (1789–1970)* (Paris, 1970).

desires and fears common to all its citizens. He believed that, in France, political ideologies rather than a knowledge of social facts prevailed in all discussion of the nation's past and future. He hoped that through his history France could move beyond ideology to an understanding of the historical contradictions that explained her existing problems, conflicts, and passionate disagreements.

France's polarization occurred, Taine believed, when those having power, honor, and wealth in the Old Regime failed in their obligations toward the disinherited and thus irrevocably prepared the collapse of the ancient system. The Revolution was, however, unable to reverse the social hierarchies of the past; neither anarchy nor terror succeeded in founding a new society. In turn, Napoleon's imposition of order on the privileged and underprivileged denied to both the conditions for independent private and public life. After Napoleon the unresolved discordancies burdened France with a state that promiscuously extended its powers; an educational system that suppressed rather than liberated the intellect; and a religion locked into historical compromises that hastened the seepage of its members and enfeebled the imagination of the faithful and their leaders. *L'Ancien régime, La Révolution,* and *Le Régime moderne,* the three main sections making up *Les Origines de la France contemporaine,* were designed to present the paradoxes and contradictions of this long historical experience in such a fashion that they could no longer be subsumed as part of the past, but would have to be viewed as the continuing actuality of the present.

From the beginning to the end of his history Taine labored to create an acceptance of the idea that a *juste milieu* could be established for France in which inherited position, possessions, and prestige would enable rural France to incrementally open opportunity to men of merit, while keeping the state under proper restraint but giving it enough authority to curb revolutionary challenges to the social order. Yet Taine's own tensions and doubts concerning the fragility of the settlement in France after the Commune communicated to his history and readers an anxiety that could not be assuaged.

L'Ancien régime was published in December 1875 at the end of the first year of the "constitution" of the Third Republic. René

Rémond has astutely noted that this constitution was the most Orleanist of all France's fundamental laws.[64] The founding legislation of the Third Republic sanctioned a *juste milieu* between a return to the old order and a plunge into an unknown future. The Republican system based on universal suffrage and a bicameral legislature tipped the balance of social power in favor of the provincial notables; it rejected in law and by its promises the inequalities of the ancient regime while retaining an overt fear of possible violent threats from the masses. Rémond suggests that perhaps Orleanism satisfies best the political temperament of the French.[65] Taine's *Origines* thus perfectly fitted his own moment in history, the political and social milieu of his audience, and their psychological needs. In the hands of another writer, a less intense historian, his work would have been flawed by triumphalism, or been a kind of Whig history celebrating the victory of his class. Taine, however, misread his own hour; or more precisely his profound distress over his nation's capacity for failure gave his history a tension disproportionate to the crises of his time. Corrections of his mistakes by red or blue pencil cannot lighten the apprehension he created concerning France's ability to adjust to modernity.

When in 1889 France commemorated the hundreth anniversary of the Revolution, despite the Exposition Universelle and the Eiffel Tower, that fete was surrounded by a strained and unnatural gloom. At this time the historian Ernest Lavisse (1842–1922), who represented the Third Republic's first generation of professional historians, observed that the public ceremonies were more funereal than joyous. He found particularly frustrating the paucity of references to the Revolution's promise of fraternity, "the most neglected member of the Republican trinity."[66] Taine's three volumes on the Revolution, completed and published five years before its centenary, may well have made it all but impossible for the Right or the Radical Republicans to find any common ground; the historical

64. René Rémond, *La Vie politique en France depuis 1789,* 2 vols. (Paris, 1965–69), 2:320.
65. Ibid., p. 320.
66. Ernest Lavisse, "De Paris à Versailles: Souvenirs du 5 Mai 1889," *Revue bleue* 17 (11 May 1889): 598.

memories he reinforced seemed to assure their continuing division. Taine was not guilty of leading France to the prefascism of the Action française, but he was responsible for depriving Frenchmen of joy in their historical image. His ideas would have to be rejected and he anticipated this turnabout when replying in 1889 to the insensitivity and antiscientism of Paul Bourget's play *The Disciple:* "I can only conclude one thing, that taste has changed, that my generation is finshed."[67]

Rival artisans have altered the form, details, and colors of Taine's tapestry; seams have been separated, holes torn in the wool. This destruction and wear has occurred most often in those parts of the cloth where Taine thought he was using his most precious threads, doing his finest work. Contemplation of the defects of his favorite panels has made possible the masterpieces of his competitors. The most vigorous parts of his design continue, however, to impose their impressions on his successors—historians such as Paul Hazard, Daniel Mornet, Georges Lefebvre, and George Rudé. The cartoons of these weavers bear the tracings of the lines he drew so firmly.

Taine endlessly insisted, for example, that the classical reasoning of the seventeenth century functioned only in an aristocratic and insulated culture; in this closed company, judgements, arguments, and propositions were perfected in proportion to their author's ignorance of the actual world. Playwrights, preachers, and philosophers discoursed on man's needs, but had never experienced hunger. The eighteenth-century philosophes who criticized the old order were themselves, Taine suggested, captives of its methods of reasoning; their impact was possible only because the finesse of the classical modes of discourse released them from any dependency on the concrete as long as their logical constructions remained elegant. Men trained in this precious school could be expected as legislators to consider offensive to reason and humanity any challenges to their theories and practices. The perfection of their use of *raison* excluded counterpropositions, facts, and history. Paul Hazard, Daniel Mornet, and Peter Gay among others have

67. Taine, *Sa vie et sa correspondance*, 4:293 (Taine to Paul Bourget, 29 September 1889).

reestablished the autocritical capacity of Enlightened thinkers.[68] Yet at this moment, when they are most appreciated, new reflection suggests that Taine's bold and heavy line may have been close to the truth. Michel Foucault, in his much praised *The Order of Things*, appears to have joined Taine by arguing that the classical mind claimed for reason and language representative verisimilitude that cannot be delivered by human mental components, and that the classical period invented a man who must be denied existence by all the standards of modernity.[69]

Richard Cobb and George Rudé have properly objected to Taine's emphasis on the "crapulous," felonious character of the revolutionary militants as violating historical truth and destroying his reputation rather than that of those he sought to defame.[70] Yet problems persist in identifying those who participated in the revolutionary *journées*. Rudé presents unimpeachable evidence that few of those arrested or of those who came under official notice were beggars or vagabonds, and that the participants in the crowds were men of fixed abodes and artisan occupations. The limited number of socially marginal persons uncovered by Rudé's documents raises, however, the question how this sizable class of the *ancien régime* disappeared during the Revolution. No one arrested would willingly admit to having begged or to having no visible means of support; the law treated such offenders very harshly, and public opinion endorsed severe punishments. The Revolution brought little or no change in public attitude or official practice in this regard. During the Convention the beggar was still regarded with dread, and it seemed natural for Jacobin supporters of The Rights of Man to declare: "There is no fatherland for the wretch

68. Paul Hazard, *The European Mind: The Critical Years, 1680-1715* (New Haven, Conn., 1953); idem, *European Thought in the Eighteenth Century from Montesquieu to Lessing* (New Haven, Conn., 1954); Mornet, *Les Origines intellectuelles*; Peter Gay, *The Enlightenment: An Interpretation*, 2 vols. (New York, 1966-69).

69. Michel Foucault, *The Order of Things* (New York, 1970).

70. Richard Cobb, *Les Armeés révolutionnaires: Instrument de la terreur dans les départements, avril 1793 (floréal an II)*, 2 vols. (Paris, 1961-63), 1:220; Rudé, *The Crowd.*

who has nothing."[71] In the last pages of *L'Ancien régime* Taine observed that the fear caused by imagined or real threats from beggars and vagabonds was a significant part of the complaints directed against the shaky monarchy. He therefore continued to watch for the face of the beggar in the crowds of the Revolution, while today's scholarship proposes that they vanished and dropped out during that period. They live on in Taine's history, frightening the upright and eluding those sent to find them.

The distrust of Taine by professional scholars has also centered on his overreaction to the violence of the Revolution. He considered this "patriotic gore" largely the work of a minority imposing their will on French society, and he overlooked the outrages committed by counterrevolutionaries. Yet Taine's partisan and emotional response enabled him to raise questions that have been avoided by less prejudiced historians. Georges Lefebvre, for example, when describing the September massacres, wrote:"the blood letting did not cease until the countryside was purged. The collective mentality is sufficient explanation for the killing."[72] Taine's revulsion, however, led him to probe deeply into the nature of the violence committed by the defenders of the Revolution. He believed that the defensive character of their action still left unresolved an explanation as to how ordinary, average, hardworking citizens bring themselves to the point of choking, stabbing, disembering their neighbors. How do they sustain their fury? His answer is so disturbing that it might lead even the most ardent supporter of the Revolution and its place in history to pray that he might avoid the occasions for such violence. "Observe children drowning a dog or killing a snake. Tenacity of life irritates them, as if it were a rebellion against their despotism, the effect of which is to render them only the more violent against their victims."[73]

71. "Rapport et projet de décret sur l'extinction de la mendicité, présenté à la Convention Nationale, au nom du comité de secours public, par Jean-Baptiste Bo, député du département de l'Aveyron," in *Archives parlementaires*, 1st ser., 76: 443–49.
72. Georges Lefebvre, *The French Revolution from Its Origins to 1793*, trans. E. M. Evanson (New York, 1962), p. 244.
73. Taine, *The French Revolution*, trans. John Durand, 3 vols. (New York, 1931), 2:225.

Though he admitted that he was antirevolutionary, Taine refused to be described as reactionary. In a rare moment of intimacy, he confessed that he thought it was indecent for an author to expose his innermost feelings in public. He had a horror of what he described as *sensibilité affichée"* and concurred with Gautier that "One must never grieve" before others. And he felt he was not being dishonest in believing that his history had judged the action of any man by one criterion: "has he diminished, or at least not added to, the sum total of human suffering in his own time and for the future?"[74] Taine undertook to keep this test in mind when writing his chapter on "The People" in *The L'Ancien régime* and those on the Jacobins in *La Révolution*.

When Taine was admitted to the Académie française in 1880, he made a final effort to express his understanding of the historian's art and responsibility.[75] He proposed that it would be well for historians to give less attention to the role of great men and to concentrate instead on the great social groups within which the mass of men live out their lives. The historian was urged to find a place on his canvas for the members of every class, profession, and occupation. He will deal with princes, aristocrats, parliamentarians, financiers, country gentlemen, curés, employers, tenant farmers, and occasional beggars and bandits. What matters is to describe their lives within the circle of their society. The individual must be protrayed from the moment of his birth until his death, and the historian must know how the hours, the days, and the weeks of the most obscure are spent. He must ask of each class and its members: What do they produce? What do they consume? What luxuries and privations do they experience? At what cost? How do the different classes regard the family and the nation? How do they love, marry, beget, and rear children? What do they make of the state? Do they accept or reject the social hierarchies of their world? What aspects of existence bolster the confidence of a class,

74. Taine, *Sa vie et sa correspondance*, 4:236 (Taine to Jules Lemaître, 28 March 1887).
75. Taine, "M. Louis de Loménie" (Discours de réception prononcé a l'Académie française), in *Derniers essais de critique et d'histoire*, 16th ed. (Paris, 1923), pp. 281–84.

evoke their resignation, and try their patience? How do men of
every class and occupation touch the beautiful and give coherence
to their universe? How does the brief life of any generation flow
into the stream of History and the ocean of Time?

By this profession of faith and by his example Taine honored all
who had attended his investiture into the historian's high office: La
Fontaine, Saint-Simon, Montesquieu, Hegel, Guizot, Michelet,
Stendhal, Balzac, and Sainte-Beuve. He recapitulated in his history
a fair portion of what had been accomplished by his art before him
and anticipated a goodly part of its future.

I have sought in this edition of *The Origins of Contemporary
France* to represent the scope and development of Taine's whole
history. His prefaces are included as valuable statements of his
historical credo. Taine's picture of the people from *The Ancient
Regime* is chosen because it best illustrates how he wrote concrete
social history and his sensitivity to the injustices of prerevolutionary
France. The selections from *The Revolution* convey Taine's contro-
versial historical view of the anarchical opening of the Revolution,
his impassioned description of the Jacobin rise to power, and his
vitriolic treatment of the personalities of the Jacobin leaders. Taine
believed that Napoleon Bonaparte "made modern France," and his
historical and psychological portrait of Bonaparte remains central
to any discussion of Napoleon's place in history. The debate on
Taine as a historian has rarely focused on his *Modern Regime*. Yet
his knowing, perceptive, and detailed historical and sociological
examination of local society, the Church, and education in nineteenth-century France is as important as his treatment of the Old
Regime or the Revolution. The chapters offered here from *The
Modern Regime* are critical to any consideration of Hippolyte
Taine as a classic European historian.

The translations from *Les Origines de la France contemporaine*
were made by the American John Durand (1822–1908). Taine
considered Durand a good friend and a fine translator, and he
helped in every way to make possible the prompt English translation of the six volumes of *Les Origines*. As a result of this coopera-
tion, H. Holt and Company of New York brought out from 1876 to

Introduction

1894 the American edition of each volume within a year of their
initial publication in Paris by Taine's publisher Hachette. My selections are from the Holt edition, reprinted by P. Smith in 1931. In
France *Les Origines de la France contemporaine* went through
twenty-two editions by 1899, but no significant changes were made
in the text and the Durand translation remains faithful to Taine's
original work.

EDWARD T. GARGAN

THE ANCIENT REGIME

PREFACE.

In 1849, being twenty-one years of age, and an elector, I was very much puzzled, for I had to vote for fifteen or twenty deputies, and, moreover, according to French custom, I had not only to determine what candidate I would vote for, but what theory I should adopt. I had to choose between a royalist or a republican, a democrat or a conservative, a socialist or a bonapartist; as I was neither one nor the other, nor even anything, I often envied those around me who were so fortunate as to have arrived at definite conclusions. After listening to various doctrines, it seemed to me that I was laboring under some mental defect. The motives that influenced others did not influence me. I could not comprehend how, in political matters, a man should be governed by his preferences. My affirmative friends planned a constitution the same as a house, according to the latest, simplest, and most complete notion of it, and many were offered for acceptance—the mansion of a marquis, the house of a common citizen, the tenement of a laborer, the barracks of a soldier, the philanstery of a socialist, and even the camp of savages. Each claimed that his was "the true habitation for man, the only one in which a sensible person could live." I was not satisfied with such reasons, for I did not regard personal tastes as authoritative. It seemed to me that a house should not be built for the architect alone, nor for itself, but for the owner who was to occupy it.—Referring to the owner for his advice, submitting to the French people the plans of its future habitation, would evidently be either for show or to deceive them; such a question, in such a case, answers itself, and, besides, were the answer allowable, France was scarcely better prepared for it than myself; the combined ignorance of

3

ten millions is not the equivalent of one man's wisdom. A
people may be consulted and, in an extreme case, may declare
what form of government it would like best, but not that which
it most needs.   Nothing but experience can determine this; it
must have time to ascertain whether the political structure is
convenient, substantial, able to withstand inclemencies, and
adapted to customs, habits, occupations, characters, peculiarities
and caprices.   For example, the one we have tried has never
satisfied us; we have demolished it thirteen times in twenty
years that we might set it up anew, and always in vain, for never
have we found one that suited us.   If other people have been
more fortunate, or if various political structures abroad have
proved stable and enduring, it is because these have been erected
in a special way, around some primitive, massive pile, supported
by an old central edifice, often restored but always preserved,
gradually enlarged, and, after numerous trials and additions,
adapted to the wants of its occupants.   Never has one been put
up instantaneously, after an entirely new design, and according
to the measurements of pure reason.   It is well to admit, perhaps, that there is no other way of erecting a permanent building,
and that the sudden contrivance of a new, suitable, and enduring
constitution is an enterprise beyond the forces of the human
mind.

In any event, I concluded for myself that, if we ever discover
the one we want, it will not be through the processes now in
vogue.   In effect, the point is, to *discover* it, whether it exists,
and not to submit it to a vote.   Our preferences, in this respect,
would be vain; nature and history have elected for us in advance;
we must accommodate ourselves to them as it is certain that they
will not accommodate themselves to us.   The social and political
forms into which a people may enter and *remain* are not open to
arbitration, but are determined by its character and its past.   All,
even down to the minutest details, should be moulded on the
living features for which they are designed; otherwise, they will
break and fall to pieces.   Hence it is that, if we succeed in
finding our constitution, it will come to us only through a study
of ourselves, and the more thoroughly we know ourselves, the
greater our certainty in finding the one that suits us.   We must,
accordingly, set aside the usual methods and have a clear con-

ception of the nation before drawing up its constitution. The former is, undoubtedly, a more serious and more difficult task than the latter. What time, what study, what observations correcting each other, what researches into the past and the present, in all the domains of thought and of action, what manifold, secular efforts are necessary for acquiring a full and precise idea of a great people, which has already lived to a great age, and which still lives on ! Only in this way, however, can what is sound be established after having resorted to empty theories, and I resolved, for my own part, at least, that, should I ever attempt to form a political opinion, it would be only after studying France.

What is contemporary France? To answer this question, requires a knowledge of how France was formed, or, what is much better, being present at her formation, as if a spectator. At the close of the last century she undergoes a transformation, like that of an insect shedding its coat. Her ancient organization breaks up; she herself rends the most precious tissues and falls into convulsions which seem mortal. And then, there is recovery, after multiplied throes and a painful lethargy. But her organization is no longer what it was; a new being, after terrible internal travail, is substituted for the old one. In 1808, all her leading features are definitely established: departments, *arrondissements*, cantons and communes—no change has since taken place in her outward divisions and adjunctions; the Concordat, the Code, the tribunals, the University, the Institute, the prefects, the Council of State, the imposts, the tax-collectors, the Cour des Comptes, with a centralized and uniform administration—its principal organs remain the same; henceforth, every class, the nobles, the commonalty, the laboring class, and the peasants—each has the place, interests, sentiments and traditions that we now observe at the present day. Thus, the new organism is at once stable and complete. Its structure, its instincts, and its faculties indicate beforehand the circle within which its thought or action will be exercised. Surrounding nations, some precocious, others backward, all with greater caution, and many with more success, effect the same transformation in passing from the feudal to the modern State; the parturition is universal and nearly simultaneous. But in the new, as well as under the old form, the weak are always the prey of the strhng. Woe to those whose too tardy evolution has sub-jected them to the neighbor suddenly emerged from his chrysalis state fully armed! Woe likewise to him whose too violent and too brusque evolution has disturbed the balance of internal economy, and who, exaggerating his governing means, radically changing fundamental organs, impoverishing by degrees his vital substance, is condemned to rash undertakings, to debility and to impotence, surrounded by better proportioned and healthier neighbors! In the organization effected by France at the beginning of the century all the main lines of her contempo-raneous history are traceable, — political revolutions, social utopias, the divisions of classes, the rôle of the Church, the con-duct of the nobles, of the bourgeoisie and of the people, and the development, direction or deviation of philosophy, literature and science. Hence it is that, in striving to comprehend our actual situation, we constantly revert back to the terrible and fruitful crisis by which the Ancient Régime produced the Revo-lution, and the Revolution the Modern Régime.

The Ancient Régime, the Revolution, the Modern Régime, are the three conditions of things which I shall strive to describe with exactitude. I have no hesitation in stating that this is my sole object. A historian may be allowed the privilege of a natu-ralist; I have regarded my subject the same as the metamor-phosis of an insect. The event, furthermore, is so interesting as to render it worthy of study for itself alone; no effort is neces-sary to exclude mental reservations. Without taking any side, curiosity becomes scientific and centres on the secret forces which direct the wonderful process. These forces consist of the situation, the passions, the ideas, and the wills of each group of actors, and which can be defined and almost measured. They are in full view; we need not resort to conjecture about them, to doubtful surmises, to vague indications. We enjoy the singu-lar good fortune of seeing the men themselves, their exterior and their interior. The Frenchmen of the ancient régime are still within visual range. All of us, in our youth, have encountered one or more of the survivors of this vanished society. Many of their dwellings, with the furniture, still remain intact. Their pic-tures and engravings enable us to take part in their domestic life,

see how they dress, observe their attitudes and follow their movements. Through their literature, philosophy, scientific pursuits,
gazettes, and correspondence, we can reproduce their feeling and
thought, and even enjoy their familiar conversation. The multitude of memoirs, issuing during the past thirty years from public
and private archives, lead us from one drawing-room to another,
as if we bore with us so many letters of introduction. The independent descriptions by foreign travellers, in their journals and
correspondence, correct and complete the portraits which this
society has traced of itself. Everything that it could state has
been stated, except what was commonplace and well-known to
contemporaries, whatever seemed technical, tedious and vulgar,
whatever related to the provinces, to the bourgeoisie, to the peasant, to the laboring man, to the government, and to the household. It has been my aim to supply these omissions, and make
France known to others outside the small circle of the literary
and the cultivated. Owing to the kindness of M. Maury and the
valuable indications of M. Boutaric I have been able to examine
a mass of manuscript documents, consisting of the correspondence of numerous intendants, customs-directors, farmers-general,
magistrates, employees and private individuals, of every kind and
degree, during the last thirty years of the ancient regime, including reports and memorials belonging to the various departments
of the royal household, the *procès-verbaux* and *cahiers* of the
States-General, contained in one hundred and seventy-six volumes, the despatches of military officers in 1789 and 1790, the
letters, memoirs and detailed statistics, preserved in the one hundred boxes of the ecclesiastical committee, the correspondence,
in ninety-four files, of the department and municipal authorities,
with the ministries from 1790 to 1799, the reports of the Councillors of State on mission at the end of 1801, the reports of prefects under the Consulate, the Empire, and the Restoration down
to 1823, and such a quantity of unknown and instructive documents besides these that the history of the Revolution seems,
indeed, to be still unwritten. In any event, it is only such documents which can portray to us all these animated figures, the
lesser nobles, the curates, the monks, the nuns of the provinces,
the aldermen and bourgeoisie of the towns, the attorneys and
syndics of the country villages, the laborers and artisans, the offi-

cers and the soldiers. These alone enable us to contemplate and appreciate in detail the various conditions of humanity, the interior of a parsonage, of a convent, of a town-council, the wages of a workman, the produce of a farm, the taxes levied on a peasant, the duties of a tax-collector, the expenditure of a noble or prelate, the budget, retinue and ceremonial of a court. Thanks to such resources, we are able to give precise figures, to know hour by hour the occupations of a day and, better still, read off the bill of fare of a grand dinner, and recompose all parts of a full-dress costume. We have again, on the one hand, samples of the materials of the dresses worn by Marie Antoinette, pinned on paper and classified by dates, and, on the other, we can tell what clothes were worn by the peasant, describe the bread he ate, specify the flour it was made of, and state the cost of a pound of it in *sous* and *deniers*. With such resources one becomes almost contemporary with the men whose history one writes and, more than once, in the Archives, I have found myself speaking almost aloud with them while tracing their old handwriting on the time-stained paper before me.

August, 1875.

BOOK FIFTH.

The People.

CHAPTER I.

I. Privations.—Under Louis XIV.—Under Louis XV.—Under Louis XVI.—II. The condition of the peasant during the last thirty years of the Ancient Régime.—His precarious subsistence.—State of agriculture.—Uncultivated farms.—Poor cultivation.—Inadequate wages.—Lack of comforts.—III. Aspects of the country and of the peasantry.—IV. How the peasant becomes a proprietor.—He is no better off.—Increase of taxes.—He is the "mule" of the Ancient Régime.

I.

LA BRUYÈRE wrote, just a century before 1789,[1] "Certain savage-looking beings, male and female, are seen in the country, black, livid and sunburnt, and belonging to the soil which they dig and grub with invincible stubbornness. They seem capable of articulation, and, when they stand erect, they display human lineaments. They are, in fact, men. They retire at night into their dens where they live on black bread, water and roots. They spare other human beings the trouble of sowing, ploughing and harvesting, and thus should not be in want of the bread they have planted." They continue in want of it during twenty-five years after this and die in herds. I estimate that in 1715 more than one-third of the population, six millions, perish with hunger and of destitution. The picture, accordingly, for the first quarter of the century preceding the Revolution, far from being overdrawn, is the reverse; we shall see that, during more than half a century, up to the death of Louis XV. it is exact; perhaps instead of weakening any of its points, they should be strengthened.

---

[1] La Bruyère, edition of Destailleurs, II. 97. Addition to the fourth ed. (1689).

"In 1725," says St. Simon, "with the profuseness of Stras
bourg and Chantilly, the people, in Normandy, live on the grass
of the fields. The first king in Europe is great simply by being
a king of beggars of all conditions, and by turning his kingdom
into a vast hospital of dying people of whom their all is taken
without a murmur." [1] In the most prosperous days of Fleury
and in the finest region in France, the peasant hides "his wine on
account of the excise and his bread on account of the *taille*," [2]
convinced "that he is a lost man if any doubt exists of his dying
of starvation." [3] In 1739 d'Argenson writes in his journal: [4]
"The famine has just occasioned three insurrections in the provinces, at Ruffec, at Caen, and at Chinon. Women carrying their
bread with them have been assassinated on the highways. . . .
M. le Duc d'Orléans brought to the Council the other day a
piece of bread, and placed it on the table before the king; 'Sire,'
said he, 'there is the bread on which your subjects now feed
themselves.'" "In my own canton of Touraine men have been
eating herbage more than a year." Misery finds company on
all sides. "It is talked about at Versailles more than ever. The
king interrogated the bishop of Chartres on the condition of his
people; he replied that 'the famine and the mortality were such
that men ate grass like sheep and died like so many flies.'" In
1740, [5] Massillon, bishop of Clermont-Ferrand, writes to Fleury:
"The people of the rural districts are living in frightful destitution, without beds, without furniture; the majority, for half the
year, even lack barley and oat bread, their sole food, and which
they are compelled to take out of their own and their childrens'
mouths to pay the taxes. It pains me to see this sad spectacle
every year on my visits. The negroes of our colonies are, in this

[1] Oppression and misery begin about 1672. At the end of the seventeenth century (1698),
the reports made up by the intendants for the Duc de Bourgogne, state that many of the
districts and provinces have lost one-sixth, one-fifth, one-quarter, the third and even the
half of their population. (See details in the "Correspondance des contrôleurs-généraux
from 1683 to 1698," published by M. de Boislisle). According to the reports of intendants,
(Vauban, "Dime Royale," ch. vii. § 2.), the population of France in 1698 amounted to
19,994,146 inhabitants. From 1698 to 1715 it decreases. According to Forbonnais, there
were but 16 or 17 millions under the Regency. After this epoch the population no longer
diminishes but, for forty years, it hardly increases. In 1753 (Voltaire, "Dict. Phil.," article
Population), there are 3,550,499 firesides, besides 700,000 souls in Paris, which makes from
16 to 17 millions of inhabitants if we count four and one-half persons to each fireside, and
from 18 to 19 millions if we count five persons.
[2] Floquet, "Histoire du Parlement de Normandie," VII. 402.
[3] Rousseau, "Confessions," 1st part, ch. iv. (1732).
[4] D Argenson, 19th and 24th May, July 4, and Aug. 1, 1739.
[5] "Résumé de l'histoire d'Auvergne par un Auvergnat" (M. Tallandier), p. 313.

respect, infinitely better off, for, while working, they are fed and clothed along with their wives and children, while our peasantry, the most laborious in the kingdom, cannot, with the hardest and most devoted labor, earn bread for themselves and their families, and at the same time, pay the subsidies." In 1740,[1] at Lille, the people rebel against the export of grain. "An intendant informs me that the misery increases from hour to hour, the slightest danger to the crops resulting in this for three years past. . . Flanders, especially, is greatly embarrassed; there is nothing to live on until the harvesting, which will not take place for two months. The provinces the best off are not able to help the others. Each bourgeois in each town is obliged to feed one or two poor persons and provide them with fourteen pounds of bread per week. In the little town of Chatellerault, (of four thousand inhabitants), eighteen hundred poor, this winter, are on that footing. . . . The poor outnumber those able to live without begging . . . while prosecutions for unpaid dues are carried on with unexampled rigor. The clothes of the poor are seized and their last measure of flour, the latches on their doors, etc. . . . The abbess of Jouarre told me yesterday that, in her canton, in Brie, most of the ground had not been planted." It is not surprising that the famine spreads even to Paris. "Fears are entertained of next Wednesday. There is no more bread in Paris, except that of the damaged flour which is brought in and which burns (when baking). The mills are working day and night at Belleville, regrinding old damaged flour. The people are ready to rebel; bread goes up a *sol* a day; no merchant dares, or is disposed, to bring in his wheat. The market on Wednesday was almost in a state of revolt, there being no bread in it after seven o'clock in the morning. . . . The poor creatures at Bicêtre were put on short allowance, three *quarterons* (twelve ounces), being reduced to only half a pound. A rebellion broke out and they forced the guards. Numbers escaped and they have inundated Paris. The watch, with the police of the neighborhood, were called out and an attack was made on these poor wretches with bayonet and sword. About fifty of them were left on the ground; the revolt was not suppressed yesterday morning."

Ten years later the evil is greater.[2] "In the country around

---

[1] D'Argenson, 1740, Aug. 7 and 21, September 19 and 24, May 28, November 7.
[2] D'Argenson, October 4, 1749; May 20, Sept. 12, Oct. 28, Dec. 28, 1750; June 16, Dec. 22, 1751, etc.

me, ten leagues from Paris, I find increased privation and constant complaints. What must it be in our wretched provinces in the interior of the kingdom? . . . My curate tells me that eight families, supporting themselves on their labor when I left, are now begging their bread. There is no work to be had. The wealthy are economizing like the poor. And with all this the *taille* is exacted with military severity. The collectors, with their officers, accompanied by locksmiths, force open the doors and carry off and sell furniture for one-quarter of its value, the expenses exceeding the amount of the tax. . . ." " I am at this moment on my estates in Touraine. I encounter nothing but frightful privations; the melancholy sentiment of suffering no longer prevails with the poor inhabitants but rather one of utter despair; they desire death only and avoid increase. . . . It is estimated that one-quarter of the working-days of the year go to the *corvées*, the laborers feeding themselves, and with what? . . . I see poor people dying of destitution. They are paid fifteen sous a day, equal to a crown, for their load. Whole villages are either ruined or broken up, and none of the households recover. . . . Judging by what my neighbors tell me the inhabitants have diminished one-third. . . . The daily laborers are all leaving and taking refuge in the small towns. In many villages everybody leaves. I have several parishes in which the *taille* for three years is due, the proceedings for its collection always going on. . . . The receivers of the *taille* and of the fisc add one-half each year in expenses above the tax. . . . An assessor, on coming to the village where I have my country-house, states that the *taille* this year will be much increased; he noticed that the peasants here were fatter than elsewhere; that they had chicken feathers before their doors, and that the living here must be good, everybody doing well, etc. This is the cause of the peasant's discouragement, and likewise the cause of misfortune throughout the kingdom." "In the country where I am staying I hear that marriage is declining and that the population is decreasing on all sides. In my parish, with a few firesides, there are more than thirty single persons, male and female, old enough to marry and none of them having any idea of it. On being urged to marry they all reply alike that it is not worth while to bring unfortunate beings like themselves into the world. I have myself tried to induce some of the women to marry by offering them assistance, but they all reason in this way as if they

had consulted together." [1]   "One of my curates sends me word
that, although he is the oldest in the province of Touraine, and
has seen many things, including excessively high prices for wheat,
he remembers no misery so great as that of this year, even in
1709. . . . Some of the seigniors of Touraine inform me that,
being desirous of setting the inhabitants to work by the day, they
found very few of them and these so weak that they were unable
to use their arms."

Those who are able to leave, emigrate.   "A person from Languedoc tells me of vast numbers of peasants deserting that province and taking refuge in Piedmont, Savoy, and Spain, tormented
and frightened by the measures resorted to in collecting tithes.
. . . The extortioners sell everything and imprison everybody as
if prisoners of war, and even with more avidity and malice in
order to gain something themselves."   "I met an intendant of
one of the finest provinces in the kingdom, who told me that no
more farmers could be found there; that parents preferred to send
their children to the towns; that living in the surrounding country
was daily becoming more horrible to the inhabitants. . . . A
man, well-informed in financial matters, told me that over two
hundred families in Normandy had left this year, fearing the collections in their villages."   At Paris, "the streets swarm with
beggars.   One cannot stop before a door without a dozen mendicants besetting him with their importunities.   They are said to
be people from the country who, unable to endure the persecutions they have to undergo, take refuge in the cities . . . preferring mendicity to labor."   And yet the people of the cities are
not much better off.   "An officer of a company in garrison at
Mezières tells me that the poverty of that place is so great that,
after the officers had dined in the inns, the people rush in and pillage the remnants."   "There are more than twelve thousand begging workmen in Rouen, quite as many in Tours, etc.   More
than twenty thousand of these workmen are estimated as having
left the kingdom in three months for Spain, Germany, etc.   At
Lyons twenty thousand workers in silk are watched and kept in
sight for fear of their going abroad."   At Rouen,[2] and in Normandy, "those in easy circumstances find it difficult to get bread,

---

[1] D'Argenson, June 21, 1749; May 22, 1750; March 19, 1751; February 14, April 14
1752, etc.
[2] Floquet, *ibid.* VII. 410 (April, 1752, an address to the Parliament of Normandy).

the bulk of the people being entirely without it, and, to ward off starvation, providing themselves with food that shocks humanity." "Even at Paris," writes d'Argenson,[1] "I learn that on the day M. le Dauphin and Mme. la Dauphine went to Notre Dame, on pass- ing the bridge of the Tournelle, more than two thousand women assembled in that quarter crying out, 'Give us bread, or we shall die of hunger.' . . . A vicar of the parish of Saint-Marguerite affirms that over eight hur dred persons died in the faubourg St. Antoine between January 20th and February 20th; that the poor expire with cold and hunger in their garrets, and that the priests, arriving too late, see them expire without any possible relief." Were I to enumerate the riots, the seditions of the famished, and the pillagings of storehouses, I should never end; these are the convulsive twitchings of exhaustion; the people have fasted as long as possible, and instinct, at last, rebels.   In 1747,[2] "exten- sive bread-riots occur in Toulouse, and in Guyenne they take place on every market-day."   In 1750, from six to seven thousand men gather in Bearn behind a river to resist the clerks; two companies of the Artois regiment fire on the rebels and kill a dozen of them.   In 1752, a sedition at Rouen and in its neigh- borhood lasts three days; in Dauphiny and in Auvergne riotous villagers force open the grain warehouses and take away wheat at their own price; the same year, at Arles, two thousand armed peasants demand bread at the town-hall and are dispersed by the soldiers.   In one province alone, that of Normandy, I find insurrec- tions in 1725, in 1737, in 1739, in 1752, in 1764, 1765, 1766, 1767 and 1768,[3] and always on account of bread.   "Entire hamlets," writes the Parliament, "being without the necessities of life, want compels them to resort to the food of brutes. . . . Two days more and Rouen will be without provisions, without grain, with- out bread."   Accordingly, the last riot is terrible; on this occa- sion, the populace, again masters of the town for three days, pil- lage the public granaries and the stores of all the communities. Up to the last and even later, in 1770 at Rheims, in 1775 at Dijon, at Versailles, at St. Germain, at Pontoise and at Paris, in 1772 at Poitiers, in 1785 at Aix in Provence, in 1788 and 1789 in Paris and throughout France. similar eruptions are visible.[4]   Undoubt-

[1] D'Argenson, November 26, 1751; March 15, 1753.

[2] D'Argenson, IV. 124; VI. 165; VII. 194, etc.

[3] Floquet, *ibid.* VI. 400-430

[4] "Correspondance," by Métra, I. 338, 341.   Hippeau, "Le Gouvernement de Norman die." IV. 6a, 199, 258.

:dly the government under Louis XVI. is milder; tne intendant: ire more humane, the administration is less rigid, the *taille* becomes less unequal, and the *corvée* is less onerous through its transformation, in short, misery has diminished, and yet this is greater than human nature can bear.

Examine administrative correspondence for the last thirty years preceding the Revolution. Countless statements reveal excessive suffering, even when not terminating in fury. Life to a man of the lower class, to an artisan, or workman, subsisting on the labor of his own hands, is evidently precarious; he obtains simply enough to keep him from starvation and he does not always get that.[1] Here, in four districts, "the inhabitants live only on buckwheat," and for five years, the apple crop having failed, they drink only water. There, in a country of vineyards,[2] "the vine-dressers each year are reduced, for the most part, to begging their bread during the dull season." Elsewhere, several of the day-laborers and mechanics, obliged to sell their effects and household goods, die of the cold; insufficient and unhealthy food generates sickness, while, in two districts, thirty-five thousand persons are stated to be living on alms.[3] In a remote canton the peasants cut the grain still green and dry it in the oven, because they are too hungry to wait. The intendant of Poitiers writes that "as soon as the workhouses open, a prodigious number of the poor rush to them, in spite of the reduction of wages and of the restrictions imposed on them in behalf of the most needy." The intendant of Bourges notices that a great many métayers have sold off their furniture and that "entire families pass two days without eating," and that in many parishes the famished stay in bed most of the day because they suffer less. The intendant of Orleans reports that "in Sologne, poor widows have burned up their wooden bedsteads and others have consumed their fruit trees," to preserve themselves from the cold, and he adds, "nothing is exaggerated in this statement; the cries of want cannot be expressed; the misery of the rural

---

[1] "Procès-verbaux de l'assemblée provinciale de Basse Normandie" (1787), p. 151.

[2] Archives nationales, G, 319. Condition of the directory of Issoudun, and H, 1149, 612, 1418.

[3] *Ibid.* The letters of M. de Crosne, intendant of Rouen (February 17, 1784); of M. de Blossac, intendant of Poitiers (May 9, 1784); of M. de Villeneuve, intendant of Bourges (March 28, 1784); of M. de Cypièrre, intendant of Orleans (May 28, 1784); of M de Maziron, intendant of Moulins (June 28, 1786); of M. Dupont, intendant of Moulins (Nov 6, 1779), etc.

districts must be seen with one's own eyes to obtain an idea of
it." From Rioni, from La Rochelle, from Limoges, from Lyons,
from Montauban, from Caen, from Alençon, from Flanders, from
Moulins come similar statements by other intendants. One
might call it the interruptions and repetitions of a funeral knell;
even in years not disastrous it is heard on all sides. In Burgundy, near Chatillon-sur-Seine, "taxes, seigniorial dues, the
tithes, and the expenses of cultivation, divide up the productions
of the soil into thirds, leaving nothing for the unfortunate cultivators, who would have abandoned their fields, had not two
Swiss manufacturers of calicoes settled there and distributed
about the country forty thousand francs a year in cash."[1] In
Auvergne, the country is depopulated daily; many of the villages
have lost, since the beginning of the century, more than one-
third of their inhabitants.[2] "Had not steps been promptly taken
to lighten the burden of a down-trodden people," says the provincial assembly in 1787, "Auvergne would have forever lost its
population and its cultivation." In Comminges, at the outbreak
of the Revolution, certain communities threaten to abandon their
possessions, should they obtain no relief.[3] "It is a well-known
fact," says the assembly of Haute-Guyenne, in 1784, "that the lot
of the most severely taxed communities is so rigorous as to have
led their proprietors frequently to abandon their property.[4] Who
is not aware of the inhabitants of Saint-Servin having abandoned
their possessions ten times and of their threats to resort again to
this painful proceeding in their recourse to the administration?
Only a few years ago an abandonment of the community of
Boisse took place through the combined action of the inhabitants, the seignior and the *décimateur* of that community;" and
the desertion would be still greater if the law did not forbid persons liable to the *taille* abandoning over-taxed property, except
by renouncing whatever they possessed in the community. In
the Soissonais, according to the report of the provincial assembly,[5] "misery is excessive." In Gascony the spectacle is "heart-

---

[1] Archives nationales, H, 200 (A memorial by M. Amelot, intendant at Dijon, 1786).
[2] Gautier de Bianzat, "Doléances sur les surcharges que portent les gens du Tiers-Etat,"
etc. (1789), p. 188. "Procès-verbaux de l'assemblée provinciale d'Auvergne" (1787), p. 175
[3] Théron de Montaugé, "L'Agriculture et les chores rurales dans le Toulousain," 112.
[4] "Procès-verbaux de l'assemblée provinciale de la Haute-Guyenne," I. 47, 79.
[5] "Procès-verbaux de l'assemblée provinciale du Soissonais" (1787), p. 857; "de l'assemblée provinciale d'Auch," p. 24.

rending." In the environs of Toule, the cultivator after paying his taxes, tithes and other dues, remains empty-handed. "Agriculture is an occupation of steady anxiety and privation, in which thousands of men are obliged to painfully vegetate." [1]   In a village in Normandy, "nearly all the inhabitants, not excepting the farmers and proprietors, eat barley bread and drink water, living like the most wretched of men, so as to provide for the payment of the taxes with which they are overburdened." In the same province, at Forges, "many poor creatures eat oat bread, and others bread of soaked bran, this nourishment causing many deaths among infants." [2]   People evidently live from day to day; whenever the crop proves poor they lack bread. Let a frost come, a hailstorm, an inundation, and an entire province is incapable of supporting itself until the coming year; in many places even an ordinary winter suffices to bring on distress. On all sides hands are seen outstretched to the king, who is the universal almoner. The people may be said to resemble a man attempting to wade through a pool with the water up to his chin, and who, losing his footing at the slightest depression, sinks down and drowns. Existent charity and the fresh spirit of humanity vainly strive to rescue them; the water has risen too high. It must subside to a lower level and the pool be drawn off through some adequate outlet. Thus far the poor man catches breath only at intervals, running the risk of drowning at every moment.

II.

Between 1750, and 1760,[3] the idlers who eat suppers begin to regard with compassion and alarm the laborers who go without dinners. Why are the latter so impoverished, and by what mischance, on a soil as rich as that of France, do those lack bread who grow the grain? In the first place many farms remain uncultivated, and, what is worse, many are deserted. According to the best observers "one-quarter of the soil is absolutely lying waste; . . . Hundreds and hundreds of *arpents* of heath and moor form extensive deserts." [4]   "Let a person traverse Anjou,

---

[1] "Résumé des cahiers," by Prud'homme, III. 271.

[2] Hippeau, *ibid.* VI. 74, 243 (Complaints drawn up by the Chevalier de Bertin).

[3] See the article "Fermiers et Grains," in the Encyclopedia, by Quesnay, 1756.

[4] Théron de Montaugé, p. 25. "Ephémérides du citoyen," III. 190 (1766); IX. 15 (an article by M. de Butré, 1767)

Maine, Brittany, Poitou, Limousin, la Marche, Berry, Nivernais, Bourbonnais and Auvergne, and he finds one-half of these provinces in heaths, forming immense plains all of which might be cultivated." In Touraine, in Poitou and in Berry they form solitary expanses of thirty thousand *arpents*. In one canton alone, near Preuilly, forty thousand *arpents* of good soil consist of heath. The agricultural society of Rennes declares that two-thirds of Brittany is lying waste. This is not sterility but decadence. The régime invented by Louis XIV. has produced its effect; the soil for a century past, is reverting back to a wild state. "We see only abandoned and ruinous chateaux; the principal towns of the fiefs, in which the nobility formerly lived at their ease, are all now occupied by poor métayer herdsmen whose scanty labor hardly suffices for their subsistence and a remnant of tax ready to disappear through the ruin of the proprietors and the desertion of the settlers." In the election-district of Confolens a piece of property rented for 2,956 livres in 1665, brings in only 900 livres in 1747. On the confines of la Marche and of Berry a domain which, in 1660, honorably supported two seigniorial families is now simply a small unproductive métayer-farm; "the traces of the furrows once made by the ploughshare being still visible on the surrounding heaths." Sologne, once flourishing,[1] becomes a marsh and a forest; a hundred years earlier it produced three times the quantity of grain; two-thirds of its mills are gone; not a vestige of its vineyards remains; "grapes have given way. to the heath." Thus abandoned by the spade and the plough, a vast portion of the soil ceases to feed man, while the rest, poorly cultivated, scarcely provides the simplest necessities.[2]

In the first place, on the failure of a crop, this portion remains untilled; its occupant is too poor to purchase seed; the intendant is often obliged to distribute seed, without which the disaster of the current year would be followed by sterility the following year.[3] Every calamity, accordingly, in these days affects the future as

---

[1] "Procès-verbaux de l'assemblée provinciale de l'Orléanais" (1787), in a memoir by M. d'Autroche.

[2] One is surprised to see so many supported where one-half, or one-quarter of the arable ground is sterile wastes.--ARTHUR YOUNG.

[3] Archives nationales, H, 1149. A letter of the Comtesse de Saint-Georges (1772) on the effects of frost. "The ground this year will remain uncultivated, there being already much land in this condition and especially in our parish." Théron de Montaugé, *ibid.* 45, 80.

well as the present; during the two years of 1784 and 1785, around Toulouse, the drought having caused the loss of all draft animals, many of the cultivators are obliged to let their fields lie fallow.   In the second place, cultivation, when it does take place, is carried on according to mediæval modes.   Arthur Young, in 1789, considers that French agriculture has not progressed beyond that of the tenth century.[1]   Except in Flanders and on the plains of Alsace, the fields lie fallow one year out of three and oftentimes one year out of two.   The implements are poor; there are no ploughs made of iron; in many places the plough of Virgil's time is still in use.   Cart-axles and wheel-tires are made of wood, while a harrow often consists of the trestle of a cart.   There are few animals and but little manure; the capital bestowed on cultivation is three times less than that of the present day.   The yield is slight: "our ordinary farms," says a good observer, "taking one with another return about six times the seed sown."[2]   In 1778, on the rich soil around Toulouse, wheat returns about five for one, while at the present day it yields eight to one and more.   Arthur Young estimates that, in his day, the English acre produces twenty-eight bushels of grain, and the French acre eighteen bushels, and that the value of the total product of the same area for a given length of time is thirty-six pounds sterling in England and only twenty-five in France.   As the parish roads are frightful, and transportation often impracticable, it is clear that, in remote cantons, where poor soil yields scarcely three times the seed sown, food is not always obtainable.   How do they manage to live until the next crop?   This is the question always under consideration previous to, and during, the Revolution.   I find, in manuscript correspondence, the syndics and mayors of villages estimating the quantities for local subsistence at so many bushels in the granaries, so many sheaves in the barns, so many mouths to be filled, so many days to wait until the August wheat comes in, and concluding on short supplies for two, three and four months.   Such a state of inter-communication and of agriculture condemns a country to periodical famines, and I venture to state that, alongside of the small-pox which, out of eight deaths, causes one, another endemic disease exists, as prevalent and as destructive, and this disease is starvation.

---

[1] Arthur Young, II. 112, 115.   Théron de Montaugé, 52, 61.
[2] The Marquis de Mirabeau, "Traité de la population," p. 29.

We can easily imagine the people as sufferers by it and, especially, the peasant. An advance in the price of bread prevents him from getting any, and even without that advance, he obtains it with difficulty. Wheat bread cost, as at the present day, three *sous* per pound,[1] but as the average day's work brought only nineteen *sous* instead of forty, the day-laborer, working the same time, could buy only the half of a loaf instead of a full loaf.[2] Taking everything into account, and wages being estimated according to the price of grain, we find that the husbandman's manual labor then procured him 959 *litres* of wheat, while nowadays it gives him 1,851 *litres*; his well-being, accordingly, has advanced ninety-three per cent., which suffices to show to what extent his predecessors suffered privations. And these privations are peculiar to France. Through analogous observations and estimates Arthur Young shows that in France those who lived on field labor, and they constituted the great majority, are seventy-six per cent. less comfortable than the same laborers in England, while they are seventy-six per cent. less well fed and well clothed, besides being worse treated in sickness and in health. The result is that, in seven-eighths of the kingdom, there are no farmers but simply métayers.[3] The peasant is too poor to undertake cultivation on his own account, possessing no agricultural capital.[4] "The proprietor, desirous of improving his land, finds no one to cultivate it but miserable creatures possessing only a pair of hands; he is obliged to advance everything for its cultivation at his own expense, animals, implements and seed, and even to advance the wherewithal to this métayer to feed him until the first crop comes in." "At Vatan, for example, in Berry, the métayers, almost every year, borrow bread of the proprietor in order to await the harvesting." "Very rarely is one found who is not indebted to his master at least one hundred livres a year." Frequently the latter proposes to abandon the entire crop to them on condition that they demand nothing of him during the year; "these miserable creatures" have refused;

---

[1] Cf. Galiani, "Dialogues sur le commerce des blés" (1770), p. 193. Wheat bread at this time cost four *sous* per pound.

[2] Arthur Young, II. 200, 201, 260-265. Théron de Montaugé, 59, 68, 75, 79, 81, 84.

[3] "The poor people who cultivate the soil here are *métayers*, that is, men who hire the land without ability to stock it; the proprietor is forced to provide cattle and seed and he and his tenants divide the produce."—Arthur Young.

"Ephémérides du citoyen," VI. 81-94 (1767), and IX. 99 (1767).

left to themselves, they would not be sure of keeping themselves alive.   In Limousin and in Angoumois their poverty is so great[1] "that, deducting the taxes to which they are subject, they have no more than from twenty-five to thirty livres each person per annum to spend; and not in money, it must be stated, but counting whatever they consume in kind out of the crops they produce.   Frequently they have less, and when they cannot possibly make a living the master is obliged to support them. . . . The métayer is always reduced to just what is absolutely necessary to keep him from starving."   As to the small proprietor, the villager who ploughs his land himself, his condition is but little better.   "Agriculture,[2] as our peasants practise it, is a veritable drudgery; they die by thousands in childhood, and in maturity they seek places everywhere but where they should be."   In 1783, throughout the plain of the Toulousain they eat only maize, a mixture of flour, common seeds and very little wheat; those on the mountains feed, a part of the year, on chestnuts; the potato is hardly known, and, according to Arthur Young, ninety-nine out of a hundred peasants would refuse to eat it.   According to the reports of intendants, the basis of food, in Normandy, is oats; in the election-district of Troyes, buckwheat; in the Marche and in Limousin, buckwheat with chestnuts and radishes; in Auvergne, buckwheat, chestnuts, milk-curds and a little salted goat's meat; in Beauce, a mixture of barley and rye; in Berry, a mixture of barley and oats.   There is no wheat bread; the peasant consumes inferior flour only because he is unable to pay two sous a pound for his bread.   There is no butcher's meat; at best he kills one pig a year   His dwelling is built of clay *(pise)*, roofed with thatch, without windows, and the floor is the beaten ground.   Even when the soil furnishes good building materials, stone, slate and tile, the windows have no sashes.   In a parish in Normandy, in 1789, "most of the dwellings consist of four posts."   They are often mere stables or barns "to which a chimney has been added made of four poles and some mud."   Their clothes are rags, and often, in winter these are muslin rags.   In Quercy and elsewhere, they have no stockings, or shoes or *sabots* (wooden shoes).   "It is not in the power of an English imagination," says Arthur Young, "to figure

[1] Turgot, "Collections des économistes," I. 544, 549.
[2] Marquis de Mirabeau, "Traité de la population," 83.

the animals that waited on us here at the *Chapeau Rouge*
Some things that called themselves by courtesy Souillac women,
but in reality walking dung-hills. But a neatly dressed, clean
waiting-girl at an inn, will be looked for in vain in France."
On reading descriptions made on the spot we see in France a
similar aspect of country and of peasantry as in Ireland, at least
in its broad outlines.

III.

In the most fertile regions, for instance, in Limagne, both cot-
tages and faces denote " misery and privation."[1] " The peasants
are generally feeble, emaciated and of slight stature." Nearly all derive wheat and wine from their homesteads but they are forced to sell
this to pay their rents and imposts; they eat black bread, made
of rye and barley, and their sole beverage is water poured on the
lees and the husks. " An Englishman[2] who has not travelled can
not imagine the figure made by infinitely the greater part of the
countrywomen in France." Arthur Young, who stops to talk
with one of these in Champagne, says that " this woman, at no
great distance, might have been taken for sixty or seventy, her figure was so bent and her face so hardened and furrowed by labor,—
but she said she was only twenty-eight." This woman, her husband and her household, afford a sufficiently accurate example of
the condition of the small proprietary husbandmen. Their property
consists simply of a patch of ground, with a cow and a poor little
horse; their seven children consume the whole of the cow's milk.
They owe to one seignior a *franchard* (forty-two pounds) of flour,
and three chickens; to another three *franchards* of oats, one chicken
and one *sou*, to which must be added the *taille* and other imposts.
" God keep us ! " she said, " for the *tailles* and the dues crush us."
What must it be in districts where the soil is poor ! " From Ormes,
(near Chatellerault), as far as Poitiers," writes a lady,[3] " there is a
good deal of ground which brings in nothing, and from Poitiers
to my residence (in Limousin) twenty-five thousand *arpents* of
ground consist wholly of heath and sea-grass. The peasantry live
on rye, of which they do not remove the bran, and which is as black
and heavy as lead. In Poitou, and here, they plough up only the

---

[1] Dulau e, "Description de l'Auvergne," 1789.

[2] Arthur Young, I. 235.

[3] " Ephémérides du citoyen," XX. 146, a letter of the Marquis de ——, August 17 1767

skin of the ground with a miserable little plough without wheels. . . .
From Poitiers to Montmorillon it is nine leagues, equal to sixteen
of Paris, and I assure you that I have seen but four men on the
road and, between Montmorillon and my own house, which is
four leagues, but three; and then only at a distance, not having
met one on the road.   You need not be surprised at this in such
a country. . . . Marriage takes place as early as with the grand
seigniors," doubtless for fear of the militia.   "But the population of
the country is no greater because almost every infant dies.   Mothers
having scarcely any milk, their infants eat the bread of which I
spoke, the stomach of a girl of four years being as big as that of a pregnant woman. . . . The rye crop this year was ruined by the frost
on Easter day; flour is scarce; of the twelve *métairies* owned by
my mother, four of them may, perhaps, have some on hand.
There has been no rain since Easter; no hay, no pasture, no vegetables, no fruit.   You see the lot of the poor peasant.   There is
no manure, and there are no cattle. . . . My mother, whose granaries used to be always full, has not a grain of wheat in them,
because, for two years past, she has fed all her métayers and the
poor."

"The peasant is assisted," says a seignior of the same province, "protected, and rarely maltreated, but he is looked upon
with disdain.   If kindly and pliable he is made subservient, but
if ill-disposed he becomes soured and irritable. . . . He is kept
in misery, in an abject state, by men who are not at all inhuman
but whose prejudices, especially among the nobles, lead them to
regard him as of a different species of being. . . . The proprietor gets all he can out of him; in any event, looking upon him
and his oxen as domestic animals, he puts them into harness and
employs them in all weathers for every kind of journey, and for
every species of carting and transport.   On the other hand, this
métayer thinks of living with as little labor as possible, converting as much ground as he can into pasturage, for the reason that
the product arising from the increase of stock costs him no labor.
The little ploughing he does is for the purpose of raising low-
priced provisions suitable for his own nourishment, such as
buckwheat, radishes, etc.   His enjoyment consists only of his
own idleness and sluggishness, hoping for a good chestnut year
and doing nothing voluntarily but procreate;" unable to hire
farming hands he begets children.   The rest, ordinary laborers,

have small supplies, " living on the spontaneous and on a few goats which devour everything." Often again, these, by order of Parliament, are killed by the keepers. A woman, with two children in swaddling clothes, having no milk, " and without an inch of ground," whose two goats, her sole resource, had thus been slain, and another, with one goat slain in the same way, and who begs along with her boy, present themselves at the gate of the chateau; one receives twelve livres, while the other is admitted as a domestic, and henceforth, " this village is all bows and smiling faces." In short, they are not accustomed to benefactions; the lot of all these poor people is to endure. " As with rain and hail, they regard as inevitable the necessity of being oppressed by the strongest, the richest, the most skilful, the most in repute," and this stamps on them, " if one may be allowed to say so, an air of painful suffering."

In Auvergne, a feudal country, covered with extensive ecclesiastic and seigniorial domains, the misery is the same. At Clermont-Ferrand,[1] " there are many streets that can for blackness, dirt and scents only be represented by narrow channels cut in a night dunghill." In the inns of the largest bourgs, " closeness, misery, dirtiness and darkness." That of Pradelles is " one of the worst in France." That of Aubenas, says Young, " would be a purgatory for one of my pigs." The senses, in short, are paralyzed. The primitive man is content so long as he can sleep and get something to eat. He gets something to eat, but what kind of food? To put up with the indigestible mess a peasant here requires a still tougher stomach than in Limousin; in certain villages where, ten years later, every year twenty or twenty-five hogs are to be slaughtered, they now slaughter but three.[2] On contemplating this temperament, rude and intact since Vercingétorix, and, moreover, rendered more savage by suffering, one cannot avoid being somewhat alarmed. The Marquis de Mirabeau describes " the votive festival of Mont-Dore, savages descending from the mountain in torrents,[3] the curate with stole and surplice, the justice in his wig, the police corps with sabres drawn, all guarding the open square before letting the bagpipers play; the dance interrupted in a quarter of an hour

---

[1] Arthur Young, I. 280, 289, 294.
[2] Lafayette, " Mémoires," V. 533.
[3] Lucas de Montigny, *ibid.* (a letter of August 18, 1777).

by a fight; the hootings and cries of children, of the feeble and other spectators, urging them on as the rabble urge on so many fighting dogs; frightful-looking men, or rather wild beasts covered with coats of coarse wool, wearing wide leather belts pierced with copper nails, gigantic in stature, which is increased by high *sabots*, and making themselves still taller by standing on tiptoe to see the battle, stamping with their feet as it progresses and rubbing each other's flanks with their elbows, their faces haggard and covered with long matted hair, the upper portion pallid, and the lower distended, indicative of cruel delight and a sort of ferocious impatience. And these folks pay the *taille !* And now they want to take away their salt! And they know nothing of those they despoil, of those whom they think they govern, believing that, by a few strokes of a cowardly and care less pen, they may starve them with impunity up to the final catastrophe! Poor Jean-Jacques, I said to myself, had any one despatched you, with your system, to copy music amongst these folks he would have had some sharp replies to make to your discourses!" Prophetic warning and admirable foresight in one whom an excess of evil does not blind to the evil of the remedy! Enlightened by his feudal and rural instincts, the old man at once judges both the government and the philosophers, the Ancient Régime and the Revolution.

IV.

Misery begets bitterness in a man; but ownership coupled with misery renders him still more bitter. He may have submitted to indigence but not to spoliation—which is the situation of the peasant in 1789, for, during the eighteenth century, he had become the possessor of land. But how could he maintain himself in such destitution ? The fact is almost incredible, but it is nevertheless true. We can only explain it by the character of the French peasant, by his sobriety, his tenacity, his rigor with himself, his dissimulation, his hereditary passion for property and especially for that of the soil. He had lived on privations, and economized *sou* after *sou*. Every year a few pieces of silver are added to his little store of crowns buried in the most secret recess of his cellar; Rousseau's peasant, conceal ing his wine and bread in a pit, assuredly had a yet more secret hiding-place; a little money in a woollen stocking or in a jug escapes, more readily than elsewhere, the search of the clerks.   Dressed in rags, going barefoot, eating nothing but coarse black bread, but cherishing the little treasure in his breast on which he builds so many hopes, he watches for the opportunity which never fails to come.   "In spite of privileges," writes a gentleman in 1755, "the nobles are daily being ruined and reduced, the Third-Estate making all the fortunes."   A number of domains, through forced or voluntary sales, thus pass into the hands of financiers, of men of the quill, of merchants, and of the well-to-do bourgeois.   Before undergoing this total dispossession, however, the seignior, involved in debt, is evidently resigned to partial alienations of his property.   The peasant who has bribed the steward is on hand with his hoard.   "It is poor property, my lord, and it costs you more than you get from it." This may refer to an isolated patch, one end of a field or meadow, sometimes a farm whose farmer pays nothing, and generally worked by a métayer whose wants and indolence make him an annual expense to his master.   The latter may say to himself that the alienated parcel is not lost since, some day or other, through his right of repurchase, he may take it back, while in the meantime, he enjoys a *cens*, drawbacks, and the lord's dues Moreover, there is on his domain and around him, extensive open spaces which the decline of cultivation and depopulation have left a desert.   To restore the value of this he must surrender its proprietorship.   There is no other way by which to attach man permanently to the soil.   And the government helps him along in this matter.   Obtaining no revenue from the abandoned soil, it assents to a provisional withdrawal of its too weighty hand.   By the edict of 1766, a piece of cleared waste land remains free of the *taille* for fifteen years, and, thereupon, in twenty-eight provinces four hundred thousand *arpents* are cleared in three years.

This is the mode by which the seigniorial domain gradually crumbles away and decreases.   Towards the last, in many places, with the exception of the chateau and the small adjoining farm, which brings in two or three thousand francs a year, nothing is left to the seignior but his feudal dues;[2] the rest of the soil

---

[1] "Procès-verbaux de l'assemblée provinciale de Basse Normandie" (1787), p. 205.

[2] Léonce de Lavergne, p. 26 (according to the tables of indemnity granted to the *emigrés* in 1825). In the estate of Blet (see note 2 at the end of the volume), twenty-two parcels are alienated in 1760.   Arthur Young, I. 308 (the domain of Tour-d'Aigues, in Provence), and II. 198, 214.   Doniol, "Histoire des classes rurales," p. 450.   De Tocqueville, p. 36.

belongs to the peasantry. Forbonnais already remarks, towards
1750, that many of the nobles and of the ennobled "reduced to
extreme poverty but with titles to immense possessions," have
sold off portions to small cultivators at low prices, and often for
the amount of the *taille.* Towards 1760, one-quarter of the soil
is said to have already passed into the hands of agriculturists.
In 1772, in relation to the *vingtième,* which is levied on the net
revenue of real property, the intendant of Caen, having completed the statement of his quota, estimates that out of one
hundred and fifty thousand "there are perhaps fifty thousand
whose liabilities did not exceed five *sous* and perhaps still as
many more not exceeding twenty *sous.*"[1] Contemporary observers authenticate this passion of the peasant for real property.
"The savings of the lower classes, which elsewhere are invested
with individuals and in the public funds, are wholly destined in
France to the purchase of land." "Accordingly the number of
small rural holdings is always on the increase. Necker says that
there is an *immensity* of them." Arthur Young, in 1789, is astonished at their great number and "inclines to think that they
form one third of the kingdom." That would already be about
the proportion, and the proportion would still be the same,
were we to compare the number of proprietors with the number of inhabitants.

The small cultivator, however, in becoming a possessor of the
soil assumed its charges. Simply as day-laborer, and with his
arms alone, he was only partially affected by the taxes; "where
there is nothing the king loses his dues." But now, vainly is he
poor and declaring himself still poorer; the fisc has a hold on
him and on every portion of his new possessions. The collectors, peasants like himself, and jealous, by virtue of being his

---

[1] Archives nationales, H, 1463 (a letter by M. de Fontette, November 16, 1772). Cf.
Cochut, "Revue des Deux Mondes," September, 1848. The sale of the national property
seems not to have sensibly increased small properties nor sensibly diminished the number of the
large ones. The Revolution developed moderate sized properties. In 1848, the large estates
numbered 183,000 (23,000 families paying 300 francs taxes, and more, and possessing on the
average 260 *hectares* of land, and 160,000 families paying from 250 to 500 francs taxes and
possessing on the average 75 *hectares*). These 183,000 families possess 18,000,000 *hectares*.
There are besides 700,000 medium sized estates (paying from 50 to 250 francs tax), and comprising 15,000,000 *hectares*. And finally 3,900,000 small properties comprising 15,000,000
hectares (900,000 paying from 25 to 50 francs tax averaging five and one-half *hectares* each,
and 3,000,000 paying less than 25 francs, averaging three and one-ninth *hectares* each).
According to the partial statements of De Tocqueville the number of holders of real property
had increased, on the average, to five-twelfths; the population, at the same time, having increased five-thirteenths (from 26 to 36 millions).

neighbors, know how much his property, exposed to view, brings in; hence they take all they can lay their hands on. Vainly has he labored with renewed energy; his hands remain as empty, and, at the end of the year, he discovers that his field has produced him nothing. The more he acquires and produces the more burdensome do the taxes become. In 1715, the *taille* and the poll-tax, which he alone pays, or nearly alone, amounts to sixty-six millions of livres; the amount is ninety-three millions in 1759 and one hundred and ten millions in 1789.[1] In 1757, the imposts amount to 283,156,000 livres; in 1789 to 476,294,000 livres.

Theoretically, through humanity and through good sense, there is, doubtless, a desire to relieve the peasant and pity is felt for him. But, in practice, through necessity and routine, he is treated according to Cardinal Richelieu's precept, as a beast of burden to which oats are measured out for fear that he may become too strong and kick, "a mule which, accustomed to his load, is spoiled more by long repose than by work."

---

[1] "Compte-général des revenus et dépenses fixes au 1er Mai, 1789 (Imprimerie Royale, 1789). De Luynes, XVI. 49. Roux and Buchez, I. 206, 374. (This relates only to the countries of *election;* in the provinces, with assemblies, the increase is no less great). Archives nationales, H². 1610 (the parish of Bourget, in Arjou). Extracts from the *taille* rolls of three *métayer*-farms belonging to M. de Ruillé. The imposts in 1762 are 334 *livres* 3 *sous;* in 1783, 372 *livres* 15 *sous.*

CHAPTER II.

I.

LET us closely examine the extortions he has to endure, which are very great, much beyond any that we can imagine. Economists had long prepared the budget of a farm and shown by statistics the excess of charges with which the cultivator is overwhelmed.—If he continues to cultivate, they say, he must have his share in the crops, an inviolable portion, equal to one-half of the entire production and from which nothing can be deducted without ruining him. This portion, indeed, accurately represents, and not a *sou* too much, in the first place, the interest of the capital first expended on the farm in cattle, furniture, and implements of husbandry; in the second place, the maintenance of this capital, every year depreciated by wear and tear; in the third place, the advances made during the current year for seed, wages, and food for men and animals; and, in the last place, the compensation due him for the risks he takes and his losses. Here is a first lien which must be satisfied beforehand, taking precedence of all others, superior to that of the seignior, to that of the titheowner *(décimateur)*, to even that of the king, for it is an indebtedness due to the soil.[1] After this is paid back, then, and only then

---

[1] "Collection des économistes," II. 832. See a tabular statement by Beaudan

that which remains, the *net product,* can be touched. Now, in the then state of agriculture, the tithe-owner and the king appropriate one-half of this net product, when the estate is large, and the whole, if the estate is a small one.[1] A certain large farm in Picardy, worth to its owner 3,600 livres, pays 1,800 livres to the king, and 1,311 livres to the tithe-owner; another, in the Soissonnais, rented for 4,500 livres, pays 2,200 livres taxes and more than 1,000 livres to the tithes. An ordinary métayer-farm near Nevers pays into the treasury 138 livres, 121 livres to the church, and 114 livres to the proprietor. On another, in Poitou, the fisc absorbs 348 livres, and the proprietor receives only 238. In general, in the regions of large farms, the proprietor obtains ten livres the *arpent* if the cultivation is very good, and three livres when ordinary. In the regions of small farms, and of the métayer system, he gets fifteen sous the *arpent,* eight sous and even six sous. The entire net profit may be said to go to the church and into the State treasury.

Hired labor, meantime, is no less costly. On this métayer-farm in Poitou, which brings in eight sous the *arpent,* thirty-six laborers consume each twenty-six francs per annum in rye, two francs respectively in vegetables, oil and milk preparations, and two francs ten sous in pork, amounting to a sum total, each year, for each person, of sixteen pounds of meat at an expense of thirty-six francs. In fact they drink water only, use rape-seed oil for soup and for light, never taste butter, and dress themselves in materials made of the wool and hair of the sheep and goats they raise. They purchase nothing save the tools necessary to make the fabrics of which these provide the material. On another métayer-farm, on the confines of la Marche and Berry, forty-six laborers cost a smaller sum, each one consuming only the value of twenty-five francs per annum. We can judge by this of the exorbitant share appropriated to themselves by the Church and State since, at so small a cost of cultivation, the proprietor finds in his pocket, at the end of the year, six or eight sous per *arpent,* out of which, if plebeian, he must still pay the dues to his seignior, contribute to the common purse for the militia, buy his taxed salt and work out his *corvée* and the rest. Towards the end of the reign of Louis XV. in Limousin, says

---

[1] "Ephémérides du citoyen," IX 15; an article by M. de Butré, 1767

Turgot,[1] the king derives for himself alone "about as much from the soil as the proprietor." A certain election-district, that of Tulle, where he abstracts fifty-six and one-half per cent. of the product, there remains to the latter forty-three and one-half per cent. thus accounting for "a multitude of domains being abandoned."

It must not be supposed that time renders the tax less onerous or that, in other provinces, the cultivator is better treated. In this respect the documents are authentic and almost up to the latest hour. We have only to take up the official statements of the provincial assemblies held in 1787, to learn by official figures to what extent the fisc may abuse the men who labor, and take bread out of the mouths of those who have earned it by the sweat of their brows.

II.

Direct taxation alone is here concerned, the *tailles*, collateral imposts, poll-tax, *vingtièmes*, and the pecuniary tax substituted for the *corvée*.[2] In Champagne, the tax-payer pays on 100 livres income fifty-four livres fifteen sous, on the average, and in many parishes,[3] seventy-one livres thirteen sous. In the Ile-de-France, "if a taxable inhabitant of a village, the proprietor of twenty *arpents* of land which he himself works, and the income of which is estimated at ten livres per *arpent*, it is supposed that he is likewise the owner of the house he occupies, the site being valued at forty livres."[4] This tax-payer pays for his real *taille*, personal and industrial, thirty-five livres fourteen sous, for collateral taxes seventeen livres seventeen sous, for the poll-tax twenty-one livres eight sous, for the *vingtièmes* twenty-four livres four sous, in all ninety-nine livres three sous, to which must be added about five livres as the substitution for the *corvée*, in all 104 livres on a piece of property which he rents for 240 livres, and which amounts to five-twelfths of his income.

It is much worse on making the same calculation for the

---

[1] "Collection des économistes," I. 551, 562.

[2] "Procès-verbaux de l'assemblée provinciale de Champagne" (1787), p. 240.

[3] Cf. "Notice historique sur la Révolution dans le département de l'Eure," by Boivin-Champeaux, p. 37. A memorial of the parish of Epreville; on 100 francs income the Treasury takes 22 for the *taille*, 16 for collaterals, 15 for the poll-tax, 11 for the *vingtièmes*, total 67 livres.

[4] "Procès-verbaux de l'assemblée provinciale de l'Ile-de-France" (1787), p. 131.

poorer generalities. In Haute-Guyenne,[1] "all property in land is taxed, for the *taille*, the collateral imposts, and the *vingtièmes*, more than one-quarter of its revenue, the only deduction being the expenses of cultivation; also dwellings, one-third of their revenue, deducting only the cost of repairs and of maintenance; to which must be added the poll-tax, which takes about one-tenth of the revenue; the tithe, which absorbs one-seventh; the seigniorial rents which take another seventh; the tax substituted for the *corvée;* the costs of compulsory collections, seizures, sequestrations and constraints, and all ordinary and extraordinary local charges. This being subtracted, it is evident that, in communities moderately taxed, the proprietor does not enjoy a third of his income, and that, in the communities wronged by the assessments, the proprietors are reduced to the status of simple farmers scarcely able to get enough to restore the expenses of cultivation." In Auvergne,[2] the *taille* amounts to four sous on the livre net profit; the collateral imposts and the poll-tax take off four sous three deniers more; the *vingtièmes*, two sous and three deniers; the contribution to the royal roads, to the free gift, to local charges and the cost of levying, take again one sou one denier, the total being eleven sous and seven deniers per livre on income, without counting seigniorial dues and the tithe. "The bureau, moreover, recognizes with regret, that several of the collections pay at the rate of seventeen sous, sixteen sous, and the most moderate, at the rate of fourteen sous the livre. The evidence of this is in the bureau; it is on file in the registry of the court of excise, and of the election-districts. It is still more apparent in parishes where an infinite number of assessments are found, laid on property that has been abandoned, which the collectors lease, and the product of which is often inadequate to pay the tax."—Statistics of this kind are terribly eloquent. They may be summed up in one word. Putting together Normandy, the Orleans region, that of Soissons, Champagne, Ile-de-France, Berry, Poitou, Auvergne, the Lyons region, Gascony, and Haute-Guyenne, in brief the principal *election* sections, we find that out of every hundred francs of revenue the direct tax on the tax-payer is fifty-three francs, or more than one-half.[3] This is about five times as much as at the present day.

[1] "Procès-verbaux de l'ass. prov. de la Haute-Guyenne" (1784), II. 17, 40, 47.

[2] "Procès-verbaux de l'ass. prov. d'Auvergne" (1787), p. 253.

[3] See note 5 at the end of the volume.

III.

The fisc, however, in thus bearing down on taxable property has not released the taxable person without property. In the absence of land it seizes on men. In default of an income it taxes a man's wages. With the exception of the *vingtièmes*, the preceding imposts not only bore on those who possessed something but, again, on those who possessed nothing. In the Toulousain,[1] at St. Pierre de Barjouville, the poorest day-laborer, with nothing but his hands by which to earn his support, and getting ten sous a day, pays eight, nine and ten livres poll-tax. "In Burgundy[2] it is common to see a poor mechanic, without any property, taxed eighteen and twenty livres for his poll-tax and the *taille*." In Limousin,[3] all the money brought back by the masons in winter serves "to pay the imposts charged to their families." As to the rural day-laborers and the settlers *(colons)* the proprietor, even when privileged, who employs them, is obliged to take upon himself a part of their quota; otherwise, being without anything to eat, they cannot work,[4] even in the interest of the master; man must have his ration of bread the same as an ox his ration of hay. "In Brittany,[5] it is notorious that nine-tenths of the artisans, though poorly fed and poorly clothed, have not a crown free of debt at the end of the year," the poll-tax and others carrying off this only and last crown. At Paris[6] "the dealer in ashes, the buyer of old bottles, the gleaner of the gutters, the peddlers of old iron and old hats," the moment they obtain a shelter pay the poll-tax of three livres and ten sous each. To ensure its payment the occupant of a house who sub-lets to them is made responsible. Moreover, in case of delay, a "blue man," a bailiff's subordinate, is sent who installs himself on the spot and whose time they have to pay for. Mercier cites a mechanic, named Quatremain, who, with four small children, lodged in the sixth story, where he had arranged a chimney as a sort of alcove in which he and his family slept.

"Théron de Montaugé," p. 109 (1763). Wages at this time are from 7 to 12 sous a day in summer.

[2] Archives nationales, procès-verbaux and memorials of the States-General, v. LIX. p. 6. A memorial to M. Necker, by M. d'Orgeux, honorary counsellor to the Parliament of Burgundy, Oct 25, 1788.

[3] *Ibid.* H, 1418. A letter of the intendant of Limoges, Feb. 26, 1784.

[4] Turgot, II. 259.

[5] Archives nationales, H, 426 (remonstrances of the Parliament of Brittany, F+b. 1783)

[6] Mercier, XI. 59; X. 262.

"One day I opened his door, fastened with a latch only, the room presenting to view nothing but the walls and a vice; the man coming out from under his chimney, half sick, says to me, 'I thought it was the blue man for the poll-tax.'" Thus, whatever the condition of the person subject to taxation, however stripped and destitute, the dexterous hands of the fisc take hold of him. Mistakes cannot possibly occur: it puts on no disguise, it comes on the appointed day and rudely lays its hand on his shoulder. The garret and the hut, as well as the farm and the farm-house know the collector, the constable and the bailiff; no hovel escapes the detestable brood. The people sow, harvest their crops, work and undergo privation for their benefit; and, should the farthings so painfully saved each week amount, at the end of the year, to a piece of silver, the mouth of their pouch closes over it.

IV.

Observe the system actually at work. It is a sort of shearing machine, clumsy and badly put together, of which the action is about as mischievous as it is serviceable. The worst feature is, that, in its grinding cog-wheels, those who are subject to taxation, the last tool employed, must shear and fleece themselves. In each parish, there are two, three, five or seven of these who, under the name of collectors and authorized by the *elu*, must apportion and collect the taxes. "No duty is more onerous;"[1] everybody, through patronage or favor, tries to get rid of it. The communities are constantly pleading against the refractory, and, that nobody may escape under the pretext of ignorance, the table of future collectors is made up for ten and fifteen years in advance. In parishes of the second class these consist of "small proprietors, each of whom becomes a collector about every six years." In many of the villages the artisans, day-laborers, and métayer-farmers perform the service, although requiring all their time to earn their own living. In Auvergne, where the able-bodied men expatriate themselves in winter to find work, the women are taken;[2] in the election-district of Saint-Flour, a cer-

[1] Archives nationales, H, 1422, a letter by M. d'Aine, intendant of Limoges (February 17, 1782); one by the intendant of Moulins (April, 1779) the trial of the community of Mollon (Bordelais), and the tables of its collectors.
[2] "Procès-verbaux de l'ass. prov. d'Auvergne," p. 266.

tain village has four collectors in petticoats. They are responsible for all claims entrusted to them, their property, their furniture
and their persons; and, up to the time of Turgot, each is bound
for the others. We can judge of their risks and sufferings. In
1785,[1] in one single district in Champagne, eighty-five are imprisoned and two hundred of them are on the road every year. "The
collector, says the provincial assembly of Berry,[2] usually passes
one-half of the day for two years running from door to door to
see delinquent tax-payers." "This service," writes Turgot,[3] "is the
despair and almost always the ruin of those obliged to perform
it; all families in easy circumstances in a village are thus suc-
cessively reduced to want." In short, there is no collector who
is not forced to act and who has not each year "eight or ten
writs" served on him.[4] Sometimes he is imprisoned at the expense of the parish. Sometimes proceedings are instituted against
him and the tax-contributors by the installation of "'blue men'
and seizures, seizures under arrest, seizures in execution and
sales of furniture." "In the single district of Villefranche," says
the provincial Assembly of Haute-Guyenne, "a hundred and six
warrant officers and other agents of the bailiff are counted always
on the road."

The thing becomes customary and the parish suffers in vain,
for it would suffer yet more were it to do otherwise. "Near
Aurillac," says the Marquis de Mirabeau,[5] "there is industry,
application and economy without which there would be only
misery and want. This produces a partially insolvent people
with timorous rich ones who, for fear of overcharge, produce the
impoverished. The *taille* once assessed, everybody groans and
complains and nobody pays it. The term having expired, at the
hour and minute, constraint begins, the collectors, although able,
taking no trouble to arrest this by making a settlement, notwithstanding the installation of the bailiff's men is costly. But this
kind of expense is habitual and people expect it instead of fearing
it, for, if it were less rigorous, they would be sure to be additionally burdened the following year." The receiver, indeed, who

[1] Albert Babeau, "Histoire de Troyes," I. 72.

[2] "Procès-verbaux de l'ass. prov. de Berry" (1778), I. pp. 72, 80.

[3] De Tocqueville, 187.

[4] Archives nationales, H, 1417. (A letter of M. de Cypièrre, intendant at Orléans April
17, 1765).

[5] "Traité de Population," 2d part, p. 26.

OOK./

pays the bailiff's officers a franc a day, makes them pay two francs and appropriates the difference. Hence "if certain parishes venture to pay promptly, without awaiting constraint, the receiver, who sees himself deprived of the best portion of his gains, becomes ill-humored, and, at the next department (meeting), an arrangement is made between himself, messieurs the elected, the subdelegate and other shavers of this species, for the parish to bear a double load, to teach it how to behave itself."

A population of administrative blood-suckers thus lives on the peasant. " Lately," says an intendant, "in the district of Romorantin,[1] the collectors received nothing from a sale of furniture amounting to six hundred livres, because the proceeds were absorbed by the expenses. In the district of Chateaudun the same thing occurred at a sale amounting to nine hundred livres and there are other transactions of the same kind of which we have no information, however flagrant." Besides this, the fisc itself is pitiless. The same intendant writes, in 1784, a year of famine:[2] " People have seen, with horror, the collector, in the country, disputing with heads of families over the costs of a sale of furniture which had been appropriated to stopping their children's cry of want." Were the collectors not to make seizures they would themselves be seized. Urged on by the receiver we see them, in the documents, soliciting, prosecuting and persecuting the tax-payers. Every Sunday and every fête-day they are posted at the church door to warn delinquents; and then, during the week they go from door to door to obtain their dues. " Commonly they cannot write and take a scribe with them." Out of six hundred and six traversing the district of Saint-Flour not ten of them are able to read the official summons and sign a receipt; hence innumerable mistakes and frauds. Besides a scribe they take along the bailiff's subordinates, persons of the lowest class, laborers without work, conscious of being hated and who act accordingly. " Whatever orders may be given .hem not to take anything, not to make the inhabitants feed them, or to enter taverns with collectors," habit is too strong " and the abuse continues."[3] But, burdensome as the bailiff's

[1] Archives nationales, H, 1417. (A letter of M. de Cypièrre, intendant at Orleans, April 17, 1765)
[2] *Ibid.* H, 1418. (Letter of May 28, 1784).
[3] *Ibid.* (Letter of the intendant of Tours, June 15, 1765.)

men may be, care is taken not to evade them. In this respect, writes an intendant, " their obduracy is strange." " No person," a receiver reports,[1] " pays the collector until he sees the bailiff's man in his house." The peasant resembles his ass, refusing to go without being beaten, and, although in this he may appear stupid, he is politic. For the collector, being responsible, " naturally inclines to an increase of the assessment on prompt payers to the advantage of the negligent. Hence the prompt payer becomes, in his turn, negligent and, although with money in his chest, he allows the process to go on."[2] Summing all up, he calculates that the process, even if expensive, costs less than extra taxation, and of the two evils he chooses the least. He has but one resource against the collector and receiver, his simulated or actual poverty, voluntary or involuntary. " Every one subject to the *taille*," says, again, the provincial assembly of Berry, " dreads to expose his resources; he avoids any display of these in his furniture, in his dress, in his food, and in everything open to another's observation." " M. de Choiseul-Gouffier,[3] willing to roof his peasants' houses, liable to take fire, with tiles, they thanked him for his kindness but begged him to leave them as they were, telling him that if these were covered with tiles, instead of with thatch, the subdelegates would increase their taxation." " People work, but merely to satisfy their prime necessities. . . . The fear of paying an extra crown makes an average man neglect a profit of four times the amount."[4] ". . . Accordingly, lean cattle, poor implements, and bad manure-heaps when they might have others."[5] " If I earned any more," says a peasant, " it would be for the collector." Annual and illimitable spoliation " takes away even the desire for comforts." The majority, pusillanimous, distrustful, stupefied, " debased," " differing little from the old serfs,"[6] resemble Egyptian fellahs and Hindoo pariahs. The fisc, indeed, through the absolutism and enormity of its indebtedness, renders property of all kinds precarious, every acquisition vain, every accumulation derisive; in fact, proprietors are possessors only of that which they can sequestrate from it.

---

[1] Archives Nationales, H, 1417. A report by Raudon, receiver of *tailles* in the election of Laon, January, 1764.

[2] " Procès-verbaux de l'ass. prov. de Berry " 1778), I. p 72.

[3] Champfort, 93.

[4] " Procès-verbaux de l'ass. prov. de Berry," I. 77.

[5] Arthur Young, II. 205.

[6] " Procès-verbaux of the ass. prov. of the generalship of Rouen " (1787), p. 271.

V.

The fisc, in every country, has two hands, one, which visibly and directly searches the coffers of tax-payers, and the other, which covertly employs the hand of an intermediary so as not to incur the odium of fresh extortions. Here, no precaution of this kind is taken, the claws of the latter being as visible as those of the former; according to its structure and the complaints made of it, I am tempted to believe it more offensive than the other.

In the first place, the salt-tax, the excises and the customs are annually estimated and sold to adjudicators who, purely as a business matter, make as much profit as they can by their bargain. In relation to the tax-payer they are not administrators but speculators; they have bought him up. He belongs to them by the terms of their contract; they will squeeze out of him, not merely their advances and the interest on their advances, but, again, every possible benefit. This suffices to indicate the mode of levying indirect imposts. In the second place, by means of the salt-tax and the excises, the inquisition enters each household. In the provinces where these are levied, in Ile-de-France, Maine, Anjou, Touraine, Orléanais, Berry, Bourbonnais, Burgogne, Champagne, Perche, Normandy and Picardy, salt costs thirteen sous a pound, four times as much as at the present day, and, considering the standard of money, eight times as much.[1] And, furthermore, by virtue of the ordinance of 1680, each person over seven years of age is expected to purchase seven pounds per annum, which, with four persons to a family, makes eighteen francs a year, and equal to nineteen days' work: a new direct tax, which, like the *taille*, is a fiscal hand in the pockets of the tax-payers, and compelling them, like the *taille*, to torment each other. Many of them, in fact, are officially appointed to assess this obligatory use of salt and, like the collectors of the *taille*, these are "corporately responsible for the price of the salt." Others below them, ever following the same course as in collecting the *taille*, are likewise responsible. "After the former have been distrained in their persons and property, the speculator *fermier* is authorized to commence action, under the principle of

---

[1] Letrosne (1779). "De 'administration provinciale et de la reforme de l'impôt," pp. 39, 262 and 138. Archives nationales, H. 138 (1782). Cahier de Bugey, "Salt costs the countryman purchasing it of the retailers from 15 to 17 sous a pound, according to the way of measuring it."

mutual responsibility, against the principal inhabitants of the parish." The effects of this system have just been described. Accordingly, "in Normandy," says the Rouen parliament,[1] "unfortunates without bread are daily objects of seizure, sale and execution."

But if the rigor is as great as in the matter of the *taille*, the vexations are ten times greater, for these are domestic, minute and of daily occurrence. It is forbidden to divert an ounce of the seven obligatory pounds to any use but that of the "pot and the salt-cellar." If a villager should economize the salt of his soup to make brine for a piece of pork, with a view to winter consumption, let him look out for the collecting-clerks! His pork is confiscated and the fine is three hundred livres. The man must come to the warehouse and purchase other salt, make a declaration, carry off a certificate and show this at every visit of inspection. So much the worse for him if he has not the wherewithal to pay for this supplementary salt; he has only to sell his pig and abstain from meat on Christmas. This is the more frequent case and I dare say that, for the métayers who pay twenty-five francs per annum, it is the usual case. It is forbidden to make use of any other salt for the pot and salt-cellar than that of the seven pounds. "I am able to cite," says Letrosne, "two sisters residing one league from a town in which the warehouse is open only on Saturday. Their supply was exhausted. To pass three or four days until Saturday comes they boil a remnant of brine from which they extract a few ounces of salt. A visit from the clerk ensues and a *procès-verbal*. Having friends and protectors this costs them only forty-eight livres." It is forbidden to take water from the ocean and from other saline sources, under a penalty of from twenty to forty livres fine. It is forbidden to water cattle in marshes and other places containing salt, under penalty of confiscation and a fine of three hundred livres. It is forbidden to put salt into the bellies of mackerel on returning from fishing, or between their superposed layers. An order prescribes one pound and a half to a barrel. Another order prescribes the destruction annually of the natural salt formed in certain cantons in Provence. Judges are prohibited from moderating or reducing the penalties imposed in salt

---

[1] Floquet, VI. 367 (May 10, 1760).

cases, under penalty of accountability and of deposition.   I pass over quantities of orders and prohibitions, existing by hundreds. This legislation encompasses tax-payers like a net with a thou-sand meshes, while the official who casts it is interested in find-ing them at fault.   We see the fisherman, accordingly, unpack-ing his barrel, the housewife seeking a certificate for her hams, the exciseman inspecting the buffet, testing the brine, peering into the salt-box and, if it is of good quality, declaring it contra-band because that of the *ferme*, the only legitimate salt, is usually adulterated and mixed with plaster.

Meanwhile, other officials, those of the excise, descend into the cellar.   None are more formidable, nor who more eagerly seize on pretexts for delinquency.[1]   "Let a citizen charitably bestow a bottle of wine on a poor feeble creature and he is liable to prosecution and to excessive penalties. . . . The poor invalid that may interest his curate in the begging of a bottle of wine for him will undergo a trial ruining, not alone the unfortunate man that obtains it, but again the benefactor who gave it to him. This is not a fancied story."   By virtue of the right of deficient revenue the clerks may, at any hour, take an inventory of wine on hand, even the stores of a vineyard proprietor, indicate what he may consume, tax him for the rest and for the surplus quantity already drunk, the *ferme* thus associating itself with the wine-producer and claiming its portion of his production.   In a vine-yard at Epernay[2] on four casks of wine, the average product of one *arpent*, and worth six hundred francs, it levies, at first, thirty francs, and then, after the sale of the four casks, seventy-five francs additionally.   Naturally, "the inhabitants resort to the shrewdest and best planned artifices to escape" such potent rights.[3]   But the clerks are alert, watchful, and well-informed, and they pounce down unexpectedly on every suspected domicile; their instructions prescribe frequent inspections and exact regis-tries "enabling them to see at a glance the condition of the cellar of each inhabitant."[4]   The manufacturer having paid up, the merchant now has his turn.   The latter, on sending the four casks to the consumer again pays seventy-five francs to the *ferme*.

[1] Boivin-Champeaux, p. 44.   (Cahiers of Bray and of Gamaches).
[2] Arthur Young, II. 175-178.
[3] Archives nationales, G, 300; G, 319.   (Memorials and instructions of various local directors of the Excise to their successors).
[4] Letrosne, *ibid.* 523.

The wine is despatched and the *ferme* prescribes the roads by
which it must go; should others be taken it is confiscated and,
at every step on the way some payment must be made.   "A
boat laden with wine from Languedoc, Dauphiny or Roussillon,
ascending the Rhone and descending the Loire to reach Paris,
through the Briare canal, pays on the way, leaving out charges
on the Rhone, from thirty-five to forty kinds of duty not comprising the charges on entering Paris."   It pays these "at fifteen
or sixteen places, the multiplied payments obliging the carriers
to devote twelve or fifteen days more to the passage than they
otherwise would if their duties could be paid at one bureau."
The charges on the routes by water are particularly heavy.
"From Pontarlier to Lyons there are twenty-five or thirty tolls;
from Lyons to Aigues-Mortes there are others, so that whatever
costs ten sous in Burgundy amounts to fifteen and eighteen sous at
Lyons and to over twenty-five sous at Aigues-Mortes."   The
wine at last reaches the barriers of the city where it is to be
drunk.   Here it pays an *octroi* of forty-seven francs per hogshead.
Entering Paris it goes into the tapster's or innkeeper's cellar
where it again pays from thirty to forty francs for the duty on
selling it at retail; at Rethel the duty is from fifty to sixty francs
per puncheon, Rheims gauge.   The total is exorbitant.   "At
Rennes,[1] the dues and duties on a barrel of Bordeaux wine, together with a fifth over and above the tax, local charges, eight
sous per pound and the *octroi*, amount to more than seventy-two
livres exclusive of the purchase money; to which must be added
the expenses and duties advanced by the Rennes merchant and
which he recovers from the purchaser, Bordeaux drayage, freight,
insurance, tolls of the flood-gate, entrance duty into the town,
hospital dues, fees of gaugers, brokers and inspectors.   The total
outlay for the tapster who sells a barrel of wine amounts to two
hundred livres."   We may imagine whether, at this price, the
people of Rennes drink it, while these charges fall on the wine-
grower, since, if consumers do not purchase, he is unable to sell.

Accordingly, among the small growers, he is the most to be
pitied; according to the testimony of Arthur Young, wine-
grower and misery are two synonymous terms.   The crop often
fails, "every doubtful crop ruining the man without capital."   In

---

[1] Archives nationales, H, 426 (Papers of the Parliament of Brittany, February, 1783)

Burgundy, in Berry, in Soisonnais, in the Trois-Evêchés, in
Champagne,[1] I find in every report that he lacks bread and lives
on alms.   In Champagne, the syndics of Bar-sur-Aube write[2]
that the inhabitants, to escape duties, have more than once
emptied their wine into the river, the provincial assembly declaring that "in the greater portion of the province the slightest
augmentation of duties would cause the cultivators to desert the
soil."   Such is the history of wine under the ancient régime.
From the producer who grows to the tapster who sells what
extortions and what vexations! As to the salt-tax, according
to the comptroller-general,[3] this annually produces four thousand domiciliary seizures, three thousand four hundred imprison-
ments, five hundred sentences to flogging, exile and the galleys.
If ever two imposts were well combined, not only to despoil,
but to irritate the peasantry, the poor and the people, here they
are.

VI.

Evidently the burden of taxation forms the chief cause of
misery; hence an accumulated, deep-seated hatred against the
fisc and its agents, receivers, store-house keepers, excise officials.
customs officers and clerks.   But why is taxation so burdensome?
The answer is not doubtful, the communes which annually plead
against certain persons to subject them to the *taille* writing it out
fully in their demands.   What renders the charge overwhelming
is the fact that the strongest and those best able to bear taxation
succeed in evading it, the prime cause of misery being their ex-
emption.

Let us follow up the matter impost after impost.   In the first
place, not only are nobles and ecclesiastics exempt from the
personal *taille* but again, as we have already seen, they are
exempt from the cultivator's *taille*, through cultivating their domains themselves or by a steward.   In Auvergne,[4] in the single
election-district of Clermont, fifty parishes are enumerated in

---

[1] "Procès-verbaux de l'ass. prov. de Soissonnais" (1787), p. 45.   Archives nationales, H,
1515 (Remonstrances of the Parliament of Metz, 1768).   "The class of indigents form more
than twelve-thirteenths of the whole number of villages of laborers and generally those of the
wine-growers."   *Ibid.* G, 319 (Tableau des directions of Chateaudun and Issoudun).
[2] Albert Babeau, I. 89. p. 21.
[3] "Mémoires," presented to the Assembly of Notables, by M. de Calonne (1787), p. 67.
[4] Gautier de Bianzat, "Doléances," 193, 225.   "Procès-verbaux de l'ass. prov. de Poitou"
(1787), p. 99.

which, owing to this arrangement, every estate of a privileged
person is exempt, the *taille* falling wholly on those subject to it.
Furthermore, it suffices for a privileged person to maintain that
his farmer is only a steward, which is the case in Poitou in several
parishes, the subdelegate and the *élu* not daring to look into the
matter too closely.   In this way the privileged classes escape the
taille, they and their property, including their farms.   Now, the
taille, ever augmenting, is that which provides, through its special
delegations, such a vast number of new offices.   A man of the
Third-Estate has merely to run through the history of its periodical increase to see how it alone, or almost alone, paid and is paying [1] for the construction of bridges, roads, canals and courts of justice, for the purchase of offices, for the establishment and support
of houses of refuge, insane asylums, nurseries, post-houses for
horses, fencing and riding schools, for paving and sweeping Paris,
for salaries of lieutenants-general, governors, and provincial commanders, for the fees of bailiffs, seneschals and vice-bailiffs, for
the salaries of financial and election officials and of commissioners despatched to the provinces, for those of the police of the
watch and I know not how many other purposes.   In the provinces which hold assemblies, where the *taille* would seem to be
more justly apportioned, the like inequality is found.   In Burgundy [2] the expenses of the police, of public festivities, of keeping horses, all sums appropriated to the courses of lectures on
chemistry, botany, anatomy and parturition, to the encourage-
ment of the arts, to subscriptions to the chancellorship, to frank-
ing letters, to presents given to the chiefs and subalterns of commands, to salaries of officials of the provincial assemblies, to the
ministerial secretaryship, to expenses of levying taxes and even
alms, in short, 1,800,000 livres expended in the public service at
the charge of the Third-Estate, the two higher orders not paying
a cent.

In the second place, with respect to the poll-tax, originally distributed among twenty-two classes and intended to bear equally
on all according to fortunes, we know that, from the first, the
clergy buy themselves off, and, as to the nobles, they manage

---

[1] Gautier de Bianzat, *ibid.*

[2] Archives nationales, the procès-verbaux and cahiers of the States-General, V. 59. p. 6.
(Letter of M. Orgeux to M Necker), t. 27. p. 560–573.   (Cahiers of the Third-Estate of
Arnay-le-Duc).

so well as to have their tax reduced proportionately with its in-crease at the expense of the Third-Estate. A count or a marquis, an intendant or a master of requests, with 40,000 livres income, who, according to the tariff of 1695,[1] should pay from 1,700 to 2,500 livres, pays only 400 livres, while a bourgeois with 6,000 livres income and who, according to the same tariff should pay 70 livres, pays 720. The poll-tax of the privileged individual is thus diminished three-quarters or five-sixths, while that of the *taille*-payer has increased tenfold. In the Ile-de-France,[2] on an income of 240 livres, the *taille*-payer pays twenty-one livres eight sous, and the nobles three livres, and the intendant himself states that he taxes the nobles only an eightieth of their revenue; that of Orléanais taxes them only a hundredth, while, on the other hand, those subject to the *taille* are assessed the eleventh. If other privileged parties are added to the nobles, such as officers of justice, employés of the *fermes*, and exempted townsmen, a group is formed embracing nearly everybody rich or well-off and whose revenue certainly greatly surpasses that of those who are subject to the *taille*. Now, the budgets of the provincial as-semblies inform us how much each province levies on each of the two groups: in the Lyonnais district those subject to the *taille* pay 898,000 livres, the privileged, 190,000; in the Ile-de-France, the former pay 2,689,000 livres and the latter 232,000; in the generalship of Alençon, the former pay 1,067,000 livres and the latter 122,000; in Champagne, the former pay 1,377,000 livres, and the latter 199,000; in Haute-Guyenne, the former pay 1,268,000 livres, and the latter 61,000; in the generalship of Auch, the former pay 797,000 livres, the privileged 21,000; in Auvergne the former pay 1,753,000 livres and the latter 86,000; in short, summing up the total of ten provinces, 11,636,000 livres paid by the poor group and 1,450,000 livres by the rich group, the latter paying eight times less than it ought to pay.

With respect to the *vingtièmes*, the disproportion is less, the pre-cise amounts not being attainable; we may nevertheless assume that the assessment of the privileged class is about one-half of

---

[1] In these figures the rise of the money standard has been kept in mind, the silver "marc," worth 29 francs in 1695, being worth 49 francs during the last half of the eighteenth century.

[2] "Procès-verbaux de l'ass. prov. de l'Ile-de-France," 132, 158; "—— de l'Orléanais," 36, 367.

what it should be. "In 1772," says M. de Calonne, "it was admitted that the *vingtièmes* were not carried to their full value. False declarations, counterfeit leases, too favorable conditions granted to almost all the wealthy proprietors gave rise to inequalities and countless errors. A verification of 4,902 parishes shows that the product of the two *vingtièmes* amounting to 54,000,000 should have amounted to 81,000,000." A seigniorial domain which, according to its own return of income, should pay 2,400 livres, pays only 1,216. The case is much worse with the princes of the blood; we have seen that their domains are exempt and pay only 188,000 livres instead of 2,400,000. Under this system, which crushes the weak to relieve the strong, the more capable one is of contributing, the less one contributes. The same story characterizes the fourth and last direct impost, namely, the tax substituted for the *corvée*. This tax attached, at first, to the *vingtièmes* and consequently extending to all proprietors, through an act of the Council is attached to the *taille* and, consequently, bears on those the most burdened.[2] Now this tax amounts to an extra of one-quarter added to the principal of the *taille*, of which one example may be cited, that of Champagne, where, on every 100 livres income the sum of six livres five sous devolves on the *taille*-payer. "Thus," says the provincial assembly, "every road impaired by active commerce, by the multiplied coursings of the rich, is repaired wholly by the contributions of the poor."

As these figures spread out before the eye we involuntarily recur to the two animals in the fable, the horse and the mule travelling together on the same road; the horse, by right, may prance along as he pleases; hence his load is gradually transferred to the mule, the beast of burden, which finally sinks beneath the extra load.

Not only, in the corps of tax-payers, are the privileged disburdened to the detriment of the taxable, but again, in the corps of the taxable, the rich are relieved to the injury of the poor, to such an extent that the heaviest portion of the load finally falls on the most indigent and most laborious class, on the small proprietor

---

1 "Mémoire," presented to the Assembly of Notables (1787), p. 1. See note 2 at the end of the volume, on the domain of Blet.

2 "Procès-verbaux de l'ass. prov. d'Alsace" (1787), p. 116; "—— of Champagne," 192. (According to a declaration of June 2, 1787, the tax substituted for the *corvée* may be extended to one-sixth of the *taille*, with accessory taxes and the poll-tax combined). "De la généralité d'Alençon," 179; "—— du Berry," I. 218.

cultivating his own field, on the simple artisan with nothing but
his tools and his hands, and, in general, on the inhabitants cf vi'
lages.   In the first place, in the matter of imposts, a numbe· of
the towns are " abonnées," or free.   Compiègne, for the *taille* and
its accessories, with 1,671 firesides, pays only 8,000 francs, whilst
one of the villages in its neighborhood, Canly, with 148 firesides,
pays 4,475 francs.[1]   In the poll-tax, Versailles, Saint-Germain
Beauvais, Etampes, Pontoise, Saint-Denis, Compiègne, Fontainebleau, taxed in the aggregate at 169,000 livres, are two-thirds exempt, contributing but little more than one franc, instead of three
francs ten sous, per head of the population; at Versailles it is still
less, since for 70,000 inhabitants the poll-tax amounts to only
51,600 francs.[2]   Besides, in any event, on the apportionment of
a tax, the bourgeois of the town is favored above his rural neighbors.   Accordingly, " the inhabitants of the country, who depend
on the town and are comprehended in its functions, are treated
with a rigor of which it would be difficult to form an idea. . . .
Town influence is constantly throwing the burden on those who
are trying to be relieved of it, the richest of citizens paying less
taille than the most miserable of the peasant farmers."   Hence,
" a horror of the *taille* depopulates the rural districts, concentrating in the towns both capacity and capital."[3]   Outside of the towns
there is the same inequality.   Each year, the *élus* and their collectors, exercising arbitrary power, fix the *taille* of the parish and
of each inhabitant.   In these ignorant and partial hands the scales
are not held by equity but by self-interest, local hatreds, the desire
for revenge, the necessity of favoring some friend, relative, neighbor, protector, or patron, some powerful or some dangerous person.   The intendant of Moulins, on visiting his generalship, finds
" people of influence paying nothing, while the poor are overcharged."   That of Dijon writes that " the basis of apportionment
is arbitrary, to such an extent that the people of the province must
not be allowed to suffer any longer."   In the generalship of Rouen
" some parishes pay over four sous the livre and others scarcely
one sou."[4]   " For three years past that I have lived in the coun-

[1] Archives nationales, G, 322 (Memoir on the excise dues of Compiègne and its neighbor-hood, 1786).
[2] "Procès-verbaux de l'ass. prov. de l'Ile-de-France," p. 104.
[3] "Procès-verbaux de l'ass. prov. de Berry, I. 85, II. 91. "—— de l'Orléanais, p. 225."
"Arbitrariness, injustice, inequality, are inseparable from the *taille* when any change of col-lector takes place."
[4] "Procès-verbaux de l'ass. prov. de la généralité de Rouen," p. 91.

try," writes a lady of the same district, "I have remarked that most of the wealthy proprietors are the least pressed; they are selected to make the apportionment and the people are always abused." [1] "I live on an estate ten leagues from Paris," wrote d'Argenson, "where an effort is made to assess the *taille* proportionately, but only injustice has prevailed; the seigniors have succeeded in relieving their farmers." [2] Besides those who, through favor, diminish their *taille*, others buy themselves off entirely. An intendant, visiting the subdelegation of Bar-sur-Seine, observes " that the rich cultivators succeed in obtaining petty commissions in connection with the king's household and enjoy the privileges attached to these, which throws the burden of taxation on the others." [3] " One of the leading causes of our prodigious taxation," says the provincial assembly of Auvergne, "is the inconceivable number of the privileged, which daily increases through traffic in and the assignment of offices; cases occur in which these have ennobled six families in less than twenty years." Should this abuse continue "in a hundred years· every tax-payer the most capable of supporting taxation will be ennobled." [4] Observe, moreover, that an infinity of offices and functions, without conferring nobility, exempt their titularies from the personal *taille* and reduce their poll-tax to the fortieth of their income; at first, all public functionaries, administrative or judicial, and next all employments in the salt-department, in the customs, in the post-office, in the royal domains, and in the excise. [5] "There are few parishes," writes an intendant, "in which these employés are not found, while several contain as many as two or three." [6] A postmaster is exempt from the *taille*, in all his possessions and offices, and even on his farms to the extent of a hundred *arpents*. The notaries of Angoulême are exempt from the *corvée*, from collections, and the lodging of soldiers, while neither their sons or chief clerks can be drafted in the militia. On closely examining the great fiscal net in administrative correspondence, we detect at every step some

---

[1] Hippeau, VI. 22 (1788).

[2] D'Argenson, VI. 37.

[3] Archives nationales, H. 200 (Memoir of M. Amelot, 1785).

[4] " Procès-verbaux de l'ass. prov. d'Auvergne," 253.

[5] Boivin-Champeaux, "Doléances de la parvisse de Tilleul-Lambert " (Eure). "Numbers of privileged characters, Messieurs of the elections, Messieurs the post-masters, Messieurs the presidents and other attachés of the salt-warehouse, every individual possessing extensive property pays but a third or a half of the taxes they ought to pay."

[6] De Tocqueville, 385. " Procès-verbaux de l'ass. prov. de Lyonnais," p. 56.

meshes by which, with slight effort and industry, all the big and
average-sized fish escape; the small fry alone remain at the bot-
:om of the scoop.   A surgeon not an apothecary, a man of good
family forty-five years old, in commerce, but living with his parent and in a province with a written code, escapes the collector.
The same immunity is extended to the begging agents of the
monks of "la Merci" and " L'Etroite Observance."   Throughout
the South and the East individuals in easy circumstances purchase
this commission of beggar for a *"louis*," or for ten crowns, and,
putting three livres in a cup, go about presenting it in this or that
parish : [1] ten of the inhabitants of a small mountain village and
five inhabitants in the little village of Treignac obtain their discharge in this fashion.   Consequently, "the collections fall on the
poor, always powerless and often insolvent," the privileged who
effect the ruin of the tax-payer causing the deficiencies of the
treasury.

VII.

One word more to complete the picture.   People take refuge
in the towns and, indeed, compared with the country, the towns
are a refuge.   But misery accompanies the poor, for, on the one
hand, they are involved in debt, and, on the other, the coterie
administering municipal affairs imposes taxation on the indigent.
The towns being oppressed by the fisc, they oppress the people
by throwing on these the load which the king imposes on
them.   Seven times in twenty-eight years [2] he withdraws and
re-sells the right of appointing their municipal officers, and, to get
rid of "this enormous financial burden," the towns double their
octrois.   At present, although liberated, they still make payment;
the annual charge has become a perpetual charge; never does
the fisc release its hold; once beginning to suck it continues to
suck.   "Hence, in Brittany," says an intendant, "not a town is
there whose expenses are not greater than its revenue." [3]   They
are unable to mend their pavements, and repair their streets, "the
approaches to them being almost impracticable."   What could

[1] Archives nationales, H, 1422.   (Letters of M. d'Aine, intendant, also of the receiver for
the *election* of Tulle, February 23, 1783).
[2] De Tocqueville, 64, 363.
[3] Archives nationales, H, 612, 614.   (Letters of M. de la Bove, September 11, and Dec. 2
1774; June 28, 1777).

the*y* do for self-support, obliged, as they are, to pay over
again after having already paid ?   Their augmented *octrois*, in
1748, ought to furnish in eleven years the 606,000 livres agreed
upon ; but, the eleven years having lapsed, the satisfied fisc still
maintains its exigencies, and to such an extent that, in 1774, they
have contributed 2,071,052 livres, the provisional *octroi* being
still maintained.   Now, this exorbitant *octroi* bears heavily everywhere on the most indispensable necessities, the artisan being
more heavily burdened than the bourgeois.   In Paris, as we have
seen above, wine pays forty-seven livres a puncheon entrance
duty which, at the present standard of value, must be doubled.
"A turbot, taken on the coast at Harfleur and brought by post,
pays an entrance duty of eleven times its value ; the people of the
capital, consequently, are condemned to dispense with fish from
the sea." [1]   At the gates of Paris, in the little parish of Aubervilliers, I find "excessive duties on hay, straw, seeds, tallow, candles,
eggs, sugar, fish, faggots and firewood." [2]   Compiègne pays the
whole amount of its *taille* by means of a tax on beverages and
cattle.[3]   "In Toul and in Verdun the taxes are so onerous that
but few consent to remain in the town, except those kept there by
their offices and by old habits." [4]   At Coulommiers, "the merchants
and the people are so severely taxed they dread undertaking any
enterprise."   Popular hatred everywhere is profound against oc
troi, barrier and clerk.   The bourgeois oligarchy everywhere
first cares for itself before caring for those it governs.   At Nevers
and at Moulins,[5] "all rich persons find means to escape the collections by different commissions, or through their influence with
the *élus*, to such an extent that the collectors of Nevers, of the
present and preceding year, would be considered true beggars :
there are no small villages whose collectors are solvent, since the
métayers have to be taken."   At Angers, "independent of presents and candles, which annually consume 2,172 livres, the public
pence are employed and wasted in clandestine outlays according
to the fancy of the municipal officers."   In Provence, where the
communities are free to tax themselves and where they ought,
apparently, to consider the poor, "most of the towns, and notably

[1] Mercier, II. 62.
[2] "Doléances" of the parish of Aubervilliers.
Archives nationales, G, 300; G, 322 ("Mémoires" on the excise duties).
[4] "Procès-verbaux de l'ass. prov. des Trois-Evêchés," p. 442.
Archives nationales, H, 1422 (Letter of the intendant of Moulins, April 1779).

Aix, Marseilles and Toulon,[1] pay their impositions," local and general, "only by the duty of *piquet*." This is a tax "on all species of flour belonging to and consumed on the territory;" for example, on 254,897 livres, which Toulon expends, the *piquet* furnishes 233,405. Thus the taxation falls wholly on the people, while the bishop, the marquis, the president, the merchant of importance pay less on their dinner of delicate fish and becaficos than the caulker or porter on his two pounds of bread rubbed with a piece of garlic! Bread in this country is already too dear! And the quality is so poor that Malouet, the intendant of the marine, refuses to let his workmen eat it! "Sire," said M. de la Fare, bishop of Nancy, from his pulpit, May 4th, 1789, "Sire, the people over which you reign has given unmistakable proofs of its patience. . . . They are martyrs in whom life seems to have been allowed to remain to enable them to suffer the longer."

VIII.

"I am miserable because too much is taken from me. Too much is taken from me because not enough is taken from the privileged. Not only do the privileged force me to pay in their place, but, again, they previously deduct from my earnings their ecclesiastic and feudal dues. When, out of my income of 100 francs, I have parted with fifty-three francs, and more, to the collector, I am obliged again to give fourteen francs to the seignior, also more than fourteen for tithes,[2] and, out of the remaining eighteen or nineteen francs, I have additionally to satisfy the excisemen. I alone, a poor man, pay two governments, one the old government, local and now absent, useless, inconvenient and humiliating, and active only through annoyances, exemptions and taxes; and the other, recent, centralized, everywhere present, which, taking upon itself all functions, has vast needs and makes my meagre shoulders support its enormous weight." These, in precise terms, are the vague ideas beginning to ferment in the popular brain

---

[1] Archives nationales, H, 1312 (Letters of M. d'Antheman procureur-général of the excise court (May 19, 1783), and of the Archbishop of Aix (June 15, 1783).) Provence produced wheat only sufficient for seven and a half months' consumption.

[2] The feudal dues may be estimated at a seventh of the net income and the *dime* also at a seventh. These are the figures given by the ass. prov. of Haute-Guyenne (Procès-verbaux, p. 47). Isolated instances, in other provinces, indicate similar results. The *dime* ranges from a tenth to the thirteenth of the gross product, and commonly the tenth. I regard the average as about the fourteenth, and as one-half of the gross product must be deducted for expenses of cultivation, it amounts to one-seventh. Letrosne says a fifth and even a quarter

and encountered on every page of the records of the States-General. "Would to God," says a Normandy village,[1] "the monarch might take into his own hands the defence of the miserable citizen pelted and oppressed by clerks, seigniors, justiciary and clergy!" "Sire," writes a village in Champagne,[2] "the only message to us on your part is a demand for money. We were led to believe that this might cease, but every year the demand comes for more. We do not hold you responsible for this because we love you, but those whom you employ, who better know how to manage their own affairs than yours. We believed that you were deceived by them and we in our chagrin said to ourselves, If our good king only knew of this! . . . We are crushed down with every species of taxation; thus far we have given you a part of our bread and, should this continue, we shall be in want. . . . Could you see the miserable tenements in which we live, the poor food we eat, you would feel for us; this would prove to you better than words that we can support this no longer and that it must be lessened. . . . That which grieves us is that those who possess the most, pay the least. We pay the *tailles* and for our implements, while the ecclesiastics and nobles who own the best land pay nothing. Why do the rich pay the least and the poor the most? Should not each pay according to his ability? Sire, we entreat that things may be so arranged, for that is just. . . . Did we dare, we should undertake to plant the slopes with vines; but we are so persecuted by the clerks of the excise we would rather pull up those already planted; the wine that we could make would all go to them, scarcely any of it remaining for ourselves. These exactions are a great scourge and, to escape them, we would rather let the ground lie waste. . . . Relieve us of all these extortions and of the excisemen; we are great sufferers through all these devices; now is the time to change them; never shall we be happy as long as these last. We entreat all this of you, Sire, along with others of your subjects as wearied as ourselves. . . . We would entreat yet more but you cannot do all at one time." Imposts and privileges, in the really popular memorials, are the two enemies against which complaints everywhere arise.[3] " We are overwhelmed by

---

[1] Boivin-Champeaux, 72.

[2] Grievances of the community of Culmon (Election de Langres.)

[3] Boivin-Champeaux, 34, 36, 41, 48. Périn ("Doléances de sparoisses rurales de l'Artois," 301, 308). Archives nationales, procès-verbaux and cahiers of the States-Généraux, v. XVII. p. 12 (Letter of the inhabitants of Darcy-de-Viteux).

demands for subsidies, . . . we are burdened with taxes beyond our strength, . . . we do not feel able to support any more, . . . we perish, overpowered by the sacrifices demanded of us. . . . Labor is taxed while indolence is exempt. . . . Feudalism is the most disastrous of abuses, the evils it causes surpassing those of hail and lightning. . . . Subsistence is impossible if three-quarters of the crops are to be taken for field-rents, *terrage*, etc. . . . The proprietor has a fourth part, the *décimateur* a twelfth, the harvester a twelfth, taxation a tenth, not counting the depredations of vast quantities of game which devour the growing crops : nothing is left for the poor cultivator but pain and sorrow." Why should the Third-Estate alone pay for roads on which the nobles and the clergy drive in their carriages ? Why are the poor alone subject to militia draftings ? Why does "the subdelegate cause only the defenceless and the unprotected to be drafted ? " Why does it suffice to be the servant of a privileged person to escape this service ? Destroy those dove-cotes, formerly only small pigeon-pens and which now contain as many as five thousand pairs. Abolish the barbarous rights of " *motte, quevaise* and *domaine congéable* [1] under which more than five hundred thousand persons still suffer in Lower Brittany." "You have in your armies, Sire, more than thirty thousand Franche-Comté serfs ; " should one of these become an officer and be pensioned out of the service he would be obliged to return to and live in the hut in which he was born ; otherwise, at his death, the seignior will take his pittance. Let there be no more absentee prelates, nor abbés-commendatory. "The present deficit is not to be paid by us but by the bishops and beneficiaries ; deprive the princes of the church of two-thirds of their revenues." " Let feudalism be abolished. Man, the peasant especially, is tyrannically bowed down to the impoverished ground on which he lies exhausted. . . . There is no freedom, no prosperity, no happiness where the soil is enthralled. . . . Let the lord's dues, and other odious taxes not feudal, be abolished, a thousand times returned to the privileged. Let feudalism content itself with its iron sceptre without adding the poniard of the revenue speculator." [2] Here,

---

[1] *Motte :* a mound indicative of seigniorial dominion ; *quevaise :* the right of forcing a resident to remain on his property under penalty of forfeiture ; *domaine congéable :* property held subject to capricious ejection.

[2] Prud'homme, " Résumé des cahiers," III. *passim.*, and especially from 317 to 340.

and for some time before this, it is not the countryman who speaks but the *procureur*, the lawyer, who places professional metaphors and theories at his service.   But the lawyer has simply translated the countryman's sentiments into literary dialect.

CHAPTER III.

I.

To comprehend their actions we ought now to look into the condition of their minds, to know the current train of their ideas, their mode of thinking. But, is it really essential to draw this portrait, and are not the details of their mental condition we have just presented sufficient? We shall obtain a knowledge of them later, and through their actions, when, in Touraine, they come to bestowing kicks with their *sabots* on a mayor and his assistant chosen by themselves, because, in obeying the National Assembly, these two unfortunate men prepared a table of imposts; or when, at Troyes, they drag through the streets and tear to pieces the venerable magistrate who was nourishing them at that very moment, and who had just dictated his testament in their favor.

Take the still rude brain of one of our peasants and deprive it of the ideas which, for eighty years past, have entered it by so many channels, through the primary school of each village, through the return home of the conscript after his seven years' service, through the prodigious multiplication of books, newspapers, roads, railroads, foreign travel and every other species of communication.[1] Try to imagine the peasant of that epoch,

---

[1] Théron de Montaugé, 102, 113. In the Toulousain ten parishes out of fifty have schools In Gascony, says the ass. prov. of Auch (p. 24), "most of the rural districts are without schoolmasters or parsonages." In 1778, the post between Paris and Toulouse runs only three

penned and sh.t up from father to son in his hamlet, without parish highways, deprived of news, with no instruction but the Sunday sermon, solicitous only for his daily bread and the imposts, " with his wretched, dried-up aspect,"[1] not daring to repair his house, always persecuted, distrustful, his mind contracted and stinted, so to say, by misery. His condition is almost that of his ox or his ass, while his ideas are those of his condition. He has been a long time stolid; " he lacks even instinct,"[2] mechanically and fixedly regarding the ground on which he drags along his hereditary plough. In 1751, d'Argenson wrote in his journal: "nothing in the news from the court affects them; the reign is indifferent to them. . . . The distance between the capital and the province daily widens. . . . Here they are ignorant of the striking occurrences that most impressed us at Paris. . . . The inhabitants of the country are merely poverty-stricken slaves, draft cattle under a yoke, moving on as they are goaded, caring for nothing and embarassed by nothing, provided they can eat and sleep at regular hours." They make no complaints, " they do not even dream of complaining;"[3] their wretchedness seems to them natural like winter or hail. Their minds, like their agriculture, still belong to the middle ages. In the Toulousain,[4] to ascertain who committed a robbery, to cure a man or a sick animal, they resort to a sorcerer who divines this by means of a sieve. The countryman fully believes in ghosts and, on All Saints' eve, he lays the cloth for the dead. In Auvergne, at the outbreak of the Revolution, on a contagious fever making its appearance, M. de Montlosier, declared to be a sorcerer, is the cause of it and two hundred men assemble together to demolish his dwelling. Their religious belief is on the same level.[5] " Their priests drink with them and sell them absolution. On Sundays, at the sermon, they put up lieutenancies and sub-lieutenancies (among the saints) for sale: so much for a lieutenant's place under St. Peter! If the peasant hesitates in his bid a eulogy of

---

times a week; that of Toulouse by way of Alby, Rodez, etc., twice a week for Beaumont, Saint-Girons, etc., once a week. "In the country," says Théron de Montaugé, "one may be said to live in solitude and exile." In 1789 the Paris post reaches Besançon three times a week. (Arthur Young, 1. 257).

[1] One of the Marquis de Mirabeau's expressions.

[2] Archives nationales, G, 300, letter of an excise director at Coulommiers, Aug. 13, 1781.

[3] D'Argenson, VI. 425 (June 16, 1751).

[4] De Montlosier, I. 102, 146.

[5] Théron de Montaugé 102.

St. Peter at once begins and then our peasants run it up fast enough." To intellects in a primitive state, barren of ideas and crowded with images, idols on earth are as essential as idols in heaven. " No doubt whatever existed in my mind," says Rétif de la Bretonne,[1] " of the power of the king to compel any man to bestow his wife or daughter on me, and my village (Sacy, in Burgundy) thought as I did."[2] There is no room in minds of this description for abstract conceptions, for any idea of social order; they are submissive to it and that is all. " The mass of the people," writes Gouverneur Morris in 1789, " have no religion but that of their priests, no law but that of those above them, no morality but that of self-interest; these are the beings who, led on by drunken curates, are now on the high road to liberty, and the first use they make of it is to rebel on all sides because there is a dearth."[3]

How could things be otherwise? Every idea, previous to taking root in their brain, must possess a legendary form, as absurd as it is simple, adapted to their experiences, their faculties, their fears and their aspirations. Once planted in this unculti- vated and fertile soil it vegetates and becomes transformed, de- veloping into gross excrescences, sombre foliage and poisonous fruit. The more monstrous the greater its vigor, clinging to the slightest of probabilities and tenacious against the most certain of demonstrations. Under Louis XV., in an arrest of vagabonds, a few children having been carried off wilfully or by mistake, the rumor spreads that the king takes baths in blood to restore his exhausted functions, and, so true does this seem to be, the women, horrified through their maternal instincts, join in the riot; a policeman is seized and knocked down, and, on his demanding a confessor, a woman in the crowd picking up a stone, cries out that he must not have time to go to heaven, and smashes his head with it, believing that she is performing an act of justice.[4] Under Louis XVI. evidence is presented to the people that there is no scarcity: in 1789,[5] an officer, listening to the conversation of his soldiers, hears them state " with full belief that the princes

---

[1] Monsieur Nicolas, I. 448.

[2] "Tableaux de la Révolution," by Schmidt, II. 7 (Report by the agent Perriere who lived in Auvergne.

[3] Gouverneur Morris, II. 69, April 29, 1789.

[4] Mercier, "Tableau de Paris," XII. 83.

[5] De Vaublanc, 209.

and courtiers, with a view to starve Paris out, are throwing flour into the Seine." Turning to a quarter-master he asks him how he can possibly believe such an absurd story. "Lieutenant," he replies, "'tis time—the bags were tied with *blue strings (cordons bleus)*." To them this is a sufficent reason and no argument could convince them to the contrary. Thus, among the dregs of society, foul and horrible romances are forged, in connection with famine and the Bastille, in which Louis XVI., the queen Marie Antoinette, the Comte d'Artois, Madame de Lamballe, the Polignacs, the revenue farmers, the seigniors and ladies of high rank are portrayed as vampires and ghouls. I have seen many editions of these in the pamphlets of the day, in the engravings not exhibited and among popular prints and illustrations, the latter the most efficacious since they appeal to the eye. They surpass the stories of Mandrin and Cartouche, being exactly suitable for men whose literature consists of the complaints of Mandrin and Cartouche.

II

By this we can judge of their political intelligence. Every object appears to them in a false light; they are like children who, at each turn of the road, see in each tree or bush some frightful hobgoblin. Arthur Young, on visiting the springs near Clermont, is arrested,[1] and the people want to imprison a woman, his guide, some of the bystanders regarding him as "an agent of the Queen, who intended to blow the town up with a mine, and send all that escaped to the galleys." Six days after this, beyond Puy, and notwithstanding his passport, the village guard come and take him out of bed at eleven o'clock at night, declaring that "I was undoubtedly a conspirator with the Queen, the Count d'Artois and the Count d'Entragues (who has property here), who had employed me as *arpenteur* to measure their fields in order to double their taxes." We here take the unconscious, apprehensive, popular imagination in the act; a slight indication, a word, prompting the construction of either airy castles or fantastic dungeons, and seeing these as plainly as if they were so many substantial realities. They have not the inward resources that render them capable of separating and discerning; their

---

[1] Arthur Young, I. 183 (Aug. 13, 1789); I. 289 (Aug. 19, 1789).

conceptions are formed *in a lump ;* both object and fancy appear together and are united in one single perception. At the moment of electing deputies the report is current in Provence [1] that "the best of kings desires perfect equality, that there are to be no more bishops, nor seigniors, nor tithes, nor seigniorial dues, no more titles or distinctions, no more hunting or fishing rights, . . . that the people are to be wholly relieved of taxation, and that the first two orders alone are to provide the expenses of the government." Whereupon forty or fifty riots take place in one day. "Several communities refuse to make any payments to their treasurer outside of royal requisitions." Others do better: "on pillaging the strong-box of the receiver of the tax on leather at Brignolles, they shout out *Vive le Roi !* " "The peasant constantly asserts his pillage and destruction to be in conformity with the king's will." A little later, in Auvergne, the peasants who burn castles are to display "much repugnance" in thus maltreating "such kind seigniors," but they allege "imperative orders, having been advised that the king wished it." [2] At Lyons, when the tapsters of the town and the peasants of the neighborhood pass over the bodies of the customs officials they believe that the king has suspended all customs dues for three days.[3] The scope of their imagination is proportionate to their shortsightedness. " Bread, no more rents, no more taxes!" is the sole cry, the cry of want, while exasperated want plunges ahead like a famished bull. Down with the monopolist!—storehouses are forced open, convoys of grain are stopped, markets are pillaged, bakers are hung, and the price of bread is fixed so that none is to be had or is concealed. Down with the *octroi !*—barriers are demolished, clerks are beaten, money is wanting in the towns for urgent expenses. Burn tax registries, account-books, municipal archives, seigniors' charter-safes, convent parchments, every detestable document creative of debtors and sufferers! The village itself is no longer able to preserve its parish property. The rage against any written document, against public officers, against any

---

[1] Archives nationales, H, 274. Letters respectively of M. de Caraman (March 18 and April 12, 1789); M. d'Eymar de Montmegran (April 2); M. de la Tour (March 30). "The sovereign's greatest benefit is interpreted in the strangest manner by an ignorant populace."

[2] Doniol, " Hist. des classes r rales," 495. (Letter of Aug. 3, 1789, to M. de Clermont-Tonnerre).

[3] Archives nationales, H, 1453. (Letter of Imbert Colonnès, prévôt des marchands, dated July 5, 1789)

man more or less connected with grain, is blind and determined
The furious animal destroys all, although wounding himself, driv
ing and roaring against the obstacle that ought to be outflanked

III.

This is owing to the absence of leaders and to the absence of
organization, a multitude being simply a herd. Its mistrust of
its natural leaders, of the great, of the wealthy, of persons in office and clothed with authority, is inveterate and incurable.
Vainly do these wish it well and do it good; it has no faith in
their humanity or disinterestedness. It has been too down-trodden;
it entertains prejudices against every measure proceeding from
them, even the most liberal and the most beneficial. "At the
mere mention of the new assemblies," says a provincial commission in 1787,[1] "we heard a workman exclaim, 'What, more new
extortioners!'" Superiors of every kind are suspected, and from
suspicion to hostility the road is not long. In 1788[2] Mercier declares that "insubordination has been manifest for some years, especially among the trades. . . . Formerly, on entering a printing-
office the men took off their hats. Now they content themselves
with staring and leering at you; scarcely have you crossed the
threshold than you hear yourself more lightly spoken of than if
you were one of them " The same attitude is taken by the peasants in the environs of Paris; Madame Vigée-Lebrun,[3] on going
to Romainville to visit Marshal de Ségur, remarks: "Not only
do they not remove their hats but they regard us insolently; some
of them even threatened us with clubs." In March and April
following this, her guests arrive at her concert in consternation.
"In the morning, at the promenade of Longchamps, the populace,
assembled at the barrier of l'Etoile, insulted the people passing by
in carriages in the grossest manner; some of these wretches jumped
on the footsteps exclaiming: 'Next year you shall be behind the
carriage and we inside.'" At the close of the year 1788, the
stream becomes a torrent and the torrent a cataract. An intendant[4] writes that, in his province, the government must decide, and

---

[1] "Procès-verbaux de l'ass. prov. de l'Orléanais," p. 296. "Distrust still prevails throughout the rural districts. . . . Your first orders for departmental assemblies only awakened
suspicion in certain quarters."

[2] "Tableau de Paris," XII. 186.

[3] Mme. Vigée-Lebrun, I. 158 (1788); I. 183 (1789).

[4] Archives nationales, H, 723. (Letter of M. de Caumartin, intendant at Besançon, Dec.
5, 1788).

in the popular sense, to separate from privileged classes, abandon old forms and give the Third-Estate a double vote. The clergy and the nobles are detested, and their supremacy is a yoke. " Last July," he says, " the old States-General would have been received with transport and there would have been few obstacles to its formation. During the past five months minds have become enlightened; respective interests have been discussed, and leagues formed. You have been kept in ignorance of the fermentation which is at its height among all classes of the Third-Estate, and a spark will kindle the conflagration. If the king's decision should be favorable to the first two orders a general insurrection will occur throughout the province, 600,000 men in arms and the horrors of the Jacquerie." The word is spoken and the reality is coming. An insurrectionary multitude rejecting its natural leaders must elect or submit to others. It is like an army which, entering on a campaign, should depose its officers; the new grades are for the boldest, most violent, most oppressed, for those who, putting themselves ahead, cry out " march " and thus form advanced bands. In 1789, the bands are ready; for, below the mass that suffers another suffers yet more, with which the insurrection is permanent, and which, repressed, persecuted, and obscure, only awaits an opportunity to issue from its hiding-place and ravage in the open daylight.

IV.

Vagrants, every species of refractory spirit, victims of the law and of the police, mendicants, deformities, foul, filthy, haggard and savage, are engendered by the abuses of the system, and, upon each social ulcer they gather like vermin.

Four hundred leagues of guarded captainries and the security enjoyed by vast quantities of game feeding on crops under their owners' eyes, give rise to thousands of poachers, the more dangerous that they are armed and defy the most terrible laws. Already in 1752 [1] are seen around Paris " gatherings of fifty or sixty, all fully armed and acting as if on regular foraging campaigns, with the infantry at the centre and the cavalry on the wings. . . They live in the forests behind retired and guarded entrenchments, paying exactly for what they take to

---

[1] D'Argenson, March 13, 1752.

live on." In 1777, at Sens in Burgundy, the procureur-général,
M. Terray, hunting on his own property with two officers, meets
a gang of poachers who fire on the game under his own eye and
soon afterwards fire on them. M. Terray is wounded and one
of the officers has his coat pierced; guards arrive, but the poachers stand firm and repel them; dragoons are sent for, at Provins,
and the poachers kill one of these, along with three horses, and
are attacked with sabres; four of them are brought to the ground
and seven are captured. Reports of the States-General show
that every year, in each extensive forest, murders occur, sometimes at the hands of a poacher and again, and the most frequently, by the shot of a gamekeeper. Domestic warfare is organized; every vast domain thus harbors its rebels provided
with powder and ball and knowing how to use them.

Other recruits for turbulence are found in smugglers and in
dealers in contraband salt.[1] A tax, as soon as it becomes exorbitant, invites fraud, and raises up a population of delinquents
against its army of clerks. The number of defrauders of this
species may be estimated by the number of their supervisors.
twelve hundred leagues of interior custom districts are guarded by
50,000 men of which 23,000 are soldiers not in uniform.[2] "In
the chief provinces of the salt-tax and in the provinces of the
five great *fermes*, four leagues one way and another along the
line of defence," cultivation is abandoned; everybody is either a
customs official or a smuggler.[3] The more excessive the tax the
higher the premium offered to the violators of the law; at every
place on the boundaries of Brittany with Normandy, Maine and
Anjou, four *sous* per pound added to the salt-tax multiplies beyond any conception the already enormous number of contraband dealers. "Numerous bands of men,[4] armed with *frettes*, or
long sticks pointed with iron, and often with pistols or guns,
attempt to force a passage. A multitude of women and of children, quite young, cross the lines of the brigades while, on the

---

[1] Beugnot, I. 142. "No inhabitant of the barony of Choiseul mingled with any of the bands composed of the patriots of Montigny, smugglers and outcasts of the neighborhood." See, on the poachers of the day, "Les deux amis de Bourbonne," by Diderot.

[2] De Calonne, "Mémoires presentés à l'ass. des notables," No. 8. Necker, "De l'Ad-ministration des Finances," I. 195.

[3] Letrosne, "De l'Administration des Finances," 59.

[4] Archives nationales, H. 426. (Memorials of the farmers-general, Jan. 13, 1781; Sept 15, 1782). H, 614. (Letter of M. de Coetlosquet, April 25, 1777). H, 1431. Report by the farmers-general, March 9, 1787.

other hand, troops of dogs brought upon the free soil and kept
there a certain time without food, are loaded with salt and this,
urged by their hunger, they immediately transport to their masters."
Vagabonds, outlaws, the famished, sniff this lucrative occupation
from afar and run to it like so many packs of hounds. "The
outskirts of Brittany are filled with a population of emigrants,
mostly outcasts from their own districts, and who, after a year's
sojourn here in domicile, enjoy the privileges of the Bretons:
their occupation is limited to collecting piles of salt to re-sell to
the contraband dealers." We obtain a glimpse, as in a flash of
lightning, of this long line of restless, hunted, midnight rovers, a
male and female population of savage wanderers, accustomed to
blows, hardened to the inclemencies of the weather, ragged,
"almost all with an obstinate itch;" and I find similar bodies in
the vicinity of Morlaix, Lorient, and other ports on the frontiers
of other provinces and on the frontiers of the kingdom. From
1783 to 1787, in Quercy, two allied bands of smugglers, sixty
and eighty each, defraud the revenue of forty thousands of
tobacco, kill two customs officers and, with their guns, defend
their magazine in the mountains; to suppress them soldiers are
requisite, which their military commander will not furnish. In
1789,[1] a large troop of smugglers carry on operations permanently
on the frontiers of Maine and Anjou; the military commander
writes that "their chief is an intelligent and formidable bandit,
that he already has under him fifty-five men, that he will soon
have a corps, embarrassing through misery and through the disposition of minds;" it would be well, possibly, to corrupt some of
his men so as to have him betrayed since they cannot capture
him. These are the means resorted to in regions where brigandage is endemic. Here, indeed, as in Calabria, the people are on
the side of the brigands against the gendarmes. The exploits
of Mandrin in 1754,[2] may be remembered: his company of sixty
men who bring in contraband goods and ransom only the clerks,
his expedition, lasting nearly a year, across Franche-Comté, Lyonnais, Bourbonnais, Auvergne and Burgundy, the twenty-seven
towns he enters making no resistance, delivering prisoners and
making sale of his merchandise; to overcome him a camp had
to be formed at Valence and two thousand men sent against him;

---

[1] Archives nationales, H, 1453. (Letter of the Baron de Bezenval, June 19, 1789.
[2] "Mandrin," by Paul Simian, *passim.* "Histoire de Bearme," by Rossègnol, p. 453).

ne was taken through treachery and still at the present day certain families are proud of their relationship to him, declaring him a liberator.—No symptom is more alarming: on the enemies of the law being preferred by the people to its defenders, society disintegrates and the worms begin to work.   Add to these the veritable brigands, assassins and robbers.   "In 1782,[1] the provost's court of Montargis is engaged on the trial of Hulin and two hundred of his accomplices who, for ten years, by means of joint enterprises, have desolated a portion of the kingdom." Mercier enumerates in France "an army of more than 10,000 brigands and vagabonds" against which the police, composed of 3,756 men, is always on the march.   "Complaints are daily made," says the provincial assembly of Haute-Guyenne, "that there is no police in the country."   The absentee seignior pays no attention to this matter; his judges and officials take good care not to operate gratuitously against an insolvent criminal, while " his estates become the refuge of all the rascals of the canton."[2]   Every abuse thus engenders a danger, ill-placed neglect equally with excessive rigor, relaxed feudalism equally with a too-exacting monarchy.   All institutions seem under agreement to multiply or tolerate the abettors of disorder and to prepare, outside the social pale, the executive agents who are to carry it by storm.

But the total effect of all this is yet more pernicious, for, out of the vast numbers of laborers it ruins it forms mendicants unwilling to work, dangerous sluggards going about begging and extorting bread from peasants who have not too much for themselves. "The vagabonds about the country," says Letrosne,[3] "are a terrible pest; they are like an enemies' force which, distributed over the territory, obtains a living as it pleases, levying veritable contributions. . . . They are constantly roving around the country, examining the approaches to houses, and informing themselves about their inmates and of their habits. Woe to those supposed to have money ! . . . What numbers of highway robberies and what burglaries !   What numbers of travellers assassinated, and houses and doors broken into !   What assassinations of curates, farmers and widows, tormented to discover money and afterwards killed ! "   Twenty-five years anterior

---

[1] Mercier, XI. 116
[2] See *ante*, book I. p 55.
[3] Letrosne, *ibid.* (1779,, p. 539.

:o the Revolution it was not infrequent to see fifteen or twenty
of these "invade a farm-house to sleep there, intimidating the
farmers and exacting whatever they pleased." In 1764, the government takes measures against them which indicates the magnitude of the evil.[1]   "Are held to be vagabonds and vagrants, and
condemned as such, those who, for a preceding term of six
months, shall have exercised no trade or profession, and who,
having no occupation or means of subsistence, can procure no
persons worthy of confidence to attest and verify their habits and
mode of life. . . . The intent of His Majesty is not merely to arrest vagabonds traversing the country but, again, all mendicants
whatsoever, who, without occupations, may be regarded as suspected of vagabondage." The penalty for able-bodied men is three
years in the galleys; in case of a second conviction, nine years; in
case of a third conviction, the galleys for life. For invalid culprits,
three years imprisonment; in case of a second conviction, nine
years, and for a third, imprisonment for life.   Under the age of
sixteen, they are put in a hospital.   "A mendicant who has made
himself liable to arrest by the police," says the circular, "is not to
be released except under the most positive assurance that he will
no longer beg; this course will be followed only in case of persons worthy of confidence and *solvent*, guaranteeing the mendicant and engaging to provide him with employment or to support
him, and they shall indicate the means by which they are to prevent him from begging." This being furnished, the special author
ization of the intendant must be obtained in addition.   By virtue
of this law, 50,000 beggars are said to have been arrested at
once, and, as the ordinary hospitals and prisons were not large
enough to contain them, jails had to be constructed.   Up to the
end of the ancient régime this measure is carried out with occasional intermissions: in Languedoc, in 1768, arrests were still
made of 433 in six months, and, in 1785, 205 in four months.
About the same epoch 300 were confined in the depot of Besançon, 500 in that of Rennes and 650 in that of St. Denis.   It cost
the king a million a year to support them, and God knows how
they were supported!   Water, straw, bread, and two ounces of

---

[1] Archives nationales, F16, 965, and H, 892.   (Ordinance of August 4, 1764; a circular of
instructions of July 20, 1767; a letter of a police lieutenant of Toulouse, September 21, 1787).

[2] Archives nationales, H, 724; H, 554; F4, 2397; F16, 965.   Letters of the jail-keepers of
Carcassonne (June 22, 1789); of Béziers (July 19, 1786); of Nimes (July 1, 1786); of the
intendant, M. d'Aine (March 19, 1786).

salted grease, the whole at an expense of five *sous* a day; and, as the price of provisions for twenty years back had increased more than a third, the keeper who had them in charge was obliged to nake them fast or ruin himself. With respect to the mode of filling the depots, the police are Turks in their treatment of the lower class; they strike into the heap, their broom bruising as many as they sweep out. According to the ordinance of 1778, writes an intendant,[1] "the police must arrest, not only beggars an l vagabonds whom they encounter but, again, those denounced as such or as suspected persons. The citizen, the most ir-reproachable in his conduct and the least open to suspicion of vagabondage, is not sure of not being shut up in the depot, as his freedom depends on a policeman who is constantly liable to be deceived by false denunciation or corrupted by a bribe. I have seen in the depot at Rennes several husbands arrested solely through the denunciation of their wives, and as many women through that of their husbands; several children by the first wife at the solicitation of their step-mothers; many female domestics pregnant by the masters they served, shut up at their instigation, and girls in the same situation at the instance of their seducers; children denounced by their fathers, and fathers de-nounced by their children; all without the slightest evidence of vagabondage or mendicity. . . . No decision of the provost's court exists restoring the incarcerated to their liberty, notwith-standing the infinite number arrested unjustly." Suppose that a humane intendant, like this one, sets them at liberty : there they are in the streets, mendicants through the action of the law which proscribes mendicity and which adds to the wretched it prose-cutes the wretched it creates, still more embittered and corrupt in body and in soul. "It nearly always happens," says the same in-tendant, "that the prisoners, arrested twenty-five or thirty leagues from the depot, are not confined there until three or four months after their arrest and sometimes longer. Meanwhile, they are transferred from brigade to brigade, in the prisons found along the road, where they remain until the number increases sufficiently to form a convoy. Men and women are confined in the same prison, the result of which is, the females not pregnant on enter-ing it are always so on their arrival at the depot. The prisons are

---

[1] Archives nationales, H, 554. (Letter of M. de Bertrand, intendant of Rennes, August 7, 1785).

generally unhealthy; frequently, the majority of the prisoners are
sick on leaving it;" and many become rascals on coming in con
tact with rascals. Moral contagion and physical contagion, the
ulcer thus increasing through the remedy, centres of repression
becoming centres of corruption.

And yet with all its rigors the law does not attain its ends.
"Our towns," says the parliament of Brittany,[1] "are so filled
with beggars it seems as if the measures taken to suppress mendicity only increase it." "The principal highways," writes the
intendant, "are infested with dangerous vagabonds and vagrants,
actual beggars, which the police do not arrest, either through
negligence or because their interference is not provoked by special
solicitations." What would be done with them if they were
arrested? There are too many, and there is no place to put
them. And, moreover, how prevent people who live on alms from
demanding alms? The effect, undoubtedly, is lamentable but
inevitable. Poverty, to a certain extent, is a slow gangrene
in which the morbid parts consume the healthy parts, the man
scarcely able to subsist being eaten up alive by the man who has
nothing to live on. "The peasant is ruined, perishing, the victim
of oppression by the multitude of the poor that lay waste the
country and take refuge in the towns. Hence the mobs so prej-
udicial to public safety, that crowd of smugglers and vagrants,
that large body of men who have become robbers and assassins,
solely because they lack bread. This gives but a faint idea
of the disorders I have seen with my own eyes.[2] The poverty
of the rural districts, excessive in itself, becomes yet more so
through the disturbances it engenders; we have not to seek elsewhere for frightful sources of mendicity and for all the vices."[3]
Of what avail are palliatives or violent proceedings against an
evil which is in the blood and which belongs to the very constitution of the social organism? What police force could effect
anything in a parish in which one-quarter or one-third of its inhabitants have nothing to eat but that which they beg from door
to door? At Argentré,[4] in Brittany, "a town without trade or

---

[1] Archives nationales, H, 426. (Remonstrance, Feb. 4, 1783). H, 554. (Letter of M. de
Bertrand, Aug. 17, 1785).

[2] *Ibid.* H, 614. (Memorial by René de Hauteville, parliamentary advocate, St. Brieuc,
Dec. 25, 1776).

[3] "Procès-verbaux de l'ass. prov. de Soissonnais" (1787) p. 457.

[4] Archives nationales, H, 616. (A letter of M. de Bo es, intendant of Rennes, April 23,
1774).

industry, out of 2,300 inhabitants, more than one-half are any-thing else but well-off, and over 500 are reduced to beggary." At Dainville, in Artois, "out of 130 houses sixty are on the poor-list."[1] In Normandy, according to statements made by the curates, "of 900 parishioners in Saint-Malo, three-quarters can barely live and the rest are in poverty."   "Of 1,500 inhabitants in Saint-Patrice, 400 live on alms; of 500 inhabitants in Saint-Laurent three-quarters live on alms. "   At Marbœuf, says a report, "of 500 persons inhabiting our parish, 100 are reduced to men-dicity and besides these, thirty and forty a day come to us from neighboring parishes."[2]   At Bolbone in Languedoc[3] daily at the convent gate is "general alms-giving to 300 or 400 poor people, independent of that for the aged and the sick which is more numerously attended."   At Lyons, in 1787, "30,000 workmen depend on public charity for subsistence;" at Rennes, in 1788, after an inundation, "two-thirds of the inhabitants are in a state of destitution;"[4] at Paris, out of 650,000 inhabitants, the census of 1791 enumerates 118,784 as indigent.[5] Let frost or hail come, as in 1788, let a crop fail, let bread cost four *sous* a pound, and let a workman in the charity-workshops earn only twelve *sous* a day,[6] can one imagine that people will resign themselves to death by starvation?   Around Rouen, during the winter of 1788, the forests are pillaged in open day, the woods at Baguères are wholly cut away, the fallen trees are publicly sold by the ma-rauders.[7]   Both the famished and the marauders go together, necessity making itself the accomplice of crime.   From province to province we can follow up their tracks: four months later, in the vicinity of Etampes, fifteen brigands break into four farm-houses during the night, while the farmers, threatened by incen-diaries, are obliged to give, one three hundred francs, another five hundred, all the money, probably, they have in their coffers[8]

---

[1] Périn, "La Jeunesse de Robespierre," 301. (Doléances des parvisses rurales in 1789).

[2] Théron de Montaugé, p. 87. (Letter of the prior of the convent, March, 1789).

[3] Hippeau, "Le Gouvern. de Normandie," VII. 147–177 (1789). Boivin-Champeaux, "Notice hist. sur la Révolution dans le département de l'Eure," p. 83 (1789).

[4] "Procès-verbaux de l'ass. prov. de Lyonnais," p. 57.   Archives nationales, F⁴, 2073. Memorial of Jan. 24, 1788.   "Charitable assistance is very limited, the provincial authorities providing no resources for such accidents."

[5] Levasseur, "La France industrielle," 119.   In 1862, the population being almost triple (1,696,000), there are but 90,000.

[6] Albert Babeau, "Hist. de Troyes," I. 91.   (Letter of the mayor Huez, July 30, 1788).

[7] Floquet, VII. 506.

[8] Archives nationales, H, 1453. Letter of M. de Saint-Suzanne, April 29, 1789).

"Robbers, convicts, the worthless of every species," are to form
the advance guard of insurrections and lead the peasantry to the
extreme of violence.[1] After the sack of the Reveillon house in
Paris it is remarked that "of the forty ringleaders arrested, there
was scarcely one who was not an old offender, and either flogged
or branded."[2] In every revolution the lees of society come to
the surface.   Never had these been visible before; like badgers
in the woods, or rats in the sewers, they had remained in their
burrows or in their holes.   They issue from these in swarms,
while, in Paris, what figures suddenly come to light![3] "Never
had any like them been seen in open day. . . . Where do they
come from ? who has brought them out of their obscure hiding-
places ? . . . Foreigners from every country, armed with clubs,
ragged, . . . some almost naked, others oddly dressed" in incongruous patches and "frightful to look at," constitute the riotous chiefs or their subordinates, at six francs per head, behind
which the people are to march.

"In Paris," says Mercier,[4] "the people are weak, pallid, dimin-
utive, stunted," maltreated, "and, apparently, a class apart from
other classes in the State.   The rich and the great who possess
equipages, enjoy the privilege of crushing them or of mutilating
them in the streets. . . . There is no convenience for foot-pas-
sengers, no sidewalks.   Hundreds of victims die annually under
the carriage wheels." "I saw," says Arthur Young, "a poor
child run over and probably killed, and have been myself many
times blackened with the mud of the kennels. . . . If young noblemen at London were to drive their chaises in streets without
foot-ways, as their brethren do at Paris, they would speedily and
justly get very well threshed or rolled in the kennel." Mercier
grows uneasy in the face of the immense populace.   "In Paris
there are, probably, two hundred thousand individuals with no
property intrinsically worth fifty crowns, and yet the city subsists!"   Order, consequently, is maintained only through fear
and by force, owing to the soldiery of the watch who are called

---

[1] Arthur Young, I. 256.

[2] "Corresp. secrète inédite," from 1777 to 1792, published by M. de Lescure, II. 351
(May 8, 1789). Cf. C. Desmoulins, "La Lanterne," of 100 rioters arrested at Lyons 96 were
branded.

[3] De Bezenval, II. 344, 350. Dussault, "La Prise de la Bastille," 352. Marmontel II
ch. xiv. 249. Mme. Vigée-Lebrun, I. 177, 188.

[4] Mercier, I. 32; VI. 15; X. 179; XI. 59; XII. 83. Arthur Young, I. 122.

tristes-à-patte by the masses. "This appellation excites the rage of this species of militia who then deal heavier blows around them, wounding indiscriminately all they encounter. The low class is always ready to make war on them because it has never been fairly treated by them." In fact, "a squad of the guard often scatters, with no trouble, platoons of five or six hundred men, at first greatly excited, but melting away in the twinkling of an eye, after the soldiery have distributed a few blows and handcuffed two or three of the ringleaders." Nevertheless, "were the people of Paris abandoned to their first transports, did they not feel the horse and foot guards behind them, the commissary and policeman, they would set no limits to their disorder. The populace, delivered from its accustomed restraint, would give itself up to violence of so cruel a stamp as not to know when to stop. . . . As long as white bread[1] lasts, the commotion will not prove general ; the flour market[2] must interest itself in the matter, if the women are to remain tranquil. . . . Should white bread be wanting for two market days in succession, the uprising would be universal, and it is impossible to foresee the lengths this multitude at bay will go to escape famine, they and their children." In 1789 white bread proves to be wanting throughout France.

---

[1] In the original, *pain de Gonesse*, — bread made in a village of this name near Paris, and renowned for its whiteness.—TR.

[2] "Dialogues sur le commerce des blés," by Galiani (1770). "If the powerful of the markets are content, no misfortune will happen to the administration. The great conspire and rebel ; the bourgeois murmurs and lives a celibate ; peasants and artisans despair and go away ; porters get up riots."

THE REVOLUTION

VOLUME I

PREFACE.

THIS second part of "Les Origines de la France Contemporaine" will consist of two volumes.—Popular insurrections and the laws of the Constituent Assembly end in destroying all government in France; this forms the subject of the present volume.—A party arises around an extreme doctrine, gets possession of the power, and exercises it in conformity with that doctrine; this will form the subject of the second volume.

A third volume would be required to criticize authorities. For this I have no room, and I merely state the rule that I have observed. The most trustworthy testimony is that of the eye-witness, especially when this witness is an honourable, attentive, and intelligent man, writing on the spot, at the moment, and under the dictation of the facts themselves—if it is manifest that his sole object is to preserve or furnish information, if his work is not a piece of polemics planned for the needs of a cause, or a passage of eloquence arranged for popular effect, but a legal deposition, a secret report, a confidential dispatch, a private letter, or a personal memento. The nearer a document approaches this type, the more it merits confidence, and supplies superior materials.—I have found many of this character in the national archives, principally in the manuscript correspondence of ministers, intendants, sub-delegates, magistrates, and other functionaries; of military commanders, officers in the army, and gendarmerie; of royal commissioners, and of the Assembly; of administrators of departments, districts, and municipalities, besides persons in private life who address the King, the National Assembly, or the ministry. Among these are men of every rank, profession, education, and party. They are distributed by hundreds and thousands over the whole surface of the territory. They write apart, without

73

being able to consult each other, and without even knowing each other. No one is so well placed for collecting and transmitting accurate information. None of them seek literary effect, or even imagine that what they write will ever be published. They draw up their statements at once, under the direct impression of local events. Testimony of this character, of the highest order, and at first hand, provides the means by which all other testimony ought to be verified. The foot notes at the bottom of the pages indicate the condition, office, name, and dwelling-place of those decisive witnesses. For greater certainty I have transcribed as often as possible their own words. In this way the reader, confronting the texts, can interpret them for himself, and form his own opinions; he will have the same documents as myself for arriving at his conclusions, and, if he is pleased to do so, he will conclude otherwise. As for allusions, if he finds any, he himself will have introduced them, and if he applies them he is alone responsible for them. To my mind, the past has features of its own, and the portrait here presented resembles only the France of the past. I have drawn it without concerning myself with the discussions of the day; I have written as if my subject were the revolutions of Florence or Athens. This is history, and nothing more, and, if I may fully express myself, I esteem my vocation of historian too highly to make a cloak of it for the concealment of another.

December, 1877.

THE REVOLUTION.

BOOK FIRST.

Spontaneous Anarchy.

CHAPTER I.

I. The beginnings of anarchy.—Dearth the first cause.—Bad crops.—The winter of 1788 and 1789.—Dearness and poor quality of bread.—In the provinces.—At Paris.—II. Hopefulness the second cause.—Separation and laxity of the Administrative forces.—Investigations of local Assemblies.— The people become awake to their condition.—Convocation of the States-General.—Hope is born.—The coincidence of early Assemblies with early difficulties.—III. The provinces during the first six months of 1789.—Effects of the famine.—IV. Intervention of ruffians and vagabonds.—V. The first *jacquerie* in Provence.—Feebleness or ineffectiveness of repressive measures.

DURING the night of July 14-15, 1789, the Duc de la Roche-foucauld-Liancourt caused Louis XVI. to be aroused to inform him of the taking of the Bastille. "It is a revolt, then?" exclaimed the King. "Sire!" replied the Duke, "it is a revolution!" The event was even more serious. Not only had power slipped from the hands of the King, but it had not fallen into those of the Assembly; it lay on the ground, ready to the hands of the unchained populace, the violent and over-excited crowd, the mobs which picked it up like some weapon that had been thrown away in the street. In fact, there was no longer any government; the artificial structure of human society was giving way entirely; things were returning to a state of nature. This was not a revolution, but a *dissolution*.

Two causes excite and maintain the universal upheaval. The first one is a dearth, which, being constant, lasting for ten years, and aggravated by the very disturbances which it excites, bids fair to

75

inflame the popular passions to madness, and change the whole course of the Revolution into a series of spasmodic stumbles.

When a stream is brimful, a slight rise suffices to cause an over-flow. So was it with the extreme distress of the eighteenth century. A poor man who finds it difficult to live when bread is cheap, sees death staring him in the face when it is dear. In this state of suffering the animal instinct revolts, and the universal obedience which constitutes public peace depends on a degree more or less of dryness or damp, heat or cold. In 1788, a year of severe drought, the crops had been poor; in addition to this, on the eve of the harvest,[1] a terrible hail-storm burst over the region around Paris, from Normandy to Champagne, devastating sixty leagues of the most fertile territory, and causing damage to the amount of one hundred millions of francs. Winter came on, the severest that had been seen since 1709 : at the close of December the Seine was frozen over from Paris to Havre, while the thermo-meter stood at 18¾° below zero. A third of the olive-trees died in Provence, and the rest suffered to such an extent that they were considered incapable of bearing fruit for two years to come. The same disaster befell Languedoc. In Vivarais, and in the Cevennes, whole forests of chestnuts had perished, along with all the grain and grass crops on the uplands; on the plain the Rhone remained in a state of overflow for two months. After the spring of 1789 the famine spread everywhere, and it increased from month to month like a rising flood. In vain did the Government order the farmers, proprietors, and corn-dealers to keep the markets supplied ; in vain did it double the bounty on im-portations, resort to all sorts of expedients, involve itself in debt, and expend over forty millions of francs to furnish France with wheat. In vain do individuals, princes, noblemen, bishops, chapters, and communities multiply their charities, the Archbishop of Paris incurring a debt of 400,000 livres, one rich man distributing 40,000 francs the morning after the hail-storm, and a convent of Bernardins feeding twelve hundred poor persons for six weeks.[2]

---

[1] Marmontel, " Mémoires," ii. 221.—Albert Babeau, " Histoire de la Révolution Française," i. 91, 187 (Letter by Huez, Mayor of Troyes, July 30, 1788.)—Archives Nationales, H. 1274. (Letter by M. de Caraman, April 22, 1789.) H. 942 (Cahier des demandes des Etats du Languedoc).—Buchez et Roux, " Histoire Parlementaire," i. 283.

[2] See " The Ancient Régime," p. 34. Albert Babeau, i. 91. (The Bishop of Troyes gives 12,000 francs, and the chapter 6,000, for the relief workshops.)

All was not sufficient. Neither public measures nor private charity could meet the overwhelming need. In Normandy, where the last commercial treaty had ruined the manufacture of linen and of lace trimmings, forty thousand workmen were out of work. In many parishes one-fourth of the population[1] are beggars. Here, "nearly all the inhabitants, not excepting the farmers and landowners, are eating barley bread and drinking water;" there, "many poor creatures have to eat oat bread, and others soaked bran, which has caused the death of several children."— "Above all," writes the Rouen Parliament, "let help be sent to a perishing people. . . . . Sire, most of your subjects are unable to pay the price of bread, and what bread is given to those who do buy it ! "—Arthur Young,[2] who was travelling through France at this time, heard of nothing but the dearness of bread and the distress of the people. At Troyes bread costs four sous a pound— that is to say, eight sous of the present day; and artisans unemployed flock to the relief works, where they can earn only twelve sous a day. In Lorraine, according to the testimony of all observers, "the people are half dead with hunger." In Paris the number of paupers has been trebled ; there are thirty thousand in the Faubourg Saint-Antoine alone. Around Paris there is a short supply of grain, or it is spoilt.[3] In the beginning of July, at Montereau, the market is empty. "The bakers could not have baked " if the police officers had not fixed the price of bread at five sous per pound ; the rye and barley which the *intendant* is able to send " are of the worst possible quality, rotten and in a condition to produce dangerous diseases ; nevertheless, most of the small consumers are reduced to the hard necessity of using this spoilt grain." At Villeneuve-le-Roi, writes the mayor, "the rye of the two lots last sent is so black and poor that it cannot be retailed without wheat." At Sens the barley " tastes musty " to such an extent that buyers of it throw the detestable bread which it makes in the face of the sub-delegate. At Chevreuse the

[1] "The Ancient Régime," 350, 387.--Floquet, " Histoire du Parlement de Normandie," vii. 505—518. (Reports of the Parliament of Normandy, May 3, 1788. Letter from the Parliament to the King, Ju'y 15, 1789.)

[2] Arthur Young, " Voyages in France," June 29th, July 2nd and 18th.—" Journal de Paris," January 2, 1789. Letter of the curé of Sainte-Marguerite.

[3] Roux and Buchez, iv. 79—82. (Letter from the intermediary bureau of Montereau, July 9, 1789; from the *maire* of Villeneuve-le-Roi, July 10th ; from M. Baudry, July 10th; from M. Jamin, July 11th ; from M. Prioreau, July 11th, &c.) Montjoie, " Histoire de la Révolution de France," 2nd part, ch. xxi. p. 5.

barley has sprouted and smells bad ; the " poor wretches," says an employé, " must be hard pressed with hunger to put up with it." At Fontainebleau " the barley, half eaten away, produces more bran than flour, and to make bread of it, one is obliged to work it over several times." This bread, such as it is, is an object of savage greed ; " it has come to this, that it is impossible to distribute it except through wickets ; " those, again, who thus obtain their ration, " are often attacked on the road and robbed of it by the more vigorous of the famished people." At Nangis " the magistrates prohibit the same person from buying more than two bushels in the same market." In short, provisions are so scarce that there is a difficulty in feeding the soldiers ; the minister dispatches two letters one after another to order the cutting down of 250,000 bushels of rye before the harvest.[1] Paris thus, in a perfect state of tranquillity, appears like a famished city put on rations at the end of a long siege, and the dearth will not be greater nor the food worse in December, 1870, than in July, 1789.

" The nearer the 14th of July approached," says an eye-witness,[2] " the more did the dearth increase. Every baker's shop was surrounded by a crowd, to which bread was distributed with the most grudging economy. . . . This bread was generally blackish, earthy, and bitter, producing inflammation of the throat and pain in the bowels. I have seen flour of detestable quality at the military school and at other depôts. I have seen portions of it yellow in colour, with an offensive smell ; some forming blocks so hard that they had to be broken into fragments by repeated blows of a hatchet. For my own part, wearied with the difficulty of procuring this poor bread, and disgusted with that offered to me at the tables d'hôte, I avoided this kind of food altogether. In the evening I went to the Café du Caveau, where, fortunately, they were kind enough to reserve for me two of those rolls which are called *flutes*, and this is the only bread I have eaten for a week at a time." But this resource is only for the rich. As for the people, to get bread fit for dogs,

---

[1] Roux et Buchez, ibid. "It is very unfortunate," writes the Marquis d'Autichamp, "to be obliged to cut down the standing crops ready to be gathered in ; but it is dangerous to let the troops die of hunger."

[2] Montjoie, " Histoire de la Révolution de France," ch. xxix. v. 37. De Goncourt, " La Société Française pendant la Révolution," p. 53. Deposition of Maillard (Criminal Inquiry of the Châtelet concerning the events of October 5th and 6th).

they must stand in a line for hours. And here they fight for it ;
"they snatch food from one another." There is no more work to
be had ; " the work-rooms are deserted ;" often, after waiting a
whole day, the workman returns home empty-handed, and when
he does bring back a four-pound loaf it costs him 3 francs 12
sous ; that is, 12 sous for the bread, and 3 francs for the lost day.
In this long line of unemployed, excited men, swaying to and
fro before the shop-door, dark thoughts are fermenting : " if the
bakers find no flour to-night to bake with, we shall have nothing
to eat to-morrow." An appalling idea ;—in presence of which the
whole power of the Government is not too strong ; for to keep
order in the midst of famine nothing avails but the sight of an
armed force, palpable and threatening. Under Louis XIV. and
Louis XV. there had been even greater hunger and misery ; but the
outbreaks, which were roughly and promptly put down, were only
partial and passing disorders. Some rioters were at once hung,
and others were sent to the galleys : the peasant or the workman,
convinced of his impotence, at once returned to his stall or his
plough. When a wall is too high one does not even think of
scaling it.—But now the wall is cracking—all its custodians, the
clergy, the nobles, the Third-Estate, men of letters, the politicians,
and even the Government itself, making the breach wider. The
wretched, for the first time, discover an issue : they dash through
it, at first in driblets, then in a mass, and rebellion becomes as
universal as resignation was formerly.

II.

It is because through this opening hope steals like a beam of
light, and gradually finds its way down to the depths below. For
the last fifty years it has been rising, and its rays, which first
illuminated the upper class in their splendid apartments in the first
story, and next the middle-class in their entresol and on the
ground floor, have now for two years penetrated to the cellars
where the people toil, and even to the deep sinks and obscure
corners where rogues and vagabonds and malefactors, a foul and
swarming herd, crowd and hide themselves from the persecution
of the law. To the first two provincial assemblies instituted by
Necker in 1778 and 1779, Loménie de Brienne has in 1778 just
added nineteen others ; under each of these are assemblies of the
arrondissement; under each assembly of the *arrondissement* are

parish assemblies.[1] Thus the whole machinery of administration
has been changed. It is the new assemblies which assess the
taxes and superintend their collection ; which determine upon and
direct all public works ; and which form the court of final appeal
in regard to matters in dispute. The *intendant*, the *sub-delegate*,
the *élu*,[2] thus lose three-quarters of their authority. Conflicts
arise, consequently, between rival powers whose frontiers are not
clearly defined ; command shifts about, and obedience is diminished. The subject no longer feels on his shoulders the commanding weight of the one hand which, without possibility of
interference or resistance, held him in, urged him forward, and
made him move on. Meanwhile, in each assembly of the parish
arrondissement, and even of the province, plebeians, " husbandmen," [3] and oftentimes common farmers, sit by the side of lords
and prelates. They listen to and remember the vast figure of
the taxes which are paid exclusively, or almost exclusively, by
them—the *taille* and its accessories, the poll-tax and road dues,
and assuredly on their return home they talk all this over with
their neighbour. These figures are all printed ; the village attorney
discusses the matter with his clients, the artisans and rustics,
on Sunday as they leave the mass, or in the evening in the
large public room of the tavern. These little gatherings, moreover, are sanctioned, encouraged by the powers above. In the
earliest days of 1788 the provincial assemblies order a board
of inquiry to be held by the syndics and inhabitants of each
parish. Knowledge is wanted in detail of their grievances—what
part of the revenue is chargeable to each impost, what the cultivator pays and how much he suffers, how many privileged persons
there are in the parish ; the amount of their fortune, whether they
are residents, what their exemptions amount to ; and, in the replies,
the attorney who holds the pen, names and points out with his
finger each privileged individual, criticizes his way of living, and
estimates his fortune, calculates the injury done to the village by
his immunities, inveighs against the taxes and the tax-collectors.
On leaving these assemblies the villager broods over what he has

---

[1] De Tocqueville, "L'Ancien Régime et la Révolution," 272—290. De Lavergne,
"Les Assemblées provinciales," 109. Procès-verbaux des assemblées provinciales,
passim.

[2] A magistrate who gives judgment in a lower court in cases relative to taxation. These
terms are retained because there are no equivalents in English.

[3] "*Laboureurs*,"—this term, at this epoch, is applied to those who till their own land.

just heard. He sees his grievances no longer singly as before, but in mass, and coupled with the enormity of evils under which his fellows suffer. Besides this, they begin to disentangle the causes of their misery: the King is good—why then do his collectors take so much of our money? This or that canon or nobleman is not unkind—why then do they make us pay in their place?—Suppose a beast of burden to which a sudden gleam of reason should reveal the equine species contrasted with the human species; and imagine, if you can, what his first ideas would be in relation to the postillions and drivers who bridle and whip him, and again in relation to the good-natured travellers and sensitive ladies who pity him, but who to the weight of the vehicle add their own and that of their luggage.

So, in the mind of the peasant, athwart his perplexed broodings, a new idea, slowly, little by little, is unfolded;—that of an oppressed multitude of which he makes one, a vast herd scattered far beyond the visible horizon, everywhere ill used, starved, and fleeced. Towards the end of 1788 we begin to detect in the correspondence of the *intendants* and military commandants the dull universal muttering of coming wrath. Men's characters seem to change; they become suspicious and restive.—And just at this moment, the Government, dropping the reins, calls upon them to direct themselves.[1] In the month of November, 1787, the King declared that he would convoke the States-General. On the 5th of July, 1788, he calls for memorials on this subject from every competent person and body. On the 8th of August he fixes the date of the session. On the 5th of October he convokes the notables, in order to consider the subject with them. On the 27th of December he grants a double representation to the Third-Estate, because "its cause is allied with generous sentiments, and it will always obtain the support of public opinion." The same day he introduces into the electoral assemblies of the clergy a majority of *curés*, "because good and useful pastors are daily and closely associated with the indigence and relief of the people," from which it follows "that they are much more familiar with their sufferings" and necessities. On the 24th January, 1789, he prescribes the procedure and method of the meetings. After the 7th of February writs of summons are sent out one after the

---

[1] Duvergier, "Collection des lois et décrets," i. 1 to 23, and particularly p. 15.

other.   Eight days after, each parish assembly begins to draw up
its memorial of grievances, and becomes excited over the detailed
enumeration of all the miseries which it sets down in writing.—All
these appeals and all these acts are so many strokes which reverberate in the popular imagination.   " It is the desire of His
Majesty," says the order issued, "that every one, from the extremities of his kingdom, and from the most obscure of its
hamlets, should be certain of his wishes and protests reaching
him."   Thus, it is all quite true: there can be no mistake about
it, the thing is sure.   The people are invited to speak out, they
are summoned, they are consulted.   There is a disposition to
relieve them; henceforth their misery shall be less; better times
are coming.   This is all they know about it.   A few months after,
in July,[1] the only answer a peasant girl can make to Arthur Young
is, "something was to be done by some great folks for such poor
ones, but she did not know who nor how;" the thing is too
complicated, beyond the reach of a stupefied and mechanical
brain.   One idea alone emerges—the hope of immediate relief, the
persuasion that right is on their side, the resolution to aid it with
every possible means; and, consequently, an anxious waiting, a
ready impulse, a tension of the will which simply stays for the
opportunity to relax and launch forth like a resistless arrow
towards the unknown end which will reveal itself all of a sudden.
It is hunger that so suddenly marks out for them this aim:
the market must be supplied with grain; the farmers and
owners must bring it; wholesale buyers, whether the Government
or individuals, must not transport it elsewhere; it must be sold at
a low price; the price must be cut down and fixed, so that the
baker can sell bread at two sous the pound; grain, flour, wine,
salt, and provisions must pay no more duties; seignorial dues and
claims, ecclesiastical tithes, and royal or municipal taxes must no
longer exist.   On the strength of this idea disturbances broke out
on all sides in March, April, and May; contemporaries "do not
know what to think of such a scourge;[2] they cannot comprehend
how such a vast number of criminals, without visible leaders,
agree amongst themselves everywhere to commit the same excesses
just at the time when the States-General are going to begin their

---

[1] Arthur Young, July 12th, 1789 (in Champagne).
[2] Montjoie, 1st part, 102.

sittings." The reason is that, under the ancient régime, the conflagration was smouldering in a closed chamber; the great door is suddenly opened, the air enters, and immediately the flame breaks out.

III.

At first there are only intermittent, isolated fires, which are extinguished or go out of themselves; but, a moment after, in the same place, or very near it, the sparks again appear, and their number, like their recurrence, shows the vastness, depth, and heat of the combustible matter which is about to explode. In the four months which precede the taking of the Bastille, over three hundred outbreaks may be counted in France. They take place from month to month, and from week to week, in Poitou, Brittany, Touraine, Orléanais, Normandy, Ile-de-France, Picardy, Champagne, Alsace, Burgundy, Nivernais, Auvergne, Languedoc, and Provence. On the 28th of May the parliament of Rouen announces robberies of grain, " violent and bloody tumults, in which men on both sides have fallen," throughout the province, at Caen, Saint-Lô, Mortain, Granville, Evreux, Bernay, Pont-Andemer, Elbœuf, Louviers, and in other sections besides. On the 20th of April, Baron de Bezenval, military commander in the central provinces, writes : " I once more lay before M. Necker a picture of the frightful condition of Touraine and of Orléanais. Every letter I receive from these two provinces is the narrative of three or four riots, which are put down with difficulty by the troops and constabulary,"[1]—and throughout the whole extent of the kingdom a similar state of things is seen.

The women, as is natural, are generally at the head of these outbreaks. It is they who, at Montlhéry, rip open the sacks of grain with their scissors. On learning each week, on market-day, that the price of a loaf of bread advances three, four, or seven sous, they break out into shrieks of rage : at this rate for bread, with the small salaries of the men, and when work fails,[2] how can a family be fed ? Crowds gather around the sacks of flour and the doors of the bakers ; amidst outcries and reproaches some one in the crowd makes a push ; the proprietor

---

[1] Floquet, " Histoire du Parlement de Normandie," vii. 508.—" Archives Nationales," H. 1453.

[2] Arthur Young, June 29th (at Nangis).

or dealer is hustled and knocked down, the shop is invaded, the commodity is in the hands of the buyers and of the famished, each one grabbing for himself, pay or no pay, and running away with the booty.—Sometimes a party is made up beforehand.[1]   At Bray-sur-Seine, on the 1st of May, the villagers for four leagues around, armed with stones, knives, and cudgels, to the number of four thousand, compel the husbandmen and farmers who have brought grain with them to sell it at 3 livres, instead of 4 livres 10 sous the bushel; and threaten to do the same thing on the following market-day.   The farmers will not come again, the storehouse will be empty, and soldiers must be at hand, or the inhabitants of Bray will be pillaged.   At Bagnols, in Languedoc, on the 1st and 2nd of April, the peasants, armed with cudgels and assembled by tap of drum, "traverse the town, threatening to burn and destroy everything if flour and money are not given to them:" they go to private houses for grain, divide it amongst themselves at a reduced price, "promising to pay when the next crop comes round," and force the Consuls to put bread at two sous the pound, and to increase the day's wages four sous.— Indeed this is now the regular thing; it is not the people who obey the authorities, but the authorities who•obey the people.   Consuls, sheriffs, mayors, municipal officers, town-clerks, become confused and hesitating in the face of this huge clamour; they feel that they are likely to be trodden under foot or thrown out of the windows.   Others, with more firmness, are aware that a riotous crowd is mad, and scruple to spill blood; at least, they yield for the time, hoping that at the next market-day there will be more soldiers and better precautions taken.   At Amiens, "after a very violent outbreak,"[2] they decide to take the wheat belonging to the Jacobins, and, protected by the troops, to sell it to the people at a third below its value.   At Nantes, where the town-hall is attacked, they are forced to lower the price of bread one sou per pound.   At Angoulême, to avoid a recourse to arms, they request the Comte d'Artois to renounce his dues on flour for two months, reduce the price of bread, and compensate the

---

[1] " Archives Nationales," H. 1453.   Letter of the Duc de Mortemart, Seigneur of Bray, May 4th; of M. de Ballainvilliers, intendant of Languedoc, April 15th.

[2] " Archives Nationales," H. 1453.   Letter of the intendant, M. d'Agay, April 30th; of the municipal officers of Nantes, January 9th; of the intendant, M. Meulan d'Ablois, June 22nd; of M. de Ballainvilliers, April 15th.

bakers. At Cette they are so maltreated they let everything take its course; the people sack their dwellings and get the upper hand; they announce by sound of trumpet that all their demands are granted. On other occasions, the mob dispenses with their services and acts for itself. If there happens to be no grain on the market-place, the people go after it wherever they can find it—to proprietors and farmers who are unable to bring it for fear of pillage; to convents, which by royal edict are obliged always to have one year's crop in store; to granaries where the Government keeps its supplies; and to convoys which are dispatched by the *intendants* to the relief of famished towns. Each for himself—so much the worse for his neighbour. The inhabitants of Fougères beat and drive out those who come from Ernée to buy in their market; like violence is shown at Vitré to the inhabitants of Maine.[1] At Sainte-Léonard the people stop the grain started for Limoges; at Bost that intended for Aurillac; at Saint-Didier that ordered for Moulins; and at Tournus that dispatched to Macon. In vain are escorts added to the convoys; troops of men and women, armed with hatchets and guns, put themselves in ambush in the woods along the road, and seize the horses by their bridles; the sabre has to be used to secure any advance. In vain are arguments and kind words offered, " and in vain even is wheat offered for money; they refuse, shouting out that the convoy shall not go on." They have taken a stubborn stand, their resolution being that of a bull planted in the middle of the road and lowering his horns. Since the wheat is in the district, it is theirs; whoever carries it off or withholds it is a robber. This fixed idea cannot be driven out of their minds. At Chantenay, near Mans,[2] they prevent a miller from carrying that which he had just bought to his mill; at Montdragon, in Languedoc, they stone a dealer in the act of sending his last waggon-load elsewhere; at Thiers, workmen go in force to gather wheat in the fields; a proprietor with whom some is found is nearly killed; they drink wine in the cellars, and leave the taps running. At Nevers, the bakers not having put bread on their counters for

---

1 " Archives Nationales," H. 1453. Letter of the Count de Langeron, July 4th; of M. de Meulan d'Ablois, June 5th; " Procès-verbal de la Maréchaussée de Bost," April 29th. Letters of M. de Chazerat, May 29th; of M. de Bezenval, June 2nd; of the intendant, M. Amelot, April 25th.

2 " Archives Nationales," H. 1453. Letter of M. de Bezenval, May 27th; of M. de Ballainvilliers, April . 5th; of M. de Foullonde, April 19th.

four days, the populace force the granaries of private persons,
of dealers and religious communities. " The frightened corn-
dealers part with their grain at any price ; most of it is stolen in
the face of the guards," and, in the tumult of these domiciliary
visits, a number of houses are sacked.—In these days woe to all
who are concerned in the acquisition, commerce, and manipulation
of grain ! Popular imagination requires living beings to whom it
may impute its misfortunes, and on whom it may gratify its resent-
ments. To it, all such persons are monopolists, and, at any rate,
public enemies. Near Angers the Benedictine establishment is
invaded, and its fields and woods are devastated.[1] At Amiens
" the people are arranging to pillage and perhaps burn the houses
of two merchants, who have built labour-saving mills ; " restrained
by the soldiers, they confine themselves to breaking windows ; but
other " groups come to destroy or plunder the houses of two or
three persons whom they suspect of being monopolists." At
Nantes, a *sieur* Geslin, being deputed by the people to inspect a
house, and finding no wheat, a shout is set up that he is a receiver,
an accomplice ! The crowd rush at him, and he is wounded and
almost cut in pieces.—It is very evident that there is no more
security in France ; property, even life, is in danger. The first
of all property, that of provisions, is violated in hundreds of places,
and everywhere is menaced and precarious. The *intendants* and
sub-delegates everywhere call for aid, declare the constabulary
incompetent, and demand regular troops. And mark how public
authority, everywhere inadequate, disorganized, and tottering, finds
stirred up against it not only the blind madness of hunger, but, in
addition, the evil instincts which profit by every disorder and the
inveterate lusts which every political commotion frees from
restraint.

IV.

We have seen how numerous the smugglers, dealers in contraband salt, poachers, vagabonds, beggars, and escaped convicts[2]
have become, and how a year of famine increases the number.
All are so many recruits for the mobs, and whether in a disturb-

[1] " Archives Nationales," H. 1453. Letter of the intendant, M. d'Aine, March 12th ; of
M. d'Agay, April 30th ; of M. Amelot, April 25th ; of the municipal authorities of Nantes,
January 9th, &c.
[2] " The Ancient Régime," pp. 380—389.

ance or by means of a disturbance each one of them fills his pouch. Around Caux,[1] even up to the environs of Rouen, at Roncherolles, Quévrevilly, Préaux, Saint-Jacques, and in all the surrounding neighbourhood bands of armed ruffians force their way into the houses, particularly the parsonages, and lay their hands on whatever they please. To the south of Chartres "three or four hundred woodcutters, from the forests of Bellème, chop away everything that opposes them, and force grain to be given up to them at their own price." In the vicinity of Étampes, fifteen bandits enter the farmhouses at night and put the farmer to ransom, threatening him with a conflagration. In Cambrésis they pillage the abbeys of Vauchelles, of Verger, and of Guillemans, the château of the Marquis de Besselard, the estate of M. Doisy, two farms, the waggons of wheat passing along the road to Saint-Quentin, and, besides this, seven farms in Picardy. "The seat of this revolt is in some villages bordering on Picardy and Cambrésis, familiar with smuggling operations and to the license of that pursuit." The peasants allow themselves to be enticed away by the bandits. Man slips rapidly down the incline of dishonesty; one who is half-honest, and takes part in a riot inadvertently or in spite of himself, repeats the act, allured on by impunity or by gain. In fact, "it is not dire necessity which impels them;" they make a speculation of cupidity, a new sort of illicit trade. An old carabinier, sabre in hand, a forest-keeper, and "about eight persons sufficiently lax, put themselves at the head of four or five hundred men, go off each day to three or four villages, and force everybody who has any wheat to give it to them at 24 livres," and even at 18 livres, the sack. Those among the band who say that they have no money carry away their portion without payment. Others, after having paid what they please, re-sell at a profit, which amounts to even 45 livres the sack; a good business, and one in which greed takes poverty for its accomplice. At the next harvest the temptation will be similar: "they have threatened to come and do our harvesting for us, and also to take our cattle and sell the meat in

---

1 Floquet, vii. 508 (Report of February 27th). Hippeau, "Le Gouvernement de Normandie," iv. 377. (Letter of M. Perrot, June 23rd.)—"Archives Nationales," H. 1453. Letter of M. de Sainte-Suzanne, April 29th. Ibid. F. 7, 3250. Letter of M. de Rochambeau, May 16th. Ibid. F. 7, 3185. Letter of the Abbé Duplaquet, Deputy of the Third Estate of Saint-Quentin, May 17th. Letter of three husbandmen in the environs of Saint-Quentin, May 14th.

the villages at the rate of two sous the pound."—In every important insurrection there are similar evil-doers and vagabonds,
enemies to the law, savage, prowling desperadoes, who, like
wolves, roam about wherever they scent a prey. It is they who
serve as the directors and executioners of public or private
malice. Near Usès twenty-five masked men, with guns and
clubs, enter the house of a notary, fire a pistol at him, beat him,
wreck the premises, and burn his registers along with the
title-deeds and papers which he has in keeping for the Count
de Rouvres : seven of them are arrested, but the people are on
their side, and fall on the constabulary and free them.[1]—They are
known by their acts, by their love of destruction for the sake of
destruction, by their foreign accent, by their savage faces and
their rags. Some of them come from Paris to Rouen, and, for
four days, the town is at their mercy ;[2] the stores are forced open,
train waggons are discharged, wheat is wasted, and convents and
seminaries are put to ransom ; they invade the dwelling of the
attorney-general, who has begun proceedings against them, and
want to tear him to pieces ; they break his mirrors and his
furniture, leave the premises laden with booty, and go into the
town and its outskirts to pillage the manufactories and break up
or burn all the machinery.—Henceforth these constitute the new
leaders : for in every mob it is the boldest and least scrupulous
who march ahead and set the example in destruction. The
example is contagious : the beginning was the craving for bread,
the end is murder and incendiarism ; the savagery which is unchained adding its unlimited violence to the limited revolt of
necessity.

V.

Bad as it is, this savagery might, perhaps, have been overcome, in spite of the dearth and of the brigands; but what
renders it irresistible is the belief of its being authorised, and that
by those whose duty it is to repress it. Here and there words and
actions of a brutal frankness break forth, and reveal beyond
the sombre present a more threatening future.—After the 9th of
January, 1789, among the populace which attacks the Hôtel-de-

---

[1] "Archives Nationales," H. 1453. Letter of the Count de Perigord, military commandant of Languedoc, April 22nd.
[2] Floquet, vii. 511 (from the 11th to the 14th July).

Ville and besieges the bakers' shops of Nantes, " shouts of *Vive la Liberté !* [1] mingled with those of *Vive le Roi !* are heard." A few months later, around Ploërmel, the peasants refuse to pay tithes, alleging that the memorial of their seneschal's court demands their abolition. In Alsace, after March, there is the same refusal " in many places ; " many of the communities even maintain that they will pay no more taxes until their deputies to the States-General shall have fixed the precise amount of the public contributions. In Isère it is decided, by proceedings, printed and published, that " personal dues " shall no longer be paid, while the landowners who are affected by this dare not prosecute in the tribunals. At Lyons, the people have come to the conclusion " that all levies of taxes are to cease," and, on the 29th of June, on hearing of the meeting of the three orders, " astonished by the illuminations and signs of public rejoicing," they believe that the good time has come ; " they think of forcing the delivery of meat to them at four sous the pound, and wine at the same rate. The publicans insinuate to them the prospective abolition of *octrois*, and that, meanwhile, the King, in favour of the re-assembling of the three orders, has granted three days' freedom from all duties at Paris, and that Lyons ought to enjoy the same privilege." Upon this the crowd, rushing off to the barriers, to the gates of Sainte-Claire and Perrache, and to the Guillotière bridge, burn or demolish the bureaux, destroy the registers, sack the lodgings of the clerks, carry off the money and pillage the wine on hand in the depôt. In the mean time a rumour has circulated all round through the country that there is free entrance into the town for all provisions, and during the following days the peasantry stream in with enormous files of waggons loaded with wine and drawn by several oxen, so that, in spite of the re-established guard, it is necessary to let them enter all day without paying the dues ; it is only on the 7th of July that these can again be collected.—The same thing occurs in the southern provinces, where the principal imposts are levied on provisions. There also the collections are suspended in the name of public authority. At Agde,[2]

---

[1] " Archives Nationales," H. 1453. Letter of the municipal authorities of Nantes, January 9th ; of the sub-delegate of Ploërmel, July 4th ; ibid. F. 7, 2353. Letter of the intermediary commission of Alsace, September 8th ; ibid. F. 7, 3227. Letter of the intendant, Caze de la Bove, June 16th ; ibid. H. 1453. Letter of Terray, intendant of Lyons, July 4th ; of the prévot des échevins, July 5th and 7th.

[2] " Archives Nationales," H. 1453. Letter of the mayor and councils of Agde, April 21st ; of M. de Perigord, April 19th, May 5th.

" the people, considering the so-called will of the King as
to equality of classes, are foolish enough to think that they
are everything and can do everything ; " thus do they interpret in
their own way and in their own terms the double representation
which is accorded to the Third-Estate.   They threaten the town,
consequently, with general pillage if the prices of all provisions
are not reduced, and if the duties of the province on wine, fish, and
meat are not suppressed ; again, " they wish to nominate consuls
who have sprung up out of their body," and the bishop, the lord
of the manor, the mayor and the notables, against whom they
forcibly stir up the peasantry in the country, are obliged to proclaim
by sound of trumpet that their demands shall be granted.   Three
days afterwards they exact a diminution of one-half of the tax on
grinding, and go in quest of the bishop who owns the mills.   The
prelate, who is ill, sinks down in the street, and seats himself on
a stone ; they compel him forthwith to sign an act of renunciation, and hence " his mill, valued at 15,000 livres, is reduced to
7,500 livres."—At Limoux, under the pretext of searching for
grain, they enter the houses of the comptroller and tax contractors,
carry off their registers, and throw them into the water along with
the furniture of their clerks.—In Provence it is worse ; for most
unjustly, and through inconceivable imprudence, the taxes of the
towns are all levied on flour ; it is therefore to this impost that
the dearness of bread is directly attributed ; hence the fiscal agent
becomes a manifest enemy, and revolts on account of hunger are
transformed into insurrections against the State.

VI.

Here, again, political novelties are the spark that ignites the mass
of gunpowder ; everywhere, the uprising of the people takes place
on the very day on which the electoral assembly meets; from forty
to fifty riots occur in the provinces in less than a fortnight.   Popular imagination, like that of a child, goes straight to its mark ; the
reforms having been announced, people think them accomplished,
and, to make sure of them, steps are at once taken to carry them
out ; now that we are to have relief, let us relieve ourselves.
" This is not an isolated riot as usual," writes the commander of
the troops ;[1] " here the faction is united and governed by uniform

1 " Archives Nationales," H. 1453. Letters of M. de Caraman, March 23rd, 26th, 27th,
28th ; of the seneschal Missiessy, March 24th ; of the mayor of Hyères, March 25th, &c.;

principles; the same errors are diffused through all minds. . . . .
The principles impressed on the people are that the King desires
equality; no more bishops or lords, no more distinctions of rank,
no tithes, and no seignorial privileges.   Thus, these misguided
people fancy that they are exercising their rights. and obeying
the will of the King."   The effect of sonorous phrases is apparent;
the people have been told that the States-General were to bring
about the " regeneration of the kingdom ; " the inference is " that
the date of their assembly was to be one of an entire and absolute
change of conditions and fortunes."   Hence, "the insurrection
against the nobles and the clergy is as active as it is widespread."
" In many places it was distinctly announced that there was a *sort
of war declared against landowners and property*," and "in the towns
as well as in the rural districts the people persist in declaring that
they will pay nothing, neither taxes, duties, nor debts."—Naturally, the
first assault is against the *piquet*, or meal-tax.   At Aix, Marseilles,
Toulon, and in more than forty towns and market-villages, this is
summarily abolished ; at Aupt and at Luc nothing remains of the
weighing-house but the four walls ; at Marseilles the house of the
slaughter-house contractor, at Brignolles that of the director of
the leather excise, are sacked : the determination is " to purge the
land of excise-men."—This is only a beginning; bread and other
provisions must become cheap, and that without delay.   At Arles,
the corporation of sailors, presided over by M. de Barras, consul,
had just elected its representatives : by way of conclusion to the
meeting, they pass a resolution insisting that M. de Barras should
reduce the price of all comestibles, and, on his refusal, they " open
the window, exclaiming, ' We hold him, and we have only to
throw him into the street for the rest to pick him up.' "   Com-
pliance is inevitable.   The resolution is proclaimed by the town-
criers, and at each article which is reduced in price the crowd
shout, " Vive le Roi, vive M. Barras ! "—One must yield to brute
force.   But the inconvenience is great ; for, through the suppression
of the meal-tax, the towns have no longer a revenue ; and, on the
other hand, as they are obliged to indemnify the butchers and
bakers, Toulon, for instance, incurs a debt of 2,500 livres a day.

ibid. H. 1274; of M. de Montmayran, April 2nd; of M. de Caraman, March 18th, April
12th; of the intendant, M. de la Tour, April 2nd; of the procureur-général, M. d'Antheman, April 17th, and the report of June 15th ; of the municipal authorities of Toulon,
April 11th; of the sub-delegate of Manosque, March 14th ; of M. de Saint-Tropez, March
21st.—Procés-verbal, signed by 119 witnesses, of the insurrection at Aix, March 5th, &c.

In this state of disorder, woe to those who are under suspicion of having contributed, directly or indirectly, to the evils which the people endure ! At Toulon a demand is made for the head of the mayor, who signs the tax-list, and of the keeper of the records; they are trodden under foot, and their houses are ransacked. At Manosque, the Bishop of Sisteron, who is visiting the seminary, is accused of favouring a monopolist ; on his way to his carriage, on foot, he is hooted and menaced : he is first pelted with mud, and then with stones. The consuls in attendance, and the sub-delegate who come to his assistance, are mauled and repulsed. Meanwhile, some of the most furious begin, before his eyes, " to dig a ditch to bury him in."˙ Protected by five or six brave fellows, he succeeds in reaching his carriage, amidst a volley of stones, wounded on the head and on many parts of his body, and is finally saved only because the horses, which are likewise stoned, run away. Foreigners, Italians, bandits, are mingled with the peasants and artisans, and expressions are heard and acts are seen which indicate a *jacquerie.*[1] " The most excited said to the bishop, ' We are poor and you are rich, and we mean to have all your property.' "[2] Elsewhere, " the seditious mob exacts contributions from all people in good circumstances. At Brignolles, thirteen houses are pillaged from top to bottom, and thirty others half-pillaged.—At Aupt, M. de Montferrat, in defending himself, is killed and " hacked to pieces."—At La Seyne, the populace, led by a peasant, assemble by beat of drum ; some women fetch a bier, and set it down before the house of a leading bourgeois, telling him to prepare for death, and that " they will have the honour of burying him." He escapes ; his house is pillaged, as well as the bureau of the meal-tax ; and, the following day, the chief of the band " obliges the principal inhabitants to give him a sum of money to indemnify, as he states it, the peasants who have abandoned their work," and devoted the day to serving the public.—At Peinier, the Président de Peinier, an octogenarian, is " besieged in his château by a band of a hundred and fifty artisans and peasants," who bring with them a consul and a notary. Aided by these two functionaries, they force the president " to pass an act by

---

[1] A rising of the peasants. The term is used to indicate a country mob in contradistinction to a city or town mob.—Tr.

[2] " Archives Nationales," H. 1274. Letter of M. de la Tour, April 2nd (with a detailed memorial and depositions).

which he renounces his seignorial rights of every description."—At
Sollier they destroy the mills belonging to M. de Forbin-Janson,
sack the house of his business agent, pillage the château, demolish
the roof, chapel, altar, railings, and escutcheons, enter the cellars,
stave in the casks, and carry away everything that can be carried,
"the transportation taking two days ;" all of which is a damage of a
hundred thousand crowns for the marquis.—At Riez they surround
the episcopal palace with fagots, threatening to burn it, "and compromise with the bishop on a promise of fifty thousand livres," and
want him to burn his archives.—In short, the sedition is *social*, for
it singles out for attack all who profit by, or stand at the head of,
the established order of things.

Seeing them act in this way, one would say that the theory of
the *Contrat-Social* had been instilled into them.   They treat magistrates as domestics, promulgate laws, conduct themselves like
sovereigns, exercise public power, and establish, summarily, arbitrarily, and brutally, whatever they think to be in conformity with
natural right.—At Peinier they exact a second electoral assembly,
and, for themselves, the right of suffrage.—At Saint-Maximin
they themselves elect new consuls and officers of justice.—At
Solliez they oblige the judge's lieutenant to give in his resignation,
and they break his staff of office.--At Barjols " they use consuls
and judges as their town servants, announcing that they are
masters and that they will themselves administer justice."—In
fact, they do administer it as they understand it—that is to say,
through many exactions and robberies !   One man has wheat ;
he must share it with him who has none.   Another has money ;
he must give it to him who has not enough to buy bread with.
On this principle, at Barjols, they tax the Ursulin nuns 1,800
livres, carry off fifty loads of wheat from the Chapter, eighteen
from one poor artisan, and forty from another, and constrain canons
and beneficiaries to give acquittances to their farmers.   Then,
from house to house, with club in hand, they oblige some to hand
over money, others to abandon their claims on their debtors,
" one to desist from criminal proceedings, another to nullify a
decree obtained, a third to reimburse the expenses of a lawsuit
gained years before, a father to give his consent to the marriage
of his son."—All their grievances are brought to mind, and we all
know the tenacity of a peasant's memory.   Having become the
master, he redresses wrongs, and especially those of which he

thinks himself the object. There must be a general restitution ;
and first, of the feudal dues which have been collected. They
take of M. de Montmeyan's business agent all the money he has
as compensation for that received by him during fifteen years as a
notary. A former consul of Brignolles had, in 1775, inflicted
penalties to the amount of 1,500 or 1,800 francs. which had been
given to the poor ; this sum is taken from his strong box.
Moreover, if consuls and law officers are wrong-doers, the title-
deeds, rent-rolls, and other documents by which they do their
business are still worse. To the fire with all old writings—not
only office registers, but also, at Hyères, all the papers in the
town-hall and those of the principal notary.—In the matter of
papers none are good but new ones—those which convey some
discharge, quittance, or obligation to the advantage of the people.
At Brignolles the owners of the grist-mills are constrained to
execute a contract of sale by which they convey their mills to the
commune in consideration of 5,000 francs per annum, payable in
ten years without interest—an arrangement which ruins them.
On seeing the contract signed the peasants shout and cheer, and so
great is their faith in this piece of stamped paper that they at once
cause a mass of thanksgiving to be celebrated in the Cordeliers.
Formidable omens, these ! which mark the inward purpose, the
determined will, the coming deeds of this rising power. If it
prevails, its first work will be to destroy all ancient documents, all
title-deeds, rent-rolls, contracts, and claims to which force compels
it to submit. By force likewise it will draw up others to its own
advantage, and the scribes who do it will be its own deputies
and administrators whom it holds in its rude grasp.

Those who are in high places are not alarmed ; they even find
that there is some good in the revolt, inasmuch as it compels the
towns to suppress unjust taxation.[1] The new Marseilles guard,
formed of young men, is allowed to march to Aubagne, " to insist
that *M. le lieutenant criminel* and *M. l'avocat du Roi* release
the prisoners." The disobedience of Marseilles, which refuses to

---

[1] " Archives Nationales," H. 1274. Letter of M. de Caraman, April 22nd :—" One real
benefit results from this misfortune. . . . . The well-to-do class is brought to sustain that
which exceeded the strength of the poor daily labourers. We see the nobles and people in
good circumstances a little more attentive to the poor peasants : they are now habituated
to speaking to them with more gentleness." M. de Caraman was wounded, as well as his
son, at Aix, and if the soldiery, who were stoned, at length fired on the crowd, he did not
give the order.—Ibid. letter of M. d'Anthéman, April 17th ; of M. de Barentin, June 11th.

CHAP. I. *SPONTANEOUS ANARCHY.* 95

receive the magistrates sent under letters patent to take testimony, is tolerated. And better still, in spite of the remonstrances of the parliament of Aix, a general amnesty is proclaimed; "no one is excepted but a few of the leaders, to whom is allowed the liberty of leaving the kingdom." The mildness of the King and of the military authorities is admirable. It is admitted that the people are children, that they err only through ignorance, that faith must be had in their repentance, and, as soon as they return to order, they must be received with paternal effusions.—The truth is, that the child is a blind Colossus, exasperated by sufferings. Hence whatever it takes hold of is shattered—not only the local wheels of the provinces, which, if temporarily deranged, may be repaired, but even the mainspring at the centre which puts the rest in motion, and the destruction of which will throw the whole machinery into confusion.

CHAPTER II.

Paris up to the 14th of July.—I. Mob recruits in the environs.—Entry of vagabonds.—The number of paupers.—II. Excitement of the press and of opinion.—The people take part.—III. The Réveillon affair.—IV. The Palais-Royal.—Popular gatherings become a political power—Pressure on the Assembly.—V. Defection of the soldiery.—VI. July 13th and 14th.—VIII. Paris in the hands of the people.

INDEED it is in the centre that the convulsive shocks are strongest. Nothing is lacking to aggravate the insurrection—neither the most lively provocations to stimulate it, nor the most numerous bands to carry it out. The environs of Paris all furnish recruits for it; nowhere are there so many miserable wretches, so many of the famished, and so many rebellious beings. Robberies of grain take place everywhere—at Orleans, at Cosne, at Rambouillet, at Jouy, at Pont-Saint-Maxence, at Bray-sur-Seine, at Sens, at Nangis.[1] Wheaten flour is so scarce at Meudon, that every purchaser is ordered to buy at the same time an equal quantity of barley. At Viroflay, thirty women, with a rear-guard of men, stop on the main road vehicles which they suppose to be loaded with grain. At Montlhéry seven brigades of the police are dispersed by stones and clubs : an immense throng of eight thousand persons, women and men, provided with bags, fall upon the grain exposed for sale, force the delivery to them of wheat worth 40 francs at 24 francs, pillaging the half of it and conveying it off without payment. " The constabulary is disheartened," writes the sub-delegate; " the determination of the people is wonderful; I am frightened at what I have seen and heard."—After the 13th of July, 1788, the day of the hail-storm, " despair " seized the peasantry; well disposed as the proprietors may have been, it was impossible to

---

[1] " Archives Nationales," H. 1453. Letter of M. Miron, lieutenant de police, April 26th ; of M. Joly de Fleury, procureur-général, May 29th; of MM. Marchais and Berthier, April 18th and 27th, March 23rd, April 5th, May 5th.—Arthur Young, June 10th and 29th. " Archives Nationales," H. 1453. Letter of the sub-delegate of Montlhéry, April 14th.

assist them; "not a 'workshop is open;[1] the noblemen and the bourgeois, obliged to grant delays in the payment of their incomes, can give no work." Accordingly, " the famished people are on the point of risking life for life," and, publicly and boldly, they seek food wherever it can be found. At Conflans-Saint-Honorine, Eragny, Neuville, Chenevières, at Cergy, Pontoise, Ile-Adam, Presle, and Beaumont, men, women, and children, the whole parish, range the country, set snares, and destroy the burrows. " The rumour is current that the Government, informed of the damage done by the game to cultivators, allows its destruc-tion . . . . and really the hares ravaged about a fifth of the crop." At first an arrest is made of nine of these poachers ; but they are released, "taking circumstances into account," and therefore, for two months, there is a slaughter on the property of the Prince de Conti and of the Ambassador Mercy d'Argenteau ; in default of bread they eat rabbits.—Along with the abuse of property they are led, by a natural impulse, to attack property itself. Near Saint-Denis the woods belonging to the abbey are devastated ; " the farmers of the neighbourhood carry away loads of wood, drawn by four and five horses ; " the inhabitants of the villages of Ville-Parisis, Tremblay, Vert-Galant, Villepinte, sell it publicly, and threaten the wood-rangers with a beating : on the 15th of June the damage is already estimated at 60,000 livres.—It makes little difference whether the proprietor has been benevolent, like M. de Talaru,[2] who had supported the poor on his estate at Issy the preceding winter. The peasants destroy the dyke which con-ducts water to his communal mill ; condemned by the parlia-ment to restore it, they declare that not only will they not obey, but that if M. de Talaru rebuilds it they will return, to the number of three hundred armed men, and tear it away the second time.

For those who are most compromised Paris is the nearest refuge ; for the poorest and most exasperated, the door of nomadic life stands wide open. Bands rise up around the capital, just as in countries where human society has not yet been formed, or has

---

[1] " Archives Nationales," H. 1453. Letter of the sub-delegate Gobert, March 17th ; of the officers of police, June 15th :—" On the 12th, 13th, 14th, and 15th of March the inha-bitants of Conflans generally rebelled against the game law in relation to the rabbit."

[2] Montjoie, 2nd part, ch. xxi. p. 14 (the first week in June). Montjoie is a party man ; but he gives dates and details, and his testimony, when it is confirmed elsewhere, deserves to be admitted.

ceased to exist. During the first two weeks in May,[1] near Villejuif, a band of five or six hundred vagabonds strive to force Bicêtre and approach Saint-Cloud. They arrive from thirty, forty, and sixty leagues off, from Champagne, from Lorraine, from the whole circuit of country devastated by the hail-storm. All hover around Paris and are there engulfed as in a sewer, the unfortunate along with criminals, some to find work, others to beg and to rove about under the injurious promptings of hunger and the rumours of the public thoroughfares. During the last days of April,[2] the clerks at the toll-houses note the entrance of "a frightful number of poorly clad men of sinister aspect." During the first days of May a change in the appearance of the crowd is re-marked ; there mingle in it "a number of foreigners, from all countries, most of them in'rags, armed with big sticks, and whose very aspect announces what is to be feared from them." Already, before this final influx, the public sink is full to overflowing. Think of the extraordinary and rapid increase of population in Paris, the multitude of artisans brought there by recent demoli-tions and constructions, all the craftsmen whom the stagnation of manufactures, the augmentation of *octrois*, the rigour of winter, and the dearness of bread have reduced to extreme distress. Remember that in 1786 "two hundred thousand persons are enumerated whose property, all told, has not the intrinsic worth of fifty crowns ; " that, from time immemorial, they are at war with the city watchmen ; that in 1789 there are twenty thousand poachers in the capital; that, to provide them with work, it is found necessary to establish national workshops ; " that twelve thousand are kept uselessly occupied digging on the hill of Montmartre, and paid twenty sous per day ; that the wharfs and quays are covered with them, that the Hôtel-de-Ville is invested by them, and that, around the palace, they seem to be a reproach to the inactivity of disarmed justice ; " that daily they grow bitter and excited around the doors of the bakeries, where, kept waiting a long time, they are not sure of obtaining bread : you may anticipate the fury and the force with which they will storm any obstacle to which their attention may be directed.

---

[1] Montjoie, 1st part, 92—101. "Archives Nationales," H. 1453. Letter of the officer of police of Saint-Denis : "A good many workmen arrive daily from Lorraine as well as from Champagne," which increases the famine.

[2] De Bezenval, "Mémoires," i. 353. Cf. "The Ancient Régime," p. 388. Marmontel, ii. 252 and following pages. De Ferrières, i. 407.

II.

This obstacle has been pointed out to them for a couple of years : the Ministry, the Court, the Government, the ancient régime.   Whoever protests against it in favour of the people is sure to be followed as far, and farther, than he chooses to lead. The moment the Parliament of a large city refuses to register fiscal edicts it finds a riot at its service.   On the 7th of June, 1788, at Grenoble, tiles rain down on the heads of the soldiery, and the military force is powerless.   At Rennes an army is necessary to put down the rebellious city, and after this a perma- nent camp; four regiments of infantry and two of cavalry, under the command of a Marshal of France.[1]   The following year, when the Parliaments turn over to the side of the privileged class, the disturbance again begins, but this time against the Parliaments. In February, 1789, at Besançon and at Aix, the magistrates are hooted at, chased in the streets, beseiged in the town-hall, and obliged to conceal themselves or take to flight.—If such is the disposition in the provincial capitals, what must it be in the capital of the kingdom ?   To begin :—in the month of August, 1788, after the dismissal of Brienne and Lamoignon, the mob, collected on the Place Dauphine, constitutes itself judge, burns both ministers in effigy, disperses the watch, and resists the troops : no sedition, as bloody as this, had been seen for a cen- tury.   Two days later, the riot bursts out a second time ; the people are seized with a resolve to go and burn the residences of the two ministers and that of Dubois, the lieutenant of police.

Clearly a new leaven has been infused among the ignorant and brutal masses, and the new ideas are producing their effect.   They have been insensibly filtering for a long time from layer to layer, and after having gained over the aristocracy, the whole of the lettered portion of the Third-Estate, the lawyers, the schools, all the young, they have insinuated themselves drop by drop and by a thousand fissures into the class which supports itself by the labour of its own hands.   Noblemen, at their toilettes, have scoffed at Christianity, and affirmed the rights of man before their valets, hairdressers, purveyors, and all those that are in attendance upon them.   Men of letters, lawyers, and attorneys

---

[1] Arthur Young, September 1st, 1788.

have repeated, in the bitterest tone, the same diatribes and the same theories in the coffee-houses and in the restaurants, on the promenades and in all public places. They have spoken out before the lower class as if it were not present, and, from all this eloquence poured out without precaution, some bubbles besprinkle the brain of the artisan, the publican, the messenger, the shopkeeper, and the soldier.

Hence it is that a year suffices to convert mute discontent into political passion. From the 5th of July, 1787, on the invitation of the King, who convokes the States-General and demands advice from everybody, both speech and the press alter in tone.[1] Instead of general conversation of a speculative turn there is preaching, with a view to practical effect, sudden, radical, and close at hand, preaching as shrill and thrilling as the blast of a trumpet. Revolutionary pamphlets appear in quick succession : " Qu'est-ce que le Tiers ? " by Sieyes ; " Mémoire pour le Peuple Français," by Cerutti ; " Considérations sur les Intérêts des Tiers-Etat," by Rabtau Saint-Etienne; "Ma Pétition," by Target; "Les Droits des Etats-généraux," by M. d'Entraigues, and, a little later, " La France libre," par Camille Desmoulins, and others by hundreds and thousands,[2] all of which are repeated and amplified in the electoral assemblies, where new-made citizens come to declaim and increase their own excitement.[3] The unanimous, universal, and daily shout rolls along from echo to echo, into barracks and into faubourgs, into markets, workshops, and garrets. In the month of February, 1789, Necker avows " that obedience is not to be found anywhere, and that even the troops are not to be relied on." In the month of May, the fisherwomen, and next the fruite ers. of the Halle come to recommend the interests of the people to the bodies of electors, and to sing rhymes in honour of the Third-Estate. In the month of June pamphlets are in all hands ; " even lackeys are poring over them at the gates of hotels." In the month of July, as the King is signing an order, a patriotic valet becomes alarmed and reads it over his shoulder.—There is no illusion here ; it is not merely the bourgeoisie which ranges itself against the legal authorities and against the established

---

[1] Barrère, " Mémoires," i. 234.

[2] See, in the National Library. the long catalogue of those which have survived.

[3] Malouet, i. 255. Bailly, i. 43 (May 9th and 19th).—D'Hezecques, " Souvenirs d'un page de Louis XVI." 293.—De Bezenval, i. 368.

régime, but the whole people, the craftsmen, the shopkeepers and
the domestics, workmen of every kind and degree, the populace
underneath the people, the vagabonds, street rovers, and mendicants, the whole multitude, which, bound down by anxiety for its
daily bread, had never lifted its eyes to look at the great social
order of which it is the lowest stratum, and the whole weight of
which it bears.

III.

Suddenly it stirs, and the superposed scaffolding totters.   It
is the movement of a brute nature exasperated by want and
maddened by suspicion.   Have paid hands, which are invisible,
goaded it on from beneath?   Contemporaries are convinced of
this, and it is probably the case.[1]   But the uproar made around
the suffering brute would alone suffice to make it shy, and explain
its sudden start.—On the 21st of April the Electoral Assemblies
have begun in Paris; they are held in each quarter for the
clergy, the nobles, and the Third-Estate.   Every day, for almost
a month, files of electors are seen passing along the streets.   Those
of the first degree continue to meet after having nominated those
of the second : the nation must needs watch its mandatories and
maintain its imprescriptible rights.   If this exercise of their rights
has been delegated to them, they still belong to the nation, and
it reserves to itself the privilege of interposing when it pleases.
A pretension of this kind travels fast; immediately after the Third-
Estate of the Assemblies it reaches the Third-Estate of the streets.
Nothing is more natural than the desire to lead one's leaders :
the first time any dissatisfaction occurs, they lay hands on those
who halt and make them march on as directed.   On a Saturday,
April 25th,[2] a rumour is current that Réveillon, an elector and
manufacturer of wall-paper, Rue Saint-Antoine, and Lérat, a com-
missioner, have "spoken badly" at the Electoral Assembly of Sainte-
Marguerite.   To speak badly means to speak badly of the people.
What has Réveillon said ?   Nobody knows, but popular imagina-

---

[1] Marmontel, ii. 249.—Montjoie, 1st part, p. 92.—De Bezenval, i. 387 : "These spies
added that persons were seen exciting the tumult and were distributing money."
[2] "Archives Nationales," Y. 11441. Interrogatory of the Abbé Roy, May 5th. Y. 11033,
Interrogatory (April 28th and May 4th) of twenty-three wounded persons brought to the
Hôtel-Dieu. - These two documents are of prime importance in presenting the true aspect
of the insurrection ; to these must be added the narrative of M. de Bezenval, who was
commandant at this time with M. du Châtelet.   Almost all other narratives are amplified
or falsified through party spirit.

tion, with its terrible powers of invention and precision, readily fabricates or welcomes a murderous phrase. He said that "a working-man with a wife and children could live on fifteen sous a day." Such a man is a traitor, and must be disposed of at once; "all his belongings must be put to fire and sword." The rumour, it must be noted, is false.[1] Réveillon pays his poorest workman twenty-five sous a day, is the means of supporting three hundred and fifty, and, in spite of a dull season the previous winter, he kept all on at the same rate of wages. He himself was once a workman, and obtained a medal for his inventions, and is benevolent and respected by all respectable persons. All this avails nothing; bands of vagabonds and foreigners, who have just passed through the barriers, do not look so closely into matters, while the journeymen, the carters, the cobblers, the masons, the braziers, and the stone-cutters whom they entice in their lodgings are just as ignorant as they are. When irritation has accumulated, it breaks out at hap-hazard.

Just at this time the clergy of Paris renounce their privileges in the way of imposts,[2] and the people, taking friends for adversaries, add in their invectives the name of the clergy to that of Réveillon.

During the whole of the day, and also during the leisure moments of Sunday, the fermentation increases; on Monday the 27th, another day of idleness and drunkenness, the bands begin to move. Certain witnesses encounter one of these in the Rue Saint-Séverin, "armed with clubs," and so numerous as to bar the passage. "Shops and doors are closed on all sides, and the people cry out, 'There's the revolt!'" The seditious crowd belch out curses and invectives against the clergy, "and, catching sight of an abbé, shout 'Priest!'" Another band parades an effigy of Réveillon decorated with the ribbon of the order of St. Michael, which undergoes the parody of a sentence and is burnt on the Place de Grève, after which they threaten his house. Driven back by the guard, they invade that of a manufacturer of saltpetre, who is his friend, and burn and smash his effects and furniture.[3] It is only towards midnight that the crowd is dispersed and the insurrection is supposed to have ended. On the following day it begins again with greater violence; for, besides the ordinary

---

[1] De Ferrières, vol. iii. note A. (justificatory explanation by Réveillon).
[2] Bailly, i. 25 (April 26th).
[3] Hippeau, iv. 377 (Letters of M. Perrot, April 29th).

stimulants of misery [1] and the craving for license, they have a new stimulant in the idea of a cause to defend, the conviction that they are fighting " for the Third-Estate." In a cause like this each one should help himself, and all should help each other. " We should be lost," one of them exclaimed, " if we did not sustain each other." Strong in this belief, they sent deputations three times into the Faubourg Saint-Marceau to obtain recruits, and on their way, with uplifted clubs they enrol, willingly or unwillingly, all they encounter. Others, at the Porte Saint-Antoine, arrest people who are returning from the races, demanding of them if they are for the nobles or for the Third-Estate, and force women to descend from their vehicles and to cry " Vive le Tiers-Etat ! " [2] Meanwhile the crowd has increased before Réveillon's dwelling ; the thirty men on guard are unable to resist ; the house is invaded and sacked from top to bottom ; the furniture, provisions, clothing, registers, waggons, even the poultry in the back-yard, all is cast into blazing bonfires lighted in three different places ; five hundred *louis d'or*, the ready money, and the silver plate are stolen. Several roam through the cellars, drink liquor or varnish at hap-hazard until they fall down dead drunk or expire in convulsions. Against this howling horde, a corps of the watch, mounted and on foot, is seen approaching ; [3] also a hundred cavalry of the " Royal Croats," the French Guards, and later on the Swiss Guards. " Tiles and chimneys are rained down on the soldiers," who fire back four files at a time. The rioters, drunk with brandy and rage, defend themselves desperately for several hours ; more than two hundred are killed, and nearly three hundred are wounded ; they are only put down by cannon, while the mob keeps active until far into the night. Towards eight in the evening, in the Rue Vieille du Temple, the Paris Guard continue to make charges in order to

---

[1] Letter to the King by an inhabitant of the Faubourg Saint-Antoine :— ' Do not doubt, sire, that our recent misfortunes are due to the dearness of bread."

[2] Dammartin, " Événements qui se sont passés sous mes yeux," &c. i. 25 :—" We turned back and were arrested by small bands of scoundrels, who insolently proposed to us to shout ' Vive Necker ! Vive le Tiers-Etat ! ' " His two companions were knights of St. Louis, and their badges seemed an object of " increasing hatred." " The badge excited coarse mutterings, even on the part of persons who appeared superior to the agitators."

[3] Dammartin, ibid. i. 25 :—" I was dining this very day at the Hôtel d'Ecquevilly, in the Rue Saint-Louis." He leaves the house on foot and witnesses the disturbance. " Fifteen to sixteen hundred wretches, the excrement of the nation, degraded by shameful vices, covered with rags, and gorged with brandy, presented the most disgusting and revolting spectacle. More than a hundred thousand persons of both sexes and of all ages and conditions interfered greatly with the operations of the troops. The firing soon commenced and blood flowed : two innocent persons were wounded near me."

protect the doors which the miscreants try to force. Two doors
are forced at half-past eleven o'clock in the Rue Saintonge and
in the Rue de Bretagne, that of a pork-dealer and that of a
baker.—Even to this last wave of the outbreak which is sub-
siding we can distinguish the elements which have produced
the insurrection, and which are about to produce the Revolution.
Starvation is one of these : in the Rue de Bretagne the troop
which rifles the baker's shop carries bread off to the women
staying at the corner of the Rue Saintonge.   Brigandage is
another : in the middle of the night M. du Châtelet's spies, glid-
ing alongside of a ditch, "see a group of ruffians" assembled
beyond the Barrière du Trône, their leader, mounted on a little
knoll, urging them to begin again ; and the following days, on
the highways, vagabonds are saying to each other, "We can do
no more at Paris, because they are too sharp on the look-out ; let
us go to Lyons !"   There are, finally, the pa'riots : on the evening of the insurrection, between the Pont-au-Change and the Pont-
Marie, the half-naked ragamuffins, besmeared with dirt, bearing
along their hand-barrows, are fully alive to their cause ; they beg
alms in a loud tone of voice, and stretch out their hats to the
passers, saying, "Take pity on this poor Third-Estate !"—The
starving, the ruffians, and the patriots, all form one body, and
henceforth misery, crime, and public spirit unite to provide an
ever-ready insurrection for the agitators who desire to raise one.

IV.

But the agitators are already in permanent session.   The Palais-
Royal is an open-air club where, all day and even far into the
night, one excites the other and urges on the crowd to blows.
In this enclosure, protected by the privileges of the House of
Orleans, the police dare not enter.   Speech is free, and the public
who avail themselves of this freedom seem purposely chosen to
abuse it.—The public and the place are adapted to each other.[1]
The Palais-Royal, the centre of prostitution, of play, of idleness,
and of pamphlets, attracts the whole of that unrooted population
which floats about in a great city, and which, without occupation or home, lives only for curiosity or for pleasure—the fre-

---

[1] De Goncourt, "La Société Franaçise pendant la Révolution."   Thirty-one gambling-
houses are enumerated here, while a pamphlet of the day is entitled "Pétition des deux
mille cent filles du Palais-Royal."

quenters of the coffee-houses, the runners for gambling hells, adventurers, and social outcasts, the overplus or forlorn hope of literature, arts, and the bar, attorneys' clerks, students of the schools, cockneys, loungers, strangers, and the occupants of furnished lodgings, amounting, it is said, to forty thousand in Paris. They fill the garden and the galleries; " one would hardly find here one of what were called the " Six Bodies,"[1] a bourgeois settled down and occupied with his own affairs, a man whom business and family cares render serious and influential. There is no place here for industrious and orderly bees; it is the rendezvous of political and literary drones. They flock into it from every quarter of Paris, and the tumultuous, buzzing swarm covers the ground like an overturned hive. " Ten thousand people," writes Arthur Young,[2] " have been all this day in the Palais-Royal ; " the press is so great that an apple thrown from a balcony on the moving floor of heads would not reach the ground. The condition of these heads may be imagined; they are emptier of ballast than any in France, the most inflated with speculative ideas, the most excitable and the most excited. In this pell-mell of improvised politicians no one knows who is speaking ; nobody is responsible for what he says. Each is there as in the theatre, unknown among the unknown, requiring sensational impressions and transports, a prey to the contagion of the passions around him, borne along in the whirl of sounding phrases, of ready-made news, growing rumours, and other exaggerations by which fanatics keep outdoing each other. There are shoutings, tears, applause, stamping and clapping, as at the performance of a tragedy ; one or another individual becomes so inflamed and hoarse that he dies on the spot with fever and exhaustion. In vain has Arthur Young been accustomed to the tumult of political liberty ; he is dumbfounded at what he sees.[3] According to him, the excitement is " incredible. . . . We think sometimes that Debrett's or Stockdale's shops at London are crowded ; but they are mere deserts compared to Desenne's and some others here, in which one can scarcely squeeze from the door to the counter. . . . . Every hour produces its pamphlet ; thirteen came out to-day, sixteen yesterday, and

---

[1] Montjoie, 2nd part, 144. Bailly, ii. 130.

[2] Arthur Young, June 24th, 1789. Montjoie, 2nd part, 69.

[3] Arthur Young, June 9th, 24th, and 26th. " La France libre," *passim*, by C. Desmoulins.

ninety-two last week. Nineteen-twentieths of these productions
are in favour of liberty ; " and by liberty is meant the extinction
of privileges, numerical sovereignty, the application of the *Contrat-
Social*, " the Republic," and more besides, a universal levelling,
permanent anarchy, and even the *jacquerie.* Camille Desmoulins,
one of the orators commonly there, announces it and urges it in
precise terms : " Now that the animal is entrapped, let him be
knocked on the head. . . . . Never will the victors have a richer prey.
*Forty thousand palaces, mansions, and châteaux, two-fifths of the pro-
perty of France, will be the recompense of valour.* Those who pretend to be the conquerors will be conquered in turn. The nation
shall be *purged.*" Here, in advance, is the programme of the
Reign of Terror.

Now all this is not only read, but declaimed, amplified, and
turned to practical account. In front of the coffee-houses " those
who have stentorian lungs relieve each other every evening." [1]
" The coffee-houses . . . . present astonishing spectacles . . . . ex-
pectant crowds are at the doors and windows, listening *à gorge
déployée* to certain orators, who from chairs or tables harangue
each his little audience ; the eagerness with which they are
heard, and the thunder of applause they receive for every sentiment of more than common hardiness or violence against the
present Government, cannot easily be imagined." " Three days
ago a child of four years, well taught and intelligent, was promenaded around the garden, in broad daylight, at least twenty times,
borne on the shoulders of a street porter, crying out, ' Verdict of
the French people : Polignac exiled one hundred leagues from
Paris ; Condé the same ; Conti the same ; Artois the same ; the
Queen,—I dare not write it.' " A hall made of boards in the
middle of the Palais-Royal is always full, especially of young men,
who carry on their deliberations in parliamentary fashion : in the
evening the president invites the spectators to come forward and
sign motions passed during the day, and of which the originals
are placed in the Café Foy.[2] They count on their fingers the enemies of the country ; " and first two Royal Highnesses (Monsieur and
the Count d'Artois), three Most Serene Highnesses (the Prince de
Condé, Duc de Bourbon, and the Prince de Conti), one favourite

---

[1] C. Desmoulins, letters to his father, and Arthur Young, June 9th.
[2] Montjoie, 2nd part, 69, 77, 124, 144. C. Desmoulins, letters of June 24th and the following days.

(Madame de Polignac), MM. de Vandreuil, de la Trémoille, du Châtelet, de Villedeuil, de Barentin, de la Galaisière, Vidaud de la Tour, Berthier, Foulon, and also M. Linguet." Placards are posted demanding the pillory on the Pont-Neuf for the Abbé Maury. One orator proposes " to burn the house of M. d'Espréménil, his wife, children, furniture, and himself : this is passed unanimously."—No opposition is tolerated. One of those present having manifested some horror at such sanguinary motions, " is seized by the collar, obliged to kneel down, to make an apology, and to kiss the ground ; the punishment inflicted on children is given to him; he is ducked repeatedly in one of the fountain-basins, after which they hand him over to the populace, who roll him in the mud." On the following day an ecclesiastic is trodden under foot, and flung from hand to hand. A few days after, on the 22nd of June, there are two similar inflictions. The sovereign mob exercises all the functions of sovereign authority—with those of the legislator those of the judge, and those of the judge with those of the executioner. Its idols are sacred ; if any one fails to show them respect he is guilty of *lèse-majesté*, and at once punished. In the first week of July, an abbé who speaks ill of Necker is flogged ; a woman who insults the bust of Necker is stripped by the fishwomen, and beaten until she is covered with blood. War is declared against suspicious uniforms. " On the appearance of a hussar," writes Desmoulins, " they shout, ' There goes Punch ! ' and the stone-cutters fling stones at him. Last night two officers of the hussars, MM. de Sombreuil and de Polignac, came to the Palais-Royal . . . chairs were flung at them, and they would have been knocked down if they had not run away. The day before yesterday they seized a spy of the police and gave him a ducking in the fountain. They ran him down like a stag, hustled him, pelted him with stones, struck him with canes, forced one of his eyes out of its socket, and finally, in spite of his entreaties and cries for mercy, plunged him a second time in the fountain. His torments lasted from noon until half-past five o'clock, and he had about ten thousand executioners."—Consider the effect of such a focal centre at a time like this. A new power has sprung up side by side with legal powers, a legislature of the highways and public squares—anonymous, irresponsible, without restraint, driven onward by coffee-house theories, by transports of the brain and the vehemence of mountebanks, while the bare arms which have just accomplished the work of destruction in the Faubourg Saint-Antoine, form its body-guard and ministerial cabinet.

V.

This is the dictatorship of a mob, and its proceedings, conforming to its nature, consist in acts of violence ; wherever it finds resistance, it strikes.—The people of Versailles, in the streets and at the doors of the Assembly, daily " come and insult those whom they call *aristocrats.*" [1] On Monday. June 22nd, "d'Espréménil barely escapes being knocked down ; the Abbé Maury . . . owes his escape to the strength of a curé, who takes him up in his arms and tosses him into the carriage of the Archbishop of Arles." On the 23rd, "the Archbishop of Paris and the Keeper of the Seals are hooted, railed at, scoffed at, and derided, until they almost sink with shame and rage," and so formidable is the tempest of vociferation with which they are greeted, that Passeret, the King's secretary, who accompanies the minister, dies of the excitement that very day.   On the 24th, the Bishop of Beauvais is almost knocked down by a stone which strikes him on the head.   On the 25th, the Archbishop of Paris is saved only by the speed of his horses, the multitude pursuing him and pelting him with stones ; his hotel is besieged, the windows are all shattered, and, notwithstanding the intervention of the French Guards, the peril is so great that he is obliged to promise that he will join the deputies of the Third-Estate.   This is the way in which the rude hand of the people effects a reunion of the Orders. It bears as heavily on its own representatives as on its adversaries.   "Although our hall was closed to the public," says Bailly, "there were always more than six hundred spectators ; " [2] not respectful and silent, but active and noisy, mingling with the deputies, raising their hands to vote in all cases, taking part in the deliberations by their applause and hisses : a collateral Assembly which often imposes its own will on the other.   They take note of and put down the names of their opponents, which

1 Etienne Dumont, "Souvenirs," p. 72.   C. Desmoulins, letter of, June 24th.   Arthur Young, June 25th.   Roux and Buchez, ii. 28.
2 Bailly, i. 227 and 179.   Monnier, "Recherches sur les causes," &c., i. 289, 291 ; ii. 61. Malouet, i. 299 ; ii. 10.   "Actes des Apôtres," v. 4 ; (Letter of M. de Guillermy, July 31st, 1790).   Marmontel, i. 28 : "The people came even into the Assembly, to encourage their partisans, to select and indicate their victims, and to terrify the feeble with the dreadful trial of open balloting."

names, transmitted to chair-bearers in attendance at the entrance
of the hall, and from them to the populace waiting for the
departure of the deputies, are from that time regarded as the
names of public enemies.[1] Lists are made out and printed, and,
at the Palais-Royal in the evening, they become the lists of the
proscribed.—It is under this brutal pressure that many decrees
are passed, and, among them, that by which the commons
declare themselves the National Assembly and assume supreme
power. The night before, Malouet had proposed to ascertain,
by a preliminary vote, on which side the majority was : the noes
instantly gathered around him to the number of three hundred,
"upon which a man springs out from the galleries, falls upon him
and takes him by the collar exclaiming, ' Hold your tongue,
you false citizen ! '" Malouet is released and the guard comes
forward, "but terror has spread through the hall, threats are
uttered against opponents, and the next day we were only ninety."
Moreover, the lists of their names had been circulated ; some of
them, deputies from Paris, went to see Bailly that very evening :
one amongst them, " a very honest man and good patriot," had
been told that his house was to be set on fire ; now his wife had
just given birth to a child, and the slightest tumult before the
house would have been fatal. Such arguments are decisive.
Consequently, three days afterwards, at the Tennis-court, but one
deputy, Martin d'Auch, dares to write the word "opposant"
after his name. Insulted by many of his colleagues, " at once
denounced to the people who had collected at the entrance of
the building, he is obliged to escape by a side door to avoid
being cut to pieces," and, for several days, to keep away from the
meetings.[2] Owing to this intervention of the galleries the radical
minority, numbering about thirty,[3] lead the majority, and they

---

[1] Manuscript letters of M. Boullé, deputy, to the municipal authorities of Pontivy, from
May 1st, 1789, to September 4th, 1790 (communicated by M. Rosenzweig, archivist at
Vannes). June 16th, 1789: " The crowd gathered around the hall . . . . was, during these
days, from 3,000 to 4,000 persons."

[2] Letters of M. Boullé, June 23rd. " How sublime the moment, that in which we enthu-
siastically bind ourselves to the country by a new oath ! . . . . Why should this moment be
selected by one of our number to dishonour himself? His name is now blasted throughout
France. And the unfortunate man has children ! Suddenly overwhelmed by public contempt he leaves, and falls fainting at the door, exclaiming, ' Ah ! this will be my death ! '
I do not know what has become of him since. What is strange is, he had not behaved
badly up to that time, and he voted for the Constitution."

[3] De Ferrières, i. 168. Malouet, i. 298 (according to him the faction did not number
more than ten members), and ix. 10. Dumont, 250.

do not allow them to free themselves. On the 28th of May,
Malouet, having demanded a secret session to discuss the
conciliatory measures which the King had proposed, the galleries
hoot at him, and a deputy, M. Bouche, addresses him in very
plain terms. "You must know, sir, that we are deliberating
here in the presence of our masters, and that we must account
to them for our opinions." This is the doctrine of the *Contrat-
Social*, and, through timidity, fear of the Court and of the privileged class, through optimism and faith in human nature, through
enthusiasm and the necessity of adhering to previous actions, the
deputies, who are novices, provincial, and given up to theories,
neither dare nor know how to escape from the tyranny of the prevailing dogma. Henceforth it becomes the law. All the Assemblies, the Constituent, the Legislative, the Convention, submit to it
entirely. The public in the galleries are the admitted representatives of the people, under the same title, and even under a
higher title, than the deputies. Now, this public is that of the
Palais-Royal, consisting of strangers, idlers, lovers of novelties,
Paris romancers, leaders of the coffee-houses, the future pillars of
the clubs—in short, the wild enthusiasts among the middle-class,
just as the crowd which threatens doors and throws stones is
recruited from among the wild enthusiasts of the lowest class.
Thus by an involuntary selection, the faction which constitutes
itself a public power is composed of nothing but violent minds
and violent hands. Spontaneously and without previous concert
dangerous fanatics are joined with dangerous brutes, and in the
increasing discord between the legal authorities this is the illegal
league which is certain to overthrow all.

When a commanding general sits in council with his staff-
officers and his counsellors, and discusses the plan of a campaign,
the chief public interest is that discipline should remain intact, and
that intruders, soldiers, or menials, should not throw the weight of
their turbulence and thoughtlessness into the scales which have to
be cautiously and firmly held by their chiefs. This was the express
demand of the Government;[1] but the demand was not regarded; and
against the persistent usurpation of the multitude nothing is left
to it but the employment of force. But force itself is slipping from
its hands, while growing disobedience, like a contagion, after

---

[1] Declaration of June 23rd, article 15.

having gained the people is spreading among the troops. From
the 23rd of June,[1] two companies of the French Guards refused to
do duty. Confined to their barracks, they on the 27th break out,
and henceforth " they are seen every evening entering the Palais-
Royal, marching in double file." They know the place well ; it
is the general rendezvous of the abandoned women whose lovers
and parasites they are.[2] " The patriots all gather around them,
treat them to ice cream and wine, and debauch them in the face
of their officers." To this, moreover, must be added the fact that
their colonel, M. du Châtelet, has long been odious to them, that he
has fatigued them with forced drills, worried them and diminished
the number of their sergeants ; that he suppressed the school for
the education of the children of their musicians ; that he uses
the stick in punishing the men, and picks quarrels with them
about their appearance, their board, and their clothing. This
regiment is lost to discipline : a secret society has been formed in
it, and the soldiers have pledged themselves to their ensigns not
to act against the National Assembly. Thus the confederation
between them and the Palais-Royal is established.

On the 30th of June, eleven of their leaders, taken off to the
Abbaye, write to claim their assistance : a young man mounts a
chair in front of the Café Foy and reads their letter aloud ; a band
sets out on the instant, forces the gate with a sledge-hammer and
iron bars, brings back the prisoners in triumph, gives them a feast
in the garden and mounts guard around them to prevent their
being re-taken.—When disorders of this kind go unpunished,
order cannot be maintained ; in fact, on the morning of the
14th of July, five out of six battalions had gone over to the
people. As to the other corps, they are no better and are also
seduced. " Yesterday," Desmoulins writes, " the artillery regiment
followed the example of the French Guards, overpowering the sentinels and coming over to mingle with the patriots in the Palais-
Royal . . . . We see nothing but the rabble attaching themselves to soldiers whom they chance to encounter. ' Allons,
Vive le Tiers-Etat ! ' and they lead them off to a tavern to drink

[1] Montjoie, 2nd part, 118.   C. Desmoulins, letters of June 24th and the following days.
A faithful narrative by M. de Sainte-Fère, formerly an officer in the French Guard, p. 9.
De Bezenval, iii. 413.   Roux and Buchez, ii. 35.   Manuscript souvenirs of M. X.

[2] Peuchet (" Encyclopédie Méthodique," 1789, quoted by Parent Duchâtelet) : " Almost
all of the soldiers of the Guard belong to that class (the bullies of public women) : many,
indeed, only enlist in the corps that they may live at the expense of these unfortunates."

the health of the Commons." Dragoons tell the officers who are marching them to Versailles : "We obey you, but you may tell the ministers on our arrival that if we are ordered to use the least violence against our fellow-citizens, the first shot shall be for you." At the Invalides twenty men, ordered to remove the cocks and ramrods from the guns stored in a threatened arsenal, devote six hours to rendering twenty guns useless ; their object is to keep them intact for plunder and for the arming of the people.

In short, the largest portion of the army has deserted. However kind a superior officer might be, the fact of his being a superior officer secures for him the treatment of an enemy. The governor, " M. de Sombreuil, against whom these people could utter no reproach," will soon see his cannoneers point their guns at his apartment, and will just escape being hung on the iron-railings by their own hands. Thus the force which is brought forward to suppress insurrection only serves to furnish it with recruits. And even worse, for the display of arms which was relied on to restrain the mob, furnished the instigation to rebellion.

VI.

The fatal moment has arrived : it is no longer a government which falls that it may give way to another ; it is all government which ceases to exist in order to make way for an intermittent despotism, for factions blindly impelled on by enthusiasm, credulity, misery, and fear.[1] Like a tame elephant suddenly become wild again, the populace throws off its ordinary driver, and the new guides whom it tolerates perched on its neck are there simply for show ; in future it will move along as it pleases, freed from control, and abandoned to its own feelings, instincts, and appetites. Apparently, there was no desire to do more than anticipate its aberrations. The King has forbidden all violence ; the commanders order the troops not to fire ;[2] but the excited and wild animal takes all precautions for insults ; in future, it intends to be its own conductor, and, to begin, it treads its guides under foot.

[1] Gouverneur Morris. Liberty is now the general cry ; authority is a name and no longer a reality. (Correspondence with Washington, July 19th.)

[2] Bailly, i. 302. "The King was very well-disposed ; his measures were intended only to preserve order and the public peace. . . . . Du Châtelet was forced by facts to acquit M. de Bezenval of attempts against the people and the country." Cf. Marmontel, iv. 183; Mounier, ii. 40.

On the 12th of July, near noon,[1] on the news of the dismissal of
Necker, a cry of rage arises in the Palais-Royal; Camille Desmoulins, mounted on a table, announces that the Court meditates
" a St. Bartholomew of patriots." The crowd embrace him, adopt
the green cockade which he has proposed, and oblige the dancing-
saloons and theatres to close in sign of mourning : they hurry off
to the residence of Curtius, and take the busts of the Duke of
Orleans and of Necker and carry them about in triumph.   Meanwhile, the dragoons of the Prince de Lambesc, drawn up on the
Place Louis-Quinze, find a barricade of chairs at the entrance
of the Tuileries, and are greeted with a shower of stones and
bottles.[2] Elsewhere, on the Boulevard, before the Hôtel Montmorency, some of the French Guards, escaped from their barracks,
fired on a loyal detachment of the " Royal Allemand." The
tocsin is sounding on all sides, the shops where arms are sold are
pillaged, and the Hôtel-de-Ville is invaded; fifteen or sixteen
well-disposed electors, who meet there, order the districts to be
assembled and armed.—The new sovereign, the people in arms
and in the street, has declared himself.

The dregs of society at once come to the surface.   During the
night between the 12th and 13th of July,[3] " all the barriers,
from the Faubourg Saint-Antoine to the Faubourg Saint-Honoré,
besides those of the Faubourgs Saint-Marcel and Saint-Jacques, are
forced and set on fire."   There is no longer an *octroi ;* the city is
without a revenue just at the moment when it is obliged to make

---

[1] C. Desmoulins, letter of the 16th July. Roux and Buchez, ii. 83.

[2] Trial of the Prince de Lambesc (Paris, 1790), with the eighty-three depositions and the
discussion of the testimony. It is the crowd which began the attack. The troops fired in the
air. But one man, a *sieur* Chauvel, was wounded slightly by the Prince de Lambesc. (Testimony of M. Carboire, p. 84, and of Captain de Reinack, p. 101.) " M. le Prince de Lambesc,
mounted on a grey horse with a grey saddle without holsters or pistols, had scarcely
entered the garden when a dozen persons jumped at the mane and bridle of his horse and
made every effort to drag him off. A small man in grey clothes fired at him with a pistol.
. . . . The prince tried hard to free himself, and succeeded by making his horse rear up and
by flourishing his sword; without, however, up to this time, wounding any one. . . . . He
deposes that he saw the prince strike a man on the head with the flat of his sabre who was
trying to close the turning-bridge, which would have cut off the retreat of his troops. The
troops did no more than try to keep off the crowd which assailed them with stones, and
even with firearms, from the top of the terraces." The man who tried to close the bridge
had seized the prince's horse with one hand ; the wound he received was a scratch about
23 lines long, which was dressed and cured with a bandage soaked in brandy. All the
details of the affair prove that the patience and humanity of the officers were extreme.
Nevertheless " on the following day, the 13th, some one posted a written placard on the
carrefour Bussy recommending the citizens of Paris to seize the prince and quarter him at
once."—(Deposition of M. Cosson, p. 114.)

[3] Bailly, i. 336. Marmontel, iv. 310.

the heaviest expenditures; but this is of no consequence to the populace, which, above all things, wants to have cheap wine. "Ruffians, armed with pikes and sticks, proceed in several parties to give up to pillage the houses of those who are regarded as enemies to the public welfare." "They go from door to door crying, 'Arms and bread!' During this fearful night, the bourgeoisie kept themselves shut up, each trembling at home for himself and those belonging to him." On the following day, the 13th, the capital appears to be given up to bandits and the lowest of the low. One of the bands hews down the gate of the Lazarists, destroys the library and clothes-presses, the pictures, the windows and laboratory, and rushes to the cellars, where it staves in the casks and gets drunk: twenty-four hours after this, about thirty of them are found dead and dying, drowned in wine, men and women, one of these being at the point of childbirth. In front of the house [1] the street is full of the wreck, and of ruffians who hold in their hands, "some, eatables, others a jug, forcing the passers-by to drink, and pouring out wine to all comers. Wine runs down into the gutter, and the scent of it fills the air;" it is a drinking bout: meanwhile they carry away the grain and flour which the monks kept on hand according to law, fifty-two loads of it being taken to the market. Another troop comes to La Force, to deliver those imprisoned for debt; a third breaks into the Garde Meuble, carrying away valuable arms and armour. Mobs assemble before the hotel of Madame de Breteuil and the Palais-Bourbon, which they intend to ransack, in order to punish their proprietors. M. de Crosne, one of the most liberal and most respected men of Paris, but, unfortunately for himself, a lieutenant of the police, is pursued, escaping with difficulty, and his hotel is sacked. During the night between the 13th and 14th of May, the baker's shops and the wine shops are pillaged; "men of the vilest class, armed with guns, pikes, and turnspits, make people open their doors and give them something to eat and drink, as well as money and arms." Vagrants, ragged men, several of them "almost naked," and "most of them armed like savages, and of hideous appear-

---

[1] Montjoie, part 3, 86. "I talked with those who guarded the château of the Tuileries. They did not belong to Paris. . . . . A frightful physiognomy and hideous apparel." Montjoie, not to be trusted in many places, merits consultation for little facts of which he was an eye-witness. Morellet, "Mémoires," i. 374. Dussaulx, "L'œuvre des sept jours," 352. "Revue Historique," March, 1876. Interrogatory of Desnot. His occupation during the 13th of July (published by Guiffrey).

ance,"—they are " such as one does not remember to have seen in broad daylight ; " many of them are strangers, come from nobody knows where.[1] It is stated that there were fifty thousand of them, and that they had taken possession of the principal guard-houses.

During these two days and nights, says Bailly, " Paris ran the risk of being pillaged, and was only saved from the marauders by the national guard." Already, in the open street,[2] " these creatures tore off women's shoes and earrings," and the robbers were beginning to have full sway.—Fortunately the militia organized itself, and the principal inhabitants and gentlemen enrol themselves ; 48,000 men are formed into battalions and companies ; the bourgeoisie buy guns of the vagabonds for three livres apiece, and sabres or pistols for twelve sous. At last, some of the offenders are hung on the spot, and others disarmed, and the insurrection again becomes political. But, whatever its object, it remains always wild, because it is in the hands of the populace. Dussaulx, its panegyrist, confesses[3] that " he thought he was witnessing the total dissolution of society." There is no leader, no management. The electors who have converted themselves into the representatives of Paris seem to command the crowd, but it is the crowd which commands them. One of them, Legrand, to save the Hôtel-de-Ville, has no other resource but to send for six barrels of gunpowder, and to declare to the assailants that he is about to blow everything into the air. The commandant whom they themselves have chosen, M. de Salles, has twenty bayonets at his breast during a quarter of an hour, and, more than once, the whole committee is near being massacred. Let the reader imagine, on the premises where the discussions are going on, and petitions are being made, " a concourse of fifteen hundred men pressed by a hundred thousand others who are forcing an entrance," the wainscoting cracking, the benches upset one over another, the enclosure of the bureau pushed back against the president's chair, a tumult such as to bring to mind " the day of judgment," the death-

---

[1] Mathieu Dumas, " Mémoires," i. 531. " Peaceable people fled at the sight of these groups of strange, frantic vagabonds. Everybody closed their houses. . . . . When I reached home, in the Saint-Denis quarter, several of these brigands caused great alarm by firing off guns in the air."

[2] Dussaulx, 379.

[3] Dussaulx, 359, 360, 361, 288, 336. " In effect their entreaties resembled commands, and, more than once, it was impossible to resist them."

shrieks, songs, yells, and "people beside themselves, for the most part not knowing where they are nor what they want."

Each district is also a petty centre, while the Palais-Royal is the main centre. Propositions, "accusations, and deputations" travel to and fro from one to the other, along with the human torrent which is obstructed or rushes ahead with no other guide than its own inclination and the chances of the way. One wave gathers here and another there, their stategy consisting in pushing and in being pushed. Yet, their entrance is effected only because they are let in. If they get into the Invalides it is owing to the connivance of the soldiers.—At the Bastille, firearms are discharged from ten in the morning to five in the evening against walls forty feet high and thirty feet thick, and it is by chance that one of their shots reaches an *invalide* on the towers. They are treated the same as children whom one wishes to hurt as little as possible. The governor, on the first summons to surrender, orders the cannon to be withdrawn from the embrasures; he makes the garrison swear not to fire if it is not attacked; he invites the first of the deputations to lunch; he allows the messenger dispatched from the Hôtel-de-Ville to inspect the fortress; he receives several discharges without returning them, and lets the first bridge be carried without firing a shot.[1] When, at length, he does fire, it is at the last extremity, to defend the second bridge, and after having notified the assailants that he is going to do so. In short, his forbearance and patience are excessive, in conformity with the humanity of the times. The people, in turn, are infatuated with the novel sensations of attack and resistance, with the smell of gunpowder, with the excitement of the contest; all they can think of doing is to rush against the mass of stone, their expedients being on a level with their tactics. A brewer fancies that he can set fire to this block of masonry by pumping over it spikenard and poppy-seed oil mixed with phosphorus. A young carpenter, who has some archæological notions, proposes to construct a catapult. Some of them think that they have seized the governor's daughter, and want to burn her in order to make the father surrender. Others set fire to a projecting mass of buildings filled with straw, and thus close up the passage. "The Bastille was not taken by

---

[1] Dussaulx, 447 (Deposition of the *invalides*). "Revue Rétrospective," iv. 282 (Narrative of the commander of the thirty-two Swiss Guards).

main force," says the brave Elie, one of the combatants; "it
surrendered before even it was attacked,"[1] by capitulation, on the
promise that no harm should be done to anybody.   The garrison,
being perfectly secure, had no longer the heart to fire on human
beings while themselves risking nothing,[2] and, on the other hand,
they were unnerved by the sight of the immense crowd.   Eight or
nine hundred men only[3] were concerned in the attack, most of
them workmen or shopkeepers belonging to the faubourg, tailors,
wheelwrights, mercers and wine-dealers, mixed with the French
Guards.   The Place de la Bastille, however, and all the streets in
the vicinity, were crowded with the curious who came to witness
the sight; "among them," says a witness,[4] "were a number of
fashionable women of very good appearance, who had left their
carriages at some distance."   To the hundred and twenty men of
the garrison looking down from their parapets it seemed as though
all Paris had come out against them.   It is they, also, who lower
the drawbridge and introduce the enemy : everybody has lost his
head, the besieged as well as the besiegers, the latter more completely
because they are intoxicated with the sense of victory.   Scarcely
have they entered when they begin the work of destruction, and
the latest arrivals shoot at random those that come earlier ;
"each one fires without heeding where or on whom his shot tells."
Sudden omnipotence and the liberty to kill are a wine too strong
for human nature ; giddiness is the result ; men *see red*, and their
frenzy ends in ferocity.

For the peculiarity of a popular insurrection is that nobody
obeys anybody ; the bad passions are free as well as the generous
ones ; heroes are unable to restrain assassins.   Elie, who is the
first to enter the fortress, Cholat, Hulin, the brave fellows who are in
advance, the French Guards who are cognizant of the laws of war,

---

[1] Marmontel, iv. 317.

[2] Dussaulx, 454. " The soldiers replied that they would accept whatever happened rather
than cause the destruction of so great a number of their fellow-citizens."

[3] Dussaulx, 447. The number of combatants, maimed, wounded, dead, and living, is
825.   Marmontel, iv. 320.   " To the number of victors, which has been carried up to 800,
people have been added who were never near the place."

[4] Souvenirs Manuscrits de M. X., an eye-witness.   He leaned against the fence of the
Beaumarchais garden and looked on, with Mademoiselle Contat, the actress, at his side,
who had left her carriage in the Place-Royale.—Marat, " L'ami du peuple," No. 530.
" When an unheard-of conjunction of circumstances had caused the fall of the badly
defended walls of the Bastille, under the efforts of a handful of soldiers and of a troop of
unfortunate creatures, most of them Germans and almost all provincials, the Parisians
presented themselves before the fortress, curiosity alone having led them there."

try to keep their word of honour ; but the crowd pressing on behind them know not whom to strike, and they strike at random.   They spare the Swiss soldiers who have fired at them, and who, in their blue smocks, seem to them to be prisoners ; on the other hand, by way of compensation, they fall furiously on the *invalides* who opened the gates to them ; the man who prevented the governor from blowing up the fortress has his wrist severed by the blow of a sabre, is twice pierced with a sword and is hung, and the hand which had saved one of the districts of Paris is promenaded through the streets in triumph.   The officers are dragged along and five of them are killed, with three soldiers, on the spot, or on the way.   During the long hours of firing, the murderous instinct has become aroused, and the wish to kill, changed into a fixed idea, spreads afar among the crowd which has hitherto remained inactive.   It is convinced by its own clamour; a hue and cry is all that it now needs ; the moment one strikes, all want to strike. "Those who had no arms," says an officer, "threw stones at me ;[1] the women ground their teeth and shook their fists at me.   Two of my men had already been assassinated behind me.   I finally got to within some hundreds of paces of the Hôtel-de-Ville, amidst a general cry that I should be hung, when a head, stuck on a pike, was presented to me to look at, while at the same moment I was told that it was that of M. de Launay," the governor.   The latter, on going out, had received the cut of a sword on his right shoulder; on reaching the Rue Saint-Antoine "everybody pulled his hair out and struck him."   Under the arcade of Saint-Jean he was already "severely wounded."   Around him, some said, "his head ought to be struck off;" others, "let him be hung;" and others, "he ought to be tied to a horse's tail."   Then, in despair, and wishing to put an end to his torments, he cried out, "Kill me," and, in struggling, kicked one of the men who held him in the lower abdomen.   On the instant he is pierced with bayonets, dragged in the gutter, and, striking his corpse, they exclaim, "He's a scurvy wretch (*galeux*) and a monster who has betrayed us ; *the nation* demands his head to exhibit to the public," and the man who was kicked is asked to cut it off.   This man, a cook out of place, a simpleton who "went to the Bastille to see what was going on," thinks that as it is the general opinion, the act is *patriotic,*

---

[1] Narrative of the commander of the thirty-two Swiss.   Narrative of Cholat, wine-dealer, one of the victors.   Examination of Desnot (who cut off the head of M. de Launay).

and even believes that he "deserves a medal for destroying a monster." Taking a sabre which is lent to him, he strikes the bare neck, but the dull sabre not doing its work, he takes a small black-handled knife from his pocket, and, "as in his capacity of cook he knows how to cut meat," he finishes the operation successfully. Then, placing the head on the end of a three-pronged pitchfork, and accompanied by over two hundred armed men, "not counting the populace," he marches along, and, in the Rue Saint-Honoré, he has two inscriptions attached to the head, to indicate without mistake whose head it is. They grow merry over it : after filing alongside of the Palais-Royal, the procession arrives at the Pont-Neuf, where, before the statue of Henry IV., they bow the head three times, saying, " Salute thy master ! "—This ends the mockery : some of it is found in every triumph, and beneath the butcher the buffoon becomes apparent.

[Section VII of this chapter has been omitted.]

VIII.

Henceforth it is clear that no one is safe : neither the new militia nor the new authorities suffice to enforce respect for the law. "They did not dare," says Bailly,[1] " oppose the people who, eight days before this, had taken the Bastille." In vain, after the last two murders, do Bailly and Lafayette indignantly threaten to withdraw—they are forced to remain ; their protection, such as it is, is all that is left, and, if the national guard is unable to prevent every murder, it prevents some of them. People live as they can under the constant expectation of fresh popular violence. " *To every impartial man*," says Malouet, " *the Terror dates from the 14th of July.*" On the 17th, before setting out for Paris, the King attends communion and makes his will in anticipation of assassination. From the 16th to the 18th, twenty personages of high rank, among others most of those on whose heads a price is set by the Palais-Royal, leave France—the Count d'Artois, Marshal de Broglie, the Princes de Condé, de Conti, de Lambesc, de Vaudemont, the Countess de Polignac, and the Duchesses de Polignac and de Guiche. The day following the two murders, M. de Crosne, M. Doumer, M. Sureau, the most zealous and most valuable members of the committee on subsistences, all

---

[1] Bailly, ii. 95, 108. Malouet, ii. 14.

those appointed to make purchases and to take care of the storehouses, conceal themselves or fly. On the eve of the two murders, the notaries of Paris, being menaced with a riot, had to advance 45,000 francs which were promised to the workmen of the Faubourg Saint-Antoine ; while the public treasury, almost empty, is drained of 30,000 livres per day to diminish the cost of bread. Persons and possessions, great and small, private individuals and public functionaries, the Government itself, all is in the hands of the mob. " From this moment," says a deputy,[1] " liberty did not exist even in the National Assembly . . . France stood dumb before thirty factious persons. The Assembly became in their hands a passive instrument, which they forced to serve them in the execution of their projects." They themselves do not lead, although they seem to lead. The great brute, which has taken the bit in its mouth, holds on to it, and its plunging becomes more violent ; for not only do both spurs which maddened it—I mean the desire for innovation and the daily scarcity of food— continue to prick it on, but also the political hornets which, increasing by thousands, buzz around its ears, while the license in which it revels for the first time, joined to the applause lavished upon it, urges it forward more violently each day. The insurrection is glorified. Not one of the assassins is sought out. It is against the conspiracy of Ministers that the Assembly institutes an enquiry. Rewards are bestowed upon the conquerors of the Bastille ; it is declared that they have saved France. All honours are awarded to the people—to their good sense, their magnanimity, their justice. Adoration is paid to the new sovereign : he is publicly and officially told, in the Assembly and by the press, that he possesses every virtue, all rights and all powers. If he spills blood it is inadvertently, on provocation, and always with an infallible instinct. Moreover, says a deputy, " this blood, was it so pure ? " The greater number of people prefer the theories of their books to the experience of their eyes ; they persist in the idyl which they have fashioned for themselves. At the worst their dream, driven out from the present, takes refuge in the future. To-morrow, when the Constitution is complete, the people, made happy, will again become wise : let us

---

[1] De Ferrières, i. 168.

endure the storm which leads us on to so noble a harbour.

Meanwhile, beyond the King, inert and disarmed, beyond the Assembly, disobeyed or submissive, appears the real monarch, the people—that is to say, the mob of a hundred, a thousand, a hundred thousand beings gathered together haphazard, on an impulse, on an alarm, suddenly and irresistibly made legislators, judges, and executioners : a formidable power, undefined and destructive, on which no one has any hold, and which, with its mother, howling and mis-shapen Liberty, sits at the threshold of the Revolution like Milton's two spectres at the gates of Hell.

> "The one seemed woman to the waist, and fair,
> But ended foul in many a scaly fold,
> Voluminous and vast, a serpent armed
> With mortal sting. About her middle round
> A cry of hell-hounds never ceasing bark'd
> With wide Cerberean mouths full loud, and rung
> A hideous peal : and yet, when they list, would creep,
> If aught disturb'd their noise, into her womb,
> And kennel there ; yet there still bark'd and howl'd
> Within unseen. . . . .
>   . . . . The other shape,
> If shape it might be called, that shape had none
> Distinguishable in member, joint, or limb,
> Or substance might be call'd that shadow seem'd,
> For each seem'd either ; black it stood as night,
> Fierce as ten furies, terrible as hell,
> And shook a dreadful dart ; what seem'd his head
> The likeness of a kingly crown had on.
>
> The monster moving onward came as fast,
> With horrid strides."

CHAPTER III.

I.

HOWEVER bad a particular government may be, there is something still worse, and that is the suppression of all government. For, it is owing to government that human wills form a harmony instead of a chaos. It serves society as the brain serves a living being. Incapable, inconsiderate, extravagant, engrossing, it often abuses its position, overstraining or misleading the body for which it should care, and which it should direct. But, taking all things into account, whatever it may do, more good than harm is done, for through it the body stands erect, marches on and guides its steps. Without it there is no organized deliberate action, serviceable to the whole body. In it alone do we find the comprehensive views, knowledge ot the members of which it consists and of their aims, an idea of outward relationships, full and accurate information, in short, the superior intelligence which conceives what is best for the common interests, and adapts means to ends. If it falters and is no longer obeyed, if it is forced and pushed from without by a violent pressure, it ceases to control public affairs, and the social organization retrogrades by many steps. Through the dissolution of society, and the isolation of individuals, each man returns to his original feeble state, while power is vested in passing aggregates which spring up like whirling vortices amongst the human dust.—One may divine how this power, which the most competent find it difficult to apply properly, is exercised by bands of men starting up from the ground. The question is of provisions, their possession, price and distribution ; of taxation, its proportion, apportionment and collection ; of private property, its varieties, rights, and limitations ; of public authority, its province and its limits ; of all those delicate cog-wheels which, working into each other, constitute the great economic, social, and political machine. Each band in its own canton lays its rude hands on the wheels within its reach, wrenching or breaking them haphazard, under the impulse of the moment, heedless and indifferent to consequences, even when the reaction of to-morrow crushes them in the ruin which they cause to-day. Thus do unchained negroes, each pulling and hauling his own way, undertake to manage a ship of which they have just obtained the mastery.—In such a state of things white men are hardly worth more than black ones ; for, not only is the band, whose aim is violence, composed of those who are most destitute, most wildly enthusiastic, and most inclined to destructiveness and to license, but also, as this band tumultuously carries out its violent action, each individual the most brutal, the most irrational, and most corrupt, descends lower than himself, even to the darkness, the madness, and the savagery of the dregs of society. In fact, a man who in the interchange of blows, would resist the excitement of murder, and not use his strength like a savage, must be familiar with arms, accustomed to danger, cool-blooded, alive to the sentiment of honour, and, above all, sensitive to that stern military code which, to the imagination of the soldier, ever holds out to him the provost's gibbet to which he is sure to rise, should he strike one blow too many. All these restraints, inward as well as outward, are wanting to the man who plunges into insurrection. He is a novice in the acts of violence which he carries out. He has no fear of the law, because he abolishes it. The action begun carries him further than he intended to go. His anger is exasperated by peril and resistance. He catches the fever from contact with those who are fevered, and follows robbers who have become his comrades.[1] Add to

---

[1] Dussaulx, 374. " I remarked that if there were a few among the people at that time who dared commit crime, there were several who wished it, and that every one per-

this the clamours, the drunkenness, the spectacle of destruction, the nervous tremor of the body strained beyond its powers of endurance, and we can comprehend how, from the peasant, the labourer, and the bourgeois, pacified and tamed by an old civilisation, we see all of a sudden spring forth the barbarian, and, still worse, the primitive animal, the grinning, sanguinary, wanton baboon, who chuckles while he slays, and gambols over the ruin he has accomplished. Such is the actual government to which France is given up, and after eighteen months' experience, the best qualified, most judicious and profoundest observer of the Revolution will find nothing to compare to it but the invasion of the Roman Empire in the fourth century.[1] "The Huns, the Heruli, the Vandals, and the Goths will come neither from the north nor from the Black Sea ; they are in our very midst."

[Section II of this chapter has been omitted.]

III.

These people, in truth, are hungry, and, since the Revolution, their misery has increased. Around Puy-en-Velay the country is laid waste, and the soil broken up by a terrible tempest, a fierce hailstorm, and a deluge of rain. In the south, the crop proved to be moderate and even insufficient. "To trace a picture of the condition of Languedoc," writes the intendant,[2] "would be to give an account of calamities of every description. The panic which prevails in all communities, and which is stronger than all laws, stops traffic, and would cause famine even in the midst of plenty. Commodities are enormously high, and there is a lack of cash. Communities are ruined by the enormous outlays to which they are exposed,—the payment of the deputies to the seneschal's court, the establishment of the burgess guards, guardhouses for this militia, the purchase of arms, uniforms, and outlays in forming communes and permanent councils ; printing of all kinds, for the publication of the most unessential deliberations ; the loss of time

mitted it."—"Archives Nationales," D. xxix. 3. (Letter of the municipal authorities of Crémieux, Dauphiny, November 3, 1789.) "The care taken to lead them first to the cellars and to intoxicate them, can alone give a conception of the incredible excesses of rage to which they gave themselves up in the sacking and burning of the chateaux."

[1] *Mercure de France,* January 4, 1792. ("Revue politique de l'année 1791," by Mallet-Dupan.)

[2] "Archives Nationales," H. 942. (Observations of M. de Ballainvilliers, October 30, 1789.)

due to disturbances occasioned by these circumstances ; the utter
stagnation of manufactures and of trade,"—all these causes combined " have reduced Languedoc to the last extremity."—In the
Centre, and in the North, where the crops are good, provisions are
not less scarce, because wheat is not allowed a circulation, and is
kept concealed.   " For five months," writes the municipal assembly of Louviers,[1] " not a farmer has made his appearance in the
markets of this town.   Such a circumstance was never known before,
although, from time to time, high prices have prevailed to a considerable extent.   On the contrary, the markets were always well
supplied in proportion to the high price of grain."   In vain the
municipality orders the surrounding forty-seven parishes to provide
them with wheat ; they pay no attention to the mandate ; each for
himself and each for his own house ; the intendant is no longer
present to compel local interests to give way to public interests.
" In the wheat districts around us," says a letter from one of the
Burgundy towns, " we cannot rely on being able to make free
purchases.   Special regulations, supported by the burgess militia,
prevent grain from being sent out, and put a stop to its circulation.
The adjacent markets are of no use to us.   Not a sack of grain
has been brought into our market for about eight months."—At
Troyes, bread costs four sous per pound ; at Bar-sur-Aube, and in
the vicinity, four and a half sous per pound.   The artisan who is
out of work now earns twelve sous a day at the relief works, and,
on going into the country, he sees that the grain crop is good.
What conclusion can he come to but that the dearth is due to the
monopolists, and that, if he should die of hunger, it would be
because those scoundrels have starved him ?—By virtue of this
reasoning whoever has to do with these provisions, whether proprietor, farmer, merchant or administrator, all are considered
traitors.   It is plain that there is a plot against the people : the
government, the Queen, the clergy, the nobles are all parties to it ;
and likewise the magistrates and the wealthy amongst the bourgeoisie
and the rich.   A rumour is current in the Ile-de-France that sacks
of flour are thrown into the Seine, and that the cavalry horses are
purposely made to eat grain in the stalk.   In Brittany, it is main-

---

[1] " Archives Nationales," D. xxix. I.   Letter of the municipal assembly of Louviers, the
end of August, 1789.   Letter of the communal assembly of Saint-Bris (bailiwick of
Auxerre), September 25th.—Letter of the municipal officers of Ricey-Haut, near Bar-sur-
Seine, August 25th ; of the Chevalier d'Allouville, September 8th.

tained that grain is exported and stored up abroad. In Touraine, it is certain that this or that wholesale dealer allows it to sprout in his granaries rather than sell it. At Troyes, a story prevails that another has poisoned his flour with alum and arsenic, commissioned to do so by the bakers.—Conceive the effect of suspicions like these upon a suffering multitude ! A wave of hatred ascends from the empty stomach to the morbid brain. The people are everywhere in quest of their imaginary enemies, plunging forward with closed eyes no matter on whom or on what, not merely with all the weight of their mass, but with all the energy of their fury.

IV.

From the earliest of these weeks they were already alarmed. Accustomed to being led, the human herd is scared at being left to itself ; it misses its leaders whom it has trodden under foot ; in throwing off their trammels it has deprived itself of their protection. It feels lonely, in an unknown country, exposed to dangers of which it is ignorant, and against which it is unable to guard itself. Now that the shepherds are slain or disarmed, suppose the wolves should unexpectedly appear !—And there are wolves—I mean vagabonds and criminals—who have but just issued out of the darkness. They have robbed and burned, and are to be found at every insurrection. Now that the police force no longer puts them down, they show themselves instead of keeping themselves concealed. They have only to lie in wait and come forth in a band, and both life and property will be at their mercy.—Deep anxiety, a vague feeling of dread, spreads through both town and country : towards the end of July the panic, like a blinding, suffocating whirl of dust, suddenly sweeps over hundreds of leagues of territory. The brigands are coming ! they are firing the crops ! they are only six leagues off, and then only two—it is proved by the fugitives who are escaping in confusion.

On the 28th of July, at Angoulême,[1] the tocsin is heard about

---

[1] " Archives Nationales," D. xxix. I. Letter of M. Briand-Delessart (Angoulême, August 1st).—Of M. Bret, Lieutenant-General of the provostship of Mardogne, September 5th.— Of the Chevalier de Castellas (Auvergne), September 15th (relating to the night between the 2nd and 3rd of August).—Madame Campan, ii. 65.

three o'clock in the afternoon; the drums beat to arms, and cannon are mounted on the ramparts; the town has to be put in a state of defence against 15,000 bandits who are approaching; and from the walls a cloud of dust on the road is discovered with terror. It proves to be the post-waggon on its way to Bordeaux. After this the number of brigands is reduced to 1,500, but there is no doubt that they are ravaging the country. At nine o'clock in the evening 20,000 men are under arms, and thus they pass the night, always listening without hearing anything. Towards three o'clock in the morning there is a fresh alarm with the tocsin, and the people form themselves in battle array; it is certain that the brigands have burned Ruffec, Verneuil, La Rochefoucauld, and other places. The next day countrymen flock in to give their aid against bandits who are still absent. "At nine o'clock," says a witness, "we had 40,000 men in the town, to whom we had to be grateful." As the bandits do not show themselves, it must be because they are concealed; a hundred horsemen, a large number of men on foot, start out to search the forest of Braçonne, and to their great surprise they find nothing. But the terror is not allayed; "during the following days a guard is kept mounted, and companies are enrolled among the burgesses," while Bordeaux, duly informed, dispatches a courier to offer the support of 20,000 men and even 30,000. "What is surprising," adds the narrator, "is that at ten leagues off in the neighbourhood, in each parish, a similar disturbance took place, and at about the same hour."—That a girl returning to the village at night should meet two men who do not belong to the neighbourhood is sufficient to give rise to these panics. The case is the same in Auvergne. Whole parishes, on the strength of this, betake themselves at night to the woods, abandoning their houses, and carrying away their furniture; "the fugitives trod down and destroyed their own crops; pregnant women were injured in the forests, and others lost their wits." Fear lends them wings. Two years after this, Madame Campan was shown a rocky peak on which a woman had taken refuge, and from which she was obliged to be let down with ropes.—The people at last return to their homes, and their lives seem to resume the even tenor of their way. But such large masses are not unsettled with impunity; a tumult like this is, in itself, a fruitful source of alarm: as the country did rise, it must have been on account of threatened danger; and if the peril was not due to brigands, it must have come from some other quarter. Arthur Young, at Dijon and in Alsace,[1] hears at the public dinner-tables that the Queen had formed a plot to undermine the National Assembly and to massacre all Paris. Later on he is arrested in a village near Clermont, and examined because he is evidently conspiring with the Queen and the Comte d'Entraigues to blow up the town and send the survivors to the galleys.

No argument, no experience has any effect against the multiplying phantoms of an over-excited imagination. Henceforth every commune, and every man, provide themselves with arms and keep them ready for use. The peasant searches his hoard, and "finds from ten to twelve francs for the purchase of a gun." " A national militia is found in the poorest village." Burgess guards and companies of volunteers patrol all the towns. Military commanders deliver arms, ammunition, and equipments, on the requisition of municipal bodies, while, in case of refusal, the arsenals are pillaged, and, voluntarily or by force, four hundred thousand guns thus pass into the hands of the people in six months.[2] Not content with this they must have cannon. Brest having demanded two, every town in Brittany does the same thing; their *amour-propre* is excited, and also the need of feeling themselves strong. They lack nothing now to render themselves masters. All authority, all force, every means of constraint and of intimidation is in their hands, and in theirs alone ; and these sovereign hands have nothing to guide them in this actual interregnum of all legal powers, but the wild or murderous suggestions of hunger or distrust.

V.

It would take too much space to recount all the violent acts which were committed,—convoys arrested, grain pillaged, millers and corn merchants hung, decapitated, slaughtered, farmers called upon under threats of death to give up even the seed reserved

---

[1] Arthur Young, " Voyages in France," July 24th and 31st, August 13th and 19th.

[2] D. Bouillé, 108.—"Archives Nationales," KK. 1105. Correspondence of M. de Thiard, September 20, 1789 (apropos of one hundred guns given to the town of Saint-Brieuc). " They are not of the slightest use, but this passion for arms is a temporary epidemic which must be allowed to subside of itself. People are determined to believe in brigands and in enemies, whereas neither exist." September 25th, " Vanity alone impels them, and the pride of having cannon is their sole motive."

for sowing, proprietors ransomed and houses sacked.[1] These outrages, unpunished, tolerated and even excused or badly suppressed, are constantly repeated, and are, at first, directed against public men and public property. As is commonly the case, the rabble head the march and stamp the character of the whole insurrection.

[The rest of Section V has been omitted.]

VI.

We can divine, under such circumstances, whether taxes come in, and whether municipalities that sway about in every popular breeze have the power of keeping up odious revenue rights.—Towards the end of September,[2] I find a list of thirty-six committees or municipal bodies which, within a radius of fifty leagues around Paris, refuse to ensure the collection of taxes. One of them tolerates the sale of contraband salt, in order not to excite a riot. Another takes the precaution to disarm the employés in the excise department. In a third the municipal officers were the first to provide themselves with contraband salt and contraband tobacco.

At Peronne and at Ham, the order having come to restore the toll-houses, the people destroy the soldiers' quarters, conduct all the employés to their homes, and order them to leave within twenty-four hours, under penalty of death. After twenty months' resistance Paris will end the matter by forcing the National Assembly to give in and by obtaining the final suppression of its *octroi*.[3]—Of all the creditors whose hand each one felt on his shoulders, that of the exchequer was the heaviest, and now it is the weakest; hence this is the first whose grasp is to be shaken off; there is none which is more heartily detested or which receives harsher treatment. Especially against collectors of the salt-tax,

---

[1] "**Archives Nationales,**" H. 1453. Letters of M. Amelot, July 17th and 24th. " Several **wealthy private persons of the town** (Auxonne) have been put to ransom by this band, of which the largest portion consists of ruffians."—Letter of nine cultivators of Breteuil (**Picardy**), July 23rd (their granaries were pillaged up to the last grain the previous **evening**). " They threaten to pillage our crops and set our barns on fire as soon as they are full. M. Tassard, the notary, has been visited in his house by the populace, and his life has been threatened " Letter of Moreau, Procureur du Roi at the Seneschal's Court at Bar-le-Duc, September 15, 1789, D. xxix. I. " On the 27th of July the people rose and most cruelly assassinated a merchant trading in wheat. On the 27th and 28th his house and that of another were sacked," &c.

[2] " Archives Nationales," H. 1453. *Ibid.* D. xxix. I. Note of M. de la Tour-du-Pin, October 28th.

[3] Decree, February 1, 1789, enforced May 1 following.

custom-house officers, and excisemen the fury is universal. These, everywhere,[1] are in danger of their lives and are obliged to fly. At Falaise, in Normandy, the people threaten to "cut to pieces the director of the excise." At Baignes, in Saintonge, his house is devastated and his papers and effects are burned; they put a knife to the throat of his son, a child six years of age, saying, "Thou must perish that there may be no more of thy race." For four hours the clerks are on the point of being torn to pieces; through the entreaties of the lord of the manor, who sees scythes and sabres aimed at his own head, they are released only on the condition that they "abjure their employment."—Again, for two months following the taking of the Bastille, insurrections break out by hundreds, like a volley of musketry, against indirect taxation. From the 23rd of July the Intendant of Champagne reports that "the uprising is general in almost all the towns under his generalship." On the following day the Intendant of Alençon writes that, in his province, "the royal dues will no longer be paid anywhere." On the 7th of August, M. Necker states to the National Assembly that in the two intendants' districts of Caen and Alençon it has been necessary to reduce the price of salt one-half; that "in an infinity of places" the collection of the excise is stopped or suspended; that the smuggling of salt and tobacco is done by "convoys and by open force" in Picardy, in Lorraine, and in the Trois-Evêchés; that the indirect tax does not come in, that the receivers-general and the receivers of the *taille* are "at bay" and can no longer keep their engagements. The public income diminishes from month to month; in the social body, the heart, already so feeble, faints; deprived of the blood which no longer reaches it, it ceases to propel to the muscles the vivifying current which restores their waste and adds to their energy.

"All controlling power is slackened," says Necker, "everything is a prey to the passions of individuals." Where is the power to constrain them and to secure to the State its dues? The clergy,

---

[1] "Archives Nationales," D. xxix. 1. Letter of the Count de Montausier, August 8th, with notes by M. Paulian, director of the excise (an admirable letter, modest and liberal, and ending by demanding a pardon for people led astray), H. 1453. Letter of the attorney of the election district of Falaise, July 17th, &c. *Moniteur,* I. 303, 387, 505 (sessions of August 7th and 27th and of September 23rd). "The royal revenues are diminishing steadily." Roux and Buchez, III. 219 (session of October 24, 1789). Discourse of a deputation from Anjou: "Sixty thousand men are armed; the barriers have been destroyed, the clerks' horses have been sold by auction; the employés have been told to withdraw from the province within eight days. The inhabitants have declared that they will not pay taxes so long as the salt-tax exists."

the nobles, wealthy townsmen, and certain brave artisans and farmers, undoubtedly pay, and even sometimes give spontaneously. But in society those who possess intelligence, who are in easy circumstances and conscientious, form a small select class—the great mass is egotistic, ignorant, and needy, and lets its money go only under constraint ; there is but one way to collect the taxes, and that is to extort them.   From time immemorial, direct taxes in France have been collected only by bailiffs and seizures ; which is not surprising, as they take away a full half of the net income. Now that the peasants of each village are armed and form a band, let the collector come and make seizures if he dare !—" Imme-diately after the decree on the equality of the taxes," writes the provincial commission of Alsace,[1] " the people generally refused to make any payments, until those who were exempt and privi-leged should have been inscribed on the local lists."   In many places the peasants threaten to obtain the reimbursement of their instalments, while in others they insist that the decree should be retrospective and that the new rate-payers should pay for the past year.   " No collector dare send an official to distrain ; none that are sent dare fulfil their mission."—" It is not the good bourgeois " of whom there is any fear, " but the rabble who make the latter and every one else afraid of them ; " resistance and dis-order everywhere come from " people that have nothing to lose."— Not only do they shake off taxation, but they usurp property, and declare that, being the Nation, whatever belongs to the Nation belongs to them.   The forests of Alsace are laid waste, the seignorial as well as communal, and wantonly destroyed with the wastefulness of children or of maniacs.   " In many places, to avoid the trouble of removing the woods, they are burnt, and the people content themselves with carrying off the ashes."—After the decrees of August 4th, and in spite of the law which licenses the proprietor only to hunt on his own grounds, the impulse to break the law becomes irresistible.   Every man who can procure a gun begins operations ;[2] the crops which are still standing are

---

1 " Archives Nationales," F. 7, 3253 (Letter of September 8, 1789).

2 Arthur Young, September 30th.   " One would think that every rusty gun in Provence is at work, killing all sorts of birds ; the shot has fallen five or six times in my chaise and about my ears."   Reugnot, I. 141.   " Archives Nationales," D. xxix. I. Letter of the Chevalier d'Allonville, September 8, 1789 (environs of Bar-sur-Aube).   " The peasants go in armed bands into the woods belonging to the Abbey of Trois-Fontaines, which they cut down.   They saw up the oaks and transport them on waggons to Pont-Saint-Dizier, where they sell them.   In other places they fish in the ponds and break the embank-ments."

trodden under foot, the lordly residences are invaded and the palings are scaled ; the King himself at Versailles is wakened by shots fired in his park. Stags, fawns, deer, wild boars, hares, and rabbits, are slain by thousands, cooked with stolen wood, and eaten up on the spot. There is a constant discharge of musketry throughout France for more than two months, and, as on an American prairie, every living animal belongs to him who kills it. At Choiseul, in Champagne, not only are all the hares and partridges of the barony exterminated, but the ponds are exhausted of fish ; the court of the chateau even is entered, to fire on the pigeon-house and destroy the pigeons, and then the pigeons and fish, of which they have too many, are offered to the proprietor for sale.—It is " the patriots " of the village with " smugglers and bad characters " belonging to the neighbourhood who make this expedition ; they are seen in the front ranks of every act of violence, and it is not difficult to foresee that, under their leadership, attacks on public persons and public property will be followed by attacks on private persons and private property.

VII.

Indeed, a proscribed class already exists, and a name has been found for it : it is the " aristocrats." This deadly term, applied at first to the nobles and prelates in the States-General who declined to take part in the reunion of the three orders, is extended so as to embrace all whose titles, offices, alliances, and manner of living distinguish them from the multitude. That which entitled them to respect is that which marks them out as objects of ill-will ; while the people, who, though suffering from their privileges, did not regard them personally with hatred, are taught to consider them as their enemies. Each, on his own estate, is held accountable for the evil designs attributed to his brethren at Versailles, and, on the false report of a plot at the centre, the peasants range themselves on the side of the conspirators.[1] Thus does the peasant jacquerie commence, and the wild enthusiasts who have fanned

---

[1] " Archives Nationales," D. xxix. I. Letter of the assessor of the police of Saint-Flour, October 3, 1789. On the 31st of July, a report is spread that the brigands are coming. On the 1st of August the peasants arm themselves. "They amuse themselves by drinking, awaiting the arrival of the brigands; the excitement increases to such an extent as to make them believe that M. le Comte d'Espinchal had arrived in disguise the evening before at Massiac, that he was the author of the troubles disturbing the province at this time, and that he was concealed in his chateau." On the strength of this shots are fired into the windows, and there are searches, &c.

the flame in Paris are likewise fanning the flame in the provinces. " You wish to know the authors of the agitations," writes a sensible man to the committee of investigation ; " you will find them amongst the deputies of the Third-Estate," and especially among the attorneys and advocates. " These dispatch incendiary letters to their constituents, which letters are received by municipal bodies alike composed of attorneys and of advocates .... they are read aloud in the public squares, while copies of them are distributed among all the villages. In these villages, if any one knows how to read besides the priest and the lord of the manor, it is the legal practitioner," the born enemy of the lord of the manor, whose place he covets, vain of his oratorical powers, embittered by his poverty, and never failing to blacken everything.[1] It is highly probable that he is the one who composes and circulates the placards calling on the people, in the King's name, to resort to violence.—At Secondigny, in Poitou, on the 23rd of July,[2] the labourers in the forest receive a letter " which summons them to attack all the country gentlemen round about, and to massacre without mercy all those who refuse to renounce their privileges.... promising them that not only will their crimes go unpunished, but that they will even be rewarded." M. Despretz-Montpezat, correspondent of the deputies of the nobles, is seized, and dragged with his son to the dwelling of the procurator-fiscal, to force him to give his signature ; the inhabitants are forbidden to render him assistance " on pain of death and fire." " Sign," they exclaim, " or we will tear out your heart, and set fire to this house ! " At this moment the neighbouring notary, who is doubtless an accomplice, appears with a stamped paper, and says to him, " Monsieur, I have just come from Niort, where the Third-Estate has done the same thing to all the gentlemen of the town ; one, who refused, was cut to pieces before our eyes."—" We are compelled to sign renunciations of our privileges, and give our assent to one and the same taxation, as if the nobles had not already done so." The band gives notice that it will proceed in the same fashion with all

---

[1] "Archives Nationales," K. xxix. I. Letter of Etienne Fermier, Naveinne, September 18th (it is possible that the author, for the sake of caution, took a fictitious name). The manuscript correspondence of M. Boullé, deputy of Pontivy, to his constituents, is a type of this declamatory and incendiary writing. Letter of the consuls, priests, and merchants of Puy-en-Velay, September 16th.—" The Ancient Régime," p. 396.

[2] "Archives Nationales," D. xxix. I. Letter of M. Despretz-Montpezat, a former artillery officer, July 24th (with several other signatures). On the same day the tocsin is sounded in fifty villages on the rumour spreading that 7,000 brigands, English and Breton, were invading the country.

134   *THE REVOLUTION.*   BOOK I.

the chateaux in the vicinity, and terror precedes or follows them.
" Nobody dares write," M. Despretz sends word ; " I attempt it
at the risk of my life."—Nobles and prelates become objects of suspicion everywhere ; village committees open their letters, and they
have to suffer their houses to be searched.[1] They are forced to
adopt the new cockade : to be a gentleman, and not wear it, is to
deserve hanging. At Mamers, in Maine, M. de Beauvoir refuses
to wear it, and is at the point of being put into the pillory and at
once knocked on the head. Near La Flèche, M. de Brissac is
arrested, and a message is sent to Paris to know if he shall be
taken there, " or be beheaded in the meantime." Two deputies of
the nobles, MM. de Montesson and de Vassé, who had come to
ask the consent of their constituents to their joining the Third-
Estate, are recognised near Mans ; their honourable scruples and
their pledges to the constituents are considered of no importance,
nor even the step that they are now taking to fulfil them ; it suffices
that they voted against the Third-Estate at Versailles ; the populace pursues them and breaks up their carriages, and pillages their
trunks.—Woe to the nobles, especially if they have taken any part
in local rule, and if they are opposed to popular panics ! M. Cureau, deputy-mayor of Mans,[2] had issued orders during the famine,
and, having retired to his chateau of Nouay, had told the peasants
that the announcement of the coming of brigands was a false alarm ;
he thought that it was not necessary to sound the tocsin, and
all that was necessary was that they should remain quiet. Accordingly he is set down as being in league with the brigands, and
besides this he is a monopolist, and a buyer of standing crops.
The peasants lead him off, along with his son-in-law, M. de Montesson, to the neighbouring village, where there are judges. On
the way " they dragged their victims on the ground, pummelled
them, trampled on them, spit in their faces, and besmeared them
with filth." M. de Montesson is shot, while M. Cureau is killed
by degrees ; a carpenter cuts off the two heads with a double-
edged axe, and children bear them along to the sound of drums

---

[1] " Archives Nationales," D. xxix. I. Letter of Briand-Delessart, August 1st (domiciliary
visits to the Carmelites of Angoulême where it is pretended that Mme. de Polignac has
just arrived.– Beugnot, I. 140.—Arthur Young, July 20th, &c.—Roux and Buchez, iv. 166,
Letter of Mamers, July 24th ; of Mans, July 26th.

[2] Montjoie, ch. lxii. p. 93 (according to acts of legal procedure). There was a soldier in
the band who had served under M. de Montesson and who wanted to avenge himself for
the punishments he had undergone in the regiment.

and violins. Meanwhile, the judges of the place, brought by force, draw up an official report stating the finding of thirty louis and several bills of the Banque d'Escompte in the pockets of M. de Cureau, on the discovery of which a shout of triumph is set up : this evidence proves that they were going to buy up the standing wheat!—Such is the course of popular justice. Now that the Third-Estate has become the nation, every mob thinks that it has the right to pronounce sentences, which it carries out, on lives and on possessions.

These explosions are isolated in the western, central and southern provinces ; the conflagration, however, is universal in the east, on a strip of ground from thirty to fifty leagues broad, extending from the extreme north down to Provence. Alsace, Franche-Comté, Burgundy, Mâconnais, Beaujolais, Auvergne, Viennois, Dauphiny,—the whole of this territory resembles a continuous mine which explodes at the same time. The first column of flame which shoots up is on the frontiers of Alsace and Franche-Comté, in the vicinity of Belfort and Vésoul—a feudal district, in which the peasant, over-burdened with taxes, bears the heavier yoke with greater impatience. An instinctive argument is going on in his mind without his knowing it. "The good Assembly and the good King want us to be happy—suppose we help them ! They say that the King has already relieved us of the taxes—suppose we relieve ourselves of paying rents ! Down with the nobles ! They are no better than the tax-collectors ! "—On the 16th of July, the chateau of Sancy, belonging to the Princesse de Beaufremont, is sacked, and on the 18th those of Lure, Bithaine, and Molans.[1] On the 29th, an accident which occurs with some fireworks at a popular festival at the house of M. de Memmay, leads the lower class to believe that the invitation extended to them was a trap, and that there was a desire to get rid of them by treachery.[2] Seized with rage they set fire to the chateau, and during the following week[3] destroy three abbeys, ruin eleven chateaux and pillage others ; "all records are destroyed, the registers and court-rolls are carried off, and the deposits violated."—Start-

---

[1] *Mercure de France,* August 20th (Letter from Vésoul, August 13th).

[2] M. de Memmay proved his innocence later on, and was rehabilitated by a public decision after two years' proceedings (session of June 4, 1791 ; *Mercure* of June 11th).

[3] *Journal des Débats et Décrets,* i. 258. (Letter of the municipality of Vésoul, July 22nd.—Discourse of M. de Toulougeon, July 29th.)

ing from this spot, " the hurricane of insurrection " stretches over the whole of Alsace from Huningue to Landau.[1] The insurgents display placards, signed *Louis*, stating that for a certain lapse of time they shall be permitted to exercise justice themselves, and, in Sundgau, a well-dressed weaver, decorated with a blue belt, passes for a prince, the King's second son. They begin by falling on the Jews, their hereditary leeches ; they sack their dwellings, divide their money among themselves, and hunt them down like so many fallow-deer. At Bâle alone, it is said that twelve hundred of these unfortunate fugitives arrived with their families.— The distance between the Jew creditor and the Christian proprietor is not great, and this is soon cleared. Remiremont is only saved by a detachment of dragoons. Eight hundred men attack the chateau of Uberbrünn. The abbey of Neubourg is taken by storm. At Guebwiller, on the 31st of July, five hundred peasants, subjects of the abbey of Murbach, make a descent on the abbot's palace and on the house of the canons. Cupboards, chests, beds, windows, mirrors, frames, even the tiles of the roof and the hinges of the casements are hacked to pieces : " They kindle fires on the beautiful inlaid floors of the apartments, and there burn up the library and the title-deeds." The abbot's superb carriage is so broken up that not a wheel remains entire. " Wine streams through the cellars. One cask of sixteen hundred measures is half lost ; the plate and the linen are carried off."— Society is evidently being overthrown, while with the power, property is changing hands.

[A portion of the text has been omitted at this point.]

In the midst of a disintegrated society, under the semblance only of a government, it is manifest that an invasion is under way, an invasion of barbarians which will complete by terror that which it has begun by violence, and which, like the invasions of the Normans in the tenth and eleventh centuries, ends in the conquest and dispossession of an entire class. In vain the National Guard and the other troops that remain loyal succeed in stemming the first torrent ; in vain does the Assembly hollow out a bed for it and strive to bank it in by fixed boundaries. The decrees of the 4th of August and the regulations which follow

---

[1] De Rochambeau, "Mémoires," i. 353. "Archives Nationales," F. 7, 3253. (Letter of M. de Rochambeau, August 4th.)—Chronicle of Schmutz (*ibid.*), p. 284. "Archives Nationales," D. xxix. i. (Letter of Mme. Ferrette, of Remiremont, August 9th.)

are but so many spiders' webs stretched across a torrent. The peasants, moreover, putting their own interpretation on the decrees, convert the new laws into authority for continuing in their course or beginning over again. No more rents, however legitimate, however legal ! " Yesterday," [1] writes a gentleman of Auvergne, " we were notified that the fruit-tithe (*percières*) would no longer be paid, and that the example of other provinces was only being followed which no longer, even by royal order, pay tithes." In Franche-Comté " numerous communities are satisfied that they no longer owe anything either to the King or to their lords. . . . The villages divide amongst themselves the fields and woods belonging to the nobles."—It must be noted that charter-holding and feudal titles are still intact in three-fourths of France, that it is the interest of the peasant to ensure their disappearance, and that he is always armed. To secure a new outbreak of jacqueries, it is only necessary that central control, already thrown into disorder, should be withdrawn. This is the work of Versailles and of Paris ; and there, at Paris as well as at Versailles, some, through lack of foresight and infatuation, and others, through blindness and indecision—the latter through weakness and the former through violence—all are labouring to accomplish it.

---

[1] Doniol, " La Revolution et la Féodalité," p. 60 (a few days after the 4th of August).— " Archives Nationales," H. 784. Letters of M. de Langeron, military commander at Besançon, October 16th and 18th. *Ibid.*, D. xxix. I. Letter of the same, September 3rd. Arthur Young (in Provence, at the house of Baron de la Tour-d'Aignes). " The baron is an enormous sufferer by the Revolution ; a great extent of country which belonged in absolute right to his ancestors, has been granted for quit-rents, *ceus*, and other feudal payments, so that there is no comparison between the lands retained and those thus granted by his family. . . . The solid payments which the Assembly have declared to be redeemable are every hour falling to nothing, without a shadow of recompense. . . . The situation of the nobility in this country is pitiable ; they are under apprehensions that nothing will be left them, but simply such houses as the mob allows to stand unburnt; that the small farmers will retain their farms without paying the landlord his half of the produce ; and that, in case of such a refusal, there is actually neither law nor authority in the country to prevent it. This chateau, splendid even in ruins, with the fortune and lives of the owners, is at the mercy of an armed rabble."

CHAPTER IV.

I. Paris.—Powerlessness and discords of the authorities.—The people, King.—II. Their distress.—The dearth and the lack of work.—How men of executive ability are recruited.—III. The new popular leaders.—Their ascendency.—Their education.—Their sentiments.—Their situation.—Their councils.—Their denunciations.—V. The 5th and 6th of October.

I.

THE powerlessness, indeed, of the heads of the Government, and the lack of discipline among all its subordinates, are much greater in the capital than in the provinces.—Paris possesses a mayor, Bailly; but "from the first day, and in the easiest manner possible,"[1] his municipal council, that is to say, "the assembly of the representatives of the commune, has accustomed itself to carry on the government alone, overlooking him entirely."— There is a central administration—the municipal council, presided over by the mayor ; but, "at this time, authority is everywhere except where the preponderating authority should be ; the districts have delegated it and at the same time retained it ;" each of them acts as if it were alone and supreme. There are secondary powers—the district-committees, each with its president, its clerk, its offices, and commissioners ; but the mobs of the street march on without awaiting their orders ; while the people, shouting under their windows, impose their will on them ; in short, says Bailly again, "everybody knew how to command, but nobody knew how to obey."

"Imagine," writes Loustalot himself, "a man whose feet, hands, and limbs possessed intelligence and a will, whose one leg would wish to walk when the other one wanted to rest, whose throat

---

1 Bailly, " Mémoires," ii. 195, 242.

would close when the stomach demanded food, whose mouth would sing when the eyelids were weighed down with sleep ; and you will have a striking picture of the condition of things in the capital."

There are " sixty Republics " in Paris ; each district is an independent, isolated power, which receives no order without criticizing it, always in disagreement and often in conflict with the central authority or with the other districts.   It receives denunciations, orders domiciliary visits, sends deputations to the National Assembly, passes resolutions, posts its bills, not only in its own quarter but throughout the city, and sometimes even extends its jurisdiction outside of Paris.   Everything comes within its province, and particularly that which ought not to do so.—On the 18th of July, the district of Petits-Augustins[1] " decrees in its own name the establishment of justices of the peace," under the title of tribunes, and proceeds at once to elect its own, nominating the actor Molé.   On the 30th, that of the Oratoire annuls the amnesty which the representatives of the commune in the Hôtel-de-Ville had granted, and orders two of its members to go to a distance of thirty leagues to arrest M. de Bezenval.   On the 19th of August, that of Nazareth issues commissions to seize and bring to Paris the arms deposited in strong places.   From the beginning each assembly sent to the Arsenal in its own name, and " obtained as many cartridges and as much powder as it desired."   Others claim the right of keeping a watchful eye over the Hôtel-de-Ville and of reprimanding the National Assembly.   The Oratoire decides that the representatives of the commune shall be invited to deliberate in public. Saint-Nicholas des Champs deliberates on the veto and begs the Assembly to suspend its vote.—It is a strange spectacle, that of these various authorities each contradicting and destroying the other.   To-day the Hôtel-de-Ville appropriates five loads of cloth which have been dispatched by the Government, and the district of Saint-Gervais opposes the decision of the Hôtel-de-Ville.   To-morrow Versailles intercepts grain destined for Paris, while Paris threatens, if it is not restored, to march on Versailles.   I omit the incidents that are ridiculous :[2] anarchy in its essence is both

---

[1] Bailly, ii. 74, 174, 242, 261, 282, 345, 392.

[2] Such as domiciliary visits and arrests apparently made by lunatics. (" Archives de la Préfecture de Police de Paris.")—And Montjoie, ch. lxx. p. 67. Expedition of the

tragic and grotesque, and, in this universal breaking up of things, the capital, like the kingdom, resembles a bear-garden when it does not resemble a Babel.

But behind all these discordant authorities the real sovereign, who is the mob, is very soon apparent.   On the 15th of July it undertakes the demolition of the Bastille of its own accord, and this popular act is sanctioned ; for it is necessary that appearances should be kept up ; even to give orders after the blow is dealt, and to follow when it is impossible to lead.[1]   A short time after this the collection of the *octroi* at the barriers is ordered to be resumed ; forty armed individuals, however, present themselves in their district and say, that if guards are placed at the *octroi* stations, " they will resist force with force, and even make use of their cannon."   On the false rumour that arms are concealed in the Abbey of Montmartre, the abbess, Madame de Montmorency, is accused of treachery, and twenty thousand persons invade the monastery.—The commander of the National Guard and the mayor are constantly expecting a riot ; they hardly dare absent themselves a day to attend the King's *fête* at Versailles.   As soon as the multitude can assemble in the streets, an explosion is imminent.   " On rainy days," says Bailly, " I was quite at my ease."—It is under this constant pressure that the Government is carried on ; and the elect of the people, the most esteemed magistrates, those who are in best repute, are at the mercy of the throng who clamour at their doors.   In the district of St. Roch,[2] after many useless refusals, the General Assembly, notwithstanding all the reproaches of its conscience and the resistance of its reason, is obliged to open letters addressed to Monsieur, to the Duke of Orleans, and to the Ministers of War, of Foreign Affairs, and of the Marine.   In the committee on subsistences, M. Serreau, who is indispensable and who is confirmed by a public proclamation, is denounced, threatened, and constrained to leave Paris.   M. de la Salle, one of the strongest patriots among the nobles, is on the point of being murdered for having signed an order for the transport of gunpowder ;[3] the multitude, in pursuit of him, attach a

---

National Guard against imaginary brigands who are cutting down the crops at Montmorency and the volley fired in the air.—Conquest of Ile-Adam and Chantilly.

[1] Bailly, ii. 46, 95, 232, 287, 296.

[2] " Archives de la Préfecture de Police," *procès-verbal* of the section of Butte des Moulins, October 5, 1789.

[3] Bailly, ii. 224.—Dussaulx, 418, 202, 257, 174, 158.   The powder transported was called

rope to the nearest street-lamp, ransack the Hôtel-de-Ville, force every door, mount into the belfry, and seek for the traitor even under the carpet of the bureau and between the legs of the electors, and are only stayed in their course by the arrival of the National Guard.

The people not only sentence but they execute, and, as is always the case, blindly. At Saint-Denis, Chatel, the mayor's lieutenant, whose duty it is to distribute flour, had reduced the price of bread at his own expense : on the 3rd of August his house is forced open at two o'clock in the morning, and he takes refuge in a steeple ; the mob follow him, cut his throat and drag his head along the streets.—Not only do the people execute, but they pardon—and with equal discernment. On the 11th of August, at Versailles, as a parricide is about to be broken on the wheel, the crowd demand his release, fly at the executioner, and set the man free.[1] Veritably this is sovereign power like that of the oriental sovereign who arbitrarily awards life or death ! A woman who protests against this scandalous pardon is seized and comes near being hung ; for the new monarch considers as a crime whatever is offensive to his new majesty. Again, he receives public and humble homage. The Prime Minister, on imploring the pardon of M. de Bezenval at the Hôtel-de-Ville, in the presence of the electors and of the public, has said in set terms : " It is before the most unknown, the obscurest citizen of Paris that I prostrate myself, at whose feet I kneel." A few days before this, at Saint-Germain-en-Laye, and at Poissy, the deputies of the National Assembly not only kneel down in words, but actually, and for a long time, on the pavement in the street, and stretch forth their hands, weeping, to save two lives of which only one is granted to them.—Behold the monarch by these brilliant signs ! Already do the young, who are eager imitators of all actions that are in fashion, ape them in miniature ; during the month which follows the murder of Berthier and

---

poudre de traite (transport); the people understood it as *poudre de traître* (traitor). **M** de la Salle was near being killed through the addition of an *r*. It is he who had **taken** command of the National Guard on the 13th of July.

[1] Floquet, vii. 54. There is the same scene at Granville, in Normandy, on the 16th of October. A woman had assassinated her husband, while a soldier who was her lover is her accomplice ; the woman was about to be hung and the man broken on the wheel, **when** the populace shout, " The nation has the right of pardon," overset the scaffold, and **save the two assassins.**

Foulon, Bailly is informed that the *gamins* in the streets are parading about with the heads of two cats stuck on the ends of two poles.[1]

II.

A pitiable monarch, whose recognised sovereignty leaves him more miserable than he was before ! Bread is always scarce, and before the baker's doors the row of waiting people does not diminish. In vain Bailly passes his nights with the committee on supplies ; they are always in a state of terrible anxiety. Every morning for two months there is only one or two days' supply of flour, and often, in the evening, there is not enough for the following morning.[2] The life of the capital depends on a convoy which is ten, fifteen, twenty leagues off, and which may never arrive : one convoy of twenty carts is pillaged on the 18th of July, on the Rouen road ; another, on the 4th of August, in the vicinity of Louviers. Were it not for Salis' Swiss regiment, which, from the 14th of July to the end of September, marches day and night as an escort, not a boat-load of grain would reach Paris from Rouen.[3] —The commissaries charged with making purchases or with supervising the expeditions are in danger of their lives. Those who are sent to Provins are seized, and a column of four hundred men with cannon has to be dispatched to deliver them. The one who is sent to Rouen learns that he will be hung if he dares to enter the place. At Mantes a mob surrounds his cabriolet, the people regarding whoever comes there for the purpose of carrying away grain as a public pest ; he escapes with difficulty out of a back door and returns on foot to Paris.—From the very beginning, according to a universal rule, the fear of a short supply helps to augment the famine. Every one lays in a stock for several days ; on one occasion sixteen loaves of four pounds each are found in an old woman's garret. The bakings, consequently, which are estimated according to the quantity needed for a sin le day, become inadequate, and the last of those who wait at the bakers' shops for bread return home empty-handed.—On the other hand the appropriations made by the city and the State to diminish the price of bread simply serve to leng hen the rows of those who wait for it ; the countrymen flock in thither,

---

[1] Bailly, ii. 274 (August 17th).   [2] Bailly, ii. 83, 202, 230, 235, 283, 299.
[3] *Mercure de France*, the number for September 26th.   De Goncourt p. 111.

and return home loaded to their villages.   At Saint-Denis, bread having been reduced to two sous the pound, none is left for the inhabitants.   To this constant anxiety add that of a slack season. Not only is there no certainty of there being bread at the bakers' during the coming week, but many know that they will not have money in the coming week with which to buy bread. Now that security has disappeared and the rights of property are shaken, work is wanting.   The rich, deprived of their feudal dues, and, in addition thereto of their rents, have reduced their expenditure ; many of them, threatened by the committee of investigation, exposed to domiciliary visits, and liable to be informed against by their servants, have emigrated.   In the month of September M. Necker laments the delivery of six thousand passports in fifteen days to the wealthiest inhabitants.   In the month of October ladies of high rank, refugees in Rome, send word that their domestics should be discharged and their daughters placed in convents.   Before the end of 1789 there are so many fugitives in Switzerland that a house, it is said, brings in more rent than it is worth as capital.   With this first emigration, which is that of the chief spendthrifts—Count d'Artois, Prince de Conté, Duc de Bourbon, and so many others—the opulent foreigners have left, and, at the head of them, the Duchesse de l'Infantado, who spent 800,000 livres a year.   There are only three Englishmen in Paris.

It was a city of luxury, the European hot-house of costly and refined pleasures : the glass once broken, the amateurs leave and the delicate plants perish ; there is no employment now for the innumerable hands which cultivated them.   Fortunate are they who at the relief works obtain a miserable sum by handling a pickaxe !   " I saw," says Bailly, " mercers, jewellers, and merchants implore the favour of being employed at twenty sous the day." Enumerate, if you can, in one or two recognised callings, the hands which are doing nothing :[1] 1,200 hair-dressers keep about 6,000 journeymen ; 2,000 others follow the same calling in private houses ; 6,000 lackeys do but little else than this work.   The body of tailors is composed of 2,800 masters, who have under them 5,000 workmen.   " Add to these the number privately employed—the refugees in privileged places like the abbeys of Saint-Germain and Saint-Marcel, the vast enclosure of the Temple, that

---

[1] Mercier, "Tableau de Paris," i. 58 ; x. 151.

of Saint-John the Lateran, and the Faubourg Saint-Antoine, and you will find at least 12,000 persons cutting, fitting, and sewing." How many in these two groups are now idle ! How many others are walking the streets, such as upholsterers, lace-makers, embroiderers, fan-makers, gilders, carriage-makers, binders, engravers, and all the other producers of Parisian nick-nacks ! For those who are still at work how many days are lost at the doors of bakers' shops and in patrolling as National Guards ! Gatherings are formed in spite of the prohibitions of the Hôtel-de-Ville,[1] and the crowd openly discuss their miserable condition : 3,000 journeymen-tailors near the Colonnade, as many journeymen-shoemakers in the Place Louis XV., the journeymen-hairdressers in the Champs-Elysées, 4,000 domestics without places on the approaches to the Louvre,—and their propositions are on a level with their intelligence. Servants demand the expulsion from Paris of the Savoyards who enter into competition with them. Journeymen-tailors demand that a day's wages be fixed at forty sous, and that the old-clothes dealers shall not be allowed to make new ones. The journeymen-shoemakers declare that those who make shoes below the fixed price shall be driven out of the kingdom. Each of these irritated and agitated crowds contains the germ of an outbreak—and, in truth, these germs are found on every pavement in Paris : at the relief works, which at Montmartre collect 17,000 paupers ; in the Market, where the bakers want to "lantern" the flour commissioners, and at the doors of the bakers, of whom two, on the 14th of September and on the 5th of October, are conducted to the street-lamp and barely escape with their lives.—In this suffering, mendicant crowd, enterprising men become more numerous every day : they consist of deserters, and from every regiment ; they reach Paris in bands, often 250 in one day. There, "caressed and fed to the top of their bent,"[2] having received from the National Assembly 50 livres each, maintained by the King in the enjoyment of their advance-money, regaled by the districts, of which one alone incurs

---

[1] De Ferrières, i. 178.—Roux and Buchez, ii. 311, 316.—Bailly, ii. 104, 174, 207, 246, 257. 282.

[2] *Mercure de France*, September 5th, 1789. Horace Walpole's Letters, September 5, 1789.—M. de Lafayette, "Memoires," i. 272. During the week following the 14th of July, 6,000 soldiers deserted and went over to the people, besides 400 and 500 Swiss Guards and six battalions of the French Guards, who remain without officers and do as they please. Vagabonds from the neighbouring villages flock in, and there are more than "30,000 foreigners and vagrants" in Paris.

a debt of 14,000 livres for wine and sausages furnished to them, "they accustom themselves to greater expense," to greater license, and are followed by their companions. " During the night of the 31st of July the French Guards on duty at Versailles abandon the custody of the King and betake themselves to Paris, without their officers, but with their arms and baggage," that " they may take part in the cheer which the city of Paris extends to their regiment." At the beginning of September, 16,000 deserters of this stamp are counted.[1] Now, among those who commit murder these are in the first rank; and this is not surprising when we take the least account of their antecedents, education, and habits. It was a soldier of the " Royal Croat" who tore out the heart of Berthier. They were three soldiers of the regiment of Provence who forced the house of Chatel at Saint-Denis, and dragged his head through the streets. It is Swiss soldiers who, at Passy, knock down the commissioners of police with their guns. Their headquarters are at the Palais-Royal, amongst women whose instruments they are, and amongst agitators from whom they receive the word of command. Henceforth, all depends on this word, and we have only to contemplate the new popular leaders to know what it will be.

III.

Administrators and members of district assemblies, agitators of barracks, coffee-houses, clubs and public thoroughfares, writers of pamphlets, penny-a-liners are multiplying as fast as buzzing insects are hatched on a sultry night. After the 14th of July thousands of places have presented themselves to unrestrained ambitions ; "attorneys, notaries' clerks, artists, merchants, shopmen, comedians, and especially advocates ;[2] each wants to be either an officer, a director, a councillor, or a minister of the new reign ; while the

---

[1] Bailly, ii. 282. The crowd of deserters was so great that Lafayette was obliged to place a guard at the barriers to keep them from entering the city. " Without this precaution the whole army would have come in."

[2] De Ferrières, i. 103.—De Lavalette, i. 39.—Bailly, i. 53 (on the lawyers). "It may be said that the success of the Revolution is due to this class." Marmontel, ii. 243 " Since the first elections of Paris, in 1789, I remarked," he says, " this species of restless intriguing men, contending with each other to be heard, impatient to make themselves prominent. . . . It is well known what interest this body (the lawyers) had to change Reform into Revolution, the Monarchy into a Republic ; the object was to organize for itself a perpetual aristocracy."—Roux and Buchez, ii. 358 (article by C. Desmoulins). " In the districts everybody exhausts his lungs and his time in trying to be president, vice-president, secretary or vice-secretary."

journals, which are established by dozens,[1] form a permanent tribune, where orators come to court the people to their personal advantage." Philosophy, fallen into such hands, seems to parody itself, and nothing equals its emptiness, unless it be its mischievousness and success. Lawyers, in the sixty assembly districts, roll out the high-sounding dogmas of the revolutionary catechism. This or that one, passing from the question of a party wall to the constitution of empires, becomes the improvised legislator, so much the more inexhaustible and the more applauded as his flow of words, showered upon his hearers, proves to them that every capacity and every right are naturally and legitimately theirs. " When that man opened his mouth," says a cool-blooded witness, " we were sure of being inundated with quotations and maxims, often apropos of lanterns, or of the stall of a herb-dealer. His stentorian voice made the vaults ring ; and after he had spoken for two hours, and his breath was completely exhausted, the admiring and enthusiastic shouts which greeted him amounted almost to phrensy. Thus the orator fancied himself a Mirabeau, while the spectators imagined themselves the Constituent Assembly, deciding the fate of France." The journals and pamphlets are written in the same style. Every brain is filled with the fumes of conceit and of big words ; the leader of the crowd is he who raves the most, and he guides the wild enthusiasm which he increases.

Let us consider the most popular of these chiefs ; they are the green or the dry fruit of literature, and of the bar. The newspaper is the shop which every morning offers them for sale, and if

---

[1] Eugène Hatin, "Histoire de la Presse," vol. v.—*Le Patriote français* by Brissot, July 28, 1789.—*L'Ami du Peuple* by Marat, September 12, 1789.—*Annales patriotiques et littéraires* by Carra and Mercier, October 5, 1789.—*Les Révolutions de Paris*, chief editor Loustalot, July 17, 1789.—*Le Tribun du Peuple*, letters by Fauchet (middle of 1789).—*Révolutions de France et de Brabant* by C. Desmoulins, November 28, 1789 ; his *France libre* (I believe of the month of August, and his *Discours de la Lanterne*, of the month of September). The *Moniteur* does not make its appearance until November 24, 1789. In the seventy numbers which follow, up to February 3, 1790, the debates of the Assembly were afterwards written out, amplified, and put in a dramatic form. All numbers anterior to February 3, 1790, are the result of a compilation executed in the year iv. The narrative part during the first six months of the Revolution is of no value. The report of the sittings of the Assembly is more exact, but should be revised sitting by sitting and discourse by discourse for a detailed history of the National Assembly. The principal authorities which are really contemporary are, *Le Mercure de France, Le Journal de Paris, Le Point du Jour* by Barrère, the *Courrier de Versailles* by Gorsas, the *Courrier de Provence* by Mirabeau, the *Journal des Débats et Décrets*, the official reports of the National Assembly, the *Bulletin de l'Assemblée Nationale* by Marat, besides the newspapers above cited for the period following the 14th of July, and the speeches, which are printed separately.

they suit the over-excited public it is simply owing to their acid or bitter flavour. Their empty, unpractised minds are wholly void of political conceptions ; they have no capacity or practical experience. Desmoulins is twenty-nine years of age, Loustalot twenty-seven, and their intellectual ballast consists of college reminiscences, souvenirs of the law schools, and the common-places picked up in the houses of Raynal and his associates. As to Brissot and Marat, who are ostentatious humanitarians, their knowledge of France and of foreign countries consists in what they have seen through the dormer windows of their garrets, and through utopian spectacles. To minds of this class, empty or led astray, the *Contrat-Social* could not fail to be a gospel ; for it reduces political science to a strict application of an elementary axiom which relieves them of all study, and hands society over to the caprice of the people, or, in other words, delivers it into their own hands.—Hence they demolish all that remains of social insti-tutions, and push on equalisation until everything is brought down to a dead level. " With my principles," writes Desmoulins,[1] " is associated the satisfaction of putting myself where I belong, of show-ing my strength to those who have despised me, of lowering to my level all whom fortune has placed above me : my motto is that of all honest people—No superiors!" Thus, under the great name of Liberty, each vain spirit seeks its revenge and finds its nourish-ment. What. is sweeter and more natural than to justify passion by theory, to be factious in the belief that this is patriotism, and to cloak the interests of ambition with the interests of humanity ?

Let us picture to ourselves these directors of public opinion as we find them three months before this : Desmoulins, a briefless bar-rister, living in furnished lodgings with petty debts, and on a few louis extracted from his relations. Loustalot, still more unknown, was admitted the previous year to the Parliament of Bordeaux, and has landed at Paris in search of a career. Danton, another second-rate lawyer, coming out of a hovel in Champagne, borrowed the money to pay his expenses, while his stinted household is kept up only by means of a louis which is given to him weekly by his father-in-law, who is a coffee-house keeper. Brissot, a strolling

---

[1] C. Desmoulins, letters of September 20th and of subsequent dates. (He quotes a passage from Lucan in the sense indicated).– Brissot, " Mémoires," *passim.*—Biography of Danton by Robinet. (See the testimony of Madame Roland and of Rousselin de Saint-Albin.)

Bohemian, formerly employé of literary pirates, has roamed over the world for fifteen years, without bringing back with him either from England or America anything but a coat out at elbows and false ideas ; and, finally, Marat—a writer that has been hissed, an abortive scholar and philosopher, a misrepresenter of his own experiences, caught by the natural philosopher Charles in the act of committing a scientific fraud, and fallen from the top of his inordinate ambition to the subordinate post of doctor in the stables of the Comte d'Artois. At the present time, Danton, President of the Cordeliers, can arrest any one he pleases in his district, and his violent gestures and thundering voice secure to him, till something better turns up, the government of his section of the city. A word of Marat's has just caused Major Belzunce at Caen to be assassinated. Desmoulins announces, with a smile of triumph, that "a large section of the capital regards him as one among the principal authors of the Revolution, and that many even go so far as to say that he is *the* author of it." Is it to be supposed that, borne so high by such a sudden jerk of fortune, they wish to put on the drag and again descend? and is it not clear that they will aid with all their might the revolt which hoists them towards the loftiest summits? Moreover, the brain reels at a height like this ; suddenly launched in the air and feeling as if everything was tottering around them, they utter exclamations of indignation and terror, they see plots on all sides, imagine invisible cords pulling in an opposite direction, and they call upon the people to cut them. With the full weight of their inexperience, incapacity, and improvidence, of their fears, credulity, and dogmatic obstinacy, they urge on popular attacks, and their newspaper articles or discourses are all summed up in the following phrases: "Fellow-citizens, you, the people of the lower class, you who listen to me, you have enemies in the Court and the aristocracy. The Hôtel-de-Ville and the National Assembly are your servants. Seize your enemies with a strong hand, and hang them, and let your servants know that they must quicken their steps ! "

Desmoulins styles himself "Solicitor-General of the Lantern,"[1] and if he at all regrets the murders of Foulon and Berthier, it is because this too expeditious judgment has allowed the proofs of conspiracy to perish, thereby saving a number of traitors : he him-

---

[1] "Discours de la Lanterne."   See the epigraph of the engraving.

self mentions twenty of them haphazard, and little does he care whether he makes mistakes. "We are in the dark, and it is well that faithful dogs should bark, even at all who pass by, so that there may be no fear of robbers."

From this time forth Marat[1] denounces the King, the ministers, the administration, the bench, the bar, the financial system and the academies, all as " suspicious ; " at all events the people only suffer on their account. "The Government is monopolizing grain, so as to force us to buy bread which poisons us for its weight in gold." The Government, again, through a new conspiracy is about to blockade Paris, so as to starve it with greater ease. Utterances of this kind, at such a time, are firebrands thrown upon fear and hunger to kindle the flames of rage and cruelty. To this frightened and fasting crowd the agitators and newspaper writers continue to repeat that it must act, and act alongside of the authorities, and, if need be, against them. In other words, We will do as we please ; we are the sole legitimate masters ; " *in a well-constituted government, the people as a body are the real sove-reign :* our delegates are appointed only to execute our orders ; what right has the clay to rebel against the potter ? "

On the strength of such principles, the tumultuous club which occupies the Palais-Royal substitutes itself for the Assembly at Versailles. Has it not all the titles for this office ? The Palais-Royal " saved the nation " on the 12th and 13th of July. The Palais-Royal, " through its spokesmen and pamphlets," has made everybody and even the soldiers " philosophers." It is the house of patriotism, " the rendezvous of the select among the patriotic," whether provincials or Parisians, of all who possess the right of suffrage, and who cannot or will not exercise it in their own district. " It saves time to come to the Palais-Royal. There is no need there of appealing to the President for the right to speak, or to wait one's time for a couple of hours. The orator proposes his motion, and, if it finds supporters, mounts a chair. If he is applauded, it is put into proper shape. If he is hissed, he goes away. This was the way of the Romans." Behold the

---

[1] Roux and Buchez, iii. 55 ; article of Marat, October 1st. "Sweep all the suspected men out of the Hôtel-de-Ville. . . . Reduce the deputies of the communes to fifty ; do not let them remain in office more than a month or six weeks, and compel them to transact business only in public." And ii. 412, another article by Marat.—*Ibid.* iii. 21. An article by Loustalot.—C. Desmoulins, " Discours de la Lanterne," *passim.*—Bailly, ii. 326.

veritable National Assembly ! It is superior to the other semi-feudal affair, encumbered with " six hundred deputies of the clergy and nobility," who are so many intruders and who " should be sent out into the galleries."—Hence the pure Assembly rules the impure Assembly, and " the Café Foy lays claim to the government of France."

[Section IV of this chapter has been omitted.]

V.

Two distinct currents again combine in one torrent to hurry the crowd onward to a common end. On the one hand are the cravings of the stomach, and women excited by the famine : " Now that bread cannot be had in Paris, let us go to Versailles and demand it there ; once we have the King, Queen, and Dauphin in the midst of us, they will be obliged to feed us ; " we will bring back " the Baker, the Bakeress, and the Baker's boy." On the other hand, there is fanaticism, and men who are pushed on by the lust of dominion.   " Now that our chiefs yonder disobey us, let us go and make them obey us forthwith; the King is quibbling over the Constitution and the Rights of Man—let him give them his sanction ; his guards refuse to wear our cockade—let them accept it ; they want to carry him off to Metz—let him come to Paris ; here, under our eyes and in our hands, he, and the lame Assembly too, will march straight on, and quickly, whether they like it or not, and always on the right road."—Under this confluence of ideas the expedition is arranged.[1] Ten days before this, it is publicly alluded to at Versailles.   On the 4th of October, at Paris, a woman proposes it at the Palais-Royal ; Danton roars at the Cordeliers ; Marat, "alone, makes as much noise as the four trumpets on the Day of Judgment." Loustalot writes that " a second revolutionary paroxysm is necessary." " The day passes," says Desmoulins, " in holding councils at the Palais-Royal, and in the Faubourg Saint-Antoine, on the ends of the bridges, and on the quays. . . . in pulling off the cockades of but one colour. . . . These are torn off and trampled under foot with threats of the lantern, in case of fresh offence ; a soldier who is

---

[1] " Procédure criminelle du Châtelet," Deposition 148.—Roux and Buchez, iii. 67, 65. (Narrative of Desmoulins, article of Loustalot.) *Mercure de France,* number for September 5, 1789. " Sunday evening, August 30, at the Palais-Royal, the expulsion of several deputies of every class was demanded, and especially some of those from Dauphiny. . . . They spoke of bringing the King to Paris as well as the Dauphin. All virtuous citizens, every incorruptible patriot, was exhorted to set out immediately for Versailles."

trying to refasten his, changes his mind on seeing a hundred sticks raised against him."[1] These are the premonitory symptoms of a crisis ; a huge ulcer has formed in this feverish, suffering body, and it is about to break.

But, as is usually the case, it is a purulent concentration of the most poisonous passions and the foulest motives. The vilest of men and women were engaged in it. Money was freely distributed. Was it done by intriguing subalterns who, playing upon the aspirations of the Duke of Orleans, extracted millions from him under the pretext of making him lieutenant-general of the kingdom? Or is it due to the fanatics who, from the end of April, clubbed together to debauch the soldiery, and stir up a body of ruffians for the purpose of levelling and destroying everything around them?[2] There are always Machiavellis of the highways and of houses of ill-fame ready to excite the foul and the vile of both sexes. On the first day that the Flemish regiment goes into garrison at Versailles an attempt is made to corrupt it with money and women. Sixty abandoned women are sent from Paris for this purpose, while the French Guards come and treat their new comrades. The latter have been regaled at the Palais-Royal, while three of them, at Versailles, exclaim, showing some crown pieces of six livres, "What a pleasure it is to go to Paris ! one always comes back with money !" In this way, resistance is overcome beforehand. As to the attack, women are to be the advanced guard, because the soldiers will scruple to fire at them ; their ranks, however, will be reinforced by a number of men disguised as women. On looking closely at them they are easily recognised, notwithstanding their rouge, by

---

[1] These acts of violence were not reprisals ; nothing of the kind took place at the banquet of the body-guards (October 1st). "Amidst the general joy," says an eye-witness, "I heard no insults against the National Assembly, nor against the popular party, nor against anybody. The only cries were ' *Vive le Roi! Vive la Reine!* We will defend them to the death !' " (Madame de Larochejacquelein, p. 40. *Ibid.* Madame Campan, another eye-witness.) It appears to be certain, however, that the younger members of the National Guard at Versailles turned their cockades so as to be like other people, and it is also probable that some of the ladies distributed white cockades. The rest is a story made up before and after the event to justify the insurrection. Cf. Leroi, " Histoire de Versailles," ii. 20—107. *Ibid.* p. 141. "As to that proscription of the national cockade, all witnesses deny it." The originator of the calumny is Gorsas, editor of the *Courrier de Versailles.*

[2] "Procédure Criminelle du Châtelet." Depositions 88, 110, 120, 126, 127, 140, 146, 148. —Marmontel, " Mémoires," a conversation with Champfort, in May, 1789.—Morellet, " Mémoires," i. 398. (According to the evidence of Garat, Champfort gave all his savings, 3,000 livres, to defray the expenses of manœuvres of this description.)—Malouet (ii. 2). knew four of the deputies " who took direct part in this transaction."

their badly-shaven beards, and by their voices and gait.[1] No
difficulty has been found in obtaining men and women among the
prostitutes of the Palais-Royal and the military deserters who
serve them as bullies. It is probable that the former lent their
lovers the cast-off dresses they had to spare. At night all will
meet again at the common rendezvous, on the benches of the
National Assembly, where they are quite as much at home as in
their own houses.[2]—In any event, the first band which marches
out is of this stamp, displaying the finery and the gaiety of the
profession ; " most of them young, dressed in white, with powdered
hair and a sprightly air ; " many of them " laughing, singing, and
drinking," as they would do at setting out for a picnic in the
country. Three or four of them are known by name—one brandishing a sword, and another, the notorious Théroigne. Madeleine
Chabry Louison, who is selected to address the King, is a pretty
grisette who sells flowers, and something else doubtless, at the
Palais-Royal. Some appear to belong to the first rank in their
calling, and to have tact and the manners of society—suppose,
for instance, that Champfort and Laclos sent their mistresses. To
these must be added washerwomen, beggars, bare-footed women,
and fishwomen, enlisted for several days before and paid accordingly.
This is the first nucleus, and it keeps on growing ; for, by com-
pulsion or consent, the troop incorporates into it, as it passes
along, all the women it encounters—seamstresses, portresses,
housekeepers, and even respectable females, whose dwellings are
entered with threats of cutting off their hair if they do not fall in.
To these must be added vagrants, street-rovers, ruffians and robbers
—the lees of Paris, which accumulate and come to the surface
every time agitation occurs : they are to be found already at the
first hour, behind the troop of women at the Hôtel-de-Ville.
Others are to follow during the evening and in the night. Others
are waiting at Versailles. Many, both at Paris and Versailles,
are under pay : one, in a dirty whitish vest, chinks gold and silver
coin in his hand.—Such is the foul scum which, both in front and

---

[1] " Procédure Criminelle du Châtelet." 1st. On the Flemish soldiers. Depositions 17,
20, 24, 35, 87, 89, 98.—2nd. On the men disguised as women. Depositions 5, 10, 14, 44, 49,
59, 60, 110, 120, 139, 145, 146, 148. The prosecutor designates six of them to be seized.—
3rd. On the condition of the women of the expedition. Depositions 35, 83, 91, 98, 146,
and 24.—4th. On the money distributed. Depositions 49, 56, 71, 82, 110, 126.
[2] " Procédure Criminelle du Châtelet." Deposition 61. " During the night scenes, not
very decent, occurred among these people, which the witness thought it useless to
relate."

in the rear, rolls along with the popular tide ; whatever is done to stem the torrent, it widens out and will leave its mark at every stage of its overflow.

The first troop, consisting of four or five hundred women, begin operations by forcing the guard of the Hôtel-de-Ville, which is unwilling to make use of its bayonets. They spread through the rooms and try to burn all the written documents they can find, declaring that there has been nothing but scribbling since the Revolution began.[1] A crowd of men follow after them, bursting open doors, and pillaging the magazine of arms. Two hundred thousand francs in Treasury notes are stolen or disappear; several of the ruffians set fire to the building, while others hang an abbé. The abbé is cut down, and the fire extinguished only just in time: such are the interludes of the popular drama. In the meantime, the crowd of women increases on the Place de Grève, always with the same unceasing cry, " Bread !" and "To Versailles !" One of the conquerors of the Bastille the usher Maillard, offers himself as a leader. He is accepted, and taps his drum ; on leaving Paris, he has seven or eight thousand women with him, and, in addition, some hundreds of men ; by dint of remonstrances, he succeeds in maintaining some kind of order amongst this rabble as far as Versailles.—But it is a rabble notwithstanding, and consequently so much brute force, at once anarchical and imperious. On the one hand, each, and the worst among them, does what he pleases— which will be quite evident this very evening. On the other hand, its ponderous mass crushes all authority and overrides all rules and regulations—which is at once apparent on reaching Versailles. Admitted into the Assembly, at first in small numbers, the women crowd against the door, push in with a rush, fill the galleries, then the hall, the men along with them, armed with clubs, halberds, and pikes, all pell-mell, side by side with the deputies, taking possession of their benches, voting along with them, and gathering about the President, who, surrounded, threatened, and insulted, finally abandons the position, while his chair is taken by a woman.[2]

---

[1] " Procédure Criminelle du Châtelet." Depositions 35, 44, 81.—Roux and Buchez, iii. 120. (Procès-verbal of the Commune, October 5th.) *Journal de Paris*, October 12th. A few days after, M. Pic, clerk of the prosecutor, brought " a package of 100,000 francs which he had saved from the enemies' hands," and another package of notes was found thrown, in the hubbub, into a receipt-box.

[2] " Procédure Criminelle du Châtelet." Depositions 61, 77, 81, 148, 154.—Dumont, 181. —Mounier, " Exposé justificatif," *passim*.

A fishwoman commands in a gallery, and about a hundred women around her shout or keep silence at her bidding, while she interrupts and abuses the deputies : " Who is that spouter ? Silence that babbler ; he does not know what he is talking about. The question is how to get bread. Let papa Mirabeau speak—we want to hear him." A decree on subsistences having been passed, the leaders demand something in addition ; they must be allowed to enter all places where they suspect any monopolizing to be going on, and the price of " bread must be fixed at six sous the four pounds, and meat at six sous per pound." " You must not think that we are children to be played with. We are ready to strike. Do as you are bidden."—All their political injunctions emanate from this central idea. " Send back the Flemish regiment—it is a thousand men more to feed, and they take bread out of our mouths." " Punish the aristocrats, who hinder the bakers from baking." " Down with the skull-cap—the priests are the cause of our trouble ! " " Monsieur Mounier, why did you advocate that villainous veto ? Beware of the lantern ! " Under this pressure, a deputation of the Assembly, with the President at its head, sets out on foot, in the mud, through the rain, and watched by a howling escort of women and men armed with pikes : after five hours of waiting and entreaty, it wrings from the King, besides the decree on subsistences, about which there was no difficulty, the acceptance, pure and simple, of the Declaration of Rights, and his sanction to the constitutional articles.—Such is the independence of the King and the Assembly.[1]   Thus are the new principles of justice established, the grand outlines of the Constitution, the abstract axioms of political truth under the dictation of a crowd which extorts not only blindly, but which is half-conscious of its blindness.   " Monsieur le Président," some among the women say to Mounier, who returns with the Royal sanction, " will it be of any real use to us ? will it give poor folks bread in Paris ? "

Meanwhile, the scum has been bubbling up around the chateau ; and the abandoned women subsidised in Paris are pursuing their

---

[1] " Procédure Criminelle du Châtelet." Deposition 168. The witness sees on leaving the King's apartment " several women dressed as fish-dealers, one of whom, with a pretty face, has a paper in her hand, and who exclaims as she holds it up, ' Heh ! we forced him to sign.' "

calling.[1]   They slip through into the lines of the regiment drawn
up on the square, in spite of the sentinels.   Théroigne, in an
Amazonian red vest, distributes money among them.   " Side with
us," some say to the men ; " we shall soon beat the King's Guards,
strip off their fine coats and sell them."   Others lie sprawling on
the ground, alluring the soldiers, and make such offers as to lead
one of them to exclaim, " We are going to have a jolly time of
it ! "   Before the day is over, the regiment is seduced ; the women
have, according to their own idea, acted for a good motive.   When
a political idea finds its way into such heads, instead of ennobling
them, it becomes degraded there ; its only effect is to let loose
vices which a remnant of modesty still keeps in subjection, and
full play is given to luxurious or ferocious instincts under cover
of the public good.—The passions, moreover, become intensified
through their mutual interaction ; crowds, clamour, disorder, long-
ings, and fasting, end in a state of phrensy, from which nothing
can issue but dizzy madness and rage.—This phrensy began to
show itself on the way.   Already, on setting out, a woman had
exclaimed, " We shall bring back the Queen's head on the end of
a pike ! "[2]   On reaching the Sevres bridge others added, " Let us
cut her throat, and make cockades of her entrails ! "   Rain is falling ; they are cold, tired, and hungry, and get nothing to eat but
a bit of bread, distributed at a late hour, and with difficulty, on
the Place d'Armes.   One of the bands cuts up a slaughtered
horse, roasts it, and consumes it half raw, after the manner of
savages.   It is not surprising that, under the names of patriotism
and " justice," savage ideas spring up in their minds against
"members of the National Assembly who are not with the principles of the people," against " the Bishop of Langres, Mounier,
and the rest."   One man in a ragged old red coat declares that
" he must have the head of the Abbé Maury to play nine-pins
with."   But it is especially against the Queen, who is a woman,
and in sight, that the feminine imagination is the most aroused.
" She alone is the cause of the evils we endure .... she must be

---

[1] " Procédure Criminelle du Châtelet."   Depositions 89, 91, 98.   " Promising all, even
raising their petticoats before them."
[2] " Procédure Criminelle du Châtelet."   Depositions 9, 20, 24, 30, 49, 61, 82, 115, 149,
155.

killed, and quartered."—Night advances ; there are acts of violence, and violence engenders violence. " How glad I should be," says one man, " if I could only lay my hand on that she-devil, and strike off her head on the first curbstone ! " Towards morning, some cry out, " Where is that cursed cat ? We must eat her heart out. ...We'll take off her head, cut her heart out, and fry her liver ! "—With the first murders the appetite for blood has been awakened ; the women from Paris say that " they have brought tubs to carry away the stumps of the Royal Guards," and at these words others clap their hands. Some of the riff-raff of the crowd examine the rope of the lantern in the court of the National Assembly, and judging it not to be sufficiently strong, are desirous of supplying its place with another " to hang the Archbishop of Paris, Maury, and d'Esprémenil."—This murderous, carnivorous rage penetrates even among those whose duty it is to maintain order, one of the National Guard being heard to say that " the body-guards must be killed to the last man, and their hearts torn out for a breakfast."

Finally, towards midnight, the National Guard of Paris arrives; but it only adds one insurrection to another, for it has likewise mutinied against its chiefs.[1] " If M. de Lafayette is not disposed to accompany us," says one of the grenadiers, " we will take an old grenadier for our commander." Having come to this de-cision, they go after the general at the Hôtel-de-Ville, while delegates of six of the companies make known their orders to him. " General, we do not believe that you are a traitor, but we think that the Government is betraying us. . . . The committee on subsistences is deceiving us, and must be removed. We want to go to Versailles to exterminate the body-guard and the Flemish regiment who have trampled on the national cockade. If the King of France is too feeble to wear his crown, let him take it off ; we will crown his son and things will go better." In vain Lafayette refuses, and harangues them on the Place de Grève ; in vain he resists for hours, now addressing them and now imposing silence. Armed bands, coming from the Faubourgs Saint-Antoine and Saint-Marceau, swell the crowd ; they take aim at him ; others prepare the lantern. He then dismounts and endeavours to return to the Hôtel-de-Ville, but his grenadiers bar the way:

---

[1] " Procédure Criminelle du Châtelet." Depositions 7, 30, 35, 40.—Cf. Lafayette, " Mémoires," and Madame Campan, " Mémoires."

" *Morbleu*, General, you will stay with us ; you will not abandon us ! " Being their chief it is pretty plain that he must follow them ; which is also the sentiment of the representatives of the commune at the Hôtel-de-Ville, who send him their authorisation, and even the order to march, " seeing that it is impossible for him to refuse."

Fifteen thousand men thus reach Versailles, and in front of and along with them thousands of ruffians, protected by the darkness. On this side the National Guard of Versailles, posted around the chateau, together with the people of Versailles, who bar the way against vehicles, have closed up every outlet.[1] The King is prisoner in his own palace, he and his, with his ministers and his court, and with no defence. For, with his usual optimism, he has confided the outer posts of the chateau to Lafayette's soldiers, and, through a humanitarian obstinacy which he is to maintain up to the last,[2] he has forbidden his own guards to fire on the crowd, so that they are only there for show. With common right in his favour, the law, and the oath which Lafayette had just obliged his troops to renew, what could he have to fear ? What could be more effective with the people than trust in them and prudence ? And by playing the sheep one is sure of taming brutes !

From five o'clock in the morning they prowl around the palace-railings. Lafayette, exhausted with fatigue, has taken an hour's repose,[3] which hour suffices for them.[4] A populace armed with pikes and clubs, men and women, surrounds a squad of eighty-eight National Guards, forces them to fire on the King's Guards, bursts open a door, seizes two of the guards and chops their heads off. The executioner, who is a studio model, with a heavy beard, stretches out his blood-stained hands and glories in the act ; and so great is the effect on the National Guard that they move off,

---

[1] " Procédure Criminelle du Châtelet." Deposition 24. A number of butcher-boys run after the carriages issuing from the *Petite-Ecurie* shouting out, " Don't let the curs escape ! "

[2] " Procédure Criminelle du Châtelet." Depositions 101, 91, 89, and 17. M. de Miomandre, a body-guard, mildly says to the ruffians mounting the staircase : " My friends, you love your King, and yet you come to annoy him even in his palace ! "

[3] Malouet, II. 2. " I felt no distrust," says Lafayette in 1798 ; " the people promised to remain quiet."

[4] " Procédure Criminelle du Châtelet." Depositions 9, 16, 60, 128, 129, 130, 139, 158, 168, 170. M. du Repaire, body-guard, being sentry at the railing from two o'clock in the morning, a man passes his pike through the bars saying, " You embroidered —— ——, your turn will come before long." M. du Repaire, " retires within the sentry-box without saying a word to this man, considering the orders that have been issued not to act."

through sensibility, in order not to witness such sights : such is the resistance ! In the meantime the crowd invade the staircases, beat down and trample on the guards they encounter, and burst open the doors with imprecations against the Queen. The Queen runs off, just in time, in her underclothes ; she takes refuge with the King and the rest of the royal family, who have in vain barricaded themselves in the Œil-de-Bœuf, a door of which is broken in : here they stand, awaiting death, when Lafayette arrives with his grenadiers and saves all that can be saved—their lives, and nothing more. For, from the crowd huddled in the marble court the shout rises, " To Paris with the King ! " a command to which the King submits.

Now that the great hostage is in their hands, will they deign to accept the second one ? This is doubtful. On the Queen approaching the balcony with her son and daughter, a howl arises of " No children ! " She is the one they want to cover with their guns—and this she comprehends. At this moment M. de Lafayette, throwing the shield of his popularity over her, appears on the balcony at her side and respectfully kisses her hand. The reaction is instantaneous in this over-excited crowd. Both man and woman, in such a state of nervous tension, readily jump from one extreme to another, rage bordering on tears. A portress, who is a companion of Maillard's,[1] imagines that she hears Lafayette promise in the Queen's name " to love her people and be as much attached to them as Jesus Christ to his Church." People sob and embrace each other ; the grenadiers shift their caps to the heads of the body-guard. The good time has come : " the people have got back their King." Nothing is to be done now but to rejoice ; and the cortège moves on. The royal family and a hundred deputies, in carriages, form the centre, and then comes the artillery, with a number of women bestriding the cannons ; next, a convoy of flour. Round about are the King's Guards, each with a National Guard mounted behind him ; then comes the National Guard of Paris, and after them men with pikes and women on foot, on horseback, in cabs, and on carts ; in front is a band bearing two severed heads on the ends of two poles, which halts at a hairdresser's, in Sèvres, to have these

---

[1] "Procédure Criminelle du Châtelet." Depositions 82, 170.—Madame Campan. ii. 87 —De Lavalette, i. 33.—Cf. Bertrand de Molleville, " Mémoires."

heads powdered and curled ;[1] they are made to bow by way of salutation, and are daubed all over with cream ; there are jokes and shouts of laughter ; the people stop to eat and drink on the road, and oblige the guards to clink glasses with them ; they shout and fire salvos of musketry ; men and women hold each other's hands and sing and dance about in the mud.—Such is the new fraternity—a funeral procession of legal and legitimate authorities, a triumph of brutality over intelligence, a murderous and political Mardi-gras, a formidable masquerade which, preceded by the insignia of death, drags along with it the heads of France, the King, the ministers, and the deputies, that it may constrain them to rule according to its phrensy, that it may hold them under its pikes until it is pleased to slaughter them.

[Section VI of this chapter has been omitted.]

---

[1] Duval, " Souvenirs de la Terreur," i. 78. (Doubtful in almost everything, but here he is an eye-witness. He dined opposite the hair-dresser's, near the railing of the Park of Saint-Cloud.) M. de Lally-Tollendal's second letter to a friend. " At the moment the King entered his capital with two bishops of his council with him in the carriage, the cry was heard, "Off to the lantern with the bishops ! "

THE REVOLUTION

VOLUME II

PREFACE.

In this volume, as in those preceding it and in those to come, there will be found only the history of Public Powers. Other historians will write that of diplomacy, of war, of the finances, of the Church: my subject is a limited one. To my great regret, however, this new part fills an entire volume; and the last part, on the revolutionary government, will be as long.

I have again to regret the dissatisfaction which I foresee this work will cause to many of my countrymen. My excuse is, that almost all of them, more fortunate than myself, have political principles which serve them in forming their judgments of the past. I had none; if, indeed, I had any motive in undertaking this work, it was to seek for political principles. Thus far I have attained to scarcely more than one; and this is so simple that it will seem puerile, and that I hardly dare enunciate it. Nevertheless I have adhered to it, and in what the reader is about to peruse my judgments are all derived from that; its truth is the measure of theirs. It consists wholly in this observation: that *human society, especially a modern society, is a vast and complicated thing.* Hence the difficulty in knowing and comprehending it. For the same reason it is not easy to handle the subject well. It follows that a cultivated mind is much better able to do this than an uncultivated mind, and a man specially qualified than one who is not. From these two last truths flow many other consequences, which, if the reader deigns to reflect on them, he will have no trouble in defining.

BOOK FOURTH.

The Jacobin Conquest.

CHAPTER II.

I. Formation of the party.—Its recruits.—These are rare in the upper class and amongst the masses.—They are numerous in the low bourgeois class and in the upper stratum of the people.—The position and education which enroll a man in the party.—II. Spontaneous associations after July 14, 1789.—How these dissolve.—Withdrawal of people of sense and occupation.—Number of those absent at elections.—Birth and multiplication of Jacobin societies.—Their influence over their adherents—Their manoeuvres and despotism.—V. Small number of Jacobins.—Sources of their power.—They form a league.—They have faith.—Their unscrupulousness.—The power of the party vested in the group which best fulfills these conditions.

I.

CHARACTERS of this sort are found in all classes of society ; no situation or position in life protects one from wild Utopias or frantic ambition. We find among the Jacobins a Barras and a Châteauneuf-Randon, two nobles of the oldest families, Condorcet, a marquis, mathematician, philosopher and member of two renowned academies, Gobel, bishop of Lydda and suffragan to the bishop of Bâle, Hérault de Séchelles, a protégé of the Queen's and attorney-general to the Paris parliament, Lepelletier de St. Fargeau, chief-justice and one of the richest land-owners in France, Charles de Hesse, major-general, born in a royal family, and, last of all, a prince of the blood and fourth personage in the realm, the Duke of Orleans.—But, with the exception of these rare deserters, neither the hereditary aristocracy nor the upper magistracy, nor the highest of the middle class, none of the land-owners who live on their estates, or the leaders of industrial and commercial enterprises, no one belonging to the administration, none of those, in general, who are or deserve to

be considered social authorities, furnish the party with recruits;
all have too much at stake in the political edifice, shattered as it
is, to wish its entire demolition; their political experience, brief
as it is, enables them to see at once that a habitable house is not
built by merely tracing a plan of it on paper according to the
theorems of school geometry.—On the other hand, the theory in
the lower class, among the mass of rustics and the populace,
unless transformed into a shibboleth, finds no listeners. Métayers, farmers, and small cultivators looking after their own plots
of ground, peasants and craftsmen who work too hard to think
and whose minds never range beyond a village horizon, busy
only with that which brings them in their daily bread, find
abstract doctrines unintelligible; should the dogmas of the new
catechism arrest their attention the same thing happens as with
the old one, they do not understand them; that mental faculty
by which an abstraction is reached is not yet formed in them.
On being taken to a political club they fall asleep; they open
their eyes only when some one announces that tithes and feudal
privileges are to be restored; they can be depended on for
nothing more than a broil and a *jacquerie;* later on, when their
grain comes to be taxed or is taken, they prove as refractory
under the republic as under the monarchy.

The adepts in this theory come from other quarters, from the
two extremes of the lower stratum of the middle class and the
upper stratum of the low class. Again, in these two contiguous
groups, which merge into each other, those must be left out who,
absorbed in their daily occupations or professions, have no time
or thought to give to public matters, who have reached a fair
position in the social hierarchy and are not disposed to run
risks, almost all of them well-established, steady-going, mature,
married folks who have sown their wild oats and whom some
experience in life has rendered distrustful of themselves and of
theories. Overweening conceit is average in average human
nature at all times, and with most men speculative ideas obtain
but a loose, transient and feeble hold. Moreover, in this society
which, for many centuries consists of people accustomed to being
ruled, the hereditary spirit is *bourgeoi* , that is to say, used to discipline, fond of order, peaceable and even timid. There
remains a minority, a very small one,[1] innovating and restless

[1] See the figure further on.

consisting. on the one hand, of people who are discontented with their calling or profession, because they are of secondary or subaltern rank in it,[1] debutants not fully employed and aspirants for careers not yet entered upon; and, on the other hand, of men of unstable character, all who are uprooted by the immense upheaval of things; in the Church, through the suppression of convents and through schism; in the judiciary, in the administration, in the financial departments, in the army, and in various private and public careers, through the reorganisation of institutions, through the novelty of fresh resources and occupations, and through the disturbance caused by the changed relationships of patrons and clients.   Many who, in ordinary times, would otherwise remain quiet, become in this way nomadic and extravagant in politics.   Among the foremost of these are found those who, through a classical education, can take in an abstract proposition and deduce its consequences, but who, for lack of special preparation for it, and confined to the narrow circle of local affairs, are incapable of forming accurate conceptions of a vast, complex social organisation, and of the conditions which enable it to subsist.   Their talent lies in making a speech, in dashing off an editorial, in composing a pamphlet, and in drawing up reports in more or less pompous and dogmatic style, and, if we accept the kind, a few of them who are gifted become eloquent, but that is all.   Those who take leading parts, lawyers, notaries, bailiffs and former petty provincial judges and attorneys, are of this class, two-thirds of the members of the Legislative Assembly and of the Convention, surgeons and doctors in small towns, like Bo, Levasseur, and Baudot, second and third-rate literary characters, like Barrère, Louvet, Garat, Manuel, and Ronsin, college professors like Louchet and Romme, schoolmasters like Leonard Bourdon, journalists like Brissot, Desmou-

---

[1] Mallet-Dupan, II. 491.   Danton, in 1793, said one day to one of his former brethren, an advocate to the Council: "The old régime made a great mistake. It brought me up on a scholarship in Plessis College. I was brought up with nobles, who were my comrades, and with whom I lived on familiar terms. On completing my studies, I had nothing; I was poor, and tried to get a place. The Paris bar was unapproachable, and it required an effort to be accepted. I could not get into the army, without either rank or a patron. There was no opening for me in the Church. I could purchase no employment, for I hadn't a cent. My old companions turned their backs on me. I remained without a situation, and only after many long years did I succeed in buying the post of advocate in the Royal Council. The Revolution came, when I, and all like me, threw themselves into it. The ancient régime forced us to do so, by providing a good education for us, without providing an opening for our talents."   This applies to Robespierre, C. Desmoulins, Brissot, Vergniaud, and others.

iins and Fréron, actors like Collot d Herbois, artists like **Sergent,** *Oratoriens* like Fouché, capuchins like Chabot, more or less secularised priests like Lebon, Chasles, Lakanal, and Grégoire, students scarcely out of school like St. Just, Monet of Strasbourg, Rousselin of St. Albin, and Julien of the Drôme—in short, badly-cultivated minds sown with poor seed, and in which the theory had only to fall to kill out every good seed and thrive like nettles. Add to these the charlatans and others who live by their wits, the visionary and morbid of all sorts, from Fanchet and Klootz to Châlier or Marat, the whole of that needy, chattering, irresponsible crowd, ever swarming about large cities ventilating its shallow conceits and abortive pretensions. Farther in the background appear those whose scanty education qualifies them to half understand an abstract principle and imperfectly deduce its consequences, but whose roughly-polished instinct atones for the feebleness of a coarse argumentation; through cupidity, envy and rancor, they divine a rich pasture-ground behind the theory, and Jacobin dogmas become dearer to them, because the imagination sees untold treasures beyond the mists in which they are shrouded. They can listen to a club harangue without falling asleep, applaud its tirades in the right place, offer a resolution in a public garden, shout in the tribunes, pen affidavits for arrests, compose orders-of-the-day for the national guard, and lend their lungs, arms, and sabres to whoever bids for them. But here their capacity ends. In this group merchants' and notaries' clerks abound, like Hébert and Henriot, Vincent, and Chaumette, butchers like Legendre, postmasters like Drouet, boss-joiners like Duplay, school-teachers like that Buchot who becomes a minister, and many others of the same sort, accustomed to jotting down ideas, with vague notions of orthography and who are apt in speech-making,[1] foremen, sub-officers, former mendicant monks, pedlars, tavern-keepers, retailers, market-porters,[2] and city-journeymen from Gouchon, the

---

[1] Dauban, "La Demagogie à Paris en 1793," and "Paris in 1794." Read General Henriot's orders of the day in these two works. Compardon, "Histoire du Tribunal Révolutionnaire de Paris," a letter by Trinchard, I. 306 (which is here given in the original, on account of the orthography): "Si tu nest pas toute seulle et que le compagnion soit a trᵃvalier tu peus ma chaire amie venir voir juger 24 mesieurs tous si devent président ou corᵃselier au parlement de Paris et de Toulouse. Je t'ainvite a prendre quelque choge aven de venu parcheque nous naurons pas fini de 3 heures. et embrase ma chaire amie et epouge." *Ibid.*, II, 350, examination of André Chenier.—Wallon, "Hist. du Trib. Rév.", I, 316 Letter by Simon. "Je te coitte le bonjour mois est mon est pousse."

[2] "Forts de la Halle." They assumed the title of "Les forts pour la patrie."

orator of the faubourg St. Antoine, down to Simon, the cobbler of the Temple, from Trinchard, the juryman of the Revolutionary Tribunal, down to grocers, tailors, shoemakers, tapsters, waiters, barbers, and other shopkeepers or artisans who do their work at home, and who are yet to do the work of the September massacres. Add to these the foul remnants of every popular insurrection and dictatorship, beasts of prey like Jourdain of Avignon, and Fournier the American, women like Théroigne, Rose Lacombe, and the *tricoteuses* of the Convention who have unsexed themselves, the amnestied bandits and other gallows-birds who, for lack of a police, have a wide range, street-strollers and vagabonds, rebels against labor and discipline, the whole of that class in the centre of civilisation which preserves the instincts of savages, and asserts the sovereignty of the people to glut a natural appetite for license, laziness, and ferocity.

Thus is the party recruited through an enlisting process that gleans its subjects from every station in life, but which reaps them down in great swaths, and gathers them together in the two groups to which dogmatism and presumption naturally belong. Here, education has brought man to the threshold, and even to the heart of general ideas; consequently, he feels hampered within the narrow bounds of his profession or occupation, and aspires to something beyond. But as his education has remained superficial or rudimentary, consequently, outside of his narrow circle he feels out of his place. He has a perception or obtains a glimpse of political ideas and, therefore, assumes that he has capacity. But his perception of them is confined to a formula, or he sees them dimly through a cloud; hence his incapacity, and the reason why his mental *lacunæ* as well as his attainments both contribute to make him a Jacobin.

II.

Men thus disposed cannot fail to draw near each other, to understand each other, and combine together; for, in the principle of popular sovereignty, they have a common dogma, and, in the conquest of political supremacy, a common aim. Through a common aim they form a faction, and through a common dogma they constitute a sect, the league between them being more easily effected because they are a faction and sect at the same time.—

At first, their association is not distinguishable in the multitude of other associations. Political societies spring up on all sides after the taking of the Bastille. Some kind of organisation had to be substituted for the deposed or tottering government, in order to provide for urgent public needs, to secure protection against ruffians, to obtain supplies of provisions, and to guard against the probable machinations of the court. Committees installed themselves in the Hotels-de-ville, while volunteers formed bodies of militia : hundreds of local governments, almost independent, arose in the place of the central government, almost destroyed.[1]   For six months everybody attended to matters of common interest, each individual getting to be a public person-age and bearing his quota of the government load—a heavy load at all times, but heavier in times of anarchy ; this, at least, is the opinion of the greatest number, but not the opinion of some of them.   Consequently, a division arises amongst those who had assumed this load, and two groups are formed, one huge, inert and disintegrating, and the other small, compact and ener-getic, each taking one of two ways which diverge from each other, and which keep on diverging more and more.

On the one hand are the ordinary, sensible people, those who are busy, and who are, to some extent, not over-conscientious, and not over-conceited.   The power in their hands is assumed by them because they find it prostrate, lying abandoned in the street ; they hold it provisionally only, for they knew before-hand, or soon discover, that they are not qualified for the post, it being one of those which, to be properly filled, needs some preparation and fitness for it.   A man does not become legislator or administrator in one day, any more than he suddenly becomes a physician or surgeon.   If an accident obliges me to act in the latter capacity, I yield, but against my will, and I do no more than is necessary to save my patients from hurting themselves ; my fear of their dying under the operation is very great, and, as soon as some other person can be got to take my place, I go home.[2]   I should be glad, like everybody else, to have my vote in the selection of this person, and, among the candidates, I should designate, to the best of my ability, one who seemed to

---

[1] Cf. "The Revolution," page 60.
[2] Cf. on this point the admissions of the honest Bailly ("Mémoires," *passim*)

me the ablest and most conscientious.   Once selected, however,
and installed, I should not attempt to dictate to him; his cabinet is private, and I have no right to run there constantly and
cross-question him, as if he were a child or under suspicion.   It
does not become me to tell him what to do; he probably knows
more about the case than I do; in any event, to keep a steady
hand, he must not be threatened, and, to keep a clear head, he
must not be disturbed.—Nor must I be disturbed; my office and
books, my shop, my customers must be attended to as well.
Everybody has to mind his own business, and whoever would
attend to his own and another's too, spoils both.

This way of thinking prevails with most healthy minds towards
the beginning of the year 1790, all whose heads are not turned
by insane ambition and the mania for theorising, especially after
six months of practical experience and knowing the dangers,
miscalculations, and vexations to which one is exposed in trying
to lead an eager, over-excited population.—Just at this time,
December, 1789, municipal law becomes established throughout
the country; all the mayors and municipal officers are elected
almost immediately, and in the following months, all administrators of districts and departments.   The interregnum has at length
come to an end.   Legal authorities now exist, with legitimate and
clearly-determined functions.   Reasonable, honest people gladly
turn power over to those to whom it belongs, and certainly do
not dream of resuming it.   All associations for temporary purposes are at once disbanded for lack of an object, and if others
are formed, it is for the purpose of defending established
institutions.   This is the object of the Federation, and, for six
months, people embrace each other and exchange oaths of
fidelity.   After this, July 14, 1790, they retire into private life,
and I have no doubt that, from this date, the political ambition
of a large plurality of the French people is satisfied, for, although
Rousseau's denunciations of the social hierarchy are still cited
by them, they, at bottom, desire but little more than the suppression of administrative brutality and state favoritism.[1]   All this
is obtained, and plenty of other things besides; the august title

---

[1] Rétif de la Bretonne: "Nuits de Paris," 11ème nuit, p. 36.   "I lived in Paris twenty-
five years as free as air.   All could enjoy as much freedom as myself in two ways—by
living uprightly, and by not writing pamphlets against the ministry.   All else was permitted, my freedom never being interfered with.   It is only since the Revolution that a
scoundrel could succeed in having me arrested twice."

of sovereign, the deference of the public authorities, the salutations of all who wield a pen or make a speech, and, still better,
actual sovereignty in the appointment to office of all local and
national administrators; not only do the people elect their deputies, but every species of functionary of every degree, those of
commune, district, and department, officers in the national guard,
civil and criminal magistrates, bishops and curés. Again, to
ensure the responsibility of the elected to their electors, the term
of office fixed by law is a short one,[1] the electoral machine which
summons the sovereign to exercise his sovereignty being set
agoing about every four months.

This was a good deal, and too much, as the sovereign himself
soon discovers. Voting so frequently becomes unendurable; so
many prerogatives end in getting to be drudgery. Early in
1790, and after this date, the majority forego the privilege of
voting and the number of absentees becomes enormous. At
Chartres, in May, 1790,[2] 1,447 out of 1,551 voters do not attend
preliminary meetings. At Besançon, in January, 1790, on the
election of mayor and municipal officers, 2,141 out of 3,200
registered electors are recorded as absent from the polls, and
2,900 in the following month of November.[3] At Grenoble, in
August and November of this year, out of 2,500 registered
voters, more than 2,000 are noted as absent.[4] At Limoges, out
of about the same number, there are only 150 voters. At Paris,
out of 81,400 electors, in August, 1790, 67,200 do not vote,
and, three months later, the number of absentees is 71,408.[5]

---

[1] Cf. "The Revolution," Vol. I. p. 264.

[2] *Moniteur*, IV. 495. (Letter from Chartres, May 27, 1790.)

[3] Sauzay, I. 147, 195; 218, 711.

[4] *Mercure de France*, numbers of August 7, 14, 26, and Dec. 18, 1790.

[5] *Ibid.*, number f November 26, 1790. Pétion is elected mayor of Paris by 6,728 out
of 10,632 voters.   'Only 7,000 voters are found at the election of the electors who elect
deputies to the legislature. Primary and municipal meetings are deserted in the same proportion."—*Moniteur*, X. 529 (Number of Dec. 4, 1791). Manuel is elected Attorney of the
Commune by 3,770 out of 5,311 voters.—*Ibid.* XI. 378. At the election of municipal officers
for Paris, Feb. 10 and 11, 1792, only 3,787 voters present themselves; Dussault, who obtains
the most votes, has 2,588; Sergent receives 1,648.—Buchez et Roux, XI. 238 (session of
Aug. 12, 1791). Speech by Chapelier; "Archives Nationales," F. 6 (*carton*), 21. Primary
meeting of June 13, 1791, canton of Bèze (Côte d'Or). Out of 460 active citizens, 157 are
present, and, on the final ballot, 58.—*Ibid.*, F. 3,235 (January, 1792). Lozerre: "1,000
citizens, at most, out of 25,000, voted in the primary meetings. At. Saint-Chèly, capital of
the district, a few armed ruffians succeed in forming the primary meeting and in substitut-
ing their own election for that of eight parishes, whose frightened citizens withdrew from
t. . . . At Langogne, chief town of the canton and district, out of more than 400 active
citizens, 22 or 23 at most—just what one would suppose them to be when their presence
drove away the rest—alone formed the meeting."

Thus for every elector that votes, there are four, six, eight, ten, and even sixteen that abstain from voting.—In the election of deputies, the case is the same. At the primary meetings of 1791, in Paris, out of 81,200 registered names more than 74,000 fail to respond. In the Doubs, three out of four voters stay away. In one of the cantons of the Côte d'Or, at the close of the polls, only one-eighth of the electors remain at the counting of the votes, while in the secondary meetings the desertion is not less. At Paris, out of 946 electors chosen only 200 are found to give their suffrage; at Rouen, out of 700 there are but 160, and on the last day of the ballot, only 60. In short, "in all departments," says an orator in the tribune, "scarcely one out of five electors of the second degree discharges his duty."

In this manner the majority hands in its resignation. Through inertia, want of forethought, lassitude, aversion to the electoral hubbub, lack of political preferences, or dislike of all the political candidates, it shirks the task which the constitution imposes on it. Its object is not to take up the burden of a collateral task in addition—a weightier task, namely, that of devoted labor to a new league. Men who cannot find time once in three months to drop a ballot in the box, will not come three times a week to attend the meetings of a club. Far from meddling with the government, they abdicate, and as they refuse to elect it, they will not undertake to control it.

It is just the opposite with the upstarts and dogmatists who regard their royal privileges seriously. They not only vote at the elections, but they mean to keep in their own hands the authority they delegate. In their eyes every magistrate is one of their creatures, and remains accountable to them, for, in point of law, the people may not part with their sovereignty, while, as a fact, power has proved so sweet that they are not disposed to part with it.[1] During the six months preceding the regular elections, they have come to know, comprehend, and test each other; they have held conventicles; a mutual understanding is arrived at,

[1] This power, with its gratifications, is thus shown, Beugnot, I. 140, 147. "On the publication of the decrees of August 4, the committee of overseers of Montigny, reinforced by all the patriots of the country, came down like a torrent on the barony of Choiseul, and exterminated all the hares and partridges. . . They fished out the ponds. . . At Mandre we happen to be in the front room of the inn, with a dozen peasants gathered around a table decked with tumblers and bottles, amongst which we noticed an inkstand, pens, and something resembling a register. 'I don't know what they are about,' said the landlady, but there they are, from morning till night, drinking, swearing, and storming away at everybody, and they say that they are a *committee.*'"

and henceforth, as other associations disappear like scanty vegetation, theirs [1] rise vigorously on the abandoned soil.   A club is
established at Marseilles before the end of 1789; each large
town has one within the first six months of 1790, Aix in February, Montpellier in March, Nismes in April, Lyons in May, and
Bordeaux in June.[2]   But their greatest increase takes place
after the Federation festival.   Just when local gatherings merge
into that of the whole country, the sectaries keep aloof, and
form leagues of their own.   At Rouen, July 14, 1790, two
surgeons, a printer, a chaplain at the Conciergerie, a widowed
Jewess, and four women or children living in the house,—eight
persons in all, pure and not to be confounded with the mass,[3]—
bind themselves together, and form a distinct association.   Their
patriotism is of superior quality, and they take a special view of
the social compact; [4] in swearing fealty to the constitution they
reserve to themselves the Rights of Man, and they mean to
maintain not only the reforms already effected, but to complete
the Revolution just begun.—During the Federation they have
welcomed and indoctrinated their fellows who, on quitting the
capital or large cities, become bearers of instructions to the small
towns and hamlets; they are told what the object of a club is,
and how to form one, and, everywhere, popular associations
arise on the same plan, for the same purpose, and bearing the
same name.   A month later, sixty of these associations are in
operation; three months later, one hundred; in March, 1791,
two hundred and twenty-nine, and in August, 1791, nearly four
hundred.[5]   After this date a sudden increase takes place, owing
to two simultaneous impulses, which scatter their seeds broad-
cast over the entire territory.—On the one hand, at the end of
July, 1791, all moderate men, the friends of law and order, who
still hold the clubs in check, all constitutionalists, or *Feuillants,*

---

[1] Albert Babeau, I. 206, 242.—The first meeting of the revolutionary committee of Troyes,
in the cemetery of St. Jules, August, 1789. This committee becomes the only authority in
the town, after the assassination of the mayor, Huez (Sept. 10, 1790).

[2] "The French Revolution," Vol. I. pp. 235, 242, 251.—Buchez et Roux, VI. 179.—Guillon
de Montléon, "Histoire de la Ville de Lyon pendant la Révolution," I. 87.—Guadet, "Les
Girondins."

[3] Michelet, "Histoire de la Révolution," II. 47.

[4] The rules of the Paris club state that members must "labor to establish and strengthen
the constitution, *according to the spirit of the club.*"

[5] *Mercure de France,* Aug. 11, 1790.—"Journal de la Société des Amis de la Constitu
tion," Nov. 21, 1790.—*Ibid.,* March, 1791.—*Ibid,* Aug. 14, 1791 (speech by Roederer).
Buchez et Roux, XI. 481.

withdraw from them and leave them to the ultraism or triviality of the *motionnaires ;*[1] the political tone immediately falls to that of the tavern and guard-house, so that wherever one or the other of these is found, there is a political club.   On the other hand, a convocation of the electoral body is held at the same date for the election of a new National Assembly, and for the renewal of local governments; the prey being in sight, hunting-parties are everywhere formed to capture it.   In two months,[2] six hundred new clubs spring up; by the end of September they amount to one thousand, and in June, 1792, to twelve hundred—as many as there are towns and walled boroughs.   On the fall of the throne, and at the panic caused by the Prussian invasion, during a period of anarchy which equalled that of July, 1789, there were, according to Rœderer, almost as many clubs as there were communes, 26,000, one for every village containing five or six hot-headed, boisterous fellows, or roughs, (*tape-durs*), with a copyist able to pen a petition.

After November, 1790,[3] "every street in every town and hamlet," says a journal of large circulation, "must have a club of its own.   Let some honest mechanic invite his neighbors to his house, where, with a light at the common expense, he may read aloud the decrees of the National Assembly, on which he and his neighbors may comment.   Before the meeting closes, in order to enliven the company, which may feel a little gloomy on account of Marat's articles, let him read the patriotic, amusing imprecations of Père Duchesne."[4]—The advice is followed.   At these meetings are read aloud pamphlets, newspapers, and catechisms despatched from Paris, the "Gazette Villageoise," the "Journal du Soir," the "Journal de la Montagne," "Père Duchesne," the "Révolutions de Paris," and "Laclos' Gazette." Revolutionary songs are sung, and, if a good speaker happens to be present, a former *oratorien,* lawyer, or pedagogue, he empties his declamatory budget by expatiating on the Greeks

---

[1] So called from certain individuals seizing every opportunity at political meetings to make motions and offer resolutions.—TR.

[2] Michelet, II. 407.—*Moniteur,* XII 347 (May 11, 1792), article by Marie Chénier, according to whom 800 Jacobin clubs exist at this date.—*Ibid.,* XII. 753 (speech by M. Delfaux session of June 25, 1792).—Rœderer, preface to his translation of Hobbes.

[3] "Les Révolutions de Paris," by Prudhomme, number 173.

[4] Constant, "Histoire d'un Club Jacobin en province," *passim* (Fontainbleau Club, founded May 5, 1791).—Albert Babeau, I. 434 and following pages (foundation of the Troyes Club, Oct. 1790). Sauzay, I. 206 and following pages (foundation of the Besançon Club Aug. 28, 1790). *Ibid.,* 214 (foundation of the Pontarlier Club, March, 1791).

and Romans and proclaiming the regeneration of the human species. Another, appealing to women, wants to see "the declaration of the Rights of Man suspended on the walls of their bedrooms as their principal ornament, and, should war break out, these virtuous patriots, marching at the head of our armies like new bacchantes with dishevelled locks, brandishing the thyrsus." Shouts of applause greet this sentiment. The minds of the listeners, swept away by this gale of declamation, become overheated and ignite through mutual contact; like half-consumed embers that would die out if let alone, they kindle into a blaze when gathered together in a heap.—Their convictions, at the same time, gain strength. There is nothing like a coterie to make these take root. In politics, as in religion, faith generating the church, the latter, in its turn, nourishes faith; in the club, as in the conventicle, each derives authority from the common unanimity, every word and action of the whole tending to prove each in the right. And all the more because a dogma which remains uncontested, ends in seeming incontestable; as the Jacobin lives in a narrow circle, carefully guarded, no contrary opinions find their way to him. The public, in his eyes, seems two hundred persons; their opinion weighs on him without any counterpoise, and, outside of their belief, which is his also, every other belief is absurd and even culpable. Moreover, he discovers through this constant system of preaching, which is nothing but flattery, that he is patriotic, intelligent, virtuous, of which he can have no doubt, because, before being admitted into the club, his civic virtues have been verified and he carries a printed certificate of them in his pocket.—Accordingly, he is one of an élite corps, a corps which, enjoying a monopoly of patriotism, holds itself aloof, talks loud, and is distinguished from ordinary citizens by its tone and way of conducting things. The club of Pontarlier, from the first,[1] prohibits its members from using the common forms of politeness. "Members are to abstain from saluting their fellow-citizens by removing the hat, and are to avoid the phrase, 'I have the honor to be,' and others of like import, in addressing persons." A proper idea of one's importance is indispensable. "Does not the famous tribune of the Jacobins in Paris inspire traitors and impostors with fear? And do not anti-Revolutionists return to dust on beholding it?"

---

[1] Sauzay, I. 214 (April 2, 1791).

True enough, and in the provinces as well as at the capital, for, scarcely is a club organised when it sets to work on the population generally. In many of the large cities, in Paris, Lyons, Aix and Bordeaux, there are two clubs in partnership,[1] one, more or less respectable and parliamentary, "composed partly of the members of the different branches of the administration and specially devoted to purposes of general utility," and the other, practical and active, made up of bar-room politicians and club-haranguers, who indoctrinate workmen, market-gardeners and the rest of the lower bourgeois class. The latter is a branch of the former, and, in urgent cases, supplies it with rioters. "We are placed amongst the people," says one of these subaltern clubs, "we read to them the decrees, and, through lectures and counsel, we warn them against the publications and intrigues of the aristocrats. We ferret out and track plotters and their machinations. We welcome and advise all complainants; we enforce their demands, when just; finally, we, in some way, attend to all details." Thanks to these vulgar auxiliaries, but whose lungs and arms are strong, the party soon becomes dominant; it has force and uses it, and, denying that its adversaries have any rights, it re-establishes privileges of every kind for its own advantage.

[Sections III and IV of this chapter have been omitted.]

V.

At first sight their success seems doubtful, for they are in a minority, and a very small one. At Besançon, in November, 1791, the revolutionists of every shade of opinion and degree, whether Girondists or Montagnards, consist of about 500 or 600 out of 3,000 electors, and, in November, 1792, of not more than the same number out of 6,000 and 7,000.[2] At Paris, in November, 1791, there are 6,700 out of more than 81,000 on the rolls; in October, 1792, there are less than 14,000 out of 160,000.[3]

---

[1] "Journal des Amis de la Constitution," I. 534 (Letter of the "Café National" Club of Bordeaux, Jan. 29, 1791). Guillon de Montléon, I. 88.—"The French Revolution," vol. I. 128, 242.

[2] Sauzay, II. 79 (municipal election, Nov. 15, 1791).—III. 221 (mayoralty election, November, 1792). The half-way moderates had 237 votes, and the *sans-culottes*, 310.

[3] *Mercure de France*, Nov. 26, 1791 (Pétion was elected mayor, Nov. 17, by 6,728 votes out of 10,682 voters).—Mortimer-Ternaux, V. 95. (Oct. 4, 1792, Pétion was elected mayor

At Troyes, in 1792, there are found only 400 or 500 out of 7,000 electors, and at Strasbourg the same number out of 8,000 electors.[1] Accordingly only about one-tenth of the electoral population are revolutionists, and if we leave out the Girondists and the semi-conservatives, the number is reduced by one-half. Towards the end of 1792, at Besançon, scarcely more than 300 pure Jacobins are found in a population of from 25,000 to 30,000, while at Paris, out of 700,000 inhabitants only 5,000 are Jacobins. It is certain that in the capital, where the most excitement prevails, and where more of them are found than elsewhere, never, even in a crisis and when vagabonds are paid and bandits recruited, are there more than 10,000.[2] In a large town like Toulouse a representative of the people on missionary service wins over only about 400 persons.[3] Counting fifty or so in each small town, twenty in each large borough, and five or six in each village, we find, on an average, but one Jacobin to fifteen electors and National Guards, while, taking the whole of France, all the Jacobins put together do not amount to 300,000.[4]—This is a small number for the enslavement of six millions of able-bodied men, and for installing in a country of twenty-six millions inhabitants a more absolute despotism than that of an Asiatic sovereign. Force, however, is not measured by numbers; they form a band in the midst of a crowd and, in this disorganised, inert crowd, a band that is determined to push its way like an iron wedge splitting a log.

by 13,746 votes out of 14,137 voters. He declines.—Oct. 21, d'Ormessan, a moderate, who declines to stand, has, nevertheless, 4,910 votes. His competitor, Lhuillier, a pure Jacobin, obtains only 4,896.)

[1] Albert Babeau, II. 15. (The 32,000 inhabitants of Troyes indicate about 7,000 electors in December, 1792, Jacquet is elected mayor by 400 votes out of 555 voters. A striking coincidence is found in there being 400 members of the Troyes club at this time.)—Carnot, 'Mémoires,' I. 181. "Dr. Bollmann, who passed through Strasbourg in 1792, relates that, out of 8,000 qualified citizens, only 400 voters presented themselves."

[2] Mortimer-Ternaux, VI. 21. In February, 1793, Pache is elected mayor of Paris by 11,881 votes.—*Journal de Paris,* number 185. Henriot, July 2, 1793, is elected commander-in-chief of the Paris national guard, by 9,084, against 6,095 votes given for his competitor, Raffet. The national guard comprises at this time 110,000 registered members, besides 10,000 gendarmes and federates. Many of Henriot's partisans, again, voted twice. (Cf. on the elections and the number of Jacobins at Paris, chapters xi. and xii. of this volume.)

[3] Michelet, VI. 95. "Almost all (the missionary representatives) were supported by only the smallest minority. Baudot, for instance, at Toulouse, in 1793, had but 400 men for him."

[4] For example, "Archives Nationales," F 1 6, *carton* 3. Petition of the inhabitants of Arnay-le-Duc to the king (April, 1792), very insulting, employing the most familiar language; about fifty signatures.—*Ibid.,* VII. 687 (letter of Grégoire, Dec. 24, 1796).—Malouet, II. 531 (letter by Malouet, July 22, 1779). Malouet and Grégoire agree on the number 300,000. Marie Chénier (*Moniteur,* XII. 695, April 20, 1792) carries it up to 400,000.

The only defense a nation has against inward usurpation as well as invasion from without is its government. Government is t⁾e indispensable instrument of common action. Let it fail or falter and the great majority, otherwise employed, undecided what to do and lukewarm, disintegrates and falls to pieces. Of the two governments around which the nation might have rallied, the first one, after July 14, 1789, lies prostrate on the ground where it slowly crumbles away; its phantom which rises up is still more odious; the latter not only brings with it the same senseless abuses and intolerable burdens, but, in addition to these, a yelping pack of claimants and recriminators; after 1790 it appears on the frontier more arbitrary than ever at the head of a coming invasion of angry *émigrés* and grasping foreigners.—The other government, that just constructed by the Constituent Assembly, it is so badly put together that the majority cannot use it. It is not adapted to its hand; no political instrument at once so ponderous and so powerless was ever seen. An enormous effort is needed to set it agoing; every citizen is obliged to give to it about two days labor per week.[1] Thus laboriously started and but half in motion, it poorly meets the various tasks imposed upon it—the collection of taxes, public order in the streets, the circulation of supplies, and security for consciences, lives and property. Toppled over by its own action, another rises out of it, illegal and serviceable, which takes its place and stands.

In a great centralised state whoever possesses the head possesses the body. By virtue of being led, the French have contracted the habit of letting themselves be led.[2] People in the provinces involuntarily turn their eyes to the capital, and, on a crisis occurring, run out to stop the mail-carrier to know what government they are under. Into whatever hands this central government happens to have fallen, the majority accepts or submits to it. —Because, in the first place, most of the isolated groups which would like to overthrow it dare not engage in the struggle—*it seems too strong;* through inveterate routine they imagine behind it that great, distant France which, under its impulsion, will

[1] Cf. "The French Revolution," Vol. I. book ii. ch. iii.
[2] Cf. "The Ancient Régime," p. 352.

crush them with its mass.[1] In the second place, should a few
isolated groups undertake to overthrow it, they are not in a condition to keep up the struggle — *it is too strong.* They are,
indeed, not yet organised while it is fully so, owing to the
docile set of officials inherited from the government overthrown.
Under monarchy or republic the government clerk comes
to his office regularly every morning to despatch the orders
transmitted to him.[2] Under monarchy or republic the police
man daily makes his round to arrest those against whom he
has a warrant. So long as instructions come from above in the
hierarchical order of things, they are obeyed. From one end
of the territory to the other, therefore, the machine, with its
hundred thousand arms, works efficaciously in the hands of
those who have seized the lever at the central point. Resolution, audacity, rude energy, are all that are needed to make the
lever act, and none of these are wanting in the Jacobin.

First, he has faith, and faith at all times "moves mountains."
Take any ordinary party recruit, an attorney, a second-rate
lawyer, a shopkeeper, an artisan, and conceive, if you can, the
extraordinary effect of this doctrine on a mind so poorly prepared for it, so narrow, so out of proportion with the gigantic
conception which has mastered it. Formed for routine and the
limited views of one in his position, he is suddenly carried away
by a complete system of philosophy, a theory of nature and of
man, a theory of society and of religion, a theory of universal
history,[3] conclusions about the past, the present, and the future

[1] "Mémoires de Madame de Sapinaud," p. 18. Reply of M de Sapinaud to the peasants
of La Vendée, who wished him to act as their general: "My friends, it is the earthen pot
against the iron pot. What could we do? One department against eighty-two—we should
be smashed!"

[2] Malouet, II. 241. "I knew a clerk in one of the bureaus, who, during these sad days
(September, 1792), never missed going, as usual, to copy and add up his egisters. Ministerial correspondence with the armies and the provinces followed its regular course in regular form. The Paris police looked after supplies and kept its eye on sharpers, while blood
ran in the streets."—Cf. on this mechanical need and inveterate habit of receiving orders
from the central authority, Mallet-Dupan, "Mémoires," 490. "Dumouriez' soldiers said
to him: 'F——, papa general, get the Convention to order us to march on Paris and you'll
see how we will make mince-meat of those b—— in the Assembly!'"

[3] Buchez et Roux, XXVIII. 55. Letter by Brun-Lafond, a grenadier in the national
guard, July 14, 1793, to a friend in the provinces, in justification of the 31st of May. The
whole of this letter requires to be read. In it are found the ordinary ideas of a Jacobin in
relation to history. "Can we lose sight of this, that it is ever the people of Paris which,
through its murmurings and righteous insurrections against the oppressive system of many
of our kings, has forced them to entertain milder sentiments regarding the relief of the French
people, and principally of the tiller of the soil? . . Without the energy of Paris, Paris

of humanity, axioms of absolute right, a system of perfect and final truth, the whole concentrated in a few rigid formulæ as, for example: "Religion is superstition, monarchy is usurpation, priests are impostors, aristocrats are vampires, and kings are so many tyrants and monsters." These ideas flood a mind of .his stamp like a vast torrent precipitating itself into a narrow gorge; they upset it, and, no longer under self-direction, they sweep it away. The man is beside himself. A plain bourgeois, a common laborer is not transformed with impunity into an apostle or liberator of the human species.—For, it is not his country that he would save, but the entire race. Roland, just before the 10th of August, exclaims "with tears in his eyes, should liberty die in France, she is lost to the rest of the world forever! The hopes of philosophers will perish! the whole earth will succumb to the cruellest tyranny!"[1]—Grégoire, on the meeting of the Convention, obtained a decree abolishing royalty, and seemed overcome with the thought of the immense benefit he had conferred on the human race. "I must confess," said he, "that for days I could neither eat nor sleep for excess of joy!" One day a Jacobin in the tribune declared: "We shall be a nation of gods!"—Fancies like these bring on lunacy, or, at all events, they create disease. "Some men are in a fever all day long," said a companion of St. Just; "I had it for twelve years."[2] Later on, "when advanced in life and trying to analyse their experiences, they cannot comprehend it." Another states that, in his case, on a "crisis occurring, there was only a hair's breadth between reason and mad-

---

and France would now be inhabited solely by slaves, while this beautiful soil would present an aspect as wild and deserted as that of the Turkish empire or that of Germany," which has led us "to confer still greater lustre on this Revolution, by re-establishing on earth the ancient Athenian and other Grecian republics in all their purity. Distinctions among the early people of the earth did not exist; early family ties bound people together who had no ancient founders or origin; they had no other laws in their republics but those which, so to say, inspired them with those sentiments of fraternity experienced by them in the cradle of primitive populations."

[1] Barbaroux, "Mémoires" (Ed. Dauban), 336.—Grégoire, "Mémoires," I. 410.

[2] "La Révolution Française," by Quinet (extracts from the inedited "Mémoires" of Baudot), II. 209, 211, 421, 620.—Guillon de Montléon I. 445 (speech by Chalier, in the Lyons Central Club, March 23, 1793). "They say that the *sans-culottes* will go on spilling their blood. This is only the talk of aristocrats. Can a *sans-culotte* be reached in that quarter? Is he not invulnerable, like the gods whom he replaces on this earth?"—Speech by David, in the Convention, on Barra and Viala. "Under so fine a government woman will bring forth without pain."—Mercier, "Le Nouveau Paris," I. 13. "I heard (an orator) exclaim in one of the sections, to which I bear witness: 'Yes, I would take my own head by the hair, cut it off, and, presenting it to the despot, I would say to him: *Tyrant, behold the act of a free man!*'"

ness." "When St. Just and myself," says Baudot, "discharged the batteries at Wissenbourg, we were most liberally thanked for it. Well, there was no merit in that; we knew perfectly well that the shot could not reach us and do us harm."—Man, in this exalted state, is unconscious of obstacles, and, according to circumstances, rises above or falls below himself, freely spilling his own blood as well as the blood of others, heroic as a soldier and atrocious as a civilian; he is not to be resisted in either direction for his strength increases a hundredfold through his fury, and, on his tearing wildly through the streets, people get out of his way as on the approach of a mad bull.

If they do not jump aside of their own accord, he will run at them, for he is unscrupulous as well as furious.—In every polit ical struggle certain kinds of actions are prohibited; at all events, if the majority is sensible and wishes to act fairly, it repudiates them for itself. It will not violate any particular law, for, if one law is broken, this tends to the breaking of others. It is opposed to overthrowing an established government because every interregnum is a return to barbarism. It is opposed to the element of popular insurrection because, in such a resort, public power is surrendered to the irrationality of brutal passion. It is opposed to a conversion of the government into a machine for confiscation and murder because it deems the natural function of government to be the protection of life and property.—The majority, accordingly, in confronting the Jacobin, who allows himself all this, is like a man deprived of his arms in close con- flict with one in full panoply.[1] The Jacobin, through principle, holds law in contempt, for the only law which he accepts is the arbitrament of the people. He has no hesitation in proceeding against the government because, in his eyes, the government is a clerk which the people always has a right to remove. He welcomes insurrection because, through it, the people recover their inalienable sovereignty. A dictatorship suits him because by this means the people recover their sovereignty with no limita- tions.—Moreover, as with casuists, "the end justifies the means."[2]

---

[1] Lafayette, "Mémoires," I. 467 (on the Jacobins of August 10, 1792). "This sect, the destruction of which was desired by nineteen-twentieths of France."—Durand-Maillan, 49. The aversion to the Jacobins after June 20, 1792, was general. "The communes of France, everywhere wearied and dissatisfied with popular clubs, would gladly have got rid of them, that they might no longer be under their control."

[2] The words of Leclerc, a deputy of the Lyons committee in the Jacobin Club at Paris, May 12, 1793. "Popular machiavelianism must be established. . . Everything impure

"Let the colonies perish," exclaims a Jacobin in the Constituent Assembly, "rather than sacrifice a principle." "When the day comes," says St. Just, "which satisfies me that I cannot endow the French with mild, vigorous, and rational ways, inflexible against tyranny and injustice, that day I will stab myself," and in the mean time, he uses the guillotine against others. "We will convert France into a graveyard," exclaimed Carrier, "rather than not regenerate it our own way!" [1] To place themselves at the helm of the government, they are ready to scuttle the ship and sink it. From the first, they let loose on society street riots and *jacqueries* in the rural districts, prostitutes and ruffians, the foul and the savage. Throughout the struggle they profit by the coarsest and most destructive passions, by the blindness, credulity, and rage of an infatuated crowd, by dearth, by the fear of bandits, by rumors of conspiracy, by threats of invasion. At last, attaining to power through a general upheaval, they hold on to it through terror and executions.—Straining will to the utmost, with no curb to check it, steadfastly believing in its own right and with utter contempt for the rights of others, with fanatical energy and the expedients of scoundrels, a minority employing such forces may easily overcome a majority. So true is it that, with faction itself, victory is always on the side of the few whose faith is greatest and who are the least unscrupulous. Four times between 1789 and 1794, political gamesters take their seats at a table whereon the stakes consist of supreme power,

---

must disappear off the French soil. . . I shall doubtless be regarded as a brigand, but there is one way to get ahead of calumny, and that is, to exterminate the calumniators."

[1] Buchez et Roux, XXXIV. 204 (testimony of François Lameyrie). "Collection of authentic documents for the History of the Revolution at Strasbourg," II. 210 (speech by Baudot, Frimaire 19, year II., in the Jacobin Club at Strasbourg). "Egoists, the heedless, the enemies of liberty, the enemies of all nature should not be regarded as her children. Are not all who oppose the public good, or who do not share it, in the same case? Let us, then, utterly destroy them. . . Were they a million, would not one sacrifice the twenty-fourth part of one's self to get rid of a gangrene which might infect the rest of the body? . . " For these reasons, the orator thinks that every man who is not wholly devoted to the Republic must be put to death. He states that the Republic should at one blow cause the instant disappearance of every friend to kings and feudalism.—Beaulieu, "Essai," V. 200. M. d'Antonelle thought, "like most of the revolutionary clubs, that, to constitute a republic, an approximate equality of property should be established; and to do this, a third of the population should be suppressed."—"This was the general idea among the fanatics of the Revolution."—Larevellière-Lépaux, "Mémoires," I. 150 "Jean Bon St. André . . . suggested that for the solid foundation of the Republic in France, the population should be reduced one-half." He is violently interrupted by Larevellière-Lépaux, but continues and insists on this.—Guffroy, deputy of the Pas-de-Calais, proposed in his journal a still large amputation; he wanted to reduce France to five millions of inhabitants.

and four times in succession the " Impartiaux," the " Feuillants,"
the " Girondists," and the " Dantonists," form the majority and
lose the game.   Four times in succession the majority has no
desire to break customary rules, or, at the very least, to infringe
on any rule universally accepted, to wholly disregard the teachings of experience, the letter of the law, the precepts of humanity, the suggestions of pity.   The minority, on the contrary, is
determined beforehand to win at all hazards; its opinion is the
right one, and if rules are opposed to that, so much the worse
for the rules.   At the decisive moment, it claps a pistol to its
adversary's head, turns the table upside down, and decamps with
the stakes.

CHAPTER III.

The Jacobins in power.—The elections of 1791.—Proportion of p».·es gained by them.—I. Their siege operations.—Means used by them to discourage the majority of electors and conservative candidates.—Frequency of elections.—Effect of the oath.—II. Annoyances and dangers of public offices.—The Constituents excluded from the Legislative body.—III. The friends of order deprived of the right of free assemblage.—Violent treatment of their clubs in Paris and the provinces.—Legal prevention of conservative associations.—IV. Turmoil at the elections of 1790.—Elections in 1791.—Effect of the King's flight.—Domiciliary visits.—Mortagne during the electoral period.—V. Intimidation and withdrawal of the Conservatives.—Popular outbreaks in Burgundy, Lyonnais, Provence, and the large cities.—Electoral proceedings of the Jacobins; examples at Aix, Dax, and Montpellier.— Agitators go unpunished.— Denunciations by name.— Manœuvres with the peasantry.—General tactics of the Jacobins.

In June, 1791, and during the five following months, the class of active citizens[1] are convoked to elect their elective representatives, which, as we know, according to the law, are of every kind and degree; in the first place, there are 40,000 electors of the second degree and 745 deputies; next, one-half of the administrators of 83 departments, one-half of the administrators of 544 districts, one-half of the administrators of 41,000 communes, and finally, in each municipality, the mayor and syndic-attorney; in each department, the president of the criminal court and the prosecuting-attorney, and, throughout France, officers of the National Guard; in short, almost the entire body of the agents and depositaries of legal authority. The garrison of the public citadel is to be renewed, which is the second and even the third time since 1789.—At each time the Jacobins have crept into the place, in small bands, but this time they enter in large bodies. Pétion becomes mayor of Paris, Manuel, syndic-

---

[1] Law of May 28, 29, 1791 (according to official statements, the total of active citizens amounted to 4,288,360).—Laws of July 23, Sept. 12, Sept. 29, 1791.—Buchez et Roux, XII. 310.

attorney, and Danton the deputy of Manuel; Robespierre is elected prosecuting-attorney in criminal cases. The very first week,[1] 136 new deputies enter their names on the club's register. In the Assembly the party numbers about 250 members. On passing all the posts of the fortress in review, we may estimate the besiegers as occupying one-third of them, and perhaps more. Their siege for two years has been carried on with unerring instinct, the extraordinary spectacle presenting itself of an entire nation legally overcome by a troop of factionists.

I.

First of all, they clear the ground, and through the decrees forced out of the Constituent Assembly, they keep most of the majority away from the polls.—On the one hand, under the pretext of better ensuring popular sovereignty, the elections are so multiplied, and held so near together, as to demand of each active citizen one-sixth of his time; such an exaction is very great for hard-working people who have a trade or any occupation,[2] which is the case with the great mass; at all events, with the useful and healthy portion of the population. Accordingly, as we have seen, it stays away from the polls, leaving the field open to idlers or fanatics.

On the other hand, by virtue of the constitution, the civic oath, which includes the ecclesiastical oath, is imposed on all electors, for, if any one takes the former and reserves the latter, his vote is thrown out; in November, in the Doubs, the municipal elections of thirty-three communes are invalidated solely on this pretext.[3] Not only forty thousand ecclesiastics are thus

---

[1] Buchez et Roux, XII. 33.—Mortimer-Ternaux, "Histoire de la Terreur," II. 205, 348. —Sauzay, II. ch. xviii.—Albert Babeau, I. ch. xx.

[2] The following letter, by Camille Desmoulins (April 3, 1792), shows at once the time consumed by public affairs, the sort of attraction they had, and the kind of men which they diverted from their business. "I have gone back to my old profession of the law, to which I give nearly all the time which my municipal or electoral functions, and the Jacobins (club), allow me—that is to say, very little. It is very disagreeable to me to come down to pleading bourgeois cases after having managed interests of such importance, and the affairs of the government, in the face of all Europe."

[3] Sauzay, II. 83–89 and 123. A resolution of the inhabitants of Chalèze, who, headed by their municipal officers, declare themselves unanimously "non-conformists," and demand "the right of using a temple for the exercise of their religious opinions, belonging to them and built with their contributions." On the strength of this, the municipal officers of Chalèze are soundly rated by the district administration, which thus states what principles are: "Liberty, indefinite for the private individual, must be restricted for the public man whose opinions must conform to the law; otherwise, . . . he must renounce all public functions."

tendered unsworn (*insermentés*), but again, all scrupulous Catholics lose the sight of suffrage, these being by far the most
numerous in Artois, Doubs and the Jura, in the Lower and
Upper Rhine district,[1] in the two Sévres and la Vendée, in the
Lower Loire, Morbihan, Finisterre and Côtes du Nord, in
Lozère and Ardèche, without mentioning the southern departments.[2] Thus, aided by the law which they have rendered
impracticable, the Jacobins, on the one hand, are rid of all
sensible voters in advance, counting by millions; and, on the
other, aided by a law which they have rendered intolerant, they
are rid of the Catholic vote which counts by hundreds of
thousands. On entering the electoral lists, consequently, thanks
to this double exclusion, they find themselves confronted by only
the smallest numbers of electors.

II.

Operations must now be commenced against these, and a first
expedient consists in depriving them of their candidates. The
obligation of taking the oath has already partly provided for
this; in Lozère all the officials send in their resignations rather
than take the oath;[3] here are men who will not be candidates
at the coming elections, for nobody covets a place which he
had to abandon; in general, the suppression of all party candidatures is effected in no other way than by making the post of
a magistrate distasteful.—On this principle the Jacobins have
labored successfully by promoting and taking the lead in innu-

---

[1] Archives Nationales," F⁷, 3,253 (letter of the department directory, April 7, 1792). "On
the 25th of January, in our report to the National Assembly, we stated the almost general
opposition which the execution of the laws relating to the clergy has found in this department . . . nine-tenths, at least, of the Catholics refusing to recognise the sworn priests.
The teachers, influenced by their old curés or vicars, are willing to take the civic oath, but
they refuse to recognise their legitimate pastors and attend their services. We are, therefore, obliged to remove them, and to look out for others to replace them. The citizens of a
large number of the communes, persisting in trusting these, will lend no assistance whatever
to the election of the new ones; the result is, that we are obliged, in selecting these people,
to refer the matter to persons whom we scarcely know, and who are scarcely better known
to the directories of the district. As they are elected against the will of the citizens, they do
not gain their confidence, and draw their salaries from the commune treasury, without any
advantage to public instruction."

[2] *Mercure de France*, Sept. 3, 1791. "The right of attending primary meetings is that
of every citizen who pays a tax of three livres; owing to the violence to which opinions are
subject, *more than one-half of the French* are compelled to stay away from these reunions,
which are abandoned to persons who have the least interest in maintaining public order and
in securing stable laws, with the least property, and who pay the fewest taxes."

[3] "The French Revolution," Vol. I. p. 182 and following pages.

merable riots against the King, the officials and the clerks, against
nobles, ecclesiastics, corn-dealers and land-owners, against every
species of public authority whatever its origin.   Everywhere the
authorities are constrained to tolerate or excuse murders, pillage
and incendiarism, or, at the very least, insurrections and disobedience.   For two years a mayor runs the risk of being hung
on proclaiming martial law; a captain is not sure of his men on
marching to protect a tax levy; a judge on the bench is threatened if he condemns the marauders who devastate the national
forests.   The magistrate, whose duty it is to see that the law is
respected, is constantly obliged to strain the law, or allow it to be
strained; if refractory, a summary blow dealt by the local Jacobins forces his legal authority to yield to their illegal dictation, so
that he has to resign himself to being either their accomplice or
their puppet.   Such a rôle is intolerable to a man of feeling
or conscience.   Hence, in 1790 and 1791, nearly all the prominent and reputable men who, in 1789, had seats in the Hotels-
de-villes, or held command in the National Guard, all country-
gentlemen, chevaliers of St. Louis, old parliamentarians, the
upper *bourgeoisie* and large landed-proprietors, retire into private
life and renounce public functions which are no longer tenable.
Instead of offering themselves to public suffrage they avoid it,
and the party of order, far from electing the magistracy, no
longer even finds candidates for it.

Through an excess of precaution, its natural leaders have been
legally disqualified, the principal offices, especially those of deputy
and minister, being interdicted beforehand to the influential men
in whom we find the little common sense gained by the French
people during the past two years.—In the month of June, 1791,
even after the irreconcilables had parted company with the
"Right," there still remained in the Assembly about 700 members who, adhering to the constitution but determined to repress
disorder, would have formed a sensible legislature had they been
re-elected.   All of these, except a very small group of revolutionists, had learned something by experience, and, in the last
days of their session, two serious events, the king's flight and the
riot in the Champ de Mars, had made them acquainted with the
defects of their machine.   With this executive instrument in their
hands for three months, they see that it is racked, that things are

tottering, and that they themselves are being run over by fanatics and the populace.   They accordingly attempt to put on a drag, and several even think of retracing their steps.[1]   They cut loose from the Jacobins; of the three or four hundred deputies on the club list in the Rue St. Honoré [2] but seven remain; the rest form at the Feuillants a distinct opposition club, and at their head are the first founders, Duport, the two Lameths, Barnave, the authors of the constitution, all the fathers of the new régime.   In the last decree of the Constituent Assembly they loudly condemn the usurpations of popular associations, and not only interdict to these all meddling in administrative or political matters, but likewise any collective petition or deputation.[3]—Here may the friends of order find candidates whose chances are good, for, during two years and more, each in his own district is the most conspicuous, the best accredited, and the most influential man there; he stands well with his electors on account of the popularity of the constitution he has made, and it is very probable that his name would rally to it a majority of votes.—The Jacobins, however, have foreseen this danger.   Four months previous to this,[4] with the aid of the Court, which never missed an opportunity to ruin itself and everything else,[5] they made the most of the rancors of the "Right" and the lassitude of the Assembly; fagged and disgusted, in a fit of mistaken disinterestedness, the Assembly, through impulse and taken by surprise, passes an act declaring all its members ineligible for election to the following Assembly, which is tantamount to the displacement in advance of the staff of honest men.

---

[1] "Correspondence of M. de Staël " (manuscript), Swedish ambassador, with his court, Sept. 4, 1791.   " The change in the way of thinking of the democrats is extraordinary; they now seem convinced that it is impossible to make the Constitution work.   Barnave, to my own knowledge, has declared that the influence of assemblies in the future should be limited to a council of notables, and that all   power   should be in the government."

[2] *Ibid.*, Letter of July 17, 1791.   " All the members of the Assembly, with the exception of three or four, have passed a resolution to separate from the Jacobins; they number about 300."—The seven deputies who remain at the Jacobin Club, are Robespierre, Pétion, Grégoire, Buzot, Coroller, and Abbé Royer.

[3] Decree of Sept. 29, 30, 1791, with report and instructions of the Committee on the Constitution.

[4] Decree of May 17, 1791.—Malouet, XII. 161.   ' There was nothing left to us but to make one great mistake, which we did not fail to do."

[5] A few months after this, on the election of a mayor for Paris, the court voted against Lafayette, and for Pétion

III.

If the latter, in spite of so many drawbacks, attempt a strug
gle, they are arrested at the very first step.   For, to enter upon
an electoral campaign, requires preliminary meetings for conference and to understand each other, while the faculty of form
ing an association, which the law grants them as a right, is
actually withheld from them by their adversaries.   As a beginning, the Jacobins hooted at and "stoned" the members of the
" Right "[1] holding their meetings in the *Salon français* of the
Rue Royale, and, according to the prevailing rule, the police
tribunal, "considering that this assemblage is a cause of disturbance, that it produces gatherings in the street, that only violent
means can be employed to protect it," orders its dissolution.—
Towards the month of August, 1790, a second club is organised,
and, this time, composed of the wisest and most liberal men.
Malouet and Count Clermont-Tonnerre are at the head of it.   It
takes the name of "Friends of a Monarchical Constitution," and
is desirous of restoring public order by maintaining the reforms
which have been reached.   All formalities on its part have been
complied with.   There are already about 800 members in Paris.
Subscriptions flow into its treasury.   The provinces send in
numerous adhesions, and, what is worse than all, bread is distributed by them at a reduced price, by which the people, probably,
will be conciliated.   Here is a centre of opinion and influence,
analogous to that of the Jacobin club, which the Jacobins cannot
tolerate.[2]   M. de Clermont-Tonnerre having leased the summer
Vauxhall, a captain in the National Guard notifies the proprietor
of it that if he rents it, the patriots of the Palais-Royal will
march to it in a body, and close it; fearing that the building
will be damaged, he cancels the lease, while the municipality,
which fears skirmishes, orders a suspension of the meetings.
The club makes a complaint and follows it up, while the letter
of the law is so plain that an official authorisation of the club is
finally granted.   Thereupon the Jacobin newspapers and stump-

---

[1] M. de Montlosier, "Mémoires," II. 309.   "As far as concerns myself, truth compels me
to say, that I was struck on the head by three carrots and two cabbages only."—Archives o
the prefecture of police (decisions of the police court, May 15, 1790). *Moniteur,* V. 427.
"The prompt attendance of the members at the hour of meeting, in spite of the hootings and
murmurings of the crowd, seemed to convince the people that this was yet another conspiracy against liberty."

[2] Malouet, II. 50.—*Mercure de France,* Jan. 7, Feb. 5, and April 9, 1791 (letter of a member of the Monarchical Club).

speakers let loose their fury against a future rival that threatens to dispute their empire.   On the 23d of January, 1791, Barnave, in the National Assembly, employing metaphorical language apt to be used as a death-shout, accuses the members of the new club "of giving the people bread that carries poison with it." Four days after this, M. Clermont-Tonnerre's dwelling is assailed by an armed throng.   Malouet, on leaving it, is almost dragged from his carriage, and the crowd around him cry out, "There goes the b—— who denounced the people!"—At length, its founders, who, out of consideration for the municipality, have waited two months, hire another hall in the Rue des Petites-Ecuries, and on the 28th of March begin their sessions.   "On reaching it," writes one of them, "we found a mob composed of drunkards, screaming boys, ragged women, soldiers exciting them on, and especially those frightful hounds, armed with stout, knotty cudgels, two feet long, which are excellent skull-crackers."[1] The thing was made up beforehand.   At first there were only three or four hundred of them, and, ten minutes after, five or six hundred; in a quarter of an hour, there are perhaps four thousand flocking in from all sides; in short, the usual make-up of an insurrection.   "The people of the quarter certified that they did not recognise one of the faces."   Jokes, insults, cuffings, clubbings, and sabre-cuts,—the members of the club "who agreed to come unarmed" being dispersed, while several are knocked down, dragged by the hair, and a dozen or fifteen more are wounded.   To justify the attack, white cockades are shown, which, it is pretended, were found in their pockets. Mayor Bailly arrives only when it is all over, and, as a measure of "public order," the municipal authorities have the club of Constitutional Monarchists closed for good.

Owing to these outrages by the faction, with the connivance of the authorities, other similar clubs are suppressed in the same way.   There are a good many of them, and in the principal towns —"Friends of Peace," "Friends of the Country," "Friends of the King, of Peace, and of Religion," "Defenders of Religion, Persons, and Property."   Magistrates and officers, the most cultivated and polished people, are generally members; in short, the élite of the place.   Formerly, meetings took place for conversa-

---

[1] Ferrières, II. 222.   "The Jacobin Club sent five or six hundred trusty men, armed with clubs," besides "about a hundred national guards, and some of the Palais-Royal prostitutes."

tion and debate, and, being long-established, the club naturally
passes over from literature to politics.—The watch-word against
all these provincial clubs is given from the Rue St. Honoré.[1]
" They are centres of conspiracy, and must be looked after"
forthwith, and be at once trodden out.—At one time, as at
Cahors,[2] a squad of the National Guard, on its return from an
expedition against the neighboring gentry, and to finish its task.
breaks in on the club, "throws its furniture out of the win
dows, and demolishes the house."—At another time, as at
Perpignan, the excited populace surrounds the club, dancing a
fandango, and yell out, *to the lantern!* The club-house is
sacked, while eighty of its members, covered with bruises, are
shut up in the citadel for their safety.[3]   At another time, as a
Aix, the Jacobin club insults its adversaries on their own prem
ises and provokes a scuffle, whereupon the municipality causes
the doors of the assailed club to be walled up and issues war
rants of arrest against its members.—Always punishment awaits
them for whatever violence they have to submit to.   Their mere
existence seems an offence.   At Grenoble, they scarcely assemble
before they are dispersed.   The fact is, they are suspected of
"*incivism;*" their intentions may not be right; in any event,
they cause a division of the place into two camps, and that is
enough.—In the department of Gard, their clubs are all broken
up, by order of the department, because "they are centres of
malevolence."   At Bordeaux, the municipality, considering that
"alarming reports are current of priests and privileged persons
returning to town," prohibits all reunions, except that of the
Jacobin club.—Thus, "under a system of liberty of the most
exalted kind, in the presence of that famous Declaration of the
Rights of Man which legitimates whatever is not unlawful,"
and which postulates equality as the principle of the French
constitution, whoever is not a Jacobin is excluded from common

---

[1] " Journal des Amis de la Constitution."   Letter of the *Café National* Club at Bordeaux,
Jan. 20, 1791.—Letters of the " Friends of the Constitution," at Brives and Cambray, Jan.
19, 1791.
[2] "The French Revolution," I. pp. 243, 324.
[3] *Mercure de France*, Dec. 18, 1770, Jan. 17, June 8, and July 14, 1791.—*Moniteur*, VI.
697.—" Archives Nationales," F⁷, 3,193.   Letter from the Directory of the department of
Aveyron, April 20, 1792.   Narrative of events after the end of 1790.—May 22, 1791, the
club of "The Friends of Order and Peace" is burnt by the Jacobins, the fire lasting all
night and a part of the next day.   (Official report of the Directory of Milhau, May 22,
1791).

rights.   An intolerant club sets itself up as a holy church, and
proscribes others which have not received from it "orthodox
baptism, civic inspiration, and the gift of tongues."   To her
alone belongs the right of assemblage, and the right of making
proselytes.   Conservative, thoughtful men in all towns throughout the kingdom are forbidden to form electoral committees, to
possess a tribune, a fund, subscribers and adherents, to cast the
weight of their names and common strength into the scale of public
opinion, to gather around their permanent nucleus the scattered
multitude of sensible people, who would like to escape from the
Revolution without falling back into the ancient régime.   Let
them whisper amongst themselves in corners, and they may still
be tolerated, but woe to them if they would leave their lonely
retreat to act in concert, to canvass voters, and support a candidate.   Up to the day of voting they must remain in the
presence of their combined, active, and obstreperous adversaries,
scattered, inert, and mute.

IV.

Will they at least be able to vote freely on that day ?   They
are not sure of it, and, judging by occurrences during the past
year, it is doubtful.—In the month of April, 1790, at Bois d'Aisy,
in Burgundy, M. de Bois d'Aisy, a deputy, who had returned
from Paris to deposit his vote,[1] was publicly menaced; he was
given to understand that nobles and priests must take no part in
the elections, while many were heard to say, in his hearing, that
in order to prevent this it would be well to hang him.   Not far
off, at Ste. Colombe, M. de Viteaux was driven out of the electoral assembly, and then put to death after three hours of torture.
The same thing occurred at Semur ; two gentlemen were knocked
down with clubs and stones, another saved himself with difficulty, and a curé died after being stabbed six times.—This is a
warning for ecclesiastics and for gentlemen ; they will do well to
abstain from voting, and the same good advice may be given to
dealers in grain, to land-owners, and every other suspected person.   For this is the day on which the people recover their sovereignty ; the violent believe that they have the right to do exactly what suits them, nothing being more natural than to ex-

---

[1] "The French Revolution," I. p. 256, 307.

clude candidates in advance who are distrusted, or electors who do not vote as they ought to.—At Villeneuve-St.-Georges, near Paris,[1] a barrister, a man of austere and energetic character, is about to be elected judge by the district electors; the populace, however, mistrust a judge likely to condemn marauders, and forty or fifty vagabonds collect together under the windows and cry out: "We don't want him elected." The curé of Crosne, president of the electoral assembly, informs them in vain that the assembled electors represent 90 communes, nearly 100,000 inhabitants, and that "40 persons should not prevail against 100,000." Shouts redouble and the electors renounce their candidate.—At Pau, patriots among the militia[2] forcibly release one of their imprisoned leaders, circulate a list for proscriptions, attack a poll-teller with their fists and afterwards with sabres, until the proscribed hide themselves away; on the following day "nobody is disposed to attend the electoral assembly."—Things are much worse in 1791. In the month of June, just at the time of the opening of the primary meetings, the king has fled to Varennes, the Revolution seems compromised, civil war and a foreign war loom up on the horizon like two spectres; the National Guard had everywhere taken up arms, and the Jacobins were making the most of the universal panic for their own advantage. To dispute their votes is no longer the question; it is not well to be seen now; among so many turbulent gatherings a popular execution is soon over. The best thing now for royalists, constitutionalists, conservatives and moderates of every kind, for the friends of law and order, is to stay at home—too happy if they may be allowed to remain there, to which the armed commonalty assents only on the condition of making them frequent visits.

Consider their situation during the whole of the electoral period, in a tranquil district, and judge of the rest of France by this corner of it. At Mortagne,[3] a small town of 6,000 souls, the laudable spirit of 1789 still existed up to the journey to

---

[1] *Mercure de France*, Dec. 14, 1790 (letter from Villeneuve-St.-Georges, Nov. 29).

[2] "Archives Nationales," II. 1,453. Correspondence of M. Bercheny. Letter from Pau, Feb. 7, 1790. "No one has any idea of the actual state of things, in this once delightful town. People are cutting each other's throats. Four duels have taken place within 48 hours, and ten or a dozen good citizens have been obliged to hide themselves for three days past."

[3] Archives Nationales," F[7], 3,249. Memorial on the actual condition of the town and district of Mortagne, department of Orne (November, 1791).

Varennes.   Among the forty or fifty families of nobles were a
good many liberals.   Here, as elsewhere among the gentry, the
clergy and the middle class, the philosophic education of the
eighteenth century had revived the initiative spirit of old provincial times, while the entire upper class had zealously and
gratuitously undertaken public duties which it alone could well
perform.   District presidents, mayors, and municipal officers,
were all chosen from among ecclesiastics and the nobles; the
three principal officers of the National Guard were chevaliers of
St. Louis, while other grades were filled by the leading people
of the community.   Thus had the free elections placed authority
in the hands of the socially superior, the new order of things
resting on the legitimate hierarchy of conditions, educations, and
capacities.—For six months, however, the club, formed out of
"a dozen hot-headed, turbulent fellows, under the presidency
and in the hands of a certain Rattier, formerly a cook," worked
upon the populace and the rural districts.   Immediately on the
receipt of the news of the King's flight, the Jacobins "give out
that nobles and priests had supplied him with money for his departure, to bring about a counter-revolution."   One family had
given such an amount, and another so much; there was no doubt
about it; the precise figures are given, and given for each family
according to its known resources.—Forthwith, "the principal
clubbists, associated with the suspicious portion of the National
Guard," spread through the streets in squads, and enter the
houses of the nobles and of other suspected persons; all the
arms, "guns, pistols, swords, hunting-knives, and sword-canes,"
are carried off.   Every hole and corner is ransacked; they make
the inmates open, or they force open, secretaries and clothes-
presses in search of ammunition, the search extending "even to
the ladies' toilette-tables"; by way of precaution "they break
sticks of pomatum in two, presuming that musket-balls are concealed in them, and they take away hair-powder under the pretext that it is either colored or masked gunpowder."   Then,
without disbanding, the troop betakes itself to the environs and
into the country, where it operates with the same celerity in the
châteaux, so that "in one day all honest citizens, those with the
most property and furniture to protect, are left without arms at
the mercy of the first robber that comes along."   All reputed

aristocrats are disarmed. Those are reputed aristocrats who
"disapprove of the enthusiasm of the day, or who do not attend
the club, or who harbor any unsworn ecclesiastic," and, first of
all, "the officers of the National Guard who are nobles, begin-
,ing with the commander and his entire staff."—The latter allow
their swords to be taken without resistance, and with a forbearance and patriotic spirit of which their brethren everywhere
furnish an example, "they are obliging enough to remain at their
posts so as not to disorganise the army, hoping that this frenzy
will soon come to an end," contenting themselves with making
their complaint to the department.—But in vain the department
orders their arms to be restored to them.   The clubbists refuse
to give them up so long as the king refuses to accept the Constitution; meanwhile they do not hesitate to say that "at the
very first gun on the frontier, they will cut the throats of all the
nobles and unsworn priests."—After the royal oath to the Constitution is taken, the department again insists, but no attention
is paid to it.   On the contrary, the National Guard, dragging
cannons along with them, purposely station themselves before
the mansions of the unarmed gentry; the ladies of their families
are followed in the streets by urchins who sing *ça ira* in their
faces, and, in the final refrain, they mention them by name and
promise them the lantern; " not one of them could invite a dozen
of his friends to supper without incurring the risk of an ebulli-
tion."—On the strength of this, the old chiefs of the National
Guard resign, and the Jacobins turn the opportunity to account.
In contempt of the law the whole body of officers is renewed,
and, as peaceable folks dare not deposit their votes, the new
staff "is composed of infuriated men, taken for the most part,
from the lowest class."   With this purged militia the club expels
nuns, drives off unsworn priests, organises expeditions in the
neighborhood, and goes so far as to purify suspected municipalities.[1]—So many acts of violence committed in town and country,
render town and country uninhabitable, and for the élite of the
proprietors, or for well-bred persons, there is no longer any

[1] On the 15th of August, 1791, the mother-superior of the Hotel-Dieu hospital is forcibly
.rried off and placed in a tavern, half a league from the town, while the rest of the nuns
..re driven out and replaced by eight young girls. Among other motives that require notice
is the hostility of two apothecaries belonging to the club; in the Hotel-Dieu the nuns, keeping a pharmacy, by which they defrayed expenses through the sale of drugs, brought them
selves into competition with the two apothecaries.

asylum but Paris. After the first disarmament seven or eight families take refuge there, and a dozen or fifteen more join them after a threat of having their throats cut; after the religious persecution, unsworn ecclesiastics, the rest of the nobles, and countless other townspeople, "even with little means," betake themselves there in a mass. There, at least, one is lost in the crowd; one is protected by an incognito against the outrages of the commonalty; one can live there as a private individual. In the provinces even civil rights do not exist; how could any one there exercise political rights? "All honest citizens are kept away from the primary meetings by threats or maltreatment. . . . The battle-field remains with those who pay forty-five sous of taxes, more than one-half of them being registered on the poor list."—See how the elections are decided beforehand! The old cook is the one who authorises or creates candidatures, and on the election of the department deputies at the county town, the electors elected are veritably, like himself, Jacobins.[1]

V.

Such is the pressure under which voting takes place in France during the summer and fall of 1791. Domiciliary visits and disarmament everywhere force nobles and ecclesiastics, landed proprietors and people of culture, to abandon their homes, to seek refuge in the large towns and to emigrate,[2] or, at least, confine themselves strictly to private life, to abstain from all propagandism, from every candidature, and from all voting. It would be madness to be seen in so many cantons where perquisitions terminate in a *jacquerie;* in Burgundy and the Lyonnais, where castles are sacked, where aged gentlemen are mauled and left for dead, where M. de Guillin has just been assassinated and cut to pieces ; at Marseilles, where conservative party leaders are im-

---

[1] Cf. "Archives Nationales," DXXIX. 13. Letter of the municipal officers and notables of Champneuil, to the administrators of Seine-et-Oise, concerning elections, June 17, 1791.— Similar letters, from various other parishes, among them that of Charcon, June 16: They "have the honor to inform you that, at the time of the preceding primary meetings, they were exposed to the greatest danger; that the curé of Charcon, their pastor, was repeatedly stabbed with a bayonet, the marks of which he will carry to his grave. The mayor, and several other inhabitants of Charcon, escaped the same peril with difficulty."—*Ibid.*, letters from the administrators of Hautes-Alpes to the National Assembly (September, 1791), on the disturbances in the electoral assembly of Gap, August 29, 1791.

[2] "The French Revolution," pp. 159, 160, 310, 323, 324.—Lauvergne, "Histoire du département du Var," 104 (August 23).

prisoned, where a regiment of Swiss guards under arms scarcely
suffices to enforce the verdict of the court which sets them at liberty, where, if any indiscreet person opposes Jacobin resolutions
his mouth is closed by being notified that he will be buried alive;
at Toulon, where the Jacobins shoot down all conservatives and
the regular troops, where M. de Beaucaire, captain in the navy,
is killed by a shot in the back, where the club, supported by the
needy, by sailors, by navvies, and "vagabond pedlars," maintains a dictatorship by right of conquest; at Brest, at Tulle, at
Cahors, where at this very moment gentlemen and officers are
massacred in the street. It is not surprising that honest people
turn away from the ballot-box as from a centre of cut-throats.—
Nevertheless, let them come if they like; it will be easy to get rid
of them. At Aix, the assessor whose duty it is to read the electors' names is informed that "the names should be called out by
an unsullied mouth, that, being an aristocrat and fanatical, he
could neither speak nor vote," and, without further ceremony,
they put him out of the room.[1] The process is an admirable one
for converting a minority into a majority and yet here is another,
still more effectual.—At Dax, the Feuillants, taking the title of
"Friends of the French Constitution," separate from the Jacobins,[2] and, moreover, insist on excluding from the National Guard
"foreigners without property or position," the passive citizens
who are admitted into it in spite of the law, who usurp the right
of voting and who "daily affront tranquil inhabitants." Consequently, on election day, in the church where the primary

---

[1] "Archives Nationales," F 7, 3,198, deposition of Vérand Jcard, an elector at Arles, Sept. 8,
1791.—*Ibid.*, F 7, 3,195. Letter of the administrators of the Tarascon district, Dec. 8, 1791.
Two parties confront each other at the municipal elections of Barbantane, one headed by the
Abbé Chabaud, brother of one of the Avignon brigands, composed of three or four townsmen,
and of "the most impoverished in the country," and the other, three times as numerous, comprising all the land-owners, the substantial métayers and artisans, and all "who are most
interested in a good administration." The question is, whether the Abbé Chabaud is to be
mayor. The elections took place Dec. 5, 1791. Here is the official report of the acting
mayor: "We, Pierre Fontaine, mayor, addressed the rioters, to induce them to keep the
peace. At this very moment, the said Claude Gontier, *alias* Baoque, struck us with his fist
on the left eye, which bruised us considerably, and on account of which we are almost blind,
and, conjointly with others, jumped upon us, threw us down, and dragged us by the hair,
continuing to strike us, from in front of the church door, till we came in front of the door of
the town hall."

[2] *Ibid.*, F 7, 3,229. Letters of M. de Laurède, June 18, 1791; from the directory of the
department, June 8, July 31, and Sept. 22, 1791; from the municipality, July 15, 1791. The
municipality "leaves the release of the prisoners in suspense," for six months, because, it
says, the people is disposed to "insurrectionise against their discharge."—Letters of many of
the national guard, stating that the factions form only a part of it.

meeting is held, two of the Feuillants, Laurède, formerly collector of the *vingtièmes,* and Brunache, a glazier, propose to exclude an intruder, a servant on wages.   The Jacobins at once rush forward. Laurède is pressed back on the holy-water basin and wounded on the head ; on trying to escape he is seized by the hair, thrown down, pierced in the arm with a bayonet, put in prison, and Brunache along with him.   Eight days afterwards, at the second meeting none are present but Jacobins; naturally, "they are all elected" and form the new municipality, which, notwithstanding the orders of the department, not only refuses to liberate the two prisoners, but consigns them to a dungeon.—At Montpellier, the delay in the operation is greater, but it is only the more complete. The votes are deposited, the ballot-boxes closed and sealed up and the conservatives obtain a majority.   Thereupon the Jacobin club, with the band of "iron-clubs," calling itself the *Executive power,* betake themselves in force to the sectional meetings, burn one of the ballottings, use firearms and kill two men.   To restore order the municipality stations each company of the National Guard at its captain's door, and the moderates among them naturally obey orders, but the violent party do not.   They overrun the town, numbering about 2,000 inhabitants, enter the houses, kill three men in the street or in their domiciles, and force the administrative body to suspend its electoral assemblies.   In addition to this they require the disarmament "of the aristocrats," and this not being done soon enough, they kill an artisan who is walking in the street with his mother, cut off his head, bear it aloft in triumph, and suspend it in front of his dwelling.   The authorities, thus persuaded, accordingly decree a disarmament, and the victors parade the streets in a body.   Either on account of their jollity, or as a precaution, they fire at the windows of suspected houses as they pass along and happen to kill an additional man and woman.   During the three following days six hundred families emigrate, while the authorities report that everything is going on well, and that order is restored ; "the elections," they say, "are now proceeding in the quietest manner on account of the ill-intentioned voluntarily keeping away from them, a large number having left the town."[1]   A void is created around the ballot-box and this is called the unanimity of voters.

---

[1] *Mercure de France,* Dec. 10, 1791, letter from Montpellier, dated Nov. 17, 1791.—"Ar chives Nationales," F⁷, 3,223.   Extracts from letters, on the incidents of Oct. 9 and 12, 179:

The effect of such executions is great and not many of them are requisite; a few suffice when successful and when they go un-punished, which is always the case. Henceforth all that the Jar obins have to do is to threaten; people no longer resist them for they know that it costs too much to face them down; they do not care to attend electoral meetings and there meet insult and danger; they acknowledge defeat at the start. Have not the Jacobins irresistible arguments, without taking blows into account? At Paris,[1] Marat in three successive numbers of his paper has just denounced by name "the rascals and thieves" who canvass for electoral nominations, not the nobles and priests but ordinary citizens, lawyers, architects, physicians, jewellers, stationers, print-ers, upholsterers and other mechanics, each name being given in full with the professions, addresses and one of the following quali-fications, "hypocrite (*tartufe*), immoral, dishonest, bankrupt, in-former, usurer, cheat," not to mention others that I cannot trans-cribe. It must be noted that this slanderous list may become a proscriptive list, and that in every town and village in France similar lists are constantly drawn up and circulated by the local club, which enables us to judge whether the struggle between it and its adversaries is a fair one.—As to rural electors, it has suit-able means for persuading them, especially in the innumerable cantons ravaged or threatened by the *jacqueries*, or, for example, in Corrèze, where "the whole department is overspread with in-surrections and devastations, and where nobody talks of anything but of hanging the officers who serve papers."[2] Through-out the electoral operations the sittings of the club are perma-nent; "its electors are incessantly summoned to its meetings;" at each of these "the main question is the destruction of fish-ponds and rentals, their principal speakers summing it all up by saying that none ought to be paid." The majority of electors, composed of rustics, are found to be sensitive to eloquence of this kind; all its candidates are obliged to express themselves against

---

Petition by Messrs. Théri and Devon, Nov. 17, 1791. Letter addressed by them to the Min-ister, Oct. 25. Letters of M. Dupin, syndical attorney of the department, to the Minister, Nov. 14 and 15, and Dec. 26, 1791 (with official reports).—Among those assassinated on the 14th and 15th of November, we find a jeweller, an attorney, a carpenter, and a dyer. "This painful scene," writes the syndic attorney, "has restored quiet to the town."

[1] Buchez et Roux, X. 223 (*L'Ami du Peuple*, June 17, 19, 21, 179.).

[2] "Archives Nationales,' F7, 3,204, letter by M. Melon Pradon, royal commissary at Tulle, Sept. 8, 1791.

fishponds and rentals; its deputies and the public prosecuting attorney are nominated on this profession of faith; in other words, to be elected, the Jacobins promise to greedy tenants the incomes and property of their owners.—We already see in the proceedings by which they secure one-third of the offices in 1791 the germ of the proceedings by which they will secure the whole of them in 1792; in this first electoral campaign their acts indicate not merely their maxims and policy but, again, the condition, education, spirit and character of the men whom they place in power locally as well as at the capital.

CHAPTER IX.

I.

THE worst feature of anarchy is not so much the absence of the overthrown government as the rise of new governments of an inferior grade. Every fallen State produces bands which conquer and which are sovereign; it was so in Gaul on the fall of the Roman empire, also under the latest of Charlemagne's successors; the same state of things exists now in Roumelia and in Mexico. Adventurers, malefactors, men in bad repute, social outcasts, men overwhelmed with debts and lost to honor, vagabonds, deserters, dissolute troopers—born enemies of work, of subordination, and of the law—form leagues for breaking down the worm-eaten barriers which still surround the sheep-like masses; and as they are unscrupulous, they slaughter on all occasions. On this foundation their authority rests; each in turn reigns in its own canton, and their government, in keeping with its brutal masters, consists in robbery and murder; nothing else can be looked for from barbarians and brigands.

But never are they so dangerous as when, in a great State

recently fallen, a sudden revolution places the central power in their hands; for they then regard themselves as the legitimate inheritors of the shattered government, and, under this title, they undertake to manage the commonwealth. Now in times of anarchy the ruling power does not proceed from above, but from below; and the chiefs, therefore, who would remain such, are obliged to follow the blind impulsion of their flock.[1] Hence the important and dominant personage, the one whose ideas prevail, the veritable successor of Richelieu and of Louis XIV., is here the subordinate Jacobin, the pillar of the club, the maker of motions, the street rioter, Panis, Sergent, Hébert, Varlet, Henriot, Maillard, Fournier, Lazowski, or, still lower in the scale, the Marseilles "rough," the faubourg cannoneer, the drinking market-porter who elaborates his political conceptions in the interval between his hiccoughs.[2]—For information he has the rumors circulating in the streets which assign a traitor to each domicile, and for other acquisitions the club bombast, through which he becomes the leader of the great machine. This machine so vast, so complex, such a complete whole of entangled services ramifying in innumerable offices, with so much apparatus of special import, so delicate as to require constant adaptation to changing circumstances, diplomacy, finances, justice, army administration—all this transcends his limited comprehension; a bottle cannot be made to contain the bulk of a hogshead.[3] In his

---

[1] Thierry, son of Clovis, unwilling to take part in an expedition of his brothers into Burgundy, was told by his men: "If thou art unwilling to march into Burgundy with thy brothers, we will leave thee and follow them in thy place."—Clotaire, another of his sons, disposed to make peace with the Saxons, "the angry Francs rush upon him, revile him, and threaten to kill him if he declines to accompany them. Upon which he puts himself at their head."

[2] Social condition and degree of culture are often indicated orthographically.—Granier de Cassagnac, II. 480. Bécard, commanding the expedition which brought back the prisoners from Orleans, signs himself: "Bécard, commandant congointement aveque M. Fournier generalle."—"Archives Nationales," F 7, 4,426. Letter of Chemin, commissioner of the Gravilliers section, to Santerre, Aug. 11, 1792. "Mois Charles Chemin commissaire . . . fait part à Monsieur Santaire générale de la troupe parisiene que le nommé Hingray caviliers de la gendarmeris nationalle . . ma déclarés qu'ille sestes trouvés aux jourduis 11 aoux avec une home attachés à la cours aux Equris: quille lui aves dis quiere 800 home a peupres des sidevant garde du roy étes tous près a fondre sure Paris pour donaire du sécour a naux rébelle et a signer avec moi la presente."

[3] On the 19th of March, 1871, I met in the Rue de Varennes a man with two guns on his shoulder wno had taken part in the pillage of the Ecole d'Etat-major and was on his way home. I said to him: "But this is civil war, and you will let the Prussians in Paris." "I'd rather have the Prussians than Thiers. Thiers is the inside Prussian!"

narrow brain, perverted and turned topsy-turvy by the dis
proportionate notions put into it, only one idea suited to his
gross instincts and aptitudes finds a place there, and that is the
desire to kill his enemies; and these are also the State's enemies,
however open or concealed, present or future, probable or even
possible. He carries this savagery and bewilderment into politics,
and hence the evil arising from his usurpation. Simply a brigand, he would have murdered only to rob, and his murders
would have been restricted. As representing the State, he undertakes wholesale massacres, of which he has the means ready at
hand.—For he has not yet had time enough to take apart the
old administrative implements; at all events the minor wheels,
gendarmes, jailers, employees, book-keepers, and accountants, are
always in their places and under control. There can be no resistance on the part of those arrested; accustomed to the protection
of the laws and to peaceable ways and times, they have never
relied on defending themselves nor ever could imagine that any
one could be so summarily slain. As to the mass, rendered
incapable of any effort of its own by ancient centralisation, it
remains inert and passive and lets things go their own way.—
Hence, during many long, successive days, without being hurried
or impeded, with official papers quite correct and accounts in
perfect order, a massacre can be carried out with the same impunity and as methodically as cleaning the streets or clubbing
stray dogs.

II.

Let us trace the progress of the homicidal idea in the mass of
the party. It lies at the very bottom of the revolutionary creed.
Collot d'Herbois, two months after this, aptly says in the Jacobin
tribune: "The second of September is the great article in the
credo of our freedom." [1] It is peculiar to the Jacobin to consider
himself as a legitimate sovereign, and to treat his adversaries not
as belligerents, but as criminals. They are guilty of *lèse-nation ;*
they are outlaws, fit to be killed at all times and places, and deserve extinction, even when no longer able or in a condition to
do any harm.—Consequently, on the 10th of August the Swiss
Guards, who do not fire a gun and who surrender, the wounded

---

[1] *Moniteur,* Nov 14, 1792.

lying on the ground, their surgeons, the palace domestics, are killed; and, worse still, persons like M. de Clermont-Tonnerre who pass quietly along the street.   All this is now called in official phraseology the justice of the people.—On the 11th the Swiss Guards, collected in the Feuillants building, come near being massacred; the populace on the outside of it demand their heads; "it conceives the project of visiting all the prisons in Paris to take out the prisoners and administer prompt justice on them."—On the 12th in the markets[2] "divers groups of the low class call Pétion a scoundrel," because "he saved the Swiss in the Palais Bourbon"; accordingly, "he and the Swiss must be hung to-day."—In these minds turned topsy-turvy the actual, palpable truth gives way to its opposite; "the attack was not begun by them; the order to sound the tocsin came from the palace; it is the palace which was besieging the nation, and not the nation which was besieging the palace."[3]   The vanquished "are the assassins of the people," caught in the act; and on the 14th of August the Federates demand a court-martial "to avenge the death of their comrades."[4]   And even a court-martial will not answer: "It is not sufficient to mete out punishment for crimes committed on the 10th of August, but the vengeance of the people must be extended to all conspirators;" to that "Lafayette, who probably was not in Paris, *but who may have been there;*" to all the ministers, generals, judges, and other officials guilty of maintaining legal order wherever it had been maintained, and of not having recognised the Jacobin government before it came into being. Let them be brought before, not the ordinary courts, which are not to be trusted because they belong to the defunct régime, but before a specially organised tribunal, a sort of "*chambre ardente,*"[5] elected by the sections, that is to say, by a Jacobin minority. These improvised judges must give judgment on conviction, without appeal; there must be no preliminary examinations, no interval of time between arrest and execution, no dilatory and

[1] Buchez et Roux, XVII. 31.

[2] "Archives Nationales," F⁷, 4,426.   Letter of the police administrators, Aug. 11.   Declaration of Delaunay, Aug. 12.

[3] Buchez et Roux, XVII. 59 (session of Aug. 12).   Speech by Leprieur at the bar of the house.

[4] Buchez et Roux, XVII. 47.—Mortimer-Ternaux, III. 31.   Speech by Robespierre at the bar of the Assembly in the name of the commune, Aug. 15.

[5] Brissot, in his report on Robespierre's petition.—The names of the principal judges elected show its character: Fouquier-Tinville, Osselin, Coffinhal.

protective formalities. And above all, the Assembly must be expeditious in passing the decree; "otherwise," it is informed by a delegate from the Commune, "the tocsin will be rung at midnight and the general alarm sounded; for the people are tired of waiting to be avenged. Look out lest they do themselves justice!"[1]—A moment more, new threats and at a shorter date. "If the juries are not ready to act in two or three hours . . . great misfortunes will overtake Paris."

In vain the new tribunal, instantly installed, hastens its work and guillotines three innocent persons in five days; it does not move fast enough. On the 23d of August one of the sections declares to the Commune in furious language that the people themselves, "wearied and indignant" with so many delays, mean to force open the prisons and massacre the inmates.[2]—Not only do they harass the judges, but they force the accused into their presence. A deputation from the Commune and the Federates summons the Assembly "to transfer the criminals at Orleans to Paris to undergo the penalty of their heinous crimes," "otherwise," says the orator, "we will not answer for the vengeance of the people."[3] And in a still more imperative manner: "You have heard and you know that insurrection is a sacred duty," a sacred duty towards and against all: against the Assembly if it refuses, and against the tribunal if it acquits. They dash at their prey athwart all legislative and judicial formalities, like a kite across the web of a spider, while nothing diverts them from their fixed conceptions. On the acquittal of M. Luce de Montmorin[4] the brutal audience, mistaking him for his cousin the former minister of Louis XVI., break out in murmurings. The president tries to enforce silence, which increases the uproar, and M. de Montmorin is in danger. On this the president, discovering a side issue, announces that one of the jurors is related to the accused, and that in such a case a new jury must be impanelled and a new trial take place; that the matter will be enquired into, and meanwhile the prisoner will be returned to the Conciergerie. Thereupon he takes M. de Montmorin by the arm and leads him out of the court-room, amidst the yells of the audience and not

[1] Buchez et Roux, XVII. 91 (Aug. 17).
[2] Stated by Pétion in his speech (*Moniteur*, Nov. 10, 1792).
[3] Buchez et Roux, XVII. 116 (session of Aug. 23).
[4] Mortimer-Ternaux, III. 461.—Moore, I. 273 (Aug. 31).

Guards peril to himself; in the outside court one of the National without strikes at him with a sabre, and the following day the court is obliged to authorise eight delegates from the audience to go and see with their own eyes that M. de Montmorin is safe under lock and key.

At the moment of his acquittal a tragic exclamation is heard: "You discharge him to-day and in two weeks he will cut our throats!" Fear is evidently an adjunct of hatred. The Jacobin rabble is vaguely conscious of its inferior numbers, of its usurpation, of its danger, which increases in proportion as Brunswick draws near. It feels itself encamped over a mine, and if the mine should explode!—Since its adversaries are scoundrels they are capable of a sudden blow, of a plot, of a massacre; never itself having done anything else, it conceives no other idea; and, through an inevitable transposition of thought, it imputes to them the murderous intentions obscurely wrought out in the dark recesses of its own disturbed brain.—On the 27th of August, after the funeral procession gotten up by Sergent expressly to excite popular resentment, its suspicions, at once direct and pointed, begin to take the form of certainty. Ten "commemorative" banners,[1] each borne by a volunteer on horseback, have paraded before all eyes the long list of massacres "by the court and its agents"; the massacre at Nancy, the massacre at Nismes, the massacre at Montauban, the massacre at Avignon, the massacre at La Chapelle, the massacre at Carpentras, the massacre of the Champ de Mars, etc. Hesitation, in the face of such processions, is out of the question; henceforth, to women in the galleries, to the frequenters of the clubs, and to pikemen in the suburbs it is proved beyond any doubt that aristocrats are old offenders.

And on the other side there is another sign equally alarming "This lugubrious ceremony, which ought to inspire by turns both reflection and indignation, . . . did not generally produce that effect." The National Guard in uniform, who came "apparently to compensate themselves for not appearing on the day of action," did not comport themselves with civic propriety, but, on the contrary, put on "an air of dissipation and even of noisy gaiety"; they come out of curiosity, like so many Parisian cockneys, and

---

[1] Buchez et Roux, XVII. 267 (article by Prudhomme in the "Révolutions de Paris").

are much more numerous than the *sans-culottes* with their pikes[1] The latter can count themselves and plainly see that they are in a minority, and a very small one, and that their rage finds no echo; none but supernumeraries and the contrivers of the fête are there to hasten sentences and call for death-penalties. A foreigner, a good observer, who questions the shop-keepers of whom he makes purchases, the tradesmen he knows, and the company he finds in the coffee-houses, writes that he never had " seen any symptom of a sanguinary disposition except in the galleries of the National Assembly and at the Jacobin Club." Now the galleries are full of paid " applauders," especially " females, who are more noisy and to be had cheaper than males "; at the Jacobin Club are " the leaders, who dread what may be divulged against them or who have private hatreds to gratify";[2] thus the only infuriates are the leaders and the populace of the suburbs.—Lost in the crowd of this vast city, in the face of a National Guard still armed and three times their own number, confronting an indifferent or discontented bourgeoisie, the patriots are alarmed. In this state of anxiety a feverish imagination, exasperated by delays, involuntarily gives birth to fancies passionately accepted as truths, while an incident now occurs which suffices to complete the story, the germ of which has grown in their minds without their knowing it.

On the 1st of September a poor waggoner, Jean Julien,[3] condemned to chains for twelve years with exposure in the pillory, becomes furious after a couple of hours of this latter penalty, probably on account of the jeers of the by-standers; with the usual coarseness of people of his stamp he vents his impotent rage by ridding himself of his clothes and exposing his person, and naturally uses insulting language to the people who look at him: " Hurrah for the King! Hurrah for the Queen! Hurrah for Lafayette! Let the nation go to the devil!" It is also natural that he should be nearly cut to pieces. He is at once led away to the Conciergerie, where he is at once condemned, and guillo-

---

[1] "Les Révolutions de Paris," *Ibid.*, "A number of *sans-culottes* were there with their pikes; but these were *largely outnumbered* by the multitude of uniforms of the various battalions." Moore, Aug, 31: "At present the inhabitants of the faubourgs Saint-Antoine and Saint-Marceau are all that is felt of the sovereign people in Paris."

[2] Moore, Aug. 26.

[3] Mortimer-Ternaux, III. 471. Indictment against Jean-Julien.—In referring to M. Mortimer-Ternaux we do so because, like a true critic, he cites authentic and frequently unedited documents.

tined as soon as possible, for being a promoter of sedition in connection with the conspiracy of August the 10th.—The conspiracy, accordingly, is still in existence. It is so declared by the tribunal, which makes no declaration without evidence. Jean Julien has certainly confessed; now what has he revealed?—On the following day, like a crop of poisonous mushrooms, the growth of a single night, the story obtains general credence. "Jean Julien has declared that all the prisons in Paris thought as he did, that there would soon be fine times, that the prisoners were armed, and that as soon as the volunteers cleared out they would be let loose on all Paris."[1] The streets are full of anxious countenances. "One says that Verdun had been betrayed like Longwy. Others shook their heads and said it was the traitors within Paris and not the declared enemies on the frontier that were to be feared."[2] On the following day the story grows: "There are royalist officers and soldiers hidden away in Paris and in the outskirts. They are going to open the prisons, arm the prisoners, set the King and his family free, put the patriots in Paris to death, also the wives and children of those in the army. . . . It is natural for men to secure their wives and children when they are going to be separated from them, and to use the most efficient means of preventing their being opposed to the assassin's dagger."[3] The popular conflagration is lighted, and all that remains for those who kindled the flame is to mark out the path for it.

III.

It is a long time that they have fanned the flame. Already, on the 11th of August, the new Commune had announced, in a proclamation,[4] that "the guilty should perish on the scaffold," while its threatening deputations force the National Assembly into the immediate institution of a bloody tribunal. Carried into

---

[1] Rétif de la Bretonne, "Les Nuits de Paris," 11th night, p. 372.

[2] Moore, Sept. 2.

[3] Moore, Sept. 3.—Buchez et Roux, XVI. 159 (narrative by Tallien).—Official report of the Paris Commune, Sept. 4 (in the collection of Barrière and Berville, the volume entitled " Mémoires sur les journées de Septembre "). The commune adopts and expands the fable, probably invented by it. Prudhomme well says that the story of the prison plot, so scandalously circulated during the Reign of Terror, appears for the first time on the 2d of September. The same report was spread through the rural districts. At Gennevilliers, a peasant, while lamenting the massacres, said to Malouet: "It is, too, a terrible thing for the aristocrats to want to kill all the people by blowing up the city " (Malouet, II. 244).

[4] Official reports of the commune, Aug. 11

power by brutal force, it must perish if it does not maintain itself, and this can be done only through terror.—Consider for one moment, indeed, this singular situation. Installed in the Hôtel-de-ville by a bold nocturnal enterprise, about one hundred unknown individuals, delegated by a party which thinks or asserts itself to be the peoples' delegates, have overthrown one of the two great powers of the State, mangled and enslaved the other, and now rule in a capital of 700,000 souls, by the grace of eight or ten thousand fanatics and cut-throats. Never did change so sudden take men from so low a point and raise them so high! The basest of newspaper scribblers, penny-a-liners out of the gutters, bar-room oracles, unfrocked monks and priests, the refuse of the literary guild, of the bar, and of the clergy, carpenters, turners, grocers, locksmiths, shoemakers, common laborers, many with no profession at all,[1] strolling politicians and public brawlers, who, like the sellers of counterfeit wares, have speculated for the past three years on popular credulity; among them a number of men in bad repute, of doubtful honesty or of proven dishonesty, having led shiftless lives in their youth and still besmirched with old slime, put outside the pale of useful labor by their vices, driven out of inferior stations even into prohibited occupations, bruised by the perilous leap, with consciences distorted like the muscles of a tight-rope dancer, and who, were it not for the Revolution, would still grovel in their native filth, awaiting Bicêtre or the bagnios to which they were destined—can one imagine their growing intoxication as they drink deep draughts from the bottomless cup of absolute power?—For it is absolute power which they demand and which they exercise.[2] Raised by a special delegation above the regular authorities, they put up with these only as subordinates, and tolerate none among them who may become their rivals. Consequently, they reduce the Legis-

---

[1] Mortimer-Ternaux, II. 446. List of the section commissioners sitting at the Hôtel-de-ville, Aug. 10, before 9 o'clock in the morning.

[2] Official reports of the commune, Aug. 21. "Considering that, to ensure public safety and liberty, the council-general of the commune *required all the power delegated to it by the people,* at the time it was compelled to resume the exercise of its rights," sends a deputation to the National Assembly to insist that "the new department be converted, pure and simple, into a tax-commissioners' office."—Mortimer-Ternaux, III. 25. Speech of Robespierre in the name of the commune : "After the people have saved the country, after decreeing a National Convention to replace you, what remains for you to do but to gratify their wishes ? . . The people, forced to see to its own salvation, has provided for this through its delegates. . . It is essential that those chosen by itself for its magistrates *should enjoy the plenary powers befitting the sovereign.*"

lative body simply to the function of editor and herald of their decrees; they have forced the new department electors to "abjure their title," to confine themselves to tax assessments, while they lay their ignorant hands daily on every other service, on the finances, the army, supplies, the administration, justice, at the risk of breaking the administrative wheels or of interrupting their action.

One day they summon the Minister of War before them, or, for lack of one, his chief clerk; another day they keep the whole body of officials in his department in arrest for two hours, under the pretext of finding a suspected printer.[1] At one time they affix seals on the funds devoted to extraordinary expenses; at another time they do away with the commission on supplies; at another they meddle with the course of justice, either to aggravate proceedings or to impede the execution of sentences rendered.[2] There is no principle, no law, no regulation, no verdict, no public man or establishment that is not subject to the risk of their arbitrament.—And, as they have laid hands on power, they do the same with money. Not only do they extort from the Assembly 850,000 francs a month, with arrears from the 1st of January, 1792, more than six millions in all, to defray the expenses of their military police, which means to pay their bands,[3] but again, "invested with the municipal scarf," they seize, "in the public edifices belonging to the nation, all furniture, and whatever is of most value." "In one building alone, they carry off to the value of 100,000 crowns."[4] Elsewhere, in the hands of the treasurer of the civil list, they appropriate to themselves a box of jewels, other precious objects, and 340,000 francs.[5] Their commissioners bring in from Chantilly three three-horse

---

[1] Official reports of the commune, Aug. 10.—Mortimer-Ternaux, III. 155. Letter of the Minister Servan, Aug. 30.—*Ibid.*, 149.—*Ibid.*, 148. The commission on supplies having been broken up by the commune, Roland, the Minister of the Interior, begs the Assembly to act promptly, for "he will no longer be responsible for the supplies of Paris."

[2] Official reports of the commune, Aug. 21. A resolution requiring that, on trials for *lèse-nation*, those who appear for the defendants should be provided with a certificate of their integrity, issued by their assembled section, and that the interviews between them and the accused be public.—*Ibid.*, Aug. 17, a resolution to suspend the execution of the two assassins of mayor Simonneau, condemned to death by the tribunal of Seine-et-Oise.

[3] Mortimer-Ternaux, III. 11. Decree of Aug. 11.

[4] Prudhomme, "Révolutions de Paris" (number for Sept. 22). Report by Roland to the National Assembly (Sept. 16, at 9 o'clock in the morning).

[5] Madame Roland, "Mémoires," II. 414 (Ed. Barrière et Berville). Report by Roland Oct. 29. The seizure in question took place Aug. 27.

vehicles "loaded with the spoils of M. de Condé," and they un
dertake "removing the contents of the houses of the *émigrés*." [1]
They confiscate in the churches of Paris "the crucifixes, music-
stands, bells, railings, and every object in bronze or of iron,
chandeliers, cups, vases, reliquaries, statues, every article of
plate," as well "on the altars as in the sacristies," [2] and we can
imagine the enormous booty obtained; to cart away the silver
plate belonging to the single church of Madeleine-de-la-ville
required a vehicle drawn by four horses.—Now they use all this
money, so freely seized, as freely as they do power itself.
One fills his pockets in the Tuileries without the slightest concern; another, in the Garde-Meuble, rummages secretaries, and
carries off a wardrobe with its contents. [3] We have already seen
that in the depositories of the Commune "most of the seals are
broken," that enormous sums in plate, in jewels, in gold and
silver coin have disappeared. Future inquests and accounts will
charge on the Committee of Supervision, "abstractions, dilapi-
dations, and embezzlements," in short, "a mass of violations and
breaches of trust."—When one is king, one easily mistakes the
money-drawer of the State for the drawer in which one keeps
one's own money.

Unfortunately, this full possession of public power and of the
public funds holds only by a slender thread. Let the evicted
and outraged majority dare, as subsequently at Lyons, Marseilles, and Toulon, to return to the section assemblies and revoke the false mandate which they have arrogated to themselves
through fraud and force, and, on the instant, they again become,
through the sovereign will of the people, and by virtue of their
own creed, what they really are, usurpers, extortioners, and robbers; there is no middle course for them between a dictatorship
and the galleys.—The mind, before such an alternative, unless
extraordinarily well-balanced, loses its equilibrium; they have no
difficulty in deluding themselves with the idea that the State is
menaced in their persons, and, in postulating the rule, that all is

---

[1] Mémoires sur les journées de Septembre" (Ed. Barrière et Berville, pp. 307-322). List
of sums paid by the treasurer of the commune.—See, on the prolongation of this plundering,
Roland's report, Oct. 29, of money, plate, and assignats taken from the Senlis Hospital (Sept.
13), the Hotel de Coigny emptied, and sale of furniture in the Hotel d'Egmont, etc.

[2] Official reports of the commune, Aug. 17 and 20.—List of sums paid by the treasurer of
the commune, p. 3, 1.—On the 28th of August a "St. Roch" in silver is brought to the bar
of the National Assembly.

[3] Mortimer-Ternaux, III. 150, 161, 511.—Report by Roland, Oct. 29, p. 414.

allowable for them, even massacre. Has not **Bazire** stated in the tribune that, against the enemies of the nation, "all means are fair and justifiable?" Has not another deputy, Jean Debry, proposed the formation of a body of 1,200 volunteers, who "will sacrifice themselves," as formerly the assassins of the Old Man of the Mountain, in "attacking tyrants, hand to hand, individually," as well as generals?[1] Have we not seen Merlin de Thionville insisting that "the wives and children of the *émigrés* should be kept as hostages," and declared responsible, or, in other words, ready for slaughter if their relatives continue their attacks?[2]

This is all that can be done, for other measures have not proved sufficient.—In vain has the Commune decreed the arrest of journalists belonging to the opposite party, and distributed their presses amongst patriotic printers.[3] In vain has it declared the members of the Sainte-Chapelle club, the National Guards who have sworn allegiance to Lafayette, the signers of the petition of 8,000, and of that of 20,000, disqualified for any service whatever.[4] In vain has it multiplied domiciliary visits, even to the residence and carriages of the Venetian ambassador. In vain, through insulting and repeated examinations, does it keep at its bar, under the hootings and death-cries of its tribunes, the most honorable and most illustrious men, Lavoisier, Dupont de Nemours, the eminent surgeon Desault, the most harmless and most refined ladies, Madame de Tourzel, Mademoiselle de Tourzel, and the Princesse de Lamballe.[5] In vain, after a profusion of arrests during twenty days, it envelopes all Paris in one cast of its net for a nocturnal search:[6] the barriers closed and doubly

---

[1] *Moniteur*, XIII. 514, 542 (sessions of Aug. 23 and 26).

[2] Mortimer-Ternaux, III. 99 (sessions of Aug. 15 and 23). "Procès-verbaux de la Commune," Aug. 18, a resolution to obtain a law authorising the commune "to collect together the wives and children of the *émigrés* in places of security, and to make use of the former convents for this purpose."

[3] "Procès-verbaux de la Commune," Aug. 12.—*Ibid.*, Aug. 18. Not being able to find M. Geoffroy, the journalist, the commune "passes a resolution that seals be affixed to Madame Geoffroy's domicile and that she be placed in arrest until her husband appears to release her."

[4] "Procès-verbaux de la Commune," Aug. 17 and 18. Another resolution, again demanding of the National Assembly a list of the signers for publication.

[5] "Procès-verbaux de la Commune," Aug. 18, 19, 20.—On the 20th of August the commune summons before it and examines the Venetian Ambassador. "A citizen claims to be heard against the ambassador, and states that several carriages went out of Paris in his name. The name of this citizen is Chevalier, a horse-shoer's assistant . . The Council decrees that honorable mention be made of the affidavits brought forward in the accusation." On the tone of these examinations read Weber (" Mémoires," II. 245), who narrates his own.

[6] Buchez et Roux, XVII. 215. Narration by Peltier.—In spite of the orders of the Na.

guarded, sentinels on the quays and boats stationed on the Seine to prevent escape by water, the city divided beforehand into circumscriptions, and for each section, a list of suspected persons, the circulation of vehicles stopped, every citizen ordered to stay at home, the silence of death after six o'clock in the evening, and then, in each street, a patrol of sixty pikemen, seven hundred squads of *sans-culottes*, all working at the same time, and with their usual brutality, doors burst in with pieces of timber, wardrobes picked by locksmiths, walls sounded by masons, cellars searched even to digging in the ground, papers seized, arms confiscated, three thousand persons arrested and led off,[1] priests, old men, the infirm, the sick, and from ten in the evening to five o'clock in the morning, the same as in a city taken by assault, the screams of women rudely treated, the cries of prisoners compelled to march, the oaths of the guards, cursing and drinking at each grog-shop; never was there such an universal, methodical execution, so well calculated to suppress all inclination for resistance in the silence of general stupefaction.

And yet, at this very moment, there are those who act in good faith in the sections and in the Assembly, and who rebel at being under such masters. A deputation from the Lombards section, and another from the Corn-market, come to the Assembly and protest against the Commune's usurpations.[2] Choudieu, the *Montagnard*, denounces its glaring prevarications. Cambon, a stern financier, will no longer consent to have his accounts tampered with by thieving tricksters.[3] The Assembly at last seems to have recovered itself. It extends its protection to Géray, the journalist, against whom the new pachas had issued a warrant;

---

tional Assembly the affair is repeated on the following day, and it lasts from the 19th to the 31st of August, in the evening.—Moore, Aug. 31. The stupid, sheep-like vanity of the bourgeois enlisted as a gendarme for the *sans-culottes* is here well depicted. The keeper of the Hôtel Meurice, where Moore and Lord Lauderdale put up, was on guard and on the chase the night before: "He talked a good deal of the fatigue he had undergone, and hinted a little of the dangers to which he had been exposed in the course of this severe duty. Being asked if he had been successful in his search after suspected persons—'Yes, my lord, infinitely; our battalion arrested four priests.' He could not have looked more lofty if he had taken the Duke of Brunswick."

[1] According to Rœderer, the number arrested amounted to from 5,000 to 6,000 persons.

[2] Mortimer-Ternaux, III. 147, 148, Aug. 28 and 29.—*Ibid.*, 176. Other sections complain of the Commune with some bitterness.—Buchez et Roux, XVII. 358.—"Procès-verbaux de la Commune," Sept. 1. "The section of the Temple sends a deputation which declares that by virtue of a decree of the National Assembly it withdraws its powers entrusted to the commissioners elected by it to the council-general."

[3] Mortimer-Ternaux, III. 154 (session of Aug. 30)

it summons to its own bar the signers of the warrant, and orders them to confine themselves in future to the exact limits of the law which they transgress.   Better still, it dissolves the interloping Council, and substitutes for it ninety-six delegates, to be elected by the sections in twenty-four hours.   And, even still better, it orders an account to be rendered within two days of the objects it has seized, and the return of all gold or silver articles to the Treasury.   Quashed, and summoned to disgorge their booty, the autocrats of the Hôtel-de-ville come in vain to the Assembly in force on the following day[1] to extort from it a repeal of its decrees; the Assembly, in spite of their threats and those of their satellites, maintains its ground.—So much the worse for the stubborn; if they are not disposed to regard the flash of the sabre, they will feel its sharp edge and point.   The Commune, on the motion of Manuel, decides that, so long as public danger continues, they will stay where they are; it adopts an address by Robespierre to "restore sovereign power to the people," which means to fill the streets with armed bands;[2] it collects together its brigands by g'ving them the ownership of all that they stole on the 10th of August.[3] The session, prolonged into the night, does not terminate until one o'clock in the morning.   Sunday has come and there is no time to lose, for, in a few hours, the sections, by virtue of the decree of the National Assembly, and following the example of the Temple section the evening before, may revoke the pretended representatives at the Hôtel-de-ville.   To remain at the Hôtel-de-ville, and to be elected to the convention, demands on the part of the leaders some striking action, and this they require that very day.—That day is the the second of September.

IV.

Since the 23d of August their resolution is taken.[4] They have

---

[1] Mortimer-Ternaux, III. 171 (session of Aug. 31).—*Ibid.*, 208.—On the following day, Sept. 1, at the instigation of Danton, Thuriot obtains from the National Assembly an ambiguous decree which seems to allow the members of the commune to keep their places, provisionally at least, at the Hôtel-de-ville.

[2] "Procès-verbaux de la Commune," Sept. 1.

[3] "Procès-verbaux de la Commune," Sept. 1. "It is resolved that whatever effects fell into the hands of the citizens who fought for liberty and equality on the 10th of August shall remain in their possession; M. Tallien, secretary-general, is therefore authorised to return a gold watch to M. Lecomte, a gendarme."

[4] Four circumstances, simultaneous and in full agreement with each other, indicate this

arranged in their minds a plan of the massacre, and each one, little by little, spontaneously, according to his aptitudes, takes the part that suits him or is assigned to him.

Marat, foremost among them all, is the proposer and preacher of the operation, which, for him, is a perfectly natural one. It is an abridgment of his political system: a dictator or tribune, with full power to slay, and with no other power but that; a good master executioner, responsible, and "tied hand and foot"; this is his programme for a government since July the 14th, 1789, and he does not blush at it: "so much the worse for those who are not on a level with it!"[1] He appreciated the character of the Revolution from the first, not through genius, but sympathetically, he himself being equally as one-sided and monstrous; crazy with suspicion and beset with a homicidal mania for the past three years, reduced to one idea through mental impoverishment, that of murder, having lost the faculty for even the lowest order of reasoning, the poorest of journalists, save for pikemen and Billingsgate market-women, so monotonous in his constant paroxysms that the regular reading of his journal is like listening to hoarse cries from the cells of a madhouse. From the 19th of

---

date: 1. On the 23d of August the council-general resolves "that a tribune shall be arranged in the chamber for a journalist (M. Marat), whose duty it shall be to conduct a journal giving the acts passed and what goes on in the commune" ("Procès-verbaux de la Commune," Aug. 23).—2. On the same day, "on the motion of a member with a view to separate the prisoners of *lèse-nation* from those of the nurse's hospital and others of the same stamp in the different prisons, the council has adopted this measure" (Granier de Cassagnac, II. 100).—3. The same day the commune applauds the deputies of a section, which "in warm terms" denounce before it the tardiness of justice and declare to it that the people will "immolate" the prisoners in their prisons (*Moniteur*, Nov. 10, 1793, Narrative of Pétion).—4. The same day it sends a deputation to the Assembly to order a transfer of the Orleans prisoners to Paris (Buchez et Roux, XVII. 116). The next day, in spite of the prohibitions of the Assembly, it sends Fournier and his band to Orleans (Mortimer-Ternaux, III. 364), and each knows beforehand that Fournier is commissioned to kill him on the way. (Balleydier, "Histoire politique et militaire du peuple de Lyon," I. 79. Letter of Laussel, dated at Paris, Aug. 28:) "Our volunteers are at Orleans for the past two or three days to bring the anti-revolutionary prisoners here, who are treated too well there." On the day of Fournier's departure (Aug. 24) Moore observes in the Palais Royal and at the Tuileries "a greater number than usual of itinerant haranguers of the populace, hired for the purpose of inspiring the people with a horror of monarchy."

[1] *Moniteur*, Sept. 25, 1792, speech by Marat in the Convention.

[2] See his two journals, "L'Ami du peuple" and the "Journal de la Républic Française," especially for July and October, 1792.—The number for August 16 is headed: "Development of the vile plot of the court to destroy all patriots with fire and sword."—That of August 19: "The infamous conscript Fathers of the Circus, betraying the people and trying to delay the conviction of traitors until Mottié arrives, is marching with his army on Paris to destroy all patriots!"—That of Aug. 21: "The *gangrenés* of the Assembly, the perfidious accomplices of Mottié arranging for flight. . . The conscript Fathers, the assassins of patriots at Nancy in the Champ de Mars and in the Tuileries," etc.—All this was yelled out daily every morning by those who hawked these journals through the streets.

August he excites people to attack the prisons.   " The wisest and best course to pursue," he says, " is to go armed to the Abbaye, drag out the traitors, especially the Swiss officers and their ac- complices, and put them to the sword.   What folly it is to give them a trial !   That is already done.   You have massacred the soldiers, why should you spare the officers, ten times guiltier ? "— Also, two days later, his brain teeming with an executioner's fancies, insisting that " the soldiers deserved a thousand deaths As to the officers, they should be drawn and quartered, like Louis Capet and his tools of the *Manège*."[1]—On the strength of this the Commune adopts him as its official editor, assigns him a tribune in its assembly room, entrusts him to report its acts, and soon puts him on its supervisory or executive com mittee.

A fanatic of this stamp, however, is good for nothing but as a mouthpiece or instigator; he may, at best, figure in the end among the subordinate managers.—The chief of the enterprise,[2] Danton, is of another species, and of another stature, a veritable leader of men.   Through his past career and actual position, through his popular cynicism, ways and language, through his capacity for taking the initiative and for command, through his excessive corporeal and intellectual vigor, through his physical ascendency due to his ardent, absorbing will, he is well calculat- ed for his terrible office.—He alone of the Commune has become Minister, and there is no one but him to screen municipal out- rages with the patronage or inertia of the central authority.—He alone of the Commune and of the ministry is able to push things on and harmonise action in the pell-mell of the revolutionary chaos, and now, in the councils of the ministry, as formerly at the Hôtel-de ville, he governs.   In the constant uproar of incoherent discussions,[3] athwart "propositions *ex abrupto*, shouts, impreca- tions, the going and coming of questioning petitioners," he is seen mastering his new colleagues with his "stentorian voice, his gest-

[1] *L' Ami du Peuple*, Aug. 19 and 21.

[2] "Lettres autographs de Madame Roland," published by Madame Bancal des Issarts, Sept. 9.   " Danton leads all ; Robespierre is his puppet ; Marat holds his torch and dagger."

[3] Madame Roland "Mémoires," II. 19 (note by Roland).—*Ibid.*, 21, 23, 24.   Monge says: " Danton wants to have it so ; if I refuse he will denounce me to the Commune and at the Cordeliers, and have me hung."   Fournier's commission to Orleans was all in order, Roland probably having signed it unawares, like those of the commissioners sent into the departments by the executive council (Cf. Mortimer-Ternaux, III. 368.)

ures of an athlete, his fearful threats," taking upon himself their
duties, dictating to them what and whom he chooses, "fetching in
commissions already drawn up," taking charge of everything,
"making propositions, arrests, and proclamations, issuing brevets,"
and drawing millions out of the public treasury, casting a sop to
his dogs in the Cordeliers and the Commune, "to one 20,000
francs, and to another 10,000," "for the Revolution, and on account of their patriotism,"—such is a summary report of his doings.
Thus gorged, the pack of hungry "brawlers" and grasping intriguers, the whole serviceable force of the sections and of the
clubs, is in his hands. One is strong in times of anarchy at the
head of such a herd. Indeed, during the months of August and
September, Danton was king, and, later on, he may well say of
the 2d of September, as he did of the 10th of August, "I did it!"[1]

Not that he is naturally vindictive or sanguinary: on the con-
trary, with a butcher's temperament, he has a man's heart, and, at
the risk of compromising himself, against the wills of Marat and
Robespierre, he will, by-and-by, save his political adversaries,
Duport, Brissot, and the Girondists, the old party of the "Right."[2]
Not that he is blinded by fear, enmities, or the theory; furi-

---

[1] The person who gives me the following had it from the king, Louis Philippe, then an officer in Kellerman's corps:

On the evening of the battle of Valmy the young officer is sent to Paris to carry the news.
On his arrival (Sept. 22 or 23. 1792) he learns that he is removed from his post and appointed
governor of Strasbourg. He goes to Servan's house, Minister of War, and at first they refuse
to let him in. Servan is unwell and in bed, with the ministers in his room. The young man
states that he comes from the army and is the bearer of despatches. He is admitted, and
finds, indeed, Servan in bed with various personages around him, and he announces the victory.—They question him and he gives the details.—He then complains of having been displaced, and, stating that he is too young to command with any authority at Strasbourg,
requests to be reinstated with the army in the field. "Impossible," replies Servan; "your
place is given to another." Thereupon one of the personages present, with a peculiar visage
and a rough voice, takes him aside and says to him: "Servan is a fool! Come and see me
to-morrow and I will arrange the matter." "Who are you?" "I am Danton, the Minister
of Justice."—The next day he calls on Danton, who tells him: "It is all right; you shall
have your post back—not under Kellerman, however, but under Dumouriez; are you content?" The young man, delighted, thanks him. Danton resumes: "Let me give you one
piece of advice before you go: You have talent and will succeed. But get rid of one fault—
you talk too much. You have been in Paris twenty-four hours, and already you have repeatedly criticised the affair of September. I know this; I have been informed of it." "But that
was a massacre; how can one help calling it horrible?" "I did it," replies Danton. "The
Parisians are all so many j—— f——. A river of blood had to flow between them and the
émigrés. You are too young to understand these matters. Return to the army; it is the
only place nowadays for a young man like you and of your rank. You have a future before
you; but mind this—keep your mouth shut!"

[2] Hua, 167. Narrative by his guest, the physician Lambry, an intimate friend of Danton,
ultra-fanatical and member of a committee in which the question came up whether the mem
bers of the "Right" should likewise be put out of the way. "Danton had energetically

ous as a clubbist, he has the clear-sightedness of the politician ; he is not the dupe of the sonorous phrases he utters, he knows the value of the rogues he employs ;[1] he has no illusions about men or things, about other people or about himself; if he slays, it is with a full consciousness of what he is doing, of his party, of the situation, of the revolution, while the crude expressions which, in the tones of his bull's voice, he flings out as he passes along, are but a vivid statement of the precise truth : " We are the rabble ! We spring from the gutters ! " With the ordinary feeling of humanity, " we should soon get back into them. We can only rule through fear ! "[2] " The Parisians are so many —— —— ; a river of blood must flow between them and the *émigrés*."[3] "The tocsin about to be rung is not a signal of alarm, but a charge on the enemies of the country. . . . What is necessary to overcome them ? Boldness, boldness, always boldness !"[4] I have brought my mother here, seventy years of age ; I have sent for my children, and they came last night. Before the Prussians enter Paris, I want my family to die with me. Let twenty thousand torches be applied, and Paris instantly reduced to ashes ! "[5] " We must maintain ourselves in Paris at all hazards. Republicans are in an extreme minority, and, for fighting, we can rely only on them. The rest of France is devoted to royalty. The royalists must be terrified ! "[6]—It is

repelled this sanguinary proposal. ' Everybody knows,' he said, ' that I do not shrink from a criminal act when necessary ; but I disdain to commit a useless one.' "

[1] Mortimer-Ternaux, IV. 437. Danton exclaims, in relation to the "effervescent" commissioners sent by him into the department : " Eh ! d——n it, do you suppose that we would send you young ladies ? "

[2] Philippe de Ségur, " Mémoires," I. 12. Danton, in a conversation with his father, a few weeks after the 2d of September.

[3] See above, narrative of the king, Louis Philippe.

[4] Buchez et Roux, XVII. 347. The words of Danton in the National Assembly, Sept. 2, a little before two o'clock, just as the tocsin and cannon gave the signal of alarm agreed upon. Already on the 31st of August, Tallien, his faithful ally, had told the National Assembly : " We have arrested the priests who make so much trouble. They are in confinement in a certain domicile, and in a few days the soil of liberty will be purged of their presence."

[5] Meillan, " Mémoires," 325 (Ed. Barrière et Berville). Speech by Fabre d'Eglantine at the Jacobin Club, sent around among the affiliated clubs, May 1, 1793.

[6] Robinet, " Procès des Dantonistes," 39, 45 (words of Danton in the committee on general defense).—Madame Roland, " Mémoires," II. 30. On the 2d of September Grandpré, ordered to report to the Minister of the Interior on the state of the prisons, waits for Danton as he leaves the council and tells him his fears. " Danton, irritated by the description, exclaims in his bellowing way, suiting the word to the action. ' J—— the prisoners ! Let them take care of themselves ! ' and he proceeded on in an angry mood. This took place in the second ante-room, in the presence of twenty persons."—Arnault, II. 101. About the time of the September massacres " Danton, in the presence of one of my friends, replied to some one that urged him to use his authority in stopping the spilling of blood : ' Isn't it time for the people to take their revenge ? ' "

he who, on the 28th of August, obtains from the Assembly the great domiciliary visit, by which the Commune fills the prisons It is he who, on the 2d of September, to paralyse the resistance of honest people, causes the penalty of death to be decreed against whoever, "directly or indirectly shall, in any manner whatsoever, refuse to execute, or who shall interfere with the orders issued, or with the measures of the executive power." It is he who, on that day, informs the journalist Prudhomme of the pretended prison plot, and who, the second day after, sends his secretary, Camille Desmoulins, to falsify the report of the massacres.[1] It is he who, on the 3d of September, at the office of the Minister of Justice, before the battalion officers and the heads of the service, before Lacroix, president of the Assembly, and Pétion, mayor of Paris, before Clavières, Servan, Monge, Lebrun, and the entire Executive Council, except Roland, reduces at one stroke the head men of the government to the position of passive accomplices, replying to a man of feeling, who rises to stay the slaughter, "Sit down—it was necessary!"[2] It is he who, the same day, despatches the circular, countersigned by him, by which the Committee of Supervision announces the massacre, and invites "their brethren of the departments" to follow the example of Paris.[3] It is he who, on the 10th of September, "not as Minister of Justice, but as Minister of the People," is to

---

[1] Prudhomme, "Crimes de la Révolution," IV. 90. On the 2d of September, at the alarm given by the tocsin and cannon, Prudhomme calls on Danton at his house for information. Danton repeats the story which has been gotten up, and adds: "The people, who are now aroused and know what to do, want to administer justice themselves on the worthless scamps now in prison." Camille Desmoulins enters. "Look here," says Danton, "Prudhomme has come to ask what is going to be done?" "Didn't you tell him that the innocent would not be confounded with the guilty? All those that are demanded by their sections will be given up." On the 4th, Desmoulins calls at the office of the journal and says to the editors: "Well, everything has gone off in the most perfect order. The people even set free a good many aristocrats against whom there was no direct proof. . . I trust that you will state all this exactly, because the *Journal des Révolutions* is the compass of public opinion."

[2] Prudhomme, "Crimes de la Révolution," 123. According to the statements of Theophile Mandar, vice-president of a section, witness and actor in the scene; he authorises Prudhomme to mention his name.—Afterwards, in the next room, Mandar proposes to Pétion and Robespierre to attend the Assembly the next day and protest against the massacre; if necessary, the Assembly may appoint a director for one day. "Take care not to do that," replied Robespierre; "Brissot would be the dictator."—Pétion says nothing. "The ministers were all agreed to let the massacres continue."

[3] Madame Roland, II. 37.—"Angers et le départment de Maine-et-Loire de 1787 à 1830," by Blordier Langlois. Appended to the circular was a printed address bearing the title of *Comte rendu au peuple souverain*, "countersigned by the Minister of Justice and with the Minister's seal on the package," and addressed to the Jacobin Clubs of the departments, that hey, too, might preach massacre

congratulate and thank the slaughterers of Versailles.[1]—After the 10th of August, through Billaud-Varennes, his former secre tary, Fabre d'Eglantine, his secretary as Keeper of the Seals Tallien, secretary of the Commune, and his most trusty hench man, he is present at all deliberations in the Hôtel-de-ville, and, at the last hour, is careful to put on the Committee of Super vision one of his own men, the head clerk, Desforges.[2]—Not only was the mowing-machine constructed under his own eye, and with his assent, but, again, at the moment of starting it, he holds the handle, so as to guide the blade.

It is well that he does; if he did not sometimes put on the brake, it would go to pieces through its own action. Introduced into the Committee as professor of political blood-letting, Marat, stubbornly following out a fixed idea, cuts down deep, much be low the designated line; warrants of arrest were already out against thirty deputies, Brissot's papers were rummaged, Roland's house was surrounded, while Duport, seized in a neighboring de partment, is brought to the shambles. The latter is saved with the utmost difficulty; many a blow is necessary before he can be wrested from the maniac who had seized him. With a surgeon like Marat, and apprentices like the four or five hundred leaders of the Commune and of the sections, it is not essential to guide the knife, for a large amputation is certain beforehand. Their names alone tell the story,—in the Commune, Manuel, the syndic-attorney; Hébert and Billaud-Varennes, his two depu ties; Huguenin, Lhuillier, Marie Chénier, Audouin, Léonard Bourdon, Boula and Truchon, presidents in succession; in the Commune and the sections, Panis, Sergent, Tallien, Rossignol, Chaumette, Fabre d'Eglantine, Pache, Hassenfratz, the cobbler Simon, and the printer Momoro; in the National Guard, San terre, commanding-general, Henriot, brigadier-general, and, un der them, the herd of demagogues belonging to the district, the supernumeraries of Danton, Hébert, or Robespierre, and who are afterwards guillotined with their file-leaders, in brief, the

---

[1] Mortimer-Ternaux, III. 398, 391. Warned by Alquier, president of the criminal court of Versailles, of the danger to which the Orleans prisoners were exposed, Danton replied: "What is that to you? That affair does not concern you. Mind your own business, and do not meddle with things outside of it!" "But, Monsieur, the law says that prisoners must be protected." "What do you care? Some among them are great criminals, and nobody knows yet how the people will regard them and how far their indignation will carry them." Alquier wished to pursue the matter, but Danton turned his back on him.

[2] Mortimer-Ternaux, III. 217

flower of the future terrorists.[1]—They are taking the first step in
blood, each in the attitude and under impulses peculiar to himself, Chénier denounced as a member of the Sainte-Chapelle
club, and with the more exaggeration because he is suspected;[2]
Manuel, a poor little excitable fellow, dazed, dragged along, and
afterwards shuddering at the sight of his own work; Santerre, a
fine circumspect figure-head, who, on the 2d of September, under
pretence of watching the baggage, climbs on the seat of a berlin
standing on the street, where he remains a couple of hours, to
get rid of doing his duty as commanding-general;[3] Panis, president of the Committee of Supervision, a good subordinate, his
born disciple and train-bearer, an admirer of Robespierre's
whom he proposes for the dictatorship, as well as of Marat,
whom he extols as a prophet;[4] Henriot, Hébert, and Fossi-
gnol, simple malefactors in uniform or in their scarfs; Collot
d'Herbois, a stage poetaster, whose theatrical imagination delights in a combination of melodramatic horrors;[5] Billaud-Varennes, a former *oratorien*, bilious and sombre, as cool before a
murder as an inquisitor at an *auto da fé;* finally, the wily Robespierre, pushing others without committing himself, never signing
his name, giving no orders, haranguing a great deal, always
advising, showing himself everywhere, getting ready to reign,
and suddenly, at the last moment, pouncing like a cat on his
prey, and trying to slaughter his rivals, the Girondists.[6]

[1] Madame Roland, "Lettres autographes, etc.," Sept. 5, 1792. "We are here under the knives of Marat and Robespierre. These fellows are striving to excite the people and turn them against the National Assembly and the Council. They have organised a Star Chamber and they have a small army under pay, aided by what they found or stole in the palace and elsewhere, or by supplies purchased by Danton, who is underhandedly the chieftain of this horde."—Dusaulx, "Mémoires," 441. "On the following day (Sept. 3) I went to see one of the personages of most influence at this epoch. 'You know,' said I to him, 'what is going on?' 'Very well; but keep quiet; it will soon be over. A little more blood is still neces-sary.' I saw others who explained themselves much more definitely."—Mortimer-Ternaux, II. 445.

[2] "Procès-verbaux de la Commune," Aug. 17.—Buchez et Roux, XII. 206. Account of the fête of Aug. 27; a denunciation against Chénier, "who is now called simply Chénier the chaplain."—Weber, II. 274, 275.

[3] Madame de Staël, "Considérations sur la Révolution Française," 3d part, ch. x.

[4] Prudhomme, "Les Révolutions de Paris" (number for Sept. 22). At one of the last sessions of the commune "M. Panis spoke of Marat as of a prophet, another Simeon Sty-lites. 'Marat,' said he, 'remained six weeks sitting on one thigh in a dungeon.'"—Bar-baroux, 64.

[5] Weber, II. 348. Collot dwells at length, "in cool-blooded gaiety," on the murder of Madame de Lamballe and on the abominations to which her corpse was subjected. "He added, with a sigh of regret, that if he had been consulted he would have had the head of Madame de Lamballe served in a covered dish for the queen's supper."

[6] On the part played by Robespierre and his presence constantly at the Commune, see

Up to this time, in slaughtering or having it done, it was always as insurrectionists in the street; now, it is in places of imprisonment, as magistrates and functionaries, according to the registers of a lock-up, after proofs of identity and on snap judgments, by paid executioners, in the name of public security, methodically, and in cool blood, almost with the same regularity as subsequently under "the revolutionary government." September, indeed, is the beginning of it, the abridgment of it and the type; they will not do otherwise or better in the best days of the guillotine. Only, as they are as yet poorly supplied with tools, they are obliged to use pikes instead of the guillotine, and, as diffidence is not yet entirely gone, the chiefs conceal themselves behind manœuvrings. Nevertheless, we can track them, take them in the act, and we possess their autographs; they planned commanded, and conducted the operation. On the 30th of August, the Commune decided that the sections should try accused persons, and, on the 2d of September, five trusty sections reply to it by resolving that the accused shall be murdered.[1] The same day, September 2, Marat takes his place on the Committee of Supervision. The same day, September 2, Panis and Sergent sign the commissions of "their comrades," Maillard and associates, for the Abbaye, and "order them to judge," that is to say, kill the prisoners.[2] The same and the following days, at La Force, three members of the Commune, Hébert, Monneuse, and Rossignol, preside in turn over the assassin court.[3] The same day, a commissary of the Committee of Supervision comes and demands a dozen men of the Sans-Culottes section to help massacre the priests of Saint Firmin.[4] The same day, a com-

---

Granier de Cassagnac, II. 55.—Mortimer-Ternaux, III. 205. Speech by Robespierre at the commune, Sept 1. "No one dares name the traitors. Well, I give their names for the safety of the people: I denounce the *liberticide* Brissot to the Girondist factionists, the rascally commission of the Twenty-One in the National Assembly; I denounce them for having sold France to Brunswick, and for having taken in advance the reward for their dastardly act." On the 2d of September he repeats his denunciation, and consequently on that day warrants are issued by the committee of supervision against thirty deputies and against Brissot and Roland (Mortimer-Ternaux, III. 216, 247).

[1] "Procès-verbaux de la Commune," Aug. 30.—Mortimer-Ternaux, III. 217 (resolutions of the sections Poissonnière and Luxembourg).—Granier de Cassagnac, II. 104 (adhesion of the sections Mauconseil, Louvre, and Quinze-Vingt).

[2] Granier de Cassagnac, II. 156.

[3] Mortimer-Ternaux, III. 265.—Granier de Cassagnac, XII. 402. (The other five judges were also members of the commune.)

[4] Granier de Cassagnac, II. 313. Register of the General Assembly of the *sans-culotta* section, Sept. 2. Mémoires sur les journées de Septembre," 151 (declaration of Jourdan).

missary of the Commune visits the different prisons during the slaughterings, and finds that "things are going on well in all of them." [1]   The same day, at five o'clock in the afternoon, Billaud-Varennes, deputy-attorney for the Commune, "in his well-known puce-colored coat and black perruque," walking over the corpses, says to the Abbaye butchers : " Fellow-citizens, you are immolating your enemies, you are performing your duty ! "   That night he returns, highly commends them, and ratifies his promise of the wages "agreed upon"; on the following any at noon, he again returns, congratulates them more warmly, allows each one twenty francs, and urges them to keep on.[2]—In the mean time, Santerre, summoned to the staff-office by Roland, hypocritically deplores his voluntary inability, and persists in not giving the orders, without which the National Guard cannot stir a step.[3] At the sections, the presidents, Chénier, Ceyrat, Boula, Momoro, Collot d'Herbois, send away or fetch their victims under pikes. At the Commune, the council-general votes 12,000 francs, to be taken from the dead, to defray the expenses of the operation.[4] In the Committee of Supervision, Marat sends off despatches to spread murder through the departments.—It is evident that the leaders and their subordinates are unanimous, each at his post and in the service he performs; through the spontaneous co-operation of the whole party, the command from above meets the impulse from below; [5] both unite in a common murderous disposition, the work being done with the more precision in pro-

---

[1] " Mémoires sur les journées de Septembre," narrative of Abbé Sicard, 111

[2] Buchez et Roux, XVIII. 109, 178. ("La vérité tout entière," by Méhée, Jr.)—Narrative of Abbé Sicard, 132, 134.

[3] Granier de Cassagnac, II. 92, 93.—On the presence and complicity of Santerre. *Ibid.*, 89–99.

[4] Mortimer-Ternaux, III. 277 and 299 (Sept. 3).—Granier de Cassagnac, II. 257.   A commissary of the section of the Quatre-Nations states in his report that " the section authorised them to pay expenses out of the affair."—Declaration of Jourdan, 151.—Lavalette, " Mémoires," I. 91.   The initiative of the commune is further proved by the following detail : " Towards five o'clock (Sept. 2) city officials on horseback, carrying a flag, rode through the streets crying: 'To arms! to arms!'   They added: 'The enemy is coming; you are all lost; the city will be burnt and given up to pillage.   Have no fear of the traitors and conspirators behind your backs.   They are in the hands of the patriots, and before you leave *the thunderbolts of national justice will fall on them ! '*—Buchez et Roux, XXVIII. 105.   Letter of Chevalier Saint-Dizier, member of the first committee of supervision, Sept. 10. " Marat, Duplain, Fréron, etc., generally do no more in their supervision of things than wreak private vengeance. . .   Marat states openly that 40,000 heads must still be knocked off to ensure the success of the Revolution."

[5] Buchez et Roux, XVIII. 146. " Ma Résurrection," by Mathon de la Varenne. " The evening before half-intoxicated women said publicly on the Feuillants terrace: 'To-morrow is the day when their souls will be turned inside out in the prisons "

portion to its being easily done.—Jailers have received orders to open the prison doors, and give themselves no concern. Through an excess of precaution, the knives and forks of the prisoners have been taken away from them.[1]   One by one, on their names being called, they will march out like oxen in a slaughter-house, while about twenty butchers to each prison, from to two to three hundred in all,[2] will suffice to do the work.

V.

Two classes of men furnish recruits, and here we have to admire the effect of the revolutionary creed on crude intellects.—First, there are the Federates of the South, lusty fellows, former soldiers or old bandits, deserters, bohemians, and bullies of all lands and from every source, who, after finishing their work at Marseilles and Avignon, have come to Paris to begin over again. " *Triple nom de Dieu !* " exclaims one of them, "I didn't come a hundred and eighty leagues to stop with a hundred and eighty heads on the end of my pike!"[3]   Accordingly, they form in themselves a special, permanent, resident body, allowing no one to divert them from their adopted occupation. "They turn a deaf ear to the excitements of spurious patriotism";[4] they are not going to be sent off to the frontier.   Their post is at the capital; they have sworn "to defend liberty"; neither before nor after September could they be got out of it.   When, at last, after having drawn on every treasury for their pay, and under every pretext, they consent to leave Paris, it is only that they may return to Marseilles; their operations are limited to the interior, and to political adversaries.   But their zeal in this direction is only the greater; it is their band which, first of all, takes the twenty-four priests from the mayoralty, and, on the way, begins the massacre

---

[1] " Mémoires sur les journées de Septembre.   Mon agonie," by Journiac de Saint-Méard. —Madame de la Fausse-Landry, 72.   The 29th of August she obtained permission to join her uncle in prison: "M. Sergent and others told me that I was acting imprudently; that *the prisons were not safe.*"

[2] Granier de Cassagnac, — II. 27.   According to Roch Marcandier their number "did not exceed 300."   According to Louvet there were " 200, and perhaps not that number."   According to Brissot, the massacres were committed by about "a hundred unknown brigands." —Pétion, at La Force (*ibid.,* 75), on September 6, finds about a dozen executioners.   According to Madame Roland (II. 35), "there were not fifteen at the Abbaye."   Lavalette the first day finds only about fifty at the La Force prison.

[3] Mathon de la Varenne, *ibid.,* 137.

[4] Buchez et Roux, XVII. 183 (session of the Jacobin Club, Aug. 27). speech by a federate from Tarn.—Mortimer-Ternaux, III. 126.

with their own hands.[1]—After these come the infuriates of the
Paris commonalty, many of them clerks or shopmen, most of
them artisans, and others belonging to every trade, locksmiths,
masons, butchers, cartmen, tailors, shoemakers, waggoners, especially boat-loaders, dock-hands, and market-porters, and, above
all, journeymen and apprentices of all kinds, in short, men
accustomed to hand-labor, and who occupy the lowest grade in
the scale of professions.[2] Among these we find beasts of prey,
murderers by instinct, or simple robbers.[3] Others who, like one
of the disciples of Abbé Sicard, whom he loves and venerates,
confess that they never stirred except under constraint.[4] Others
are simple machines, who let themselves be driven; for instance,
a corner "commissionaire," a good sort of man, but who, dragged
along, plied with liquor, and then made crazy, kills twenty priests
for his share, and dies at the end of the month, still drinking,
unable to sleep, frothing at the mouth and trembling in every
limb.[5] Others, finally, who, coming with good intentions, are
seized with vertigo in contact with the bloody whirl, and, through
a sudden stroke of revolutionary grace, are converted to the
religion of slaughter; a certain Grapin, deputed by his section
to save two prisoners, seats himself alongside of Maillard, joins
him in his decisions during sixty-three hours, and demands a
certificate from him.[6] The majority, however, entertain the same
opinions as the cook, who, after taking the Bastille, finding him-

---

[1] Sicard, 80.—Méhée, 187.—Weber, II. 279.—Cf., in Journiac de Saint-Méard, his conver
sation with a Provençal.—Rétif de la Bretonne, "Les Nuits de Paris," 375. "About 2
o'clock in the morning (Sept. 3) I heard a troop of cannibals passing under my window, none
of whom appeared to have the Parisian accent; they were all foreign."

[2] Granier de Cassagnac, II. 164, 502.—Mortimer-Ternaux, III. 530.—Maillard's assessors
at the Abbaye were a watchmaker living in the Rue Childebert, a fruit-dealer in the Rue
Mazarine, a keeper of a public house in the Rue du Four-Saint-Germain, a journeyman hat-
ter in the Rue Sainte-Marguerite, and two others whose occupation is not mentioned.—On
the composition of the tribunal at La Force, Cf. Journiac de Saint-Méard, 120, and Weber,
II. 261.

[3] Granier de Cassagnac, II. 507 (on Damiens), 513 (on L'empereur).—Meillan, 388 (on
Laforet and his wife, old-clothes dealers on the Quai du Louvre, who on the 31st of May
prepare for a second blow, and calculate this time on having for their share the pillaging of
fifty houses).

[4] Sicard, 98.

[5] De Ferrières (Ed. Berville et Barrière), III. 486.—Rétif de la Bretonne, 381. At the end
of the Rue des Ballets a prisoner had just been killed, while the next one slipped through the
railing and escaped. "A man not belonging to the butchers, but one of those thoughtless
machines of which there are so many, interposed his pike and stopped him. . . The poor
fellow was arrested by his pursuers and massacred. The pikeman coolly said to us: 'I didn't
know they wanted to kill him.'"

[6] Granier de Cassagnac, II. 511.

self on the spot and having cut off M. de Launay's head, regards it as a "patriotic" action, and deems himself worthy of a "medal for having destroyed a monster." These people are not common malefactors, but well-disposed persons living in the vicinity, who, seeing a public service established in their neighborhood,[1] issue from their domiciles to give it a lift; their dose of probity is about the same as we find nowadays among people of the same condition in life.

At the outset, especially, no one dreams of filling his pockets. At the Abbaye, they come honorably and place on the table in the room of the civil committee the purses and jewels of the dead.[2] If they appropriate anything to themselves, it is shoes to cover their naked feet, and then only after asking permission. As to pay, all rough work deserves it, and, moreover, between them and their enticers, their compensation is understood. With nothing but their own hands to rely on, they cannot give their time gratis,[3] and, as the work is hard, it ought to count for two days. They require six francs a day, besides their meals and wine as much as they want. One keeper of a cook-shop alone furnished the men at the Abbaye with 346 pints: with uninterrupted work that lasts all day and all night, and which is like that of sewer-cleaners and miners, nothing else will keep their spirits up.—Food and wages must be paid for by the nation; the work is done for the nation, and, naturally, on interposing formalities, they get out of temper and betake themselves to Roland, to the city treasurer, to the section committees, to the Committee of Supervision,[5] murmuring, threatening, and show-

---

[1] The judges and slaughterers at the Abbaye, discovered in the trial of the year IV., almost all lived in the neighborhood, in the rues Dauphine, de Nevers, Guénégaud, de Bussy, Childebert, Taranne, de l'Egoût, du Vieux Colombier, de l'Echaudé-Saint-Benoit, du Four-Saint-Germain, etc.

[2] Sicard, 86, 87, 101.—Jourdan, 123. "The president of the committee of supervision replied to me that these were very honest persons; that on the previous evening or the evening before that, one of them, in a shirt and *sabots*, presented himself before their committee all covered with blood, bringing with him in his hat twenty-five *louis* in gold, which he had found on the person of a man he had killed."—Another instance of probity may be found in the " Procès-verbaux du conseil-général de la Commune de Versailles," 367, 371.—On the following day, Sept. 3, robberies commence and go on increasing.

[3] Méhée, 179. "'Would you believe that I have earned only twenty-four francs?' said a baker's boy armed with a club. 'I killed more than forty for my share.'"

[4] Granier de Cassagnac. II. 153.—Cf. *Ibid.*, 202–209, details on the meals of the workmen and on the more delicate repast of Maillard and his assistants.

[5] Mortimer-Ternaux, III. 175–176.—Granier de Cassagnac, II. 84.—Jourdan, 222.—Méhée, 179. "At midnight they came back swearing, cursing, and foaming with rage, threatening to cut the throats of the committee in a body if they were not instantly paid."

ing their bloody pikes. That is the evidence of having done their work well. They boast of it to Pétion, impress upon him how "just and attentive" they were,[1] their discernment, the time given to the work, so many days and so many hours; they ask only for what is "due to them"; when the treasurer, on paying them, demands their names, they give them without the slightest hesitation. Those who escort a prisoner let off, masons, hair-dressers, federates, require no recompense but "something to drink"; "we do not carry on this business for money," they say; "here is your friend; he promised us a glass of brandy, which we will take and then go back to our work." [2]—Outside of their business they possess the expansive sympathy and ready sensi-bility of the Parisian workman. At the Abbaye, a federate,[3] on learning that the prisoners had been kept without water for twenty-six hours, wanted to "exterminate" the turnkey for his negligence, and would have done it if "the prisoners them-selves had not pleaded for him." On the acquittal of a prisoner, the guards and the butchers, everybody, embraces him with transports; Weber is greeted again and again for more than a hundred yards; they cheer to excess. Each wants to escort the prisoner; the cab of Mathon de la Varenne is invaded; "they perch themselves on the driver's seat, at the doors, on top, and behind." [4]—Some of them display extraordinary phases of feel-ing Two of the butchers, still covered with blood, who lead the chevalier de Bertrand home, insist on going up stairs with him to witness the joy of his family; after their terrible task they need the relaxation of tender emotion. On entering, they wait discreetly in the drawing-room until the ladies are prepared for the meeting; the happiness of which they are witnesses melts them; they remain some time, refuse money tendered to them and leave, with many acknowledgments.[5]—Still more extraordi-

[1] Mortimer-Ternaux, III. 320. Speech by Pétion on the charges preferred against Robes-pierre.

[2] Mathon de la Varenne, 156.—Journiac de Saint-Méard, 129.—Moore, 267.

[3] Journiac de Saint-Méard, 115.

[4] Weber, II. 265.—Journiac de Saint-Méard, 129.—Mathon de la Varenne, 155.

[5] Moore, 267.—Cf. Malouet, II. 240. Malouet, on the evening of Sept. 1, was at his sister-in-law's; there is a domiciliary visit at midnight; she faints on hearing the patrol mount the stairs. "I begged them not to enter the drawing-room, so as not to disturb the poor suf ferer. The sight of a woman in a swoon and pleasing in appearance affected them, and they at once withdrew, leaving me alone with her."—Beaulieu, "Essais," I. 108. (*Apropos* of two of the Abbaye butchers he meets in the house of Journiac de Saint-Méard, and who chat with him in giving him a safe-conduct.) "What struck me was to detect generous senti-

nary are the vestiges of innate politeness.   A market-porter,
desirous of embracing a discharged prisoner, first asks his permission.   Old "hags," who had just clapped their hands at the
slaughterings, stop the guards "violently" as they hurry Weber
along, in white silk stockings, across pools of blood : "Heigh,
guard, look out, you are making Monsieur walk in the gutter!"[1]
In short, they display the permanent qualities of their race and
class; they seem to be neither above nor below the average of
their brethren.   Most of them, probably, would never have done
anything very monstrous had a rigid police, like that which
maintains order in ordinary times, kept them in their shops or at
home in their lodgings or in their tap-rooms.

But, in their own eyes, they are so many kings; "sovereignty
is committed to their hands,"[2] their powers are unlimited ; whoever doubts this is a traitor, and is properly punished; he must
be put out of the way ; while, for royal councillors, they take
maniacs and knaves, who, through monomania or calculation,
preach that doctrine, just the same as a negro king surrounded
by white slave-dealers, who urge him into raids, and by black
sorcerers, who prompt him to massacre.   How could such a man
with such guides, and in such an office, be retarded by the formalities of justice, or by the distinctions of equity ?   Equity and
justice are the elaborate products of civilisation, while he is
merely a political savage.   In vain are the innocent recom-
mended to his mercy !   "Look here, citizen,[3] do you, too, want
to set us to sleep ?   Suppose that those cursed Prussian and
Austrian beggars were in Paris, would they pick out the guilty ?
Wouldn't they strike right and left, the same as the Swiss did on
the 10th of August ?   Very well, I can't make speeches, but I
don't set anybody to sleep.   I say, I am the father of a family—
I have a wife and five children that I mean to leave here for the
section to look after, while I go and fight the enemy.   But I
have no idea that while I am gone these villains here in prison,

---

ments through their ferocity, those of men determined to protect any one whose cause they
adopted."

[1] Weber, II. 264, 348.

[2] Sicard, 101.   Billaud-Varennes, addressing the slaughterers.—*Ibid.*, 75.   "Greater
power," replied a member of the committee of supervision, "what are you thinking of ?   To
give you greater power would be limiting those you have already.   Have you forgotten that
you are sovereigns ?   that the sovereignty of the people is confided to you, and that you are
now in full exercise of it ?"

[3] Méhée, 171.

and other villains who would come and let them out, should cut the throats of my wife and children. I have three boys who I hope will some day be more useful to their country than those rascals you want to save. Anyhow, all that can be done is to let 'em out and give them arms, and we will fight 'em on an equal footing. Whether I die here or on the frontiers, scoundrels would kill me all the same, and I will sell my life dearly. But, whether it is done by me or by some one else, the prison shall be cleaned out of those cursed beggars, there, now!" At this a general cry is heard: "He's right! No mercy! Let us go in!" All that the crowd assent to is an improvised tribunal, the reading of the jailer's register, and prompt judgment; condemnation and slaughter must follow, according to the famous Commune, which simplifies things.—There is another simplification still more formidable, which is the condemnation and slaughter by categories. Any title suffices, Swiss, priest, officer, or servant of the King, "the moths of the civil list"; wherever a lot of priests or Swiss are found, it is not worth while to have a trial, as they can be killed in a heap.—Reduced to this, the operation is adapted to the operators; the arms of the new sovereign are as strong as his mind is weak, and, through an inevitable adaptation, he degrades his work to the level of his faculties.

His work, in its turn, degrades and perverts him. No man, and especially a man of the people, rendered pacific by an old civilisation, can, with impunity, become at one stroke both sovereign and executioner. In vain does he work himself up against the condemned and heap insult on them to augment his fury;[1] he is dimly conscious of committing a great crime, and his soul, like that of Macbeth, "is full of scorpions." Through a terrible self-shrinking, he hardens himself against the inborn, hereditary impulses of humanity; these resist while he becomes exasperated, and, to stifle them, there is no other way but to "sup on horrors,"[2] by adding murder to murder. For murder, especially as he practices it, that is to say, with a naked sword on defenceless people, introduces into his animal and moral machine two extraordinary and disproportionate emotions which unsettle it,

---

[1] Sicard, 81. At the beginning the Marseilles men themselves were averse to striking the disarmed, and exclaimed to the crowd: "Here, take our swords and pikes and kill the monsters!"

[2] Macbeth.

on the one hand, a sensation of omnipotence exercised uncontrolled, unimpeded, without danger, on human life, on throbbing flesh,[1] and, on the other hand, an interest in bloody and diversified death, accompanied with an ever new series of contortions and exclamations;[2] formerly, in the Roman circus, one could not tear one's self away from it; the spectacle once seen, the spectator always returned to see it again. Just at this time each prison court is a circus, and what makes it worse is that the spectators are likewise actors.—Thus, for them, two fiery liquids mingle together in one draught. To moral intoxication is added physical intoxication, wine in profusion, bumpers at every pause, revelry over corpses; and we see rising out of this unnatural creature the demon of Dante, at once brutal and refined, not merely a destroyer, but, again, an executioner, contriver and calculator of suffering, and radiant and joyous over the evil it accomplishes.

They are joyous. They dance around each new corpse, and sing the *carmagnole*;[3] they arouse the people of the quarter "to amuse them," and that they may have their share of "the fine fête."[4] Benches are arranged for "gentlemen" and others for "ladies": the latter, with greater curiosity, are additionally anxious to contemplate at their ease "the aristocrats" already slain; consequently, lights are required, and one is placed on the breast of each corpse.

Meanwhile, slaughter continues, and is carried to perfection. A butcher at the Abbaye[5] complains that "the aristocrats die too quick, and that those only who strike first have the pleasure of it"; henceforth they are to be struck with the backs of the swords only, and made to run between two rows of their butch-

---

[1] Observe children drowning a dog or killing a snake. Tenacity of life irritates them, as if it were a rebellion against their despotism, the effect of which is to render them only the more violent against their victim.

[2] One may recall to mind the effect of bull-fights, also the irresistible fascination which St. Augustin experienced on first hearing the death-cry of a gladiator in the amphitheatre.

[3] Mortimer-Ternaux, III. 131. Trial of the September actors; the judge's summing up. "The third and forty-sixth witnesses stated that they saw Monneuse (member of the commune) go to and come from La Force, express his delight at those sad events that had just occurred, acting very immorally in relation thereto, adding that there was violin playing in his presence, and that his colleague danced."—Sicard, 88.

[4] Sicard, 91, 87. So called by a wine-dealer, who wants the custom of the murderers.— Granier de Cassagnac, II. 197-200. The original bills for wine, straw, and lights are presented.

[5] Sicard, 91.—Mathon de la Varenne, 150.

ers, like soldiers formerly running a gauntlet.　If there happers to be a person well-known, it is agreed to take more care in prolonging the torment.　At La Force, the Federates who come for M. de Rulhières swear "with frightful imprecations that they will cut off the first man's head who gives him a thrust with a pike"; the first thing is to strip him naked, and then, for half an hour, with the flat of their sabres, they cut and slash him until he drips with blood and is "skinned to his entrails."—All the unfettered instincts that live in the lowest depths of the heart start from the human abyss at once, not alone the heinous instincts with their fangs,[1] but likewise the foulest with their slaver, both becoming more furious against women whose noble or infamous repute makes them conspicuous; on Madame de Lamballe, the Queen's friend; on Madame Desrues, widow of the famous poisoner; on the flower-girl of the Palais-Royal, who, two years before, had mutilated her lover, a French guardsman, in a fit of jealousy. Ferocity here is associated with lubricity to add profanation to torture, while life is attacked through outrages on modesty.　In Madame de Lamballe, killed too quickly, the libidinous butchers could outrage only a corpse, but for the widow,[2] and especially the flower-girl, they revive, like so many Neros, the fire-circle of the Iroquois.[3]　From the Iroquois to the cannibal, the interval is narrow, and some of them spring across it.　At the Abbaye, an old soldier named Damiens, buries his sabre in the side of the adjutant-general Laleu, thrusts his hand into the opening, tears out the heart "and puts it to his mouth as if to eat it"; "the blood," says an eye-witness, "trickled from his mouth and formed a sort of moustache for him."[4]　At La Force, Madame de Lamballe is cut to pieces.　I cannot transcribe what Charlot, the hair-dresser, did with her head.　I merely state that another

---

[1] Mathon de la Varenne, 154.　A man of the suburbs said to him (Mathon is an advocate): "All right, Monsieur Fine-skin; I shall treat myself to a glass of your blood!"

[2] Rétif de la Bretonne, "Les Nuits de Paris," 9th night, p. 388.　"She screamed horribly, whilst the brigands amused themselves with their disgraceful acts.　Her body even after death was not exempt.　These people had heard that she had been beautiful."

[3] Prudhomme, "Les Révolutions de Paris," number for Sept. 8, 1792.　"The people subjected the flower-girl of the Palais-Royal to the law of retaliation."—Granier de Cassagnac, II. 329.　According to the bulletin of the revolutionary tribunal, number for Sept. 3.—Mortimer-Ternaux, III. 291.　Deposition of the concierge of the Conciergerie.—Buchez et Roux, XVII. 198.　"Histoire des hommes de proie," by Roch Marcandier.

[4] Mortimer-Ternaux, III 257.　Trial of the September murderers; deposition of Roussel *Ibid.* 628.

wretch, in the Rue Saint-Antoine, bore off her heart and " ate it."[1]

They kill and they drink, and drink and kill again. Weariness comes and stupor begins. One of them, a wheelwright's apprentice, has despatched sixteen for his share; another " has labored so hard at this merchandise as to leave the blade of his sabre sticking in it "; " I was more tired," says a Federate, " with two hours pulling limbs to pieces, right and left, than any mason any two days plastering a wall."[2] The first excitement is gone, and now they strike automatically.[3] Some of them fall asleep stretched out on benches. Others, huddled together, sleep off the fumes of their wine, removed on one side. The exhalation from the carnage is so strong that the president of the civil committee faints in his chair,[4] while the odor of the drinking-bout is equal to that of the charnel-house. A heavy, dull state of torpor gradually overcomes their clouded brains, the last glimmerings of reason dying out one by one, like the smoky lights on the already cold breasts of the corpses lying around them. Through the stupor spreading over the faces of butchers and cannibals, we see appearing that of the idiot. It is the revolutionary idiot, in which all conceptions, save two, have vanished, two fixed, rudimentary, and mechanical ideas, one destruction and the other that of public safety. With no others in his empty head, these blend together through an irresistible attraction, and the effect proceeding from their contact may be imagined. " Is there anything else to do?" asks one of these butchers in the deserted court. " If that is all," reply a couple of women at the gate, "*you must start something more*,"[5] and, naturally, this is done.

As the prisons are to be cleaned out, it is as well to clean them all out, and do it at once. After the Swiss, priests, the aristo-

[1] Deposition of the woman Millet, *ibid.*, 63.—Weber, II. 350.—Roch Marcandier, 197, 198. —Rétif de la Bretonne, 381.

[2] Mathon de la Varenne, 150.—Granier de Cassagnac, 515, 508. Trial of the September murderers, cases of Sainte-Foye, Debèche.—*Ibid.*, 507, 513 (cases of Corlet, Crapier, Ledoux).

[3] On this mechanical and murderous action Cf. Dusaulx, " Mémoires," 440. He addresses the bystanders in favor of the prisoners, and, affected by his words, they hold out their hands to him. " But before this the executioners had struck me on the cheeks with the points of their pikes, from which hung pieces of flesh. Others wanted to cut off my head, which would have been done if two gendarmes had not kept them back."

[4] Jourdan, 219.

[5] Méhée, 179.

crats, and the "white-skin gentlemen," there remain convicts
and those confined through the ordinary channels of justice,
robbers, assassins, and those sentenced to the galleys in the
Conciergerie, in the Châtelet, and in the Tour St. Bernard, with
branded women, vagabonds, old beggars, and boys confined in
Bicêtre and the Salpétrière. They are good for nothing, cost
something to feed,[1] and, probably, cherish evil designs. At the
Salpétrière, for example, the wife of Desrues, the poisoner, is,
assuredly, like himself, "cunning, wicked, and capable of anything"; she must be furious at being in prison; if she could, she
would set fire to Paris; she must have said so; she did say it [2]—
one more sweep of the broom.—This time, as the job is more
foul, the broom is wielded by fouler hands; among those who
seize the handle are the frequenters of jails. The butchers at the
Abbaye, especially towards the close, had already committed
thefts; [3] here, at the Châtelet and the Conciergerie, they carry
away "everything which seems to them suitable," even to the
clothes of the dead, prison sheets and coverlids, even the small
savings of the jailers, and, besides this, they enlist their cronies
in the service. "Out of 36 prisoners set free, many were assassins and robbers, associated with them by the butchers. There
were also 75 women, confined in part for larceny, who promised
to faithfully serve their liberators." Later on, indeed, these are
to become, at the Jacobin and Cordeliers clubs, the *tricoteuses*
who fill their tribunes.[4]—At the Salpétrière, "all the bullies of
Paris, former spies, . . . libertines, the rascals of France
and all Europe, prepare beforehand for the operation," and rape
alternates with massacre.[5]—Thus far, at least, slaughter has been
seasoned with robbery, and the grossness of eating and drinking; at Bicêtre, however, it is crude butchery, the carnivorous
instinct alone satisfying itself. Among other prisoners are 43
youths of the lowest class, from 17 to 19 years of age, placed

---

[1] Mortimer-Ternaux, III. 558. The same idea is found among the federates and Parisians
composing the company of the Egalité, which brought the Orleans prisoners to Versailles
and then murdered them. They explain their conduct by saying that they "hoped to put
an end to the excessive expenditure to which the French empire was subject through the
prolonged detention of conspirators."

[2] Rétif de la Bretonne, 388.

[3] Méhée, 177.

[4] Prudhomme, "Les Crimes de la Révolution," III. 272.

[5] Rétif de la Bretonne, 388. There were two sorts of women at the Salpétrière, those who
were branded and young girls brought up in the prison. Hence the two alternatives.

there for correction by their parents, or by those to whom they are bound;[1] one need only look at them to see that they are genuine Parisian scamps, the apprentices of vice and misery, the future recruits for the reigning band, and these the band falls on, beating them to death with clubs.   At this age life is tenacious, and, no life being harder to take, it requires extra efforts to despatch them.   "In that corner," said a jailer, "they made a mountain of their bodies.   The next day, when they were to be buried, the sight was enough to break one's heart.   One of them looked as if he were sleeping like one of God's angels, but the rest were horribly mutilated."[2]—Here, man has sunk below himself, down into the lowest strata of the animal kingdom, lower than the wolf, for wolves do not strangle their young.

VI.

There are six days and five nights of uninterrupted butchery,[3] 171 murders at the Abbaye, 169 at La Force, 223 at the Châtelet, 328 at the Conciergerie, 73 at the Tour-Saint-Bernard, 120 at the Carmelites, 79 at Saint Firmin, 170 at Bicêtre, 35 at the Salpétrière; among the dead, 250 priests, 3 bishops or archbishops, general officers, magistrates, one former minister, one royal princess, belonging to the best names in France, and, on the other side, one negro, several low class women, young scapegraces, convicts, and poor old men.   What man now, little or big, does not feel himself under the knife?—And all the more because the band has grown larger.   Fournier, Lazowski, and Bécard, the chiefs of robbers and assassins, return from Orleans with fifteen hundred cut-throats.[4]   On the way they kill M. de Brissac, M. de Lessart, and 42 others accused of *lèse-nation*, whom they wrested from their judges hands, and then, by way of surplus, "following the example of Paris," twenty-one prisoners taken from the Versailles prisons.   At Paris the Minister of Jus-

---

[1] Mortimer-Ternaux, III. 295. See list of names, ages, and occupations.

[2] Barthélemy Maurice, "Histoire politique and anecdotique des prisons de la Seine," 329.

[3] Granier de Cassagnac, II. 421. Official report of the commissary of police Auzolle. According to the declaration of the gate-keeper at La Force the massacre was prolonged up to the 7th of September.—Mortimer-Ternaux, III. 548.

[4] Mortimer-Ternaux, III. 399, 592, 602–606.—"Procès-verbal des 8, 9, 10 Septembre, extrait des registres de la municipalité de Versailles." (In the "Mémoires sur les journées de Septembre"), p. 358 and following pages.—Granier de Cassagnac, II. 483. Bonnet's exploit at Orleans, pointed out to Fournier, Sept. I. Fournier replies: "D——, I am not tc be ordered. When the heads of the cursed beggars are cut off the trial may come off!"

tice thanks them, the Commune congratulates them, and the sections feast them and embrace them.[1]—Can anybody doubt that they were ready to begin again? Can a step be taken in or out of Paris without being subject to their oppression or encountering their despotism? On leaving the city, sentinels ot their species are posted at the barriers, while the section committees on the inside are in permanent authority. Malouet, led before that of Roule,[2] sees before him a pandemonium of fanatics, at least a hundred individuals in the same room, the suspected, those denouncing them, co-laborers, attendants, a long, green table in the centre, covered with swords and daggers, with the committee around it, "twenty patriots with their shirt-sleeves rolled up, some holding pistols and others pens," signing warrants of arrest, "quarreling with and threatening each other, all talking at once, and shouting, Traitor! Conspirator! Off to prison with him! Guillotine him! and behind these, a crowd of spectators, pell-mell, yelling, and gesticulating" like wild beasts pressed against each other in the same cage, showing their teeth and trying to spring at eacn other. "One of the most excited, brandishing his sabre in order to strike an antagonist, stopped on seeing me, and exclaimed, 'There's Malouet!' The other, however, less occupied with me than with his enemy, took advantage of the opportunity, and with a blow of his club, knocked him down." Malouet is just saved, and that is all, such escapes in Paris being mere matters of chance.—If one remains in the city, one is beset with funereal imagery ;—the hurrying step of squads of men in each street, leading the suspected to prison or before the committee; around each prison the crowds that have come "to see the disasters"; in the court of the Abbaye the cry of the auctioneer selling the clothes of the dead; the rumbling of carts on the pavement bearing away 1,300 corpses; the songs of the women mounted aloft, beating time on the

---

[1] Roch Marcandier, 210. Speech by Lazowski to the section of Finistère, faubourg Saint-Marceau. Lazowski had, in addition, set free the assassins of the mayor of Etampes, and laid their manacles on the bureau table.

[2] Malouet, II. 243 (Sept. 2).—*Moniteur*, XIII. 48 (session of Sept. 27, 1792). We see in the speech of Panis that analogous scenes took place in the committee of supervision. "Imagine our situation. We were surrounded by citizens irritated against the treachery of the court. We were told: 'Here is an aristocrat who is going to fly; you must stop him, or you yourselves are traitors!' Pistols were pointed at us and we found ourselves obliged to sign warrants, not so much for our own safety as for that of the persons denounced."

naked bodies.[1]   Is there a man who, after one of these encounters, does not see himself in imagination before the green table
of the section committee, after this, in prison with sabres over
his head, and then in the cart in the midst of the bloody pile ?

Courage falters before a vision like this.   All the journals approve, palliate, or keep silent; nobody dares offer resistance.
Property as well as lives belong to whoever wants to take them.
At the barriers, at the markets, on the boulevard of the Temple,
thieves, decked with the tricolor ribbon, stop people as they pass
along, seize whatever they carry, and, under the pretext that
jewels should be deposited on the altars of Patriotism, take
purses, watches, rings, and other articles, so rudely that women
who are not quick enough, have the lobes of their ears torn in
unhooking their earrings.[2]   Others, installed in the cellars of the
Tuileries, sell the nation's wine and oil for their own profit.
Others, again, given their liberty eight days before by the people,
scent out a bigger job by finding their way into the Garde-meuble
and stealing diamonds to the value of thirty millions.[3]

Like a man struck on the head with a mallet, Paris, felled to
the ground, lets things go; the authors of the massacre have
fully attained their ends.   The faction has fast hold of power,
and will maintain its hold.   Neither in the Legislative Assembly
nor in the Convention will the aims of the Girondists be successful against its tenacious usurpation.   It has proved by a striking
example that it is capable of anything, and boasts of it; it is
still armed, it stands there ever prepared and anonymous on its
murderous basis, with its speedy modes of operation, its own
group of fanatical agents and bravos, with Maillard and Fournier, with its cannon and its pikes.   All that does not live within
it lives only through its favor from day to day, through its good
will.   Everybody knows that.   The Assembly no longer thinks
of dislodging people who meet decrees of expulsion with massa-

---

[1] Granier de Cassagnac, II. 258.—Prudhomme, "Les Crimes de la Révolution," III. 272.
—Mortimer-Ternaux, III. 631.—De Ferrière, III. 391.—(The expression quoted was recorded
by Rétif de la Bretonne.)

[2] *Moniteur*, XIII. 688, 698 (numbers for Sept. 15 and 16).   *Ibid.*, Letter of Roland, 701;
of Pétion, 711.—Buchez et Roux, XVIII. 33, 34.—Prudhomme's journal contains an engraving of this subject (Sept. 14).—" An Englishman admitted to the bar of the house denounces
to the National Assembly a robbery committed in a house occupied by him at Chaillot by
two bailiffs and their satellites.   The robbery consisted of twelve *louis*, five guineas, five thousand pounds in assignats, and several other objects."   The courts before which he appeared
did not dare take up his case (Buchez et Roux, XVII. p. 1, Sept. 18).

[3] Buchez et Roux, XVII. 461.—Prudhomme, " Les Révolution de Paris," number for
Sept. 22, 1792.

cre; it is no longer a question of auditing their accounts, or of keeping them within the confines of the law. Their dictatorship is not to be disputed, and their purifications continue. From four to five hundred new prisoners, arrested within eleven days, by order of the municipality, by the sections, and by this or that individual Jacobin, are crowded into cells still dripping with blood, and the report is spread that, on the 20th of September, the prisons will be emptied by a second massacre.[1]—Let the Convention, if it pleases, pompously install itself as sovereign, and grind out decrees—it makes no difference; regular or irregular, the government still marches on in the hands of those who hold the sword. The Jacobins, through sudden terror, have maintained their illegal authority; through a prolongation of terror they are going to establish their legal authority. A forced suffrage is going to put them in office at the Hôtel-de-ville, in the tribunals, in the National Guard, in the sections, and in the various administrations, while they have already elected to the Convention, Marat, Danton, Fabre d'Eglantine, Camille Desmoulins, Manuel, Billaud-Varennes, Panis, Sergent, Collot d'Herbois, Robespierre, Legendre, Osselin, Fréron, David, Robert, Lavicourterie, in brief, the instigators, conductors and accomplices of the massacre.[2] Nothing that could force or falsify votes was overlooked. In the first place the presence of the people is imposed on the electoral assembly, and, to this end, it is transferred to the large hall of the Jacobin club, under the pressure of the Jacobin galleries. As a second precaution, every opponent is excluded from voting, every constitutionalist, every former member of the monarchical club, of the Feuillants, and of the Sainte-Chapelle club, every signer of the petition of the 20,000, or of that of the 8,000, and, on the sections protesting

---

[1] *Moniteur*, XIII. 711 (session of Sept. 16). Letter of Roland to the National Assembly. —Buchez et Roux, XVIII. 42.—*Moniteur*, XIII. 731 (session of Sept. 17). Speech by Pétion: "Yesterday there was some talk of again visiting the prisons, and particularly the Conciergerie."

[2] "Archives Nationales," II. 58 to 76. Official reports of the Paris electoral assembly.— Robespierre is elected the twelfth (Sept. 5), then Danton and Collot d'Herbois (Sept. 6) then Manuel and Billaud-Varennes (Sept. 7), next C. Desmoulins (Sept. 8), Marat (Sept. 9), etc.—Mortimer-Ternaux, IV. 35 (act passed by the commune at the instigation of Robespierre for the regulation of electoral operations).—Louvet, "Mémoires." Louvet, in the electoral assembly asks to be heard on the candidacy of Marat, but is unsuccessful. "On going out I was surrounded by those men with big clubs and sabres by whom the future dictator was always attended, Robespierre's body-guard. They threatened me and told me in very concise terms: 'Before long you shall have your turn.' This is the freedom of that assembly in which one declared his vote under a dagger pointed at him."

against this, their protest is thrown out on the ground of its being the fruit of "an intrigue." Finally, at each ballotting, each elector's vote is called out, which ensures the right vote beforehand, the warnings he has received being very explicit. On the 2d of September, during the first meeting of the electoral body, held at the bishop's palace, the Marseilles troop, 500 yards off, came and took the twenty-four priests from the mayoralty, and, on the way, hacked them to pieces on the Pont-Neuf. Throughout the evening and all night the agents of the munici-pality carried on their work at the Abbaye, at the Carmelites, and at La Force, and, on the 3d of September, on the electoral assembly transferring itself to the Jacobin club, it passed over the Pont-au-Change between two rows of corpses, which the slaughterers had brought there from the Châtel t and the Conciergerie.

THE REVOLUTION

VOLUME III

PREFACE.

"In Egypt," says Clement of Alexandria, "the sanctuaries of the temples are shaded by curtains of golden tissue. But on going further into the interior in quest of the statue, a priest of grave aspect, advancing to meet you and chanting a hymn in the Egyptian tongue, slightly raises a veil to show you the god. And what do you behold? A crocodile, or some indigenous serpent, or other dangerous animal, the Egyptian god being a brute rolling about on a purple carpet."

We need not visit Egypt or go so far back in history to encounter crocodile worship, as this can be readily found in France at the end of the last century.—Unfortunately, a hundred years is too long an interval, too far away, for an imaginative retrospect of the past. At the present time, standing where we do and regarding the horizon behind us, we see only forms which the intervening atmosphere embellishes, shimmering contours which each spectator may interpret in his own fashion ; no distinct, animated figure, but merely a mass of moving points, forming and dissolving in the midst of picturesque architecture. I was anxious to have a nearer view of these vague points, and, accordingly, transported myself back to the last half of the eighteenth century, where I have been living with them for twelve years, and, like Clement of Alexandria, examining, first, the temple, and next the god. A passing glance at these is not sufficient ; a step further must be taken to comprehend the theology on which this cult is founded. This one, explained by a very specious theology, like most others, is composed of dogmas called the principles of 1789 ; they were proclaimed, indeed, at that date, having been previously formulated by Jean-Jacques Rousseau, the well-known sovereignty of the people, the rights of man, and the social contract. Once adopted, their practical results unfolded themselves naturally ; in three years the crocodile brought by these dogmas into the sanctuary installed himself there on the purple carpet behind the golden veil ; in effect, he was intended for the place on account of the energy of his jaws and the capacity of his stomach; he became a god through his qualities as a destructive brute and man-eater.—Comprehending this, the rites which consecrate him and the pomp which surrounds him need not give us any further concern.—We can observe him, like any ordinary animal, and study his various attitudes, as he lies in wait for his prey, springs upon it, tears it to pieces, swallows it, and digests it. I have studied the details of his structure, the play of his organs, his habits, his mode of living, his instincts, his faculties, and his appetites.—Specimens abounded. I have handled thousands of them, and have dissected hundreds of every species and variety, always preserving the most valuable and characteristic examples, but for lack of room I have been compelled to let many of them go because my collection was too large. Those that I was able to bring back with me will be found here, and, among others, about twenty individuals of different dimensions, which—a difficult undertaking—I have kept alive with great pains. At all events, they are intact and perfect, and particularly the three largest. These seem to me, of their kind, truly remarkable, and those in which the divinity of the day might well incarnate himself.—The bills of butchers, as well as housekeeping accounts, authentic and regularly kept, throw sufficient light on the cost of this cult. We can estimate about how much the sacred crocodiles consumed in ten years ; we know their bills of fare daily, their favorite morsels. Naturally, the god selected the fattest victims, but his voracity was so great that he likewise bolted down, and blindly, the lean ones, and in much greater number than the fattest. Moreover, by virtue of his instincts, and an unfailing effect of the situation, he ate his equals once or twice a year, except when they succeeded in eating him.— This cult certainly is instructive, at least to historians and men of pure science. If any believers in it still remain I do not aim

to convert them ; one cannot argue with a devotee on matters
of faith. This volume, accordingly, like the others that have
gone before it, is written solely for amateurs of moral zoology,
for naturalists of the understanding, for seekers of truth, of texts,
and of proofs—for these alone and not for the public, whose
mind is made up and which has its own opinion on the Revolution. This opinion began to be formed between 1825 and
1830, after the retirement or withdrawal of eye witnesses.
When they disappeared it was easy to convince a credulous
public that crocodiles were philanthropists ; that many possessed genius ; that they scarcely ate others than the guilty, and
that if they sometimes ate too many it was unconsciously and in
spite of themselves, or through devotion and self-sacrifice for
the common good.

MENTHON SAINT BERNARD, July, 1884.

BOOK SEVENTH.

The Governors.

CHAPTER I.

Psychology of the Jacobin leaders.—I. Marat.—Disparity between his faculties and pretensions.—The Maniac.—The Ambitious delirium.—Rage for persecution.—A confirmed nightmare insanity.—Homicidal frenzy.—II. Danton.—Richness of his faculties.—Disparity between his condition and instincts.—The Barbarian.—His work.—His weakness.—III. Robespierre. —Mediocrity of his faculties.—The *Cuistre*.—Absence of ideas.—Study of phrases.—Wounded self-esteem.—Intensity of this trait.—Satisfied self-esteem.—His infatuation.—He plays the victim.—His gloomy fancies.—His resemblance to Marat.—Difference between him and Marat.—The sincere hypocrite.—The Festival in honor of the Supreme Being, and the law of Prairial 22.—The external and internal characters of Robespierre and the Revolution.

I.

Three men among the Jacobins, Marat, Danton and Robespierre, merited distinction and possessed authority :—owing to a malformation, or distortion, of head and heart, they fulfilled the requisite conditions.—Of the three, Marat is the most monstrous ; he borders on the lunatic, of which he displays the chief characteristics—furious exaltation, constant over-excitement, feverish restlessness, an inexhaustible propensity for scribbling, that mental automatism and tetanus of the will under the constraint and rule of a fixed idea, and, in addition to this, the usual physical symptoms, such as sleeplessness, a livid tint, bad blood, foulness of dress and person,[1] with, during the last five months of his life, irritations and eruptions over his

---

[1] Harmand (de la Meuse): "Anecdotes relatives à la Révolution." " He dressed about like a cab-driver ill at his ease. He had a disturbed look and an eye always in motion ; he acted in an abrupt, quick and jerky way. A constant restlessness gave a convulsive contraction to his muscles and features which likewise affected his manner of walking so that he never stepped but jumped."

whole body.[1] Issuing from incongruous races, born of a mixed blood and tainted with serious moral commotions,[2] he harbors within him a singular germ : physically, he is an abortion, morally a pretender, and one who covet all places of distinction. His father, who was a physician, intended, from his early childhood, that he should be a savant ; his mother, an idealist, meant that he should be a philanthropist, while he himself always steered his course towards both summits. " At five years of age," he says, "it would have pleased me to be a schoolmaster, at fifteen a professor, at eighteen an author, and a creative genius at twenty,"[3] and, afterwards, up to the last, an apostle and martyr to humanity. " From my earliest infancy I had an intense love of fame which changed its object at various stages of my life, but which never left me for a moment." He rambled over Europe or vegetated in Paris for thirty years, living a nomadic life in subordinate positions, hissed as an author, distrusted as a man of science and ignored as a philosopher, a third rate political writer, aspiring to every sort of celebrity and to every honor, constantly presenting himself as a candidate and as constantly rejected,—too great a disproportion between his faculties and ambition ! Talentless,[4] possessing no critical acumen and of mediocre intelligence, he was fitted only to teach some branch of the sciences, or to practise some one of the arts, either as professor or doctor more or less bold and lucky, or to follow, with occasional slips on one side or the other, some path clearly marked out for him. " But," he says, "I never had any thing to do with a subject which did not

---

1 Chevremont, " Jean Paul Marat ; " also Alfred Bougeard, " Marat " *passim.* These two works, with numerous documents, are panegyrics of Marat.—Bougeat, i., 11 (description of Marat by Fabre d'Eglantine); ii., 259 and i., 83.—" Journal de la République Française," by Marat, No. 93, January 9, 1793. " I devote only two out of the twenty-four hours to sleep, and only one hour to my meals, toilette and domestic necessities. I have not had fifteen minutes play-spell for more than three years."

2 Chevremont, i., pp. 1 and 2. His family, on the father's side, was Spanish, long settled in Sardinia. The father, Dr. Jean Mara, had abandoned Catholicism and removed to Geneva where he married a woman of that city ; he afterwards established himself in the canton of Neufchatel.

3 " Journal de la République Française " No. 98, description of " l'Ami du peuple " by himself.

4 Read his novel " Les Aventures du jeune Comte Potowski," letter 5, by Lucile : " I think of Potowski only. My imagination, inflamed at the torch of love, ever presents to me his sweet image." Letter of Potowski after his marriage. " Lucile now grants to love all that modesty permits . . . . enjoying such transports of bliss, I believe that the gods are jealous of my lot."

hold out . . . . great results for myself, and show my originality, for I cannot make up my mind to treat a subject over
again that has been well done, or to plod over the work of
others."—Consequently, when he tries to originate he merely
imitates, or commits mistakes. His treatise on "Man" is a
jumble of physiological and moral common-places, made up of
ill-digested reading and words strung together haphazard,[1] of
gratuitous and incoherent suppositions in which the doctrines
of the seventeenth and eighteenth centuries, coupled together,
end in empty phraseology. "Soul and Body are distinct sub-
stances with no essential relationship, being connected together
solely through the nervous fluid;" this fluid is not gelatinous
for the spirituous by which it is renewed contains no gelatine ;
the soul, excited by this, excites that ; hence the place assigned
to it "in the *meninges.*"—His "Optics"[2] is the reverse of the
great truth already discovered by Newton more than a century
before, and since confirmed by more than another century of
experiment and calculation. On "Heat" and "Electricity" he
merely puts forth feeble hypotheses and literary generalisations;
one day, driven to the wall, he inserts a needle in a piece of
rosin to make this a conductor, in which piece of scientific
trickery he is caught by the physicist Charles.[3] He is not even
qualified to comprehend the great discoverers of his age, Laplace,
Monge, Lavoisier, or Fourcroy ; on the contrary, he libels them
in the style of a low rebellious subordinate, who, without the
shadow of a claim, aims to take the place of legitimate authorities. In Politics, he adopts every absurd idea in vogue growing out of the "Contrat-Social" based on natural right, and
which he renders still more absurd by repeating as his own the
arguments advanced by those bungling socialists, who, physiol-
ogists astray in the moral world, derive all rights from physical necessities. "All human rights issue from physical wants.[4]
If a man has nothing, he has a right to any surplus with which

---

1 Preface, xx. "Descartes, Helvetius, Haller, Lelat all ignored great principles ; man,
with them, is an enigma, an impenetrable secret." He says in a foot-note, "We find evidence of this in the works of Hume, Voltaire, Bonnet, *Racine* and Pascal."

2 "Mémoires Académiques sur la Lumière," pref., vii. He especially opposes "the
differential refrangibility of heterogeneous rays" which is "the basis of Newton's
theory."

3 Chevremont, i., 74. (See the testimony of Arago, Feb. 24, 1844).

4 Ibid., i., 104. (Sketch of a declaration of the rights of man and of the citizen).

another gorges himself. What do I say? He has a right
to seize the indispensable, and, rather than die of hunger, he
may cut another's throat and eat his throbbing flesh. . . .
Man has a right to self-preservation, to the property, the liberty
and even the lives of his fellow creatures. To escape oppression
he has a right to repress, to bind and to massacre. He is free
to do what he pleases to ensure his own happiness." It is plain
enough what this leads to.—But, let the consequences be what
they may, whatever he writes or does, it is always in self-admiration and always in a counter sense, being as vain-glorious
of his encyclopædic impotence as he is of his social mischievousness. Taking his word for it, his discoveries in Physics will
render him immortal.[1] " They will at least effect a complete
transformation in Optics. . . . The true primitive colors
were unknown before me." He is a Newton, and still better.
Previous to his appearance " the place occupied by the electric
fluid in nature, considered as an universal agent, was completely
ignored. . . . I have made it known in such a way as to
leave no further doubt about it."[2] As to the igneous fluid,
" that existence unknown before me, I have freed the theory
from every hypothesis and conjecture, from every alembical
argument ; I have purged it of error, I have rendered it intui-
tive ; I have written this out in a small volume which consigns
to oblivion all that scientific bodies have hitherto published on
that subject."[3] Anterior to his treatise on " Man," moral and
physical relationships were incomprehensible. " Descartes,
Helvetius, Haller, Lecat, Hume, Voltaire, Bonnet, held this to
be an impenetrable secret, 'an enigma.' " He has solved the
problem, he has fixed the seat of the soul, he has
determined the medium through which the soul com-
municates with the body.[4]—In the higher sciences, those
treating of nature generally, or of human society, he reaches
the climax. " I believe that I have exhausted every combination
of the human intellect in relation to morals, philosophy and

---

1 See the epigraph of his " Mémoires sur la Lumière." " They will force their way
against wind and tide."—Ibid., preface, vii. " Déconvertes de Monsieur Marat," 1780, 2nd
ed., p. 140.
2 " Recherches physiques sur l'electricité," 1782, pp. 13, 17.
3 Chevremont, i., 59.
4 " De l'Homme," preface vii. and book iv.

political science."[1]   Not only has he discovered the true theory of government, but he is a statesman, a practical expert, able to forecast the future and shape events.   He makes predictions, on the average, twice a week, which always turn out right ; he already claims, during the early sessions of the Convention, to have made " three hundred predictions on the leading points of the Revolution, all justified by the event."[2]   In the face of the *Constituants* who demolish and reconstruct so slowly, he is sufficiently strong to take down, put up and complete at a moment's notice.   " If I were one of the people's tribunes[3] and were supported by a few thousand determined men, I answer for it that, in six weeks, the Constitution would be perfected, the political machine well agoing, and the nation free and happy.   In less than a year there would be a flourishing, formidable government which would remain so as long as I lived."—If necessary, he could act as commander-in-chief of the army and always be victorious : having twice seen the Vendeans carry on a fight he would end the war " at the first encounter."[4]   " If I could stand the march, I would go in person and carry out my views.   At the head of a small party of trusty troops the rebels could be easily put down to the last man, and in one day.   I know something of military art, and, without boasting, I can answer for success."—On any difficulty occurring, it is owing to his advice not having been taken ; he is the great political physician : his diagnosis from the beginning of the Revolution is always correct, his prognosis infallible, his therapeutics efficacious, humane and salutary.   He furnishes the panacea and he should be allowed to prescribe it ; only, to

---

1 " Journal de la République Française," No. 98.

2 Journal de la République Française," by Marat, No. 1.

3 " L'Ami du Peuple " No. 173, (July 26, 1790). The memories of conceited persons, given to immoderate self-expansion, are largely at fault. I have seen patients in asylums who, believing in their exalted position, have recounted their successes in about the same vein as Marat. (Chevremont, i., 40, 47, 54).   " The reports of extraordinary cures effected by me brought me a great crowd of the sick. The street in front of my door was blocked with carriages. People came to consult me from all quarters.   .   .   .   The abstract of my experiments on Light finally appeared and it created a prodigious sensation throughout Europe ; the newspapers were all filled with it.   I had the court and the town in my house for six months.   .   .   .   The Academy, finding that it could not stifle my discoveries tried to make it appear that they had emanated from its body." Three academic bodies came in turn the same day to see if he would not present himself as a candidate.—" Up to the present time several crowned heads have sought me and always on account of the fame of my works."

4 " Journal de la République Française," July 6, 1793.

ensure a satisfactory operation, he should himself administer the dose.   Let the public lancet, therefore, be put in his hands that he may perform the humanitarian operation of blood-letting. "Such are my opinions. I have published them in my works. I have signed them with my name and I am not ashamed of it. . . . If you are not equal to me and able to comprehend me so much the worse for you." [1]   In other words, in his own eyes, Marat is in advance of everybody else and, through his superior genius and character, he is the veri-table saviour.

Such are the symptoms by which medical men recognise immediately one of those partial lunatics who may not be put in confinement, but who are all the more dangerous ; [2] the mal-ady, as they would express it in technical terms, may be called the *ambitious delirium*, well known in lunatic asylums.   Two propensities, one an habitually perverted judgment, and the other a colossal excess of self-esteem, [3] constitute its sources, and nowhere are both more prolific than in Marat.   Never did man with such diversified culture, possess such an incurably perverted intellect.   Never did man, after so many abortive speculations and such repeated malpractices, conceive and maintain so high an opinion of himself.   Each of these two sources in him augments the other : through his faculty of not seeing things as they are, he attributes to himself virtue and genius ; satisfied that he possesses genius and virtue, he regards his misdeeds as merits and his crotchets as truths.—Thence-forth, and spontaneously, his malady runs its own course and becomes complex ; next to the ambitious delirium comes the *mania for persecution*.   In effect, the evident or demonstrated truths which he supplies should strike the public at once ; if they burn slowly or miss fire, it is owing to their being stamped out by enemies or the envious : manifestly, they have conspired against him, and against him plots have never ceased.   First came the philosophers' plot : when his treatise on "Man"

---

[1] *Moniteur*, (Session of the Convention, Sep. 25, 1792). Marat, indeed, is constantly claiming the post of temporary dictator. (" L'Ami du peuple," Nos. 258, 268, 466, 668 and " Appel à la nation," p. 53).

[2] Cf. Moreau de Tours. " La Folie lucide."

[3] Chevremont, ii., 81.   " Shortly after the taking of the Bastille and obliged to oppose the Paris municipality, I stated that I was the eye of the people and that I was of more consequence in the triumph of liberty than an army of one hundred thousand men."

reached Paris from Amsterdam, "they felt the blow I struck at their principles and had the book stopped at the custom-house."[1] Next came the plot of the doctors, who "ruefully estimated my enormous gains. Were it necessary, I could prove that they often met together to consider the best way to destroy my reputation." Finally, came the plot of the Academicians; "the disgraceful persecution I had to undergo from the Academy of Sciences for two years, after being satisfied that my discoveries on Light upset all that it had done for a century, and that I was quite indifferent about becoming a member of its body. . . Would it be believed that these scientific charlatans succeeded in underrating my discoveries throughout Europe, in exciting every society of savants against me, and in closing against me all the newspapers!"[2] Naturally, the would-be-persecuted man defends himself, that is to say, he attacks. Naturally, as he is the aggressor, he is repulsed and put down, and, after creating imaginary enemies, he creates real ones, especially in politics where, on principle, he daily preaches insurrection and murder. Naturally, in fine, he is prosecuted, convicted at the Chatelet court, tracked by the police, obliged to fly and wander from one hiding-place to another; to live like a bat "in a cellar, underground, in a dark dungeon;"[3] once, says his friend Panis, he passed "six weeks on one of his buttocks" like a madman in his cell, face to face with his reveries.—It is not surprising that, with such a system, the reverie should become more intense, more and more gloomy, and, at last settle down into a *confirmed nightmare;* that, in his distorted brain, objects should appear distorted; that, even in full daylight men and things should seem awry, as in a magnifying, dislocating mirror; that, frequently, on the numbers (of his journal) appearing too blood-thirsty, and his chronic disease too acute, his physician should bleed him to arrest these attacks and prevent their return.[4]

---

1 Chevremont, i., 40. (Marat's letters, 1793).

2 Journal de la République Française, No. 98.

3 The words of Marat and Panes. (Chevremont, i., 197, 203; also " The Revolution " ii., 290, 2d note).

4 Michelet, " Histoire de la Révolution," ii., 89. (Narrated by M. Bourdier, Marat's physician, to M. Serre, the physiologist). Barbaroux, " Mémoires," 355, (after a visit to Marat) : " You should see how superficially Marat composed his articles. Without any knowledge of a public man he would ask the first person he met what he thought of him and this he wrote down, exclaiming ' I'll crush the rascal ! ' "

But he has taken his bent : henceforth, falsities spring up in his brain as on their native soil ; planting himself on the irrational he cultivates the absurd, even physical and mathematical. "Taking an extreme view of it," he says, "the patriotic contribution of one-quarter of one's income will produce, at the very least, four billion eight hundred and sixty million francs, and perhaps twice that sum ;" with this sum M. Necker may raise five hundred thousand men, which he calculates on for the subjugation of France.[1]—Since the taking of the Bastille, "the municipality's defalcations alone amount to two hundred millions. The sums pocketed by Bailly are estimated at more than two millions ; what 'Mottié' (Lafayette) has taken for the past two years is incalculable."[2]—On the 15th of November, 1791, the gathering of *emigrés* comprises "at least one hundred and twenty thousand gentlemen and drilled partisans and soldiers, not counting the forces of the gentlemen-princes about to join them."[3]—Consequently, as with his brethren in Bicêtre, (a lunatic asylum), he raves incessantly on the horrible and the foul : the procession of terrible or disgusting phantoms has begun.[4] According to him, the savants who do not choose to admire him are fools, charlatans and plagiarists. Laplace and Monge are even "automatons," so many calculating machines ; Lavoisier, "reputed father of every discovery that makes any noise in the world, has not an idea of his own ; " he steals from others without comprehending them, and "changes his system as he changes his shoes." Fourcroy, his disciple and horn-blower, is of still thinner stuff. All are scamps : "I could cite a hundred instances of dishonesty by the Academicians of Paris, a hundred breaches of trust ; " twelve thousand francs were entrusted to them for the purpose of ascertaining how to direct balloons, and "they divided it among themselves, squandering it at the Rapée, the opera and in brothels."[5] In

---

1 Chevremont, i., 361. (From a pamphlet against Necker, by Marat, July, 1790).

2 "L'Ami du Peuple," No. 552. (August 30, 1791).

3 Ibid., No. 626. (Dec. 15, 1791). Cf. "The Revolution," ii., 129, on the number of armed emigrés. At this date the authorised number as published is four thousand.

4 His filthy imputations cannot be quoted. See in Buchez et Roux, ix., 419 (April 26, 1791), and x., 220 (Nos. for June 17, 19 and 21), his statement against Lafayette ; again, his list with its vile qualifications of "rascals and rogues," who are canvassing for election, and his letters on the Academicians.

5 Buchez et Roux, x., 407 (Sept., 1791).—Cf. ibid., 473. According to Marat, "it is useless to measure a degree of the meridian ; the Egyptians having already given this measure.

the political world, where debates are battles, it is still worse. The " Friend of the people " has merely rascals for adversaries. Praise of Lafayette's courage and disinterestedness, how absurd ! If he went to America it was because he was jilted, " cast off by a Messalina ; " he maintained a park of artillery there as " powder-monkeys look after ammunition-wagons ; " these are his only exploits ; besides, he is a thief. Bailly is also a thief, and Malouet a " clown." Necker has conceived the " horrible project of starving and poisoning the people ; he has drawn on himself for all eternity the execration of Frenchmen and the detestation of mankind."—What is the Constituent Assembly but a set of " low, rampant, mean, stupid fellows ? "—" Infamous legislators, vile scoundrels, monsters athirst for gold and blood, you traffic with the monarch, with our fortunes, with our rights, with our liberties, with our lives ! "—" The second legislative corps is no less rotten than the first one."—In the Convention, Roland, " the officious Gilles and the forger Pasquin, is the infamous head of the monopolisers." " Isnard is a juggler, Buzot a Tartuffe, Vergniaud a police spy." [1]—When a madman sees everywhere around him, on the floor, on the walls, on the ceiling, toads, scorpions, spiders, swarms of crawling, loathsome vermin, he thinks only of crushing them, and the disease enters on its last stage : after the ambitious delirium, the mania for persecution and the settled nightmare, comes the *homicidal mania.*

With Marat, this broke out at the very beginning of the Revolution. The disease was innate ; he was inoculated with it beforehand. He had contracted it in good earnest, on principle ; never was there a plainer case of deliberate insanity.—On the one hand, having derived the rights of man from physical necessities, he concluded " that society owes to those among its members who have no property, and whose labor scarcely suffices for their support, an assured subsistence, the wherewithal to feed, lodge and clothe oneself suitably, provision for attend-

---

The Academicians obtained an appropriation of one thousand crowns for the expenses of this undertaking, a small cake which they have fraternally divided amongst themselves."

1 Chevremont, i., 238–249. " L'Ami du peuple," Nos. 419, 519, 543, 608, 641. Other falsities just as extravagant are nearly all grotesque. No. 630, (April 15, 1792). "Simonneau, mayor of d'Etampes, is an infamous ministerial monopoliser."—No. 627, (April 12, 1792). Delessart, the minister, " accepts gold to let a got-up decree be passed against him." No. 650, (May 10, 1792). " Louis XVI. desired war only to establish his despotism on an indestructible foundation."

ance in sickness and when old age comes on, and for bringing up children. Those who wallow in wealth must (then) supply the wants of those who lack the necessaries of life." Otherwise, "the honest citizen whom society abandons to poverty and despair, reverts back to the state of nature and the right of forcibly claiming advantages which were only alienated by him to procure greater ones. All authority which is opposed to this is tyrannical, and the judge who condemns a man to death (through it) is simply a cowardly assassin." [1] Thus do the innumerable riots which the dearth excites, find justification, and, as the dearth is permanent, the daily riot is legitimate.— On the other hand, having laid down the principle of popular sovereignty he deduces from this, " the sacred right of constituents to dismiss their delegates ; " to seize them by the throat if they prevaricate, to keep them in the right path by fear, and wring their necks should they attempt to vote wrong or govern badly. Now, they are always subject to this temptation. "If there is one eternal truth of which it is important to convince man, it is that the mortal enemy of the people, the most to be dreaded by them, is the Government."—"Any minister who remains twice twenty-four hours in office, when it is not impossible for the cabinet to operate against the Government is 'suspect.' " [2]—Bestir yourselves, then, ye unfortunates in town and country, workmen without work, street stragglers sleeping under bridges, prowlers along the highways, beggars without fuel or shelter, tattered vagabonds, cripples and tramps, and seize your faithless mandatories !—On July 14th and October 5th and 6th, "the people had the right not only to execute some of the conspirators in military fashion, but to immolate them all, to put to the sword the entire body of royal satellites leagued together for our destruction, the whole herd of traitors to the country, of every condition and degree." [3] Never go to the Assembly "without filling your pockets with stones and throwing them at the impudent scoundrels who preach monarchical maxims ; I recommend to you no other

---

1 Chevremont, i., 106. (Draft of a declaration of the rights of man and of the citizen, 1789).—Ibid., i., 196.

2 " L'Ami du peuple," Nos. 24 and 274.—Cf. " Placard de Marat," Sept. 18, 1792. " The National Convention should always be under the eye of the people, so that the people may stone it if it neglects its duty."

3 " L'Ami du peuple," Nos. 108–111. (May 20–23, 1790).

precaution but that of telling their neighbors to look out." [1]
" We do not demand the resignation of the ministers—we
demand their heads. `We demand the heads of all the minis-
terialists in the Assembly, your mayor's, your general's, the
heads of most of the staff-officers, of most of the municipal
council, of the principal agents of the executive power in the
kingdom."—Of what use are half-way measures, like the sack of
the hotel de Castries? [2] " Avenge yourselves wisely ! Death !
Death ! is the sole penalty for traitors raging to destroy you !
It is the only one that strikes terror into them. . . . . Follow
the example of your implacable enemies ! Keep always armed,
so that they may not escape through the delays of the law !
Stab them on the spot or blow their brains out !"—" Twenty-
four millions of men shout in unison : If the black, gangrened,
archi-gangrened ministerialists dare pass a bill reducing and
reorganising the army, citizens, do you build eight hundred
scaffolds in the Tuileries garden and hang on them every traitor
to his country—that infamous Riquetti, Comte de Mirabeau,
at the head of them—and, at the same time, erect in the middle of the fountain basin a big pile of logs to roast the ministers and their tools !" [3]—Could " the Friend of the people "
rally around him two thousand men determined " to save the
country, he would go and tear the heart out of that infernal
Mottié in the very midst of his battalions of slaves ; he would
go and burn the monarch and his imps in his palace, impale
the deputies on their benches, and bury them beneath the
flaming ruins of their den." [4]—On the first cannon shot being
fired on the frontier, " it is indispensable that the people
should close the gates of the towns and unhesitatingly make
way with every priest, public functionary and anti-revolutionist, known machinators and their accomplices."—" It would
be wise for the people's magistrates to keep constantly manu-
facturing large quantities of strong, sharp, short-bladed, double-
edged knives, so as to arm each citizen known as a friend of
his country. Now, the art of fighting with these terrible weap-
ons consists in this : Use the left arm as buckler, and cover it

---

1 *Ibid.*, No. 258. (Oct. 22, 1790).
2 *Ibid.*, No. 286 (Novem. 20, 1790.)
3 *Ibid.*, No. 198 (August 22, 1790).
4 *Ibid.*, Nos. 523 and 524 (July 19 and 20, 1791).

up to the arm-pit with a sleeve quilted with some woollen stuff,
filled with rags and hair, and then rush on the enemy, the right
hand wielding the knife."[1]—Let us use these knives as soon
as possible, for "what now remains to us to end the evils
which overwhelm us? I repeat it, nothing but executions by
the people."[2]—The Throne is at last down; but "be careful
not to give way to false pity! . . . . No quarter! I advise
you to decimate the anti-revolutionist members of the municipality, of the justices of the peace, of the members of the departments and of the National Assembly."[3]—At the outset, a
few lives would have sufficed: "five hundred heads ought to
have fallen when the Bastille was taken, and all would then
have gone on well." But, through lack of foresight and timidity, the evil was allowed to spread, and the more it spread the
larger the amputation should have been. With the sure, keen
eye of the surgeon, Marat gives its dimensions; he has made
his calculation beforehand. In September, 1792, in the Council at the Commune, he estimates approximatively forty thousand as the number of heads that should be laid low.[4] Six
weeks later, the social abscess having enormously increased,
the figures swell in proportion; he now demands two hundred
and seventy thousand heads,[5] always on the score of humanity,
"to ensure public tranquillity," on condition that the operation
be entrusted to him, as the summary, temporary justiciary.—

---

1 *Ibid.*, No. 626 (Decem. 15, 1791).

2 *Ibid.*, No. 668 (July 8, 1792).—Cf. No. 649 (May 6, 1792). He approves of the murder
of General Dillon by his men, and recommends the troops everywhere to do the same
thing.

3 *Ibid.*, No. 677 (August 10, 1792). See also subsequent numbers, especially No. 680,
Aug. 19th, for hastening on the massacre of the Abbaye prisoners. And Aug. 21st: "As
to the officers, they deserve to be quartered like Louis Capet and his *manège* toadies."

4 Buchez et Roux, xxviii., 105. (Letter of Chevalier St. Dizier, member of the first Committee of Surveillance, Sep. 10, 1792.)—Michelet, ii., 94. (In December, 1790, he already
demands twenty thousand heads).

5 *Moniteur*, Oct. 26, 1792. (Session of the Convention, Oct. 24th.) "N——: I know a
member of the Convention, who heard Marat say that, to ensure public tranquillity, two
hundred and seventy thousand heads more should fall."

Vermont: "I declare that Marat made that statement in my presence."

Marat: "Well, I did say so; that's my opinion and I say it again."

Up to the last he advocates surgical operations. (No. for July 12, 1793, the eve of his
death.) Observe what he says on the anti-revolutionists. "To prevent them from entering into any new military body I had proposed at that time, as an indispensable prudent
measure, cutting off their ears, or rather their thumbs." He likewise had his imitators.
(Buchez et Roux, xxxii., 186, Session of the Convention, April 4, 1796.) Deputies from
the popular club of Cette "regret that they had not followed his advice and cut off three
hundred thousand heads."

Save this last point, the rest is granted to him ; it is unfortunate that he could not see with his own eyes the complete fulfilment of his programme, the batches condemned by the revolutionary Tribunal, the massacres of Lyons and Toulon, the drownings of Nantes.—From first to last, he was in the right line of the Revolution, lucid on account of his blindness, thanks to his crazy logic, thanks to the concordance of his personal malady with the public malady, to the precocity of his complete madness alongside of the incomplete or tardy madness of the rest, he alone steadfast, remorseless, triumphant, perched aloft at the first bound on the sharp pinnacle which his rivals dared not climb or only stumbled up.

II.

There is nothing of the madman about Danton ; on the contrary, not only is his intellect sound, but he possesses political aptitudes to an eminent degree, and to such an extent that, in this particular, none of his associates or adversaries compare with him, while, among the men of the Revolution, only Mirabeau equals or surpasses him. He is an original, spontaneous genius and not, like most of his contemporaries, a disputatious, quill-driving theorist,[1] that is to say, a fanatical pedant, an artificial being composed of his books, a mill-horse with blinkers, and turning around in a circle without an issue. His free judgment is not hampered by abstract prejudices : he does not carry about with him a social contract, like Rousseau, nor, like Sièyes, a social art and cabinet principles or combinations ;[2] he has kept aloof from these instinctively and, perhaps, through contempt for them ; he had no need of them ; he would not have known what to do with them. Systems are crutches for the impotent, while he is able-bodied ; formulas serve as spectacles for the short-sighted, while his eyes are good. " He had read and meditated very little," says a learned and philosophical

---

1 Danton never wrote or printed a speech. " I am no writer," he says. (Garat, "Memoires," 31.)

2 Garat, Mémoires," iii. : " Danton had given no serious study to those philosophers who, for a century past, had detected the principles of social art in human nature. He had not sought in his own organisation for the vast and simple combinations which a great empire demands. He had that instinct for the grand which constitutes genius and that silent circumspection which constitutes judgment."

witness ;[1] "his knowledge was scanty and he took no pride in investigation ; but he *observed* and *saw* . . . His native capacity, which was very great and not absorbed by other things, was naturally closed to vague, complex and false notions, and naturally open to every notion of experience the truth of which was made manifest." Consequently, "his perceptions of men and things, sudden, clear, impartial and true, were instinct with solid, practical discretion." To form a clear idea of the divergent or concordant dispositions, fickle or earnest, actual or possible, of different parties and of twenty-six millions of souls, to justly estimate probable resistances, and calculate available forces, to recognise and take advantage of the one decisive moment, to combine executive means, to find men of action, to measure the effect produced, to foresee near and remote contingencies, to regret nothing and take things coolly, to accept crimes in proportion to their political efficacy, to manœuvre in the face of great obstacles, even in contempt of current maxims, to consider objects and men the same as an engineer contracting for machinery and calculating horse-power [2]—such are the faculties of which he gave proof on the 10th of August and the 2nd of September, during his effective dictatorship between the 10th of August and the 21st of September, afterwards in the Convention, on the first Committee of Public Safety, on the 31st of May and on the 2nd of June :[3] we have seen him busy at work. Up to the last, in spite of his partisans, he has tried to diminish or, at least, not add to, the resistance the government had to overcome. Nearly up to the last, in spite of his adversaries, he tried to increase or, at least, not destroy the available forces of the government. In defiance of the shoutings of the clubs, which clamor for the extermination of the Prussians, the capture of the King of Prussia, the overthrow of all thrones,

---

1 Garat, *ibid.*, 311, 312.

2 The head of a State may be considered in the same light as the superintendent of an asylum for the sick, the demented and the infirm. In the government of his asylum he undoubtedly does well to consult the moralist and the physiologist ; but, before following out their instructions he must remember that in his asylum its inmates, including the keepers and himself, are more or less ill, demented or infirm.

3 De Sybel : " Histoire de l'Europe pendant la Révolution Française," (Dosquet's translation from the German) ii., 303. " It can now be stated that it was the active operations of Danton and the first Committee of Public Safety which divided the coalition and gave the Republic the power of opposing Europe . . . We shall soon see, on the contrary, that the measures of the " Mountain " party, far from hastening the armaments, hindered them."

and the murder of Louis XVI., he negotiated the almost pacific withdrawal of Brunswick ;[1] he strove to detach Prussia from the coalition ;[2] he wanted to turn a war of propagandism into one of interests ;[3] he caused the Convention to pass the decree that France would not in any way interfere with foreign governments ; he secured an alliance with Sweden ; he prescribed beforehand the basis of the treaty of Basle, and had an idea of saving the King.[4]   In spite of the distrust and attacks of the Girondists, who strove to discredit him and put him out of the way, he persists in offering them his hand ; he declared war on them only because they refused to make peace,[5] and he made efforts to save them when they were down.   Amidst so many ranters and scribblers whose logic is mere words and whose rage is blind, who grind out phrases like a hand-organ, or are wound up for murder, his intellect, always capacious and supple, went right to facts, not to disfigure and pervert them, but to accept them, to adapt himself to them, and to comprehend them.   With a mind of this quality one goes far no matter in what direction ; nothing remains but to choose one's path.   Mandrin, under the ancient régime, was also, in a similar way, a superior man ;[6] only he chose the highway.

---

1 *Ibid.*, i., 558, 562, 585. (The intermediaries were Westermann and Dumouriez.)

2 *Ibid.*, ii., 28, 290, 291, 293.

3 Buchez et Roux, xxv., 445. (Session of April 13, 1793.)

4 According to a statement made by Count Theodore de Lameth, the eldest of the four brothers Lameth and a colonel and also deputy in the Legislative Assembly. During the Assembly he was well acquainted with Danton.   After the September massacre he took refuge in Switzerland and was put on the list of *emigrés*. About a month before the King's death he was desirous of making a last effort and came to Paris. " I went straight to Danton's house, and, without giving my name, insisted on seeing him immediately.   Finally, I was admitted and I found Danton in a bath-tub. " You here ! " he exclaimed.   " Do you know that I have only to say the word and send you to the guillotine ? " " Danton," I replied, " you are a great criminal, but there are some vile things you cannot do, and one of them is to denounce me." " You come to save the King ? " " Yes." We then began to talk in a friendly and confidential way. " I am willing," said Danton, " to try and save the King, but I must have a million to buy up the necessary votes and the money must be on hand in eight days.   I warn you that although I may save his life I shall vote for his death ; I am quite willing to save his head but not to lose mine."   M. de Lameth set about raising the money ; he saw the Spanish Embassador and had the matter broached to Pitt who refused.   Danton, as he said he would, voted for the King's death, and then aided or allowed the return of M. de Lameth to Switzerland. (I have this account through M . . . who had it from Count Theodore de Lameth's own lips.)

5 Garat. " Mémoires," 317. " Twenty times, he said to me one day, I offered them peace. They did not want it. They refused to believe me in order to reserve the right of ruining me."

6 Cf. the " Ancient Régime," p. 501.

Between the demagogue and the highwayman the resemblance is close : both are leaders of bands and each requires an opportunity to organise his band.   Danton, to organise his band, required the Revolution.—"Of low birth, without a patron," penniless, every office being filled, and "the Paris bar unattainable," admitted a lawyer after "a struggle," he for a long time strolled about the streets without a brief, or frequented the coffee-houses, the same as similar men nowadays frequent the beer-shops.   At the Café de l'Ecole, the proprietor, a good natured old fellow "in a small round perruque, grey coat and a napkin on his arm," circulated among his tables smiling blandly, while his daughter sat in the rear as cashier.[1]   Danton chatted with her and demanded her hand in marriage.   To obtain her, he had to mend his ways, purchase an attorneyship in the Court of the Royal Council and find bondsmen and endorsers in his small native town.[2]   Wedded and lodged in the gloomy Passage du Commerce, "more burdened with debts than with causes," tied down to a sedentary profession which demands vigorous application, accuracy, a moderate tone, a respectable style and blameless deportment ; obliged to keep house on so small a scale that, without the help of a *louis* regularly advanced to him each week by his coffee-house father-in-law, he could not make both ends meet ;[3] his free-and-easy tastes, his alternately impetuous and indolent disposition, his love of enjoyment and of having his own way, his rude, violent instincts, his expansiveness, creativeness and activity, all rebel : he is ill-calculated for the quiet routine of our civil careers ; it is not the steady discipline of an old society that suits him, but the tumultuous brutality of a society going to pieces, or one in a state of formation.   In temperament and character he is a *barbarian*, and a barbarian born to command his fellow-creatures, like this or that vassal of the sixth century or baron of the tenth century.   A colossus with the head of a "Tartar," pitted with the small-pox, tragically and terribly ugly, with a

---

1 "Danton," by Dr. Robinet, *passim*.   (Notices by Béon, one of Danton's fellow-disciples.—Fragment by Saint Albin.)—"The Revolution," ii., p. 35, foot-note.

2 Emile Bos, "Les Avocats du Conseil du Roi," 515, 520.   (See Danton's marriage-contract and the discussions about his fortune. From 1787 to 1791, he is found engaged as counsel only in three cases.)

3 Madame Roland, "Mémoires."   (Statement of Madame Danton to Madame Roland.)

mask convulsed like that of a growling " bull-dog," [1] with small, cavernous, restless eyes buried under the huge wrinkles of a threatening brow, with a thundering voice and moving and acting like a combatant, full-blooded, boiling over with passion and energy, his strength in its outbursts seeming illimitable like the forces of nature, roaring like a bull when speaking, and heard through closed windows fifty yards off in the street, employing immoderate imagery, intensely in earnest, trembling with indignation, revenge and patriotic sentiments, able to arouse savage instincts in the most tranquil breast and generous instincts in the most brutal,[2] profane, using emphatic terms,[3] cynical, not monotonously so and affectedly like Hébert, but spontaneously and to the point, full of crude jests worthy of Rabelais, possessing a stock of jovial sensuality and good-humor, cordial and familiar in his ways, frank, friendly in tone ; in short, outwardly and inwardly the best fitted for winning the confidence and sympathy of a Gallic, Parisian populace, and all contributing to the formation of " his inborn, practical popularity," and to make of him " a grand-seigñior of *sans-culotterie*." [4]—Thus endowed for playing a part, there is a strong temptation to act it the moment the theatre is ready, whether this be a mean one, got up for the occasion, and the actors rogues, scamps and prostitutes, or the part an ignoble one, murderous, and finally fatal to him who undertakes it.—To withstand temptation of this sort would require a sentiment of repugnance which a refined or thorough culture develops in

---

1 Expressions used by Garat and Rœderer. Larevilliere-Lepaux calls him " the Cyclop."
2 Fauchet describes him as " the Pluto of Eloquence."
3 Riouffe, " Mémoires sur les prisons." In prison " every utterance was mingled with oaths and gross expressions."
4 Terms used by Fabre d'Eglantine and Garat. Beugnot, a very good observer, had a good idea of Danton.—M. Dufort de Cheverney, (manuscript memoirs published by M. Robert de Crèvecœur), after the execution of Babœuf, in 1797, had an opportunity to hear Samson, the executioner, talk with a war commissary, in an inn between Vendôme and Blois. Samson recounted the last moments of Danton and Fabre d'Eglantine. Danton, on the way to the scaffold, asked if he might sing. " There is nothing to hinder," said Samson. " All right. Try to remember the verses I have just composed," and he sang the following to a tune in vogue :

" Nous sommes menés au trépas
Par quantité de scélérats,
C'est ce qui nous désole.
Mais bientot le moment viendra
Où chacun d'eux y passera,
C'est ce qui nous console."

both sense and soul, but which was completely wanting in Danton. Nothing disgusts him physically or morally : he embraces Marat,[1] fraternises with drunkards, congratulates the *Septembriseurs,* retorts in blackguard terms to the insults of prostitutes, treats reprobates, thieves and jail-birds as equals,— Carra, Westermann, Huguenin, Rossignol and the confirmed scoundrels whom he sends into the departments after the 2d of September. " Eh ! f——, you think we ought to send young misses." [2]—One must employ foul people to do foul work ; one cannot stop one's nose when they come for their wages ; one must pay them well, talk to them encouragingly, and leave them plenty of sea-room. Danton is willing to add fuel to the fire, and he humors vices ; he has no scruples, and lets people scratch and take.—He has taken himself as much to give as to keep, to maintain his role as much as to benefit by it, squaring accounts by spending the money of the Court against the Court, probably inwardly chuckling, the same as the peasant in a blouse on getting ahead of his well-duped landlord, or as the Frank, whom the ancient historian describes as leering on pocketing Roman gold the better to make war against Rome.—The graft on this plebeian seedling has not taken ; in our modern garden this remains as in the ancient forest ; its vigorous sap preserves its primitive raciness and produces none of the fine fruits of our civilisation, a moral sense, honor and conscience. Danton has no respect for himself nor for others ; the nice, delicate limitations that circumscribe human personality, seem to him as legal conventionality and mere drawing-room courtesy. Like a Clovis, he tramples on this, and like a Clovis, equal in faculties, in similar expedients, and with a worse horde at his back, he throws himself athwart society, to stagger along, destroy and reconstruct it to his own advantage.

At the start, he comprehended the peculiar character and

---

1 Buchez et Roux, xxi., 108. Speech (printed) by Pétion : " Marat embraced Danton and Danton embraced him. I certify that this took place in my presence."

2 Buchez et Roux, xxi., 126. (" To Maximilian Robespierre 'and his royalists," a pamphlet by Louvet.)—Beugnot, " Mémoires," i., 250, " On arriving in Paris as deputy from my department (to the Legislative Assembly) Danton sought me and wanted me to join his party. I dined with him three times, in the Cour du Commerce, and always went away frightened at his plans and energy. . . . He contented himself by remarking to his friend Courtois and my colleague : ' Thy big Beugnot is nothing but a devotee—you can do nothing with him.' "

normal procedure of the Revolution, that is to say, the useful
agency of popular brutality : in 1788 he had already figured
in insurrections.   He comprehended from the first the ultimate
object and definite result of the Revolution, that is to say, the
dictatorship of the violent minority.   Immediately after the
" 14th of July," 1789, he organised in his quarter of the city[1]
a small independent republic, aggressive and predominant, the
centre of the faction, a refuge for the riff-raff and a rendezvous for fanatics, a pandemonium composed of every available
madcap, every rogue, visionary, shoulder-hitter, newspaper
scribbler and stump-speaker, either a secret or avowed plotter
of murder, Camille Desmoulins, Fréron, Hébert, Chaumette,
Clootz, Théroigne, Marat,—while, in this more than Jacobin
State, the model in anticipation of that he is to establish later,
he reigns, as he will afterwards reign, the permanent president of the district, commander of the battalion, orator of the
club, and the concocter of bold undertakings.   Here, usurpation is the rule : there is no recognition of legal authority ;
they brave the King, the ministers, the judges, the Assembly,
the municipality, the mayor, the commandant of the National
Guard.   Nature and principle raise them above the law ; the
district takes charge of Marat, posts two sentinels at his door
to protect him from prosecutions, and uses arms against the
armed force sent with a warrant to arrest him.[2]   And yet
more, in the name of the city of Paris, " chief sentinel of the
nation," they assume to govern France : Danton betakes himself to the National Assembly and declares that the citizens of
Paris are the natural representatives of the eighty-three departments, and summons it, on their injunction, to cancel an act it
has passed.[3]—The entire Jacobin conception is therein expressed : Danton, with his keen insight, took it all in
and proclaimed it in appropriate terms ; to apply it
at the present time on a grand scale,[4] he has merely to

---

1 The Cordeliers district.   (Buchez et Roux, iv., 27.) Assembly meeting of the Cordeliers district, November 11th, 1789, to sanction Danton's permanent presidency. He is
always re-elected, and unanimously. This is the first sign of his ascendency, although
sometimes, to save the appearance of his dictatorship, he has his chief clerk Paré elected,
whom he subsequently made minister.

2 Buchez et Roux, iv., 295, 298, 401 ; v., 140.

3 *Ibid.*, viii., 28 (October, 1790).

4 *Ibid.*, ix., 408 ; x., 144, 234, 297, 417.—Lafayette " Mémoires," i., 359, 366. **Immedi-**

pass from the small theatre to the large one, from the
Cordeliers club to the Commune, to the Ministry, and the Committee of Public Safety, and, in all these theatres, he plays the
same part with the same end in view and the same results.   A
despotism formed by conquest and maintained by terror, the
despotism of the Jacobin Parisian rabble, is the end to which
he directly marches.   He employs no other means and, adapt-
ing the means to the end and the end to the means, manages
the important days and instigates the decisive measures of the
Revolution—the 10th of August,[1] the 2d of September, the
31st of May, the 2d of June ;[2] the decree providing for an army
of paid *sans-culottes* "to keep down aristocrats with their
pikes ;" the decree in each commune where grain is dear, taxing the rich to put bread within reach of the poor ;[3] the
decree giving laborers forty sous for attending the meetings of
the Section Assemblies ;[4] the institution of the revolutionary
Tribunal ;[5] the proposal to erect the Committee of Public
Safety into a provisional government ; the proclamation of
Terror ; the concentration of Jacobin zeal on useful works ;
the employment of the eight thousand delegates of the primary assemblies, who had been sent home as recruiting agents
for the universal armament ;[6] the inflammatory expressions
of young men on the frontier ; the wise resolutions for limiting
the levy *en masse* to men between eighteen and twenty-five,
which put an end to the scandalous songs and dances by the

---

ately after Mirabeau's death (April, 1791) Danton's plans are apparent, and his initiative is
of the highest importance.

1 " The Revolution," ii., 238 (Note) and 283.—Garat, 309 : " After the 20th of June
everybody made mischief at the chateau, the power of which was daily increasing. Danton
arranged the 10th of August and the chateau was thunderstruck."—Robinet : " Le Procès
des Dantonistes," 224, 229. (" Journal de la Société des amis de la Constitution," No.
214, June 5, 1792.) Danton proposes " the law of Valerius Publicola, passed in Rome after
the expulsion of the Tarquins, permitting every citizen to kill any man convicted of having
expressed opinions opposed to the law of the State, except in case of proof of the crime."
(*Ibid.*, Nos. 230 and 231, July 13, 1792.) Danton induces the federals present " to swear
that they will not leave the capital until liberty is established, and before the will of the department is made known on the fate of the executive power." Such are the principles and
the instruments, of " August 10 " and " September 2."

2 Garat, 314. " He was present for a moment on the Committee of Public Safety. The
outbreaks of May 31 and June 2 occurred ; he was the author of both these days."

3 Decrees of April 6 and 7, 1793.

4 Decree of September 5, 1793.

5 Decree of March 10, 1793.

6 August 1 and 12, 1793.

populace in the very hall of the Convention.[1]—In order to set the machine up, he cleared the ground, fused the metal, hammered out the principal pieces, filed off the blisterings, designed the action, adjusted the minor wheels, set it agoing and indicated what it had to do, and, at the same time, he forged the plating which guarded it from the foreigner and against all outward violence. The machine being his, why, after constructing it, did he not serve as its engineer ?

Because, if competent to construct it, he was not qualified to manage it. In a crisis, he may take hold of the wheel himself, excite an assembly or a mob in his favor, carry things with a high hand and direct an executive committee for a few weeks. But he dislikes regular, persistent labor ; he is not made for studying documents, for poring over papers and confining himself to administrative routine.[2] Never, like Robespierre and Billaud can he attend to both official and police duties at the same time, carefully reading minute daily reports, annotating mortuary lists, extemporising ornate abstractions, coolly enunciating falsehoods and acting out the patient, satisfied inquisitor ; and especially, he can never become the systematic executioner.—On the one hand, his eyes are not obscured by the grey veil of theory : he does not regard men through the "Contrat-Social " as a sum of arithmetical units,[3] but as they really are, living, suffering, shedding their blood, especially those he knows, each with his peculiar physiognomy and demeanor. Compassion is excited by all this when one has any feeling, and he had. Danton had a heart ; he had the quick sensibilities of a man of flesh and blood stirred by the primitive instincts, the good ones along with the bad ones, instincts which culture had neither impaired nor deadened, which

---

1 See " The Revolution," vol. iii., ch. i.—Buchez et Roux, xxv., 285. (Meeting of Nov. 26, 1793.)—*Moniteur*, xix., 726. Danton (March 16, 1794) secures the passing of a decree that " hereafter prose only shall be heard at the bar of the house."

2 Archives Nationales, Papers of the Committee of General Security, No 134.—Letter of Delacroix to Danton, Lille, March 25, 1793, on the situation in Belgium, and the retreat of Dumouriez. . . . " My letter is so long I fear that you will not read it to the end. . . . Oblige me by forgetting your usual indolence."—Letter of Chabot to Danton, Frimaire 12, year II. " I know your genius, my dear colleague, and consequently your natural indolent disposition. I was afraid that you would not read me through if I wrote a long letter. Nevertheless I rely on your friendship to make an exception in my favor."

3 Lagrange, the mathematician, and senator under the empire, was asked how it was that he voted for the terrible annual conscriptions. " It had no sensible effect on the tables of mortality," he replied.

allowed him to plan and permit the September massacre, but
which did not allow him to practise daily and blindly, systematic and wholesale murder. Already in September, "cloaking
his pity under his bellowing," [1] he had shielded or saved many
eminent men from the butchers. When the axe is about to
fall on the Girondists, he is "ill with grief" and despair. "I
am unable to save them," he exclaimed, "and big tears
streamed down his cheeks."—On the other hand, his eyes are
not covered by the bandage of incapacity or lack of forethought. He detected the innate vice of the system, the
inevitable and approaching suicide of the Revolution. "The
Girondists forced us to throw ourselves upon the *sans-culotterie*
which has devoured them, which will devour us, and which
will eat itself up." [2]—"Let Robespierre and Saint-Just alone,
and there will soon be nothing left in France but a Thebiad of
political Trappists." [3] At the end, he sees more clearly still.
"On a day like this I organised the Revolutionary Tribunal.
. . . . I ask pardon for it of God and man. . . . In Revolutions, authority remains with the greatest scoundrels. . . . It
is better to be a poor fisherman than govern men." [4]—Nevertheless, he professed to govern them ; he constructed a new machine for the purpose, and, deaf to its creaking, it worked in
conformity with its structure and the impulse he gave to it. It
towers before him, this sinister machine, with its vast wheel
and iron cogs grinding all France, their multiplied teeth pressing out each individual life, its steel blade constantly rising
and falling, and, as it plays faster and faster, daily exacting a
larger and larger supply of human material, while those who
furnish this supply are held to be as insensible and as senseless
as itself. Danton cannot, or will not, be so.—He gets out of
the way, diverts himself, gambles, [5] forgets ; he supposes that
the titular decapitators will probably consent to take no notice

---

1 Garat, 305, 310, 313. "His friends almost worshipped him."

2 *Ibid.*, 317.—Thibeaudeau, "Mémoires," i., 59.

3 Quinet, "La Révolution," ii., 304. (According to the unpublished memoirs of Baudot.)
These expressions by Danton's friends all bear the mark of Danton himself. At all events
they express exactly his ideas.

4 Riouffe, 67.

5 Miot de Melito, "Mémoires," i., 40, 42.—Michelet, "Histoire de la Révolution
Française," vi., 34 ; v. 178, 184. (On the second marriage of Danton in June, 1793, to a
young girl of sixteen. On his journey to Arcis, March, 1794.)—Riouffe, 68. In prison
"He talked constantly about trees, the country and nature."

of him ; in any event they do not pursue him ; "they would not dare do it." "No one must lay hands on me, I am the ark." At the worst, he prefers "to be guillotined rather than guillotine."—Having said or thought this, he is ripe for the scaffold.

III.

Even with the firm determination to remain decapitator-in-chief, Danton would not be the true representative of the Revolution. It is brigandage, but carried on philosophically ; its creed includes robbery and assassination, but only as a knife in its sheath ; the showy, polished sheath is for public display, and not the sharp and bloody blade. Danton, like Marat, lets the blade be too plainly visible. At the mere sight of Marat, filthy and slovenly, with his livid, frog-like face, round, gleaming and fixed eyeballs, bold, maniacal stare and steady monotonous rage, common-sense rebels ; people do not accept for their guide a homicidal bedlamite. At sight of Danton, with his billingsgate expressions, his voice like a tocsin of insurrection, his cyclopean features and air of an exterminator, humanity takes alarm ; one does not surrender oneself to a political butcher without repugnance. The Revolution demands another interpreter, wearing like itself a specious exterior, and such is Robespierre,[1] with his irreproachable attire, well-powdered hair, carefully brushed coat,[2] strict habits, dogmatic tone, and formal, studied manner of speaking. No mind, in its medi-

---

[1] We can trace the effect of his attitude on the public in the police reports, especially at the end of 1793, and beginning of the year 1794. (Archives Nationales, F 7. 3, 61, report of Charmont, Nivose 6, year II.) "Robespierre gains singularly in public estimation, especially since his speech in the Convention, calling on his colleagues to rally and crush out the monsters in the interior, also in which *he calls on all to support* the new revolutionary government with their intelligence and talents ...I have to state that I have everywhere heard his name mentioned with admiration. They wound up by saying that it would be well for all members of the Convention to adopt the measures presented by Robespierre."— (Report of Robin, Nivose 8.) "Citizen Robespierre is honored everywhere, in all groupes and in the *cafés*. At the Café Manouri it was given out that his views of the government were the only ones which, *like the magnet*, would attract all citizens to the Revolution. It is not the same with citizen Billaud-Varennes." (Report of the Purveyor, Nivose 9.) "In certain clubs and groups there is a rumor that Robespierre is to be appointed dictator.....The people do justice to his austere virtues ; it is noticed that he has never changed his opinions since the Revolution began."

[2] "Souvenirs d'un déporté" by P. Villiers, (Robespierre's secretary for seven months in 1790,) p. 2. "Of painstaking cleanliness."—Buchez et Roux, xxxiv., 94. Description of Robespierre, published in the newspapers after his death: "His clothes were exquisitely clean and his hair always carefully brushed."

ocrity and incompetence, so well harmonises with the spirit of the epoch.   The reverse of the statesman, he soars in empty space, amongst abstractions, always mounted on a principle and incapable of dismounting so as to see things practically.   " That b—— there," exclaims Danton, " doesn't even know how to boil an egg ! "   " The vague generalities of his preaching," writes another contemporary,[1] " rarely culminated in any specific measure or legal provision.   He combated everything and proposed nothing ; the secret of his policy happily accorded with his intellectual impotence and with the nullity of his legislative conceptions."   Once the thread of his revolutionary scholasticism has spun itself out, he is completely used up. —As to financial matters and military art, he knows nothing and risks nothing, except to underrate or calumniate Carnot and Cambon who did know and who took risks.[2]—In relation to a foreign policy his speech on the state of Europe is the amplification of a schoolboy ; on exposing the plans of the English minister he reaches the pinnacle of chimerical nonsense ;[3] eliminate the rhetorical passages, and it is not the head of a government who speaks, but the porter of the Jacobin club. On contemporary France, as it actually exists, he has not one just or precise idea : instead of men, he sees only twenty-six millions of automatons, who, duly penned in, work together in peace and harmony ; they are, indeed, naturally good,[4] and,

---

1 D'Hericault, " La Révolution du 9 Thermidor," (as stated by Daunou).—Meillan, " Mémoires," p. 4. " His eloquence was nothing but diffusive declamation without order or method, and especially with no conclusions. Every time he spoke we were obliged to ask him what he was driving at.....Never did he propose any remedy. He left the task of finding expedients to others, and especially to Danton."

2 Buchez et Roux, xxxiii., 437, 438, 440, 442. (Speech by Robespierre, Thermidor 8, year II.)

3 *Ibid.*, xxx., 225, 226, 227, 228 (Speech, Nov. 17, 1793), and xxxi., 255 (Speech, Jan. 26, 1794). " The policy of the London Cabinet largely contributed to the first movement of our Revolution....Taking advantage of political tempests (the cabinet) aimed to effect in exhausted and dismembered France a change of dynasty and to *place the Duke of York on the throne of Louis XVI.* ...Pitt....is an imbecile, whatever may be said of a reputation that has been much too greatly puffed up. A man who, abusing the influence acquired by him on an island *placed haphazard in the ocean*, is desirous of contending with the French people, could not have conceived of such an absurd plan elsewhere than in a madhouse."—Cf. *Ibid.*, xxx., 465.

4 *Ibid.*, xxvi., 433, 441, (Speech on the Constitution, May 10, 1793) ; xxxi., 275. " Goodness consists in the people preferring itself to what is not itself ; the magistrate, to be good, must himself immolate himself to the people."....." Let this maxim be first adopted that the people are good and that its delegates are corruptible."... xxx., 464. (Speech, Dec. 25, 1793) : " The virtues are the appanage of the unfortunate and the patrimony of the people."

after a little necessary purification, they will become good again ; accordingly, their collective will is " the voice of reason and public interest ; " hence, on meeting together, they are wise. "The people's assembly of delegates should deliberate, if possible, in the presence of the whole body of the people ; " the Legislative body, at least, should hold its sittings "in a vast, majestic edifice open to twenty thousand spectators." Note that for the past four years, in the Constituent Assembly, in the Legislative Assembly, in the Convention, at the Hotel-de-Ville, in the Jacobin Club, wherever Robespierre speaks, the galleries have kept up constant vociferations : such a positive, palpable experience would open anybody's eyes ; his are closed through prejudice or interest ; even physical truth finds no access to his mind, because he is unable to comprehend it, or because he has to keep it out.   He is, accordingly, either obtuse or a charlatan, and both in fact, for both combine to form the *cuistre*, that is to say, the hollow, inflated mind which, filled with words and imagining that these are ideas, revels in its own declamation and dupes itself that it may dictate to others.

Such is his title, character and the part he plays.   In this artificial and declamatory tragedy of the Revolution he takes the leading part ; the maniac and the barbarian slowly retire in the background on the appearance of the *cuistre ;* Marat and Danton finally become effaced, or efface themselves, and the stage is left to Robespierre who absorbs attention.[1]—If we would comprehend him we must look at him as he stands in the midst of his surroundings.   At the last stage of an intellectual vegetation passing away, he remains on the last branch of the eighteenth century, the most abortive and driest offshoot of the classical spirit.[2]   He has retained nothing of a worn-out system of philosophy but its lifeless dregs and well-conned formulæ, the formulæ of Rousseau, Mably, and Raynal, concerning "the people, nature, reason, liberty, tyrants, factions, virtue, morality," a ready-made vocabulary,[3] expressions too

---

1 Cf. *passim*, Hamel, "Histoire de Robespierre," 3 vols. An elaborate panegyric full of details. Although eighty years have elapsed, Robespierre still makes dupes of people through his attitudinising and rhetorical flourishes. M. Hamel twice intimates his resemblance to Jesus Christ. The resemblance, indeed, is that of Pascal's Jesuits to the Jesus of the Gospel.

2 " The Ancient Régime," p. 262.

3 Garat, " Mémoires," 84. Garat who is himself an ideologist, notes " his eternal twad-

ample, the meaning of which, ill-defined by the masters, evaporates in the hands of the disciple. He never tries to get at this ;
his writings and speeches are merely long strings of vague
abstract periods ; there is no telling fact in them, no distinct,
characteristic detail, no appeal to the eye evoking a living
image, no personal, special observation, no clear, frank original
impression. It might be said of him that he never saw anything with his own eyes, that he neither could nor would see,
that false conceptions have intervened and fixed themselves
between him and the object ;[1] he combines these in logical
sequence, and simulates the absent thought by an affected jargon, and this is all. The other Jacobins alongside of him likewise use the same scholastic jargon ; but none of them expati-
ate on it so lengthily. For hours, we grope after him in the
vague shadows of political speculation, in the cold and perplex-
ing mist of didactic generalities, trying in vain to make
something out of his colorless tirades, and we grasp nothing.
We then, astonished, ask what all this talk amounts to, and
why he talks at all ; the answer is, that he has said nothing and
that he talks only for the sake of talking, the same as a sec-
tary preaching to his congregation, neither the preacher nor
his audience ever wearying, the one of turning the dogmatic
crank, and the other of listening. So much the better if the
hopper is empty ; the emptier it is the easier and faster the
crank turns. And better still, if the empty term he selects is
used in a contrary sense ; the sonorous words justice, humanity, mean to him piles of human heads, the same as a text from
the gospels means to a grand inquisitor the burning of here-
tics.—Through this extreme perversity, the *cuistre* spoils his
own mental instrument ; thenceforth he employs it as he likes,
as his passions dictate, believing that he serves truth in serving
these.

Now, his first passion, his principal passion, is literary vanity. Never was the chief of a party, sect or government, even

<hr/>

dle about the rights of man, the sovereignty of the people, and other principles which he was
always talking about, and on which he never gave utterance to one precise or fresh idea."

1 Read especially his speech on the Constitution, (May 10, 1793), his report on the principles of Republican Government, (Dec. 15, 1793), his speech on the relationship between
religious and national ideas and republican principles. (May 7, 1794) and speech of Thermidor
8.—Carnot: "Mémoires," ii., 512. " He brought to bear nothing but vague generalities in all
business deliberations."

at critical moments, such an incurable, insignificant rhetorician, so formal, so pompous, and so vapid.—On the eve of the 9th of Thermidor, when it was necessary to conquer or die, he enters the tribune with a set speech, written and re-written, polished and re-polished,[1] overloaded with studied ornaments and bits for effect,[2] coated by dint of time and labor, with the academic varnish, the glitter of symmetrical antitheses, rounded periods, exclamations, preteritions, apostrophes and other tricks of the pen.[3]—In the most famous and important of his reports,[4] I have counted eighty-four instances of prosopopœia imitated from Rousseau and the antique, many of them largely expanded, some addressed to the dead, to Brutus, to young Barra, and others to absentees, priests, and aristocrats, to the unfortunate, to French women, and finally to abstract substantives like Liberty and Friendship. With unshaken conviction and intense satisfaction, he deems himself an orator because he harps on the same old tune. There is no sign of true inspiration in his elaborate eloquence, nothing but recipes and those of a worn-out art, Greek and Roman common-places, Socrates and the hemlock, Brutus and his dagger, classic metaphors like "the flambeaux of discord," and "the vessel of State,"[5] words coupled together and beauties of style which a pupil in rhetoric aims at on the college bench;[6] sometimes a grand

---

1 Buchez at Roux, xxxiii., 406. (Speech delivered Thermidor 8th.) The printed copy of the manuscript with corrections and erasures.

2 *Ibid.*, 420, 422, 427.

3 *Ibid.*, 428, 435, 436. "O day forever blessed! What a sight to behold, the entire French people assembled together and rendering to the author of nature the only homage worthy of him! How affecting each object that enchants the eye and touches the heart of man! O honored old age! O generous ardor of the young of our country! O the innocent, pure joy of youthful citizens! O the exquisite tears of tender mothers! O the divine charms of innocence and beauty! What majesty in a great people happy in its strength, power and virtue!"—"No, Charmette, No, death is not the sleep of eternity!"—"Remember, O, People, that in a republic, etc."—"If such truths must be dissembled then bring me the hemlock!"

4 Speech, May 7, 1794. (On moral and religious ideas in relation to republican principles.)

5 Buchez et Roux, xxxiii., 436. "The Verres and Catilines of our country." (Speech of Thermidor 8th.)—Note especially the speech delivered March 7, 1794, crammed full of classical reminiscences.

6 *Ibid.*, xxxiii., 421. " Truth has touching and terrible accents which reverberate powerfully in pure hearts as in guilty consciences, and which falsehood can no more counterfeit than Salome can counterfeit the thunders of heaven."—437 : " Why do those who yesterday predicted such frightful tempests now gaze only on the fleeciest clouds? Why do those who but lately exclaimed ' I affirm that we are treading on a volcano,' now behold themselves sleeping on a bed of roses ? "

bravura air, so essential for parade in public ;[1] oftentimes a delicate strain of the flute, for, in those days, one must have a tender heart ;[2] in short, Marmontel's method in " Belisarius," or
that of Thomas in his " Eloges," all borrowed from Rousseau,
but of inferior quality, like a sharp, thin voice strained to imitate a rich, powerful voice ; a sort of involuntary parody, and
the more repulsive because a word ends in a blow, because a
sentimental, declamatory Trissotin poses as statesman, because
the studied elegances of the closet become pistol shots aimed
at living breasts, because an epithet skilfully directed sends a
man to the guillotine.—The contrast is too great between his
talent and the part he plays.   With a talent as petty and false
as his intellect, there is no employment for which he is less
calculated than that of governing men ; he was cut out for
another, which, in a peaceable community, would have stood
him in stead.   Suppress the Revolution, and Marat would have
probably ended his days in an asylum.   Danton might possibly
have become a legal fillibuster, a Mandrin or bravo under
certain circumstances, and finally throttled or hung.   Robespierre, on the contrary, might have continued as he began,[3] a
busy, hard-working lawyer of good standing, member of the
Arras Academy, winner of competitive prizes, author of
literary eulogiums, moral essays and philanthropic pamphlets ;
his little lamp, lighted like hundreds of others of equal
capacity at the focus of the new philosophy, would have
burned moderately without doing harm to any one, and diffused over a provincial circle a dim, commonplace illumination
proportionate to the little oil his lamp would hold.

But the Revolution bore him into the Constituent Assembly,
where, for a long time on this great stage, the self-love that
constitutes the sensitive chord of the *cuistre,* suffered terribly.

---

1 *Ibid.,* xxxii., 360, 361. (Portraits of the encyclopædists and Hébertists.)

2 *Ibid.,* xxxiii., 408. " Here I must give vent to my feelings."—xxxii., 475-478, the concluding part.

3 Hamel: " Histoire de Robespierre," i., 34-76. An attorney at 23, a member of the
Rosati club at Arras at 24, a member of the Arras Academy at 25. The Royal Society of
Metz awarded him a second prize for his discourse against the prejudice which regards the
relatives of condemned criminals as infamous. His eulogy of Gresset is not crowned by
the Amiens Academy. He reads before the Academy of Arras a discourse against the civil
disabilities of bastards, and then another on reforms in criminal jurisprudence. In 1789, he
is president of the Arras Academy, and publishes an eulogy of Dupaty and an address to
the Artesian nation on the qualities necessary for future deputies.

He had already suffered on this score from his earliest youth, and his wounds being still fresh made him only the more sensitive. Left an orphan, poor, befriended by his bishop, becoming a bursar through favor at the college Louis-le-Grand, after this a clerk with Brissot under the revolutionary system of law-practice, and at length settled down in his gloomy rue des Rapporteurs as a pettifogger, living with a peevish sister, he adopts Rousseau, whom he had once seen and whom he ardently studies, for his master in philosophy, politics and style. Fancying, probably, like other young men of his age and condition, that he could play a similar part and thus emerge from his blind alley, he published law pleadings for effect, contended for Academy prizes, and read papers before his Arras colleagues. His success was moderate : one of his harangues obtained a notice in the Artois Almanack ; the Academy of Metz awarded him only a second prize ; that of Amiens gave him no prize, while the critic of the " Mercure " spoke of his style as smacking of the provinces.—In the National Assembly, eclipsed by men of great and spontaneous ability, he remains a long time in the shade, and, more than once, through over self-assertion or lack of tact, makes himself ridiculous. With his sharp, thin, attorney's visage, " dull, monotonous, coarse voice and wearisome delivery," " an artesian accent " and constrained air,[1] his constantly putting himself forward, his elaboration of commonplaces, his evident determination to impose on cultivated people, still a body of intelligent listeners, and the intolerable ennui he caused them—all this is not calculated to render the Assembly indulgent to errors of sense and taste.[2] One day, referring to certain acts of the " Conseil : " " It is necessary that a noble and simple formula should announce national rights and carry respect for law into the hearts of the people." Consequently, in the decrees as promulgated, after the words

---

[1] See his eulogy of Rousseau in the speech of May 7, 1794. (Buchez et Roux, xxxii., 369.)—Garat, 85. " I hoped that his selection of Rousseau for a model of style and the constant reading of his works would exert some good influence on his character."

[2] Fievée, " Correspondance " (introduction). Fievée, who heard him at the Jacobin Club, said that he resembled a " tailor of the ancient régime." Laréveillère-Lepeaux, " Mémoires. '—Buchez et Roux, xxxiv., 94.—Malouet, " Mémoires," ii., 135. (Session of May 31, 1791, after the delivery of Abbé Raynal's address.) " This is the first and only time I found Robespierre clear and even eloquent. . . . He spun out his opening phrases as usual, which contained the spirit of his discourse, and which, in spite of his accustomed rigmarole, produced the effect he intended."

" Louis, by the grace of God," etc., these words should follow :
" People, behold the law imposed on you ! Let this law be
considered sacred and inviolable for all ! " Upon this, a Gas-
con deputy arises and remarks in his southern accent, " Gentlemen, this formula is useless—we do not sing psalms
(*cantique*)." There is a general roar ; [1] Robespierre keeps silent
and bleeds internally : two or three discomfitures of this stamp
render a man sore from head to foot.

It is not that his folly is foolishness to him ; no pedant taken
in the act and hissed would avow that he deserved such treatment ; on the contrary, he is content to have spoken as becomes
a philosophic and moral legislator, and so much the worse for
the narrow minds and corrupt hearts unable to comprehend
him.—Thrown back upon himself, his wounded vanity seeks
inward nourishment and takes what it can find in the sterile
uniformity of his bourgeois moderation. Robespierre, unlike
Danton, has no cravings. He is sober ; he is not tormented
by his senses ; if he gives way to them, it is only no further than
he can help, and with a bad grace ; in the rue Saintonge in
Paris, " for seven months," says his secretary, " I knew of but
one woman that he kept company with, and he did not treat
her very well. . . . very often he would not let her enter his
room : " when busy, he must not be disturbed ; he is naturally steady, hard-working, studious and fond of seclusion, at
college a model pupil, at home in his province an attentive
advocate, a punctual deputy in the Assembly, everywhere free
of temptation and incapable of going astray.—" Irreproachable "
is the word which from early youth an inward voice constantly
repeats to him in low tones to console him for obscurity and
patience. Thus has he ever been, is now, and ever will be ; he
says this to himself, tells others so, and on this foundation, all
of a piece, he builds up his character. He is not, like Desmoulins, to be seduced by dinners, like Barnave, by flattery, like
Mirabeau and Danton, by money, like the Girondists, by the

---

[1] Courrier de Provence, iii., No. 52, (Octo. 7 and 8, 1789).—Buchez et Roux, vi., 372.
(Session of July 10, 1790.) Another similar blunder was committed by him on the occasion
of an American deputation. The president had made his response, which was " unanimously applauded." Robespierre wanted to have his say notwithstanding the objections
of the Assembly, impatient at his verbiage, and which finally put him down. Amidst the
laughter, " M. l'Abbé Maury demands ironically the printing of M. Robespierre's discourse."

insinuating charm of ancient politeness and select society, like the Dantonists, by the bait of joviality and unbounded license— he is the incorruptible. He is not to be deterred or diverted, like the Feuillants, Girondists, and Dantonists, like statesmen or specialists, by considerations of a lower order, by regard for interests or respect for acquired positions, by the danger of undertaking too much at once, by the necessity of not disor- ganising the service and of giving play to human passions, motives of utility and opportunity : he is the uncompromising champion of right.[1] "Alone, or nearly alone, I do not allow myself to be corrupted ; alone or nearly alone, I do not com- promise the right ;[2] which two merits I possess in the highest degree. A few others may live correctly, but they oppose or betray principles ; a few others profess to have principles, but they do not live correctly. No one else leads so pure a life or is so loyal to principles ; no one else joins to so fervent a wor- ship of truth so strict a practice of virtue : I am the unique."— What can be more agreeable than this mute soliloquy ? It is gently heard the first day in Robespierre's address to the Third- Estate of Arras ;[3] it is uttered aloud the last day in his great speech in the Convention ;[4] during the interval, it crops out and shines through all his compositions harangues, or reports, in exordiums, parentheses and perorations, permeating every sentence like the drone of a bag-pipe.[5]—Through the delight he

---

1 P. Villiers, p. 2.

2 Cf. his principal speeches in the Constituent Assembly ;—against martial law ; against the veto, even suspensive ; against the qualification of the silver marc and in favor of universal suffrage ; in favor of admitting into the National Guard non-acting citizens ; of the marriage of priests ; of the abolition of the death penalty ; of granting political rights to colored men ; of interdicting the father from favoring any one of his children ; of declaring the "Constituants" ineligible to the Legislative Assembly, etc. On royalty : "The King is not the representative but the clerk of the nation." On the danger of allowing political rights to colored men : "Let the colonies perish if they cost you your honor, your glory, your liberty ! "

3 Hamel, i., 76, 77, (March, 1789). "My heart is an honest one and I stand firm ; I have never bowed beneath the yoke of baseness and corruption." He enumerates the virtues that a representative of the Third Estate should possess (26, 83). He already shows his blubbering capacity and his disposition to regard himself as a victim : "They under- take making martyrs of the people's defenders. Had they the power to deprive me of the advantages they envy, could they snatch from me my soul and the consciousness of the benefits I desire to confer on them."

4 Buchez et Roux, xxxiii. "Who am I that am thus accused ? The slave of freedom, a living martyr to the Republic, at once the victim and the enemy of crime ! " See this speech in full.

5 Especially in his address to the French people, (Aug., 1791), which, in a justificatory form, is his apotheosis.—Cf. Hamel, ii., 212 ; Speech in the Jacobin Club, (April 27, 1792).

takes in this he can listen to nothing else, and it is just here that the outward echoes supervene and sustain with their accom-paniment the inward cantata which he sings to his own glory. Towards the end of the Constituent Assembly, through the withdrawal or the elimination of every man at all able or com-petent, he becomes one of the conspicuous tenors on the politi-cal stage, while in the Jacobin Club he is decidedly the tenor most in vogue.—" Unique competitor of the Roman Fabri-cius," writes the branch club at Marseilles to him ; " immor-tal defender of popular rights," says the Jacobin crew of Bourges.[1] One of two portraits of him in the exhibi-tion of 1791 bears the inscription : " The Incorruptible." At the Moliere Theatre a drama of the day represents him as launching the thunderbolts of his logic and virtue at Rohan and Condé. On his way, at Bapaume, the patriots of the place, the National Guard on the road and the authorities, come in a body to honor the great man. The town of Arras is illum-inated on his arrival. On the adjournment of the Constituent Assembly the people in the street greet him with shouts, crown him with oak wreaths, take the horses from his cab and drag him in triumph to the rue St. Honoré, where he lodges with the carpenter Duplay.—Here, in one of those families in which the semi-bourgeois class borders on the people, whose minds are unsophisticated, and on whom glittering generalities and orator-ical tirades take full hold, he finds his worshippers ; they drink in his words ; they have the same opinion of him that he has of himself ; to every soul in the house, husband, wife and daughter, he is the great patriot, the infallible sage ; he bestows benedictions night and morning ; he inhales clouds of incense ; he is a god installed in furnished apartments. The faithful, to obtain access to him form a line in the court ;[1] they are ad-mitted into the reception room, where they gather around por-traits of him drawn with pencil and stump, in sepia and in water color, and before miniature busts in red or grey plaster ; then, on the signal being given by him, they penetrate through a glass door into the sanctuary where he presides, in the private closet in which the best bust of him, with verses and mottoes,

---

[1] Hamel, i., 517, 532, 559 ; ii., 5.

[2] Laréveillère-Lepeaux, " Mémoires."—Barbaroux, " Mémoires," 358. (Both, after a visit to him.)

supplies his place during his absence.—His worshippers adore
him on their knees, and the women more than the men.   On
the day he delivers his apology before the Convention "the passages are lined with women [1] .... seven or eight hundred of
them in the galleries, and but two hundred men at most ; " and
how frantically they cheer him !   He is a priest surrounded by
devotees." [2]   On spouting his "rigmarole" at the Jacobin
Club "the most affecting sobbings, shoutings and stampings
almost make the house tumble." [3]   A looker-on who shows no
emotion is greeted with murmurs and obliged to slip out, like a
heretic that has strayed into a church on the elevation of the
Host.—The faster the revolutionary thunderbolts fall on other
heads, so does Robespierre mount higher and higher in glory
and deification.   Letters are addressed to him as "the founder
of the Republic, the incorruptible genius who foresees all and
saves all, who can neither be deceived nor seduced ; " [4] who
has "the energy of a Spartan and the eloquence of an Athenian ; " [5] "who shields the Republic with the ægis of his eloquence ; " [6] who "illuminates the universe with his writings, fills
the world with his renown and regenerates the human species
here below ;" [7] whose " name is now, and will be, held in venera-

---

1 Robespierre's devotees constantly attend at the Jacobin Club and in the Convention to
hear him speak and applaud him, and are called, from their condition and dress, " the fat
petticoats."

2 Buchez et Roux, xx., 197. (Meeting of Nov. 1, 1792.)—" Chronique de Paris," Nov. 9,
1792, article by Condorcet.   With the keen insight of the man of the world, he saw clearly
into Robespierre's character.   " Robespierre preaches, Robespierre censures ; he is animated, grave, melancholy, deliberately enthusiastic and systematic in his ideas, and conduct.   He thunders against the rich and the great ; he lives on nothing and has no physical necessities.   His sole mission is to talk, and this he does almost constantly... His
characteristics are not those of a religious reformer, but of the chief of a sect.   He has won
a reputation for austerity approaching sanctity.   He jumps up on a bench and talks about
God and Providence.   He styles himself the friend of the poor ; he attracts around him a
crowd of women and ' the poor in spirit,' and gravely accepts their homage and worship....
Robespierre is a priest and never will be anything else."   Among Robespierre's devotees
Madame de Chalabre must be mentioned, (Hamel, i., 525), a young widow (Hamel, iii.,
524), who offers him her hand with an income of forty thousand francs.   " Thou art my
supreme deity," she writes to him, " and I know no other on this earth !   I regard thee
as my guardian angel, and would live only under thy laws."

3 Fievée, " Correspondance," (introduction).

4 Report of Courtois on the papers found in Robespierre's domicile.   Justificatory documents No. 20, letter of the Secretary of the Committee of Surveillance of Saint Calais,
Nivose 15, year II.

5 *Ibid.*, No. 18.   Letter of V——, former inspector of " droits reservés," Feb. 5, 1792.

6 *Ibid.*, No. 8.   Letter of P. Brincourt, Sedan, Aug. 29, 1793.

7 *Ibid.*, No. 1.   Letter of Besson, with an address of the popular club of Menosque,
Prairial 23, year II.

tion for all ages, present and to come ;" [1] who is "the Messiah promised by the Eternal for universal reform." [2]—"An extraordinary popularity," says Billaud-Varennes,[3] a popularity which, founded under the Constituent Assembly, "only increased during the Legislative Assembly," and, later on, so much more, that, "in the National Convention he soon found himself the only one able to fix attention on his person.... and control public opinion.... With this ascendency over public opinion, with this irresistible preponderance, when he reached the Committee of Public Safety, he was already the most important being in France." In three years, a chorus of a thousand voices,[4] which he formed and led indefatigably, rehearses to him in unison his own litany, his most sacred creed, the hymn of three stanzas composed by him in his own honor, and which he daily recites to himself in a low tone of voice, and often in a loud one : "Robespierre alone has discovered the ideal citizen ! Robespierre alone attains to it without exaggeration or shortcomings ! Robespierre alone is worthy of and able to lead the Revolution !" [5]—Cool infatuation carried thus far is equivalent to a raging fever, and Robespierre almost attains to the ideas and the ravings of Marat.

First, in his own eyes, he, like Marat, is a persecuted man, and, like Marat, he poses himself as a "martyr," but more skilfully and keeping within bounds, affecting the resigned and tender air of an innocent victim, who, offering himself as a sacrifice, ascends to Heaven, bequeathing to mankind the imperishable souvenir of his virtues.[6] "I excite against me the self-love of everybody ; [7] I sharpen against me a thou

---

1 *Ibid.*, No. 14. Letter of D——, member of the Cordeliers Club, and former mercer, Jan. 31, 1792.

2 *Ibid.*, No. 12. Letter by C——, Chateau Thierry, Prairial 30, year II.

3 Hamel, iii., 682. (Copied from Billaud-Varennes' manuscripts, in the Archives Nationales).

4 *Moniteur*, xxii., 175. (Session of Vendémiaire 18, year III. Speech by Laignelot.) "Robespierre had all the popular clubs under his thumb."

5 Garat, 85. "The most conspicuous sentiment with Robespierre, and one, indeed, of which he made no mystery, was that the defender of the people could never see amiss."— (Bailleul, quoted in Carnot's Memoirs, i., 516.) "He regarded himself as a privileged being, destined to become the people's regenerator and instructor."

6 Speech of May 16, 1794, and of Thermidor 8, year II.

7 Buchez et Roux, x., 295, 296. (Session June 22, 1791, of the Jacobin Club.)—*Ibid.*, 294.—Marat spoke in the same vein : "I have made myself a curse for all good people in France." He writes, the same date : "Writers in behalf of the people will be dragged to dungeons. ' The friend of the people,' whose last sigh is given for his country, and whose

sand daggers.   I am a sacrifice to every species of hatred. ....
It is certain that my head will atone for the truths I have
uttered.   I have given my life, and shall welcome death almost
as a boon.   It is, perhaps, Heaven's will that my blood
should indicate the pathway of my country to happiness
and freedom.   With what transports I accept this glorious
destiny !"[1] —"One does not wage war against tyrants for
existence, and, what is still more dangerous, against miscreants ;
. . . . the greater their eagerness to put an end to my career
here below, the more eager I shall be to fill it with actions
serving the welfare of my fellow-creatures."[2]   "These miscreants all revile me ;[3] the most insignificant, the most legitimate actions of others are, in my case, crimes.   Whoever becomes acquainted with me is at once calumniated.   The luck
of others is pardoned, my zeal is guilt.   Deprive me of my
conscience and I am the most wretched of men.   I do not
even enjoy the rights of a citizen.   I am not even allowed to
perform my duty as a representative of the people. . . . .   To
the enemies of my country, to whom my existence seems an
obstacle to their heinous plots, I am ready to sacrifice it, if
their odious empire is to endure ; . . . . let their road to the
scaffold be the pathway of crime, ours shall be that of virtue ;
. . . . let the hemlock be got ready for me, I await it on this
hallowed spot.   I shall at least bequeath to my country an
example of constant affection for it, and to the enemies of
humanity the disgrace of my death."

Naturally, as always with Marat, he sees around him only
"evil-doers," "intriguers" and "traitors."[4]—Naturally, as
with Marat, common sense with him is perverted, and, like
Marat again, he thinks at random.   "I am not obliged to

---

faithful voice still summons you to freedom, is to find his grave in a fiery furnace." The
last expression shows the difference in their imaginations.

1 Hamel, ii., 122.   (Meeting of the Jacobin Club, Feb. 10, 1792.)   "To obtain death at
the hands of tyrants is not enough—one must deserve death.   If it be true that the earliest
defenders of liberty became its martyrs they should not suffer death without bearing tyranny
along with them into the grave."—Cf., *ibid.*, ii., 215.   (Meeting of April 27, 1792.)

2 Hamel, ii., 513.   (Speech in the Convention, Prairial 7, year II.)

3 Buchez et Roux, xxxiii., 422, 445, 447, 457.   (Speech in the Convention, Thermidor 8,
year II.)

4 Buchez et Roux, xx., 11, 18.   (Meeting of the Jacobin Club, Oct. 29, 1792.)   Speech on
Lafayette, the Feuillants and Girondists.   xxxi., 360, 363.   (Meeting of the Convention,
May 7, 1794.)   On Lafayette, the Girondists, Dantonists and Hébertists.—xxxiii., 427.
(Speech of Thermidor 8, year II.)

reflect," said he to Garat, " I always rely on first impressions."
" For him," says the same authority, "the best reasons are
suspicions," [1] and nought makes headway against suspicions,
not even the most positive evidence. On September 4, 1792,
talking confidentially with Pétion, and hard pressed with the
questions that he put to him, he ends by saying, " Very well, I
think that Brissot is on Brunswick's side."[2]—Naturally, finally,
he, like Marat, imagines the darkest fictions, but they are less
improvised, less grossly absurd, more slowly worked out and
more industriously interwoven in his calculating inquisitorial
brain. " Evidently," he says to Garat, "the Girondists are
conspiring." [3] "And where?" demands Garat. " Every
where," he replies, "in Paris, throughout France, over all
Europe. Gensonné, at Paris, is plotting in the Faubourg St.
Antoine, going about among the shopkeepers and persuading
them that we patriots mean to pillage their shops. The Gironde
(department) has for a long time been plotting its separation
from France so as to join England ; the chiefs of its deputation are at the head of the plot, and mean to carry it out at
any cost. Gensonné makes no secret of it ; he tells all among
them who will listen to him that they are not representatives
of the nation, but plenipotentiaries of the Gironde. Brissot is
plotting in his journal, which is simply a tocsin of civil war ;
we know of his going to England, and why he went ; we know
all about his intimacy with that Lebrun, minister of foreign
affairs, a *Liegois* and creature of the Austrian house. Brissot's
best friend is Clavière, and Clavière has plotted wherever he
could breathe. Rabaut, treacherous like the Protestant and
philosopher that he is, was not clever enough to conceal his
correspondence with that courtier and traitor Montesquiou ;
six months ago they were working together to open Savoy and
France to the Piedmontese. Servan was made general of the
Pyrenean army only to give the keys of France to the
Spaniards."—" Is there no doubt of this in your mind?" asks
Garat. " None, whatever." [4]

---

1 Garat, " Mémoires," 87, 88.
2 Buchez et Roux, xxi., 107. (Speech of Pétion on the charges made against him by
Robespierre.) Pétion justly objects that " Brunswick would be the first to cut off Brissot's
head, and Brissot is not fool enough to doubt it."
3 Garat, 94. (After the King's death and a little before the 10th of March, 1793.)
4 *Ibid.*, 97. In 1789 Robespierre assured Garat that Necker was plundering the Treasury,

Such assurance, equal to that of Marat, is terrible and worse in its effect, for Robespierre's list of conspirators is longer than that of Marat. Political and social, in Marat's mind, the list comprehends only aristocrats and the rich ; theological and moral in Robespierre's mind, it comprehends all atheists and dishonest persons, that is to say, nearly the whole of his party. In this narrow mind, given up to abstractions and habitually classifying men under two opposite headings, whoever is not with him on the good side is against him on the bad side, and, on the bad side, the common understanding between the factious of every flag and the rogues of every degree, is natural. "All aristocrats are corrupt, and every corrupt man is an aristocrat ; " for, "republican government and public morality are one and the same thing." [1]   Not only do evil-doers of both species tend through instinct and interest to league together, but their league is already perfected.   One has only to open one's eyes to detect "in all its extent" the plot they have hatched, "the frightful system of destruction of public morality." [2] Guadet, Vergniaud, Gensonné, Danton, Hébert, "all of them artificial characters," had no other end in view : "they felt [3] that, to destroy liberty, it was necessary to favor by every means whatever tended to justify egoism, wither the heart and efface that idea of moral beauty, which affords the only rule for public reason in its judgment of the defenders and enemies of humanity."—Their heirs remain ; but let those be careful. Immorality is a political offence ; one conspires against the State merely by making a parade of materialism or by preaching indulgence, by acting scandalously, or by following evil courses, by stock-jobbing, by dining too sumptuously ; by being vicious, scheming, given to exaggeration, or "on the fence ; " by exciting or perverting the people, by deceiving the people, by finding fault with the people, by distrusting the people, [4]

---

and that people had seen mules loaded with the gold and silver he was sending off by millions to Geneva.—Carnot, "Mémoires," i., 512. "Robespierre," say Carnot and Prieur, "paid very little attention to public business, but a good deal to public officers ; he made himself intolerable with his perpetual mistrust of these, never seeing any but traitors and conspirators."

1 Buchez et Roux, xxxiii., 417. (Speech of Thermidor 8, year II.)

2 *Ibid.*, xxxii., 361, (Speech May 7, 1794,) and 359. "Immorality is the basis of despotism, as virtue is the essence of the Republic."

3 *Ibid.*, 371.

4 Buchez et Roux, xxxiii., 195. (Report of Couthon and decree in conformity therewith,

in short, when one does not march straight along on the prescribed path marked out by Robespierre according to principles : whoever stumbles or turns aside is a scoundrel, a
traitor.   Now, not counting the Royalists, Feuillantists,
Girondists, Hébertists, Dantonists, and others already decapitated or imprisoned according to their deserts, how many
traitors still remain in the Convention, on the Committees,
amongst the representatives on mission, in the administrative
bodies not properly weeded out, amongst petty tyrannic under-
lings and the entire ruling, influential class at Paris and in the
provinces ?   Outside of "about twenty political Trappists in
the Convention," outside of a small devoted group of pure
Jacobins in Paris, outside of a faithful few scattered among
the popular clubs of the departments, how many Fouchés,
Vadiers, Talliens, Bourdons, Collots, remain amongst the so-
called revolutionists ?   How many dissentients are there, disguised as orthodox, charlatans disguised as patriots, and
pachas disguised as *sans-culottes ?* [1]   Add all this vermin to
that which Marat seeks to crush out ; it is no longer by hundreds of thousands, but by millions, exclaim Baudot, Jean Bon
St. André and Guffroy, that the guilty must be counted
and heads laid low !—And all these heads, Robespierre,
according to his maxims, must strike off.   He is well aware of
this ; hostile as his intellect may be to precise ideas, he, when
alone in his closet, face to face with himself, sees clearly, as clearly
as Marat.—Marat's chimera, on first spreading out its wings, bore
its frenzied rider swiftly onward to the charnel house ; that of

---

Prairial 22, year II.) " The revolutionary tribunal is organised for the punishment of the
people's enemies . . . . The penalty for all offences within its jurisdiction is death. Those
are held to be enemies of the people who shall have misled the people, or the representatives
of the people, into measures opposed to the interests of liberty ; those who shall have
sought to create discouragement by favoring the undertakings of tyrants leagued against
the Republic ; those who shall have spread false reports to divide or disturb the people ;
those who shall have sought to misdirect opinion and impede popular instruction, produce
depravity and corrupt the public conscience, diminish the energy and purity of revolutionary and republican principles, or stay their progress. . . . . Those who, charged with public functions, abuse them to serve the enemies of the Revolution, vex patriots, oppress the
people, etc."

[1] Buchez et Roux, xxxv., 290. (" Institutions," by Saint-Just.) " The Revolution is
chilled. Principles have lost their vigor. Nothing remains but red-caps worn by intrigue."
—Report by Courtois, " Pièces justificatives " No. 20. (Letter of Pays and Rompillon,
president and secretary of the Committee of Surveillance of Saint-Calais, to Robespierre,
Nivose 15, year II.) " The Mountain here is composed of only a dozen or fifteen men on
whom you can rely as on yourself ; the rest are either deceived, seduced, corrupted or
enticed away. Public opinion is debauched by the gold and intrigues of honest folks."

Robespierre, fluttering and hobbling along, reaches the goal in its turn ; in its turn, it demands something to feed on, and the rhetorician, the professor of principles, begins to calculate the voracity of the monstrous brute on which he is mounted. Slower than the other, this one is still more ravenous, for, with similar claws and teeth, it has a vaster appetite. At the end of three years Robespierre has overtaken Marat, at the extreme point reached by Marat at the outset, and the theorist adopts the policy, the aim, the means, the work, and almost the vocabulary of the maniac :[1] armed dictatorship of the urban mob, systematic maddening of the subsidised populace, war against the bourgeoisie, extermination of the rich, proscription of opposition writers, administrators and deputies. Both monsters demand the same food ; only, Robespierre adds "vicious men" to the ration of his monster, by way of extra and preferable game. Henceforth, he may in vain abstain from action, take refuge in his rhetoric, stop his chaste ears, and raise his hypocritical eyes to heaven, he cannot avoid seeing or hearing under his immaculate feet the streaming gore, and the bones crashing in the open jaws of the insatiable monster which he has fashioned and on which he prances.[2] These ever open and hungry jaws must be daily fed with an ampler supply of human flesh ; not only is he bound to let it eat, but to furnish the food, often with his own hands, except that he must afterwards wash them, declaring, and even believing, that no spot of blood has ever

---

1 Report by Courtois, N. 43.—Cf. Hamel, iii., 43, 71.—(The following important document is on file in the Archives Nationales, F 7 4446, and consists of two notes written by Robespierre in June and July, 1793) : "Who are our enemies ? *The vicious and the rich.* How may the civil war be stopped ? Punish traitors and conspirators, especially guilty deputies and administrators ; . . . . make terrible examples ; . . . . proscribe perfidious writers and anti-revolutionists ; . . . . internal danger comes from the bourgeois ; to overcome the bourgeois, rally the people ; . . . . the present insurrection must be kept up ; . . . . It is necessary that the same plan of insurrection should go on step by step. . . . . *The sans-culottes should be paid and remain in the towns.* They ought to be armed, *worked up,* taught."

2 The Committee of Public Safety, and Robespierre especially, knew of and commanded the drownings of Nantes, as well as the principal massacres by Carrier, Turreau, etc. (De Martel, "Etude sur Fouché," 257—265.)—*Ibid.*, ("Types révolutionnaires," 41—49.)—Buchez et Roux, xxxiii., 101 (May 26, 1794.) Report by Barère and decree of the Convention ordering that "No English prisoners should be taken." Robespierre afterwards speaks in the same sense. *Ibid.*, 458. After the capture of Newport, where they took five thousand English prisoners, the French soldiers were unwilling to execute the Convention's decree, on which Robespierre (speech of Thermidor 8) said : "I warn you that your decree against the English has been cruelly violated ; England, ill-treated in our discourses, is favored by our arms."

soiled them.   He is generally content to caress and flatter the
brute, to excuse it, to let it go on.   Nevertheless, more than
once, tempted by the opportunity, he points out the prey
and gives it the rein.[1]   He is now himself starting off in
quest of living prey ; he casts the net of his rhetoric[2] around
it ; he fetches it bound to the open jaws ; he thrusts aside with
an absolute air the arms of friends, wives and mothers, the
outstretched hands of suppliants begging for lives ;[3] he suddenly throttles the struggling victims[4] and, for fear that they
might escape, he strangles them in time.   Towards the last,
this no longer suffices ; the brute must have grander quarries,
and, accordingly, a pack of hounds, beaters-up, and, willingly
or not, Robespierre must equip, direct and urge them on, at
Orange, at Paris,[5] ordering them to empty the prisons, and be
expeditious in doing their work.—Destructive instincts, long
repressed by civilisation, thus devoted to butchery, become
aroused.   His feline physiognomy, at first " that of a domestic
cat, restless but mild, changes into the savage mien of the wild-
cat, and next to the ferocious mien of the tiger.   In the Constituent Assembly he speaks with a whine, in the Convention
he froths at the mouth."[6]   The monotonous drone of
a stiff sub-professor changes into the personal accent of furious passion ; he hisses and grinds his teeth ;[7]
sometimes, on a change of scene, he affects to shed tears.[8]

---

1 On the Girondists, Cf. " The Revolution," ii., 216.

2 Buchez et Roux, xxx., 157.   Sketch of a speech on the Fabre d'Eglantine factim.—
Ibid., 336, Speech at the Jacobin Club against Clootz.—xxxii., abstract of a report on the
Chabot affair, 18.—*Ibid.*, 69, Speech on maintaining Danton's arrest.

3 *Ibid.*, xxx., 378.   (Dec. 10, 1793.)   With respect to the women who crowd the Convention in order to secure the liberty of their husbands : " Are republican women insensible
to the proprieties of citizenship by remembering that they are wives ? "

4 Hamel, iii., 196.—Michelet, v., 394, abstract of the judicial debates on the disposition of
the Girondists : " The minutes of this decree are found in Robespierre's handwriting."

5 De Martel, " Types révolutionnaires," 44.   The instructions sent to the Revolutionary
Tribunal at Orange are in Robespierre's handwriting.—(Archives Nationales, F7 4439.)

6 Merlin de Thionville.

7 Buchez et Roux, xxxii., 71.   (On Danton.)   " Before the day is over we shall see
whether the Convention will shatter an idol a long time rotten. . . . .   In what respect
is Danton superior to his fellow-citizens ? . . . .   I say that the man who now hesitates
is guilty. . . . .   The debate, just begun, is a danger to the country."—Also the speech
in full, against Clootz.

8 *Ibid.*, xxx., 338.   " Alas, suffering patriots, what can we do, surrounded by enemies
fighting in our own ranks ! . . . .   Let us watch, for the fall of our country is not far off,"
etc.—These cantatas, with the accompaniments of the celestial harp, are terrible to one who
considers the circumstances.   For instance, on the 3d of September, 1792, while the massacres are going on, Robespierre enters the tribune of the electoral assembly and " declares

But his wildest outbursts are less alarming than his affected sensibility. The festering grudges, corrosive envies and bitter schemings which have accumulated in his breast are astonishing. The gall vessels are full, and the extravasated gall overflows on the dead. He never tires of re-executing his guillotined adversaries, the Girondists, Chaumette, Hébert and especially Danton,[1] probably because Danton was the active agent in the Revolution of which he was simply the incapable pedagogue : he vents his posthumous hatred on this still warm corpse in artful insinuations and obvious misrepresentations. Thus, inwardly corroded by the venom it distils, his physical machine gets out of order, like that of Marat, but with other symptoms. When speaking in the tribune "his hands crisp with a sort of nervous contraction ; " sudden tremors agitate "his shoulders and neck, shaking him convulsively to and fro." [2] "His bilious complexion becomes livid," his eyelids quiver under his spectacles, and how he looks ! "Ah," said a *Montagnard,* "you would have voted as we did on the 9th of Thermidor, had you seen his green eyeballs !" "Physically as well as morally," he becomes a second Marat, suffering all the more because his delirium is not steady, and because his policy, being a moral one, forces him to exterminate on a grander scale.

But he is a discreet Marat, of a timid temperament, anxious,[3] keeping his thoughts to himself, made for a school-master or a pleader, but not for taking the lead or for governing, always acting hesitatingly, and ambitious to be rather the pope, than the dictator of the Revolution.[4] He would prefer to remain

---

that he will calmly face the steel of the enemies of public good, and carry with him to his grave the satisfaction of having served his country, the certainty of France having preserved its liberty.—(Archives Nationales, C. ii., 58–76.)

1 Buchez et Roux, xxxii., 360, 371. (Speech of May 7, 1794.) "Danton, the most dangerous, if he had not been the most cowardly, of the enemies of his country . . . . Danton, the coldest, the most indifferent, during his country's greatest peril."

2 *Ibid.,* xxxiv., 94.—Cf. the description of him by Fievée, who saw him in the tribune at the Jacobin Club.

3 Merlin de Thionville "A vague, painful anxiety, due to his temperament, was the sole source of his activity."

4 Barère, "Mémoires." "He wanted to rule France influentially rather than directly." —Buchez et Roux, xiv., 188. (Article by Marat.) During the early sessions of the Legislative Assembly, Marat saw Robespierre on one occasion, and explained to him his plans for exciting popular outbreaks, and for his purifying massacres. "Robespierre listened to me with dismay, turned pale and kept silent for some moments. This interview confirmed me in the idea I always had of him, that he combined the enlightenment of a wise senator with the uprightness of a genuine good man and the zeal of a true patriot, but that he

288 *THE REVOLUTION.* BOOK VII.

a political Grandison ; he keeps the mask on to the very last, not only to the public and to others, but to himself and in his inmost conscience. The mask, indeed, has adhered to his skin ; he can no longer distinguish one from the other ; never did impostor more carefully conceal intentions and acts under sophisms, and persuade himself that the mask was his face, and that in telling a lie, he told the truth.

Taking his word for it, he had nothing to do with the September events.[1] " Previous to these occurrences, he had ceased to attend the General Council of the Commune . . . He no longer went there." He was not charged with any duty, he had no influence there ; he had not provoked the arrest and murder of the Girondists.[2] All he did was to "speak frankly concerning certain members of the Committee of Twenty-one ;" as " a magistrate " and "one of a municipal assembly." Should he

---

equally lacked the views and boldness of a statesman."—Thibaudeau, " Mémoires," 58.—He was the only member of the Committee of Public Safety who did not join the department missions.

1 Buchez et Roux xx., 198. (Speech of Robespierre in the Convention, November 5, 1792.)

2 All these statements by Robespierre are opposed to the truth.—("Procès-verbaux des Séances de la Commune de Paris.") Sep. 1, 1792, Robespierre *speaks twice at the evening session.*—The testimony of two persons, both agreeing, indicate, moreover, that he *spoke at the morning session*, the names of the speakers not being given. " The question," says Pétion (Buchez et Roux, xxi., 103), " was the decree opening the barriers." This decree is under discussion at the Commune at the morning session of September 1 : " Robespierre, on this question, spoke in the most animated manner, wandering off in sombre flights of imagination ; he saw precipices at his feet and plots of *liberticides ;* he designated *the pretended conspirators.*"—Louvet (*ibid.*, 130), assigns the same date, (except that he takes the evening for the morning session), for Robespierre's first denunciation of the Girondists: " Nobody, then," says Robespierre, " dare name the traitors ? Very well, I denounce them. I denounce them for the security of the people. I denounce the *liberticide* Brissot, the Girondist faction, the villainous committee of twenty-one in the National Assembly. I denounce them for having sold France to Brunswick and for having received pay in advance for their baseness."—Sep. 2, (" Procès verbaux de la Commune," evening session), " MM. Billaud-Varennes and Robespierre, in developing their civic sentiments, . . . denounce to the Conseil-Général the conspirators in favor of the Duke of Brunswick, whom a powerful party want to put on the throne of France."—September 3, at 6 o'clock in the morning, (Buchez et Roux, 16, 132, letter of Louvet), commissioners of the Commune present themselves at Brissot's house with an order to inspect his papers ; one of them says to Brissot that he has eight similar orders against the Gironde deputies and that he is to begin with Guadet. (Letter of Brissot complaining of this visit, *Moniteur*, Sep. 7, 1792.) This same day, Sep. 3, Robespierre presides at the Commune. (Granier de Cassagnac, " Les Girondins " ii., 63.) It is here that a deputation of the Mauconseil section comes to find him, and he is charged by the " Conseil" with a commission at the Temple.—Septem. 4 (Buchez et Roux, xxi., 106, Speech of Pétion), the Commune issues a warrant of arrest against Roland ; Danton comes to the Mayoralty with Robespierre and has the warrant revoked ; Robespierre ends by telling Pétion : " I believe that Brissot belongs to Brunswick."—*Ibid.*, 506. " Robespierre (before Septem. 2), took the lead in the Conseil."—*Ibid.*, 107. " Robespierre," I said, " you are making a good deal of mischief. Your denunciations, your fears, hatreds and suspicions, excite the people."

not " explain himself freely on the authors of a dangerous plot ? "
Besides, the Commune " far from provoking the 2d of September did all in its power to prevent it." In fine, but one innocent person perished, "which is undoubtedly one too many. Citizens, mourn over this cruel mistake ; we too have long mourned over it ! But, as all things human come to an end, let your tears cease to flow." When the sovereign people resumes its delegated power and exercises its inalienable rights, we have only to bow our heads.—Moreover, it is just, wise and good : " in all that it undertakes, all is virtue and truth ; nothing can be excess, error or crime." [1] It must intervene when its true representatives are hampered by the law : " let it assemble in its sections and compel the arrest of faithless deputies." [2] What is more legal than such a motion, which is the only part Robespierre took on the 31st of May. He is too scrupulous to commit or prescribe an illegal act. That will do for the Dantons, the Marats, men of relaxed morals or excited brains, who if need be, tramp in the gutters and roll up their shirt-sleeves ; as to himself, he can do nothing that would ostensibly derange or soil the dress proper to an honest man and irreproachable citizen. In the Committee of Public Safety, he merely executes the decrees of the Convention, and the Convention is always free. He a dictator ! He is merely one of seven hundred deputies, and his authority, if he has any, is simply the legitimate ascendency of reason and virtue.[3] He a murderer ! If he has denounced conspirators, it is the Convention which summons these before the revolutionary Tribunal,[4] and the revolutionary Tribunal pronounces judgment on them. He a terrorist ! He merely seeks to simplify the established proceedings, so as to secure a speedier release of the innocent, the punishment of the guilty, and the final purgation that is to render liberty and morals the order of the day.[5]—Before uttering all this he almost believes it, and, when he has uttered it he believes it fully.[6]

---

1 Garat, 86.—Cf. Hamel, i., 264. (Speech, June 9, 1791.)

2 " The Revolution," ii., 338, 339. (Speech, Aug. 3, 1792.)

3 Buchez et Roux, xxxiii., 420. (Speech, Thermidor 8.)

4 *Ibid.*, xxxii., 71. (Speech against Danton.) " What have you done that you have not done freely ? "

5 *Ibid.*, xxxiii., 199 and 221. (Speech on the law of Prairial 22.)

5 Mirabeau said of Robespierre : " Whatever that man has said, he believes in it."— Robespierre, Duplay's guest, dined every day with Duplay, a juryman in the revolutionary

When nature and history combine, to produce a character, they succeed better than man's imagination. Neither Molière in his " Tartuffe," nor Shakespeare in his " Richard III.," dared bring on the stage a hypocrite believing himself sincere, and a Cain that regarded himself as an Abel. There he stands on a colossal stage, in the presence of a hundred thousand spectators, on the 8th of June, 1794, the most glorious day of his life, at that fête in honor of the Supreme Being, which is the glorious triumph of his doctrine and the official consecration of his popedom. Two characters are found in Robespierre, as in the Revolution which he represents : one, apparent, paraded, external, and the other hidden, dissembled, inward, the latter being overlaid by the former.—The first one all for show, fashioned out of purely cerebral cogitations, is as artificial as the solemn farce going on around him. According to David's programme, the cavalcade of supernumeraries who file in front of an allegorical mountain, gesticulate and shout at the command, and under the eyes, of Henriot and his gendarmes,[1] manifesting at the appointed time the emotions which are prescribed for them. At five o'clock in the morning "friends, husbands, wives, relations and children will embrace. . . . . The old man, his eyes streaming with tears of joy, feels himself rejuvenated." At two o'clock, on the turf-laid terraces of the sacred mountain " all will show a state of commotion and excitement : mothers here press to their bosoms the infants they suckle, and there offer them up in homage to the author of Nature, while youths, aglow with the ardor of battle, simultaneously draw their swords and hand them to their venerable fathers. Sharing in the enthusiasm of their sons, the transported old men embrace them and bestow on them the paternal benediction. . . . . All the

---

tribunal and co-operator for the guillotine, at eighteen francs a day. The talk at the table probably turned on the current abstractions ; but there must have been frequent allusions to the condemnations *of the day*, and, even when not mentioned, they were in their minds. Only Robert Browning, at the present day, could imagine and revive what was spoken and thought in those evening conversations before the mother and daughters.

1 Buchez et Roux, xxxiii., 151 .—Cf. Dauban, " Paris en 1794," p. 386 (illustration), and 392, Fête de l'Etre Suprême à Sceaux," according to the programme drawn up by the patriot Palloy. " All citizens are requested to be at their windows or doors, even those occupying lodgings in by-streets."—*Ibid.*, 399. " Youthful citizens will strew flowers at each station, fathers will embrace their children and mothers turn their eyes upward to heaven." —*Moniteur*, xxx., 653. " Plan of the fête in honor of the Supreme Being, drawn up by David, and decreed by the National Convention."

men distributed around the ' Field of Reunion' sing in chorus the (first) refrain. . . . . All the women distributed around the ' Field of Reunion' sing in unison the (second) refrain. . . . . All Frenchmen partake of each other's sentiments in one grand fraternal embrace." Such an idyl, performed to the beating of drums, in the presence of moral symbols and colored pasteboard divinities, what could better please the counterfeit moralist, unable to distinguish the false from the true, and whose skin-deep sensibility is borrowed from sentimental authors ! " For the first time " his glowing countenance beams with joy, while " the enthusiasm " [1] of the scribe overflows, as usual, in book phraseology : " Behold ! " he exclaims, " that which is most interesting in humanity ! The Universe is here assembled ! O, Nature, how sublime, how exquisite is thy power ! How tyrants must quail at the contemplation of this festival ! " Is not he himself its most dazzling ornament ? Was not he unanimously chosen to preside over the Convention and conduct the ceremonies ? Is he not the founder of the new cult, the only pure worship on the face of the earth, approved of by morality and reason ? Wearing the uniform of a representative, nankeen breeches, blue coat, tri-colored sash and plumed hat,[2] holding in his hand a bouquet of flowers and grain, he marches at the head of the Convention and officiates on the platform ; he sets fire to the veil which hides from view the idol representing " Atheism," and suddenly, through an ingenious contrivance, the majestic statue of " Wisdom" appears in its place. He then addresses the crowd, over and over again, exhorting, apostrophising, preaching, elevating his soul to the Supreme Being, and with what oratorical combinations ! What an academic swell of bombastic cadences, strung together to enforce his tirades ! How cunning the even balance of adjective and substantive ! [3] From these faded rhetorical flowers, arranged as if for a prize distribution or a funeral oration, exhales a sanctimonious, collegiate odor which he complacently breathes, and which intoxicates him. At this moment, he must certainly be in earnest ; there is no hesitation or reserve in his self-admiration ; he is

---

1 Buchez et Roux, xxxiii., 176. (Narrative by Valate.)
2 Hamel, iii., 541.
3 Buchez et Roux, xxviii., 178, 180.

not only in his own eyes a great writer and great orator, but a great statesman and great citizen : his artificial, philosophic conscience awards him only praise.—But look underneath, or rather wait a moment. Signs of impatience and antipathy appear behind his back : Lecointre has braved him openly ; numerous insults, and, worse than these, sarcasms, reach his ears. On such an occasion, and in such a place ! Against the pontiff of Truth, the apostle of Virtue ! The miscreants, how dare they ! Silent and pale, he suppresses his rage, and,[1] losing his balance, closing his eyes, he plunges headlong on the path of murder : cost what it will, the miscreants must perish and without loss of time. To expedite matters, he must get their heads off quietly, and as " up to this time things have been managed confidentially in the Committee of Public Safety," he, alone with Couthon, two days after, without informing his colleagues,[2] draws up, brings to the Convention, and has passed the terrible act of Prairial which places everybody's life at his disposal.—In his crafty, blundering haste, he has demanded too much ; each one, on reflection, becomes alarmed for himself ; he is compelled to back out, to protest that he is misunderstood, admit that representatives are excepted, and, accordingly, to sheathe the knife he has already applied to his adversaries' throats. But he still holds it in his grasp. He watches them, and, pretending to retreat, affects a renunciation, crouched in his corner,[3] waiting until they discredit themselves, so as to spring upon them a second time.

---

1 *Ibid.*, 177 (Narrative by Vilate.) *Ibid.*, 170, Notes by Robespierre on Bourdon (de l'Oise) 417. Passages erased by Robespierre in the manuscript of his speech of Thermidor 8.—249. Analogous passages in his speech as delivered,—all these indications enable us to trace the depths of his resentment.

2 *Ibid.*, 183. Memoirs of Billaud-Varennes, Collot d'Herbois, Vadier and Barère. " The next day after Prairial 22, at the morning session (of the Committee of Public Safety) . . . I now see, says Robespierre, that I stand alone, with nobody to support me, and, getting violently excited, he launched out against the members of the Committee who had conspired against him. He shouted so loud as to collect together a number of citizens on the Tuileries terrace." Finally, " he pushed hypocrisy so far as to shed tears." The nervous machine, I imagine, broke down.—Another member of the Committee, Prieur, (Carnot, " Mémoires," ii., 525), relates that, in the month of Floréal, after another equally long and violent session, " Robespierre, exhausted, became ill."

3 Carnot, " Mémoires," ii., 526. " As his bureau was in a separate place, where none of us set foot, he could retire to it without coming in contact with any of us, as in effect, he did. He even made a pretence of passing through the committee rooms, after the session was over, and he signed some papers ; but he really neglected nothing, except our common discussions. He held frequent conferences in his house with the presidents of the revolutionary tribunals, over which his influence was greater than ever."

He has not to wait long, for the exterminating machine he set up on the 22d of Prairial, is in their hands, and it has to work as he planned it, namely, by making rapid turns and almost haphazard : the odium of a blind sweeping massacre rests with them ; he not only makes no opposition to this, but, while pretending to abstain from it, he urges it on. Secluded in the private office of his secret police, he orders arrests ;[1] he sends out his principal bloodhound, Herman ; he first signs and then despatches the resolution by which it is supposed that there are conspirators among those in confinement and which, authorising spies or paid informers, is to provide the guillotine with those vast batches which " purge and clean prisons out in a trice."[2]—" I am not responsible," he states later on.... " My lack of power to do any good, to arrest the evil, forced me for more than six weeks to abandon my post on the Committee of Public Safety."[3] To ruin his adversaries by murders committed by him, by those which he makes them commit and which he imputes to them, to whitewash himself and blacken them with the same stroke of the brush, what intense delight ! If the natural conscience murmurs in whispers at moments, the acquired superposed conscience immediately imposes silence, conceal-

---

1 Dauban, " Paris en 1794," 563.—Archives Nationales, AF.II., 58. The signature of Robespierre, in his own handwriting, is found affixed to many of the resolutions of the Committee of Public Safety, passed Thermidor 5 and 7, and those of St. Just and Couthon after this, up to Thermidor 3, 6 and 7. On the register of the minutes of the Committee of Public Safety, Robespierre is always recorded as present at all meetings between Messidor 1 and Thermidor 8, inclusive.

2 Archives Nationales, F.7, 4438. Report to the Committee of Public Safety by Herman, Commissioner of the Civil and Police administrations and of the Courts, Messidor 3, year II. " The Committee charged with a general surpervision of the prisons, and obliged to recognise that all the rascals mostly concerned with *liberticide* plots are....still in the prisons, forming a band apart, and rendering surveillance very troublesome ; they are a constant source of disorder, always getting up attempts to escape, being a daily assemblage of persons devoting themselves wholly to imprecations against liberty and its defenders.... *It would be easy to point out in each prison, those who have served, and are to serve, the diverse factions, the diverse conspiracies....It may be necessary, perhaps, to purge the prisons at once and free the soil of liberty of their filth, the refuse of humanity.*" The Committee of Public Safety consequently " charges the Commission to ascertain in the prisons of Paris... who have been more specially concerned in the diverse factions and conspiracies that the National Convention has destroyed." The word " approved " appears at the foot of the resolution in Robespierre's handwriting, then the signature of Robespierre, and lower down, those of Billaud and Barère. A similar resolution providing for the 7th of Messidor, signed by the same parties and five others, is despatched the same day. (M. de Martel came across and made use of this conclusive document before I did, most of it being quoted in " Les Types Révolutionnaires.")

3 Buchez et Roux, xxxiii., 434.

ing personal hatreds under public pretexts : the guillotined, after all, were aristocrats, and whoever comes under the guillotine is immoral. Thus, the means are good and the end better ; in employing the means, as well as in pursuing the end, the function is sacerdotal.

Such is the scenic exterior of the Revolution, a specious mask with a hideous visage beneath it, under the reign of a nominal humanitarian theory, covering over the effective dictatorship of evil and low passions. In its true representative, as in itself, we see ferocity issuing from philanthropy, and, from the *cuistre*, the executioner.

THE MODERN REGIME

VOLUME I

PREFACE.

THE following third and last part of the *Origins of Contemporary France* is to consist of two volumes ; after the present volume, the second is to treat of the Church, the School and the Family, describe the modern *milieu* and note the facilities and obstacles which a society like our own encounters in this new *milieu ;* here, the past and the present meet, and the work already done is continued by the work which is going on under our eyes.—The undertaking is hazardous and more difficult than with the two preceding parts. For the Ancient Régime and the Revolution are henceforth complete and finished periods ; we have seen the end of both and are thus able to comprehend their entire course. On the contrary, the end of the ulterior period is still wanting ; the great institutions which date from the Consulate and the Empire, either consolidation or dissolution, have not yet reached their historic term ; since 1800, the social order of things, notwithstanding eight changes of political form, has remained almost intact. Our children or grandchildren will know whether it will finally succeed or miscarry ; witnesses of the denouement, they will have fuller light by which to judge of the entire drama. Thus far four acts only have been played ; of the fifth act, we have simply a presentiment.—On the other hand, by dint of living under this social system, we have become accustomed to it ; it no longer excites our wonder ; however artificial it may be it seems to us natural ; we can scarcely conceive of another that is healthier ; and what is much worse, it is repugnant to us to do so. For, such a conception would soon lead to comparisons, and hence to a judgment and, on many points, to an unfavorable judgment, one which would be a censure, not only of our institutions but of ourselves. The machine of the year VIII, applied to us for three generations, has shaped and fixed us as we are, for good or for ill ; if, for a century, it sustains us, it represses us for a century ; we have contracted the infirmities it imports—stoppage of development, instability of internal balance, disorders of the intellect and of the will, fixed ideas and ideas that are false. These ideas are *ours ;* therefore we hold on to them, or, rather, they have taken hold of us. To get rid of them, to impose the necessary recoil on our mind, to transport us to a distance and place us at a critical point of view, where we can study ourselves, our ideas and our institutions as scientific objects, requires a great effort on our part, many precautions, and long reflection.—Hence, the delays of this study ; the reader will pardon them on considering that an ordinary opinion, caught on the wing, on such a subject, does not suffice ; in any event, when one presents an opinion on such a subject one is bound to believe it. I can believe in my own only when it has become precise and seems to me proven.

MENTHON SAINT-BERNARD,
   September, 1890.

THE MODERN RÉGIME.

BOOK FIRST.
Napoleon Bonaparte.

CHAPTER I.

Historical importance of his character and genius.—I. He is of another race and another century.—Origin of his paternal family.—Transplanted to Corsica.—His maternal family.—Lætitia Ramolino.—Persistence of Corsican souvenirs in Napoleon's mind.—His youthful sentiments regarding Corsica and France.—Indications found in his early compositions and in his style.—Current monarchical or democratic ideas have no hold on him.—His impressions of the 10th of June and 10th of August after the 31st of May.—His associations with Robespierre and Barras without committing himself.—His sentiments and the side he takes Vendémiaire 13th.—The great *Condottière*.—His character and conduct in Italy.—Description of him morally and physically in 1798.—His precocious and sudden ascendency.—Analogous in spirit and character to his Italian ancestors of the XVth century.—II. Intelligence during the Italian Renaissance and at the present day.—Integrity of Bonaparte's mental machinery.—Flexibility, force, and tenacity of his attention.—Another difference between Napoleon's intellect and that of his contemporaries.—He thinks objects and not words.—His antipathy to Ideology.—Little or no literary or philosophical education.—Self-taught through direct observation and technical instruction.—His fondness for details.—His inward vision of physical objects and places.—His mental portrayal of positions, distances, and quantities.—His psychological faculty and way of getting at the thought and feeling of others.—His self-analysis.—How he imagines a general situation by a particular case, also the invisible inward by the visible outward.—Originality and superiority of his style and discourse.—His adaptation of these to his hearers and to circumstances.—His notation and calculation of serviceable motives.—His three atlases.—Their scale and completeness.—His constructive imagination.—His projects and dreams.—Manifestation of the master faculty and its excesses.

IN trying to explain to ourselves the meaning of an edifice we must take into account whatever has opposed or favored its construction, the kind and quality of its available materials, the time, the opportunity, and the demand for it ; but, still more important, we must consider the genius and taste of the architect, especially whether he is the proprietor, whether he

built it to live in himself, and, once installed in it, whether
he took pains to adapt it to his own way of living, to his
own necessities, to his own use.—Such is the social edifice erected by Napoleon Bonaparte, its architect, proprietor,
and principal occupant from 1799 to 1814 ; it is he who has
made modern France ; never was an individual character so
profoundly stamped on any collective work, so that, to comprehend the work, we must first study the character of the
man.[1]

I.

Disproportionate in all things, but, stranger still, he is not
only out of the common run, but there is no standard of
measurement for him ; through his temperament, instincts,
faculties, imagination, passions, and moral constitution he
seems cast in a special mould, composed of another metal than
that which enters into the composition of his fellows and contemporaries.   Evidently he is not a Frenchman, nor a man of
the eighteenth century ; he belongs to another race and
another epoch ;[2] we detect in him, at the first glance, the
foreigner, the Italian,[3] and something more, apart and beyond

---

1 The main authority is, of course, the " Correspondance de l'Empereur Napoléon I.,"
in thirty-two volumes.   This " Correspondance," unfortunately, is still incomplete, while,
after the sixth volume, it must not be forgotten that much of it has been purposely stricken
out.   " In general," say the editors (xvi., p. 4), " we have been governed simply by this plain
rule, that we were required to publish only *what the Emperor himself would have given to
the public* had he survived himself, and, anticipating the verdict of time, exposed to posterity his own personality and system."—The savant who has the most carefully examined
this correspondence, entire in the French archives, estimates that it comprises about 80,000
pieces, of which 30,000 have been published in the collection referred to; passages in 20,000 of
the others have been stricken out on account of previous publication, and about 30,000
more, through considerations of propriety or policy.   For example, but little more than one-
half of the letters from Napoleon to Bigot de Préameneu on ecclesiastical matters have been
published ; many of these omitted letters, all important and characteristic, may be found in
" L'Église romaine et le Premier Empire," by M. d'Haussonville.

2 " Mémorial de Sainte Hélène," by Las Casas (May 29, 1816).—" In Corsica, Paoli,
on a horseback excursion, explained the positions to him, the places where liberty found
resistance or triumphed.   Estimating the character of Napoleon by what he saw of it
through personal observation, Paoli said to him, " Oh, Napoleon, there is nothing modern
in you, you belong wholly to Plutarch ! "—Antonomarchi, " Mémoires," Oct. 25, 1819.
The same account, slightly different, is there given : " Oh, Napoleon," said Paoli to me,
" you do not belong to this century ; you talk like one of Plutarch's characters.   Courage,
you will take flight yet ! "

3 De Ségur, " Histoire et Mémoires," i., 150.   (Narrative by Pontécoulant, member of
the Committee in the war, June, 1795.)   " Boissy d'Anglas told him that he had seen the

these, surpassing all similitude or analogy.—Italian he was
through blood and lineage ; first, through his paternal family,
which is Tuscan,[1] and which we can follow down from the
twelfth century, at Florence, then at San Miniato ; next at
Sarzana, a small, backward, remote town in the state of Genoa,
where, from father to son, it vegetates obscurely in provincial
isolation, through a long line of notaries and municipal syndics.
" My origin," says Napoleon himself,[2] " has made all Italians
regard me as a compatriot. . . . When the question of the
marriage of my sister Pauline with Prince Borghèse came up
there was but one voice in Rome and in Tuscany, in that
family, and with all its connections : ' *It will do,*' said all of
them, ' *it's amongst ourselves, it's one of our own families.* ' "
When the Pope hesitated about coming to Paris to crown
Napoleon, " the Italian party in the Conclave prevailed against
the Austrian party by supporting political arguments with the
following slight tribute to national *amour propre : ' After all,
we are imposing an Italian family on the barbarians, to govern
them.   We are revenging ourselves on the Gauls.*"   This significant expression throws light into the depths of the Italian
nature, the eldest daughter of modern civilization, imbued
with its right of primogeniture, persistent in its grudge against
the transalpines, the rancorous inheritor of Roman pride and
of antique patriotism.[3]

From Sarzana, a Bonaparte emigrates to Corsica, where he
establishes himself and lives after 1529.   The following year

---

evening before *a little Italian*, pale, slender, and puny, but singularly audacious in his
views and in the vigor of his expressions."—The next day, Bonaparte calls on Pontécoulant, " Attitude rigid through a morbid pride, poor exterior, long visage, hollow and
bronzed. . . . He is just from the army and talks like one who knows what he is talking
about."

1 Coston, " Biographie des premières années de Napoléon Buonaparte," 2 vols. (1840),
passim.—Yung, " Bonaparte et son Temps," i., 300, 302. (Pièces généalogiques.)—King
Joseph, " Mémoires," i., 109, 111. (On the various branches and distinguished men of the
Bonaparte family.)—Miot de Melito, " Mémoires," ii., 30. (Documents on the Bonaparte
family, collected on the spot by the author in 1801.)

2 " Mémorial," May 6, 1816.—Miot de Melito, ii., 30. (On the Bonapartes of San
Miniato) : " The last offshoot of this branch was a canon then still living in this same
town of San Miniato, and visited by Bonaparte in the year IV, when he came to
Florence."

3 " Correspondance de l'Empereur Napoléon I." (Letter of Bonaparte, Sept. 29, 1797, in
relation to Italy) : " A people at bottom inimical to the French through the prejudices,
character, and customs of centuries."

Florence is taken and completely subjugated ; henceforth, in Tuscany, under Alexander de Medici, then under Cosmo I. and his successors, in all Italy under Spanish rule, municipal independence, private feuds, the great exploits of political adventures and successful usurpations, the system of ephemeral principalities, based on force and fraud, all give way to permanent repression, monarchical discipline, external order, and a certain species of public tranquillity. Thus, just at the time when the energy and ambition, the vigorous and free sap of the Middle Ages begins to run down and then dry up in the shriveled trunk,[1] a small detached branch takes root in an island, not less Italian but almost barbarous, amidst institutions, customs, and passions belonging to the primitive mediæval epoch,[2] and in a social atmosphere sufficiently rude for the maintenance of all its vigor and harshness.—Grafted, moreover, by frequent marriages, on the wild stock of the island, Napoleon, on the maternal side, through his grandmother and mother, is wholly indigenous. His grandmother, a Pietra-Santa, belonged to Sartène,[3] a Corsican canton *par excellence* where, in 1800, hereditary vendettas still maintained the régime of the eleventh century ; where the permanent strife of inimical families was suspended only by truces; where, in many villages, nobody stirred out of doors except in armed bodies, and where the houses were crenellated like fortresses. His mother, Lætitia Ramolini, from whom, in character and in will, he derived much more than from his father,[4] is a primi-

---

1 Miot de Melito, i., 126, (1796): " Florence, for two centuries and a half, had lost that antique energy which, in the stormy times of the Republic, distinguished this city. Indolence was the dominant spirit of all classes. . . . Almost everywhere I saw only men lulled to rest by the charms of the most exquisite climate, occupied solely with the details of a monotonous existence, and tranquilly vegetating under its beneficent sky."—(On Milan, in 1796, cf. Stendhal, introduction to the " Chartreuse de Parme.")

2 " Miot de Melito, i., 131 : " Having just left one of the most civilized cities in Italy, it was not without some emotion that I found myself suddenly transported to a country (Corsica) which, in its savage aspect, its rugged mountains, and its inhabitants uniformly dressed in coarse brown cloth, contrasted so strongly with the rich and smiling landscape of Tuscany, and with the comfort, I should almost say elegance, of costume worn by the happy cultivators of that fertile soil."

3 Miot de Melito, ii., 30 : " Of a not very important family of Sartène."—ii., 143. (On the canton of Sartène and the Vendettas of 1796).—Coston, i., 4 : " The family of Madame Lætitia, sprung from the counts of Cotalto, came originally from Italy."

4 His father, Charles Bonaparte, weak and even frivolous, "too fond of pleasure to care about his children," and to see to his affairs, tolerably learned and an indifferent

tive soul on which civilization has taken no hold ; simple, all
of a piece, unsuited to the refinements, charms, and graces of
a worldly life ; indifferent to comforts, without literary culture,
as parsimonious as any peasant woman, but as energetic as the
leader of a band ; powerful, physically and spiritually, accustomed to danger, ready in desperate resolutions ; in short, a
" rustic Cornelia," who conceived and gave birth to her son
amidst the risks of battle and of defeat, in the thickest of the
French invasion, amidst mountain rides on horseback, nocturnal surprises, and volleys of musketry.[1]   " Losses, privations,
and fatigue," says Napoleon, " she endured all and braved all.
Hers was a man's head on a woman's shoulders."—Thus
fashioned and brought into the world, he felt that, from first
to the last, he was of his race and country.

   " Everything was better there," said he, at Saint Helena,[2]
" even the very smell of the soil, which he could have detected
with his eyes shut ; nowhere had he found the same thing.
He imagined himself there again in early infancy, and lived
over again the days of his youth, amidst precipices, traversing
lofty peaks, deep valleys, and narrow defiles, enjoying the
honors and pleasures of hospitality," treated everywhere as a

---

head of a family, died at the age of thirty-nine of a cancer in the stomach, which seems to
be the only bequest he made to his son Napoleon.—His mother, on the contrary, serious,
authoritative, the true head of a family, was, said Napoleon, " hard in her affections : she
punished and rewarded without distinction, good or bad ; she made us all feel it."—On becoming head of the household, " she was too parsimonious—even ridiculously so. This
was due to excess of foresight on her part ; she had known want, and her terrible sufferings were never out of her mind. . . . Paoli had tried persuasion with her before resorting
to force. . . . Madame replied heroically, as a Cornelia would have done. . . . From
twelve to fifteen thousand peasants poured down from the mountains of Ajaccio ; our
house was pillaged and burnt, our vines destroyed, and our flocks. . . . In other respects,
this woman, from whom it would have been so difficult to extract five francs, would have
given up everything to secure my return from Elba, and after Waterloo she offered me
all she possessed to restore my affairs." (" Mémorial," May 29, 1816, and " Mémoires
d'Antonomarchi," Nov. 18, 1819.—On the ideas and ways of Bonaparte's mother, read her
" Conversation " in " Journal et Mémoires," vol. iv., by Stanislas Girardin.) Duchesse
d'Abrantès, " Mèmoires," ii., 318, 319. " Avaricious out of all reason except on a few
grave occasions. . . . No knowledge whatever of the usages of society. . . . Very ignorant, not alone of our literature, but of her own."—Stendhal, " Vie de Napoléon ": " The
character of her son is to be explained by the perfectly Italian character of Madame
Lætitia."

   1 The French conquest is effected by armed force between July 30, 1768, and May 22,
1769. The Bonaparte family submitted May 23, 1769, and Napoleon was born on the following 15th of August.

   2 Antonomarchi, " Mémoires," October 4, 1819. " Mémorial," May 29, 1816.

brother and compatriot, " without any accident or insult ever
suggesting to him that his confidence was not well grounded."
At Bocognano,[1] where his mother, pregnant with him, had taken
refuge, " where hatred and vengeance extended to the seventh
degree of relationship, and where the dowry of a young girl
was estimated by the number of her cousins, I was feasted
and made welcome, and everybody would have died for me."
Forced to become a Frenchman, transplanted to France, educated at the expense of the king in a French school, he
became rigid in his insular patriotism, and loudly extolled
Paoli, the liberator, against whom his relations had declared
themselves. " Paoli," said he, at the dinner table,[2] " was a
great man. He loved his country. My father was his adju-
tant, and never will I forgive him for having aided in the
union of Corsica with France. He should have followed her
fortunes and have succumbed only with her." Throughout
his youth he is at heart anti-French, morose, "bitter, liking
very few and very little liked, brooding over resentment," like
a vanquished man, always moody and compelled to work
against the grain. At Brienne, he keeps aloof from his comrades, takes no part in their sports, shuts himself in the library,
and unbosoms himself only to Bourrienne in explosions of
hatred : " I will do you Frenchmen all the harm I can ! "—
" Corsican by nation and character," wrote his professor of
history in the Military Academy, " he will go far if circumstances favor him." [3]—Leaving the Academy, and in garrison
at Valence and Auxonne, he remains always hostile, dena-
tionalized ; his old bitterness returns, and, addressing his letters to Paoli, he says : " I was born when our country perished.

---

1 Miot de Melito, ii., 33 : " The day I arrived at Bocognano two men lost their lives
through private vengeance. About eight years before this one of the inhabitants of the
canton had killed a neighbor, the father of two children. . . . On reaching the age of
sixteen or seventeen years these children left the country in order to dog the steps of the
murderer, who kept on the watch, not daring to go far from his village. . . . Finding him
playing cards under a tree, they fired at and killed him, and besides this accidentally shot
another man who was asleep a few paces off. The relatives on both sides pronounced the
act justifiable and according to rule." *Ibid.*, i., 143 : " On reaching Bastia from Ajaccio
the two principal families of the place, the Peraldi and the Visuldi, fired at each other, in
disputing over the honor of entertaining me."

2 Bourrienne, " Mémoires," i., 18, 19.

3 De Ségur, " Histoire et Mémoires," i., 74.

Thirty thousand Frenchmen vomited on our shores, drowning the throne of liberty in floods of blood—such was the odious spectacle on which my eyes first opened ! The groans of the dying, the shrieks of the oppressed, tears of despair, surrounded my cradle from my birth. . . . I will blacken those who betrayed the common cause with the brush of infamy . . . vile, sordid souls corrupted by gain ! " [1] A little later, his letter to Buttafuoco, deputy in the Constituent Assembly and principal agent in the annexation to France, is one long strain of renewed, concentrated hatred, which, after at first trying to restrain it within the bounds of cold sarcasm, ends in boiling over, like red-hot lava, in a torrent of scorching invective.—From the age of fifteen, at the Academy and afterwards in his regiment, he finds refuge in imagination in the past of his island ; [2] he recounts its history, his mind dwells upon it for many years, and he dedicates his work to Paoli. Unable to get it published, he abridges it, and dedicates the abridgment to Abbé Raynal, recapitulating in a strained style, with warm, vibrating sympathy, the annals of his small community, its revolts and deliverances, its heroic and sanguinary outbreaks, its public and domestic tragedies, ambuscades, betrayals, revenges, loves, and murders,—in short, a history similar to that of the Scottish highlanders, while the style, still more than the sympathies, denotes the foreigner. Undoubtedly, in this work, as in other youthful writings, he follows as well as he can the authors in vogue—Rousseau, and especially Raynal ; he gives a schoolboy imitation of their tirades, their sentimental declamation, and their humanitarian grandiloquence. But these borrowed clothes, which incommode him, do not fit him ; they are too tight, and the cloth is too fine ; they require too much circumspection in walking ; he does not know how to put them on, and they rip at every seam. Not only has he never learned how to spell, but he does not know the true

1 Yung, i., 195. (Letter of Bonaparte to Paoli, June 12, 1789) ; i., 250 (Letter of Bonaparte to Buttafuoco, January 23, 1790).

2 Yung, i., 107 (Letter of Napoleon to his father, Sept. 12, 1784) ; i., 163 (Letter of Napoleon to Abbé Raynal, July, 1786) ; i., 197 (Letter of Napoleon to Paoli, June 12, 1789). The three letters on the history of Corsica are dedicated to Abbé Raynal in a letter of June 24, 1790, and may be found in Yung, i., 434.

meaning, connections, and relations of words, the propriety
or impropriety of phrases, the exact significance of imagery ;[1]
he strides on impetuously athwart a pell-mell of incongruities,
incoherences, Italianisms, and barbarisms, undoubtedly stum-
bling along through awkwardness and inexperience, but also
through excess of ardor and of heat ;[2] his jerking, eruptive
thought, overcharged with passion, indicates the depth and
temperature of its source.   Already, at the Academy, the professor of belles-lettres[3] notes down that "in the strange and
incorrect grandeur of his amplifications he seems to see granite
fused in a volcano."   However original in mind and in sensibility, ill-adapted as he is to the society around him, different
from his comrades, it is clear beforehand that the current ideas
which take such hold on them will obtain no hold on him.

Of the two dominant and opposite ideas which clash with
each other, it might be supposed that he would lean either to
one or to the other, although accepting neither.—Pensioner of
the king, who supported him at Brienne, and afterwards in the
Military Academy ; who also supported his sister at St. Cyr ;
who, for twenty years, is the benefactor of his family ; to
whom, at this very time, he addresses entreating or grateful
letters over his mother's signature—he does not regard him as
his born general ; it does not enter his mind to take sides and

---

1 Read especially his essay " On the Truths and Sentiments most important to inculcate
on Men for their Welfare " (a subject proposed by the Academy of Lyons in 1790).
" Some bold men *impulsed* by genius. . . . Perfection grows out of reason as fruit out of
a tree. . . . Reason's eyes guard man from the precipice of the passions. . . . *The spectacle of the strength of virtue* was what the Lacedæmonians principally felt. . . . Must
men then be lucky in the means by which they are led on to happiness ? . . . . My rights
(to property) are renewed along with my transpiration, circulate in my blood, are written
on my nerves, on my heart. . . . Proclaim to the rich—your wealth is your misfortune,
withdrawn *within the latitude of your senses.* . . . Let the enemies of nature at thy
voice keep silence and swallow their rabid serpents' tongues. . . . The wretched shun the
society of men, the *tapestry of gayety* turns to mourning. . . . Such, gentlemen, are the
sentiments which, *in animal relations*, mankind should have taught it for its welfare."

2 Yung, i., 252 (Letter to Buttafuoco). " Dripping with the blood of his brethren, sul-
lied by every species of crime, he presents himself with confidence under *his vest of a
general,* the sole reward of his criminalities."—i., 192 (Letter to the Corsican Intendant,
April 2, 1879). " Cultivation is what ruins us".—See various manuscript letters, copied by
Yung, for innumerable and gross mistakes in French.—Miot de Melito, i., 84 (July, 1796).
" He spoke curtly and, at this time, very incorrectly".—Madame de Rémusat, i., 104.
" Whatever language he spoke it never seemed familiar to him ; he appeared to force him-
self in expressing his ideas."

3 De Ségur, i., 174.

draw his sword in his patron's behalf ; in vain is he a gentleman, to whom d'Hozier has certified ; reared in a school of
noble cadets, he has no noble or monarchical traditions.[1]—Poor
and tormented by ambition, a reader of Rousseau, patronized
by Raynal, and tacking together sentences of philosophic
fustian about equality, if he speaks the jargon of the day, it is
without any belief in it ; the phrases in vogue form a decent,
academical drapery for his ideas, or serve him as a red cap for
the club ; he is not bewildered by democratic illusions, and
entertains no other feeling than disgust for the revolution
and the sovereignty of the populace.—At Paris, in April, 1792,
when the struggle between the monarchists and the revolutionists is at its height, he tries to find "some successful speculation,"[2] and thinks he will hire and sublet houses at a profit.
On the 20th of June he witnesses, only as a matter of curiosity, the invasion of the Tuileries, and, on seeing the king at
a window place the red cap on his head, exclaims, so as to be
heard, " *Che Coglione !* "   Immediately after this : " How
could they let that rabble enter ! Mow down four or five
hundred of them with cannon-balls and the rest would run
away."   On August 10, when the tocsin sounds, he regards
the people and the king with equal contempt ; he rushes to a
friend's house on the Carrousel and there, still as a looker-on,
views at his ease all the occurrences of the day ;[3] finally, the
chateau is forced and he strolls through the Tuileries, looks
in at the neighboring cafés, and that is all : he is not disposed
to take sides, he has no Jacobin or royalist impulse.   His
features, even, are so calm as to provoke many hostile remarks,

---

[1] Cf. the " Mémoires " of Marshal Marmont, i., 15, for the ordinary sentiments of the
young nobility. " In 1792 I had a sentiment for the person of the king, difficult to define,
of which I recovered the trace, and to some extent the power, twenty-two years later ; a
sentiment of devotion almost religious in character, an innate respect as if due to a being
of a superior order. The word King then possessed a magic, a force, which nothing had
changed in pure and honest breasts. . . . This religion of royalty still existed in the mass
of the nation, and especially amongst the *well-born*, who, sufficiently remote from power,
were rather struck with its brilliancy than with its imperfections. . . . This love became a sort of worship."

[2] Bourrienne, " Mémoires," i. 27.—Ségur, i. 445. In 1795, at Paris, Bonaparte, being
out of military employment, enters upon several commercial speculations, amongst which
is a bookstore, which does not succeed. (Stated by Sebastiani and many others.)

[3] " Mémorial," Aug. 3, 1816.

"and distrustful, as if unknown and suspicious."—Similarly, after the 31st of May and the 2d of June, his "Souper de Beaucaire" shows that if he condemns the departmental insurrection it is mainly because he deems it fruitless ; on the side of the insurgents, a defeated army, no position tenable, no cavalry, raw artillerymen, Marseilles reduced to its own troops, full of hostile *sans-culottes* and sore besieged, taken and pillaged ; chances are against it. "Poor sections of the country, the people of Vivaris, of the Cevennes, of Corsica, may fight to the last extremity, but you lose a battle and the fruit of a thousand years of fatigue, hardship, economy, and happiness become the soldier's prey."[1] And this for the conversion of the Girondists !—None of the political or social convictions which then exercise such control over men's minds have any hold on him. Before the 9th of Thermidor he seemed to be a "republican montagnard," and we follow him for months in Provence "the favorite and confidential adviser of young Robespierre," "admirer" of the elder Robespierre,[2] intimate at Nice with Charlotte Robespierre. After the 9th of Thermidor has passed, he frees himself with bombast from this compromising friendship : "I thought him sincere," says he of the younger Robespierre, in a letter intended to be shown, "but were he my father and had aimed at tyranny, I would have stabbed him myself." On returning to Paris, after having knocked at several doors, he takes Barras for a patron. Barras, the most brazen of the corrupt, Barras, who has overthrown and contrived the death of his two former protectors.[3] Among the contending parties and fanaticisms which succeed each other he keeps cool and free to dispose of himself as he pleases, indifferent to every cause and concerning himself only

---

1 Bourrienne, i., 171. (Original text of the " Souper de Beaucaire.")

2 Yung, ii., 430, 431. (Words of Charlotte Robespierre.) Bonaparte. as a souvenir of his acquaintance with her. granted her a pension, under the consulate, of 3600 francs.—*Ibid.* (Letter of Tilly, chargé d'affaires at Genoa, to Buchot, commissioner of foreign affairs.)— Cf. in the " Mémorial," Napoleon's favorable judgment of Robespierre.

3 Yung, ii., 455. (Letter from Bonaparte to Tilly, Aug. 7, 1794.) *Ibid.*, iii., 120. (Memoirs of Lucien.) " Barras has charge of Josephine's dowry, which is the command of the army in Italy." *Ibid.*, ii., 477. (Grading of general officers, notes by Schérer on Bonaparte.) " He knows all about artillery, but is rather too ambitious, and too intriguing for promotion."

with his own interests.—On the evening of the 12th of Vendémiaire, on leaving the Feydeau theatre, and noticing the
preparations of the sectionists,[1] he said to Junot, "Ah, if the
sections would only let me lead them ! I would guarantee to
place them in the Tuileries in two hours and have all those
Convention rascals driven out ! " Five hours later, denounced
by Barras and the Conventionalists, he takes " three minutes "
to make up his mind, and, instead of " blowing up the representatives," he shoots down the Parisians like any other good
condottière, who, holding himself in reserve, inclines to the first
that offers and then to who offers the most, except to back
out afterwards, and finally, seizing the opportunity, grabs anything.—Likewise, a veritable *condottière*, that is to say, leader
of a band, more and more independent, pretending to submit
under the pretext of the public good, looking out solely for
his own interest, centering all on himself, general on his own
account and for his own advantage in his Italian campaign
before and after the 18th of Fructidor,[2] but a *condottière* of the
first class, already aspiring to the loftiest summits, "with no
stopping-place but the throne or the scaffold,"[3] "determined[4]
to master France, also Europe through France, ever occupied
with his own plans, and without distraction, sleeping three
hours during the night," making playthings of ideas, people,
religions, and governments, managing mankind with incomparable dexterity and brutality, in the choice of means as of

---

1 De Ségur, i., 162.—La Fayette, " Mémoires," ii., 215. " Mémorial " (note dictated
by Napoleon). He states the reasons for and against, and adds, speaking of himself :
" These sentiments, twenty-five years of age, confidence in his strength, his destiny, determined him." Bourrienne, i., 51: " It is certain that he has always bemoaned that day ;
he has often said to me that he would give years of his life to efface that page of his
history."

2 " Mémorial," i., Sept 6, 1815. " It is only after Lodi that the idea came to me that I
might, after all, become a decisive actor on our political stage. Then the first spark of lofty
ambition gleamed out." On his aim and conduct in the Italian campaign of Sybel, " Histoire de l'Europe pendant la Révolution Française " (Dosquet translation), vol. iv., books
ii. and iii., especially pp. 182, 199, 334, 335, 406, 420, 475, 489.

3 Yung, iii., 213. (Letter of M. de Sucy, August 4, 1797.)

4 *Ibid.*, iii., 214. (Report of d'Entraigues to M. de Mowikinoff, Sept., 1797.) " If there
was any king in France which was not himself, he would like to have been his creator,
with his rights at the end of his sword, this sword never to be parted with, so that he
might plunge it in the king's bosom if he ever ceased to be submissive to him."—Miot de
Melito, i., 154. (Bonaparte to Montebello, before Miot and Melzi, June, 1797.) *Ibid*, i.,
184. (Bonaparte to Miot, Nov. 18, 1797, at Turin.)

ends, a superior artist, inexhaustible in prestiges, seductions, corruption, and intimidation, wonderful, and yet more terrible than any wild beast suddenly turned in on a herd of browsing cattle. The expression is not too strong and was uttered by an eye-witness, almost at this very date, a friend and a competent diplomat : " You know that, while I am very fond of the dear general, I call him to myself *the little tiger*, so as to properly characterize his figure, tenacity, and courage, the rapidity of his movements, and all that he has in him which may be fairly regarded in that sense." [1]

At this very date, previous to official adulation and the adoption of a recognized type, we see him face to face in two portraits drawn from life, one physical, by a truthful painter, Guérin, and the other moral, by a superior woman, Madame de Staël, who to the best European culture added tact and worldly perspicacity. Both portraits agree so perfectly that each seems to interpret and complete the other. " I saw him for the first time," [2] says Madame de Staël, " on his return to France after the treaty of Campo-Formio. After recovering from the first excitement of admiration there succeeded to this a decided sentiment of fear." And yet, " at this time he had no power, for it was even then supposed that the Directory looked upon him with a good deal of suspicion." People regarded him sympathetically, and were even prepossessed in his favor ; " thus the fear he inspired was simply due to the singular effect of his person on almost all who approached him. I had met men worthy of respect and had likewise met men of ferocious character ; but nothing in the impression which Bonaparte produced on me reminded me of either. I soon found, in the various opportunities I had of meeting him during his stay in Paris, that *his character was not to be described in terms commonly employed;* he was neither mild nor

1 D'Haussonville, " L'Église Romaine et la Premier Empire," i., 405. (Words of M. Cacault, signer of the Treaty of Tolentino, and French Secretary of Legation at Rome, at the commencement of negotiations for the Concordat.) M. Cacault says that he used this expression, " After the scenes of Tolentino and of Leghorn, and the fright of Man fredini, and Matéi threatened, and so many other vivacities."

2 Madame de Staël, " Considérations sur la Révolution Française," 3d part, ch. xxvi., and 4th part, ch. xviii.

violent, nor gentle nor cruel, like certain personages one happens to know. *A being like him, wholly unlike anybody else,* could neither feel nor excite sympathy ; he was *both more and less than a man ;* his figure, intellect, and language bore the impress of a foreign nationality . . . . far from being reassured on seeing Bonaparte oftener, he intimidated me more and more every day. I had a confused impression that he was not to be influenced by any emotion of sympathy or affection. *He regards a human being as a fact, an object, and not as a fellow-creature.* He neither hates nor loves, *he exists for himself alone ;* the rest of humanity are so many ciphers. The force of his will consists in the imperturbable calculation of his egoism ; he is a skillful player who has the human species for an antagonist, and whom he proposes to checkmate. . . . Every time that I heard him talk I was struck with *his superiority;* it bore no resemblance to that of men informed and cultivated through study and social intercourse, such as we find in France and England ; his conversation indicated the *tact of circumstances,* like that of the hunter in pursuit of his prey. His spirit seemed a cold, keen sword-blade, which freezes while it wounds. I felt a profound irony in his mind, which nothing great or beautiful could escape, not even his own fame, for he despised the nation whose suffrages he sought."—"With him, everything was means to ends ; the involuntary, whether for good or for evil, was entirely absent." No law, no ideal and abstract rule, existed for him ; " he examined things only with reference to their immediate usefulness ; a general principle was repugnant to him, either as so much nonsense or as an enemy."

Now, contemplate in Guérin [1] the spare body, those narrow shoulders under the uniform wrinkled by sudden movements, that neck swathed in its high twisted cravat, those temples covered by long, smooth, straight hair, exposing only the mask, the hard features intensified through strong contrasts of light and shade, the cheeks hollow up to the inner angle of the eye, the projecting cheek-bones, the massive, protuberant jaw, the

---

[1] Portrait of Bonaparte in the " Cabinet des Etampes," "drawn by Guérin, engraved by Fiesinger, deposited in the National Library, Vendémiaire 29, year VII."

sinuous, mobile lips, pressed together as if attentive, the large, clear eyes, deeply sunk under the broad, arched eyebrows, the fixed, oblique look, as penetrating as a rapier, and the two creases which extend from the base of the nose to the brow, as if in a frown of suppressed anger and determined will. Add to this the accounts of his contemporaries [1] who saw or heard the curt accent or the sharp, abrupt gesture, the interrogating, imperious, absolute tone of voice, and we comprehend how, the moment they accosted him, they felt the dominating hand which seizes them, presses them down, holds them firmly and never relaxes its grasp.

Already, at the receptions of the Directory, when conversing with men, or even with ladies, he puts questions " which prove the superiority of the questioner to those who have to answer them." [2] " Are you married ? " says he to this one, and " How many children have you ? " to another. To that one, " When did you come here ? " or, again, " When are you going away ? " He places himself in front of a French lady, well known for her beauty and wit and the vivacity of her opinions, " like the stiffest of German generals, and says : ' Madame, I don't like women who meddle with politics ! ' " Equality, ease, and familiarity—all fellowship vanishes at his approach. Eighteen months before this, on his appointment as commander-in-chief of the army in Italy, Admiral Decrès, who had known him well at Paris, [3] learns that he is to pass through Toulon :

" I at once propose to my comrades to introduce them, venturing to do so on my acquaintance with him in Paris. Full of eagerness and joy, I start off. The door opens and I am about to press forwards," he afterwards wrote, " when the attitude, the look, and the tone of voice suffice to arrest me. And yet there was nothing offensive about him ; still, this was enough. I never tried after that to overstep the line thus imposed on me." A few days later, at Alberga, [4] certain

---

1 Madame de Rémusat, " Mémoires, " i., 104.—Miot de Melito, i., 84.

2 Madame de Staël, " Considérations," etc., 3d part,ch. xxv.—Madame de Rémusat, ii., 77.

3 Stendhal, " Mémoires sur Napoléon," narration of Admiral Decrès.—Same narration in the " Mémorial."

4 De Ségur, i., 193.'

generals of division, and among them Augereau, a vulgar, heroic old soldier, vain of his tall figure and courage, arrive at headquarters, not well disposed toward the little parvenu sent out to them from Paris. Recalling the description of him which had been given to them, Augereau is abusive and insubordinate beforehand. "One of Barras's favorites! The Vendémiaire general! A street general! Never in action! Hasn't a friend! Looks like a bear because he always thinks for himself! An insignificant figure! He is said to be a mathematician and dreamer!"[1] They enter, and Bonaparte keeps them waiting. At last he appears, with his sword and belt on, explains the disposition of the forces, gives them his orders, and dismisses them. Augereau is thunderstruck. Only when he gets out of doors does he recover himself and fall back on his accustomed oaths. He agrees with Massena that "that little —— of a general frightened him." He cannot comprehend the ascendency "which overawes him at the first glance."[2]

Extraordinary and superior, made for command[3] and for conquest, singular and of an unique species, is the feeling of all his contemporaries; those who are most familiar with the histories of other nations, Madame de Staël and, after her, Stendhal, go back to the right sources to comprehend him, to the "petty Italian tyrants of the fourteenth and fifteenth centuries," to Castruccio-Castracani, to the Braccio of Mantua, to the Piccinino, the Malatestas of Rimini, and the Sforzas of Milan. In their opinion, however, it is only a chance analogy, a psychological resemblance. Really, however, and histori-

---

1 Roederer, "Œuvres Complètes," ii., 560. (Conversations with General Lasalle in 1809, and Lasalle's judgment on the débuts of Napoleon).

2 Another instance of this commanding influence is found in the case of General Vandamme, an old revolutionary soldier still more brutal and energetic than Augereau. In 1815, Vandamme said to Marshal d'Ornano, one day, on ascending the staircase of the Tuileries together : "My dear fellow, that devil of a man (speaking of the Emperor) fascinates me in a way I cannot account for. I, who don't fear either God or the devil, when I approach him I tremble like a child. He would make me dash through the eye of a needle into the fire !" ("Le Général Vandamme," by du Casse, ii., 385).

3 Roederer, iii., 356. (Napoleon himself says, February 11, 1809): "I, military! I am so, because I was born so ; it is my habit, my very existence. Wherever I have been I have always had command. I commanded at twenty-three, at the siege of Toulon ; I commanded at Paris in Vendémiaire ; I won over the soldiers in Italy the moment I presented myself. I was born for that."

cally it is a positive relationship. He is a descendant of the great Italians, the men of action of the year 1400, the military adventurers, usurpers, and founders of life-governments ; he inherits in direct affiliation their blood and inward organization, mental and moral.[1] A sprout has been transplanted from their forest, before the age of refinement, impoverishment, and decay, to a similar and remote nursery, where the tragic and militant régime is permanently established ; the primitive germ is preserved there intact and transmitted from one generation to another, renewed and invigorated by interbreeding. Finally, at the last stage of its growth, it springs out of the ground and develops magnificently, blooming the same as ever, and producing the same fruit as on the original stem ; modern cultivation and French gardening have pruned away but very few of its branches and blunted a few of its thorns : its original texture, inmost substance, and spontaneous devel-

---

[1] Observe various traits of the same mental and moral structure among different members of the family. (Speaking of his brothers and sisters in the " Mémorial " Napoleon says): " What family as numerous presents such a splendid combination ?"—" Mémoires " (unpublished), by M. X——, fourteen manuscript volumes, vol. ii., 543. (This author, a young magistrate under Louis XVI., a high functionary under the Empire, an important political personage under the restoration and the July monarchy, is probably the best informed and most judicious of eye-witnesses during the first half of our century.) " Their vices and virtues surpass ordinary proportions and have a physiognomy of their own. But what especially distinguishes them is a stubborn will, and inflexible resolution. . . . All possessed the instinct of their greatness." They readily accepted " the highest positions; they even got to believing that their elevation was inevitable. . . . Nothing in the incredible good fortune of Joseph astonished him; often in January, 1814, I heard him say over and over again that if his brother had not meddled with his affairs after the second entry into Madrid, he would still be on the throne of Spain. As to determined obstinacy we have only to refer to the resignation of Louis, the retirement of Lucien, and the resistances of Fesch ; they alone could stem the will of Napoleon and sometimes break a lance with him.—Passion, sensuality, the habit of considering themselves outside of rules, and self-confidence combined with talent, superabound among the women, as in the fifteenth century. Elisa, in Tuscany, had a vigorous brain, was high spirited and a genuine sovereign, notwithstanding the disorders of her private life, in which even appearances were not sufficiently maintained." Caroline at Naples, " without being more scrupulous than her sisters," better observed the proprieties ; none of the others so much resembled the Emperor ; "with her, all tastes succumbed to ambition "; it was she who advised and prevailed upon her husband, Murat, to desert Napoleon in 1824. As to Pauline, the most beautiful woman of her epoch, " no wife, since that of the Emperor Claude, surpassed her in the use she dared make of her charms ; nothing could stop her, not even a malady attributed to her dissipation and for which we have so often seen her borne in a litter."—Jerome, " in spite of the uncommon boldness of his debaucheries, maintained his ascendancy over his wife to the last."—On the " pressing efforts and attempts " of Joseph on Maria Louise in 1814, M. X——, after Savary's papers and the evidence of M. de Saint-Aignan, gives extraordinary details. (Vol. iv., 112.)

opment have not changed.   The soil of France and of Europe,
however, broken up by revolutionary tempests, is more favorable to its roots than the worn-out fields of the Middle Ages ;
and there it grows by itself, without being subject, like its
Italian ancestors, to rivalry with its own species ; nothing
checks the growth ; it may absorb all the juices of the ground,
all the air and sunshine of the region, and become the Colossus which the ancient plants, equally deep-rooted and
certainly as absorbent, but born in a less friable soil and
more crowded together, could not provide.

II.

" The man-plant," says Alfieri, " is in no country born more
vigorous than in Italy "; and never, in Italy, was it so vigorous
as from 1300 to 1500, from the contemporaries of Dante down
to those of Michael Angelo, Cæsar Borgia, Julius II., and
Macchiavelli.[1]   The first distinguishing mark of a man of
those times is *the integrity of his mental instrument.*   Nowadays, after three hundred years of service, ours has lost somewhat of its temper, sharpness, and suppleness ; in general, a
compulsory, special application of it has rendered it one-sided ;
the multiplication, besides, of ready-made ideas and acquired
methods incrusts it and reduces its play to a sort of routine ;
finally, it is much worn through excess of cerebral action,
weakened by the continuity of sedentary habits.   It is just the
opposite with those impulsive spirits of new blood and of a
new race.

Roederer, a competent and independent judge, who, at the
beginning of the consular government, sees Bonaparte daily
at the meetings of the Council of State, and who notes down
every evening the impressions of the day, is carried away with
admiration.[2]   " Punctual at every sitting, prolonging the session five or six hours, discussing before and afterwards the
subjects brought forward, always returning to two questions,
' Is that *just ?* '   ' Is that *useful ?* ' examining each question in

---

1 Burkhardt, " Die Renaissance in Italien," *passim.*—Stendhal, " Histoire de la pein-
ture en Italie " (introduction), and " Rome, Naples, et Florence," *passim.*
2 Roederer, iii., 380 (1802).

itself, under both relations, after having subjected it to a
most exact and elaborate analysis ; next, consulting the best
authorities, the times, experience, and obtaining information
about bygone jurisprudence, the laws of Louis XIV. and of
Frederick the Great. . . . Never did the council adjourn
without its members knowing more than the day before ; if not
through knowledge derived from him, at least through the
researches he obliged them to make.   Never did the members
of the Senate and the Corps Législatif, or of the tribunals, pay
their respects to him without being rewarded for their homage
by valuable instructions.   He cannot be surrounded by public
men without being the statesman, all forming for him a council of state."   "What characterizes him above them all,"
is not alone the penetration and universality of his comprehension, but likewise and especially "the force, flexibility, and
constancy of his attention.   He can work eighteen hours at a
stretch, on one or on several subjects.   I never saw him tired.
I never found his mind lacking in inspiration, even when
weary in body, nor when violently exercised, nor when angry.
I never saw him diverted from one matter by another, turning
from that under discussion to one he had just finished or was
about to take up.   The news, good or bad, he received from
Egypt, did not divert his mind from the civil code, nor the
civil code from the combinations which the safety of Egypt
required.   Never did man more wholly devote himself to the
work in hand, nor better devote his time to what he had to do.
Never did mind more inflexibly set aside the occupation or
thought which did not come at the right day or hour, never
was one more ardent in seeking it, more alert in its pursuit,
more capable of fixing it when the time came to take
it up."—He himself said later on :[1]   "Various subjects
and affairs are stowed away in my brain as in a chest of
drawers.   When I want to take up any special business I
shut one drawer and open another.   None of them ever
get mixed, and never does this incommode me or fatigue
me.   If I feel sleepy I shut all the drawers and go to sleep."
Never has brain so disciplined and under such control been

---

[1] " Mémorial."

seen, one so ready at all times for any task, so capable of immediate and absolute concentration. Its flexibility [1] is wonderful, "in the instant application of every faculty and energy, and bringing them all to bear at once on any object that concerns him, on a mite as well as on an elephant, on any given individual as well as on an enemy's army. . . . When specially occupied, other things do not exist for him ; it is a sort of chase from which nothing diverts him." And this hot pursuit, which nothing arrests save capture, this tenacious hunt, this headlong course by one to whom the goal is never other than a fresh starting-point, is the spontaneous gait, the natural, even pace which his mind prefers. "I am always at work," says he to Roederer.[2] "I meditate a great deal. If I seem always equal to the occasion, ready to face what comes, it is because I have thought the matter over a long time before undertaking it. I have anticipated whatever might happen. It is no genius which suddenly reveals to me what I ought to do or say in any unlooked-for circumstance, but my own reflection, my own meditation. . . . I work all the time, at dinner, in the theatre. I wake up at night in order to resume my work. I got up last night at two o'clock. I stretched myself on my couch before the fire to examine the army reports sent to me by the Minister of War. I found twenty mistakes in them, and made notes which I have this morning sent to the minister, who is now engaged with his clerks in rectifying them." His fellow-workmen break down and sink under the burden imposed on them and which he supports without feeling the weight. When Consul,[3] "he sometimes presides at special meetings of the section of the interior from ten o'clock in the evening until five o'clock in the morning. . . . Often, at Saint-Cloud, he keeps the counsellors of state from nine o'clock in the morning until five in the evening, with fifteen minutes' intermission, and seems no more fatigued at the close of the session than when it began."

---

1 De Pradt, "Histoire de l'Ambassade dans la grande-duché de Varsovie en 1812," preface, p. x, and 5.

2 Roederer, iii., 544 (February 24, 1809). Cf. Meneval, "Napoléon et Marie-Louise, souvenirs historiques," i., 210–213.

3 Pelet de la Lozère," Opinions de Napoléon au conseil d'état," p.8.—Roederer, iii., 380.

During the night sessions " many of the members succumb through lassitude, while the Minister of War falls asleep "; he gives them a shake and wakes them up, " Come, come, citizens, let us bestir ourselves, it is only two o'clock and we must earn the money the French people pay us." Consul or Emperor,[1] " he demands of each minister an account of the smallest details. It is not rare to see them leaving the council room overcome with fatigue, due to the long interrogatories to which he has subjected them; he disdains to take any notice of this, and talks about the day's work simply as a relaxation which has scarcely given his mind exercise." And what is worse, " it often happens that on returning home they find a dozen of his letters requiring immediate answer, for which the whole night scarcely suffices." The quantity of facts he is able to retain and store away, the quantity of ideas he elaborates and produces, seems to surpass human capacity, and this insatiable, inexhaustible, unmovable brain thus keeps on working uninterruptedly for thirty years.

Through another result of the same mental organization, *it demands material to work on;* and this, at the present day, is our great danger. For the past three hundred years we have more and more lost sight of the exact and direct meaning of things; subject to the constraints of a domestic, many-sided, and prolonged education we fix our attention on the symbols of objects rather than on the objects themselves; instead of on the ground

---

1 Mollien, " Mémoires," i., 379 ; ii., 230 —Roederer, iii., 434. " He is at the head of all things. He governs, administrates, negotiates, works eighteen hours a day, with the clearest and best organized head ; he has governed more in three years than kings in a hundred years."—Lavalette, " Mémoires," ii., 75. (The words of Napoleon's secretary on Napoleon's labor in Paris, after Leipsic) : " He retires at eleven, but gets up at three o'clock in the morning, and until the evening there is not a moment he does not devote to work. It is time this stopped, for he will be used up, and myself before he is."—Gaudin, Duc de Gaëte, " Mémoires," iii. (supplement), p. 75. Account of an evening in which, from eight o'clock to three in the morning, Napoleon examines with Gaudin his general budget, during seven consecutive hours, without stopping a minute.—Sir Neil Campbell, " Napoléon at Fontainebleau and at Elbe," p. 243. " Journal de Sir Neil Campbell à l'île d'Elbe " : " I never saw any man, in any station in life, so personally active and so persistent in his activity. He seems to take pleasure in perpetual motion and in seeing those who accompany him completely tired out, which frequently happened in my case when I accompanied him. . . . Yesterday, after having been on his legs from eight in the morning to three in the afternoon, visiting the frigates and transports, even to going down to the lower compartments among the horses, he rode on horseback for three hours, and, as he afterwards said to me, to *rest himself.*"

itself, on a map of it ; instead of on animals struggling for existence,[1] on nomenclatures and classifications, or, at best, on stuffed specimens displayed in a museum ; instead of on men who feel and act, on statistics, codes, histories, literatures, and philosophies ; in short, on printed words, and, worse still, on abstract terms, which from century to century have become more abstract and therefore further removed from experience,. more difficult to understand, less adaptable and more deceptive, especially in all that relates to human life and society. In this domain, owing to extended governments, to the multiplication of services, to the entanglement of interests, the object, indefinitely expanded and complex, now eludes our grasp; our vague, incomplete, incorrect idea of it badly corresponds with it, or does not correspond at all ; in nine minds out of ten, or perhaps ninety-nine out of a hundred, it is but little more than a word; the rest, if they desire some significant indication of what society actually is beyond the teachings of books, require ten or fifteen years of close observation and study to re-think the phrases with which these have filled their memory, to interpret them anew, to make clear their meaning, to get at and verify their sense, to substitute for the more or less empty and indefinite term the fullness and precision of a personal impression. We have seen how ideas of Society, State, Government, Sovereignty, Rights, Liberty, the most important of all ideas, were, at the close of the eighteenth century, curtailed and falsified ; how, in most minds, simple verbal reasoning combined them together in dogmas and axioms; what an offspring these metaphysical simulacra gave birth to, how many lifeless and grotesque abortions, how many monstrous and destructive chimeras. There is no place for any of

---

1 The starting-point of the great discoveries of Darwin is the physical, circumstantial fact of which he has made account in his study of animals and plants, as *living, during the whole course of life*, subject to innumerable difficulties and to such rude competition ; this study is wholly lacking in the ordinary zoologist or botanist, whose mind is busy only with anatomical preparations or collections of plants. In every science, the difficulty lies in arriving at a reduction in brief of the real object through significant specimens, just as it exists before us, and its true history. Claude Bernard one day remarked to me, "We shall know physiology when we are able to follow step by step a molecule of carbon or azote in the body of a dog, give its history, and describe its passage from its entrance to its exit."

these chimeras in the mind of Bonaparte ; they cannot arise
in it, nor find access to it ; his aversion to the unsubstantial
phantoms of political abstraction extends beyond disdain, even
to disgust ;[1] the ideology of that day, as it is called, is his
particular bugbear ; he loathes it not alone through calculation,
but still more through an instinctive demand for what is real,
as a practical man and statesman, always keeping in mind, like
the great Catherine, " that he is operating, not on paper, but
on the human hide, which is ticklish." Every idea entertained
by him had its origin in his personal observation, and it was
his personal observation which controlled it.

If books are useful to him it is to suggest questions, which he
never answers but through his own experience. He read very
little, and hastily ;[2] his classical education was rudimentary ; in
the way of Latin, he remained in the lower class. The instruction he got at the Military Academy as well as at Brienne was
below mediocrity, while, after Brienne, it is stated that " for
the languages and belles-lettres, he had no taste." Next
to this, the literature of elegance and refinement, the philosophy of the closet and drawing-room, with which his contemporaries are imbued, glided over his intellect as over a rock ;
none but mathematical truths and positive notions about
geography and history found their way into his mind and
deeply impressed it. Everything else, as with his predecessors
of the fifteenth century, comes to him through the original,

---

1 Thibaudeau, "Mémoires sur le Consulat," 204. (Apropos of the tribunate) : " They
consist of a dozen or fifteen metaphysicians who ought to be flung into the water ; they
crawl all over me like vermin."

2 Madame de Rémusat, i., 115 : " He is really ignorant, having read very little and always
hastily."—Stendhal, " Mémoires sur Napoléon": " His education was very defective. . . .
He knew nothing of the great principles discovered within the past one hundred years,"
and just those which concern man or society. " For example, he had not read Montesquieu as this writer ought to be read, that is to say, in a way to accept or decidedly reject each of the thirty-one books of the ' Esprit des lois.' He had not thus read Bayle's
Dictionary nor the Essay on the Wealth of Nations by Adam Smith. This ignorance of
the Emperor's was not perceptible in conversation, and first, because he led in conversation,
and next, because with Italian finesse no question put by him, or careless supposition thrown
out, ever betrayed that ignorance."—Bourrienne. i., 19,21 : ³ t Brienne, " unfortunately for
us, the monks to whom the education of youth was confided knew nothing, and were too
poor to pay good foreign teachers. . . . It is inconceivable how any capable man ever
graduated from this educational institution." —Yung. i., 125 (Notes made by him on
Bonaparte, when he left the Military Academy) : " Very fond of the abstract sciences,
indifferent to others, well grounded in mathematics and geography."

direct action of his faculties in contact with men and things, through his prompt and sure tact, his indefatigable and minute attention, his indefinitely repeated and rectified divinations during long hours of solitude and silence. Practice, and not speculation, is the source of his instruction, the same as with a mechanic brought up amongst machinery. " There is nothing relating to warfare that I cannot make myself. If nobody knows how to make gunpowder, I do. I can construct gun-carriages. If cannon must be cast, I will see that it is done properly. If tactical details must be taught, I will teach them."[1] Hence his competency at the outset—general in the artillery, major-general, diplomatist, financier and adminis-trator, all at once and in every direction. Thanks to this fecund apprenticeship, beginning with the Consulate, he shows cabinet clerks and veteran ministers who send in their reports to him what to do. " I am a better administrator than they are ;[2] when one has been obliged to rack his brains to find out how to feed, maintain, control, and animate with the same spirit and will two or three hundred thousand men, a long distance from their country, one soon gets at the secrets of administration." He takes in at a glance every part of the human machine he fashions and manipulates, each in its proper place and function ; the generators of power, the organs of its transmission, the extra working gear, the com-posite action, the speed which ensues, the final result, the complete effect, the net product ; never is he content with a superficial and summary inspection ; he penetrates into obscure corners and to the lowest depths " through the technical pre-

---

1 Roederer, iii., 544 (March 6, 1809), 26, 563 (Jan. 23, 1811, and Nov. 12, 1813).

2 Mollien, i., 348 (a short time before the rupture of the peace of Amiens), iii., 16 : " It was at the end of January, 1809, that he wanted a full report of the financial situation on the 31st of December, 1808. . . . This report was to be ready in two days."—iii., 34 :' ' A complete balance sheet of the public treasury for the first six months of 1812 was under Napoleon's eyes at Witepsk, the 11th of August, eleven days after the close of these first six months. What is truly wonderful is, that amidst so many different occupations and preoccupations . . . . he could preserve such an accurate run of the proceedings and methods of the administrative branches about which he wanted to know at any moment. Nobody had any excuse for not answering him, for each was *questioned in his own terms ;* it is that singular aptitude of the head of the State, and *the technical precision of his questions,* which alone explains how he could maintain such a remarkable *ensemble* in an adminis-trative system of which the smallest threads centred in himself."

cision of his questions," with the lucidity of a specialist, and in this way, borrowing an expression from the philosophers, his idea is found *adequate to its object.*

Hence his eagerness for details, for these form the body and substance of the object ; the hand that has not grasped these, or lets them go, retains only the shell, an envelope. With respect to these his curiosity is "insatiable." [1] In each ministerial department he knows more than the ministers, and in each bureau he knows as much as the clerks. " On his table [2] lie reports of the positions of his forces on land and on water ; he has furnished the plans of these, and fresh ones are issued every month "; such is the daily reading he likes best. " I have my reports on positions always at hand ; my memory for an Alexandrine is not good, but I never forget a syllable of my reports on positions. I shall find them in my room this evening, and I shall not go to bed until I have read them." He always knows " his position " on land and at sea better than is known in the War and Navy departments ; better even than his staff-officers the number, size, and qualities of his ships in or out of port, the present and future state of vessels under construction, the composition and strength of their crews, the formation, organization, staff of officers, material, stations, and enlistments, past and to come, of each army corps and of each regiment.

---

1 An expression of Mollien.

2 Meneval, i., 210, 213.—Roederer, iii., 537, 545 (February and March, 1889) : Words of Napoleon : " At this moment it was nearly midnight." *Ibid.*, iv., 55 (November, 1809). Read the admirable examination of Roederer by Napoleon on the Kingdom of Naples. His queries form a vast systematic and concise network, embracing the entire subject, leaving no physical or moral data, no useful circumstance not seized upon.—Ségur, ii., 231 : M. de Ségur, ordered to inspect every part of the coast-line, had sent in his report : " ' I have seen your reports,' said the First Consul to me, ' and they are exact. Nevertheless, you forgot two cannon at Ostend,' and he pointed out the place. ' in a road behind the town.' I went out overwhelmed with astonishment that among thousands of cannon distributed among the mounted batteries or light artillery on the coast, two pieces should not have escaped his recollection."—" Correspondance," letter to King Joseph, August 6, 1806 : " The admirable condition of my armies is due to this, that I give attention to them every day for an hour or two, and, when the monthly reports come in, to the state of my troops and fleets, all forming about *twenty large volumes.* I leave every other occupation to read them over in detail, to see what difference there is between one month and another. I take more pleasure in reading those than any young girl does in a novel."—Cadet de Gassicourt, " Voyage en Autriche " (1809). On his reviews at Schoenbrunn and his verification of the contents of a pontoon-wagon, taken as an example.

It is the same in the financial and diplomatic services, in every branch of the adminstration, laic or ecclesiastical, in the physical order and in the moral order. His topographical memory and his geographical conception of countries, places, ground, and obstacles culminate in an inward vision which he evokes at will, and which, years afterwards, revives as fresh as on the first day. His calculation of distances, marches, and manœuvres is so rigid a mathematical operation that, frequently, at a distance of two or four hundred leagues, his military foresight, calculated two or four months ahead, turns out correct, almost on the day named, and precisely on the spot designated.[1] Add to this one other faculty, and the rarest of all ; for, if things turn out as he foresaw they would, it is because, as with famous chess-players, he has accurately measured not alone the mechanical moves of the pieces, but the character and talent of his adversary, " sounded his draft of water," and divined his probable mistakes ; he has added the calculation of physical quantities and probabilities to the calculation of moral quantities and probabilities, thus showing himself as great a psychologist as he is an accomplished strate-

---

[1] Bourrienne, ii., 116; iv., 238 : " He had not a good memory for proper names, words, and dates, but it was prodigious for *facts and localities.* I remember that, on the way from Paris to Toulon, he called my attention to ten places suitable for giving battle. . . . It was a souvenir of his youthful travels, and he described to me the lay of the ground, designating the positions he would have taken even before we were on the spot." March 17, 1800, puncturing a card with a pin, he shows Bourrienne the place where he intends to beat Mélas, at San Juliano. " Four months after this I found myself at San Juliano with his portfolio and despatches, and, that very evening, at Torre-di-Gafolo, a league off, I wrote the bulletin of the battle under his dictation" (of Marengo).—De Ségur, ii., 30 (Narrative of M. Daru to M. de Ségur: Aug. 13, 1805, at the headquarters of La Manche, Napoleon dictates to M. Daru the complete plan of the campaign against Austria) : " Order of marches, their duration, places of convergence or meeting of the columns, attacks in full force, the various movements and mistakes of the enemy, all, in this rapid dictation, was foreseen two months beforehand and at a distance of two hundred leagues. . . . The battle-field, the victories, and even the very days on which we were to enter Munich and Vienna were then announced and written down as it all turned out. . . . Daru saw these oracles fulfilled on the designated days up to our entry into Munich ; if there were any differences of time and not of results between Munich and Vienna, they were all in our favor."—M. de La Vallette, " Mémoires," ii., p. 35. (He was postmaster-general) : " It often happened to me that I was not as certain as he was of distances and of many details in my administration on which he was able to set me straight."—On returning from the camp at Bologna, Napoleon encounters a squad of soldiers who had got lost, asks what regiment they belong to, calculates the day they left, the road they took, what distance they should have marched. and then tells them, " You will find your battalion at such a halting place."—At this time, " the army numbered 200,000 men."

gist. In fact, no one has surpassed him in the art of defining the various states and impulses of one or of many minds,
either prolonged or for the time being, which impel or restrain
man in general, or this or that individual in particular ; what
springs of action may be touched, and the kind and degree of
pressure that may be applied to them. ˙ This central faculty
rules all the others, and in the art of mastering man his genius
is found supreme.

No faculty is more precious for a political engineer ; for the
forces he acts upon are never other than human passions.
But how, except through divination, can these passions, which
grow out of the deepest sentiments, be reached ; and how, save
by conjecture, can forces be estimated which seem to defy all
measurement? On this dark and uncertain ground, where
one has to grope one's way, Napoleon moves with almost
absolute certainty ; he moves promptly, and, first of all, he
studies himself ; indeed, to find one's way into another's soul
requires, preliminarily, that one should dive deep into one's
own.[1] " I have always delighted in analysis," said he, one day,
" and should I ever fall seriously in love I would take my sentiment to pieces. *Why* and *How* are such important questions
one cannot put them to one's self too often." " It is certain,"
writes an observer, " that he, of all men, is the one who has
most meditated on the *why* which controls human actions."
His method, that of the experimental sciences, consists
in testing every hypothesis or deduction by some positive
fact, observed by him under definite conditions ; a physical
force being ascertained and accurately measured through
the deviation of a needle, or through the rise and fall
of a fluid, this or that invisible moral force can likewise
be ascertained and approximately measured through some
emotional sign, some decisive manifestation, consisting of a
certain word, tone, or gesture. It is these words, tones,
and gestures which he dwells on ; he detects inward sentiments by the outward expression ; he figures to himself the
internal by the external, by some physiognomical trait, some
striking attitude, some summary and topical circumstance, so

---

1 Madame de Rémusat, i., 103, 268.

pertinent and with such particulars as will afford a complete indication of the innumerable series of analogous cases. In this way, the vague, fleeting object is suddenly arrested, brought to bear, and then gauged and weighed, like some impalpable gas collected and kept in a graduated transparent glass tube.—Accordingly, at the Council of State, while the others, either legists or administrators, adduce abstractions, articles of the code and precedents, he looks into natures as they are—the Frenchman's, the Italian's, the German's ; that of the peasant, the workman, the *bourgeois*, the noble, the returned *emigré*,[1] the soldier, the officer and the functionary— everywhere the individual man as he is, the man who ploughs, manufactures, fights, marries, generates, toils, enjoys himself, and dies.

Nothing is more striking than the contrast between the dull, grave arguments advanced by the wise official editor, and Napoleon's own words caught on the wing, at the moment, vibrating and teeming with illustrations and imagery.[2] Apropos of divorce, the principle of which he wishes to maintain : " Consult, now, national manners and customs. Adultery is no phenomenon ; it is common enough—*une affaire de canapé.* . . . There must be some curb on women who commit adultery for trinkets, poetry, Apollo, and the muses, etc." But if divorce

---

1 Thibaudeau, p. 25, 1 (on the Jacobin survivors) : " They are nothing but common artisans, painters, etc., with lively imaginations, a little better instructed than the people, living amongst the people and exercising influence over them."—Madame de Rémusat, i., 271 (on the royalist party) : " It is very easy to deceive that party because its starting-point is not what it is, but what it would like to have."—i., 337 : " The Bourbons will never see anything except through the *Œil de Bœuf.*"—Thibaudeau, p. 46: " Insurrections and emigrations are skin diseases ; terrorism is an internal malady." *Ibid.*, 75 : " What now keeps the spirit of the army up is the idea soldiers have that they occupy the places of former nobles."

2 Thibaudeau, pp. 419 to 452. (Both texts are given in separate columns.) And *passim*, for instance, p. 84, the following portrayal of the decadal system of worship under the Republic : " It was imagined that citizens could be got together in churches, to freeze with cold and hear, read, and study laws, in which there was already but little fun for those who executed them." Another example of the way in which his ideas expressed themselves through imagery (Pelet de la Lozère, p. 242) : " I am not satisfied with the customs regulations on the Alps. They show no life. We don't hear the *rattle of crown pieces* pouring into the public treasury." To appreciate the vividness of Napoleon's expressions and thought the reader must consult, especially, the five or six long conversations, noted on the very evening of the day they occurred by Roederer ; the two or three conversations likewise noted by Miot de Melito ; the scenes narrated by Beugnot ; the notes of Pelet de la Lozère and by Stanislas de Girardin, and nearly the entire volume by Thibaudeau.

be allowed for incompatibility of temper you undermine marriage ; the fragility of the bond will be apparent the moment the obligation is contracted ; " it is just as if a man said to himself, ' I am going to marry until I feel different.' " Nullity of marriage must not be too often allowed ; once a marriage is made it is a serious matter to undo it. " Suppose that, in marrying my cousin just arrived from the Indies, I wed an adventuress. She bears me children, and I then discover she is not my cousin—is that marriage valid ? Does not public morality demand that it should be so considered ? There has been a mutual exchange of souls, of transpiration." On the right of children to be supported and fed although of age, he says : " Will you allow a father to drive a girl of fifteen out of his house ? A father worth 60,000 francs a year might say to his son, ' You are stout and fat ; go and turn ploughman.' The children of a rich father, or of one in good circumstances, are always entitled to the paternal porridge. Strike out their right to be fed, and you compel children to murder their parents."—As to adoption : " You regard this as law-makers and not as statesmen. It is not a civil contract nor a judicial contract. The analysis (of the jurist) leads to vicious results. Man is governed by imagination only ; without imagination he is a brute. It is not for five cents a day, simply to distinguish himself, that a man consents to be killed ; if you want to electrify him touch his heart. A notary, who is paid a fee of twelve francs for his services, cannot do that. It requires some other process, a legislative act. Adoption, what is that ? An imitation by which society tries to counterfeit nature. It is a new kind of sacrament. . . . Society ordains that the bones and blood of one being shall be changed into the bones and blood of another. It is the greatest of all legal acts. It gives the sentiments of a son to one who never had them, and reciprocally those of a parent. Where ought this to originate ? Above, like a clap of thunder ! "

All his expressions are bright flashes one after another.[1]

---

[1] Pelet de la Lozère, 63, 64. (On the physiological differences between the English and the French.)—Madame de Rémusat, i., 273, 392 : " You, Frenchmen, are not in earnest about anything, except, perhaps, equality, and even here you would gladly give this up if

Nobody, since Voltaire and Galiani, has launched forth such a profusion of them ; some of them, like those of Montesquieu, on society, laws, government, France and the French, penetrate to and suddenly illuminate the darkest recesses ; he does not hammer them out laboriously, but they burst forth, the outpourings of his intellect, its natural, involuntary, constant action. And what adds to their value is that, outside of councils and private conversations, he abstains from them, employing them only in the service of thought ; at other times he subordinates them to the end he has in view, which is always the practical effect ; ordinarily, he writes and speaks in a different language, in a language suited to his audience ; he retrenches the singularities, the fits and starts of the imagination and of improvisation, the outbursts of genius and inspiration. All that he retains and allows himself the use of are merely those which are intended to impress the personage whom he wishes to dazzle with a great idea of himself, a Pius VII., or the Emperor Alexander ; in this case, his conversational tone is that of a caressing, expansive, amiable familiarity ; he is then before the footlights, and when he acts he can play all parts, tragedy or comedy, with the same life and spirit whether he fulminates, insinuates, or even affects simplicity. When with his generals, ministers, and head clerks,

---

you were sure of being the foremost. . . . The hope of advancement in the world should be cherished by everybody. . . . Keep your vanity always alive. The severity of the republican government would have worried you to death. What started the Revolution? Vanity. What will end it? Vanity, again. Liberty is merely a pretext."—iii., 153 : " Liberty is the craving of a small and privileged class by nature, with faculties superior to the common run of men ; this class, therefore, may be put under restraint with impunity; equality, on the contrary, catches the multitude."—Thibaudeau, 99: "What do I care for the opinions and cackle of the drawing-room ? I never heed it. I pay attention only to what rude peasants say." His estimates of certain situations are masterpieces of picturesque concision. "Why did I stop and sign the preliminaries of Leoben? Because I played *vingt-et-un* and was satisfied with twenty." His insight into (dramatic) character is that of the most sagacious critic. "The 'Mahomet' of Voltaire is neither a prophet nor an Arab, only an impostor graduated out of the École Polytechnique."—"Madame de Genlis tries to define virtue as if she were the discoverer of it."—(On Madame de Staël): " This woman teaches people to think who never took to it, or have forgotten how."— (On Chateaubriand, one of whose relations had just been shot) : " He will write a few pathetic pages and read them aloud in the faubourg Saint-Germain ; pretty women will shed tears, and that will console him."—(On Abbé Delille) : " He is wit in its dotage."— (On Pasquier and Molé) : "I make the most of one, and made the other."—Madame de· Rémusat., ii., 389, 391, 394, 399, 402 ; iii., 67.

he falls back on the concise, positive, technical business style ; any other would interfere with that ; the impassioned soul re- veals itself only through the brevity and imperious strength and rudeness of the accent.   For his armies and the common run of men, he has his proclamations and bulletins, that is to say, sonorous phrases composed for effect, a statement of facts purposely simplified and falsified,[1] in short, an excellent effer- vescent wine, good for exciting enthusiasm, and an equally excellent narcotic for maintaining credulity,[2] a sort of popular mixture retailed out by him just at the proper time, and whose ingredients are so well proportioned that the public drinks it with delight, and becomes at once intoxicated.   His style on every occasion, whether affected or spontaneous, shows his wonderful knowledge of the masses and of individuals ; ex- cept in two or three cases, on one exalted domain, of which he always remains ignorant, he has ever hit the mark, applying the appropriate lever, giving just the push, weight, and de- gree of impulsion which best accomplishes his purpose.   A series of brief, accurate memoranda, corrected daily, enables him to frame for himself a sort of psychological tablet whereon he notes down and sums up, in almost numerical valuation, the mental and moral dispositions, characters, faculties, pas- sions, and aptitudes, the strong or weak points, of the innum- erable human beings, near or remote, on whom he acts.

Let us try for a moment to form some idea of the grasp and capacity of this intellect ; we should probably have to recur to Cæsar to find its counterpart ; but, for lack of documents, we have nothing of Cæsar but general features—a summary out- line ; of Napoleon we have, besides the perfect outline, the features in detail.   Read his correspondence, day by day, then chapter by chapter ;[3] for example, in 1806, after the battle of

---

1 Bourrienne, ii., 281, 342 : " It pained me to write official statements under his dicta- tion, of which each was an imposture."   He always answered : " My dear sir, you are a simpleton—you understand nothing ! "—Madame de Rémusat, ii., 205, 209.

2 See especially the campaign bulletins for 1807, so insulting to the king and queen of Prussia, but, owing to that fact, so well calculated to excite the contemptuous laughter and jeers of the soldiers.

3 In " La Correspondance de Napoléon," published in thirty-two volumes, the letters are arranged under dates.—In his " Correspondance avec Eugène, vice-roi d'Italie," they are arranged under chapters ; also with Joseph, King of Naples and after of Spain.   It is easy

Austerlitz, or, still better, in 1809, after his return from Spain, up to the peace of Vienna ; whatever our technical shortcomings may be, we shall find that his mind, in its comprehensiveness and amplitude, largely surpasses all known or even credible proportions.

He has mentally within him three principal atlases, always at hand, each composed of "about twenty note-books," each distinct and each regularly posted up.—The first one is military, forming a vast collection of topographical charts as minute as those of an *état-major*, with detailed plans of every stronghold, also specific indications and the local distribution of all forces on sea and on land—crews, regiments, batteries, arsenals, storehouses, present and future resources in supplies of men, horses, vehicles, arms, munitions, food, and clothing. The second, which is civil, resembles the heavy, thick volumes published every year, in which we now read the state of the budget, and comprehend, first, the innumerable items of ordinary and extraordinary receipt and expenditure, internal taxes, foreign contributions, the products of the domains in France and out of France, the fiscal services, pensions, public works, and the rest ; next, all administrative statistics, the hierarchy of functions and of functionaries, senators, deputies, ministers, prefects, bishops, professors, judges, and those under their orders, each where he resides, with his rank, jurisdiction, and salary.—The third is a vast biographical and moral dictionary, in which, as in the pigeon-holes of the Chief of Police, each notable personage and local group, each professional or

---

to compose other chapters not less instructive : one on foreign affairs (letters to M. de Champagny, M. de Talleyrand, and M. de Bassano) ; another on the finances (letters to M. Gaudin and to M. Mollien) ; another on the navy (letters to Admiral Decrès) ; another on military administration (letters to General Clarke) ; another on the affairs of the Church (letters to M. Portalis and to M. Bigot de Préameneu) ; another on the Police (letters to Fouché), etc. Finally, by dividing and distributing his letters according as they relate to this or that grand enterprise, especially to this or that military compaign, a third classification could be made. In this way we can form a conception of the vastness of his positive information, also of the ordinary play of his intellect. Cf. especially the following letters to Prince Eugène, June 11, 1806 (on the supplies and expenses of the Italian army) ; June 1 and 18, 1806 (on the occupation of Dalmatia, and on the military situation, offensive and defensive). To Gen. Dejean, April 28, 1806 (on the war supplies) ; June 27, 1806 (on the fortifications of Peschiera) ; July 20, 1806 (on the fortifications of Wesel and of Juliers).

social body, and even each population, has its label, along with
a brief note on its situation, needs, and antecedents, and, therefore, its demonstrated character, eventual disposition, and
probable conduct. Each label, card, or strip of paper has
its summing-up ; all these partial summaries, methodically
classified, terminate in totals, and the totals of the three atlases,
combined together, thus furnish their possessor with an estimate of his disposable forces.—Now, in 1809, however full
these atlases, they are clearly imprinted on Napoleon's mind ;
he knows not only the total and the partial summaries, but
also the slightest details : he reads them readily and at every
hour ; he comprehends in a mass, and in all particulars, the
various nations he governs directly, or through some one else;
that is to say, 60,000,000 men, the different countries he has
conquered or overrun, consisting of 70,000 square miles ; at
first, France increased by the addition of Belgium and Piedmont ; next Spain, from which he is just returned, and where
he has placed his brother Joseph ; southern Italy, where, after
Joseph, he has placed Murat ; central Italy, where he occupies
Rome ; northern Italy, where Eugène is his delegate ; Dalmatia
and Istria, which he has joined to his empire ; Austria, which
he invades for the second time ; the Confederation of the
Rhine, which he has made and which he directs ; Westphalia
and Holland, where his brother sare only his lieutenants ;
Prussia, which he has subdued and mutilated and which he
oppresses, and the strongholds of which he still retains ; and,
add a last mental tableau, that which represents the northern
seas, the Atlantic and the Mediterranean, all the fleets of the
continent at sea and in port from Dantzic to Flessingen and
Bayonne, from Cadiz to Toulon and Gaëta, from Tarentum to
Venice, Corfu, and Constantinople. [1]—On the psychological and

---

[1] Cf. in the " Correspondance " the letters dated at Schoenbrunn near Vienna, during
August and September, 1809, and especially: 1st, the great number of letters and orders
relating to the English expeditions to Walcheren ; 2d, the letters to chief-judge Regnier and
to the arch-chancellor Cambacérès on expropriations for public benefit (Aug. 21, Sept. 7
and 29) ; 3d, the letters and orders to M. de Champagny to treat with Austria (Aug. 19,
and Sept. 10, 15, 18, 22, and 23) ; 4th, the letters to Admirable Decrès, to despatch naval
expeditions to the colonies (Aug. 17 and Sept. 26) ; 5th, the letter to Mollien on the budget
of expenditure (Aug. 8) ; 6th, the letter to Clarke on the statement of guns in store
throughout the empire (Sept. 14).—Other letters, ordering the preparation of two treatises

moral atlas, besides a primitive gap which he will never fill up, because this is a characteristic trait, there are some estimates which are wrong, especially with regard to the Pope and to Catholic conscience ; in like manner he rates the energy of national sentiment in Spain and Germany too low ; he rates too high his own prestige in France and in the countries annexed to her, the balance of confidence and zeal on which he may rely. But these errors are rather the product of his will than of his intelligence , he recognizes them at intervals; if he has illusions it is because he forges them ; left to himself his good sense would rest infallible, it is only his passions which blurred the lucidity of his intellect. As to the other two atlases, the topographical and the military, they are as complete and as exact as ever ; it is in vain that the reality which they present to him has become swollen and complex ; however monstrous at this date, they correspond to it in their fulness and precision, trait for trait.

But this multitude of notations forms only the smallest portion of the mental population swarming in this immense brain ; for, on his idea of the real, germinate and swarm his conceptions of the possible ; without these conceptions there would be no way to handle and transform things, and that he did handle and transform them we all know. Before acting, he has decided on his plan, and if this plan is adopted, it is one among several others,[1] after examining, comparing, and giving it the preference ; he has accordingly thought over all the others. Behind each combination adopted by him we detect those he has rejected , there are dozens of them behind each of his decisions, each manœuvre effected, each treaty signed, each decree promulgated, each order issued, and I venture to say, behind almost every improvised action or word spoken ; for calculation enters into everything he does, even into his

on military art (Oct. 1), two works on the history and encroachments of the Holy See (Oct. 3), prohibiting conferences at Saint-Sulpice (Sept. 15), and forbidding priests to preach outside the churches (Sept. 24).—From Schoenbrunn, he watches the details of public works in France and Italy ; for instance, the letters to M. le Montalivet (Sept. 30), to send an auditor post to Parma, to have a dyke repaired at once, and (Oct. 8) to hasten the building of several bridges and quays at Lyons.

1 He says himself : " I pose my theme always in many ways."

seeming expansiveness, also into his outbursts when in earnest ; if he gives way to these, it is on purpose, foreseeing the effect, with a view to intimidate or to dazzle ; he turns everything in others as well as in himself to account—his passion, his vehemence, his weaknesses, his fondness for talking out, and all for the advancement of the edifice he is constructing.[1] Certainly among his diverse faculties, however great, that of the *constructive imagination* is the most powerful. At the very beginning we feel its heat and boiling intensity beneath the coolness and rigidity of his technical and positive instructions. " When I plan a battle," said he to Roederer, " no man is more pusillanimous than I am. I magnify to myself all the dangers and all the evils that are possible under the circumstances. I am in a state of agitation that is really painful. But this does not prevent me from appearing quite composed to people around me ; *I am like a woman giving birth to a child.*" [2] Passionately, in the throes of the creator, he is thus absorbed with his coming creation ; he already anticipates and enjoys living in his imaginary edifice. " General," said Madame de Clermont-Tonnerre to him, one day, " you are building behind a scaffolding which you will take down when you have done with it." " Yes, madame, that's it," replied Bonaparte ; " you are right. I am always living two years in advance." [3] His response came with " incredible vivacity," as if a sudden inspiration, that of a soul stirred in its innermost fibre. Accordingly, on this side, the power, alertness, fecundity, play,

---

1 Madame de Rémusat, i., 117, 120. " I heard M. de Talleyrand exclaim one day, somewhat out of humor, ' This devil of a man misleads you in all directions. Even his passions escape you,for he finds some way to counterfeit them, although they really exist.' " Thus, just as he was about to confer with Lord Whitworth, and the violent scene took place which put an end to the treaty of Amiens, he was chatting and amusing himself with the women and the infant Napoleon, his nephew, in the gayest and most unconcerned manner : " He is suddenly told that the company had assembled. His countenance changes like that of an actor when the scene shifts. He seems to turn pale at will and his features contract "; he rises, steps up precipitately to the English ambassador, and fulminates for two hours before two hundred persons. (Hansard's Parliamentary History, vol. xxvi, despatches of Lord Whitworth, pp. 1798, 1302, 1310.)—" He often observes that the politician should calculate every advantage that could be gained by his defects." One day, after an explosion he says to Abbé de Pradt : " You thought me angry ! you are mistaken. Anger with me never mounts higher than here (pointing to his neck)."

2 Roederer, iii. (The first days of Brumaire, year VIII.)

3 Bourrienne, iii., 114.

and jet of his thought seem illimitable.   What he has accomplished is astonishing, but what he has undertaken is more so ; and whatever he may have undertaken is far surpassed by what he has imagined.   However vigorous his practical faculty, his poetical faculty is stronger ; it is even too vigorous for a statesman ; its grandeur is exaggerated into enormity, and its enormity degenerates into madness.   In Italy, after the 18th of Fructidor, he said to Bourrienne : "Europe is a molehill ; never have there been great empires and great revolutions, except in the Orient, with its 600,000,000 of men."[1]   The following year at St. Jean d'Acre, on the eve of the last assault, he added : " If I succeed I shall find in the town the pacha's treasure and arms for 300,000 men.   I stir up and arm all Syria. . . . I march on Damascus and Aleppo ; as I advance in the country my army will increase with the discontented.   I proclaim to the people the abolition of slavery, and of the tyrannical government of the pachas.   I reach Constantinople with armed masses.   I overthrow the Turkish Empire ; I found in the East a new and grand empire, which fixes my place with posterity, and perhaps I return to Paris by the way of Adrianople, or by Vienna, after having annihilated the house of Austria."[2]

Become consul, and then emperor, he often recurs to this happy period, when, " rid of the restraints of a troublesome civilization," he could imagine at will and construct at pleasure.[3]—" I created a religion ; I saw myself on the road to Asia, mounted on an elephant, with a turban on my head, and in my hand a new Koran, which I composed to suit myself."— Confined to Europe, he thinks, after 1804, that he will reorganize Charlemagne's empire.   " The French Empire will become the

<hr>

1 Bourrienne, ii., 228. (Conversation with Bourrienne in the park at Passeriano.)
2 *Ibid.*, ii., 331. (Written down by Bourrienne the same evening.)
3 Madame de Rémusat, i., 274.—De Ségur, ii., 459. (Napoleon's own words on the eve of the battle of Austerlitz): " Yes, if I had taken Acre, I would have assumed the turban, I would have put the army in loose breeches ; I would no longer have exposed it, except at the last extremity ; I would have made it my sacred battalion, my immortals. It is with Arabs, Greeks, and Armenians that I would have ended the war against the Turks. Instead of one battle in Moravia I would have gained a battle of Issus ; I would have made myself emperor of the East, and returned to Paris by the way of Constantinople."—De Pradt, p. 19 (Napoleon's own words at Mayence, September, 1804): " Since two hundred years there is nothing more to do in Europe ; it is only in the East that things can be carried out on a grand scale."

mother country of other sovereignties. . . . I mean that every king in Europe shall build a grand palace at Paris for his own use ; on the coronation of the Emperor of the French these kings will come and occupy it ; they will grace this imposing ceremony with their presence, and honor it with their salutations." [1]   The Pope will come ; he came to the first one ; he must necessarily return to Paris, and fix himself there permanently. Where could the Holy See be better off than in the new capital of Christianity, under Napoleon, heir to Charlemagne, and temporal sovereign of the Sovereign Pontiff ? Through the temporal the emperor will control the spiritual,[2] and through the Pope, consciences." In November, 1811, unusually excited, he says to De Pradt : " In five years I shall be master of the world ; only Russia will remain, but I will crush her.' . . . Paris will extend out to St. Cloud." To render Paris the physical capital of Europe is, through his own confession, " one of his constant dreams." "At times," he says,[4] " I would like to see her a city of two, three, four millions of inhabitants, something fabulous, colossal, unknown down to our day, and its public establishments adequate to its population. . . . Archimedes proposed to lift the world if he could be allowed to place his lever ; for myself, I would have changed it wherever I could have been allowed to exercise my energy, perseverance, and budgets." At all events, he believes so ; for however lofty and badly supported the next story of his structure may be, he has always ready a new story, loftier and

---

1 Madame de Rémusat, i., 407.—Miot de Melito, ii., 214 (a few weeks after his coronation): " There will be no repose in Europe until it is under one head, under an Emperor, whose officers would be kings, who would distribute kingdoms to his lieutenants, who would make one of them King of Italy, another King of Bavaria, here a *landmann* of Switzerland, and here a stadtholder of Holland, etc."

2 "Correspondance de Napoléon I.," vol. xxx., 550, 558. (Memoirs dictated by Napoleon at Saint Hélène.)—Miot de Melito, ii., 290.—D'Haussonville, "l'Église Romaine et le Premier Empire," *passim.*—" Mémorial. " " Paris would become the capital of the Christian world, and I would have governed the religious world as well as the political world."

3 De Pradt, 23.

4 "Mémoires et Mémorial." " It was essential that Paris should become the unique capital, not to be compared with other capitals. The masterpieces of science and of art, the museums, all that had illustrated past centuries, were to be collected there. Napoleon regretted that he could not transport St. Peter's to Paris ; the meanness of Notre Dame dissatisfied him."

more unsteady, to put above it.   A few months before launching himself, with all Europe at his back, against Russia, he
said to Narbonne : [1]   " After all, my dear sir, this long road is
the road to India.   Alexander started as far off as Moscow to
reach the Ganges ; this has occurred to me since St. Jean
d'Acre. . . . To reach England to-day I need the extremity
of Europe, from which to take Asia in the rear. . . . Suppose
Moscow taken, Russia subdued, the czar reconciled, or dead
through some court conspiracy, perhaps another and dependent
throne, and tell me whether it is not possible for a French
army, with its auxiliaries, setting out from Tiflis, to get as far
as the Ganges, where it needs only a thrust of the French
sword to bring down the whole of that grand commercial scaffolding throughout India.   It would be the most gigantic expedition, I admit, but practicable in the nineteenth century.
Through it France, at one stroke, would secure the independence of the West and the freedom of the seas."

While uttering this his eyes shone with strange brilliancy,
and he keeps on accumulating motive after motive, in calculating obstacles, means, and chances : the inspiration is under
full headway, and he gives himself up to it.   The master faculty finds itself suddenly free, and it takes flight ; the artist,[2]
sheathed in the political scabbard, has escaped from it ; he is
creating out of the ideal and the impossible.   We take him
for what he is, a posthumous brother of Dante and Michael

---

[1] Villemain, " Souvenir contemporaines," i., 175.   Napoleon's statement to M. de Narbonne early in March, 1812, and repeated by him to Villemain an hour afterwards.   The
wording is at second hand and merely a very good imitation, while the ideas are substantially
Napoleon's.   Cf. his reveries about Italy and the Mediterranean, equally exaggerated (" Correspondance," xxx., 548), and an admirable improvisation on Spain and the colonies at Bayonne.—De Pradt, " Mémoires sur les révolutions d'Espagne," p. 130: "Therefore Napoleon talked, or rather poetized ; he *Ossianized* for a long time, ... like a man full of a
sentiment which oppressed him, in an animated, picturesque style, and with the impetuosity,
imagery, and originality which were familiar to him, ... on the vast throne of Mexico and
Peru, on the greatness of the sovereigns who should possess them . . . . and on the results
which these great foundations would have on the universe.   I had often heard him, but
under no circumstances had I ever heard him develop such a wealth and compass of imagination.   Whether it was the richness of his subject, or whether his faculties had become
excited by the scene he conjured up, and all the chords of the instrument vibrated at
once, he was sublime."

[2] Roederer, iii., 541 (February 2, 1809): " I love power.   But I love it *as an artist.*
. . . . I love it *as a musician loves his violin,* for the tones, chords, and harmonies he can
get out of it."

Angelo ; in the clear outlines of his vision, in the intensity, coherency, and inward logic of his reverie, in the profundity of his meditations, in the superhuman grandeur of his conceptions, he is, indeed, their fellow and their equal. His genius is of the same stature and the same structure ; he is one of the three sovereign minds of the Italian Renaissance. Only, while the first two operated on paper and on marble, the latter operates on the living being, on the sensitive and suffering flesh of humanity.

BOOK FOURTH.

𝕮𝖍𝖊 𝕯𝖊𝖋𝖊𝖈𝖙 𝖆𝖓𝖉 𝕰𝖋𝖋𝖊𝖈𝖙𝖘 𝖔𝖋 𝖙𝖍𝖊 𝕾𝖞𝖘𝖙𝖊𝖒.

CHAPTER II.

I. Local society since 1830.—Introduction of a new internal motor.—
Subordinate to the external motor.—Advantageous under the system of
universal suffrage.—II. Application of universal suffrage to local society.—
Two assessments for the expenses of local society.—The fixed amount of
one should in equity be equal to the average sum of the other.—Practically,
the sum of one is kept too low.—How the new régime provides for local
expenditure.—The "additional centimes."—How the small taxpayer is
relieved in town and country.—His quota in local expenditure reduced to
the minimum.—His quota of local benefits remains intact.—Hence the large
or average taxpayer bears, beside his own burden, that of the relieved senate
taxpayer.—Number of those relieved.—The extra burden of the large and
average taxpayer is alms-giving.—The relief of the small taxpayer is a levy
of alms.—III. Possible compensation in the other side of the scale.—What
the distribution of rights should be according to the principle of distributive
justice.—In every association of stock-owners.—In local society confined to
its natural object.—In local society charged with supplementary functions.—
The local statute in England and Prussia.—The exchange equitable when
burdens are compensated by rights.—IV. How unlimited universal suffrage
found its way into local society.—Object and mode of the French legislator.—V. No distinction between the rural and the urban commune.—
Effects of the law on the rural commune.—Disproportion between the intelligence of its elected representatives and the work imposed on them.—The
mayor and the municipal council.—Lack of qualified members.—The secretary of the mayoralty.—The chief or under-chief of the prefectorial bureau.—
VI. Effects of the law on the urban commune —Disproportion between the
administrative capacity of its elected representatives and the work imposed
on them.—Lack of a special and permanent manager.—The municipal
council and the mayor.—The general council and the intermediary committee.—The prefect.—His dominant rule.—His obligatory concessions.—
His principal aim.—Bargains between the central authority and the local
Jacobins.—Effect of this on local government, on the officials, and in local
finances.—VII. Present state of local society.—Considered as an organism,
it is stillborn.—Considered as a mechanism, it gets out of order.—Two
successive and false conceptions of local government.—In theory, one
excludes the other.—Practically, their union ends in the actual system.—
Powers of the prefect.—Restrictions on these through subsequent changes.—
Give and take.—Bargaining.—Supported by the government and cost to the
State.—VIII. Final result in a tendency to bankruptcy.

I.

AFTER thirty years of silence, neither feeling nor thought
are any longer capable of uttering this vivifying and decisive
phrase : those who ought to be interested in local society as a
private association care but little for it, while the State does
not admit of it.   Indeed, after the year VIII, the State introduces into the machine a new mainspring.   After the revolution of 1830,[1] the municipal and general councilors become
elective and are appointed by a limited suffrage ; after the
revolution of 1848,[2] they are elected by universal suffrage.
After the revolution of 1870,[3] each municipal council elects its
own mayor, while the council-general, whose powers are enlarged, leaves in its place, during its vacations, a standing committee who arrange with, and govern along with, the prefect.
Here, in local society, is a superadded internal motor, working
from below, whilst the first one is external and works from
above ; henceforth, both are to work together and in accord.—
But, in reality, the second remains subordinate ; moreover, it
does not suit the machine and the machine does not suit it ;
it was not made for the machine, nor the machine for it ; it is
only a superfetation, an inconvenient and cumbersome intruder, nearly always useless, and often mischievous.   Its impulse
is feeble and of little effect ; too many brakes are attached to
it ; its force diminishes through the complexity of its numerous wheels ; it fails in giving action ; it cannot but little more
than impede or moderate other impulsions, those of the external motor, sometimes as it should, and sometimes the contrary.   Most frequently, even nowadays, it is of no efficiency

---

1 Laws of March 21, 1831, and July 18, 1837, June 22, 1833, and May 10, 1838. The
municipal electors number about 2,250,000 and form the superior third of the adult masculine population ; in the choice of its notables and semi-notables, the law takes into account not only wealth and direct taxation, but likewise education and services rendered to
the public.—The department electors number about 200,000, about as many as the political electors. The reporter observes that "an almost complete analogy exists between the
choice of a deputy and the choice of a department councilor, and that it is natural to confide the election to the same electoral body otherwise divided, since the object is to afford
representation to another order of interests."

2 Law of July 3, 1848.

3 Laws of Aug. 12, 1876, March 28, 1882, and April 5, 1884 ; law of Aug. 10, 1871.

whatever.   Three-quarters of the municipal councils, for three-fourths of their business, hold sessions only to give signatures. Their pretended deliberations are simply a parade formality ; the impulsion and direction continue to come from without, and from above ; under the third Republic, as under the Restoration and the first Empire, it is always the central State which governs the local society ; amid all the wranglings and disputes, in spite of passing conflicts it is, and remains, the initiator, proposer, leader, controller, accountant, and executor of every undertaking, the preponderating power in the department as well as in the commune, and with what deplorable results we all know.—There is still another and more serious result.   Nowadays, its interference is an advantage, for should it renounce its preponderance this would pass over to the other power which, since this has become vested in a numerical majority, is mere blind and brutal force ; abandoned to itself and without any counter-weight, its ascendency would be disastrous ; we would see reappearing along with the blunders of 1789, the outrages, usurpations, and distress of 1790, 1791, and 1792.[1]—In any event, there is this advantage in despotic centralization, that it still preserves us from democratic autonomy. In the present state of institutions and minds, the former system, objectionable as it may be, is our last retreat against the greater evil of the latter.

II.

In effect, direct universal suffrage, counted by heads, is in local society an incongruous element, a monstrous contrivance, to which it is adverse.   Constituted as this is, not by human arbitrament, but by physical conditions, its mechanism is determined beforehand ; it excludes certain wheels and connections ; the legislator must write out in the law what is written out by things, or, at least, translate this as closely as he can, without any gross contradiction.   Nature herself presents him with ready-made statutes.   His business is to read these prop-

---

[1] " The Revolution," vol. i., book viii.

erly ; he has already transcribed the apportionment of burdens ; he can now transcribe the apportionment of rights.

So we have seen, local society renders two distinct services,
which, that the expenses of both may be met, require two distinct assessments, one personal and the other real, one levied
on everybody and of which the amount is alike for all, and the
other levied only on those whose amount is based on what he
spends, on the importance of his business, and on the income
from his real property.—In strict equity, the amount of the
former should be equal to the average amount of the latter ;
in effect, as has been shown, the services defrayed by the former are as many, as diverse, and as precious, still more vital,
and not less costly than those of which the latter is the price.
Of the two interests which they represent, each, did it stand
alone, would be obliged to secure the same services, to take
upon itself the whole of the work ; neither would obtain more
in the dividend, and each would have to pay the whole of the
expense. Accordingly, each gains as much as the other in
the physical solidarity which binds them together. Hence, in
the legal bond which unites them they enter into it on an equal
footing, on condition that each is burdened or relieved as
much as the other, on condition that if the latter assumes one-
half of the expense the former shall assume the other half, on
condition that if the latter quota on each one hundred francs
expended against calamities and for public roads is fifty francs,
the former quota shall also be fifty francs.—Practically, however, this is impossible. Three times out of four the former
levy with this apportionment would not be returned ; through
prudence as well as humanity, the legislator is bound not to
overburden the poor. Recently, in organizing the general tax
and the revenue of the State, he has looked out for them ;
now, in organizing the local tax and the revenue of the department or of the commune, he looks out for them to a still
greater extent.

In the new financial scheme, so many centimes, added to
each franc of direct tax, form the principal resource of the
department and commune, and it is through this extra charge
that each taxpayer pays his quota of local expenditure. Now,

there is no surcharge on the personal tax, no additional centimes.   Under this heading, the laborer without any property
or income, the workman who lives in lodgings, on his wages,
and from day to day, contributes nothing to the expenses of
his commune or department.   In vain do "additional centimes" pour down on other branches of direct taxation ; they
are not grafted on this one, and do not suck away the substance of the poor.[1]—There is the same regard for the half
poor, in relation to the artisan who furnishes his own room,
but who lodges in an upper story, and in relation to the
peasant whose hovel or cottage has but one door and one window.[2]   Their rate of taxation on doors and windows is very
low, purposely reduced, kept below one franc a year, while the
rate of their personal tax is scarcely higher.   "Additional
centimes" may be imposed on so small a principal and be
multiplied in vain, never will they reach more than an insignificant sum.—Not only are the indigent relieved of both
principal and "additional centimes," the verified indigent,
those who are registered and are helped, or should be, that is
to say 2,470,000 persons ;[3] but, again, others, by hundreds of
thousands, whom the municipal council judges incapable of
paying.—Even when people possess but a small piece of land,
they are also relieved of the land tax and of the numerous additional centimes which increase it.   Such is the case with those
who are infirm or burdened with a family.   The exchequer,
so as not to convert them into beggars and vagabonds, avoids
expropriation, selling out their concrete hovel, vegetable gar-

---

1 Paul Leroy-Beaulieu, "Traité de la science des finances," 4th edition, i., p. 303:
"The personal tax, levied only as principal, oscillates between the minimum of 1 fr. 50
and the maximum of 4 fr. 50 per annum, according to the communes.—*Ibid.*, 304: " In
1806 the personal tax produced in France about sixteen millions of francs, a little less than
0 fr. 50 per head of the inhabitants."

2 *Ibid.*, i., 367 (on the tax on doors and windows).   According to the population of the
commune, this is from 0 fr. 30 to 1 fr. for each opening, from 0 fr. 45 to 1 fr. 50 for two
openings, from 0 fr. 90 to 4 fr. 50 for three openings, from 1 fr. 60 to 6 fr. 40 for four
openings, and from 2 fr. 50 to 8 fr. 50 for five openings.   The first of these rates is applied
to all communes of less than 5000 souls.   We see that the poor man, especially the poor
peasant, is considered ; the tax on him is progressive in an inverse sense.

3 De Foville, "La France Economique" (1887), p. 59: "Our 14,500 charity bureaux
gave assistance in 1883 to 1,405,500 persons ; . . . . as, in reality, the population of the
communes aided (by them) is only 22,000,000, the proportion of the registered poor
amounts to over six per cent."

den, and small field of potatoes or cabbages; it gives them
receipts gratis, or, at least, refrains from prosecuting them.[1]
In this way the poor peasant, although a land-owner, again
exempts himself, or is exempted from his local indebtedness.
In truth, he pays nothing, or nearly nothing, otherwise than
by *prestations* in money or in kind ; that is to say, by three days'
work on the district roads, which, if he pays in kind, are not
worth more than fifty sous.[2] Add to this his portion, very
small and often null, of the additional centimes on the tax on
doors and windows, on the personal tax, and on the tax on real
estate, in all four or five francs a year. Such is the amount
by which the poor or half-poor taxpayer in the villages libe-
rates himself toward his department and commune.—In the
towns, he apparently pays more, owing to the *octroi*. But, at
first, there are only one thousand five hundred and twenty-
five communes out of thirty-six thousand in which the
octroi[3] has been established ; while in the beginning, under
the Directory and Consulate, it was revived only on his
account, for his benefit, in behalf of public charity, to defray
the expenses of asylums and hospitals ruined by revolutionary
confiscation. It was then " an octroi for charity," in fact as
well as in name, like the surplus tax on theater seats and
tickets, established at the same time and for the same purpose ; it still to-day preserves the stamp of its first institution.
Bread, the indispensable provision for the poor, is not subjected
to the *octroi*, nor the materials for making it, either grain or
flour, nor milk, fruits, vegetables, or codfish, while there is
only a light tax on butcher's meat. Even on beverages, where
the *octroi* is heavier, it remains, like all indirect taxes, nearly
proportional and semi-optional. In effect, it is simply an increase of the tax on beverages, so many additional centimes
per franc on the sum of indirect taxation, as warrantable as

---

1 Paul Leroy-Beaulieu, " Essai sur la répartition des richesses," p. 174, *et seq.*—In 1851,
the number of land-owners in France was estimated at 7,800,000. Out of these, three
millions were relieved of the land tax, as indigent, and their quotas were considered as
irrecoverable.

2 Paul Leroy-Beaulieu, " Traité de la science des finances," p. 721.

3 De Foville, p. 419. (In 1889.)

the impost itself, as tolerable, and for the same motives.[1] For
the greater the sobriety of the taxpayer, the less is he affected
by this tax. At Paris, where the increase is excessive, and
adds to the six centimes paid to the state, on each quart of
wine, twelve centimes paid to the city ; if he drinks but one
quart a day, he pays, under this heading, into the city treasury
forty-three francs eighty centimes per annum ; but, as compensation for this, he is free of personal tax, of the eleven and
three-quarters per centum which this adds to the amount of
each rental, of the eleven and three-quarters per centum
whereby this would have added to his rent, and therefore
forty-seven francs per annum on a rent of four hundred francs.
Thus what he has paid with one hand he gets back with the
other. Now, at Paris, all rentals under four hundred francs [2]
are thus free of any personal tax ; all rentals between four
hundred and one thousand francs are more or less free, and,
in the other *octroi* towns, an analogous discharge reimburses
to the small taxpayers a portion more or less great of the sum
they pay to the *octroi.*—Accordingly, in the towns as in the
country, they are favored at one time through fiscal relief and
at another through administrative favor, now through compulsory deduction and now through total or partial reimbursement. Always, and very wisely, the legislator apportions the
burden according to the strength of the shoulders ; he relieves
them as much as he can, at first, of the general tax, and next,
which is still better, of the local tax. Hence, in local expenditure, their quota diminishes out of all proportion and is
reduced to the minimum. Nevertheless, their quota of local
benefit remains full and entire ; at this insignificant price
they enjoy the public highways and profit by all the precautions taken against physical ills ; each profits by this personally, equally with any millionaire. Each personally receives
as much in the great dividend of security, health, and convenience, in the fruit of the vast works of utility and enjoyment due to improved communications, which preserve health,

---

[1] Cf. *ante*, on the characteristics of indirect taxation.
[2] Here it is the estimated rent, which stands to the real rent as four to five ; an esti-
nated rent of 400 francs indicates a real rent of 500 francs.

promote intercourse, and beautify the locality, and without
which, in town as well as in the country, life would be impossible or intolerable.

But these works which cost so much, these defensive operations and apparatus against inundations, fires, epidemics, and
contagions, these 500,000 kilometres of district and department
roads, these dikes, quays, bridges, public gardens, and promenades, this paving, drainage, sweeping and lighting, these
aqueducts and supplies of drinkable water, all this is paid for
by somebody, and, since it is not done by the small taxpayer,
it is the large or average taxpayer who pays for it. The
latter then, bears, besides his obligatory weight, a gratuitous
surplus burden, consisting of the weight of which the other is
relieved.

Evidently the greater the number of the relieved, the heavier
will be this overweight, and the relieved count by millions.
Two millions and a half of declared poor[1] are relieved of any
direct tax, and, therefore, of all the centimes which have just
increased the burden. Out of eight millions of real estate
owners,[2] three millions, considered as insolvent, pay neither
the real estate tax nor the centimes which it comprises. In
the *octroi* towns, it is not the minority but the majority of the
inhabitants who are relieved in the way just described ; in
Paris,[3] out of 685,000 rentals, 625,000, in other terms twelve
out of thirteen lodgings, are exempt, wholly or in part, from
the personal tax, the principal and " additional centimes." On

---

1 De Foville, p. 57.

2 Paul Leroy-Beaulieu, " Essai sur la répartition de richesses," p. 174.

3 *Ibid.*, p. 209: In 1878, in Paris, 74,000 houses with 1,022,539 rentals, 337,587 being for
trade and commerce, and 684,952 for dwelling purp ses. Among the latter, 468,641 have a
locative value interior to 300 francs a year ; 74,360 are between 500 and 750 francs ; 21,147
are between 750 and 1000 francs. All these lodgings are more or less exempt from the personal tax : those between 1000 and 400 francs pay it wit'ı a more or less great reduction :
those under 400 francs pay nothing. Above 1000 francs, we find 17,202 apartments from
between 1000 and 1250 francs ; 6198 from between 1250 and 1500 francs ; 21,453 from 1500 to
3000 francs. These apartments are occupied by more or less well-to-do people.—14,858
apartments above 3000 francs are occupied by the richer or the wealthy class. Among the
latter 9985 are from 3000 to 6000 ; 3040 are from 6000 to 10,000 ; 1443 are from 10.000 to
20,000 ; 421 are under 20,000 francs. These two latter categories are occupied by the really
opulent class.—According to the latest statistics, instead of 684,952 dwelling rentals there
are 806,187, of which 727,419 are wholly or partly free of the personal tax. (" Situation au
1ère Janvier, 1888," report by M. Lamouroux, conseiller-municipal.)

each franc of this principal there are ninety-six of these super-added centimes for the benefit of the town and department ; and because the department and the town expend a good deal, and because receipts are essential for the settlement of these accounts, this or that sum is noted beforehand in every chapter of receipts, and the main thing now is to have this paid in, and it must be paid by somebody ; it matters little whether the peasants are few or numerous ; if among thirteen taxable persons there is only one that pays, so much the worse for him, for he must pay for himself and the other twelve.   Such is the case in Paris, which accounts for the "additional centimes" here being so numerous,[1] owing to there being less than 60,000 rentals for the acquittance of the entire tax, and, besides paying their own debt, they must discharge the indebtedness of six hundred and twenty-five thousand other rentals, the tax on which is reduced or null.—Frequently, before the Revolution, some rich convent or philanthropic seignior would pay the taxes of his poor neighbors out of his own pocket; willingly or not, sixty thousand Parisians, more or less well lodged, now hand over the same sum, bestow the same charity, on six hundred and twenty-five thousand badly or only tolerably lodged Parisians ; among these sixty thousand benefactors whom the exchequer obliges to be benevolent, thirty-four thousand eight hundred who pay from one thousand to three thousand francs rent, bestow, under this heading, a pretty large sum for charitable purposes, while fourteen thousand eight hundred, who pay more than three thousand francs rent, pay a very large one.   Other branches of direct taxation, in the country as well as in the city, present the same spectacle : it is always the rich or the well-to-do taxpayers who, through their over-tax, more or less completely relieve the poor or straitened taxpayers ; it is always the owners of large or small properties, those who pay heavy or average licenses,

---

[1] The following appropriations for 1889 are printed on my tax-bill : " To the State, 51 per cent.; to the Department, 21 per cent.; to the Commune, 25 per cent."   On business permits : " To the State, 64 per cent.; to the Department, 12 per cent.; to the Commune, 20 per cent.   The surplus of taxes is appropriated to the benevolent fund and for remission of taxes,"

the occupants of lodgings with more than five openings,[1] and whose locative value surpasses 1000 francs, who in local expenditure pay besides their own dues the dues of others and, through their additional centimes, almost entirely defray the expenses of the department and commune.—This is nearly always the case in a local society, except when it chances to possess an abundant income, arising from productive real estate, and is able to provide for its wants without taxing its members ; apart from this rare exception, it is forced to tax some in order to relieve others. In other words, the same as with other enterprises, it manufactures and sells its product ; but, just the reverse of other enterprises, it sells the product, an equal quantity of the same product, that is to say, equal protection against the same calamities, and the equal enjoyment of the same public highway, at unequal prices, very dear to a few, moderately dear to many, at cost price to a large number, and with a discount to the mass ; to this last class of consumers the discount goes on increasing like the emptiness of their purse ; to the last of all, extremely numerous, the goods are delivered almost gratis, or even for nothing.

But to this inequality of prices may correspond the inequality of rights, and compensation will come, the balance may be restored, distributive justice may be applied, if, in the government of the enterprise, the parts assigned are not equal, if each member sees his portion of influence growing or diminishing along with the weight of his charge, if the statute, graduating authority according to the scale of the levies, assigns few votes to those who pay the lowest quotas of expense and receive alms, and many votes to those who give alms and pay the largest quotas of the expenditure.

---

1 Paul Leroy-Beaulieu, " Traité de la science des finances," i., pp. 367-368 : " In communes under 5000 inhabitants the principal of the tax on doors and windows is, for houses with one opening, o fr. 30 per annum ; for those with four openings, 1 fr. 60." Now, " a house with five openings pays nearly nine times as much as a house with one opening." The small taxpayers are accordingly largely relieved at the expense of those who pay heavy and average taxes, the magnitude of this relief being appreciable by the following figures : In 1885, out of 8,975,166 houses, 248,352 had one opening, 1,827,104 two openings, 1,624,516 three openings, and 1,165,902 four openings.   More than one-half of the houses, all of those belonging to the poor or straitened, are thus relieved, while the other half, since the tax is an impost, not one aliquot part, but an apportionment, is overcharged as much.

III.

Such is the rule in every association of interests, even in stock companies in which the distribution of charges allows of no favor or disfavor to any associate. It must be noted that, in these companies, co-operation is not compulsory, but voluntary ; the associates are not, as in the local society, conscripts enlisted under the constraint of physical solidarity, but subscribers bound together under the impulsion of a deliberate preference, each remaining in it of his own free will just as he entered it ; if he wishes to leave it he has only to sell his stock ; the fact of his keeping this confirms his subscription, and, thus holding on to it, he daily subscribes anew to the statute. Here, then, is a perfectly free association ; it is accordingly perfectly equitable, and its statute serves as a model for others.

Now this statute always makes a distinction between the small and the large stockholders ; it always attributes a greater share of authority and influence to those who share most largely in the risks and expenses ; in principle, the number of votes it confers on each associate is proportionate to the number of shares of which he is the owner or bearer.—All the stronger is the reason why this principle should be embodied in the statutes of a society which, like the local community, diminishes the burden of the small taxpayer through its reductions, and increases by its extra taxation the burden of the large or average taxpayer ; when the appointment of managers is handed over to universal suffrage, counted by heads, the large and average taxpayers are defrauded of their dues and deprived of their rights, more so by far and more deeply wronged than the bearer or owner of a thousand shares in an omnibus or gas company if, on voting at a meeting of stockholders, his vote did not count for more than that of the owner or bearer of a single share.—How is it then when a local society adds to its natural and unavoidable purpose an optional and supplementary purpose ; when, increasing its load, it undertakes to defray the cost of public charity and of primary education ; when, to support this additional cost, it

multiplies the additional centimes ; when the large or average
taxpayer pays alone, or nearly alone, for this benevolent work
by which he does not benefit ; when the small taxpayer pays
nothing, or next to nothing, to this benevolent work by which
he does benefit ; when, in voting for the expense thus apportioned, each taxpayer, whatever the amount of his contribution,
has one vote and only one ? In this case, powers, benefits,
reductions, and exemptions, all the advantages are on one side,
that of the poor and half-poor forming the majority and who,
if not restrained from above, will persistently abuse their
numerical force to augment their advantages, at the increasing
expense of the rich or well-to-do minority. Thenceforth, in
the local society, the average or large taxpayer is no longer
an associate but a victim ; were he free to choose he would not
enter into it ; he would like to leave it and establish himself
elsewhere ; but were he to enter others, near or remote,
his condition would be no better. He remains, accordingly,
where he is, physically present, but absent in feeling ; he takes
no part in deliberative meetings ; his zeal has died out ; he
withholds from public affairs that surplus of vigilant attention,
that spontaneous and ready collaboration which he would have
contributed gratis ; he lets matters go along without him, just
as it happens ; he remains there just what he is, a workable,
taxable individual in capricious hands, in short, a passive subject who gives up and has become resigned.—For this reason,
in countries where an encroaching democracy has not yet
abolished or perverted the notion of equity, the local statute
applies the fundamental rule of an equitable exchange ; it lays
down the principle that *he who pays commands, and in proportion to the sum he pays.*[1] In England, a surplus of votes is

1 One result of this principle is, that the indigent who are exempt from taxation or who
are on the poor list have no vote, which is the case in England and in Prussia.—Though
another result of the same principle, the law of May 15, 1818, in France, summoned the
heaviest taxpayers, in equal number with the members of the municipal council, to deliberate
with it every time that "a really urgent expenditure" obliged the commune to raise extra
additional centimes beyond the usual o fr. 05. "Thus," says Henrion de Pancey ("Du
pouvoir municipal," p. 109), "the members of the municipal councils belonging to the
class of small land-owners, at least in a large number of communes, voted the charges
without examination which only affected them insensibly."—This last refuge of distributive justice was abolished by the law of April 5, 1882.

awarded to those most heavily taxed, even six votes to one voter ; in Prussia, local taxation is divided into thirds, and, accordingly, the taxpayers into three groups, the first one composed of heavy taxpayers, few in number, and who pay the first third, the second composed of average taxpayers, average in number, and who pay the second third, and the third composed of the great number of small taxpayers, who pay the last third.[1] To each of these groups is assigned the same number of suffrages in the commune election, or the same number of representatives in the commune representation. Though this approximative balance of legal burdens and of legal rights, the two sides of the scales are nearly at their level, the level which distributive justice demands, and the level which the state, special interpreter, sole arbiter and universal minister of distributive justice, should establish when, in the local community, it imposes, rectifies, or maintains the statute according to which it derives its income and governs.

IV.

If the state, in France, does just the contrary, it is at the height of a violent and sudden revolution, under the dictation of the master faction and of popular prejudice, logically, and through contagion. According to revolutionary and French usage, the legislator was bound to institute uniformity and to make things symmetrical ; having placed universal suffrage in political society, he was likewise determined to place it in local society. He had been ordered to apply an abstract principle, that is to say, to legislate according to a summary, superficial, and verbal notion which, purposely curtailed and simplified to excess, did not correspond with its object. He obeyed and did nothing more ; he made no effort outside of his instructions. He did not propose to himself to restore local society to its members, to revive it, to make it a living body, capable

---

1 Max Leclerc, "La Vie municipale en Prusse." (Extrait des "Annales de l'Ecole libre des sciences politique," 1889, a study on the town of Bonn.) At Bonn, which has a population of 35,810 inhabitants, the first group is composed of 167 electors : the second, of 471 ; the third, of 2607, and each group elects 8 municipal councilors out of 24.

of spontaneous, co-ordinate, voluntary action, and, to this end, provided with indispensable organs ; he did not even take the trouble to figure it to himself mentally, as it is effectively, I mean by this, complex and diverse ; inversely to his predecessors in France before 1789, and adversely to legislators before and after 1789 outside of France, against all the teachings of experience, against the evidence of nature, he refused to recognize the fact that, in France, mankind are of two species, the people of the towns and the people of the country, and that, therefore, there are two types of local society, the urban commune and the rural commune ; he was not disposed to take this capital difference into consideration ; he issued decrees for the Frenchman in general, for the citizen in himself, for fictive men, so reduced that the statute which suits them can nowhere suit the actual and complete man.   At one stroke, the legislative shears cut out of the same stuff, according to the same pattern, thirty-six thousand examples of the same coat, one coat indifferently for every commune, whatever its shape, a coat too small for the city and too large for the village, disproportionate in both cases, and useless beforehand, because it could not fit very large bodies, nor very small ones.   Nevertheless, once dispatched from Paris, people had to put the coat on and wear it ; it must answer for good or for ill, each donning his own for lack of another better adjusted ; hence the strangest attitudes for each, and, in the long run, a combination of consequences which neither governors nor the governed had foreseen.

V.

Let us consider these results in turn in the small and in the great communes ; clear enough and distinct at the two extremities of the scale, they blend into each at intermediate degrees, because here they combine together, but in different proportions, according as the commune, higher or lower in the scale, comes nearer to the village or to the city.—On this territory, too, subdivided since 1789, and, so to say, crumbled to pieces by the Constituent Assembly, the small communes are enormous in number ; among thirty-six thousand, more

than twenty-seven thousand have less than one thousand
inhabitants, and of these, more than sixteen thousand have
less than five hundred inhabitants.[1]   Whoever has traveled
over France, or lived in this country, sees at once what
sort of men compose such purely rustic groups ; he has
only to recall physiognomies and attitudes to know to what
extent in these rude brains, rendered torpid by the routine of manual labor and oppressed by the cares of daily
life, how narrow and obstructed are the inlets to the mind ;
how limited is their information in the way of facts; how, in
the way of ideas, the acquisition of them is slow ; what hereditary distrust separates the illiterate mass from the lettered
class ; what an almost insurmountable wall the difference of
education, of habits, and of manners interposes in France
between the blouse and the dress-coat ; why, if each commune
contains a few cultivated individuals and a few notable proprietors, universal suffrage sets them aside, or at least does
not seek them out for the municipal council or the mayoralty.—
Before 1830, when the prefect appointed the municipal councilors and the mayor, these were always on hand ; under the
monarchy of July and a limited suffrage, they were still on
hand, at least for the most part; under the second Empire,
whatever the elected municipal council might be, the mayor,
who was appointed by the prefect, and even outside of this
council, might be one of the least ignorant and least stupid
even in the commune.   At the present day, it is only accidentally and by chance that a noble or bourgeois, in a few
provinces and in certain communes, can become mayor or
municipal councilor ; and yet more is it essential that he
should be born on the soil, long established there, resident
and popular.   Everywhere else the numerical majority, being
sovereign, tends to selecting its candidates from among its

---

1 De Foville, " La France économique," p. 16 (Census of 1881).—Number of communes,
36,097 ; number below 1000 inhabitants, 27,503 ; number below 500 inhabitants, 16,870.—
What is stated applies partly to the two following categories : 1st, communes from 1000 to
1500 inhabitants, 2982 ; 2d, communes from 1500 to 2000 inhabitants, 1917.—All the communes below 2000 inhabitants are counted as *rural* in the statistics of population, and they
number 33,402.

own set ; in the village, he is a man of average rural intelligence, and, more frequently, the village municipal councilor,
as narrow-minded as his electors, elects a mayor equally as
narrow-minded as himself.   Such are, henceforth, the representatives and directors of communal interests ; except when they
themselves are affected by personal interests in which they
are sensitive, their inertia is only equaled by their incapacity.[1]

Four times a year a bundle of elaborately drawn papers,
prepared in the prefecture bureaux, are submitted to these
paralytics, born blind, large sheets divided into columns from
top to bottom, with tabular headings from right to left, and
covered with printed texts and figures in writing—details of
receipts and expenses, general centimes, special centimes, obligatory centimes, optional centimes, ordinary centimes, extra
centimes, with their sources and employment ; preliminary
budget, final budget, corrected budget, along with legal references, regulations, and decisions bearing on each article ; in
short, a methodical table as specific as possible and highly instructive to a legist or accountant, but perfect jargon to peasants,
most of whom can scarcely write their name and who, on Sundays, are seen standing before the advertisement board [2] trying
to spell out the *Journal Officiel*, whose abstract phrases, beyond their reach, pass over their heads in aerial and transient
flight, like some confused rustling of vague and unknown
forms.   To guide them in political life, much more difficult
than in private life, they require a similar guide to the one
they take in the difficult matters of their individual life, a

---

1 See Paul Leroy-Beaulieu, "L'État moderne et ses fonctions," p. 169.   "The various
groups of inhabitants, especially in the country, do not know how to undertake or agree
upon anything of themselves.   I have seen villages of two or three hundred people belonging to a large scattered commune wait patiently for years and humbly petition for aid in
constructing an indispensable fountain, which required only a contribution of 200 or 300
francs, 5 francs per head, to put up.   I have seen others possessing only one road on which
to send off their produce and unable to act in concert, when, with an outlay of 2000 francs,
and 200 or 300 francs a year to keep it in order, it would easily suffice for all their require-
ments.   I speak of regions relatively rich, much better off than the generality of communes
in France."

2 In French villages, on one of the walls of a public building on the square are notices of all
kinds, of interest to the inhabitants, and among these, in a frame behind a wire netting, the
latest copy of the government official newspaper, giving authentic political items, those
which it thinks best for the people to read.   (Tr.)

legal or business adviser, one that is qualified and competent, able to understand the prefecture documents, sitting alongside of them to explain their budget, rights and limits of their rights, the financial resources, legal expedients, and consequences of a law ; one who can arrange their debates, make up their accounts, watch daily files of bills, attend to their business at the county town, throughout the entire series of legal formalities and attendance on the bureaux,—in short, some trusty person, familiar with technicalities, whom they might choose to select.—Such a person was found in Savoy, before the annexation to France, a notary or lawyer who, practicing in the neighborhood or at the principal town, and with five or six communes for clients, visited them in turn, helped them with his knowledge and intelligence, attended their meetings and, besides, served them as scribe, like the present secretary of the mayoralty, for about the same pay, amounting in all to about the same total of fees or salaries.[1]— At the present time, there is nobody in the municipal council to advise and give information to its members; the schoolmaster is their secretary, and he cannot be, and should not be, other than a scribe. He reads in a monotonous tone of voice the long financial enigma which French public book-keeping, too perfect, offers to their divinations, and which nobody, save one who is educated to it, can clearly comprehend until after weeks of study. They listen all agog. Some, adjusting their spectacles, try to pick out among so many articles the one they want, the amount of taxes they have to pay. The sum is too large, the assessments are excessive ; it is important that the number of additional centimes should be reduced, and

---

[1] On the communal system in France, and on the reforms which, following the example of other nations, might be introduced into it, cf. Joseph Ferrand (formerly a prefect), " Les Institutions administratives en France et à l'étranger "; Rudolph Gneist, " Les Réformes administratives en Prusse accomplies par la législation de 1872," (especially the institution of *Amts-vorsteher*, for the union of communes or circumscriptions of about 1500 souls) ; the Duc de Broglie, " Vues sur le gouvernement de la France " (especially on the reforms that should be made in the administration of the commune and canton), p. 21.—" Deprive communal magistrates of their quality as government agents ; separate the two orders of functions ; have the public functionary whose duty it is to see that the laws are executed in the communes, the execution of general laws and the decisions of the superior authority carried out, placed at the county town."

therefore that less money should be expended. Hence, if there is any special item of expense which can be got rid of by a refusal, they set it aside by voting No, until some new law or decree from above obliges them to say Yes. But, as things go, nearly all the expenses designated on the paper are obligatory; willingly or not, these must be met, and there is no way to pay them outside of the additional centimes; however numerous these are, vote them they must and sanction the centimes inscribed. They accordingly affix their signatures, not with trust but with mistrust, with resignation, and out of pure necessity. Abandoned to their natural ignorance, the twenty-seven thousand petty municipal councilors of the country are now more passive, more inert, more constrained than ever; deprived of the light which, formerly, the choice of the prefect or a restricted suffrage could still throw into the darkness around them, there remains to them only one safe tutor or conductor; and this final guide is the official staff of the bureaux, especially this or that old, permanent chief, or under clerk, who is perfectly familiar with his files of papers. With about four hundred municipal councilors to lead, one may imagine what he will do with them—nothing except to drive them like a flock of sheep into a pen of printed regulations, or urge them on mechanically, in lots, according to his instructions, he himself being as automatic and as much in a rut as they are.

VI.

Let us now look at the other side of the scale, on the side of the large urban communes, of which there are two hundred and twenty-three, with above ten thousand inhabitants, ninety of these above twenty thousand inhabitants, nine of the latter above one hundred thousand inhabitants, and Paris, which has two million three hundred thousand.[1] We see at the first glance bestowed on an average specimen of these human ant-hills, a town containing from forty to fifty thousand souls, how

1 De Foville, *ibid.*, p. 16.—The remarks here made apply to towns of the foregoing category (from 5000 to 10,000 souls), numbering 312. A last category comprises towns from 2000 to 5000 souls, numbering 2160, and forming the last class of urban populations; these, through their mixed character, assimilate to the 1817 communes containing from 1500 to 2000 inhabitants, forming the first category of the *rural* populations.

vast and complex the collective undertaking becomes, how many
principal and accessory services the communal society must
co-ordinate and unite together in order to secure to its members the advantages of public roads and insure their protection
against spreading calamities,—the maintenance and repairs
of these roads, the straightening, laying-out, paving, and drainage, the constructions and expense for sewers, quays, and
rivers, and often for a commercial harbor ; the negotiations
and arrangements with departments and with the state for
this or that harbor, canal, dyke, or insane asylum ; the contracts with cab, omnibus, and tramway companies and with
telephone and house-lighting companies ; the street-lighting,
artesian wells and aqueducts ; the city police, superintendence
and rules for using public highways, and orders and agents for
preventing men from injuring each other when collected together in large assemblies in the streets, in the markets, at the
theater, in any public place, whether coffee-houses or taverns ;
the firemen and machinery for conflagrations ; the sanitary
measures against contagions, and precautions, long beforehand,
to insure salubrity during epidemics ; and, as extra burdens
and abuses, the establishment, direction and support of primary schools, colleges, public lectures, libraries, theaters, hospitals, and other institutions which should be supported and
governed by different associations ; at the very least, the appropriations to these establishments and therefore a more or
less legitimate and more or less imperative intervention in
their internal management—such are the great undertakings
which form a whole, which bear alike on the present, past, and
future budget of the commune, and which, as so many distinct
branches of every considerable enterprise, require, for proper
execution, to have their continuity and connection always
present in the thoughtful and directing mind which has them
in charge.[1] Experience shows that, in the great industrial or

---

1 Max Leclerc, " La Vie municipale en Prusse," p. 17.—In Prussia, this directing mind
is called " the magistrate," as in our northern and northeastern communes. In eastern
Prussia, the " magistrate " is a collective body ; for example, at Berlin, it comprises 34
persons, of which 17 are specialists, paid and engaged for twelve years, and 17 without pay.
In western Prussia, the municipal management consists generally of an individual, the
burgomaster, salaried and engaged for twelve years.

financial companies, in the Bank of France, in the Crédit Lyonnais, and in the Société Générale, at Creusot, at Saint Go-
bin, in the insurance, navigation, and railroad companies,
the best way to accomplish this end is a permanent manager
or director, always present, engaged or accepted by the administrative board on understood conditions, a special, tried man
who, sure of his place for a long period, and with a reputation
to maintain, gives his whole time, faculties, and zeal to the
work, and who, alone, possessing at every moment a coherent
and detailed conception of the entire undertaking, can alone
give it the proper stimulus, and bring to bear the most eco-
nomical and the most perfect practical improvements.   Such is
also the municipal régime in the Prussian towns on the Rhine.
Then, in Bonn, for instance,[1] the municipal council, elected by
the inhabitants " goes in quest " of some eminent specialist
whose ability is well known.   It must be noted that he is taken
wherever he can be found, outside the city, in some remote
province ; they bargain with him, the same as with some famous
musician, for the management of a series of concerts ; under
the title of burgomaster, with a salary of ten thousand francs
per annum, he becomes for twelve years the director of all
municipal services, leader of the civic orchestra, solely in-
trusted with executive power, wielding the magisterial baton
which the various instruments obey, many of these being salaried functionaries and others benevolent amateurs,[2] all in harmony and through him, because they know that he is watch-

---

1 Max Leclerc, *ibid.*, p. 20.—"The present burgomaster in Bonn was burgomaster at
Münchens-Stadbach, before being called to Bonn.   The present burgomaster of Crefeld
came from Silesia. . . . . A jurist, well known for his works on public law, occupying a government position at Magdeburg," was recently called " to the lucrative position of burgomaster " in the town of Munster.   At Bonn, a town of 30,000 inhabitants, " everything
rests on his shoulders ; he exercises a great many of the functions which, with us, belong
to the prefect."

2 Max Leclerc, *ibid.*, p. 25.—Alongside of the paid town officers and the municipal councilors, there are special committees composed of benevolent members and electors " either
to administer or superintend some branch of communal business, or to study some particular question."   " These committees, subject, moreover, in all respects to the burgomaster,
are elected by the municipal council."—There are twelve of these in Bonn and over a
hundred in Berlin.   This institution serves admirably for rendering those who are well-
disposed useful, as well as for the development of local patriotism, a practical sense and
public spirit.

ful, competent, and superior, constantly occupied with the general combination, responsible, and for his own interest, as a point of honor, wholly devoted to his work which is likewise their work, that is to say, to the complete success of the concert.

Nothing in a French town corresponds to this admirable type of a municipal institution; here, also, and to a much greater extent than in the village, the effect of universal suffrage has been to discredit the true notables and to insure the abdication or exclusion of men who, by their education, the large proportion of the taxes they pay, and still greater influence or production on labor and on business, are social authorities, and who should become legal authorities; in every country where conditions are unequal, the preponderance of a numerical majority necessarily ends in the nearly general abstention or almost certain defeat of the candidates most deserving of election. But here the case is different; the elected, being towns-people (*citadins*) and not rustics, are not of the same species as in the village. They read a daily newspaper, and believe that they understand not only local matters but all subjects of national and general importance, that is to say, the highest formulæ of political economy, of philosophic history, and of public right; somewhat resembling the schoolmaster who, being familiar with the rules of arithmetic, thinks that he can teach the differential calculus, and the theory of functions. At any rate, they talk loud and argue on every subject with confidence, according to Jacobin traditions, being, indeed, so many fresh Jacobins, the heirs and continuators of the old sectarians, issuing from the same stock and of the same stamp, a few in good faith, but mainly narrow-minded, excited, and bewildered by the smoke of the glittering generalities they utter, most of them mere politicians, charlatans, and intriguers, third-class lawyers and doctors, literary failures, semi-educated stump-speakers, bar-room, club, or clique orators, and of low ambition, who, left behind in private careers, in which one is closely watched and accepted for what he is worth, launch out on a public career because, in these lists, popular suffrage at once ignorant, indifferent, and badly informed, a prejudiced and passionate judge, a moralist of easy conscience, instead of demanding unsullied integrity and proven competency, asks for nothing from candidates but oratorical "buncombe," self-pushing and self-display in public, gross flattery, a parade of zeal and promises to place the power about to be conferred on them by the people in the hands of those who will serve its antipathies and prejudices. Thus introduced into the municipal council, they constitute its majority and appoint a mayor who is their coryphæus or creature, now the bold leader and again the docile instrument of their spite, their favors, and their headlong action, of their blunders and presumption, and of their meddlesome disposition and encroachments.—In the department, the council general, also elected by universal suffrage, also savors of its origin ; its quality, without falling so low, still descends in a certain degree, and through changes which keep on increasing : politicians install themselves there and make use of their place as a stepping-stone to mount higher ; it also, with larger powers and prolonged during its vacations by its committee, is tempted to regard itself as the legitimate sovereign of the extensive and scattered community which it represents.—Thus recruited and composed, enlarged and deteriorated, the local authorities become difficult to manage, and henceforth, to carry on the administration, the prefect must come to some understanding with them.

VII.

Before 1870, when he appointed the mayors and when the council general held its sessions only fifteen days in the year, this prefect was almost omnipotent ; still, at the present day, "his powers are immense,"[1] and his power remains preponderant. He has the right to suspend the municipal council and the mayor, and to propose their dismissal to the head of the state. Without resorting to this extremity, he holds them with a strong hand, and always uplifted over the commune, for he can veto the acts of the municipal police and of the road

---

1 AUCOC, p. 283.

committee, annul the regulations of the mayor, and, through a skillful use of his prerogative, impose his own.   He holds in hand, removes, appoints or helps appoint, not alone the clerks in his office, but likewise every kind and degree of clerk who, outside his office, serves the commune or department,[1] from the archivist, keeper of the museum, architect, director, and teachers of the municipal drawing-schools, from the directors and collectors of charity establishments, directors and account-ants of almshouses, doctors of the mineral springs, doctors and accountants of the insane asylums and for epidemics, head-overseers of *octrois*, wolf-bounty guards, commissioners of the urban police, inspectors of weights and measures, town col-lectors, whose receipts do not exceed thirty thousand francs, down to and comprising the lowest employés, such as forest-guards of the department and commune, lock-keepers and navigation guards, overseers of the quays and of commercial ports, toll-gatherers on bridges and highways, field-guards of the smallest village, policemen posted at the corner of a street, and stone-breakers on the public highway.   When things and not persons are concerned, it is he, again, who, in every proj-ect, enterprise, or proceeding, is charged with the preliminary examination and final execution of it, who proposes the depart-ment budget and presents it, regularly drawn up, to the council general, who draws up the communal budget and presents that to the municipal council, and who, after the council general or municipal council have voted on it, remains on the spot the sole executor, director, and master of the operation to which they have assented.   Their total, effective part in this opera-tion is very insignificant, it being reduced to a bare act of the will ; in reaching a vote they have had in their hands scarcely any other documents than those furnished and arranged by him ; in gradually reaching their decision step by step, they have had no help but his, that of an independent collaborator who, governed by his own views and interests, never becomes the mere instrument.   They lack for their decision direct, per-

1 Paul Leroy-Beaulieu, " L'administrateur locale en France et en Angleterre," pp. 26, 28, 92.   (Decrees of March 25, 1852, and April 13, 1861.)

sonal, and full information, and, beyond this, complete, efficient power ; it is simply a dry Yes, interposed between
insufficient resources, or else cut off, and the fruit of which is
abortive or only half ripens.   The persistent will of the prefect
alone informed and who acts, must and does generally prevail
against this ill-supported and ill-furnished will.   At bottom,
and as he stands, he is, in his mental and official capacity,
always the prefect of the year VIII.

Nevertheless, after the laws lately passed, his hands are not
so free.   The competency of local assemblies is extended and
comprises not only new cases but, again, of a new species,
while the number of their executive decisions has increased
five-fold.   The municipal council, instead of holding one session a year, holds four, and of longer duration.   The council
general, instead of one session a year, holds two, and maintains itself in the interim by its delegation which meets every
month.   With these increased authorities and generally present, the prefect has to reckon, and what is still more serious,
he must reckon with local opinion ; he can no longer rule with
closed doors ; the proceedings of the municipal council, the
smallest one, are duly posted ; in the towns, they are published
and commented on by the newspapers of the locality ; the
general council furnishes reports of its deliberations.—Thus,
behind elected powers, and weighing with these on the same
side of the scales, here is a new power, *opinion*, as this grows
in a country leveled by equalized centralization, in a heaving
or stagnant crowd of disintegrated individuals lacking any
spontaneous, central, rallying point, and who, failing natural
leaders, simply push and jostle each other or stand still, each
according to personal, blind, and haphazard impressions—a
hasty, improvident, inconsequent, superficial opinion, caught
on the wing, based on vague rumors, on four or five minutes
of attention given each week, and chiefly to big words imperfectly understood, two or three sonorous, commonplace phrases,
of which the listeners fail to catch the sense, but the sound of
which, by dint of frequent repetition, becomes for them a
recognized signal, the blast of a horn or a shrieking whistle
which assembles the herd and arrests or drives it on.   No

opposition can make head against this herd as it rushes along in too compact and too heavy masses.—The prefect, on the contrary, is obliged to cajole it, yield to it, and satisfy it ; for, under the system of universal suffrage, this same herd, besides local representatives, elects the central powers, the deputies, the government ; and when the government sends a prefect from Paris into the provinces, it is after the fashion of a large commercial establishment, with a view to keep and increase the number of its customers, to stay there, maintain its credit, and act permanently as its traveling-clerk, or, in other terms, as its electoral agent, and, still more precisely, as the head-manager of coming elections for the dominant party and for the ministers in office who have commissioned and appointed him, and who, from top to bottom, constantly stimulate him to hold on to the voters already secured and to gain fresh ones.— Undoubtedly, the interests of the state, department, and commune must be seriously considered, but, first and above all, he is the recruiting officer for voters. By virtue of this position and on this point he treats with the council general and the standing committee, with the municipal councilors and mayors, with influential electors, but especially with the small active committee which, in each commune, supports the prevailing policy and offers its zeal to the government.

Give and take. These indispensable auxiliaries must obtain nearly all they ask for, and they ask for a great deal. Instinctively, as well as by doctrine and tradition, the Jacobins are exacting, disposed to regard themselves as the representatives of the real and the ideal people, that is to say, as sovereigns by right, above the law, entitled to make it and therefore to unmake it, or, at least, strain it and interpret it as they please. Always in the general council, in the municipal council, and in the mayoralty, they are tempted to usurp it ; the prefect has as much as he can do to keep them within the local bounds, to keep them from meddling with state matters and the general policy ; he is often obliged to pocket their want of respect, to be patient with them, to talk to them mildly ; for they talk loud and want the administration to reckon with them as a clerk with his master ; if they vote money for any

service it is on condition that they take part in the use of the
funds and in the details of the service, in the choice of contractors and in hiring the workmen ; on condition that their
authority be extended and their hands applied to the consecutive execution of what does not belong to them but which
belongs to the prefect.[1]   Bargaining, consequently, goes on
between them incessantly and they come to terms.—The prefect, it must be noted, who is bound to pay, can do so without
violating the letter of the law.   The stern page on which the
legislator has printed his imperative text is always provided
with an ample margin where the administrator, charged with
its execution, can write down the decisions that he is free to
make.   In relation to each departmental or communal affair,
the prefect can with his own hand write out what suits him on
the white margin, which, as we have already seen, is ample
enough ; but the margin at his disposition is wider still and
continues, beyond anything we have seen, on other pages ; for
he is *chargé d'affaires* not only of the department and commune,
but again of the State.   Titular conductor or overseer of all
general services, he is, in his circumscription, head inquisitor
of the republican faith,[2] even in relation to private life and

---

1 J. Ferrand, *ibid.*, p. 170 (Paris, 1779), and 169 : " In many cases, general tutelage and
local tutelage are paralyzed. . . . . Since 1870—1876 the mayors, to lessen the difficulties
of their task, are frequently forced to abandon any rightful authority ; the prefects are
induced to tolerate, to approve of these infractions of the law. . . . For many years one
cannot read the minutes of a session of the council general or of the municipal council
without finding numerous examples of the illegality we report. . . . . In another order of
facts, for example in that which relates to the official staff, do we not see every day agents of
the state, even conscientious, yield to the will of all-powerful political notabilities and
entirely abandon the interests of the service ? "—These abuses have largely increased
within the past ten years.

2 See " La République et les conservateurs," in the *Revue des Deux Mondes* of March 1,
1890, p. 108.—" I speak of this *de visu :* I take my own *arrondissement.* It is in one of
the eastern departments, lately represented by radicals. This time it was carried by a
conservative.   An attempt was first made to annul the election, which had to be given up
as the votes in dispute were too many.   Revenge was taken on the electors.   Gendarmes,
in the communes, investigated the conduct of the curés, forest-guard. and storekeeper.
The hospital doctor, a conservator, was replaced by an opportunist.   The tax-comptroller,
a man of the district, and of suspicious zeal, was sent far into the west.   Every functionary
who, on the eve of the election, did not have a contrite look, was threatened with dismissal.
A road-surveyor was regarded as having been lukewarm, and accordingly put on the
retired list.   There is no petty vexation that was not resorted to, no insignificant person,
whom they disdained to strike.   Stone breakers were denounced for saying that they ought
not to have had their wages reduced.   Sisters of charity, in a certain commune, dispensed

inner sentiments, the responsible director of orthodox or heretical acts or opinions, which are laudable or blamable in the innumerable army of functionaries by which the central state now undertakes the complete mastery of human life, the twenty distinct regiments of its vast hierarchy—with the staff of the clergy, of the magistracy, of the preventive and repressive police, of public education, of public charities, of direct taxation, of indirect taxation, of registration, and of the customs ; with the officials of bridges and highways, forest domains, stock-breeding establishments, postal and telegraph departments, tobacco and other monopolies ; with those of every national enterprise which ought to be private, Sèvres and Gobelins, deaf and dumb and blind asylums, and every auxiliary and special workshop for war and navigation purposes, which the state supports and manages. I pass some of them and all too many. Only remark this, that the indulgence or severity of the prefecture in the way of fiscal violations or irregularities is an advantage or danger of the highest importance to three hundred and seventy-seven thousand dealers in wines and liquors ; that an accusation brought before and admitted in the prefecture may deprive thirty-eight thousand clergymen of their bread,[1] forty-three thousand letter-carriers and telegragh messengers, forty-five thousand sellers of tobacco and collecting-clerks, seventy-five thousand stone-breakers, and one hundred and twenty thousand male and female teachers ;[2] directly or indirectly, the good or ill favor of the prefecture is

medicine to the poor ; they were forbidden to do this, to annoy the mayor living in Paris. The custodians of mortgages had an errand-boy who was guilty of distributing, not voting-tickets, but family notices (of a marriage) on the part of the new deputy ; a few days after this, a letter from the prefecture gave the custodian notice that the criminal must be replaced in twenty-four hours. A notary, in a public meeting, dared to interrupt the radical candidate ; he was prosecuted in the court for a violation of professional duties, and the judges of judiciary reforms condemned him to three months' suspension." This took place, " not in Languedoc, or in Provence, in the south among excited brains where everything is allowable, but under the dull skies of Champagne. And when I interrogate the conservators of the West and of the Center, they reply : " We have seen many beside these, but it is long since we have ceased to be astonished ! "

1 *Ibid.*, p. 105 : " Each cantonal chief town has its office of informers. The Minister of Public Worship has himself told that on the first of January, 1890, there were 300 curés deprived of their salary, about three or four times as many as on the first of January, 1889."

2 These figures are taken from the latest statistical reports. Some of them are furnished by the chief or directors of special services.

of consequence, since recent military laws, to all adults between twenty and forty-five years, and, since recent school laws, to all children between six and thirteen years of age. According to these figures, which go on increasing from year to year, calculate the breadth of the margin on which, alongside of the legal text which states the law for persons and things in general, the prefect in his turn gives the law for persons and things in particular. On this margin, which belongs to him, he writes as he pleases, at one time permissions and favors, exemptions, dispensations, leaves of absence, relief of taxes or discharges, help and subventions, preferences and gratuities, appointments and promotions, and at another time destitutions, severities, prosecutions, wrongs, and injuries. To guide his hand in each case, that is to say, to endure all the favors on one side and all the disfavors on the other, he has special informers and imperious solicitors belonging to the local set of Jacobins. If not restrained by a very strong sentiment of distributive justice and very great solicitude for the public good he can hardly resist them, and in general when he takes up his pen it is to write under the dictation of his Jacobin collaborators.

Thus has the institution of the year VIII deviated, no longer attaining its object. The prefect, formerly appointed to a department, like a *pacier* of the Middle Ages, imposed on it from above, ignorant of local passions, independent, qualified and fitted for the office, was able to remain, in general, for fifty years, the impartial minister of the law and of equity, maintaining the rights of each, and exacting from each his due, without heeding opinions and without respect to persons. Now he is obliged to become an accomplice of the ruling faction, govern for the advantage of some to the detriment of others, and to put into his scales, as a preponderating weight, every time he weighs judgment, a consideration for persons and opinions. At the same time, the entire administrative staff in his hands, and under his eye, deteriorates ; each year, on the recommendation of a senator or deputy, he adds to it, or sees, intruders there, whose previous services are null, feeble in capacity and of weak integrity who do poor work or none at all, and who, to hold their post or get promoted, count not on their merits but on their patrons. The rest, able and faithful functionaries of the old school, who are poor and to whom no path is open, become weary and lose their energy ; they are no longer even certain of keeping their place ; if they stay, it is for the dispatch of current business and because they cannot be dispensed with ; perhaps to-morrow, however, they will cease to be considered indispensable ; some political renunciation, or to give a political favorite a place, will put them by anticipation on the retired list. Henceforth they have two powers to consult, one, legitimate and natural, the authority of their administrative chiefs, and the other illegitimate and parasite, consisting of democratic influence from both above and below ; for them, as for the prefect, public good descends to the second rank and the electoral interest mounts upward to the first rank. With them as with him, self-respect, professional honor, the conscientious performance of duty, reciprocal loyalty go down ; discipline relaxes, punctuality falters, and, as the saying goes, the great administrative edifice is no longer a well-kept house, but a barracks.

Naturally, under the democratic régime, the maintenance and service of this house becomes more and more costly ; for, owing to the additional centimes, it is the rich or well-to-do minority which defrays the larger portion of the expense ; owing to universal suffrage, it is the poor or half-poor majority which preponderates in voting, while the larger number who vote can overtax the small paying number with impunity. At Paris, the parliament and the government, elected by this numerical majority, contrive demands in its behalf, force expenditure, augment public works, schools, endowments, gratuities, prizes, a multiplication of offices to increase the number of their clients, while it never tires in decreeing, in the name of principles, works for show, theatrical, ruinous, and dangerous, the cost of which they do not care to know, and of which the social import escapes them. Democracy, above as well as below, is short-sighted ; it seizes whatever food it comes across, like an animal, with open jaws and head down ; it refuses to anticipate and to calculate ; it burdens the future and

wastes every fortune it undertakes to manage, not alone that
of the central state, but, again, those of all local societies.
Up to the advent of universal suffrage, the administrators appointed above or elected below, in the department or in the
commune, kept tight hold of the purse-strings; since 1848,
especially since 1870, and still later, since the passage of the
laws of 1882, which, in suppressing the obligatory consent of
the heaviest taxed, let slip the last of these strings, this purse,
wide open, is emptied into the street.[1]   In 1851, the departments, all together, expended ninety-seven millions; in 1869,
one hundred and ninety-two millions; in 1881, three hundred
and fourteen millions.   In 1836, the communes, all together,
save Paris, expended one hundred and seventeen millions, in
1862, four hundred and fifty millions, in 1877, six hundred and
seventy-six millions.   If we examine the receipts covering this
expenditure, we find that the additional centimes which supplied the local budgets, in 1820, with eighty millions, and, in
1850, with one hundred and thirty-one millions, supplied them,
in 1870, with two hundred and forty-nine millions, in 1880,
with three hundred and eighteen millions, and, in 1887, with
three hundred and sixty-four millions.   The annual increase,
therefore, of these superadded centimes to the principal of the
direct taxes is enormous, and finally ends in an overflow.   In
1874,[2] there were already twenty-four departments in which
the sum of additional centimes reached or surpassed the sum
of the principal.   "In a very few years," says an eminent
economist,[3] "it is probable that, for nearly all of the departments," the overcharge will be similar.   Already, for a long
time, in the total of personal taxation,[4] the local budgets raised

---

1 De Foville, pp. 412, 416, 425, 455 ; Paul Leroy-Beaulieu, "Traité de la science des finances," i., p. 717.

2 "Statistiques financières des communes en 1889 ":—3539 communes pay less than 15 common centimes ; 2597 pay from 0 fr. 15 to 0 fr. 30 ; 9652 pay from 0 fr. 31 to 0 fr. 50; 11,095
from 0 fr. 51 to 1 franc, and 4248 over 1 franc.—Here this relates only to the common centimes ; to have the sum total of the *additional local centimes* of each commune would require the addition of the department centimes, which the statistics do not furnish.

3 Paul Leroy-Beaulieu, *ibid.*, i., pp. 690, 717.

4 *Ibid.:* " If the personal tax were deducted from the amount of personal and house tax
combined we would find that the assessment of the state in the product of the house tax,
that is to say the product of the tax on rentals, amounts to 41 or 42 millions, and that the

more than the state, and, in 1888, the principal of the tax on real property, one hundred and eighty-three millions, is less than the total of centimes joined with it, one hundred and ninety-six millions. Coming generations are burdened over and beyond the present generation, while the sum of loans constantly increases, like that of taxation. The communes with debts, all together save Paris, owed, in 1868, five hundred and twenty-four millions, in 1871, seven hundred and eleven millions, in 1878, thirteen hundred and twenty-two millions. Paris, in 1868, already owed thirteen hundred and seventy-six millions, March 30, 1878, it owed nineteen hundred and eighty-eight millions.[1] In this same Paris, the annual contribution of each inhabitant for local expenses was, at the end of the first Empire, in 1813, thirty-seven francs per head, at the end of the Restoration, 45 francs, after the July monarchy, in 1848, 43 francs, and, at the end of the second Empire, in 1869, 94 francs. In 1887, it is 110 francs per head.[2]

VIII.

Such, in brief, is the history of local society from 1789 down to 1889. After the philosophic demolitions of the Revolution and the practical constructions of the Consulate, it could no longer be a small patrimony, something to take pride in, an object of affection and devotion to its inhabitants. The departments and communes have become more or less vast lodging-houses, all built on the same plan and managed according to the same regulations, one as passable as the other, with apartments in them which, more or less good, are more or less dear, but at rates which, higher or lower, are

---

share of localities in the product of this tax surpasses that of the state by 8 or 9 millions." (Year 1877.)

1 " Situation financière des department et des communes," published in 1889 by the Minister of the Interior. Loans and indebtedness of the departments at the end of the fiscal year in 1886, six hundred and thirty million, sixty-six thousand, one hundred and two francs. Loans and indebtedness of the communes Dec. 30, 1886, three billion, twenty million, four hundred and fifty thousand, five hundred and twenty-eight francs.

2 De Foville, p. 148 ; Paul Leroy-Beaulieu, " L'État moderne et ses fonctions," p. 21.

fixed at a uniform tariff over the entire territory, so that the
thirty-six thousand communal buildings and the eighty-six
department hotels are about equal, it making but little difference whether one lodges in the latter rather than in the
former. The permanent taxpayers of both sexes who have
made these premises their home, have not obtained recognition for what they are, invincibly and by nature, a syndicate
of neighbors, an involuntary, obligatory and private association, in which physical solidarity engenders moral solidarity, a
natural, limited society whose members own the building in
common, and each possesses a property right more or less
great, according to the greater or lesser contribution he
makes to the expenses of the establishment. Up to this time
no room has yet been found, either in the law or in minds, for
this very plain truth; its place is taken and occupied in advance by the two errors which, in turn or both at once, have
led the legislator and opinion astray.

Taking things as a whole, it is admitted up to 1830 that the
legitimate proprietor of the local building is the central state,
that it may install its delegate therein, the prefect, with full
powers; that, for better government, he consents to be instructed by the leading interested and most capable parties on
the spot; that he should fix the petty rights he concedes to
them within the narrowest limits; that he should appoint
them; that, if he calls them together for consultation, it is
from time to time and generally for form's sake, to add the
authority of their assent to the authority of his omnipotence,
on the implied condition that he shall not give heed to their
objections if he does not like them, and not follow their advice
if he does not choose to accept it.—Taking things as a whole,
it is admitted that, since 1848, the legitimate proprietors of the
building are its adult male inhabitants, counted by heads, all
equal and all with an equal part in the common property,
comprising those who contribute nothing or nearly nothing to
the common expenditure of the house, the numerous body of
semi-poor who lodge in it at half price, and the not less
numerous body to whom administrative philanthropy furnishes
house comforts, shelter, light, and frequently provisions, gratui-

tously.—Between both these contradictory and false conceptions, between the prefect of the year VIII, and the democracy
of 1792, a compromise has been effected ; undoubtedly, the
prefect, sent from Paris, is and remains the titular director,
the active and responsible manager of the departmental or
communal building ; but, in his management of it he is bound
to keep in view the coming elections, and in such a way as
will maintain the parliamentary majority in the seats they
occupy in parliament; consequently, he must conciliate the
local leaders of universal suffrage, rule with their help, put up
with the intrusion of their bias and cupidity, take their advice
daily, follow it often, even in small matters, even in payments
day by day of sums already voted, in appointing an office-
clerk, in the appointment of an unpaid underling, who may
some day or other take this clerk's place.[1]—Hence the spectacle before our eyes : a badly kept establishment in which
profusion and waste render each other worse and worse,
where sinecures multiply and where corruption enters in ; a
staff of officials becoming more and more numerous and less
and less serviceable, harassed between two different authorities, obliged to possess or to simulate political zeal and to
neutralize an impartial law by partiality, and, besides performing their regular duties, to do dirty work ; in this staff, there
are two sorts of employés, the new-comers who are greedy
and who, through favor, get the best places, and the old ones
who are patient and pretend no more, but who suffer and
grow disheartened ; in the building itself, there is great
demolition and reconstruction, architectural fronts in monu-
mental style for parade and to excite attention, entirely new
decorative and extremely tiresome structures at extravagant
cost ; consequently, loans and debts, heavier bills at the end
of each year for each occupant, low rents, but still high, for
favorites in the small rooms and garrets, and extravagant
rents for the larger and more sumptuous apartments ; in sum,

---

[1] Paul Leroy-Beaulieu, " L'Administration locale en France et en Angleterre," p. 28.
(Decrees of March 25, 1852, and April 13, 1861.)   List of offices directly appointed by the
prefect and on the recommendation of the heads of the service, among others the supernumeraries of telegraph lines and of the tax offices.

forced receipts which do not offset the expenses ; liabilities which exceed assets ; a budget which shows only a stable balance on paper,—in short, an establishment with which the public is not content, and which is on the road to bankruptcy.

THE MODERN REGIME

VOLUME II

BOOK FIFTH.

𝕿𝖍𝖊 𝕮𝖍𝖚𝖗𝖈𝖍.

CHAPTER II.

II. The bishop in his diocese.—Change of situation and rôle.—Depreciation of other local authorities.—Diminution of other ecclesiastical authorities.—Decline of the chapter and the *officialité.*—The bishop alone dispenses rigors and favors.—Use of displacement.—Second-class clergy subject to military discipline.—Why it submits to this.—Change in the habits and ways of the bishop.—His origin, age, capability, mode of living, labor, initiative, undertakings, and moral and social ascendency.—III. The subordinates.—The secular clergy.—Its derivation and how recruited.—How prepared and led.—The lower seminary.— The higher seminary.—Monthly lectures and annual retreat.—The *Exercitia.*—The *Manreze du Prêtre.*—The curé in his parish.—His rôle a difficult one.—His patience and correct conduct.

[Section I of this chapter has been omitted.]

II.

[The first two sentences of this section have been omitted.]

In 1789, out of one hundred and thirty-four bishops or archbishops, only five were of plebeian origin; in 1889, out of ninety bishops or archbishops there are only four of them nobles; [1] previous to the Revolution, the titulary of an episcopal see enjoyed, on the average, a revenue of one hundred thousand francs; [2] at the present day, he receives only a salary of from ten to fifteen thousand francs. In place of the grand seignior, an amiable and magnificent head of a mansion, given to display and to entertaining the best company, keeping an open table in his diocese when he happens to be there, but generally absent, an *habitué* of Paris or a courtier at Versailles, we see another stepping forward to take his seat, bearing the

---

1 " Almanach national de 1889." (Among these four, one only belongs to a historic family, Mgr. de Deux-Brézé of Moulins.)

2 See ' The Ancient Régime," pp. 65, 120, 150, 292.

same title, a personage whose habits and origins are different, a resident administrator, much less ornamental but a far more active and governing spirit, provided with a more ample jurisdiction, with more absolute authority and wielding more effective influence. The final effect of the Revolution in relation to the bishop is the same as in relation to the Pope, and in the French diocese, as in the universal Church, the modern regime sets up a central, extraordinary, enormous power of which the ancient regime knew nothing.

Formerly, the bishop encountered around him, on the spot, equals and rivals, bodies of men or individuals, as independent and powerful as himself, irremovable, owners of estates, dispensers of offices and of favors, local authorities by legal sanction, permanent patrons of a permanent class of dependents.   In his own cathedral, his metropolitan chapter was, like himself, a collator of livings; elsewhere, other chapters were so likewise and knew how to maintain their rights against his supremacy.   In each body of regular clergy, every grand abbot or prior, every noble abbess was, like himself, a sort of sovereign prince ; likewise sovereign through the partial survival of the old feudal order, wholly laic, a territorial seignior and justiciary on his own domain; likewise sovereign, for its part, the parliament of the province, with its rights of registry and of remonstrance, with its administrative attributes and interferences, with its train of loyal auxiliaries and subordinates, from the judges of the presidencies and bailiwicks down to the corporations of advocates, prosecutors and other members of the bar.[1] The parliamentarians of the district capital (*chef-lieu*), purchasers and owners of their offices, magistrates from father to son, much wealthier and much prouder than nowadays, were, in their old hereditary mansions, the real chiefs of the province, its constant representatives on the spot, its popular defenders against ministerial and royal absolutism. All these powers, which once counterbalanced episcopal

---

[1] Cf. the history of the parliaments of Grenoble and Rennes on the approach of the Revolution.   Remark the fidelity of all their judicial subordinates in 1788 and 1789, and the provincial power of the league thus formed.

power, have disappeared. Restricted to their judicial office, the tribunals have ceased to be political authorities and moderators of the central government: in the town and department, the mayor and general councillors, appointed or elected for a certain time, enjoy only temporary credit ; the prefect, the military commandant, the rector, the treasurer-general are merely passing strangers. The local circumscription, for a century, is an exterior post where individuals live together in contact but not associated ; no longer does any intimate, lasting and strong bond exist between them ; n thing remains of the old province but a population of inh bitants, a given number of private persons under unstable functionaries. The bishop alone has maintained himself intact and erect, a dignitary for life, the conductor, by title and in fact, of a good many persons, the stationary and patient undertaker of a great service, the unique general and undisputed commander of a special militia which, through conscience and profession, gathers close around him and, every morning, awaits his orders. Because, in his essence, he is a governor of souls. Revolution and centralization have not encroached on his ecclesiastical prerogative. Thanks to this indelible quality he has been able to endure the suppression of the others ; these have come back to him of themselves and with others added, comprising local superiority, real importance and local ascendency ; including the various honorable appellations which, under the ancient régime, denoted his rank and preëminence ; at the present day, under the modern régime, they are no longer in use for a layman and even for a minister of state; after 1802, one of the articles of the Organic Laws,[1] interdicts them to bishops and archbishops ; they are " allowed to add to their name only the title of *citizen* and *monsieur.*" But practically, except in the official almanac, everybody addresses a prelate as " my lord," and in the clergy, among believers, in writing or in speaking to him, he is called " your Grace," under the republic as under the monarchy.

Thus, in this provincial soil where other powers have lost

---

[1] Article 12.

their roots, not only has he kept his, but he has extended them and much farther ; he has grown beyond all measure and now the whole ecclesiastical territory belongs to him. Formerly, on this territory, many portions of it, and quite large ones, were enclosures set apart, reserves that an immemorial wall prevented him from entering. It is not he who, in a great majority of cases, confers livings and offices; it is not he who, in more than one-half of them, appoints to vacant curacies. At Besançon,[1] among fifteen hundred benefices and livings, he once conferred less than one hundred of them, while his metropolitan chapter appointed as many curés as himself ; at Arras, he appointed only seventeen curés and his chapter sixty-six; at Saint-Omer, among the collators of curacies he ranked only third, after the abbey of Saint-Martin and after the chapter of the cathedral. At Troyes, he could dispose only of one hundred and ninety-seven curacies out of three hundred and seventy two ; at Boulogne, out of one hundred and eighty, he had only eighty, and this again because the chapter voluntarily abandoned to him sixteen. Naturally, the eyes of all aspirants turned towards the collator ; now, among the highest and most lucrative places, those which gave the least trouble and afforded the most satisfaction, all sinecures, ranks, simple benefices and large urban curacies, probendaries and canonicates, most of the offices, titles, and incomes that might tempt human ambition, were in the hands, not of the bishop, but of the king or of the Pope, of an abbot or prior, of an abbess, or of a certain university,[2] of this or that cathe-

---

1 "The Revolution," Vol. I.—Abbé Sicard, "Les Dispensateurs des bénéfices ecclésiastiques avant 1789." ("Correspondant" of Sep. 10, 1889, pp. 887, 892, 893.) Grosley, "Mémoires pour servir l'histoire de Troyes," ii , pp. 35, 45.

2 Abbé Elie Méric, "Le Clergé sous l'ancien régime," i., p. 26. (Ten universities conferred letters of appointment on their graduates.)—Abbé Sicard, "Les Dispensateurs," etc., p. 876.—352 parliamentarians of Paris had an *indult*, that is to say, the right of obliging collators and church patrons to bestow the first vacant benefice either on himself or on one of his children, relations or friends. Turgot gave his *indult* to his friend Abbé Morellet, who consequently obtained (in June 1788) the priory of Thimer, with 16,000 livres revenue and a handsome house.—*Ibid.*, p. 887. "The bias of the Pope, ecclesiastical or lay patrons, licensed parties, *indultaires*, graduates, the so frequent use of resignations, permutations, pensions, left to the bishop, who is

dral or college-body, of a lay seignior, of a patentee, or of an *indultaire*, and often of the titulary himself. Thus, the hold of the bishop on his *clercs* was feeble ; he did not hold them through the hope of a favor. And, on the other hand, he had still less hold on them, no hold at all, through fear of losing favor. They might displease him almost with impunity ; his faculty for punishment was much more restricted than his means of recompense. His subordinates could find shelter and refuge against his displeasure, and even against his hostility. In the first place, and as a principle, a titulary, whether ecclesiastic or laic, owned his office and hence was irremovable ; they themselves, plain vicar-curates, the humble *desservans* [1] of a rural parish, had acquired this privilege through the declarations of 1726 and 1731. [2] Moreover, in case of interdiction, suspension or of censure, a titulary could always recur to the courts against episcopal judgment and any other, against all encroachment on spiritual or temporal prerogatives, or on those which were useful or honorary belonging to his charge.

These courts were of two kinds, one ecclesiastical and the other laic, and in each an appeal could be made from a lower to a higher court, from the diocesan official to the metropolitan official, and from the *présidial* to the parliament, with a complete judicial staff, judge, assessors, public ministry, prosecutors, advocates and clerks, restricted to the observing of all judicial formalities, authentic papers, citations of witnesses and challenges of testimony, interrogatories and pleadings, allegation of canons, laws and precedents, presence of the defendant, opposing arguments, delays in procedure, publicity and scandal. Before the slow march and inconveniences of such a trial, the bishop often avoided giving judgment, and all the more because

---

now undisputed master of his diocesan appointments, but very few situations to bestow."—Grosley, " Mémoires, etc.," ii., p. 35. " The tithes followed collations. Nearly all our ecclesiastical collators are at the same time large tithe-owners."

1 An inferior class of priests, generally assigned to poor parishes.

2 Abbé Elie Méric, *ibid.*, p. 448.

his verdicts, even when confirmed by the ecclesiastical
court, might be warded off or rendered ineffective by the
lay tribunal ; for, from the former to the latter, there was
an appeal under writ of error, and the latter, a jealous rival
of the former, was ill-disposed towards the sacerdotal
authorities ;[1] besides, in the latter case, far more than in
the former, the bishop found confronting him not merely
the more or less legal right of his own party, but again the
allies and patrons of his party, corporations and individuals
who, according to an accepted usage, interfered through
their solicitations with the judges and openly placed their
credit at the service of their protégé. With so many
spokes in the wheels, the working of an administrative
machine was difficult ; to give it effective motion, it required the steady pressure, the constant starting, the watchful and persistent efforts of a laborious, energetic, and
callous hand, while, under the ancient régime, the delicate
white hands of a gentleman-prelate were ill-adapted to this
rude business ; they were too nicely washed, too soft.   To
manage personally and on the spot a provincial, complicated and rusty machine, always creaking and groaning, to
give one's self up to it, to urge and adjust twenty local
wheels, to put up with knocks and splashes, to become a
business man, that is to say a man of all work—nothing
was less desirable for a grand seignior of that epoch.   In
the Church as in the State, he made the most of his rank ;
he collected and enjoyed its fruits, that is to say money,
honors and gratifications, and, among these gratifications, the
principal one, leisure ; hence, he abandoned every special
duty, the daily manipulation of men and things, the practical direction, all effective government, to his ecclesiastical or lay intendants, to subordinates whom he scarcely
looked after and who, at his own house, on his own domain,
replaced him as fixed residents.   The bishop, in his own
diocese, left the administration in the hands of his canons

---

[1] Abbé Elie Méric, *ibid.*, pp. 392–403. (Details in support.)

and grand-vicars ; "the official decided without his meddling."[1]   The machine thus worked alone and by itself,
with very few shocks, in the old rut established by routine ;
he helped it along only by the influence he exercised at
Paris and Versailles, by recommendations to the ministers ;
in reality, he was merely the remote and worldly representative of his ecclesiastical principality at court and in the
drawing-room.[2]   When, from time to time, he made his appearance there, the bells were rung ; deputations from all
bodies hurried to his antechambers ; each authority in turn,
and according to the order of precedence, paid him its
little compliment, which compliment he graciously returned
and then, the homage being over, he distributed among
them benedictions and smiles.   After this, with equal dignity and still more graciously throughout his sojourn, he
invited the most eligible to his table and, in his episcopal
palace or in his country-house, he treated them as guests.
This done, he had performed his duty ; the rest was left to
his secretaries, ecclesiastical officials and clerks, men of the
bureaux, specialists and "plodders."   "Did you read my
pastoral letter ?" said a bishop to Piron.   And Piron, who
was very outspoken, dared reply, "Yes, my lord.   And
yourself ?"

Under the modern régime, this suzerain for show, negligent and intermittent, is succeeded by an active sovereign
whose reign is personal and constant ; the limited and easy
monarchy of the diocese is converted into an universal and
absolute monarchy.   When the bishop, once invested and
consecrated, enters the choir of his cathedral to the re-
verberations of the organ, lighted with wax candles amidst
clouds of incense, and seats himself in solemn pomp[3] "on

---

1 Abbé Richandeau, "De l'ancienne et de la nouvelle discipline de l'Église en
France," p. 281.   Cf. Abbé Elie Méric, *ibid.*, ch. ii.   (On the justice and judges
of the Church.)

2 Mercur, "Tableau de Paris," iv., chap. 345.   "The flock no longer recognize the brow of their pastor and regard him as nothing but an opulent man, enjoying himself in the capital and giving himself very little trouble about it."

3 "Le Monde" of Novem. 9, 1890.   (Details, according to the Montpellier

his throne," he is a prince who takes possession of his government, which possession is not nominal or partial, but real and complete. He holds in his hand "the splendid cross which the priests of his diocese have presented to him," in witness of and symbolizing their voluntary, eager and full obedience ; and this pastoral baton is larger than the old one. In the ecclesiastical herd, no head browses at a distance or under cover ; high or low, all are within reach, all eyes are turned towards the episcopal crook ; at a sign made by the crook, and according to the signal, each head forthwith stands, advances or recedes : it knows too well that the shepherd's hands are free and that it is subject to its will. Napoleon, in his reconstruction of the diocese, made additions to only one of the diocesan powers, that of the bishop ; he suffered the others to remain low down, on the ground. The delays, complications and frictions of a divided government were repugnant to him ; he had no taste for and no comprehension of any but a concentrated government ; he found it convenient to deal with but one man, a prefect of the spiritual order, as pliable as his colleague of the temporal order, a mitred grand functionary— such was the bishop in his eyes. This is the reason why he did not oblige him to surround himself with constitutional and moderating authorities ; he did not restore the ancient bishop's court and the ancient chapter ; he allowed his prelates themselves to pen the new diocesan statute.— Naturally, in the division of powers, the bishop reserved the best part to himself, the entire substance, and, to limit his local omnipotence, there remained simply lay authority. But, in practice, the shackles by which the civil government kept him in its dependence, broke or became relaxed one by one. Among the Organic Articles, almost all of them which subjected or repressed the bishop fell into discredit or into desuetude. Meanwhile, those which authorized and

---

newspapers, of the ceremony which had just taken place in the cathedral of that town for the remission of the pallium to Mgr. Roverié de Cabrières.

exalted the bishop remained in vigor and maintained their effect. Consequently, Napoleon's calculation, in relation to the bishop or in relation to the Pope, proved erroneous. He wanted to unite in one person two incompatible characters, to convert the dignitaries of the Church into dignitaries of the State, to make functionaries out of potentates. The functionary insensibly disappeared ; the potentate alone subsisted and still subsists.

At the present day, conformably to the statute of 1802, the cathedral chapter,[1] except in case of one interim, is a lifeless and still-born body, a vain simulachre ; it is always, by title or on paper, the Catholic "senate," the bishop's obligatory "council";[2] but he takes his councillors where he pleases, outside of the chapter, if that suits him, and he is free not to take any of them, " to govern alone, to do all himself." It is he who appoints to all offices, to the five or six hundred offices of his diocese ; he is the universal collator of these and, nine times out of ten, the sole collator; excepting eight or nine canonships and the thirty or forty cantonal curacies, which the government must approve, he alone makes appointments and without any person's concurrence. Thus, in the way of favors, his clerical body has nothing to expect from anybody but himself—while, on the other hand, they no longer enjoy any protection against his severities ; the hand which punishes is still less restrained than that which rewards ; like the cathedral chapter, the ecclesiastical tribunal has lost its consistency and

---

1 " Encyclopédie théologique," by Abbé Migne, ix., p. 465. (M. Emery, " Des Nouveaux chapitres cathédraux," p. 238.) " The custom in France at present, of common law, is that the bishops govern their dioceses without the participation of any chapter. They simply call to their council those they deem proper, and choose from these their chapter and cathedral councillors."

2 *Ibid., id.*: " Notwithstanding these fine titles, the members of the chapter take no part in the government during the life of the bishop ; all depends on this prelate, who can do everything himself, or, if he needs assistants, he may take them outside of the chapter." *Ibid.*, p. 445. Since 1802, in France, " the titular canons are appointed by the bishop and afterwards by the government, which gives them a salary. It is only the shadow of the canonical organization, of which, however, they possess all the canonical rights."

independence, its efficiency; nothing remains of the ancient bishop's court but an appearance and a name.[1]

At one time, the bishop in person is himself the whole court ; he deliberates only with himself and decides *ex informata conscientia* without a trial, without advice, and, if he chooses, in his own cabinet with closed doors, in private according to facts, the value of which he alone estimates, and through motives of which he is the sole appreciator. At another time, the presiding magistrate is one of his grand-vicars, his revocable delegate, his confidential man, his mouthpiece, in short, another self, and this official acts without the restraint of ancient regulations, of a fixed and understood procedure beforehand, of a series of judicial formalities, of verifications and the presence of witnesses, of the delays and all other legal precautions which guard the judge against prejudice, haste, error, and ignorance and without which justice always risks becoming injustice. In both cases, the head over which the sentence is suspended lacks guarantees, and, once pronounced, this sentence is definitive. For, on appeal to the court of the metropolitan bishop, it is always confirmed ;[2] the bishop's support each other, and, let the appellant be right or wrong, the appeal is in itself a bad mark against him : he did not submit at once, he stood out against reproof, he was lacking in humility, he has set an example of insubordination, and this alone is a grave fault. There remains the recourse

---

1 Abbé André, " Exposition de quelques principes fondamentaux de droit canonique," p. 187 (citing on this subject one of the documents of Mgr. Sibour, then bishop of Digne).—" Since the Concordat of 1801, the absence of all fixed procedure in the trial of priests has left nothing for the accused to depend on but the conscience and intelligence of the bishop. The bishop, accordingly, has been, in law, as in fact, the sole pastor and judge of his clergy, and, except in rare cases, no external limit has been put to the exercise of his spiritual authority."

2 Émile Ollivier, " L'Église et l'État au concile du Vatican," p 517.—Abbé André, *ibid.*, pp. 17, 19, 30, 280. (Various instances, particularly the appeal of a rural curé, Feb. 8, 1866.) " The metropolitan (bishop) first remarked that he could not bring himself to condemn his suffragan." Next (Feb. 20, 1866), judgment confirmed by the metropolitan court, declaring "that no reason exists for declaring exaggerated and open to reform the penalty of depriving the rector of the parish of X—— of his title, *a title purely conferred by and revocable at the will of the bishop.*"

to Rome ; but Rome is far off,[1] and, while maintaining her
superior jurisdiction, she does not willingly cancel an episcopal verdict ; she treats prelates with respect, she is careful of her lieutenant-generals, her collectors of Saint Peter's
pence. As to the lay tribunals, these have declared themselves incompetent,[2] and the new canon law teaches that
never, " under the pretext of a writ of error, may a priest
make an appeal to the secular magistrate ";[3] through this
appeal, " he derogates from the authority and liberty of the
Church and is liable to the gravest censures ;" he betrays his
order.

Such is now, for the lower clergy, ecclesiastical law, and
likewise laic law, both agreeing together in not affording
him protection ; add to this change in the jurisprudence
which concerns him a no less decisive change in the titles
which place and qualify him. Before 1789, there were in
France thirty-six thousand curés entitled irremovable ; at
the present day, there are only three thousand four hundred
and twenty-five ; before 1789, there were only twenty-five
hundred curés in France entitled removable, while to-day
there are thirty-four thousand and forty-two ;[4] all of the
latter, appointed by the bishop without the approbation of
the civil powers, are removable at his discretion ; their
parochial ministry is simply a provisional commission ;
they may be transferred from day to day, they may be
placed elsewhere, passing from one precarious curacy to
another no less precarious. " At Valence,[5] Mgr. Char-

1 Émile Ollivier, *ibi*, ii., 517, 516. Abbé André, *ibid.*, p. 241. " During the first
half of the nineteenth century no appeal could be had from the Church of France
to Rome."

2 Émile Ollivier, *ibid.*, i , p. 286. Abbé André, *ibid.*, p. 242: " From 1803 to 1854
thirty-eight appeals under writ of error (were presented) to the Council of State
by priests accused. . . . Not one of the thirty-eight appeals was admitted."

3 Prælectiones juris canonici habitæ in seminario Sancti Sulpicii, iii., p. 146.

4 Émile Ollivier, *ibid.*, i., 136.

5 *Id.*, *ibid.*, i., p. 285. (According to Abbé Denys, " Études sur l'administration de l'Église." p. 211.)—Cf. Abbé André, *ibid.*, and " L'État actuel du
clergé en France par les frères Allignol " (1839).—This last work, written by two
assistant-curés, well shows, article by article, the effects of the Concordat and the
enormous distance which separates the clergy of to-day from the old clergy. The

trousse, in one month transferred one hundred and fifty
priests from one parish to another. In 1835, in the diocese
of Valence, thirty-five transfers were sent out by the same
mail." No assistant-priest, however long in his parish, feels
that he is at home there, on his own domain, for the rest of his
life ; he is merely there in garrison, about the same as lay functionaries and with less security, even when irreproachable.
For he may be transplanted, not alone for spiritual reasons,
but likewise for political reasons. He has not grown less
worthy, but the municipal council or the mayor have taken
a dislike to his person ; consequently, to tranquillize things,
he is displaced. Far better, he had become worthy and is
on good terms with the municipal council and the mayor ;
wherever he has lived he has known how to mollify these,
and consequently " he is removed from parish to parish,[1]
chosen expressly to be put into those where there are
troublesome, wrangling, malevolent, and impious mayors."
It is for the good of the service and in the interest of the
Church. The bishop subordinates persons to this superior
interest. The legislation of 1801 and 1802 has conferred
full powers upon him and he exercises them ; among the
many grips by which he holds his clergy the strongest is
the power of removal, and he uses it. Into all civil or
ecclesiastical institutions Napoleon, directly or by counter-

---

modifications and additions which comport with this exposition are indicated by
Abbé Richandeau, director of the Blois Seminary, in his book, " De l'ancienne et
de la nouvelle discipline de l'Église en France " (1842). Besides this, the above
exposition, as well as what follows, is derived from, in addition to printed documents, personal observations, much oral information, and numerous manuscript
letters.

1 " Manreze du prêtre," by the R. P. Caussette, vicar-general of Toulouse, 1879,
t. ii., p. 523. (As stated by the Abbé Dubois, an experienced missionary. He
adds that these priests, " transferred to difficult posts, are always on good terms
with their mayors, . . . triumph over obstacles, and maintain peace.")—*Ibid.*, i.,
p. 312. " I do not know whether the well-informed consciences of our lords the
bishops have made any mistakes, but what pardons have they not granted ! what
scandals have they not suppressed ! what reputations have they not preserved !
What a misfortune if you have to do with a court instead of with a father ! For
the court acquits and does not pardon. . . . And your bishop may not only employ
the mercy of forgiveness, but, again, that of secrecy. How reap the advantages
of this paternal system by calumniating it !"

strokes, has injected his spirit, the military spirit ; hence the authoritative régime, still more firmly established in the Church than in the State, because that is the essence of the Catholic institution ; far from being relaxed in this, it has become stricter ; at present it is avowed, proclaimed, and even made canonical ; the bishop, in our days, in fact as in law, is a general of division, and, in law as in fact, his curés are simply sergeants or corporals.[1] Command, from such a lofty grade, falls direct, with extraordinary force, on grades so low, and, at the first stroke, is followed by passive obedience. Discipline in a diocese is as perfect as in an army corps, and the prelates publicly take pride in it. " It is an insult," said Cardinal de Bonnechose to the Senate,[2] "to suppose that we are not masters in our own house, that we cannot direct our clergy, and that it is the clergy which directs us. . . . There is no general within its walls who would accept the reproach that he could not compel the obedience of his soldiers. Each of us has command of a regiment, and the regiment marches."

III.

In order to make troops march, a baton, even when pastoral, is not sufficient ; it is still requisite that forced subordination in the men should go along with voluntary subordination ; consequently, legal authority in the chief should be accompanied with moral authority ; otherwise he

---

1 " Vie de Mgr. Dupanloup," by Abbé Lagrange, ii., p. 43 : " Mgr. Dupanloup believed that pastoral removal was very favorable, not to say necessary, to the good administration of a diocese, to the proper management of parishes, even to the honor of priests and the Church, considering the difficulties of the times we live in. Irremovability was instituted for fortunate times and countries in which the people fulfilled all their duties and in which the sacerdotal ministry could not be otherwise than a simple ministry of *conservation ;* at the present day it is a ministry of *conquest* and of apostleship. The priest, accordingly, must dispose of his priests as he thinks them fit for this work, according to their zeal and to their possible success *in a country which has to be converted.*" Against the official character and publicity of its judgments " it is important that it should not make out of a misfortune which is reparable a scandal that nothing can repair."

2 "Moniteur," session of March 11, 1865.

will not be loyally supported and to the end. In 1789, this was not the case with the bishop ; on two occasions, and at two critical moments, the clergy of the inferior order formed a separate band, at first at the elections, by select-ing for deputies curés and not prelates, and next in the national assembly, by abandoning the prelates to unite with the Third Estate. The intimate hold of the chief on his men was relaxed or broken. His ascendency over them was no longer sufficiently great ; they no longer had confidence in him. His subordinates had come to regard him as he was, a privileged individual, sprung from a dis-tinct race and furnished by a class apart, bishop by right of birth, without a prolonged apprenticeship, having ren-dered no services, without tests of merit, almost an in-terloper in the body of his clergy, a Church parasite accustomed to spending the revenues of his diocese away from his diocese, idle and ostentatious, often a shameless gallant or obnoxious hunter, disposed to be a philosopher and free-thinker, and who lacked two qualifications for a leader of Christian priests : first, ecclesiastical deportment, and next, and very often, Christian faith.[1]

All these gaps in and discrepancies of episcopal char-acter, all these differences and distances between the ori-gins, interests, habits, and manners of the lower and the

---

1 "The Ancient Régime," pp. 65, 120, 150, 292. " Memoires inédits de Madame de —— " (I am not allowed to give the author's name). The type in high relief of one of these prelates a few years before the Revolution may here be found. He was bishop of Narbonne, with an income of 800,000 livres derived from the possessions of the clergy. He passed a fortnight every other year at Narbonne, and then for six weeks he presided with ability and propriety over the provincial parliament at Montpellier. But during the other twenty-two months he gave no thought to any parliamentary business or to his diocese, and lived at Haute Fon-taine with his niece, Madame de Rothe, of whom he was the lover. Madame de Dillon, his grand-niece, and the Prince de Guémenée, the lover of Madame de Dillon, lived in the same château. The proprieties of deportment were great enough, but language there was more than free, so much so that the Marquise d'Osmond, on a visit, " was embarrassed even to shedding tears. . . . On Sunday, out of respect to the character of the master of the house, they went to Mass ; but nobody carried a prayer-book ; it was always some gay and often scandalous book, which was left lying about in the tribune of the château, open to those who cleaned the room, for their edification as they pleased."

upper clergy, all these inequalities and irregularities which
alienated inferiors from the superior, have disappeared;
the modern régime has levelled the wall of separation
established by the ancient régime between the bishop and
his priests. At the present day he is, like them, a plebeian,
of common extraction, and sometimes very low, one being
the son of a village shoemaker, another the natural son of
a poor workwoman, both being men of feeling and never
blushing at their humble origin, openly tender and respectful to their mothers,—a certain bishop lodging his
mother, formerly a servant, in his episcopal palace and giving her the first seat at his table among the most honored
and noblest of his guests.[1] He is "one of fortune's officers," that is to say, a meritorious and old officer. According to the "Almanac" of 1889, the three youngest
are from forty-seven to forty-nine years of age; all the
others are fifty and over; among the latter, three fourths
of them are over sixty. As a general rule, a priest cannot
become a bishop short of twenty or twenty-five years'
service in the lower and average grades; he must have
remained in each grade a longer or shorter period, in turn
vicar, curé, vicar-general, canon, head of a seminary, sometimes coadjutor, and almost always have distinguished himself in some office, either as preacher or catechist, professor
or administrator, canonist or theologian. His full compe-
tence cannot be contested, and he enjoys a right to exact
full obedience; he has himself rendered it up to his consecration; "he boasts of it," and the example he proposes to
his priests is the one he has himself given.[2] On the other
hand, his moderate way of living excites but little envy; it is
about like that of a general of division, or of a prefect, or of
a high civil functionary who, lacking personal fortune, has

[1] "Vie de Mgr. Dupanloup," by Abbé Lagrange.—"Histoire du Cardinal Pie,
évêque de Poitiers," by Mgr. Bannard.

[2] "Moniteur," session of March 14, 1865, speech of Cardinal de Bonnechose:
"I exact full obedience, because I myself, like those among you who belong to the
army or navy, have always taken pride in thus rendering it to my chiefs, to my
superiors."

nothing but his salary to live on.   He does not display, as
formerly, confessionals lined with satin, kitchen utensils of
massive silver, hunting accoutrements, a hierarchical staff
of major-domos, ushers, valets, and liveried lackeys, stables
and carriages, lay grand-seigniors, vassals of his suzerainty
and figuring at his consecration, a princely ceremonial of
parade and homage, a pompous show of receptions and of
hospitalities.   There is nothing but what is necessary, the
indispensable instruments of his office : an ordinary carriage for his episcopal journeys and town visits, three or
four domestics for manual service, three or four secretaries
for official writings, some old mansion or other cheaply
repaired and refurnished without ostentation, its rooms and
bureaus being those of an administrator, business man, and
responsible head of a numerous staff ; in effect, he is
responsible for a good many subordinates, he has a good
deal to attend to; he works himself, looking after the whole
and in detail, keeping classified files by means of a chrono-
logical and systematic collection,[1] like the general director
of a vast company ; if he enjoys greater honors, he is
subject to greater exigencies ; assuredly, his predecessors
under the ancient régime, delicate epicureans, would not
have wished for such a life ; they would have considered
the disagreeable as surpassing its gratifications.

Even when old, he draws on his energies ; he officiates,
he preaches, he presides at long ceremonies, he ordains
seminarians, he confirms thousands of children,[2] he visits

---

[1] " Histoire du Cardinal Pie," by M. Bannard, ii., p. 690.   M. Pie left six large
volumes in which, for thirty years, he recorded his episcopal acts, uninterruptedly,
until his last illness.

[2] *Ibid.*, ii., p. 135 : " In the year 1860 he had confirmed 11,586 belonging to his
diocese ; in 1861 he confirmed 11,845."—" Vie de Mgr. Dupanloup," by Abbé La
Grange, iii., p. 19.   (Letter to his clergy, 1863.)   He enumerates what he had
done in his diocese : " The parochial *retraites* which have amounted to nearly
one hundred ; the perpetual adoration of the Holy Sacrament established in all
the parishes; confirmation, not alone in the cantonal town but in the smallest villages and always preceded by the mission ; the canonical visit made annually in
each parish, partly by the archdeacon, partly by the dean, and partly by the
bishop ; . . . the vicarships doubled ; life in common established among the parochial clergy; sisters of charity for schools and the sick multiplied in the diocese

one after another the parishes in his diocese ; often, at the
end of his administration, he has visited them all and many
times. Meanwhile, shut up in his episcopal cabinet, he is
constantly inspecting these four or five hundred parishes ;
he reads or listens to reports, informs himself on the number of communicants, on what is required in worship, on
the financial state of the *fabrique,* on the attitude of the
inhabitants, on the good or bad dispositions of municipal
counsellors and mayors, on the local causes of dissension
and conflict, on the conduct and character of the curé or
vicar ; each resident ecclesiastic needs guidance or maintenance between intemperate zeal and inert lukewarmness,
evenly balanced according as parishes and circumstances
vary, but always in a way to prevent false steps, to turn
aside mistakes, to humor opinion, to stop scandals. For
the entire life of the clergyman, not only his public life
but again his personal, domestic, private life, belongs to
and concerns the Church : there must be no evil reports,
even without foundation, on his account ; if these occur,
the bishop summons him to headquarters, warns him, ad-
monishes him, and, without handing the matter over to a
responsible tribunal, decides himself alone, in private, and
therefore subject to the investigations, anxieties and painful, painstaking labor always attendant on direct absolute power. Likewise, in relation to his upper and his
lower seminary : here are two indispensable nurseries of
which he is the head gardener, attentive to filling annual
vacancies and seeking proper subjects for these throughout
his diocese, ever verifying and cultivating their vocations ;

---

and spread on all sides ; augmentation of everything concerning ecclesiastical
studies, the number of small and large seminaries being largely increased; examinations of young priests ; ecclesiastical lectures ; grades organized and raised;
churches and rectories everywhere rebuilt or repaired ; a great diocesan work in
helping poor parishes and, to sustain it, the diocesan lottery and fair of the ladies
of Orleans ; finally, *retraites* and communions for men established, and also in
other important towns and parishes of the diocese." (P. 46.) (Letter of January
26, 1846, prescribing in each parish the exact holding of the *status animarum,*
which *status* is his criterion for placing a curé.) "The *État de Pâques* in his
parish must always be known while he is in it, before withdrawing him and
placing him elsewhere."

he confers scholarships ; he dictates rules and regulations ; appoints and dismisses, displaces and procures as he pleases, the director and professors ; he takes them, if he chooses, out of his diocese or out of the body of regular clergy ; he prescribes a doctrine to them, methods, ways of thinking and teaching, and he keeps his eye, beyond his present or future priests, on three or four hundred monks and on four-teen hundred nuns.

As to the monks, so long as they remain inside their dwellings, in company together and at home, he has nothing to say to them ; but, when they come to preach, confess, officiate or teach in public on his ground, they fall under his jurisdiction ; in concert with their superior and with the Pope, he has rights over them and he uses them. In effect, they are auxiliaries assigned to or summoned by him, available troops and a reinforcement, so many choice com-panies expressly ready, each with its own discipline, its par-ticular uniform, its special weapon, and who bring to him in following a campaign under his orders, distinct aptitudes and a livelier zeal ; he has need of them[1] in order to make up for the insufficiency of his local clergy in arousing the spirit of devotion in his parishes and in enforcing sound doctrine in his seminaries. Now, between these two forces a common understanding is difficult ; the former, adjuncts and flying about, march in front ; the latter, holding the ground and stationary, look upon the new-comers as usurpers who lessen both their popularity and their fees ; a bishop must possess great tact as well as energy to impose on both bodies of this clergy, if not an intimate union, at least mutual aid and a collaboration without conflict.—As to the nuns,[2] he is their *ordinary*, the sole arbiter, overseer and ruler over all these cloistered lives ; he receives their vows, and renders them free of them ; it is he who, after due inquiry and examina-

---

1 " Moniteur." session of March 14. 1865. (Speech of Cardinal de Bonnechose.) "What would we do without our monks, Jesuits, Dominicans, Carmelites, etc., to preach at Advent and during Lent, and act as missionaries in the country? The (parochial) clergy is not numerous enough to do this daily work."

2 *Prælectiones juris canonici*, ii., 305 and following pages.

tion, authorizes each entrance into the community or a return to society, at first each admission or novitiate, and
next each profession of faith or assumption of the veil,
every dismissal or departure of a nun, every claim that
one makes, every grave act of severity or decision on the
part of the superior ; he approves of, or appoints, the confessor of the establishment ; he maintains seclusion in it,
he draws tighter or relaxes the observances ; he himself
enters its doors by privilege of his office, and, with his own
eyes, he inspects its régime, spiritual and temporal, through
a right of control which extends from the direction of souls
to the administration of property.

To so many obligatory matters he adds others which are
voluntary, not alone works of piety, those relating to worship, propagandism, diocesan missions, catechising adults,
brotherhoods for perpetual adoration, meetings for the
uninterrupted recital of the rosary, Peter's pence, seminary
funds, Catholic journals and reviews—but, again, institutions for charity and education.[1]   In the way of charity, he
founds or supports twenty different kinds, sixty in one
diocese alone, general and special services, infant nurseries,
clubs, asylums, lodging-houses, patronages, societies for
helping and placing the poor, for the sick at home and in
the hospitals, for suckling infants, for the deaf and dumb,
for the blind, for old men, for orphans, for repentant prostitutes, for prisoners, for soldiers in garrison, for workmen,
apprentices, youths, and quantities of others.   In the way
of education, there are yet more of them—works which the
Catholic chiefs have most at heart ; without these, it is
impossible in modern society to preserve the faith in each
new generation.   Hence, at each turning-point of political
history, we see the bishops benefiting by the toleration or
warding off the intolerance of the teaching State, competing

---

[1] " La Charité à Nancy," by Abbé Girard, 1890, 1 vol.—" La Charité à Angers,"
by Léon Cosnier, 1890, 2 vols.—" Manuel des œuvres et institutions charitable à
Paris," by Lacour, 1 vol.—" Les Congrégations religieuses en France," by Émile
Keller, 1880, 1 vol.

with it, erecting alongside of its public schools free schools of its own, directed or served by priests or religious brother-hoods;—after the suppression of the university monopoly in 1850, more than one hundred colleges[1] for secondary education; after the favorable law of 1875, four or five provincial faculties or universities for superior instruction; after the hostile laws of 1882, many thousands of parochial schools for primary instruction.

Foundation and support, all this is expensive. The bishop requires a great deal of money, especially since the State, become ill-disposed, cuts off clerical resources as much as possible, no longer maintains scholarships in the seminaries, deprives suspicious *desservans* of their small stipends, eats into the salaries of the prelates, throws ob-stacles in the way of communal liberalities, taxes and over-taxes the congregations, so that, not merely through the diminution of its allowances it relieves itself at the expense of the Church, but again, through the increase of its im-posts, it burdens the Church for its own advantage. The episcopacy obtains all necessary funds through collections in the churches and at domiciles, through the gifts and sub-scriptions of the faithful; and, every year, it needs millions, apart from the budget appropriation, for its faculties and universities in which it installs largely paid professors, for the construction, location and arrangement of its countless buildings, for the expenses of its minor schools, for the support of its ten thousand seminarists, for the general out-lay on so many charitable institutions; and it is the bishop who, their principal promoter, must provide for this, all the more because he has often taken it upon himself in advance, and made himself responsible for it by either a written or verbal promise. He responds to all these engagements; he

---

[1] "Vie de Mgr. Dupanloup," i., 506 (1853). "More than one hundred free eccle-siastical establishments for secondary education have been founded since the law of 1850."—"Statistique de l'enseignement secondaire." In 1865, there were 276 free ecclesiastical schools for secondary instruction with 34,897 pupils, of which 23.549 were boarders and 11,348 day-scholars. In 1876, there were 390 with 46,816 pupils, of which 33,092 were boarders and 13,724 day-scholars.

has funds on hand at the maturity of each contract. In 1883, the bishop of Nancy, in need of one hundred thousand francs to build a school-house with a work-room attached to it, mentions this to a number of persons assembled in his drawing-room; one of these puts his hand in his pocket and gives him ten thousand francs, and others subscribe on the spot to the amount of seventy-four thousand francs.[1] Cardinal Mathieu, during his administration, archbishop of Besançon, thus collects and expends four millions. Lately, Cardinal Lavigerie, to whom the budget allows fifteen thousand francs per annum, wrote that he had spent eighteen hundred thousand francs and had incurred no debt.[2]—Through this initiative and this ascendency the bishop becomes a central social rallying-point; there is no other in the provinces, nothing but so many disjointed lives, juxtaposed and kept together in an artificial circle prescribed from above; so that a good many of these, and of most consideration, gravitate to and group themselves, especially since 1830, around this last permanent centre and form a part of its body; he is the sole germinating, vivifying, intact centre that still agglutinates scattered wills and suitably organizes them. Naturally, class and party interests incorporate themselves additionally along with the Catholic interest which he represents, and his ecclesiastical authority becomes a political influence; besides his secular and regular clergy, over and beyond the two thousand five hundred exemplary or directorial lives which he controls, we see behind him an indefinite multitude of lay adhesions and devotedness. Consequently, every government must take him into their calculations, and all the more because his colleagues stand by him; the episcopacy, banded together, remains erect in face of the omnipotent State, under the July monarchy as claimants of free instruction and under the second empire in support of the temporal

---

1 " La Charité à Nancy," by Abbé Girard, p. 87.—" Vie du Cardinal Mathieu," by Mgr. Besson, 2 vols.

2 December, 1890.

power of the Pope.—In this militant attitude, the figure of
the bishop is fully unveiled ; the titular champion of an
infallible Church, himself a believer and submissive ; his
voice is extraordinarily proud and defiant;[1] in his own eyes,
he is the unique depository of truth and morality; in the
eyes of his followers, he becomes a superhuman personage,
a prophet of salvation or of destruction, the annunciator of
divine judgments, the dispenser of celestial anger or of
celestial pardon ; he rises to the clouds in an apotheosis of
glory ; with women especially, this veneration grows into
enthusiasm and degenerates into idolatry. Towards the
end of the second empire an eminent French bishop, on a
steamboat on Lake Leman, taking a roll of bread from his
pocket, seated himself alongside of two ladies and ate it,
handing each of them a piece of it. One of them, bowing
reverently, replied to him, " At your hands, my lord, this is
almost the holy communion ! "[2]

IV.

A clergy submissive in mind and feeling, long prepared
by its condition and education for faith and obedience,
acts under the sway of this sovereign and consecrated hand.
Among the forty thousand curés and *desservans* " more than
thirty-five thousand belong to the laboring class of workmen and peasants,"[3] not the first class of peasants, but the
second class, the poorer families earning their daily bread
and often with a good many children. Under the pressure
of the ambient atmosphere and of the modern régime, the
others keep back their sons, retaining them for the world
and denying them to the Church ; ambition, even low down

---

1 Cf., in the above-mentioned biographies, the public and political discourses of
the leading prelates, especially those of M. Mathieu (of Besançon), M. Dupanloup
(of Orleans), Mgr. de Bonnechose (of Rouen), and particularly Mgr. Pie (of Poitiers).

2 A fact told me by a lady, an eye-witness. In the seventeenth century it is
probable that Fénelon or Bossuet would have regarded such a response as extravagant and even sacrilegious.

3 Abbé Elie Méric, in the " Correspondant " of January 10, 1890, p. 18.

on the scale, has developed itself and changed its object. Nobody now aspires to make his son a curé but a schoolmaster, a railroad employé, or a commercial clerk.[1] The ground has to be dug deeper, to reach a lower stratum, in order to extract from it the priests that are lacking.

Undoubtedly, at this depth, the extraction costs more ; the family cannot afford to pay for the child's ecclesiastical education ; the State, moreover, after 1830, no longer gives anything to the lower seminary, nor to the large one after 1885.[2] The expenses of these schools must be borne by the faithful in the shape of donations and legacies ; to this end, the bishop orders collections in the churches in Lent and encourages his diocesans to found scholarships ; the outlay for the support and education, nearly gratis, of a future priest between the ages of twelve and twenty-four is very great ; in the lower seminary alone it costs from forty to fifty thousand francs over and above the net receipts ;[3] in the face of such an annual deficit, the bishop, who is responsible for the undertaking, is greatly concerned and sometimes extremely anxious.—To make amends, and as compensation, the extraction is surer ; the long process by which a child is withdrawn and instructed for the priesthood goes on and is finished with less uncertainty. Neither the light nor the murmur of the century

---

1 "De l'État actuel du clergé en France" (1839), p. 248, by the brothers Allignol. Careers of every kind are too crowded ; "only the ecclesiastical is in want of subjects ; willing youths are the only ones wanted and none are found." This is due, say these authors, to the profession of assistant-priest being too gloomy —eight years of preparatory study, five years in the seminary, 800 francs of pay with the risk of losing it any day, poor extras, a life-servitude, no retiring pension, etc.—" Le Grand Péril de l'Église en France," by Abbé Bougaud (4th ed., 1879), pp. 2–23.—"Lettre Circulaire " (No. 53) of Mgr. Thiebaut, archbishop of Rouen, 1890, p. 618.

2 There is a gradual suppression of the subvention in 1877 and 1853 and a final one in 1885.

3 Abbé Bougaud, *ibid.*, p. 118, etc.—The lower seminary contains about 200 or 250 pupils. Scarcely one of these pays full board. They pay on the average from 100 to 200 frs. per head, while their maintenance costs 400 francs.—The instructors who are priests get 600 francs a year. Those who are not priests get 300 francs, which adds 12,000 francs to the expenses and brings the total deficit up to 42,000 or 52,000 francs.

finds its way to these low depths ; nobody ever reads the
newspaper, even the penny paper; vocations can here
shape themselves and become fixed like crystals, intact and
rigid, and all of a piece ; they are better protected than in
the upper layers, less exposed to mundane infiltrations; they
run less risk of being disturbed or thwarted by curiosity,
reason and scepticism, by modern ideas ; the outside
world and family surroundings do not, as elsewhere, interfere with their silent internal workings. When the choir-
boy comes home after the service, when the seminarian returns to his parents in his vacations, he does not here encounter so many disintegrating influences, various kinds of
information, free and easy talk, comparisons between careers,
concern about advancement, habits of comfort, maternal
solicitude, the shrugs of the shoulder and the half-smile of
the strong-minded neighbor ; stone upon stone and each
stone in its place, his faith gains strength and completed-
ness without any incoherency in its structure, with no in-
congruity in the materials, without having deviated from a
plumb-line. He has been taken in hand before his twelfth
year, when very young ; his curé, who has been instructed
from above to secure suitable subjects, has singled him out
in the catechism class and again at the ceremony of confirmation ;[1] he is found to have a pious tendency and a
taste for sacred ceremonies, a suitable demeanor, a mild
disposition, complacency, and is inclined to study ; he is a
docile and well-behaved child ; whether an acolyte at the
altar or in the sacristy, he tries to fold the chasuble properly;
all his genuflexions are correct, they do not worry him, he
has no trouble in standing still, he is not excited and diverted, like the others, by the eruptions of animal spirits
and rustic coarseness. If his rude brain is open to cultivation, if grammar and Latin can take root in it, the curé or
the vicar at once take charge of him ; he studies under them,

---

[1] Circular letter (No. 53) of M. Léon, archbishop of Rouen (1890), p. 618 and
following pages.

gratis or nearly so, until he is far enough advanced, and he then enters the lower seminary.

This is a school apart, a boarding-house of picked youths, an inclosed hot-house intended for the preservation and development of special vocations. None of these schools existed previous to 1789 ; at the present day, they number eighty-six in France, and all the pupils are to become future priests. No foreign plants, no future laymen, are admitted into this preparatory nursery ; [1] for experience has shown that if the lower seminary is mixed it no longer attains its ecclesiastical purpose ; " it habitually turns over to the upper seminary only the foot of the classes ; those at the head seek fortune elsewhere " ; on the contrary, " in the lower seminaries kept pure, the entire rhetoric class passes on into the upper seminary ; not only do they obtain the foot of the classes but the head."—The culture, in this second nursery, which is prolonged during five years, becomes extreme, wholly special ; it was less so under the ancient régime, even at Saint-Sulpice ; there was breakage in the glass which let in currents of air ; the archbishop's nephews and the younger sons of nobles predestined for Church dignities had introduced into it the laxity and liberties which were then the privileges of the episcopacy. During the vacations, [2] fairy scenes and pastorals were performed there with costumes and dances, " The Enthrone-

---

1 Abbé Bougaud, *ibid.*, p. 135. (Opinion of the archbishop of Aix, *ibid.*, p. 138.) " I know a lower seminary in which a class *en quatrième* of 44 pupils furnished only 4 priests, 40 having dropped out on the way. . . . I have been informed that a large *collège* in Paris, conducted by priests and containing 400 pupils, turned out in ten years but one of an ecclesiastical calling."—" Moniteur," March, 14, 1865. (Speech in the Senate by Cardinal Bonnechose.) " With us, discipline begins at an early age, first in the lower seminary and then in the upper seminary. . . . Other nations envy us our seminaries. They have not succeeded in establishing any like them. They cannot keep pupils so long; their pupils enter their seminaries only as day scholars."

2 " Histoire de M. Emery," by Abbé Elie Méric, i., 15, 17. " From 1786 onwards, the toleration of the drama was allowed to the philosophers, the ' Robertuis' and the Laon community; it was excluded from the great seminary where it ought never to have been admitted." This reform was effected by the new director, M. Emery, and met with such opposition that it almost cost him his life,

ment of the Great Mogul," and the "Shepherds in Chains";
the seminarians took great care of their hair ; a first-class
hair-dresser came and waited on them ; the doors were not
regularly shut : the youthful Talleyrand knew how to get
out into the city and begin or continue his gallantries.[1]
From and after the Concordat, stricter discipline in the new
seminaries had become monastic ; these are practical
schools, not for knowledge, but for training, the object
being much less to make learned men than believing priests ;
education takes precedence of instruction and intellectual
exercises are made subordinate to spiritual exercises[2]—
mass every day and five visits to the *Saint-Sacrament,* with
minute or half-hour prayer stations ; rosaries of sixty-three
paters and *aves,* litanies, the *angelus,* loud and whispered
prayers, special self-examinations, meditation on the knees,
edifying readings in common, silence until one o'clock in
the afternoon, silence at meals and the listening to an edifying discourse, frequent communions, weekly confessions,
general confession at New-year's, one day of retreat at the
end of every month after the vacations and before the col-
lation of each of the four orders, eight days of retirement

1 M. de Talleyrand, "Mémoires," vol. i. (Concerning one of his gallantries.)
"The superiors might have had some suspicion, . . . but Abbé Couturier had
shown them how to shut their eyes. He had taught them not to reprove a young
seminarist whom they believed destined to a high position, who might become
coadjutor at Rheims, perhaps a cardinal, perhaps minister, minister *de la feuille*
—who knows ? "

2 "Diary in France," by Christopher Wordsworth, D.D., 1845. (Weakness of
the course of study at Saint-Sulpice.) "There is no regular course of lectures
on ecclesiastical history."—There is still at the present day no special course of
Greek for learning to read the New Testament in the original.—" Le clergé
français en 1890 " (by an anonymous ecclesiastic), pp. 24-38. "High and substantial service is lacking with us. . . . For a long time, the candidates for the
episcopacy are exempt by a papal bull from the title of doctor."—In the seminary
there are discussions in barbarous Latin, antiquated subjects, bits of text, cut out
and wire-drawn : "They have not learned how to think. . . . Their science is
good for nothing ; they have no means or methods even for learning. . . . The
Testament of Christ is what they are most ignorant of. . . . A priest who devotes
himself to study is regarded either as a pure speculator unfit for the government,
or with an ambition which nothing can satisfy, or again an odd, ill-humored, ill-
balanced person ; we live under the empire of this stupid prejudice. . . . We have
archeologists, assyriologists, geologists, philologists and other *one-sided savants.*
The philosophers, theologians, historians, and canonists have become rare."

during which a suspension of all study, morning and evening sermons, spiritual readings, meditations, orisons and
other services from hour to hour ;[1] in short, the daily and
systematic application of a wise and steadily perfected
method, the most serviceable for fortifying faith, exalt-
ing the imagination, giving direction and impulse to the
will, analogous to that of a military school, Saint-Cyr or
Saumur, to such an extent that its corporeal and mental
imprint is indelible, and that by the way in which he thinks,
talks, smiles, bows and stands in your presence we at once
recognize a former pupil of Saint-Sulpice as we do a former
pupil of Saumur and of Saint-Cyr.

Thus graduated, an ordained and consecrated priest, first
a vicar and then a curé *desservant,* the discipline which has
bound and fashioned him still keeps him erect and presenting arms. Besides his duties in church and his ministra-
tions in the homes of his parishioners, besides masses,
vespers, sermons, catechisings, confessions, communions,
baptisms, marriages, extreme unctions, funerals, visiting
the sick and suffering, he has his personal and private exercises : at first, his breviary, the reading of which demands
each day an hour and a half, no practical duty being so
necessary. Lamennais obtained a dispensation from it, and
hence his lapses and fall.[2] Let no one object that such a
recitation soon becomes mechanical[3] ; the prayers, phrases
and words which it buries deep in the mind, even wandering, necessarily become fixed inhabitants in it, and hence
occult and stirring powers banded together which encompass the intellect and lay siege to the will, which, in the

---

1 " Journal d'un voyage en France," by Th. W. Allies, 1845, p. 38. (Table of
daily exercises in Saint-Sulpice furnished by Abbé Caron, former secretary to the
archbishop of Paris.)—Cf. in "Volupté," by Saint-Beuve, the same table furnished by Lacordaire.

2 "Manreze du prêtre," by the Rev. Father Caussette, i., 82.

3 *Ibid.,* i., 48. "Out of 360 meditations made by a priest during the year, 300
of them are arid." We have the testimony of Abbé d'Astros on the efficacy of
prayers committed to memory, who was in prison for three years under the first
empire and without any books. " I knew the psalms by heart and, thanks to this
converse with God, which escaped the jailor, I was never troubled with *ennui.*"

subterranean regions of the soul, gradually extend or fortify
their silent occupation of the place, which insensibly operate on the man without his being aware of it, and which,
at critical moments, unexpectedly rise up to steady his
footsteps or to save him from temptation.   Add to this antique custom two modern institutions which contribute to
the same end.   The first one is the monthly conference,
which brings together the *desservans* curés at the residence
of the oldest curé in the canton ; each has prepared a study
on some theme furnished by the bishopric, some question of
dogma, morality or religious history, which he reads aloud
and discusses with his brethren under the presidency and
direction of the oldest curé, who gives his final decision ;
this keeps theoretical knowledge and ecclesiastical erudi-
tion fresh in the minds of both reader and hearers.   The
other institution, almost universal nowadays, is the annual
retreat which the priests in the diocese pass in the large
seminary of the principal town.   The plan of it was traced
by Saint Ignatius ; his *Exercitia* is still to-day the manual
in use, the text of which is literally,[1] or very nearly, followed.[2]   The object is to reconstitute the supernatural
world in the soul, for, in general, it evaporates, becomes
effaced, and ceases to be palpable under the pressure of the
natural world.   Even the faithful pay very little attention
to it, while their vague conception of it ends in becoming
a mere verbal belief ; it is essential to give them back the
positive sensation, the contact and feeling.   To this end, a
man retires to a suitable place, where what he does active-
ly or passively is hourly determined for him in advance—
attendance at chapel or at preaching, telling his beads, lit-

---

[1] As with the "Frères des Écoles Chrétiennes," whose society has the most
members.

[2] "Manreze du prêtre," by the Rev. Father Caussette, i., 9.   The *Manrese* is
the grotto where Saint Ignatius found the plan of his *Exercitia* and the three
ways by which a man succeeds in detaching himself from the world, "the purga-
tive, the illuminative and the unitive."   The author says that he has brought all
to the second way, as the most suitable for priests.   He himself preached pastoral
retreats everywhere in France, his book being a collection of rules for retreats of
this kind,

anies, orisons aloud, orisons in his own breast, repeated self-examination, confession and the rest—in short, an uninterrupted series of diversified and convergent ceremonies which, by calculated degrees, drive out terrestrial preoccupations and overcome him with spiritual impressions ; immediately around him, impressions of the same kind followed by the contagion of example, mutual fervor, common expectation, involuntary emulation, and that overstrained eagerness which creates its object ; with all the more certainty that the individual himself works on himself, in silence, five hours a day, according to the prescriptions of a profound psychology, in order that his bare conception may take upon itself body and substance. Whatever may be the subject of his meditations, he repeats it twice the same day, and each time he begins by "creating the scene," the Nativity or the Passion, the Day of Judgment or Hell ; he converts the remote and undefined story, the dry, abstract dogma, into a detailed and figured representation ; he dwells on it, he evokes in turn the images furnished by the five senses, visual, audible, tactile, olfactory, and even gustatory ; he groups them together, and in the evening he animates them afresh in order that he may find them more intense when he awakes the next morning. He thus obtains the complete, precise, almost physical spectacle of his aspirations ; he reaches the *alibi*, that mental transposition, that reversal of the points of view in which the order of certainties becomes inverted, in which substantial objects seem to be vain phantoms and the mystic world a world of substantial reality.—According to persons and circumstances, the theme for meditation differs, and the retreat is prolonged for a shorter or longer period. For laymen, it generally lasts for three days only ; for the Brethren of the Christian Schools it is eight days annually, and when, at the age of twenty-eight, they take their vows in perpetuity, it lasts thirty days : for the secular priests, it lasts a little less than a week, while the theme on which their meditations are concentrated is the supernatural char-

acter of the priest. The priest who is confessor and minis-
trant of the Eucharist, the priest who is the saviour and
restorer, the priest who is pastor, preacher and administrator—such are the subjects on which their imagination,
assisted and directed, must work in order to compose the
cordial which has to support them for the entire year.
None is more potent ; that which the Puritans drank at an
American camp-meeting or at a Scotch revival was stronger
but of less enduring effect.[1]

Two different cordials, one strengthening the other, are
mixed together in this drink, both being of high flavor and
so rank as to burn an ordinary mouth.—On the one hand,
with the freedom of language and the boldness of deduction characteristic of the method, the sentiment of the
priest's dignity is exalted. What is the priest? "He is, between God who is in heaven and the man who tries to find

---

[1] One of these enduring effects is the intense faith of the prelates, who in the
last century believed so little. At the present day, not made bishops until about
fifty years of age, thirty of which have been passed in exercises of this description, their piety has taken the Roman, positive, practical turn which terminates
in devotions properly so called. M. Emery, the reformer of Saint-Sulpice, gave
the impulsion in this sense. ("Histoire de M. Emery," by Abbé Elie Méric, p.
115 etc.) M. Emery addressed the seminarians thus : "Do you think that, if we
pray to the Holy Virgin sixty times a day to aid us at the hour of death, she will
desert us at the last moment ? "—"He led us into the chapel, which he had decked
with reliquaries. . . . He made the tour of it, kissing in turn each reliquary with
respect and love, and when he found one of them out of reach for this homage,
he said to us, 'Since we cannot kiss that one, let us accord it our profoundest
reverence !' . . . And we all three kneeled before the reliquary."—Among other
episcopal lives, that of Cardinal Pie, bishop of Poitiers, presents the order of
devotion in high relief. ("Histoire du Cardinal Pie," by M. Bannard, ii., 348
and *passim*.) There was a statuette of the Virgin on his bureau. After his death,
a quantity of paper scraps, in Latin or French, written and placed there by him-
were found, dedicating this or that action, journey or undertaking under the
special patronage of the Virgin or St. Joseph. He also possessed a statuette of
Our Lady of Lourdes which never was out of his sight, day or night. "One day,
having gone out of his palace, he suddenly returned, having forgotten something
—he had neglected to kiss the feet of his Heavenly Mother."—Cf. "Vie de Mgr.
Dupanloup," Abbé Lagrange, i., 524. "During his mother's illness, he multiplied the *neuvaines*, visited every altar, made vows, burnt candles, for *not only
had he devotion, but devotions*. . . . On the 2d of January, 1849, there was fresh
alarm ; thereupon, a *neuvaine* at Saint-Geneviève and a vow—no longer the chap-
let, but the rosary. Then, as the fête of Saint François de Sales drew near, a
new *neuvaine* to this great Savoyard saint ; prayers to the Virgin in Saint-Sulpice ; to the faithful Virgin ; to the most wise Virgin, everywhere."

him on earth, a being, *God and man,* who brings these
nearer by his impersonating both.[1] . . . I do not flatter
you with pious hyperboles in calling you gods; this is not a
rhetorical falsehood. . . . You are creators similar to Mary
in her coöperation in the Incarnation. . . . You are creators like God in time. . . . You are creators like God in
eternity. Our creation on our part, our daily creation, is
nothing less than the Word made flesh itself. . . . God
may create other worlds, he cannot so order it that any act
under the sun can be greater than your sacrifice; for, at
this moment, he reposes in your hands all that he has and
all that he is. . . . I am not a little lower than the cheru-
bim and seraphim in the government of the world, I am far
above them; they are only the servants of God, we are his
coadjutors. . . . The angels, who behold the vast riches
passing through our hands daily, are amazed at our prerogative. . . . I fulfil three sublime functions in relation
to the god of our altars—I cause him to descend, I administer his body, I am his custodian. . . . Jesus dwells under
your lock and key; his hours of reception begin and end
through you, he does not move without your permission,
he gives no benediction without your assistance, he bestows
nothing except at your hands, and his dependence is so
dear to him that, for eighteen hundred years, he has not
left the Church for one moment to lose himself on the
glory of his Father."—On the other hand, they are made
to drink in full draughts the sentiment of subordination,
which they imbibe to their very marrow.[2] "Ecclesiastical
obedience is . . . a love of dependence, a violation of
judgment. . . . Would you know what it is as to the extent of sacrifice ? A voluntary death, the sepulchre of the
will, says Saint Climaque. . . . There is a sort of *real presence* infused into those who command us. . . ." Let us
be careful not to fall " into the crafty opposition of lib-

1 " Manreze du prêtre," i., 27, 29, 30, 31, 35, 91, 92, 244, 246, 247, 268.
2 *Ibid.*, i., 279, 281, 301, 307, 308, 319.

eral Catholicism. . . . Liberalism, in its consequences, is
social atheism. . . . Unity, in Roman faith, is not sufficient; let us labor together in the unity of the Roman
spirit; for that, let us always judge Rome with the optimism of affection. . . . Each new dogmatic definition produces its own advantages: that of the Immaculate Conception has given us Lourdes and its truly œcumenical won-
ders."

   Nothing of all this is too much, and, in the face of the
exigencies of modern times, it scarcely suffices. Now that
society has become incredulous, indifferent or, at the least,
laic, the priest must possess the two intense and master
ideas which support a soldier abroad among insurgents or
barbarians, one being the conviction that he is of a species
and essence apart, infinitely superior to the common herd ;
and the other is the thought that he belongs to his flag, to
his chiefs, especially to the commanding general, and that
he has given himself up entirely to prompt obedience, to
obeying every order issued without question or doubt.
Thus, in that parish where the permanent curé was once
installed, especially in the rural districts,[1] the legal and
popular governor of all souls, his successor, the removable
desservant, is merely a resident bailiff, a sentry in his box, at
the opening of a road which the public at large no longer
travel. From time to time he hails you ! But scarcely
any one listens to him. Nine out of ten men pass at a distance, along a newer, more convenient and broader road.
They either nod to him afar off or give him the go-by.

---

   [1] " Le clergé française en 1890" (by an anonymous ecclesiastic), p. 72. (On the
smaller parishes.) " The task of the curé here is thankless if he is zealous, too
easy if he has no zeal. In any event, he is an isolated man, with no resources
whatever, tempted by all the demons of solitude and inactivity."—*Ibid.*, 92. "Our
authority among the common classes as well as among thinking people is held
in check; the human mind is to-day fully emancipated and society secularized."—
Ibid., 15. " Indifference seems to have retired from the summits of the nation
only to descend to the lower strata. . . . In France, the priest is the more
liked the less he is seen ; to efface himself, to disappear is what is first and often-
est demanded of him. The clergy and the nation live together side by side,
scarcely in contact, through certain actions in life, and never intermingling."

Some are even ill-disposed, watching him or denouncing him to the ecclesiastic or lay authorities on which he depends.   He is expected to make his orders respected and yet not hated, to be zealous and yet not importunate, to act and yet not efface himself: he succeeds pretty often, thanks to the preparation just described, and, in his rural sentry-box, patient, resigned, obeying his orders, he mounts guard lonely and in solitude, a guard which, for the past fifteen years, is disturbed and anxious and becoming singularly difficult.

BOOK SIXTH.

𝕻𝖚𝖇𝖑𝖎𝖈 𝕴𝖓𝖘𝖙𝖗𝖚𝖈𝖙𝖎𝖔𝖓.

——

CHAPTER I.

I. Public instruction and its three effects.—Influences of the master,
of the pupils on each other, and of discipline.—Case in which all three
tend towards producing a particular type of man. II. Napoleon's
aim.—University monopoly.—Revival and multitude of private
schools.—Napoleon regards them unfavorably.—His motives.—Private enterprises compete with public enterprise.—Measures against
them.—Previous authorization necessary and optional suppression of
them.—Taxes on free education in favor of the university.—Decree
of November, 1811.—Limitation of secondary teaching in private
schools.—How the university takes away their pupils.—Day-schools as
prescribed.—Number of boarders limited.—Measures for the restriction
or assimilation of ecclesiastical schools.—Recruits forcibly obtained
in prominent and ill-disposed families.—Napoleon the sole educator
in his empire. III. His machinery.—The educating body.—How its
members come to realize their union.—Hierarchy of rank.—How
ambition and *amour-propre* are gratified.—The monastic principle of
celibacy.—The monastic and military principle of obedience.—Obligations contracted and discipline enforced.—The École Normale and
recruits for the future university. IV. Object of the educational
corps and adaptation of youth to the established order of things.—
Sentiments required of children and adults.—Passive acceptance of
these rules.—Extent and details of school regulations.—Emulation
and the desire to be at the head.—Constant competition and annual
distribution of prizes. V. Military preparation and the cult of the
Emperor.

AT fixed intervals a man, in a room, gathers around him
children, youths, a group of young people, ten, twenty,

407

thirty or more; he talks to them for one or two hours and they listen to him. They sit alongside of each other, look in each other's faces, touch each other's elbows, feel that they are fellow-disciples, of the same age and occupied alike; they form a society and in two ways, one with another and all with the master. Hence they live under a statute: every society has one of its own, spontaneous or imposed on it; as soon as men, little or big, come together in any number, in a drawing-room, in a café, in the street, they find themselves subject to a local charter, a sort of code which prescribes to them, or interdicts a certain sort of conduct. And so with the school: positive rules along with many tacit rules are here observed and these form a mould which stamps on minds and souls a lasting imprint. Whatever a public lesson may be, whatever its object, laic or ecclesiastic, whether its subject-matter is religious or scientific, from the bottom to the top of the scale, from the primary school and the catechism up to the great seminary, in upper schools and in the faculties, we find in abridgment the academic institution. Of all social engines, it is probably the most powerful and the most efficacious; for it exercises three kinds of influence on the young lives it enfolds and directs, one through the master, another through con-discipleship and the last through rules and regulations.

On the one hand, the master, who passes for a savant, teaches with authority and the scholars, who feel that they are ignorant, learn with confidence.—On the other hand, outside of his family and the domestic circle, the pupil finds in his group of comrades a new, different and complete world which has its own ways and customs, its own sense of honor and its own vices, its own view of things (*esprit de corps*), in which independent and spontaneous judgments arise, precocious and haphazard divinations, expressions of opinion on all things human and divine. It is in this environment that he begins to think for himself, in contact with others like himself and his equals, in contact

with their ideas, much more intelligible and acceptable to
him than those of mature men, and therefore much more
persuasive, contagious and exciting ; these form for him the
ambient, penetrating atmosphere in which his thought arises,
grows and shapes itself ; he here adopts his way of looking
at the great society of adults of which he is soon to become
a member, his first notions of justice and injustice, and
hence an anticipated attitude of respect or of rebellion, in
short, a *prejudice* which, according as the spirit of the group
is reasonable or unreasonable, is either sound or unsound,
social or antisocial.—Finally, the discipline of the school has
its effect.   Whatever its rules and regulations may be,
whether liberal or despotic, lax or strict, monastic, military
or worldly, whether a boarding or a day school, mixed or
exclusive, in town or in country, with greater or less stress
no gymnastic training or on brain-work, with the mind given
to studying objects or to the study of words, the pupil enters into an order of things fashioned for him beforehand.
According to the diversities of the system (*cadre*) he practises
different exercises ; he contracts different habits ; he is
developed or stunted physically or morally, in one sense or
in a contrary sense.   Hence, just as the system is good or
bad, he becomes more or less capable or incapable of bodily
or mental effort, of reflection, of invention, of taking the
initiative, of starting an enterprise, of subordinating himself
to a given purpose, of willing, persistent association, that is
to say, in sum, of playing an active and useful part on the
stage of the world he is about to enter upon.   Observe that
this apprenticeship in common, sitting on benches according to certain regulations and under a master, lasts six, ten,
fifteen years and often twenty ; that girls are not exempt
from it ; that not one boy out of a hundred is educated to
the end at home by a private teacher ; that, in secondary
and even in superior instruction, the school wheel turns
uniformly and without stopping ten hours a day if the
scholar boards outside, and twenty-four hours a day if he
boards within ; that at this age the human clay is soft, that

it has not yet received its shape, that no acquired and re-
sistent form yet protects it from the potter's hand, against
the weight of the turning-wheel, against the friction of other
morsels of clay kneaded alongside of it, against the three
pressures, constant and prolonged, which compose public
education.

Evidently, there is here an enormous force, especially if
the three pressures, instead of opposing each other, as often
happens, combine and converge towards the production of
a certain finished type of man ; if, from infancy to youth
and from youth to adult age, the successive stages of preparation are superposed in such a way as to stamp the
adopted type deeper and with more exactness ; if all the
influences and operations that impress it, near or far, great
or small, internal or external, form together a coherent, defined, applicable and applied system.   Let the State undertake its fabrication and application, let it monopolize public education, let it become its regulator, director and contractor, let it set up and work its machine throughout the
length and breadth of the land, let it, through moral authority and legal constraint, force the new generation to enter
therein—it will find twenty years later in these minors who
have become major, the kind and number of ideas it aimed
to provide, the extent, limit and form of mind it approves
of, and the moral and social prejudice that suits its purposes.

II.

Such is the aim of Napoleon :   " In the establishment of
an educational corps," he says to himself,[1] " my principal
aim is to secure the means for directing political and moral
opinions."   Still more precisely, he counts on the new institution to set up and keep open for inspection a universal
and complete police repertory.   " This body must be orga-

---

[1] Pelet de la Lozère, 161. (Speech by Napoleon to the Council of State, March 11,
1806.)

nized in such a way as to keep notes on each child after the age of nine years." Having seized adults he wants to seize children also, watch and shape future Frenchmen in advance ; brought up by him, in his hands or in sight, they become ready-made auxiliaries, docile subjects and more docile than their parents. Amongst the latter, there are still too many unsubmissive and refractory spirits, too many royalists and too many republicans ; domestic traditions from family to family contradict each other or vary, and children grow up in their homes only to clash with each other in society afterwards. Let us anticipate this conflict; let us prepare them for concord ; all brought up in the same fashion, they will some day or other find themselves unanimous,[1] not only apparently, as nowadays through fear or force, but in fact and fundamentally, through inveterate habit and by previous adaptation of imagination and affection. Otherwise, " there will be no stable political state " in France [2] ; " so long as one grows up without knowing whether to be republican or monarchist, Catholic or irreligious, the State will never form a nation ; it will rest on uncertain and vague foundations ; it will be constantly exposed to disorder and change."—Consequently, he assigns to himself the monopoly of public instruction ; he alone is to enjoy the right to manufacture and sell this like salt and tobacco ; " public instruction, throughout the Empire, is entrusted *exclusively* to the university. No school, no establishment for instruction whatever," superior, secondary, primary, special, general, collateral, laic or ecclesiastic, " may be organized outside of the imperial university and without the authorization of its chief."[3]

---

1 A. de Beauchamp, " Recueil des lois et réglemens sur l'enseignement supérieur," vol. iv. (Report of Fourcroy to the Corps Législatif, May 6, 1806.) " How important it is . . . that the mode of education admitted to be the best should add to this advantage, that of being *uniform* for the whole Empire, teaching the same knowledge, inculcating the same principles on individuals who must live together in the same society, forming in some way but one body, possessing but one mind, and all contributing to the public good through *unanimity* of sentiment and action."

2 Pelet de la Lozère, 154.

3 A. de Beauchamp, *ibid.* (Decree of March 7, 1808.)—Special and collateral schools

Every manufactory of school product within these boundaries and operating under this direction is of two sorts. Some of them, in the best places, interconnected and skilfully grouped, are national factories founded by the government, or at its command, by the communes,—faculties, lycées, colleges, and small communal schools ; others, isolated and scattered about, are private factories founded by individuals, such as boarding-schools and institutions for secondary instruction, small free schools. The former, works of the State, ruled, managed, supported and turned to account by it, according to the plan prescribed by it and for the object it has proposed, are simply a prolongation of itself ; it is the State which operates in them and which, directly and entirely, acts through them : they enjoy therefore all its favor and the others all its disfavor. The latter, during the Consulate, revived or sprung up by hundreds, in all directions, spontaneously, under the pressure of necessity, and because the young need instruction as they need clothes, but haphazard, as required according to demand and supply, without any superior and common regulation— nothing being more antipathetic to the governmental genius of Napoleon: " It is impossible," he says,[1] " to remain longer as we are, since everybody can start an education shop the same as a cloth shop" and furnish as he pleases, or as his customers please, this or that piece of stuff, even of poor quality, and of this or that fashion, even extravagant or out of date : hence so many different dresses, and a horrible medley. One good obligatory coat, of stout cloth and suitable cut, a uniform for which the public authority supplies the pattern, is what should go on the back of every child, youth or young man ; private individuals who undertake this matter are mistrusted beforehand. Even when obedient, they are only half-docile ; they take their own course

---

which teach subjects not taught in the lycées, for example the living languages, which are confined to filling a gap, and do not compete with the lycées, are subject to previous authorization and to university pay.

[1] Pelet de la Lozère, p. 170. (Session of the Council of State, March 20, 1806.)

and have their own preferences, they follow their own taste or that of parents. Every private enterprise, simply because it exists and thrives, constitutes a more or less independent and dissentient group. Napoleon, on learning that Sainte-Barbe, restored under the direction of M. de Lanneau, had five hundred inmates, exclaims[1] : " How does it happen that an ordinary private individual has so many in his house ?" The Emperor almost seems jealous ; it seems as if he had just discovered a rival in one corner of his university domain ; this man is an usurper on the domain of the sovereign ; he has constituted himself a centre ; he has collected around him clients and a platoon ; now, as Louis XIV. said, the State must have no "platoons apart." Since M. de Lanneau has talent and is successful, let him enter the official ranks and become a functionary. Napoleon at once means to get hold of him, his house and his pupils, and orders M. de Fontaines, Grand-Master of the University, to negotiate the affair ; M. de Lanneau will be suitably compensated ; Sainte-Barbe will be formed into a lycée, and M. de Lanneau shall be put at the head of it. Let it be noted that he is not an opponent, a man that is not all right. M. de Fontaines himself praises his teaching, his excellent mind, his perfect exactitude, and calls him the *universitarian of the university*. But he does not belong to it, he stands aloof and stays at home, he is not disposed to become a mere cog-wheel in the imperial manufactory. Therefore, whether he is aware of it or not, he does it harm, and all the more according to his prosperity ; his full house empties the lycées ; the more pupils he has the less they have. Private enterprises in their essence enter into competition with public enterprise.

For this reason, if tolerated by the latter, it is reluctantly and because nothing else can be done ; there are too many of them ; the money and the means to replace them at one stroke would be wanting. Moreover, with instruction, the

[1] Quicherat, " Histoire de Sainte-Barbe," iii., 125.

consumers, as with other supplies and commodities, naturally dislike monopoly ; they must be gradually brought to
it ; resignation must come to them through habit. The
State, accordingly, may allow private enterprises to exist, at
least for the time being. But, on condition of their being
kept in the strictest dependence, of its arrogating to itself
the right over them of life and death, of reducing them to
the state of tributaries and branches, of utilizing them, of
transforming their native and injurious rivalry into a fruitful and forced collaboration. Not only must private schools
obtain from the State its express consent to be born, for lack
of which they are closed and their principals punished,[1]
but again, even when licensed, they live subject to the good-
will of the Grand-Master, who can and must close them as
soon as he recognizes in them "grave abuses and principles
contrary to those professed by the University." Meanwhile, the University supports itself with their funds ; since
it alone has the right to teach, it may profit by this right,
concede for money the faculty of teaching or of being taught
alongside of it, oblige every head of an institution to pay so
much for himself and so much for each of his pupils ; in
sum, here as elsewhere, in derogation of the university
blockade, as with the continental blockade, the State sells
licenses to certain parties. So true is this that, even with
superior instruction, when nobody competes with it, it sells
them ; every graduate who gives a course of lectures on
literature or on science must pay beforehand, for the year,
seventy-five francs at Paris and fifty francs in the provinces.
Every graduate who lectures on law or medicine must pay
beforehand one hundred and fifty francs at Paris and one

---

1 A. de Beauchamp, *ibid.* (Decrees of March 17, 1808, arts. 103 and 105, of Sep.
17, 1808, arts. 2 and 3 of Novem. 15, 1801, arts. 54, 55 and 56.) "Should any one
publicly teach and keep a school without the Grand-Master's consent, he will be
officially prosecuted by our imperial judges, who will close the school. . . . He
will be brought before the criminal court and condemned to a fine of from one
hundred to two hundred francs, without prejudice to greater penalties, should he
be found guilty of having directed instruction in a way contrary to order and to
the public interest."—*Ibid.*, art. 57. (On the closing of schools provided with prescribed authority.)

hundred francs in the provinces.[1] There is the same annual duty on the directors of secondary schools, boarding-schools and private institutions. Moreover, to obtain the indispensable license, the master of a boarding-school at Paris must pay three hundred francs, and in a province two hundred francs ; the principal of an institution in Paris pays six hundred francs, and in the provinces four hundred francs ; besides that, this license, always revocable, is granted only for ten years ; at the end of the ten years the titulary must obtain a renewal and pay the tax anew. As to his pupils, of whatever kind, boarding scholars, day scholars, or even gratis,[2] the University levies on each a tax equal to the twentieth of the cost of full board ; the director himself of the establishment is the one who fixes and levies the tax ; he is the responsible collector of it, book-keeper and the debtor. Let him not forget to declare exactly the terms of his school and the number of his pupils ; otherwise, there is investigation, verification, condemnation, restitution, fine, censure, and the possible closing of his establishment.

Regulations, stricter and stricter, tighten the cord around his neck and, in 1811, the rigid articles of the last decree draw so tight as to insure certain strangling at short date. Napoleon counts on that.[3] For his lycées, especially at the start, have not succeeded ; they have failed to obtain the confidence of families ;[4] the discipline is too military, the

---

1 A. de Beauchamp, *ibid.* (Decree of Sep. 17, 1808, arts. 27, 28, 29, 30, and act passed April 7, 1809.)

2 *Id., ibid.* (Decrees of March 17, 1808, art. 134 ; of Sep. 17, 1808, arts. 25 and 26 ; of Nov. 15, 1811, art. 63).

3 Ambroise Rendu, "Essai sur l'instruction publique," 4 vols., 1819, i., 221. (Notice to M. de Fontanes, March 24, 1808. "The university undertakes all public institutions, and *its tendency must be to have as few private institutions as possible.*"

4 Eugène Rendu, "Ambroise Rendu et l'Université de France" (1861), pp. 25, 26. (Letter of the Emperor to Fourcroy, Floreal 3, year XIII, ordering him to inspect the lycées and Report of Fourcroy at the end of four months.) " In general, the drum, the drill and military discipline prevent parents in the largest number of the towns from sending their children to the lycée. . . . Advantage is taken of this measure to make parents believe that the Emperor wants only to make soldiers." *Ibid.* (Note of M. de Champagny, Minister of the Interior, written a few months

education is not sufficiently paternal, the principals and professors are only indifferent functionaries, more or less egoist or worldly ; only former subaltern officers, rude and foul-mouthed, serve as superintendents and assistant-teachers ; the holders of State scholarships bring with them "habits fashioned out of a bad education," or by the ignorance of almost no education at all,[1] so that "for a child that is well born and well brought up," their companionship is disproportionate and their contact as baneful as it is repulsive. Consequently, the lycées during the first years,[2] solely filled with the few holders of scholarships, remain deserted or scarcely occupied, whilst "the élite of the young crowd into private schools more or less dear."

This élite of which the University is thus robbed must be got back. Since the young do not attend the lycée because they like it, they must come through necessity ; to this end, other issues are rendered difficult and several are entirely barred ; and better still, all those that are tolerated are made to converge to one sole central outlet, a university establishment, in such a way that the director of each private school, changed from a rival into a purveyor, serves

---

later.) "A large half of the heads (of the lycée) or professors is, from a moral point of view, completely indifferent. One quarter, by their talk, their conduct, their reputation, exhibit the most dangerous character to the youths. . . . The greatest defect of the principals is the religious spirit, religious zeal. . . . There are not more than two or three lycées in which this is apparent. Hence the coolness of the parents which is attributed to political prejudices ; hence the rarity of peasant pupils ; hence the discredit of the lycées. In this respect opinion is unanimous."

1 "Histoire du Collége Louis le Grand," by Esmond, emeritus censor, 1845, p. 267 : "Who were the assistant-teachers ? Retired subaltern officers who preserved the coarseness of the camp and knew of no virtue but passive obedience. . . . The age at which scholarships were given was not fixed, the Emperor's choice often falling on boys of fifteen or sixteen, who presented themselves with habits already formed out of a bad education and so ignorant that one was obliged to assign them to the lowest classes, along with children."—Fabry, "Mémoires pour servir à l'histoire de l'instruction publique depuis 1789," i., 3)1. "The kernel of boarding-scholars (holders of scholarships) was furnished by the Prytanée. Profound corruption, to which the military régime gives an appearance of regularity, a cool impiety which conforms to the outward ceremonies of religion as to the movements of a drill, . . . steady tradition has transmitted this spirit to all the pupils that have succeeded each other for twelve years."

2 Fabry, *ibid.*, vol. ii., 12, and vol. iii., 399.

the university instead of injuring it and gives it pupils instead of taking them away. In the first place, his high standard of instruction is limited;[1] even in the country and in the towns that have neither lycée nor college, he must teach nothing above a fixed degree ; if he is the principal of an institution, this degree must not go beyond the class of the humanities ; he must leave to the faculties of the State their domain intact, differential calculus, astronomy, geology, natural history and superior literature ; if he is the master of a boarding-school, this degree must not extend beyond grammar classes, nor the first elements of geometry and arithmetic ; he must leave to State lycées and colleges their domain intact, the humanities properly so called, superior lectures and means of secondary instruction.—In the second place, in the towns possessing a lycée or college, he must teach at home only what the University leaves untaught ;[2] he is not deprived, indeed, of the younger boys ; he may still instruct and keep them ; but he must conduct all his pupils over ten years of age to the college or lycée, where they will regularly follow the classes as day-scholars. Consequently, daily and twice a day, he marches them to and fro between his house and the university establishment ; before going, in the intermission, and after the class is dismissed he examines them in the lesson they have received out of his house ; apart from that, he lodges and feeds them, his office being reduced to this. He is nothing beyond a watched and serviceable auxiliary, a subaltern, a University tutor and " coach," a sort of unpaid, or rather paying, schoolmaster and innkeeper in its employ.

All this does not yet suffice. Not only does the State recruit its day-scholars in his establishment but it takes

---

1 Decree of Nov. 15, 1811, articles 15, 16, 22.

2 Quicherat, *ibid.*, iii., 93 to 105.—Up to 1809, owing to M. de Fontane's toleration, M. de Lanneau could keep one half of his pupils in his house under the name of pupils in preparatory classes, or for the lectures in French or on commerce ; nevertheless, he was obliged to renounce teaching philosophy. In 1810, he is ordered to send all his scholars to the lycée within three months. There were at this date 400 scholars in Sainte-Barbe.

from him his boarding-scholars. " On and after the first of November 1812,[1] the heads of institutions and the masters of boarding-schools shall receive no resident pupils in their houses above the age of nine years, until the lycée or college, established in the same town or place where there is a lycée, shall have as many boarders as it can take." This complement shall be three hundred boarders per lycée ; there are to be " eighty lycées in full operation " during the year 1812, and one hundred in the course of the year 1813, so that, at this last date, the total of the complement demanded, without counting that of the colleges, amounts to thirty thousand boarding-scholars. Such is the enormous levy of the State on the crop of boarding-school pupils. It evidently seizes the entire crop in advance ; private establishments, after it, can only glean, and through tolerance. In reality, the decree forbids them to receive boarding-scholars; henceforth, the University will have the monopoly of them.

The proceedings against the small seminaries, more energetic competitors, are still more vigorous. " There shall be but one secondary ecclesiastical school in each department ; the Grand-Master will designate those that are to be maintained ; the others are to be closed. None of them shall be in the country." All those not situated in a town provided with a lycée or with a college shall be closed. All the buildings and furniture belonging to the ecclesiastic schools not retained shall be seized and confiscated for the benefit of the University. " In all places where ecclesiastical schools exist, the pupils of these schools shall be taken to

---

1 Decree of Nov. 15, 1811, articles 1, 4, 5, 9, 17 to 19 and 24 to 32.—" Procès-verbaux des séances du conseil de l'Université impériale." (Manuscripts in the archives of the Ministry of Public Instruction, furnished by M. A. de Beauchamp), session of March 12, 1811, note of the Emperor communicated by the Grand-Master. " His Majesty requires that the following arrangement be added to the decree presented to him : *Wherever there is a lycée, the Grand-Master will order private institutions to be closed until the lycée has all the boarders it can contain.*" The personal intervention of Napoleon is here evident ; the decree starts with him ; he wished it at once more rigorous, more decidedly arbitrary and prohibitive.

the lycée or college and join its classes." Finally, "all
these schools shall be under the control of the University ;
they must be organized only by her ; their prospectus and
their regulations must be drawn up by the council of the
University at the suggesiton of the Grand-Master. The
teaching must be done only by members of the University
at the disposition of the Grand-Master."—In like manner,
in the lay schools, at Sainte-Barbe for example,[1] every professor, private tutor, or even common superintendent, must
be provided with a special authorization by the University.
Staff and discipline, the spirit and matter of the teaching,
every detail of study and recreation,[2] all are imposed, conducted and restrained in these so-called free establishments;
whatever they may be, ecclesiastic or laic, not only does
the University surround and hamper them, but again it absorbs and assimilates them ; it does not even leave them anything distinctly external.   It is true that, in the small seminaries, the exercises begin at the ringing of a bell, and the
pupils wear an ecclesiastic dress ; but the priest's gown,
adopted by the State that adopts the Church, is still a State
uniform.   In the other private establishments, the uniform
is that which it imposes, the lay uniform, belonging to colleges and lycées "under penalty of being closed " ; while,
in addition, there is the drum, the demeanor, the habits,
ways and regularity of the barracks.   All initiative, all invention, all diversity, every professional or local adaptation
is abolished.[3]   M. de Lanneau thus wrote [4] : " I am nothing

---

1 Quicherat, *ibid.*, iii., 95–105.—*Ibid.*, 126. After the decree of November 15,
1811, threatening circulars follow each other for fifteen months and always to hold
fast or annoy the heads of institutions or private schools. Even in the smallest
boarding-schools, the school exercises must be announced by the drum and the
uniform worn under penalty of being shut up.

2 *Ibid.*, iii., 42.—At Sainte-Barbe, before 1808, there were various sports favoring
agility and flexibility of the body, such as running races, etc. All that is suppressed by the imperial University ; it does not admit that anything can be done
better or otherwise than by itself.

3 Decree of March 17, 1808, article 38. Among " the bases of teaching," the
legislator prescribes " obedience to the statutes the object of which is the *uniformity of instruction.*"

4 Quicherat, iii., 128.

but a sergeant-major of languid and mangled classes . . . to the tap of a drum and under military colors."

There is no longer any public or even private refuge against the encroachments of this "university" institution ; for the last of all, domestic education at home, is not respected. In 1808,[1] "among the old and wealthy families which are not in the system," Napoleon selects ten from each department and fifty at Paris of which the sons from sixteen to eighteen must be compelled to go to Saint-Cyr and, on leaving it, into the army as second lieutenants.[2] In 1813, he adds ten thousand more of them, many of whom are the sons of Conventionalists or Vendéans, who, under the title of guards of honor, are to form a corps apart and who are at once trained in the barracks. All the more necessary is the subjection to this Napoleonic education of the sons of important and refractory families, everywhere numerous in the annexed countries. Already in 1802, Fourcroy had explained in a report to the legislative corps the political and social utility of the future University.[3] Napoleon, at his discretion, may recruit and select scholars among his recent subjects ; only, it is not in a lycée that he places them, but in a still more military school, at La Flèche, of which the pupils are all sons of officers and, so to say, children of the army. Towards the end of 1812, he orders the Roman prince Patrizzi to send his two sons to this school, one seventeen years of age and the other thirteen[4] ; and, to be sure of them, he has them taken from

---

1 " The Modern Régime," i., 164.

2 See, for a comprehension of the full effect of this forced education, "Les Mécontens" by Mérimée, the rôle of Lieutenant Marquis Edward de Naugis.

3 "Recueil," by A. de Beauchamp ; Report by Fourcroy, April 20, 1802 : "The populations which have become united with France and which, speaking a different language and accustomed to foreign institutions, need to abandon old habits and refashion themselves on those of their new country, cannot find at home the essential means for giving their sons the instruction, the manners and the character which should amalgamate them with Frenchmen. What destiny could be more advantageous for them and, at the same time, what a resource for the government, which desires nothing so much as to attach new citizens to France ! "

4 "Journal d'un détenu de 1807 à 1814" (1 vol., 1828, in English), p. 167. (An account given by Charles Choderlos de Laclos, who was then at La Flèche.

their home and brought there by gendarmes. Along with these, ninety other Italians of high rank are counted at La Flèche, the Dorias, the Pallavicinis, the Alfieris, with one hundred and twenty young men of the Illyrian provinces, others again furnished by the countries of the Rhine confederation, in all three hundred and sixty inmates at eight hundred francs per annum. The parents might often accompany or follow their children and establish themselves within reach of them. This privilege was not granted to Prince Patrizzi ; he was stopped on the road at Marseilles and kept there.—In this way, through the skilful combination of legislative prescriptions with arbitrary appointments, Napoleon becomes in fact, directly or indirectly, the sole head-schoolmaster of all Frenchmen old or new, the unique and universal educator in his empire.

III.

To effect this purpose, he requires a good instrument, some great human machine which, designed, put together and set up by himself, henceforth works alone and of its own accord, without deviating or breaking down, conformably to his instructions and always under his eye, but without the necessity of his lending a hand and personally interfering in its predetermined and calculated movement. The finest engines of this sort are the religious orders, masterpieces of the Catholic, Roman and governmental mind, all managed from above according to fixed rules in view of a definite object, so many kinds of intelligent automatons, alone capable of working indefinitely without loss of energy, with persistency, uniformity and precision, at the minimum of cost and the maximum of effect, and this through the simple play of their internal mechanism which, fully regulated beforehand, adapts them completely and ready-made to this special service, to the social operations which a recognized authority and a superior intelligence have assigned to them as their function.—Nothing

could be better suited to the social instinct of Napoleon, to
his imagination, his taste, his political policy and his plans,
and on this point he loftily proclaims his preferences. " I
know," says he to the Council of State, " that the Jesuits,
as regards instruction, have left a very great void. I do
not want to restore them, nor any other body that has its
sovereign at Rome."[1] Nevertheless, one is necessary.
" As for myself, I would rather confide public education to
a religious order than leave it as it is to-day," which means
free and abandoned to private individuals. " But I want
neither one nor the other." Two conditions are requisite
for the new establishment. First of all, " I want a corporation, because a corporation never dies " ; it alone, through
its perpetuity, maintains teaching in the way marked out
for it, brings up " according to fixed principles " successive
generations, thus assuring the stability of the political State,
and "inspires youth with a spirit and opinions in conformity with the new laws of the empire." But this corporation must be laic. Its members are to be State and not
Church " Jesuits ";[2] they must belong to the Emperor and
not to the Pope, and will form, in the hands of the government, a civil militia composed of "ten thousand persons,"
administrators and professors of every degree, comprehending schoolmasters, an organized, coherent and lasting
militia.

As it must be laic, there must be no hold on it through
dogma or faith, paradise or hell, no spiritual incitements ;
consequently, temporal means are to be employed, not
less efficacious, when one knows how to manage them,
—*amour propre*, emulation, imagination, ambition, the
grandiose, vague hope of indefinite promotion, in short,
the means and motives already maintaining the temper and

---

[1] Pelet de la Lozère, *ibid.*, pp. 162, 163, 167. (Speeches by Napoleon to the Council
of State, sessions of Feb. 10, March 1, 11 and 20, April 7, and May 21 and 29, 1806.)

[2] Napoleon himself said this : " I want a corporation, not of Jesuits whose
sovereign is in Rome, but Jesuits who have no ambition but to be useful and no
interest but the interest of the State."

zeal of the army. " The educational corps must copy the classification of military grades ;" an " order of promotion," a hierarchy of places is to be instituted ; no one will attain superior rank without having passed through the inferior ; " no one can become a principal without having been a teacher, nor professor in the higher classes without having taught in the lower ones."—And, on the other hand, the highest places will be within reach of all ; " the young, who devote themselves to teaching, will enjoy the perspective of rising from one grade to another, up to the highest dignities of the State." Authority, importance, titles, large salaries, preëminence, precedence,—these are to exist in the University as in other public careers and furnish the wherewithal for the most magnificent dreams.[1] " The feet of this great body[2] will be on the college benches and its head in the senate." Its chief, the Grand-Master, unique of his species, less restricted, with freer hands than the ministers themselves, is to be one of the principal personages of the empire; his greatness will exalt the condition and feeling of his subordinates. In the provinces, on every fête-day or at every public ceremony, people will take pride in seeing their rector or principal in official costume seated alongside of the general or prefect in full uniform.[3]

The consideration awarded to their chief will reflect on them ; they will enjoy it along with him ; they will say to themselves that they too, like him and those under him, all together, form an élite ; by degrees, they will feel that they are all one body ; they will acquire the spirit of the association and attach themselves to the University, the

---

[1] This intention is formally expressed in the law. (Decree of March 17, 1808, art. 30.) " Immediately after the formation of the imperial university, th · order of rank shall be followed in the appointment of functionaries, and no one can be assigned a place who has not passed through the lowest. The situations will then afford a career which offers to knowledge and good behavior the hope of reaching the highest position in the imperial university."

[2] Pelet de la Lozère, *ibid.*

[3] " Procès-verbaux des séances du conseil de l'Université." (In manuscript.) Memoir of February 1, 1811, on the means for developing the spirit of the corporation in the University. In this memoir, communicated to the Emperor, the above motive is alleged.

same as a soldier to his regiment or like a monk to his brethren in a monastery.

Thus, as in a monastic order, one must join the University by "taking the cowl." [1] "I want," says Napoleon, "some solemnity attached to this act. My purpose is that the members of the corps of instruction should contract, not as formerly, a religious engagement, but a civil engagement before a notary, or before the justice of the peace, or prefect, or other (officer). . . . They will espouse public education the same as their forerunners espoused the Church, with this difference, that the marriage will not be as sacred, as indissoluble. . . . They will engage themselves for three, six, or nine years, and not resign without giving notice a certain number of years beforehand." To heighten the resemblance, "the principle of celibacy must be established, in this sense, that a man consecrated to teaching shall not marry until after having passed through the first stages of his career;" for example, "schoolmasters shall not marry before the age of twenty-five or thirty years, after having obtained a salary of three or four thousand francs and economized something." But, at bottom, marriage, a family, private life, all natural and normal matters in the great world of society, are causes of trouble and weakness in a corps where individuals, to be good organs, must give themselves up wholly and without reserve. "In future,[2] not only must schoolmasters, but, again, the principals and censors of the lycées, and the principals and rulers of the colleges, be restricted to celibacy and a life in common."—The last complementary and significant trait, which gives to the laic institution the aspect of a convent, is this : "No woman shall have a lodging in, or be admitted into, the lycées and colleges."

Now, let us add to the monastic principle of celibacy the monastic and military principle of obedience ; the latter, in Napoleon's eyes, is fundamental and the basis of the

---

1 Pelet de la Lozère, *ibid.*
2 Decree of March 17, 1808, arts. 101, 102.

others ; this principle being accepted, a veritable corporation
exists ; members are ruled by one head and command becomes effective. " There will be," says Napoleon, " a corps
of instructors, if all the principals, censors and professors
have one or several chiefs, the same as the Jesuits had
their general and their *provincial*," like the soldiers of a
regiment with their colonel and captain. The indispensable link is found ; individuals, in this way, keep together,
for they are held by authorities, under one regulation. As
with a volunteer in a regiment, or a monk who enters a convent, the members of the University will accept its total
régime in advance, present and future, wholly and in detail,
and will subject themselves under oath. " They are to
take an engagement[1] to faithfully observe the statutes and
regulations of the University. They must promise obedience to the Grand-Master in everything ordered by him for
the service of the Emperor, and for the advantage of education. They must engage not to quit the educational
corps and abandon their functions before having obtained
the Grand-Master's consent. They are to accept no other
public or private salaried function without the authentic
permission of the Grand-Master. They are bound to give
notice to the Grand-Master and his officers of whatever
comes to their knowledge that is opposed to the doctrine
and principles of the educational corps in the establishments for public instruction." There are many other obligations, indefinite or precise,[2] of which the sanction is
not only moral, but, again, legal, all notable and lasting,
an entire surrender of the person who suffers more or less
profoundly at having accepted them, and whose forced
resignation must be insured by the fear of punishment.
" Care must be taken[3] to insure severe discipline every-

---

[1] Decree of March 20, 1808, articles 40-46.

[2] For example, act of March 31, 1812, on leaves of absence.—Cf. the regulations
of April 8, 1810, for the " École de la Maternité, titres ix, x and xi). In this
strict and special instance we see plainly what Napoleon meant by "the police"
of a school.

[3] Pelet de la Lozère, *ibid.*

where : the professors themselves are to be subject in certain cases to the penalty of arrest ; they will lose no more
consideration on this account than the colonels who are
punished in the same manner." It is the least of all penalties ; there are others of greater and greater gravity,[1]
"the reprimand in presence of an academical board, censure in presence of the University board, transfer to an
inferior office, suspension with or without entire or partial deprivation of salary, half-pay or put on the retired
list, or stricken off the University roll," and, in the latter
case "rendered incapable of obtaining employment in any
other public administration." "Every member of the University[2] who shall fail to conform to the subordination established by the statutes and regulations, or in respect due
to superiors, shall be reprimanded, censured or suspended
from his functions according to the gravity of the case."
In no case may he withdraw of his own accord, resign at
will, and voluntarily return to private life ; he is bound to
obtain beforehand the Grand-Master's assent ; and, if the
latter refuses this, he must renew his application three
times, every two months, with the formalities, the delays and
the importunacy of a long procedure ; failing in which, he
is not only stricken from the rolls, but again " condemned
to a confinement proportioned to the gravity of the circumstances," and which may last a year.

A system of things ending in a prison is not attractive,
and is established only after great resistance. " We were
under the necessity," says the superior council,[3] " of taking
candidates as they could be found, differing infinitely in

---

1 Decree of March 17, 1808, articles 47 and 48.

2 Decree of Nov. 15, 1811, articles 66 and 69.

3 Procès-verbaux et papiers du conseil supérieur de l'Université (in manuscript).—(Two memoirs submitted to the Emperor, Feb. 1, 1811, on the means of
strengthening the discipline and spirit of the body in the University.)—The
memoir requests that the sentences of the university authorities be executable on
the simple *exequatur* of the courts ; it is important to diminish the intervention of
tribunals and prefects, to cut short appeals and pleadings ; the University must
have full powers and full jurisdiction on its domain, collect taxes from its tax-
payers, and repress all infractions of those amenable to its jurisdiction.

methods, principles and sentiments, accustomed to almost unlimited pardon or, at least, to being governed by the caprices of parents and nearly all disliking the régime attempted to be enforced on them." Moreover, through this intervention of the State, "the local authorities find one of their most cherished perogatives wrested from them." In sum, "the masters detested the new duties imposed on them ; the administrators and bishops protested against the appointments not made at their suggestion ; fathers of families complained of the new taxes they had to pay. It is said that the University is known only by its imposts and by its forced regulations ; again, in 1811, most of its masters are incompetent, or indocile, and of a bad spirit.—There is still another reason for tightening the cord that binds them to the corporation. " The absolute subordination of every individual belonging to the University is its first necessity ; without discipline and without obedience, no University could exist. This obedience must be prompt, and, in grave cases, where recourse must be had to the authority of the government, obedience must always be provisional." But, on this incurably refractory staff, compression will not suffice ; it has grown old and hardened ; the true remedy, therefore, consists in replacing it with a younger one, more manageable, expressly shaped and wrought out in a special school, which will be for the University what Fontainebleau is for the army, what the grand seminaries are for the clergy, a nursery of subjects carefully selected and fashioned beforehand.

Such is the object of the "École normale."[1] Young students enter it at the age of seventeen and bind themselves to remain in the University at least ten years. It is a boarding-school (*internat*), and they are obliged to live in common : "individual exits are not allowed," while "the exits in common . . . in uniform . . . can be made only under the direction and conduct of superintendent masters.

---

[1] " Statut sur l'administration, l'enseignement et la police de l'École normale," March 30, 1810, title ii, articles 20–23.

. . . These superintendents inspect the pupils during their studies and recreations, on rising and on going to bed and during the night. . . . No pupil is allowed to pass the hours of his play-spell in his own room without permission of the superintendent. No pupil is allowed to enter the hall of another division without the permission of two superintendents. . . . The director of studies must examine the books of the pupils whenever he deems it necessary, and as often as once a month." Every hour of the day has its prescribed task ; all exercises, including religious observances, are prescribed, each in time and place, with a detail and minuteness, as if purposely to close all possible issues to personal initiation and everywhere substitute mechanical uniformity for individual diversities. " The principal duties of the pupils are respect for religion, attachment to the sovereign and the government, steady application, constant regularity, docility and submission to superiors ; whoever fails in these duties is punished according to the gravity of the offence."—In 1812,[1] the Normal School is still a small one, scarcely housed, lodged in the upper stories of the lycée Louis le Grand, and composed of forty pupils and four masters. But Napoleon has its eyes on it and is kept informed of what goes on in it. He does not approve of the comments on the " Dialogue de Sylla et d'Eucrate," by Montesquieu, on the " Éloge de Marc Aurèle," by Thomas, on the " Annales " of Tacitus : " Let the young read Cæsar's commentaries. . . . Corneille, Bossuet, are the masters worth having ; these, under the full sail of obedience, enter into the established order of things of their time ; they strengthen it, they illustrate it," they are the literary coadjutors of public authority. Let the spirit of the Normal School con-

---

[1] Villemain, " Souvenirs contemporaines," vol. i., 137-156. (" Une visite à l'École normale en 1812," Napoleon's own words to M. de Narbonne.) " Tacitus is a dissatisfied senator, an Auteuil grumbler, who revenges himself, pen in hand, in his cabinet. His is the spite of the aristocrat and philosopher both at once. . . . Marcus Aurelius is a sort of Joseph II., and, in much larger proportions, a philanthropist and sectarian in commerce with the sophists and idealogues of his time, flattering them and imitating them. . . . I like Diocletian better."—". . . Public education lies in the future and in the duration of my work after I am gone."

form to that of these great men.   The University establishment is the original, central workshop which forges, finishes
and supplies the finest pieces, the best wheels.   Just now
the workshop is incomplete, poorly fitted out, poorly directed and still rudimentary ; but it is to be enlarged and
completed and made to turn out more and better work.
For the time being, it produces only what is needed to fill
the annual vacancies in the lycées and in the colleges.
Nevertheless, the first decree states that it is "intended to
receive as many as three hundred youths." [1]   The production
of this number will fill all vacancies, however great they
may be, and fill them with products of superior and authentic
quality.   These human products thus manufactured by the
State in its own shop, these school instruments which the
State stamps with its own mark, the State naturally prefers.
It imposes them on its various branches ; it puts them by
order into its lycées and colleges ; at last, it accepts no
others ; not only does it confer on itself the monopoly of
teaching, but again the preparation of the masters who
teach.   In 1813, [2] a circular announces that "the number of
places that chance to fall vacant from year to year, in the
various University establishments, sensibly diminishes according as the organization of the teaching body becomes more complete and regular in its operation, as
order and discipline are established, and as education becomes graduated and proportionate to diverse localities.
The moment has thus arrived for declaring that the Normal
School is henceforth the only road by which to enter upon
the career of public instruction ; it will suffice for all the
needs of the service."

IV.

What is the object of this service ?—Previous to the Revolution, when directed by, or under the supervision of, the

---

1 Decree of March 17, 1808, art. 110 and the following.
2 Circular of Nov. 13, 1813.

Church, its great object was the maintenance and strengthening of the faith of the young. Successor of the old kings, the new monarch underlines[1] among " the bases of education," " the precepts of the *Catholic* religion," and this phrase he writes himself with a marked intention ; when first drawn up, the Council of State had written the *Christian* reiigion ; Napoleon himself, in the definitive and public decree, substitutes the narrowest term for the broadest.[2] In this particular, he is politic, taking one step more on the road on which he has entered through the Concordat, desiring to conciliate Rome and the French clergy by seeming to give religion the highest place.—But it is simply a place for show, similar to that which he assigns to ecclesiastical dignitaries in public ceremonies and on the roll of precedencies. He does not concern himself with reanimating or even preserving earnest belief ; far from that, " it should be so arranged," he says,[3] " that young people may be neither too bigoted nor too incredulous : they should be adapted to the state of the nation and of society." All that can be demanded of them is external deference, personal attendance on the ceremonies of worship, a brief prayer in Latin muttered in haste at the beginning and end of each lesson,[4] in short, acts like those of raising one's hat or other public marks of respect, such as the official attitudes imposed by a government, author of the Concordat, on its military and civil staff. They likewise, the lyceans and the collegians, are to belong to it and do already, Napoleon thus forming his adult staff out of his juvenile staff.

---

1 Decree of March 17, 1808, article 38.

2 Pelet de la Lozère, *ibid.*, 158.

3 *Id., ibid.*, 168. (Session of March 20, 1806.)

4 Hermann Niemeyer, " Beobactungen auf einer Deportation-Reise nach Frankreich im J. 1807 (Halle, 1824), ii., 353.—Fabry, " Mémoires pour servir à l'histoire de l'instruction publique," iii., 120. (Documents and testimony of pupils showing that religion in the lycées is only ceremonial practice.)—*Id.*, Riancey, " Histoire de l'instruction publique," ii., 378. (Reports of nine chaplains in the royal colleges in 1830 proving that the same spirit prevailed throughout the Restoration : " A boy sent to one of these establishments containing 400 pupils for the term of eight years has only eight or ten chances favoring the preservation [of his faith ; all the others are against him, that is to say, out of four hundred chances, three hundred and ninety risk his being a man with no religion."

In fact, it is for himself that he works, for himself alone, and not for the Church whose ascendency would prejudice his own ; besides, in private conversation, he declares that he wishes to supplant it ; his object in forming the University is first and especially " to take education out of the hands of the priests.[1] They consider this world only as a diligence for transportation to the other," and Napoleon " wants the diligence filled with good soldiers for his armies," good functionories for his administrations, and good, zealous subjects for his service.—And, thereupon, in the decree which organizes the University, and following after this phrase written for effect, he states the real and fundamental truth. " All the schools belonging to the University shall take for the basis of their teaching loyalty to the Emperor, to the imperial monarchy to which the happiness of the people is confided and to the Napoleonic dynasty which preserves the unity of France and of all *liberal* ideas proclaimed by the Constitutions." In other terms, the object is to plant civil faith in the breasts of children, boys and young men, to make them believe in the beauty, goodness and excellence of the established order of things, to predispose their minds and hearts in favor of the system, to adapt them to this system,[2] to the concentration of authority and to the centralization of services, to uniformity and to "falling into line " (*encadrement*), to equality in obeying, to com-

---

1 Fabry, *ibid.*, iii., 175. (Napoleon's own words to a member of his council.)—Pelet de la Lozère, *ibid.*, 161 : " I do not want priests meddling with public education."— 167 : " The establishment of a teaching corps will be a guarantee against the re-establishment of monks. Without that they would some day come back."

2 Fabry, *ibid*, iii., 120. (Abstract of the system of lycées by a pupil who passed many years in two lycées.) Terms for board 900 francs, insufficiency of food and clothing, crowded lectures and dormitories, too many pupils in each class, profits of the principal who lives well, gives one grand dinner a week to thirty persons, deprives the dormitory, already too narrow, of space for a billiard-table, and takes for his own use a terrace planted with fine trees. The censor, the steward, the chaplain, the sub-director do the same, although to a less degree. The masters are likewise as poorly fed as the scholars. The punishments are severe, no paternal remonstrance or guidance, the under-masters maltreated on applying the rules, despised by their superiors and without any influence on their pupils.—" Libertinage, idleness, self-interest animated all breasts, there being no tie of friendship uniting either the masters to the scholars nor the pupils amongst themselves."

petition, to enthusiasm, in short, to the spirit of the reign, to
the combinations of the comprehensive and calculating
mind which, claiming for itself and appropriating for its own
use the entire field of human action, sets up its corner-posts
everywhere, its barriers, its rectilinear compartments, lays
out and arranges its racecourses, brings together and introduces the runners, urges them on, stimulates them at each
stage, reduces their soul to the fixed determination of getting
ahead fast and far, leaving to the individual but one motive
for living, that of the desire to figure in the foremost rank
in the career where, now by choice and now through force,
he finds himself inclosed and launched.

For this purpose, two sentiments are essential with adults
and therefore with children : the first is the passive acceptance of a prescribed regulation, and nowhere does a rule
applied from above bind and direct the whole life by such
precise and multiplied injunctions as under the University
régime.   School life is circumscribed and marked out according to a rigid, unique system, the same for all the colleges and lycées of the Empire, according to an imperative
and detailed plan which foresees and prescribes everything
even to the minutest point, labor and rest of mind and of
body, material and method of instruction, class-books, passages to translate or to recite, a list of fifteen hundred volumes for each library with a prohibition against intro-
ducing another volume into it without the Grand-Master's
permission, hours, duration, application and sessions of
classes, of studies, of recreations and of promenades, that is
to say, the premeditated stifling of native curiosity with the
masters and still more, with the scholars, of spontaneous inquiry, of inventive and personal originality, so great that one
day, under the second Empire, a minister, drawing out his
watch, could exclaim with satisfaction, " At this very time,
in such a class, all the scholars of the Empire are studying a
certain page in Virgil."—Well-informed, judicious, impartial
and some kindly-disposed foreigners,[1] on seeing this mech-

---

[1] Hermann Niemeyer, " Beobachtungen," etc., ii., 350.   " A very worthy man, pro-

anism which everywhere substitutes for the initiative from
below the compression and impulsion from above, are very
much surprised. "The law means that the young shall never
for one moment be left to themselves ; the children are
under their masters' eyes all day " and all night.   Every
step outside of the regulations is a false one and always arrested by the ever-present authority.   And, in cases of in-
fraction, punishments are severe ; "according to the gravity
of the case,[1] the pupils will be punished by confinement
from three days to *three months* in the lycée or college, in
some place assigned to that purpose ; if fathers, mothers or
guardians object to these measures, the pupil must be sent
home and can no longer enter any other college or lycée
belonging to the university, which, as an effect of university
monopoly, thereafter deprives him of instruction, unless his
parents are wealthy enough to employ a professor in the
house.   " Everything that can be effected by rigid discipline
is thus obtained[2] and better, perhaps, in France than in any
other country," for if, on leaving the lycée, young people
have lost a will of their own, they have acquired " a love of
and habits of subordination and punctuality " which are
elsewhere wanting.

Meanwhile, on this narrow and strictly defined road,
whilst the regulation supports them, emulation pushes
them on.   In this respect, the new university corps, which,
according to Napoleon himself, must be a company of "lay
Jesuits," resumes to its advantage the double process which
its forerunners, the former Jesuits, had so well employed in
education ; on the one hand, constant direction and in-
cessant watchfulness ; on the other hand, the appeal to
amour-propre and to the excitements of parades before the
public.   If the pupil works hard, it is not for the purpose

fessor in one of the royal colleges, said to me : ' What backward steps we have been
obliged to take ! How all the pleasure of teaching, all the love for our art, has
been taken away from us by this constraint !' "

[1] *Id., ibid.*, ii., 339.—" Decree of November 15, 1811, art. 17.

[2] *Id., ibid.*, ii., 353.

of learning and knowing, but to be the first in his class ;
the object is not to develop in him the need of truthful-
ness and the love of knowledge, but his memory, taste and
literary talent ; at best, the logical faculty of arrangement
and deduction, but especially the desire to surpass his
rivals, to *distinguish himself*, to shine, at first in the little
public of his companions, and next, at the end of the year,
before the great public of grown-up men.   Hence, the
weekly compositions, the register of ranks and names,
every place being numbered and proclaimed ; hence, those
annual and solemn awards of prizes in each lycée and at
the grand competition of all lycées, along with the pomp,
music, decoration, speeches and attendance of distinguished personages.   The German observer testifies to the
powerful effect of a ceremony of this kind [1]: " One might
think one's self at the play, so theatrical was it ;" and he
notices the oratorical tone of the speakers, " the fire of
their declamation," the communication of emotion, the
applause of the public, the prolonged shouts, the ardent
expression of the pupils obtaining the prizes, their spark-
ling eyes, their blushes, the joy and the tears of the
parents.   Undoubtedly, the system has its defects ; very
few of the pupils can expect to obtain the first place ;
others lack the spur and are moreover neglected by the
master.   But the élite make extraordinary efforts and,
with this, there is success.   " During the war times," says
again another German, " I lodged a good many French
officers who knew one half of Virgil and Horace by heart."
Similarly, in mathematics, young people of eighteen, pupils
of the Polytechnic School, understand very well the differential and integral calculus, and, according to the testi-

---

1 Hermann Niemeyer, *ibid.*, 366, and following pages.   On the character,
advantages and defects of the system, this testimony of an eye-witness is very
instructive and forms an almost complete picture.   The subjects taught are
reduced to Latin and mathematics ; there is scarcely any Greek, and none of the
modern languages, hardly a tinge of history and the natural sciences, while phi-
lology is null ; that which a pupil must know of the classics is their "contents
and their spirit " (Geist und Inhalt).—Cf. Guizot, " Essai sur l'histoire et l'état
actuel de l'instruction publique," 1816, p. 103.

mony of an Englishman,[1] "they know it better than many of the English professors."

V.

This general preparation, Napoleon lays it out with precision and directs it in the sense of his policy, and, as he has special need of soldiers, the school, in his hands, becomes the vestibule of the barracks. From its origin, the institution has received the military turn and spirit, and this form, which is essential to him, becomes more and more restricted. In 1805, during four months,[2] Fourcroy, ordered by the Emperor, visits the new lycées "with an inspector of reviews and a captain or adjutant-major, who everywhere gives instruction in drill and discipline." The young have been already broke in ; " almost everywhere," he says on his return, " I saw young people obey without murmur or reflection younger and weaker corporals and sergeants than themselves, raised to a merited rank through their behavior and progress." He himself, although a liberal, finds reasons which justify to the legislative body this unpopular practice ;[3] he replies to the objections and alarm of the parents "that it is favorable to order, without which there are no good studies," and moreover " it accustoms the pupils to carrying and using arms, which shortens their work and accelerates their promotion on being summoned by the conscription to the service of the State." The tap of the drum, the attitude in presenting arms, marching at command, uniform, gold lace, and all that, in 1811, becomes obligatory, not only for the lycées and colleges, but again, and under the penalty of being closed, for private institutions.[4] At the end of the Empire,

---

[1] " Travels in France during the Years 1814 and 1815 " (Edinburgh, 1816), vol. i., p. 152.

[2] " Ambroise Rendu et l'Université de France," by E. Rendu (1861), pp. 25 and 26. (Letter of the Emperor, Floréal 3, year XIII, and report by Fourcroy.)

[3] " Recueil," etc., by de Beauchamp, i., 151. (Report to the *Corps Législatif* by Fourcroy, May 6, 1806.)

[4] " Procès-verbaux et papiers " (manuscripts) of the superior council of the Uni-

there were enumerated in the departments alone which composed old France 76,000 scholars studying under this system of excitation and constraint. "Our masters," as a former pupil is to say later on, "resembled captain-instructors, our study-rooms mess-rooms, our recreations drills, and our examinations reviews."[1] The whole tendency of the school inclines to the army and merges therein on the studies being completed—sometimes, even, it flows into it before the term is over. After 1806,[2] the anticipated conscriptions take youths from the benches of the philosophy and rhetoric classes. After 1808, ministerial circulars[3] demand of the lycées boys (*des enfans*) who are well disposed, scholars of eighteen and nineteen who "know how to manœuvre," so that they may at once be made under-officers or second-lieutenants; and these the lycées furnish without any difficulty by hundreds; in this way, the beardless volunteer entering upon the career one or two years sooner, but gaining by this one or two grades in rank.—"Thus," says a principal[4] of one of the colleges, "the brain of the French boy is full of the soldier. As far as knowledge goes there is but little hope of it, at least under existing circumstances." In the schools, says another witness of the reign,[5] "the young refuse to learn anything but mathematics and a knowledge of arms. I can

versity, session of March 12, 1811, note by the Emperor communicated by the Grand-Master: "The Grand-Master will direct that in all boarding-schools and institutions which may come into existence, the pupils shall wear a uniform, and that everything shall go on as in the lycées according to *military* discipline." In the decree in conformity with this, of Nov. 15, 1811, the word *military* was omitted, probably because it seemed too crude; but it shows the thought behind it, the veritable desire of Napoleon.—Quicherat, " Histoire de Sainte-Barbe," iii., 126. The decree was enforced "even in the smallest boarding-schools."

1 Testimony of Alfred de Vigny in " Grandeur et Servitude militaires." Alfred de Musset is of the same impression in his " Confession d'un enfant du siècle."

2 Quicherat, *ibid.*, p. 126.

3 " The Modern Régime," i.

4 Hermann Niemeyer, *ibid.*, i., 153.

5 "Travels in France," etc., ii., 123. (Testimony of a French gentleman.) "The rapid destruction of population in France caused constant promotions, and the army became the career which offered the most chances. It was a profession for which no education was necessary and to which all had access. There, Bonaparte never allowed merit to go unrecognized."

recall many examples of young lads of ten or twelve years who daily entreated their father and mother to let them go with Napoleon."—In those days, the military profession is evidently the first of all, almost the only one. Every civilian is a *pékin*, that is to say an inferior, and is treated as such.[1] At the door of the theatre, the officer breaks the line of those who are waiting to get their tickets and, as a right, takes one under the nose of those who came before him ; they let him pass, go in, and they wait. In the café, where the newspapers are read in common, he lays hold of them as if through a requisition and uses them as he pleases in the face of the patient bourgeois.

The central idea of this glorification of the army, be it understood, is the worship of Napoleon, the supreme, unique, absolute sovereign of the army and all the rest, while the prestige of this name is as great, as carefully maintained, in the school as in the army. At the start, he put his own free scholars (*boursiers*) into the lycées and colleges, about three thousand boys[2] whom he supports and brings up at his own expense, for his own advantage, destined to become his creatures, and who form the first layer of the school population; about one hundred and fifty of these scholarships to each lycée, first occupants of the lycée and still for a long time more numerous than their paying comrades, all of a more or less needy family, sons of soldiers and functionaries who live on the Emperor and rely on him only, all accustomed from infancy to regard the Emperor as the arbiter of their destiny, the special, generous and all-powerful patron who, having taken charge of them now, will also take charge of them in the future. A figure of this kind

---

1 Véron, "Mémoires d'un bourgeois de Paris," i., 127 (year 1806).

2 Guizot, *ibid.*, pp. 59 and 61.—Fabry, " Mémoires pour servir à l'histoire de l'instruction publique," iii., 102. (On the families of these favorites and on the means made use of to obtain these scholarships.)—Jourdain, " le Budget de l'instruction publique (1857), p. 144.—In 1809, in the 36 lycées, there are 9,068 pupils, boarding and day scholars, of whom 4,199 are *boursiers*. In 1811, there are 10,926 pupils, of whom 4,008 are *boursiers*. In 1813, there are 14,992 pupils, of whom 3,500 are *boursiers*. At the same epoch, in private establishments, there are 30,000 pupils.

fills and occupies the entire field of their imagination ;
whatever grandeur it already possesses it here becomes still
more grand, colossal and superhuman.   At the beginning
their enthusiasm gave the pitch to their co-disciples ;[1] the
institution, through its mechanism, labors to keep this up,
and the administrators or professors, by order or through
zeal, use all their efforts to make the sonorous and ringing
chord vibrate with all the more energy.   After 1811, even
in a private institution,[2] "the victories of the Emperor form
almost the only subject on which the imagination of the
pupils is allowed to exercise itself."   After 1807,[3] at Louis
le Grand, the prize compositions are those on the recent
victory of Jena.   "Our masters themselves," says Alfred
de Vigny, "unceasingly read to us the bulletins of the
Grande Armée, while cries of *Vive l'Empereur* interrupted
Virgil and Plato."   In sum, write many witnesses,[4] Bonaparte desired to bestow on French youths the organization
of the "Mamelukes," and he nearly succeeded.   More
exactly and in his own words, "His Majesty[5] desired to
realize in a State of forty millions of inhabitants what had
been done in Sparta and in Athens."—"But," he is to say
later, "I only half succeeded.   That was one of my finest
conceptions" ;[6] M. de Fontanes and the other university
men did not comprehend this or want to comprehend
it.   Napoleon himself could give only a moment of attention to his school work, his halting-spells between two
campaigns ;[7] in his absence, "they spoiled for him his best

---

1 Fabry, *ibid.*, ii., 391 (1819).   (On the peopling of the lycées and colleges.)
"The first nucleus of the boarders was furnished by the Prytanée. . . . Tradition
has steadily transmitted this spirit to all the pupils that succeeded each other
for the first twelve years."—*Ibid.*, iii., 112.   "The institution of lycées tends to
creating a race inimical to repose, eager and ambitious, foreign to the domestic
affections and of a military and adventurous spirit."

2 Quicherat, *ibid.*, iii., 126.

3 Hermann Niemeyer, *ibid.*, ii., 350.

4 Fabry, *ibid.*, iii., 109-112.

5 Ambroise Rendu, "Essai sur l'instruction publique," (1819), i., 221.   (Letter of
Napoleon to M. de Fontanes, March 24, 1808.)

6 "Mémorial," June 17, 1816.

7 Pelet de la Lozère, *ibid.*, 154, 157, 159.

ideas " ; " his executants " never perfectly carried out his intentions.   " He scolded, and they bowed to the storm, but
not the less continued on in the usual way."   Fourcroy
kept too much of the Revolution in mind, and Fontanes too
much of the ancient régime ; the former was too much a
man of science, and the latter too much a man of letters ;
with such capacities they laid too great stress on intellectual
culture and too little on discipline of the feelings.   In education, literature and science are " secondary " matters; the
essential thing is training, an early, methodical, prolonged,
irresistible training which, through the convergence of
every means—lessons, examples and habits—inculcates
" principles," and lastingly impresses on young souls " the
national doctrine," a sort of social and political catechism,
the first article of which enjoins fanatical docility, passionate
devotion, and the total surrender of one's self to the Emperor.[1]

---

1 " Mémorial," June 17, 1816. " This conception of the University by Napoleon
must be taken with another, of more vast proportions, which he sets forth in the
same conversation and which clearly shows his complete plan. He desired " the
military classing of the nation," that is to say *five successive conscriptions*, one
above the other. The first, that of children and boys by means of the University;
the second, that of ordinary conscripts yearly and effected by the drawing by
lot ; the third, fourth and fifth provided by three standards of national guard, the
first one comprising young unmarried men and held to frontier service, the second
comprising men of middle age, married and to serve only in the department, and
the third comprising aged men to be employed only in the defence of towns—in
all, through these three classes, two millions of classified men, enrolled and
armed, each with his post assigned him in case of invasion. " In 1810 or 1811,
this scheme was read to the Council of State up to fifteen or twenty corrections.
" The Emperor, who laid great stress on it, frequently recurred to it." We see
the place of the University in his edifice : from ten to sixty years, his universal
conscription was to take, first, children, then adults, and, with valid persons, the
semi-invalids, as, for instance, Cambacérès, the arch-chancellor, gross, impotent,
and, of all men, the least military. " There is Cambacérès," says Napoleon, " who
must be ready to shoulder his gun if danger makes it necessary. . . . Then you
will have a nation sticking together like lime and sand, able to defy time and
man." There is constant repugnance to this by the whole Council of State,
" marked disfavor, mute and inert opposition. . . . Each member trembled at
seeing himself classed, transported abroad," and, under pretext of internal defence, used for foreign wars." The Emperor, absorbed with other projects, overlooked this plan.

INDEX.